K.45'1-26-3

W9-BUL-366

9.95

THE GREAT AIR WAR

THE GREAT
AIR WAR

by AARON NORMAN

The Macmillan Company · New York

Collier–Macmillan Limited · London

ACKNOWLEDGMENT

Holt, Rinehart and Winston, Inc., has granted permission
to reprint excerpts from *One Man's War* by Lt. Bert Hall
and Lt. John J. Niles, copyright 1929, copyright © 1957
by Holt, Rinehart and Winston, Inc.

Copyright © 1968 by Aaron Norman

All rights reserved. No part of this book may be repro-
duced or transmitted in any form or by any means, electronic or mechanical, including photocopying, recording
or by any information storage and retrieval system, without permission in writing from the Publisher.

Library of Congress Catalog Card Number: 68-10180

FIRST PRINTING

The Macmillan Company, New York
Collier-Macmillan Canada Ltd., Toronto, Ontario

Printed in the United States of America

This book is affectionately dedicated
to the memory of my brother,
CHARLES SIGMUND POPOK
Captain, United States Marine Air Wing,
killed in an airplane accident
February 11, 1961

CONTENTS

PREFACE

WORLD WAR I BEGAN little more than a decade after Orville Wright skimmed above the sands of Kitty Hawk in history's first successful airplane flight. When the war did begin, the military potential of the flying machine was largely unconsidered. Those who foretold its combative uses were ridiculed as quixotic romancers and tetched visionaries. In all the armies of the world, officers of the highest rank dismissed aviation as a mere feather in the scale. The airman, they assumed, would play a negligible role. He would reconnoiter, which was something of value, and maybe he would harass troop movements to some slight degree by throwing bombs and weighted arrows. Yet, as the war progressed, the battle for the skies became an important, if not critical, factor. Tiny, platoon-sized air detachments mushroomed into huge and complex organizations. Aviation technology bloomed; the airplane, hardly more than a motorized kite in 1914, became a sophisticated, lethal weapon. Aircraft manufacture, a backshed industry when war broke out, was soon a great hive of large factories. Before hostilities ceased, all the basic strategies and tactics of aerial warfare had been established for the future. Air Power was a reality to be reckoned with. War would never be the same again.

To the people who lived through those convulsive four years, the spectacle of winged combat was an astonishing, incredible, fascinating development. It was as if, today, we were suddenly to hear of astronauts doing battle in outer space. If man persists in his belligerency towards man, he will someday, I fear, fight wars beyond the moon. It need not, and perhaps will not, be a contest involving human warriors, but rather robot machines. The supersonic, jet-powered combat planes of the present are virtually guided missiles; that flesh-and-blood pilots do the guiding, instead of some remote computer-control station doing it automatically, is due in substantial measure to economics—pilots are cheaper to employ than a vast network of cybernetic brains and relays. But it is only a matter of time and necessity before the battle flyer goes the way of the horse soldier. He is already merely an extension of his machine. His electronic gear tells him most of what he should do, or else does it for him; it can think faster, see farther, and aim truer than he. The startling fact is that man, less than fifty years after he began fighting in the sky, has become obsolescent as a sky fighter.

In the beginning, of course, the machine was an extension of the individual at its controls. It was flimsily constructed of wood, fabric, and wire, and propelled by an engine less powerful than that in the average modern automobile. Its controls consisted of the essential minimum—throttle, "joystick," and rudder bars. Its instrument panel usually had but six dials—altimeter, tachometer, airspeed indicator, and gauges for oil pressure, oil temperature, and manifold pressure. It carried a machine gun or two for armament, and a sight through which to aim. That was the typical single-seater aircraft of the 1914-1918 war. A man's skill and cunning counted for more than the machine. An expert pilot flying a mediocre plane was deadlier than a mediocre pilot in a first-rate machine. A Spad or Fokker, in the hands of a good aviator, could wreak havoc. But it soon became the coffin of a bad aviator, an unlucky aviator, or one too imprudent. It was calculated that the pilot who survived six weeks at the front was beating the odds against him.

The war in the air was a personal, man-to-man kind of war. Opposing pilots came to recognize and know one another. Men built reputations as their victories increased. Many of them emblazoned their planes with gaudy colors and personal insignia. They fought their aerial tournaments with a romantic intensity unknown since the disappearance of the medieval knight. Later generations look back and think of them almost as we see the knights of Camelot. Their names—Richthofen, Immelmann, Boelcke, Guynemer, Fonck, Nungesser, Garros, Bishop, Ball, Mannock, Rickenbacker, Luke, and many others—conjure images of immaculate valor, comparable to that of Launcelot or Gawain.

But the myths and mystique of World War I aviation, like those of ancient chivalry, are a distillation of partial truths that largely ignores the seamier and serious sides of things as they were. To explore the whole truth is attempted in this book. Some long-held notions are debunked on the pages that follow, but the light of fact does not destroy the drama and excitement that attended the high arena. Rather, I think, it adds new meaning. I have tried to portray the pilots in the round, to reveal their individual strong points and shortcomings, their motivations and problems. To know what they did is interesting, but to know why and how they did it is fascinating. In order to achieve my purpose, I have had to discuss the machines they flew, the tactics they used, their daily life at the front, their separate backgrounds and personalities, and I have also had to discuss the ground war—its effect on their actions, and the effect of their actions on it.

Writing a history of this scope and complexity has required a heavy dependence on other, earlier books, all of which are listed in the bibliography at the end of this volume. Some of these works, however, merit special mention here, for I relied most heavily on them. To their authors, whose researches I have ransacked, my gratitude is beyond expression. I find myself in much the same position as that described by the late Quentin Reynolds in the introduction to his book, *They Fought for the Sky*. "Now that the book is finished," he wrote, "I am disturbed by the thought that I didn't really write it—I merely typewrote it. I picked the brains of hundreds of men, dead and living, and this is the result. . . . This is definitely not an apology; it is an explanation and a confession."

The authors and the works to which I owe most are: W. M. Lamberton, *Fighter Aircraft of the 1914–1918 War* and *Reconnaissance and Bomber Aircraft of the 1914–1918 War;* H. J. Nowarra and Kimbrough S. Brown, *Richthofen and the Flying Circus;* Bruce Robertson (ed.), *Air Aces of the 1914–1918 War;* James Norman Hall and Charles Bernard Nordhoff, *The Lafayette Flying Corps;* James R. McConnell, *Flying for France;* R. H. Kiernan, *Captain Albert Ball;* Bert Hall and John R. Niles, *One Man's War;* Ernest Dudley, *Monsters of the Purple Twilight;* and John R. Cuneo, *Winged Mars: The German Air Weapon, 1870–1914*.

I should also like to extend my heartfelt thanks to all who assisted me in gathering the research and pictorial material for this book, including many helpful representatives of the United States Air Force, the National Archives, the National Air Museum, the Library of Congress, and the New York Public Library. To my treasured wife, Edith, I especially say thanks for her kindness and understanding.

AARON NORMAN

New York City
May 30, 1968

THE GREAT AIR WAR

CHAPTER I

America and the Air War

AT THE AIRDROME of the American 94th Pursuit Squadron near Toul, France, on April 14, 1918, a sudden alarm broke the morning stillness. Lieutenants Douglas Campbell and Alan Winslow ran to their Nieuport airplanes. They belted themselves into their cockpit seats and hurriedly tested the controls, watching the response of aileron, elevator, and rudder to each movement of the stick and pedals. Mechanics began pulling through the propellers to load the engine cylinders with fuel. Everyone, as they readied the machines for take-off, cast nervous glances upward. High overhead, specks against the gray ceiling, a pair of German fighter planes—an Albatros and a Pfalz—were flying in lazy circles, their presence above the airfield an open invitation to battle.

Neither man had ever flown against the enemy, and each suffered anxiety as he switched his magneto to the "on" position and waited for the engine to spark. When it finally did whine and belch to life, they listened critically. Since there was no time for a proper warm-up, the flyers revved the engines and watched their tachometer needles slide toward the red warning lines on the dials. The wires bracing the wings vibrated with the throbbing pulse of the engine. Oil pressure was checked. As soon as the pressure held steady, each man signaled his ground crew to yank the chocks away from the straining undercarriage. Campbell first and then Winslow swung their Nieuports into the wind and advanced the throttle to full power. The increased wash of the propeller cleared the cockpits of exhaust fumes as the planes lurched ahead to gather flying speed. In a few seconds they were airborne, grinding in a mounting spiral toward the hostile warbirds above.

Campbell, in the front-flying Nieuport, was climbing out past five thousand feet when the Germans took advantage of their superior altitude. The black-crossed planes slid into shallow dives and closed for the attack. Campbell, glancing back at Winslow, signaled that he would take on the enemy leader. Winslow waved acknowledgment, then swerved off to the west. The Pfalz immediately turned to give chase. In the best tradition of World War I aerial combat, this was to be a man-to-man encounter.

As he maneuvered for defensive position, Campbell never took his eyes from the winged menace that swooped toward him. The Albatros was approaching fast, coming down on a collision course. Sooner than he expected, Campbell heard the staccato cough of the German's twin Spandau machine guns. Before he could react, the Spandaus fired again. Bullets tore through the Nieuport's fabric. Desperate to elude his antagonist's aim, Campbell wheeled over into a twisting descent. The German, in an effort to get on the Nieuport's vulnerable tail, pitched his plane into a steep dive. Flying more by instinct than reason, Campbell zoomed upward and executed an Immelmann turn—a half-loop with a roll-out at the apex—which put him above the Albatros. While the surprised German tried to fight his plane out of its vertical plunge, Campbell slipped in behind and pressed the trigger lever on his control stick. Two Vickers .303 machine guns, both mounted on the left side of the engine cowling, spat death. After three quick bursts a plume of black smoke billowed from the stricken Albatros as it plummeted to earth.

Winslow won his duel too, that morning. But Campbell, scoring a minute or so before Winslow, was the man who made history. In that awesome instant of triumph this twenty-two-year-old Californian became the first American pilot to shoot down an enemy aircraft in the service of his country. Although other American flyers—notably those of the much-storied Lafayette Escadrille —had been fighting over the western front since 1915, and taking a heavy toll of German planes, they had been serving as free-lance volunteers in the air forces of France and, in fewer cases, England. Not until Douglas Campbell posted his initial kill could the United States Air Service claim a victory in the sky.

This first victory came a full year after America's entrance into the war, and only seven months prior to the Armistice. Its tardiness along with the fact that Campbell piloted a French plane, armed with British guns, demonstrated how ill-prepared was America for aerial warfare. In their seven remaining months of action the "flying doughboys" of the American Expeditionary Force compiled a laudable record: 781 enemy aircraft destroyed as against 289 planes lost, a kill ratio of almost three to one. No fighter plane of American creation ever reached the front. The A.E.F. pilots waged all their battles in planes of French and British design. And, except for a relatively small number of Marlin machine guns shipped to France late in the summer of 1918, no arms of American origin were used in the air.

In April 1917, when the United States formally declared war, the Aviation Section of the Signal Corps, at the time representing the bulk of the nation's air strength, possessed only fifty-five airplanes in dependable flying condition.

Most of these were antiquated and unarmed trainers, little better than powered boxkites by European standards. The most advanced American plane at this critical juncture was the Curtiss JN-4 Jenny. Three of these had seen limited reconnaissance service a year earlier in the 1916 Punitive Expedition into Mexico that was led by Brigadier General John J. Pershing against the border-raiding insurrectionist bands of Pancho Villa. Faced now with a full-scale war in Europe, the army owned a dozen Jennys and naïvely regarded them as superlative examples of modern military aircraft. They were well-constructed machines with wide wings and reliable Curtiss engines of ninety horsepower. By the end of World War I some 5500 of them would be manufactured as primary trainers, but they sorely lacked the smart performance of contemporary fighter planes abroad. Top speed of the Jennys approximated seventy-five miles an hour. In sharp contrast, the Albatros D-5 of Germany, the Royal Aircraft Factory SE-5 of England, and the Spad S-13 of France— each then making its debut at the front—did better than 115 miles an hour in flight. Moreover, each carried a pair of automatic guns with a synchronizing device that permitted firing through the propeller arc, and at least a thousand rounds of ammunition along with various other necessary accouterments. The docile Jenny had never been asked to carry a machine gun, since the added weight and wind resistance would have reduced the plane's speed and agility to that of an arthritic chicken, and the operation of such a weapon in the air would have presented too many problems to an already overworked pilot.

Along with this paucity and primitiveness of aircraft, there was a dire shortage of skilled American flyers. Of sixty-five officers in the Aviation Section, no more than half were capable of active duty as pilots. A mere five or six had attained the aerobatic proficiency required for combat flying; none had so much as seen a warplane of the sophisticated class then being flown in battle by French, British, and German airmen. The American pilots were unaware of the aeronautical progress that had been made in Europe since the outbreak of war, and they clung to the illusion that their training and equipment matched any in the world. Evidence of their virtuosity, they thought, lay in the ability to pilot the Curtiss Jenny. "If you can fly a JN-4," the saying went, "you can fly anything." Because of its inherent stability and spacious wing surfaces, the trickiest part of handling a Jenny was simply stalling the wheels to the turf in landing and keeping them there—a characteristic that reflected the plane's tameness in the air. In any case, such positive stability and abundant lift had long ago been sacrificed to rapid climb and maneuverability in the fighter craft of Europe. By comparison the Jenny was almost three years behind the times, and the American aviator, his confidence unshakable, his ignorance of the facts abysmal, was thoroughly incompetent to take the controls of a swift, temperamental pursuit plane like that being flown in life-and-death tournaments above the bleeding countryside of France.

The gap between America and Europe in aviation technology, as events would later prove, had become too great ever to be closed in the nineteen months that remained of World War I. 'Nearly three years of bitter conflict had clearly delineated the vital necessity for air power—aviation had revolutionized warfare—yet not even the prototype of an up-to-date combat plane existed on the western side of the Atlantic. The situation was such, asserted General Pershing upon his appointment as commander in chief of the A.E.F., "that every American ought to feel mortified to hear it mentioned."

The utter lack of preparedness was the painful culmination of a prolonged drought in the development of military aeronautics. The principal excuse for this dereliction, as put forth by the senior ranks, was that Congress had always been too parsimonious in appropriating funds for the furtherance of army aviation. While it was undeniable that the politicians had not satisfied all the army's requests for money, it was also true that the military had failed to impress Congress sufficiently with the urgent need for a large, modern, combat-ready air fleet. Plans for building up the aviation branch had never been accorded earnest consideration by top-echelon officers; the few men who did crusade for such a build-up were invariably muzzled and frequently reprimanded by their complacent superiors. The tight-fisted spending policy of Congress did not justify this deficiency in foresight and initiative, but rather reflected it.

There was another convenient reason cited by apologists for the backward state of aviation in the nation. The French and English had maintained, since the war's beginning, a strict censorship of aeronautical information and had refused even to allow American observers to visit military airdromes. But this was not the whole truth. At least one American officer did witness the onset of aerial combat over the battlefields of France. Colonel George O. Squier, after serving as an attaché to the British army and spending some time in front-line trenches, came home in 1916 to preach the military heresy of "winning the war in the air." Scorn, ridicule, and skepticism rewarded his enthusiasm, and his lengthy report on the rapid growth of aviation in Europe received scant notice. Less than a year after Squier's return, the nation was in the throes of mobilization for active participation in the war, and his previous judgments were belatedly vindicated. Squier was promoted to brigadier general and named chief signal officer of the army, in which capacity he had the Air Service among the departments in his aegis. Locating knowledgable personnel to supervise the aviation branch proved an impossible task for Squier, who could devote only a portion of his own energy to this one area of command. He finally turned to a civilian, Professor Hiram Bingham, the noted explorer, to organize a training program for military aviators. Bingham, at the age of forty-one, had recently acquired his pilot's license at a private flying school. He was therefore astonished at the lack-brained attitudes and prejudices he found among his uniformed associates. For example, he had to contend with officers like the one who, under Squier, had immediate charge of the Aviation Section. This officer, Bingham later wrote, "was not a pilot, had been up only once or twice, was frankly afraid to fly even as an observer, and went so far as to say to me that for the father of seven sons to take flying lessons showed that he did not love his children."

When the call to arms sounded across the land, few Americans realized that the army, right up to the highest command, knew virtually nothing about martial aviation. The general staff was in such a hopeless muddle that it issued a regulation requiring aviators to wear spurs on their boots. After the country had been at war for six months, the arbiters of punctilio authorized pilots to sport the insignia of wings, but continued to insist on boots with spurs. An entire year passed before the general staff concluded that airmen might safely be relieved of their spurs.

At the time of President Woodrow Wilson's declaration of war, and for many months after, there was not a solitary general staff officer who had attended a flying school, or who had the vaguest notion about the needs of an air service. Scarcely anyone seemed to appreciate the extent to which the United States had lagged behind the European powers in aeronautical prowess. High-spirited, intrepid young men by the tens of thousands applied for the Air Service. Flamboyant speeches were being made by Senators and Congressmen, promising to "darken the skies of Europe" with American airplanes, yet only a handful of qualified pilots and a pitiful miscellany of archaic flying machines were available to back up their thrasonic rant and bluster. It was, furthermore, too late—much too late—for all the engineering genius and industrial might of the nation to overtake the war-accelerated capabilities of the European belligerents.

The original mobilization scheme of the general staff, which called for an over-all force of a million men, relegated aviation to a minor status. Although the press and the public were enthusiastic about expanding the Air Service, it was only finally at the instigation of France and England that the aviation arm of the A.E.F. grew to become a potent combat tool. Within three weeks of the United States' renunciation of neutrality, well-staffed missions from the Allied countries arrived to encourage greater American participation in the air war. Based mainly on French recommendations, a plan was drafted for the production of 22,625 aircraft and twice that quantity of engines in eighteen months' time—this from an industry which had produced fewer than five hundred aircraft since the Wright brothers had first flown at Kitty Hawk. Secretary of War Newton D. Baker approved the plan and, on July 24, 1917, Congress voted $640,000,000 for military aeronautics, the largest sum ever appropriated for a single purpose up to that time. With sufficient funds finally at its disposal, the Aviation Section secured permission for an expansion to 345 combat squadrons, forty-five construction companies, eighty-one supply squadrons, eleven repair squadrons, and twenty-six balloon companies. Of this number, 263 squadrons were intended for use at the front by June 1918, less than a year away.[1]

[1] Robertson: *Air Aces of the 1914–1918 War.*

For a nation practically devoid of aircraft and airmen, this amounted to an extremely hopeful estimate of its engineering and industrial capacities. In the light of past neglect and disinterest in aeronautics, the huge designing, production, and training programs thrust upon the military were formidable indeed. The experience and know-how essential to such a vast undertaking were just not to be found. But these sobering realities were concealed from the public, and all during 1917 the American people confidently awaited a miracle. If enough money were spent, why couldn't the war be won in the air? That an endless wave of American airplanes would soon blot the sun from German soil seemed a foregone conclusion. The newspapers published reassuring article after reassuring article. "How United States Builds for Air Supremacy" was a typical headline; the accompanying story described in glittering generalities the "intensive development of quantity production of engines and planes." The respected magazine *Flying* predicted that the Atlantic would be bridged by air within a few months, thereby solving the "problem of delivering to England and France the thousands of warplanes needed for striking Germany." Thousands of planes could be flown to Europe. It was simple as that!

Sole justification for the tide of early optimism was the prompt development of a mass-producible aircraft engine. Late in May 1917, a group of prominent automotive designers locked themselves in a Washington hotel room with a drawing board. After four days they emerged with the assembly sketches for a new engine. Jesse G. Vincent, of the Packard Motor Car Company, and J. G. Hall, of the Hall-Scott Motor Company, codirected the fruitful collaboration. The projected engine was actually an adaptation of one formerly designed by Vincent. As originally planned, it was to be a V-eight unit furnishing three hundred horsepower at 1250 revolutions per minute. Inside of thirty-three days a hand-made test model was ready to undergo trials at Washington. After a prolonged series of modifications, the cylinders were increased in number to twelve, with a 905-cubic-inch piston displacement, which raised the horsepower rating to four hundred. This final version became the celebrated Liberty engine, so named because the first model had been inspected by government officials on Independence Day, 1917. Contracts were awarded in December to six Detroit manufacturers for 22,500 units. At the conclusion of the war, however, few more than five thousand had in fact been delivered.

The small output of planes was similarly disappointing. By the end of 1917, the ballyhooed flood of aircraft expected to stream from American factories had failed to materialize. The only planes being produced in sizable quantity were Curtiss trainers; not a single combat craft had yet been turned out. The harsh realities of building from scratch an air force to fight in Europe were at last being recognized—at no cheap cost to national morale—and the inflated quotas previously adopted were ruefully lowered to more reasonable levels. After consideration of several proposals, a program was approved for 202 squadrons to be at the front by July 1919, if hostilities endured that long. This was a drastic comedown from the original prospectus, which had 263 squadrons slated for combat a whole year sooner.

Since the Liberty engine was too heavy for use on the single-seater pursuit planes so desperately needed by the Air Service, it was deemed expedient to purchase such machines from the French and English. In order to find an aircraft that could be mated with the engine, the Aviation Production Board—an advisory body established to assist the military in aeronautical matters—brought a De Havilland DH-4 light bomber from England to the United States. The plane was fitted with the hastily fabricated twelve-cylinder Liberty and flown on October 29, 1917, and the hybrid design became the only combat plane to enter mass production in this country. After a spate of bewildering hesitations—on one day the Production Board proposed an output of six thousand DH-4's; the next day this was raised to fifteen thousand; six days later it was reduced again to six thousand; after another four days the target figure of fifteen thousand was restored—contracts were rendered to several Detroit firms for 9500 of the machines.

The first American DH-4 to become operational was completed in February 1918, and 529 were delivered to the A.E.F. in France by the end of June. Quentin Roosevelt, son of Teddy Roosevelt and a lieutenant in the 95th Pursuit Squadron until a German pilot shot him down in July, commented on the De Havilland in a letter home:

> I wish some one who did know something about flying at the front would go back [to America], just to talk for a while with the designers and builders of the Liberty motor and plane. It's going to be a long time before the thing gets to the front, and tho' I'm not crazy about the bus I'm flying [a Nieuport 28], I'd be much more comfortable in it than I would in a Liberty if I had to go across the lines. They have no right to send the things over here, tell the people in the states how wonderful they are, and then to expect us over here to work with them when each flight shows some new defect to be remedied. Of course they're all minor defects, but still they've been flying the planes over here for a month and yet she's [sic] not ready for the front yet.

When a formation of these planes crossed the German frontier on the morning of August 2, the Liberty-powered DH-4 became the one and only American-built aircraft to fly over enemy territory in World War I.[2] A thousand DH-4's per month were coming off Detroit assembly lines by October, and Armistice Day found the type equipping five bombing and seven reconnaissance squadrons of the A.E.F. Other American reconnaissance squadrons, eleven of them, were still flying the Salmson 2A2, a rugged French two-seater introduced early in 1918. And the 96th Aero Squadron, a day-bombardment

[2] Wagner: *American Combat Planes.*

unit, the first from America to taste combat, manned the French Breguet 14B2, a plane very similar to the DH-4 with its two open cockpits, a nose squared by a flat radiator for the water-cooled engine, and a pair of wide-spreading, fabric-covered wings held together with four pairs of struts and a network of crisscrossing wires. Of the three types of bombing and observation craft flown by American airmen, the DH-4 was held lowest in esteem, as Quentin Roosevelt implied it would be. The plane was commonly described as a "flaming coffin" because of its supposed readiness to catch fire, although out of the thirty-three American DH-4's lost to enemy action, only eight fell in flames—less than a fourth of them—which was no worse than the average at that time. Its bad reputation may have stemmed from the fact that the DH-4, unlike many other planes then in the air, lacked the protection of self-sealing fuel tanks. The most objectionable fault, however, was the placement of the fuel tank behind the pilot, between his and the observer's cockpits. This made the DH-4 a terrible plane for a pilot to crash because it always came down nose-first, and upon impact the gasoline tank would tear loose from its moorings and smash into the hot engine, cutting the pilot in half and then, as a rule, exploding.

Unless serving in one of the twelve squadrons provided with Liberty DH-4's, the A.E.F. pilot was obliged to do his flying and fighting entirely in airplanes supplied by America's two great allies. After the A.E.F. arrived in France, it trained its fledgling aviators on the Nieuports 17, 21, 23, 24, and 27. Fortunately the A.E.F. never had to utilize these underpowered models in battle. When Campbell and Winslow scored the first American air victories, they used the sturdier Nieuport 28. Four American squadrons flew Nieuports until July, when they were replaced by the famous Spad S-13, which did not shed its wings as readily as its predecessor. Fifteen of the sixteen A.E.F. pursuit squadrons flew Spads in the waning weeks of war.

In addition to these French planes, three single-seater types were obtained from the British. Introduced in July 1917, the redoubtable Sopwith F-1 Camel scored the highest number of enemy planes destroyed of any fighter in the war. Because of the excessive torque of its 130-horsepower Clerget rotary engine, and a low degree of lateral stability, the Camel was treacherous to fly. Two American pursuit squadrons that were often assigned to night patrol were composed of Camel pilots who had survived the training course—many did not with this airplane—and 143 Camels were received after June 1918. The Royal Aircraft Factory's SE-5, a single-bay biplane powered by the 210-horsepower Hispano-Suiza, a most praiseworthy engine, was less dangerous to fly. Thirty-eight of these husky fighters were issued to an A.E.F. unit in August.

And so, despite the ebullient assurances of Washington officialdom, the skies of Europe were never darkened by American airplanes. The "greatest of aerial fleets," foreseen in June 1917, by the New York *Herald,* never arrived "to crush the Teutons." Not a single combat plane of U.S. design went into regular production throughout the duration of the war. Some low-powered single-seaters, such as the Curtiss S-3 and the Orenco C, were built in appreciable numbers, but they were suitable only for advanced training of stateside aviation cadets who had graduated from the Curtiss Jenny. Also, private industry, speculatively and with little real encouragement from the army, did perfect four good combat machines that could have gone into mass production shortly after the November Armistice. These were the Standard E-1, the Thomas-Morse S-4 Scout, the Heinrich Pursuit, and the Packard-LePere Lusac 11 (a large two-seater designed specifically to accommodate the twelve-cylinder Liberty engine).[3] Considering the prewar blight of aeronautical progress in this country, the celerity with which these machines were developed stands as a testimonial to American technology, for each was the equal of the planes then at the front. A late start, however, meant a late attainment of goals. No sooner were twenty-five Packard-LePeres placed on government order than the war ended.

Attempts to duplicate foreign-designed fighters failed. A sample Spad was received from France in September 1917, and a contract for three thousand copies was awarded to the Curtiss Aeroplane Company. The contract was canceled in the subsequent month, when the airframe was discovered to be inadequate for the massive Liberty engine then being planned for army standardization. Several months were wasted searching for a Liberty-powered pursuit plane, but the engine was much too bulky for use on anything smaller than the De Havilland DH-4, a light bomber more than a third again the size of a compact fighter-machine. In April 1918, Curtiss was asked a second time to build fighters—a thousand facsimiles of the British SE-5. Only one Curtiss SE-5 reached completion. Delivered in August, it had a 180-horsepower Wright-Hispano engine but was on that account obsolete, since the Royal Aircraft Factory SE-5 then operational at the front had 210 horsepower.

Part of this failure to produce a decent fighter plane in the United States was due to indecision about which foreign type to manufacture—indecision caused in some measure by the intense rivalry of the Allied representatives on behalf of their respective machines. One day at the Dayton-Wright field in Ohio, for example, while a British general was showing off an SE-5, reciting its merits, a captain of the French mission sauntered up. "Have you gentlemen," he inquired, "heard of that prehistoric bird, the pterodactyl?" Casting a baleful look at the squarish SE-5, the Frenchman's insinuation was obvious. His own Spad was then rolled out to display its more graceful lines.[4]

The future fighter pilots of the A.E.F. began arriving in Europe in the summer of 1917 for flying instruction, particularly in the French schools at

[3] Two of these machines did enter mass production. Of 460 Standard E-1's ordered, 130 were built, 98 of which were delivered in November 1918. Nearly 600 Thomas Morse Scouts were built by the end of 1918 and used as trainers.

[4] The author is indebted to Ray Wagner's *American Combat Planes* for much of the material appearing between this and the earlier citation.

Tours and Clermont-Ferrand. At Issoudun the construction of a large American training center got underway. A shortage of men and material, together with a good deal of bureaucratic bungling, delayed the opening of the center at Issoudun until late in October. The newly established site was a sea of mud and makeshift barracks, and it was months before training was in full swing. An additional handicap was the shipping priority given to infantry troops, preventing practically any Air Service personnel from arriving in Europe between December 1917, and July 1918. Facilities in England and Italy were also recruited in this hurried attempt at training flyers. Approximately a third of the American pilots winging about Europe's embattled firmament at the close of the war were alumni of the British School of Military Aeronautics at Oxford. More than four hundred had received their brevets at a school in Foggia, Italy. At the Armistice, 1647 aviators and 851 observers had been taught the lessons of martial flying by experienced Allied pilots in the overseas training centers.

It was easy to prate about "turning the tide of victory," but something else again to produce qualified airmen to do the job. Seven demoralizing months passed between September 1917, when the first A.E.F. squadron commenced training, and the following March, when the outfit flew off on its initial combat assignment, an uneventful patrol over the German trenches. The 1st Aero Squadron, under Major Ralph Royce, was followed in November by other squadrons, including the 88th, 90th, 93rd, 94th, 95th and 96th. At Tours and Clermont-Ferrand, Amanty and Epiez, and subsequently at Colomby, these units practiced in antiquated aircraft until they could be furnished with the latest combat machines and groomed by veteran French aviators for action at the front.

Many young Americans had early cast their lot with the Allies, some for the sheer sake of adventure, but many for idealistic reasons. Most celebrated of these were the members of the Lafayette Escadrille, organized in March 1916, and baptized at Verdun. They flew the French cockade into the fray for nearly two years and afterward formed the nucleus of the 103rd Pursuit Squadron, the first American contingent to confront the enemy in the air. Moving to the front in February 1918, the 103rd continued fighting as an adjunct of the French army until the end of June and was then transferred to American control. In like manner, all American units were attached to Allied forces on a sort of apprenticeship basis during the spring and early summer of 1918. Two British-trained squadrons—the 17th and 148th—flew Sopwith Camels with the Royal Air Force in the field until November 1, when, with only ten days of war left, they were ordered to join the American Second Army. The first detachment of eighteen bomber pilots, commanded by Captain Fiorello La Guardia (destined later for a colorful career in New York politics), participated in sixty-five bombing missions in the Italian theater from June 20 to November 2.

In France, the quiet Toul sector afforded an opportunity for many neophyte flyers to learn the techniques of aerial warfare. By mid-March the 94th and 95th Pursuit Squadrons had begun reconnoitering enemy lines; on April 12 a formation of the 1st Squadron was set upon by hostile aircraft during a scouting patrol. Two days later, over the Toul airdrome, Lieutenants Campbell and Winslow won their twin victory. And on June 12, the 96th Squadron bowed into the war, five of its planes dropping eighty bombs with observed success on a railroad junction near Metz.

The fledgling eagles from across the ocean had their first taste of real warfare in July and August, when they were called upon to help withstand Germany's desperate, last-ditch thrusts along the Marne and Vesle. They took part in operations culminating in the momentous Château-Thierry counter-offensive. Here they found themselves caught up in a cloud-girt Armageddon, turning back wave after wave of enemy aircraft, flying around the clock in slaughterous melees of darting, looping, diving, twisting planes and barking machine guns. Through it all, the American squadrons fought under the tactical control of the British and French armies. By the middle of August the Germans had completed their disastrous retreat from the Champagne bulge and a temporary lull mercifully settled upon no-man's-land.

Readied now by this background of training and action, the air arm of the A.E.F. was considered capable of managing its own affairs in the bitter contest for control of the sky. Accordingly, when General Pershing organized the American First Army as a combat unit on August 10, the Allies relinquished command of sixteen A.E.F. squadrons to Lieutenant Colonel William (Billy) Mitchell, Pershing's tactical air chief. Ten more squadrons joined this front-line aggregation in time for the First Army's first big mission, slicing off an enemy salient east of Verdun. This was followed by the climactic offensives of Saint-Mihiel and the Meuse-Argonne which heralded the final collapse of the German army and the Armistice of November 11.

The soldier-pilots of the A.E.F., upon venturing into the skies of Europe, found themselves embroiled in an air war that had reached a furious crescendo. They acquitted themselves heroically in their French-built Nieuports and Spads, blazing away with their Vickers and Lewis guns, and they wondered how—during those many months that war had raged in Europe—their own country could have been so blind to the imperative need for air strength. Still in their teens and early twenties, most of them, they could remember a time not so long ago when it had seemed the United States would be the country to develop the world's first air weapon.

CHAPTER II

·🙟 *Evolution of a Weapon* 🙝·

O N DECEMBER 23, 1907, four years almost to the day after Orville Wright flew above Kitty Hawk in the first successful heavier-than-air flying machine, the United States Signal Corps disclosed its intention to purchase an airplane. An advertisement for bids, issued by the War Department, specified that an acceptable machine would have to be capable of carrying two men on a sustained flight of sixty minutes. Its range had to be at least 125 miles, and an average speed of forty miles per hour over a ten-mile course had to be attained. The ability to "steer in all directions without difficulty" was also prescribed. Lastly, the plane had to be constructed in such a way that it could be taken apart for transportation by truck and easily reassembled.

That same year, on August 1, the chief signal officer, Brigadier General James Allen, set up an Aeronautical Division within the Signal Corps. Placed under the command of Captain Charles DeForest Chandler, the division was charged with the responsibility for "military ballooning, air machines, and all kindred subjects."

These were extremely farsighted actions at a time when the airplane was regarded by most as merely a plaything for adventurous sportsmen and carnival daredevils. Indeed, a large segment of the population did not yet believe the Wright brothers had really flown a heavier-than-air machine at Kitty Hawk or anywhere else. From the day the advertisement for bids appeared, the Signal Corps became the butt of journalistic abuse, not because it had been slow about interesting itself in the airplane, but because it had done so at all. The New York *Globe,* in an editorial typical of many, had this to say:

> One might be inclined to assume from the following announcement, "the United States army is asking for bids for a military

airship," that the era of practical human flight had arrived, or that the government had seriously taken up the problem of developing this means of travel. A very brief examination of the conditions imposed . . . suffices, however, to prove this assumption a delusion. A machine such as is described in the Signal Corps specifications would record the solution of all the difficulties in the way of the heavier-than-air airship, and, in fact, finally give mankind almost as complete control of the air as it now has of the land and water. . . .

Nothing in any way approaching such a machine has ever been constructed.

The *Globe* brushed aside the claims of Wilbur and Orville Wright as an unconfirmed rumor.

Even the authoritative *American Magazine of Aeronautics,* in its edition of January 1908, castigated the Signal Corps for its visionary scheme. "There is not a known flying machine in the world," crowed the editor, "which could fulfill these specifications at the present moment. . . . Perhaps the Signal Corps has been too much influenced by the 'hot air' of theorizers, in which aeronautics unfortunately abounds."

Strictly speaking, the press was correct. Neither the Wrights nor any of the pioneer aviators in Europe had yet built a machine able to answer the requirements set forth by the Signal Corps. But two years earlier, in 1905, at Huffman's pasture on the outskirts of their native Dayton, Ohio, the Wright brothers had made more than forty flights in an improved model of their original biplane; with a few additional modifications this machine stood a good chance of satisfying army specifications. None but the Dayton inventors themselves seemed aware of this fact. The journalistic fraternity, in keeping with a long-standing prejudice against the Wrights, had evinced virtually no curiosity about their endeavors at Huffman's pasture and now gave no credence to their assertions of mastery of the air. On the grounds of purblind obstinacy, then, and opinionated ignorance, the press stood guilty.

In response to its advertisement, the War Department, to everyone's amazement, received forty-one bids. Most were immediately recognizable as the brainstorms of cranks and crackpots; all but three were rejected because the bidders did not put up a required 10 percent of the proposed cost of the airplane as a sign of good faith and serious intent. Two others besides the Wrights did post the necessary bond. A Chicago inventor, J. F. Scott, entered a bid of $1,000 and promised delivery in 185 days. Another was August M. Herring, a well-known experimenter who promised to deliver a plane within 180 days at a cost of $20,000 to the government. The Wrights' bid was $25,000, with delivery in two hundred days.

The War Department had anticipated only a single bid, that of the Wrights. It was a logical expectation, since no one else in America was known to have succeeded in flying a self-propelled heavier-than-air machine. Receipt of the two unforeseen bids created a problem. Chances were that neither Scott nor Herring had anything practical to offer, yet the War Department was constrained by law to accept the lowest bid and let the winner show what his machine would do. Undoubtedly, if it got off the ground at all, it would fail dismally to meet performance specifications, and a debacle at this delicate juncture would furnish an already vociferous chorus of skeptics with additional arguments against the feasibility of military aviation. Faced with this dilemma, General Allen, accompanied by Captain Chandler, called upon the Secretary of War, William Howard Taft. The latter proposed a gamble. He suggested that all proper bids be accepted, pointing out that the Wrights alone were likely to fulfill the requirements. The only difficulty now was that even if no money would ever be paid to Scott or Herring, it would be illegal to accept their bids unless sufficient capital was on hand to pay for whatever was ordered. The remote eventuality that three planes would pass the test had to be covered. Taft had a solution to this problem as well. He knew that President Theodore Roosevelt was a staunch proponent of aeronautical development; with a contingency fund at his beck, the President might agree to guarantee payment to all successful bidders. In a hastily arranged conference at the White House, Roosevelt endorsed the scheme. Legal technicalities thus settled, the War Department announced it would buy planes from each of the three bidders if they satisfied the prescribed flight requirements.

Scott thereupon removed himself from the competition by asking the government to return his 10 percent deposit. Though the money was forfeit, the War Department promptly complied with the request in order to save the trouble and possible embarrassment of testing an airplane that was nearly certain to be a total disappointment.

Herring did not give up so handily. A rather dubious character, he had a reputation for exaggerating the credit owing him for his share in the experiments of others, most notably those of Octave Chanute, whom he had assisted in building and flying gliders in the late 1890s. Herring further insisted that he had flown an airplane, powered by compressed air, some five years prior to the Wrights' initial triumph at Kitty Hawk. He had earned the enmity of the Wright brothers by afterward contesting several of their patent claims, and by threatening them with costly litigation unless they gave him a one-third interest in their invention. That had been in 1904. Now his plan was to obtain a contract from the War Department by virtue of his lower price and then to sublet it to the Wrights for a liberal commission. Considering his earlier extortion attempt against the Wrights, his effrontery was colossal when he went to Dayton and explained his preposterous proposition. The brothers, of course, were not fooled. "We refused to help him out in that matter," Orville commented in later years, "and that is the reason he was compelled to make the ridiculous 'technical delivery' of his machine." The reference was to Herring's attempt to sell the Signal Corps a suitcase containing a dismantled engine and an odd assortment of wooden spars and metal fittings, avowing them to be parts of an airplane then nearing completion in his workshop.

The Wrights' bid was accepted on February 8, 1908. The contract, signed two days later, provided that 10 percent of the $25,000 purchase price would be deducted for each mile per hour the machine fell short of the forty-mile-per-hour goal. If it flew only thirty-nine miles per hour, for instance, the Wrights could be penalized $2,500; if only thirty-eight miles per hour, another $2,500 would be subtracted from the purchase price, and so on. Should the plane not travel a minimum of thirty-six miles per hour, then the government had the option of rejecting it altogether.

The contract likewise enjoined the government to pay a 10 percent bonus for each mile per hour the plane attained above the stipulated speed. These reduced or additional payments were to be computed on the basis of full miles, not fractional miles, and this clause of the agreement was weighted in favor of the buyer. The slightest fraction less than a full mile counted against the plane's performance, whereas a fraction more than a full mile did not count to its credit. Hence, if the plane went 40.99 miles per hour, the Wrights would not be paid for more than forty; but if the plane's speed was 39.99 miles per hour, they would be docked $2,500 for a full mile.

Although they had done no flying since October 1905, the Wrights had accomplished much toward improving their machine. During all their early experiments they had continued to ride lying prone upon the lower wing and caged in by struts and wires. Sprawling out like that and directing the plane partly by shifting the hips from side to side may have been good enough in the beginning stages of aviation, but the Wrights knew that a flying machine would have no practical value until the pilot could sit upright and manipulate the controls with his hands and feet, as in an automobile. It was not easy to lie flat with your head raised for an hour at a time to see ahead. "I used to think," Orville recollected in 1917, "the back of my neck would break if I endured one more turn around the field." The brothers therefore had devised a different arrangement of the controls, for use in a sitting position. Over the leading edge of the bottom wing they installed two seats, one for the pilot and the other for a passenger. They had also perfected a new engine with vertical instead of horizontal cylinders. Capable of producing thirty-five horse-power steadily, the improved engine made possible flights of greater duration and reduced the danger of failure of the motive power.

The Wrights built two identical airplanes and tested them at Kitty Hawk. One was to be taken by Orville to Fort Myer, Virginia, there to be demonstrated before War Department officials. The other machine was to go with Wilbur to France, where a syndicate had been formed to build Wright airplanes and sell them to European governments. Wilbur, before his departure, decided to try the plane's ability to carry two men. Charles W. Furnas, a mechanic in the brothers' employ, sat beside him as they circled above the beach dunes on May 14, 1908, to win distinction as history's first airplane passenger.

Orville arrived at Fort Myer in the third week of August. On the drill field he assembled his machine, which had been christened the Wright Model A Flyer. September 3 was selected as the date for initiating his practice flights. The affair was no secret, and Orville was two weeks on the ground preparing for the trials, but the newspapers ignored his presence. Though surrounded by well-wishers and admirers at the Cosmos Club, where he resided in nearby Washington, Orville was disheartened by the lack of interest he encountered. Few people had ever seen an airplane take off, fly through the air, and land; the prospect of witnessing such a miracle attracted scarcely a hundred spectators to Fort Myer on the day of Orville's first ascent. But, those who did watch were visibly overwhelmed by the spectacle. Young Theodore Roosevelt, Jr., said in describing the event: "When the plane first rose, the crowd's gasp of astonishment was not alone at the wonder of it, but because it was so unexpected. The sound from the crowd . . . was a sound of complete surprise."

When Orville landed, three reporters rushed out to him. One, by his own story, had tears streaming down his cheeks. The sight of man invading the air on wings of his own building had touched them all. But their editors had seen nothing, and the published accounts were as indifferent as they were concise. The best notice appeared in the New York *World*—on page five. Nevertheless, several thousand onlookers thronged the field for the next day of practice flights.

Orville left the Cosmos Club every morning before dawn and rode the streetcar to Fort Myer. With each flight he increased the plane's altitude and range. Then, on September 9, he demonstrated the full capabilities of the Wright Flyer. Dressed in a gray business suit, wearing his usual starched white collar, he took off shortly after daybreak. The launching device was similar to that used at Huffman's pasture. The skids of the machine rested on a trolley to be driven along a sixty-foot monorail. A stout cable connected the trolley to a one-ton weight suspended atop a tall tripod behind the track. Upon being released, the falling weight propelled the trolley along the rail, catapulting the plane into the air. Orville circled the parade ground fifty-seven times in as many minutes.

Presumably the press was informed of this remarkable feat, for reporters flocked to the scene in time to see a second flight that lasted more than an hour. Since it was an exceptionally beautiful day for flying, Orville took his friend, Lieutenant Frank P. Lahm, a Signal Corps balloonist, for a six-minute aerial tour of the fort. Never before had an officer of any army flown in a heavier-than-air machine.

On the following day Orville broke his previous endurance record, staying airborne for one hour, ten minutes, and twenty-five seconds. On September 12, Major George Squier, the man who was to play so prominent a role in army aeronautics during the war years, made his first flight as a passenger. Squier was treated to a ride nine minutes long. Orville immediately went up again and remained aloft for one hour and fifteen minutes, reaching an estimated height of three hundred feet.

News of the flight trials had still not been featured on the front page of a single newspaper. Not until September 17, when Orville met disaster, did the events at Fort Myer reach the headlines. On that day Lieutenant Thomas E. Selfridge had been assigned at his own request to go up as a passenger. The plane was at an altitude of 125 feet, banking around the northeast corner of the field, when the starboard propeller cracked. It flattened, losing its thrust. The disparity in pitch between the two airscrews caused a terrific vibration in the eight hundred pounds of wire, cloth, spruce, glue, and metal that comprised the Wright Flyer. Orville tried an emergency landing, but the rudder collapsed. The plane, from fifty feet off the ground, crashed. Selfridge died a few hours later of head injuries, gaining a tragic place in aviation annals as the first victim of a fatal airplane accident. Orville suffered a fractured left thigh, four broken ribs, and severe shock. The mishap was given page-one. coverage in newspapers everywhere. But the press, in recounting the circumstances of the accident, could not omit details of the foregoing series of successful flights, and millions of people now learned for the first time that man had actually conquered the air.

The stunning achievements of the Wright airplane, so far as the public cared, were decidedly more significant than the smash-up at Fort Myer. Others before Selfridge, after all, had hurtled to destruction while trying to emulate the birds, if not in mechanical aircraft, then in balloons, dirigibles, and gliders. Powered flights in a controllable machine had become a reality, and that was the important revelation.

Orville did not sufficiently recover from his injuries to resume the Signal Corps trials until June 28, 1909, when he commenced another series of preliminary flights. Washington officialdom was well represented this time. Observers from every department of the government swarmed to the army base to watch the demonstrations. So did the correspondents of every major newspaper, finally awakened to the validity of the Wrights' claims and the wondrous things their invention portended.

Also present, though he did no flying himself, was Wilbur Wright, whose recently concluded exhibitions in France had thrilled the entire European continent. Huge crowds had poured into the village of Le Mans to see Wilbur show off the practicability of the airplane. His endurance, his altitude, his flawless control, and easy maneuvers electrified and delighted the spectators. Beating the French records for duration, distance, and elevation, he won valuable awards. Once he rose to a height of 380 feet, a spine-chilling spectacle to those who watched from below. On September 21, 1908, three days after hearing of his brother's misfortune at Fort Myer, Wilbur flew forty-two miles in an hour and thirty minutes; on October 11, he carried a pas-

senger for an hour and ten minutes. As a grand finale, on the last day of the
year, he traveled seventy-seven miles in two hours and twenty minutes to
collect the coveted Michelin prize of twenty thousand francs, awarded for the
longest distance flown during the year. It was an auspicious close to the most
progressive and eventful year in aviation—the first year of exhibition flying,
the inaugural year of a science pregnant with mixed blessings and calamities.

In mid-January 1909, Wilbur went to Pau in the south of France to continue his flights. Here he was joined by Orville, still recuperating from his
accident, and their sister Katherine, dragooned into service as a much-needed
social secretary. Unlike Orville in America, Wilbur was lionized by the press
in Europe. In a dozen diverse languages the newspapers reported his every
action and utterance, no matter how trivial. A hit song—"Il Vole"—was
written in his honor and sung whenever he made an appearance. Postcards
depicting him and his "clipper of the clouds" were printed by the tens of
thousands. King Edward VII of England, Dowager Queen Margherita of
Italy, and Spain's King Alfonso XIII journeyed to the plains at Pont Long,
six miles from Pau, to view Wilbur and his marvelous machine. The royal
personages, too enthralled to heed the niceties of protocol, deserted the comfort of their carriages to walk out upon the field, shake the American aviator's
hand, and inspect the wide-winged biplane they had just seen coursing through
the air. Prince Wilhelm of Germany, the Kaiser's eldest son, insisted that he
be given a ride, after which he rewarded Wilbur with an autographed picture
of his father. European enthusiasm for the Wrights, indeed European interest in solving the mysteries of dynamic flight—as contrasted with apathy and
doubt on the western side of the Atlantic—were the fundamental reasons why
the airplane was to be developed more rapidly abroad than in the United
States, its birthplace. Even as Orville prepared to finish the Signal Corps
trials at Fort Myer that summer, two companies in Europe were building
Wright flying machines under contract to various governments and commercial concerns.

Fulfilling the War Department requirements on July 27, Orville exceeded
the record for a two-man flight. With Lieutenant Lahm again his passenger,
his elapsed time in the air was clocked at one hour, twelve minutes, and forty
seconds. On a cross-country flight three days later, Orville made a speed run
with Lieutenant Benjamin D. Foulois aboard, averaging 42.5 miles per hour
over the ten-mile route. The Signal Corps took delivery of the Wright Flyer
on August 2, 1909. Having bettered the prescribed speed by two full miles
an hour, the Wrights were paid a $5,000 bonus.

Intended purely for scouting and communications work, the Wright Flyer
was the first military airplane to be put into practical service by any government. It was used that October at the newly established army airfield at
College Park, Maryland, to teach two Signal Corps officers to fly. Wilbur
Wright was their instructor.

Selected to be Army aviator number-one was Lieutenant Frederick E.

Humphreys. The toss of a coin gave him precedence over Lieutenant Lahm, although Lahm was already an experienced aeronaut in lighter-than-air craft and had twice flown as an airplane passenger. Inasmuch as they had to fly "by the seat of their pants"—relying on wits alone to navigate the machine —the aptitude of both men was rather exceptional. The plane had no instruments of any sort, save a cloth strip that dangled from the landing skid in front of the pilot. When the cloth blew out straight, the pilot could relax; when it trailed at an angle he knew the plane was off balance. With only their senses and this piece of cloth to guide them, neither Humphreys nor Lahm needed more than a half day's training before soloing.

Wilbur, in the months between October 1909, and April 1911, taught four more army officers to fly. They were Lieutenants Foulois, T. DeWitt Milling, Henry (Hap) Arnold, and Captain Chandler, the commander of the Aeronautical Division. A few months prior to his untimely death in May 1912, when he succumbed to typhoid fever, Wilbur gave Lieutenant George C. Sweet the tutoring he required to qualify as the navy's first pilot. Each of these early airmen, along with Humphreys and Lahm, was destined in oncoming decades to join the immortal names in American military aviation.

Another man, Glenn Hammond Curtiss, had meanwhile risen to challenge the preeminence of the Wright brothers. Curtiss was no stranger to the military. In 1905, this mechanical wizard installed a light, air-cooled engine of his own design in a semi-rigid airship constructed by the famed balloonist, Thomas Scott Baldwin. Subsequently purchased by the Signal Corps, it was among the first military aerostats to utilize an internal-combustion engine to overcome the vagaries of the wind. With this success under his belt, Curtiss, already a renowned motorcycle racer, concentrated his entire genius on aeronautics. Alexander Graham Bell asked him to join the Aerial Experiment Association, which Bell was at the time organizing. With $25,000 capital donated by Mrs. Bell, the A.E.A. began operations at Curtiss' hometown of Hammondsport, New York. Four aircraft were built by the small group of experimenters. The third, Curtiss' *June Bug*—whimsically named for the month of its completion—was the most airworthy of the lot, winning in 1908 a trophy from *Scientific American* magazine. This was the first aviation prize to be awarded in the United States; its presentation to Curtiss galled the Wrights, who accused their rival, with some justification, of infringing upon their patents.

After the A.E.A. was dissolved, Curtiss formed a short-lived partnership with August Herring, the Wrights' old adversary. The Herring-Curtiss Company produced the *Golden Flyer,* which in August 1909, won the first international air race at Rheims, France. Curtiss and Herring, however, terminated their relationship right after this victory, and Curtiss took over the assets of the firm. With these he formed the Curtiss Aeroplane Company early in 1910. Shortly afterward, in August, an unprecedented experiment—one that presaged the pernicious role of the airplane in warfare—was thought up by Curtiss.

The scene that summer day was an air show at the Sheepshead Bay race track on Long Island. All afternoon the tense crowd had been watching the antics of flimsily constructed flying machines. The spectators had been promised an act never before attempted, and they waited impatiently as a Curtiss-employed exhibition flyer named Charles Willard climbed into a fragile biplane. As Willard warmed the plane's engine an army officer walked out and strapped himself to the passenger's seat. The soldier was Lieutenant Jacob E. Fickel, an expert marksman. He carried with him a regulation .30-caliber Springfield infantry rifle. His intention was to fire the rifle from the machine in flight. No weapon of any description had ever previously been fired from aboard an airplane.

With Willard at the controls and Fickel clutching the rifle with one hand and a wing strut with the other, the plane took off. After gaining an altitude of three hundred feet, it circled the target that had been erected in the center-field of the race track. Four times, Fickel aimed and squeezed the trigger. Two of the four shots were bullseyes; the other two, near misses. The audience was thrilled. Perhaps there were some in the grandstand, too, who sensed the beginning of things to come.

In those days, simply to keep a machine airborne was a magnificent feat. To possess as well the means for bringing an enemy to earth goaded the imagination, and the press made the most of it. Troops were pictured being transported in giant planes and gliders; noiseless, invisible wars were envisioned by the use of smokeless power and rifle-muffling devices. The impact on the public was immediate and profound, yet the military remained impassive and incredulous as ever. The general staff published a mathematical equation to show that nothing more deadly than a rifle could safely be fired from an airplane, one shot at a time, and under certain conditions only, lest the redundant recoil of a rapid succession of shots upset the plane. And in no circumstance, said the staff, could any great weight—such as a bomb—be dropped in flight, since its sudden release would cause the plane to fall out of control. While both these hypotheses were to be confuted in the months that followed, the intransigence of army higher-ups was not diminished. Because of the obstinancy and unyielding conservatism of old-line soldiers ensconced in musty offices, military aviation remained a neglected stepchild through all the years leading up to American intervention in World War I. Army aeronautics, in fact, might have met total extinction at this infant stage of development, were it not for the relentless determination of a small clique of air-minded officers.

Accordingly, when Lieutenant Foulois flew the Signal Corps' lone airplane in winter exercises at Fort Sam Houston, Texas, in 1910, he did so at his own insistence—and largely at his own expense. At the same time Foulois was dipping into his pocket to help finance flight operations, Brigadier General Allen, in his capacity as chief signal officer, was petitioning Congress for money enough to procure twenty additional aircraft. Allen, since 1908, had annually requested an aviation fund of $250,000. His ultimate objective was to assign an aero company to every Signal Corps battalion in a field army. Had he received energetic support from the general staff in this, Allen might have realized his ambition in 1911. Though Congress did at last pass an appropriation for army aviation, it came to only $125,000, half the amount asked by the Signal Corps chief.

By this time the improved Wright Model B biplane, with wheels affixed to the landing skids, and with the empennage moved from front to rear, had been introduced. Such a plane had recently completed the initial crossing of the continent by air, negotiating the distance from New York to California in forty-nine days with protracted delays at Dayton, Chicago, Kansas City, Dallas, and Phoenix. The civilian pilot, Cal P. Rodgers, had been sponsored by a soft-drink concern, and his plane was named after a grape-flavored beverage—*Vin Fizz*. The resulting publicity sold not only more soda pop but more Wright flying machines as well. The Signal Corps, in the spring of 1911, bought four of them; a month later, two Curtiss machines were also acquired.

That October a Wright Model B was flown at College Park to test a bomb-sight devised by Lieutenant Riley B. Scott of the Coast Artillery. Earlier in the year a bombsight invented by another artilleryman, Lieutenant Myron Crissy, had failed to impress the army in an unofficial tryout at Tanforan race track, San Francisco. Scott's apparatus promised better results and, at the behest of General Allen, the War Department reluctantly agreed to a trial. The plane was piloted by Lieutenant Milling. On each pass over the 4-by-5-foot target, Scott let go a single eighteen-pound bomb from a canvas sling under his seat. From an approximate altitude of four hundred feet he plunked every projectile within ten feet of the mark. Those who witnessed this extraordinary exhibition knew immediately the ominous implications of Scott's success as an aerial bombadier; before their eyes, as all but the most unimaginative could perceive, the future pattern of war in the air had taken further shape. Scott had demonstrated the inevitability of this mode of warfare. This glaring fact did not escape the press or the more enlightened citizens of the nation. But once again the feeble-visioned administrators of the army seemed oblivious to reality. To proceed with more trials, it was reckoned, would be too costly; for that reason, all experiments involving aerial bombardment were to be abandoned.

Lieutenant Scott, too much the officer-gentleman to divulge his low opinion of desk-soldier mentality, resigned his commission and went overseas with his invention. On January 11, 1912, in France, he won the $5,000 Michelin prize for bomb-dropping accuracy, competing against highly reputed European aviators, including several from Italy who, three months before in Tripoli, had dropped live bombs on the Turkish infantry. The Italians, in their 1911 campaign against the Turks in North Africa, were the first to drop explosives on an enemy from the sky.

Soon after rejecting the Scott bombsight, the general staff, with War Department agreement, made one of the most stupid decisions to be found in military history. In a candid statement to the press, this august agency revealed that the further development of aircraft armament no longer interested the army in the least degree. All projected plans for transforming the airplane into an offensive combat vehicle were to cease immediately. "The continuance of such schemes," asserted an anonymous army spokesman, "can serve no practical purpose whatever. Any dream of aerial conflict is merely the product of a fertile imagination, a malady often encountered in younger men with insufficient service to recognize certain things as manifestly absurd."

Afterward, the general staff held tenaciously to its dogma. From 1912 right up to the nation's entanglement in war, the only experiments to merit official approval were based on the assumption that aircraft were useful strictly as mobile observation platforms. This conviction emphasized the need for a practical system of air-to-ground communication and led to a precocious experiment with radio. A wireless transmitter designed by Lieutenant Foulois for use on a Wright Model B was tested in January 1912, by the Aeronautical Division of the Signal Corps at its temporary winter headquarters near Augusta, Georgia. Unhappily, the transmitter proved too burdensome for the frail airplane. The added weight so grievously impaired the plane's flight performance that the pilot, in order to avert crashing, was forced to land before a single word could be tapped out on the transmitter key.

The army, after that, remained somewhat dilatory about accepting wireless telegraphy as the best method of air-to-ground communication. In the following months efforts were made at Fort Riley, Kansas, to establish a technique for directing artillery fire from an airplane. Most of the time was devoted to seeking a substitute for radio. It was thought impossible to devise a light enough transmitter, so two alternatives were tried. The first consisted simply of penciled notes dropped by the aerial observer to the battery command post. Though admirably uncomplicated, this procedure consumed too many precious minutes. By the time the cannoneers could effect the indicated corrections between salvos, an enemy could leisurely evacuate the positions being shelled. The next step, logically, would have been signal lights which could be flashed from the plane and instantly comprehended on the ground. When the Fort Riley aviators advocated such a system, they were aghast to learn that smoke-telegraphy had already been scheduled for trials. The airmen barely took it seriously, but the artillery officers in charge of the experiment considered the sending of smoke signals a "clever idea." The aerial observer, by working a lever alongside his seat, could release dense chemical smoke in a trail of dots and dashes behind the aircraft. While the message could be deciphered from the ground easily enough, the process wasted nearly as much time as did the note dropping.

Before the practicality of signaling by semaphore lights could be fairly assessed, news of the navy's success with airborne radio reached Fort Riley. A wireless message, on July 26, 1912, was sent from a Curtiss hydroplane to the torpedo boat *Stringham,* anchored off Annapolis, Maryland, in the Severn River. The plane was a mile from the surface vessel when the transmission was accomplished. Tapped out in Morse code by Ensign Charles H. Maddox, who had designed the remarkably compact radio set, the message said: "We are off the water, going full speed on course for [the] Naval Academy."

The timely introduction of a more efficient airplane, the Wright Model C Scout, together with some minor refinements in Lieutenant Foulois' original transmitter, afforded the Signal corps its initial mastery of air-to-ground radio. The Wright Model C had been designed to carry a greater payload, a total of 450 pounds, allowing for a two-man crew with camera and radio gear. The Aeronautical Division purchased seven of these airplanes, and two were promptly shipped to Fort Riley. The Field Artillery Board, after watching the radio-equipped aircraft fulfill expectations in November, deduced that howitzer fire could be regulated by flying observers, and that radio was indeed the most useful medium of communication. Artillery spotting thereafter became a routine duty of the army aviator.

At the same time, enthusiasm for turning the flying machine into a fighting machine had not diminished in the Aeronautical Division. Official sanction for this venture was still being withheld by general staff traditionalists, and Captain Chandler, the division's commander, did not ask for permission when he decided to demonstrate the potential efficacy of the airplane as a winged gun-carriage. Chandler succeeded on June 7, 1912, firing a fully automatic weapon from the passenger seat of a Wright Model B—an exploit often contemplated but never previously attempted. The site of the demonstration was the College Park airfield, where Chandler was conveniently in charge of flight operations. To circumvent any cease-and-desist order from the general staff, he scheduled the gunnery exhibition as though it were to be an ordinary training task. Since a regulation could not be found that specifically forbade carrying a machine gun aboard an airplane, Chandler felt he was technically within his rights. General Allen, the chief signal officer, consulted by Chandler to help interpret the regulations, tacitly approved of the undertaking by not asking pointed questions. Word of the test evidently leaked out, however, inasmuch as several uninvited general staff members showed up, along with a group of curious newspapermen on the sidelines.

Chandler's plane was armed with an air-cooled machine gun that had just been invented by the well-known ordnance expert, Colonel Isaac Newton Lewis. The gun had no sights yet, nor was there any provision for securing it to the fuselage of the plane. Its hooded muzzle rested on the crossbar on which Chandler and his pilot, Lieutenant Milling, rested their feet. The target consisted of a piece of cheesecloth, six by seven feet in size, spread out on the grass. Colonel Lewis calculated that the plane would travel over the length of the target in one-tenth of a second. Milling made three approaches at an altitude of 250 feet, with Chandler firing a short burst each time. Later examination showed five hits on the target and a tight grouping of bullet craters immediately in front of it. Chandler, though, could not see where his shots were striking and, while circling above some adjacent fishponds, he fired the remainder of the bullets into the water to judge their spacing by the splashes. This unexpected shooting caused Colonel Lewis much anguish. Thinking Chandler had discharged the weapon by mistake, he frantically herded the ground observers into a nearby hangar to take cover.

When repercussions from the higher command failed to materialize by next morning, another test was carried out. This time they used a target six feet long and eighteen inches wide. Milling took the plane up to 550 feet and there leveled off for his first pass over the cheesecloth strip. Chandler put fourteen of forty-four bullets into the target, and all hit close by.

The significance of Chandler's strafing exhibition gave rise to another epidemic of journalistic speculations concerning the future of military aviation. Most of the stories were garnished with a photograph of the flyers poised in their seats for the take-off, with the Lewis gun sitting between Chandler's feet. A typical caption posed the central question: "Tomorrow's Warriors?" The writer supplied the answer in his text with an accurate, if richly embroidered, description of aviators entangled in battles to the death, suggesting that such battles would be technologically possible "as early as 1925." But Chandler's demonstration elicited only the expected negative response from the general staff. In interviews the senior officers clearly stated that airplanes were suitable for reconnaissance and maybe for artillery observation (the Fort Riley experiments were then in progress), but certainly not for doing combat against an opposing army. Nothing had changed. Nothing would, for that matter, or could happen in the prewar interlude to alter the *idée fixe* of the old guard. Five years later, in 1917, when the United States went to war, the Air Service was still regarded merely as "the eyes of the army," in spite of overwhelming testimony from European battle zones that a smashing blow could be let loose from the air, a strategic as well as a tactical punch. So Uncle Sam meandered into the Great War with one arm tied behind his back.

Like so many American inventors before him, Colonel Lewis left for Europe. The War Department had no interest in his machine gun. In 1913, he founded the Armes Automatique Lewis Company at Liège, Belgium. The gun he had invented and that had been tested by Captain Chandler was a novel departure in automatic weaponry. Since it was air-cooled it thereby eliminated the bulky water jacket of conventional machine guns, and was marvelously light-weight. It was fed by detachable ammunition drums, which were easy to handle and protected the cartridges from dirt and oil. Besides qualifying as an excellent infantry weapon, the Lewis gun—though its invention was premature by three years—was peculiarly well suited for aerial use. The cataclysmic war in which it was to play so significant a role lay just beyond the horizon, yet no military man of stature, in Europe as well as the United States, seemed to anticipate the day when machine guns would be wed to airplanes to form lethal instruments of destruction. For centuries wars had been waged on the land and the sea—only lunatics and hyperbolic journalists contended that the heavens, too, would soon become a field of battle.

CHAPTER III

·◦❦ *Prelude in Europe* ❧◦·

MAN'S AGE-OLD DREAM of being borne aloft on wings was almost made a reality by several different aeronautical experimenters in the decades before the Wright brothers' success. Prominent among those who strove to be the first to thread the clouds in a heavier-than-air machine was the Frenchman, Clement Ader. Many in France are convinced that Ader actually did achieve flight in his grotesque machines. But the circumstantial evidences of history deny this. It is true, however, that Clement Ader very nearly made it possible for his country to have a military airplane as early as 1897—fully twelve years before the United States Signal Corps earned this distinction by placing a Wright biplane into service.

Ader, an electrical engineer associated with the development of the telephone in France, began investigating the problems of dynamic flight in 1872. After numerous discouragements with ornithopters—machines with flapping wings—he journeyed to Arabia to study the great desert vultures as they sailed majestically through the air. These creatures, he noted, worked their wings only to get off the ground, then gained altitude almost entirely by gliding and soaring, effortlessly riding the wind. Taking inspiration from what he saw, Ader decided to model his next machine after these large birds, with a stationary airfoil, but with a steam-driven propeller to furnish the forward momentum needed for the machine to rise free of the earth.

Ader finished the machine in 1886 and named it the *Eole*. To his last day he swore that he succeeded in flying this contraption during secret trials at the Château d'Armainvilliers, near Gretz. Two men professed to having watched the alleged flight, but they both were Ader's intimate friends, a circumstance which sorely strained belief in their testimony, and nobody of consequence was yet prepared to believe the boast of the self-declared conqueror of the air. When Ader tried to substantiate his contention by staging

26

an ascent before a disinterested jury of scientists and newspapermen, his fragile machine capsized and was wrecked beyond repair.

Undaunted, the inventor confined himself to his workshop for another five years and brought forth a larger version of the *Eole,* a weird tailless craft with bat-shaped wings spanning forty-six feet. A steam engine of twenty-odd horsepower actuated a pair of four-bladed propellers stuck out on long shafts in front of the enclosed cabin. Known as the *Avion* and resembling nothing more than a monstrous black vampire, this machine, too, was only privately demonstrated. Ader, producing but a single corroborating witness, again claimed a successful flight. Although unequivocal proof was still wanting, the fervency with which he pleaded his case impressed a few officials of the French War Ministry. Whether these officials were progressive thinkers, conscientiously gambling the taxpayers' money on a potentially useful device, or simply gullible victims of Ader's stubborn assertiveness, remains a matter of conjecture. In either event, the military gave Ader a sum equivalent to $100,000 to build a fleet of militarily useful airplanes.

Six years of work and every last centime of the government grant were invested in the construction of another machine, the *Avion II,* similar in conformation to the earlier ones but bigger, with a wingspan of sixty feet and a twenty-horsepower steam engine to drive each of the two propellers. October 12, 1897, was set as the day for a preliminary test, which was viewed by some half dozen army officers and a couple of professors from a polytechnic institute. One of the observers, General Mensier, afterward reported that the machine, while perhaps it did not actually fly, did execute a series of short hops. The others said nothing, choosing to defer comment until a more thorough assessment of the aircraft's performance could be made. The same group of onlookers was present two days later, when Ader conducted his first official test. Here, in his own words, is the inventor's account of what happened:

> We started off at a lively pace. In keeping the *Avion* on the white line [which he had painted on the ground] I had much difficulty, for the wind was blowing quite strongly and across our path. Finally, a harder blow caused the machine to drift to one side, though still traveling forward. I immediately put over the rudder to the left as far as it would go, at the same time increasing the steam pressure, in order to regain our course. But the wind was too much for the *Avion;* it drifted farther and farther away from the mark, and began running toward the School of Musketry. Frightened at the prospect of the machine striking the posts and barriers guarding the school, and surprised to find the wheels of the machine lifting off the ground, I hastily shut off steam and stopped the engine. Then came a great shock, a splintering, a heavy concussion, and we were in the midst of the shattered machine.

Among the observers there was a broad spectrum of opinions as to what really did occur that afternoon. General Grillon, who had been in the machine with Ader, said that the *Avion* had momentarily cleared the ground the instant before crashing. General Mensier, however, insisted he had seen the craft "leap into the air for several minutes," yet the whole calamitous event could scarcely have taken that long. Analyzing the story related by Ader himself, it seems an inescapable conclusion that General Mensier's eyesight was something less than keen. The flight he described could not have been achieved, for if the *Avion* had stayed airborne those "several minutes," then Ader would have felt the difference in his controls—a detail assuredly worth mentioning. It seems probable from reading Ader's deposition that he had, in truth, never risen above the ground in either of his other machines. Had he actually flown in his previous attempts, why should he be "surprised" to find the wheels of this machine lifting off the ground? And more than that, why did Ader, after his careful watching of birds on the wing and after having supposedly already flown in his two other quaint monoplanes, now attempt a crosswind takeoff? The wind, he said, "was blowing . . . across our path." Such circumstantial evidence seems enough to negate his pretension of being the first man ever to fly in a heavier-than-air machine.

In justice to Ader it must be noted that his winged steam machines, had they squarely stemmed the wind in taking off and if they had been equipped with the fins necessary to vertical stabilization, could possibly have labored into the air for a feeble flight of sorts. What Ader might have done with a bit more research and an internal-combustion engine, such as the Wright brothers subsequently used at Kitty Hawk, can only be guessed. He could well have changed the course of aviation, hastening its achievement and perhaps endowing France with a supremacy in the sky that no nation would dare have challenged militarily for years to come. But Clement Ader, after his failure with *Avion II,* dispirited and deprived of further government support, gave up.

News of the Wright success in America was an incentive to stepped-up activity throughout Europe and especially in France. Alberto Santos-Dumont, the millionaire scion of a Brazilian coffee dynasty, was already famed for his exploits in small dirigibles above the boulevards of Paris. On November 12, 1906, he won the prize offered by the French Aero Club for the first public airplane flight in Europe. His plane was a boxlike contrivance, typically cruci-form in layout except that it flew with the tail surfaces foremost; the pilot rode standing erect in a deep wicker basket located immediately ahead of the two main wings. Far better known was his later effort, the *Demoiselle* monoplane, an ultralight affair of bamboo construction, powered by a tiny Darracq engine. Nicknamed the "Infuriated Grasshopper," and dimensionally suited strictly for small aviators—Santos-Dumont himself weighing barely 110 pounds—the *Demoiselle* at one time held the world's altitude record.

Right after Santos-Dumont came such great names as Henri Farman, Leon

Delagrange, Hubert Latham, Louis Bleriot, and the Voisin brothers, Charles and Gabriel, whose early biplanes launched many a pioneer aviator's career in France. Farman, a painter, and Delagrange, a sculptor, created one sensation after another at the controls of Voisin-designed machines, the latter crashing to his death in 1910. On July 25, 1909, Louis Bleriot, originator of the midwing monoplane, startled the world by crossing the English Channel for the first time in a heavier-than-air machine. Just six days before, Latham had failed in the attempt, but Bleriot covered the distance from Barraques to Dover in thirty-seven minutes, landing safely on Northfall meadow. Lamed in a gasoline explosion some time earlier, Bleriot was ready with a glib explanation as to why he had undertaken the hazardous hop across twenty-two miles of open water. "If I cannot walk without crutches," said he, "I will show that I can fly." Though Bleriot's real motive was to collect a lucrative prize from the London *Daily Mail,* and everyone knew it, a wry editorialist in a competing newspaper pretended to take the aviator at his word and cavalierly inquired whether "Monsieur Bleriot had paused also to consider his inability to swim." (Bleriot had indeed, for he placed an inflated ballonet within his plane to keep it afloat in the event of being forced down.)

Others in England did not regard Bleriot's accomplishment so blithely, however. The great moat separating the British Isles from the European mainland had been bridged with almost ridiculous ease; in an island kingdom that relied for its wealth and security upon an invincible navy, the disquieting implications of this fact were missed by few. The specter of airborne attack was delineated in every fearsome aspect by the press. Much the same foreboding had gripped the English people once before, way back in 1785, when a pair of aeronauts in a hydrogen balloon drifted across the Channel in the opposite direction, from Dover to Calais. Now, in 1909, British military chiefs pooh-poohed the notion that England lay vulnerable to aerial assault. The prospect seemed so remote that the War Office and the Admiralty did absolutely nothing to offset the leadership of France in heavier-than-air craft —nor the predominance in lighter-than-air ships of Germany, where Count Ferdinand von Zeppelin had already emerged as a prophet vindicated, and where such pan-Germanists as General Friedrich von Bernhardi were writing books foretelling the raids against London and Paris by mammoth Zeppelin dirigibles sliding noiselessly through the night sky.

France at this juncture was the only country with almost a dozen different airplane engines available and had by far the most advanced flying machines. But the birth throes of French military aviation were spasmodic and disorganized until the summer of 1909. Although regular army personnel had figured actively in the development of aviation, including a number of officers training as pilots and others taking an interest in the mechanical side of flying, their efforts lacked official backing. In an obtuse but nonetheless real sense, the father of the French flying corps was Wilbur Wright, whose exhibition flights had so incisively impressed upon the French the realization that the

airplane was more than a mere experimental toy. It was in response to the
pressure of public opinion that the War Minister, on July 12, agreed to the
purchase of a Wright machine. At the same time, however, he decreed that
a search be made for a plane of French design and construction that could
be adapted to military reconnaissance. In addition to the Wright machine,
the procurement of two Farman biplanes and a Bleriot monoplane was
authorized. By the end of March 1910, all four aircraft were in government
service and ten army officers were attending flight schools at Pau and Chalons.
Yet the War Minister himself was still not convinced on the subject of aviation. "The airplane at best," he said, "might have some limited utility in
wartime as a substitute for the captive observation balloon." Four years later,
on the eve of World War I, the French Director of Military Aeronautics
voiced the same conviction, pointing out that "the airplane is almost useless
for actual combat because its requisite high speed . . . prevents the carrying
of armament except of small caliber."

But if French policy toward aviation during the prewar interval was one
of skepticism, it was a healthy skepticism and it did not prevent the early
activities of an ever-expanding flying corps. More than $2,000,000 was spent
in France on this venture in 1910 alone. Before that year was over the army
had thirty planes already in operation and another sixty-one on order. From
July onward, military pilots were taking part in all the important civil flying
displays. The September army maneuvers in Picardy really gave them the
chance to show their mettle. Regular and reserve pilots, the latter called up
especially for the occasion, gave a good account of themselves in dangerous
and unfavorable weather conditions. Seven of the thirteen participating aircraft were badly damaged, but the pilots proved themselves capable, and
successfully executed such tasks as the rapid delivery of orders and information, and the collation and checking of intelligence reports from the other
branches of service.

In 1911, the National Subscription allowed the public to contribute nearly
four million francs for the purchase of equipment by the Cinquième Arme,
as the flying corps was then popularly called. This money was used later in
the year to finance the Military Aircraft Competition, arranged for the purpose of ascertaining which of the numerous planes on the French market
were best suited to army needs. After a series of bitterly contested preliminary trials nine of the original 110 machines entered remained to compete
in November in the final trials. A trim little monoplane designed and built
by Charles and Edouard Nieuport was the top performer. It reached an average speed of about seventy miles an hour over the prescribed 186-mile course.
Second place went to a biplane designed by Louis Breguet. Finishing third
was a shoulder-wing monoplane of the Société Provisoire des Aeroplane
Deperdussin. This Deperdussin machine was steered by means of a wheel
instead of the stick control—a feature that gave rise to the term "Dep
control" as used by World War I pilots to denote any aircraft with a wheel

to turn the rudder. Afterward, Armand Deperdussin, director of the firm that manufactured this machine, became involved in a business scandal and was in prison when the company was reorganized in August 1914, under the management of Louis Bleriot. The new concern retained the initials S.P.A.D., which now stood for Société pour l'Aviation et ses Dérivés, and went on to produce the redoubtable Spad single-seater fighters.

Winning pilots in the Military Aircraft Competition received handsome prizes, and government orders were placed with the builders of their aircraft: Nieuport for ten machines, Breguet for six, and Deperdussin for four. From then till the outbreak of war, the planes of the French flying corps were all derived more or less from these designs. The Third International Aeronautical Exposition, held in Paris just a month after the close of the 1911 military trials, showed how fast the service plane was undergoing improvement in France. For example, an armored machine built by Morane-Saulnier appeared. This was the Type M, with steel plating around the engine and cockpit. Accompanying it were other machines intended solely for army aviation, with metal replacing wood as a structural material on several. There was even one all-metal plane, the so-named *Tubavion* from the workshop of Primard and Ponche.

The pessimism with which the French War Ministry viewed the likelihood of ever developing an offensive punch for its air arm did not impede the prosecution of experiments with this end in mind. It is to the credit of the men who then administered French military affairs that they refused to let their doubts dictate their decisions. When the Michelin brothers, the famous tire manufacturers, offered to underwrite the cost of an international competition for military aviators, the War Ministry gave both its consent and hearty cooperation. If nothing else, the aerial games—which ran from January through September of 1912—proved the airplane potentially useful as a substitute for artillery. Among those who collected cash awards in the bomb-dropping contest was Lieutenant Riley Scott, whose bombsight had earlier been declined by the United States War Department.

In another field, Raymond Saulnier, working as usual in collaboration with Robert and Leon Morane, was already trying to perfect a system whereby an automatic gun could be timed to fire directly through the disc of a whirling propeller. By 1914, he had devised an interrupter gear which mechanically linked the gun's trigger to a cam on the engine shaft, but in spite of the considerable advantage this would have afforded over other countries, the War Ministry was not interested. The idea was filed away and forgotten until the unhappy summer of 1915, when Germany introduced the Fokker E-1 monoplane and its synchronized guns into combat. This lethal combination proved disastrous to Allied airmen. Fewer than two dozen Fokkers—so murderously efficient were they against slower, poorly armed Allied planes—tipped the balance of power decisively in the Germans' favor almost overnight. Harassed British pilots summed up their position with laconic bitterness, referring to

themselves and their French companions as "Fokker fodder," and a whole
year passed before the belated arrival of Allied synchronizers at the front
permitted them to retaliate in kind.

Why, when they could have entered the war with such deadly aerial
ordnance, did the French high command disaffirm Saulnier's invention?

Principally to blame was the still primitive state of aviation technology and
the difficulties encountered in mounting massive, water-cooled infantry
weapons on rickety and underpowered aircraft. The French had already conducted official experiments in 1913 with machine guns on airplanes—Morane-
Saulnier Type I and Type M monoplanes—and found the added weight of the
guns a hindrance to flight performance. It was the outcome of these trials,
in fact, that brought the War Ministry's estimate of the airplane as a potential fighting craft so low and led the director of military aeronautics to state
that airplanes were "almost useless for actual combat."

The weapon used in these tests was the standard Hotchkiss 8-mm machine
gun. Weighing more than fifty pounds and further handicapped in aerial use
by a clumsy strip-feed mechanism, the Hotchkiss had been part of the French
infantry arsenal since before the turn of the century. Manufactured at the
sprawling munitions plant established in France during the Franco-Prussian
War by the American artillery engineer, Benjamin Berkeley Hotchkiss, the
gun was intrinsically unsound for air use. The Hotchkiss 8-mm, at the beginning of World War I, held a strip of only twenty-five cartridges, and it
was constantly necessary for the gunner to break off shooting and reload.
This was convenient enough on the ground; in the air it was doubly damnable.
Nevertheless, a handful of zealots in the French flying corps affixed Hotchkiss
guns to their aircraft in the opening weeks of the war, doing so with neither
the approval nor disapproval of higher authority. And on October 14, 1914,
one of these Frenchmen—anonymous in the official diaries—claimed the
first confirmed kill in the annals of aerial warfare, destroying an enemy
Taube monoplane from the forward cockpit of his Voisin pusher biplane.[1]

Though some German historians have maintained that *all* French aircraft
carried machine guns by the middle of October, not more than a dozen, and
probably less than half that number, were so armed at the time. The cavalry
carbine remained the basic French air weapon well into the following year,
when the Lewis gun was finally supplied to fighter-plane escadrilles. Despite
the merits of the Lewis—and later, the British Vickers gun—the French
never gave up trying to improve their own Hotchkiss, which saw limited
action on French aircraft throughout the war. When the Nieuport Scout
entered service in the waning days of 1914, a modified Hotchkiss of .303
caliber, with the cumbersome water jacket removed to permit air-cooling,
was fitted above the top wing to shoot straight ahead over the propeller.
The gun now had a large ammunition drum attached to the side of the

[1] Various histories have identified the vic-   or as an unranked observer named
tor as either Pilot-Sergeant Joseph Franz   Quenault.

breech, which offered a great amount of wind resistance and caused the plane to crab in flight. Furthermore, in replacing an empty cannister of ammunition, the pilot—who pulled the trigger by means of a three-foot Bowden cable—had to stand on the seat to reach the gun. While this awkward arrangement was soon altered by making it possible to slide the gun down into the cockpit for reloading, the Hotchkiss itself was never transformed into a really good piece of aerial ordnance. However, many Allied single-seater planes—in particular the French Nieuports and British SE-5's—afterward carried Lewis guns on this same sort of top-wing mounting.

It is interesting to note that the weapons which figured most prominently in air operations along the western front could all be traced back to American inventors in Europe. Besides the Lewis and the Hotchkiss, this holds true for the Vickers and even the German Parabellum and Spandau guns. These two German arms, and the Vickers shared a common ancestor in the classic Maxim gun of the 1880s. This, the first recoil-operated machine gun in history, was the brainchild of that protean inventor, Hiram Stevens Maxim, a self-expatriated American who became a British subject after finding, to his disgust, the United States War Department insensible to the tactical expedience of a fully automatic rapid-fire weapon. The British were not so short-sighted; they eagerly paid the inventor's price in 1888 and added the Maxim gun to their arms inventory to supplant the older, hand-cranked Gatling gun. In 1901, to show his nation's gratitude, King Edward conferred knighthood upon him.

Sir Hiram left his footprints in diverse fields of science. As a Maine schoolboy he assisted his father in building a helicopter. Based on the fifteenth century precepts of Leonardo da Vinci and powered by a treadle, the craft had rotors that could never be turned with sufficient speed to supply lift. The project was abandoned, but not till the young Hiram developed a profound curiosity about the mysteries of dynamic flight. He delved into them repeatedly in the years that followed, building and testing hundreds of assorted miniature planes. Finally in 1893, at the age of fifty-three, the inventor decided enough data had been accumulated to warrant construction of a full-scale flying machine.

What a machine it turned out to be! It stood almost thirty feet high, with a framework made entirely of steel tubing. The two main wings, which had a spread of 104 feet, and the stabilizers were fabricated of tautly shrunken silk. A heavy three-hundred-horsepower steam engine was geared to drive a pair of enormous, paddle-bladed propellers set behind and midway between the wings. The complete assemblage, with seventy-five gallons of water filling its boiler, weighed nearly four tons!

A man of overweening faith in his own infallibility, Maxim placed his huge contrivance on a long track, and carefully locked down the undercarriage with guard rails to insure against an unpremeditated takeoff while the engine was being tested. On one of these dry runs, however, he opened the throttle wider than usual and sent the machine scooting along the track at a speed above forty miles per hour. To Maxim's astonishment, his winged colossus tore away from its wheel supports, slanted in the air, and missed the timber barricade at the end of the track by inches. Any elation the inventor may have felt at finding himself transported aloft was quickly smothered by panic. The flight was barely five seconds old when he frantically stopped the engine and flopped back to earth. The machine collapsed, a geyser of steam shot up from the sprung boiler, and there amid the debris sat Maxim, not injured but too unnerved to budge, staring dumbly at what he had wrought.

Although his machine had shown itself capable of flight, Maxim resolved then and there to abandon his experiments. This was a strange situation, inasmuch as he was a rich man who could have easily met the expense of a second machine. Stranger still was his later comment in the *Scientific American* that he was "convinced . . . the aeroplane system is impractical for flying." Or maybe it was no so puzzling after all: further tinkering would have eventually necessitated another test flight, and any reluctance he entertained in that connection—considering the earlier episode—was pardonable.

It was another Anglo-American experimenter, Samuel Franklin Cody, who managed to sustain flight in a heavier-than-air machine for the first time in the British Isles. Cody, a colorful ex-cowboy from Fort Worth, Texas, who landed in England with a Wild West troupe, used his show business earnings to experiment with man-carrying kites. These were so successful that the British War Office hired him as a kite instructor for the balloon section of the Royal Engineers at Farnborough. While there, he took part in the designing and building of the *Nulli Secondus,* the first British dirigible. In 1908, he constructed his first flying machine—a birdcage biplane typical of the period—and in February 1909, he made a flight of about four hundred yards' distance. Algernon E. Berriman, an early aviation writer, soon afterward was one of Cody's passengers and with tongue in cheek described the experience:

> The man and his machine were unique. There was an iron seat behind the pilot, of the kind that is used on threshing machines and agricultural instruments of the vehicular kind generally. It was comfortable enough to sit on, but when we got going over the roughness of Laffan's Plain it was extraordinary how seldom the seat would hit me in the right place. How Cody himself remained secure with both hands on the control, when it was all I could do to remain in the machine by clinging with both hands on to the framework, exercised my mind even then to the comparative exclusion of the other thought of how awkward it would be for both of us if I should happen to fall out.
>
> Once in the air, and how different it was!—the extraordinary smoothness of motion and yet withal the feeling of firmness of this

aerial support. I was engaged wholly with my own sensations, and I think they are still predominated when Cody motioned to me that I was to observe how responsive was his big machine, which he thereupon proceeded to sway about in the air. On the whole, I must honestly confess that the real sense of enjoyment came afterward on that occasion.

Cody built another machine that same year and with it established a world's record for cross-country flying. In the 1912 Michelin competition he won the prize for the best British airplane, and a special award for his kites. Still an American citizen, this picturesque pioneer of British aviation lost control of his plane and was killed in August 1913.

Cody's interest in airplanes was probably originally stimulated by a young lieutenant named John W. Dunne, a co-worker of his at Farnborough. An army careerist, born in Ireland in 1875, Dunne had dreamed of sailing about in flying craft since his boyhood reading of Jules Verne's *Clipper of the Clouds*. He saw action in the Boer War, and it was then that he realized that an airplane would be of great benefit to military reconnaissance; soon thereafter he began to study the possibilities of mechanical flight. From the outset he understood that stability and control were of primary importance. By 1904, he had assembled several small flying models which convinced him he was on the right path. He talked the War Office into posting him to Farnborough for the purpose of assembling a full-sized machine.

The first Dunn airplane, tested in 1907, was a failure. Its two Buchet engines together delivered less than fifteen horsepower and were unable to lift the machine from the ground. The War Office tartly remarked that "a machine which could not fly with fifteen horsepower was of no use to the British army." A year later the Dunne D-3 was tested. Its wings had single-surface covering only, for Dunne had been denied funds sufficient to obtain the fabric needed to cover both surfaces. The D-3 was nonetheless an exceptional machine for its time. It was tailless and without a fuselage. As viewed from above, it was shaped like a broad *V* with the point foremost. The pilot sat far forward in a nacelle that protruded in front of the swept-back wings, which gave him an unobstructed field of vision. Although Dunne a couple of years later succeeded in flying a similar machine, the D-3 was another disappointment. Now thoroughly disenchanted, the War Office decided "to cease making any experiments with aeroplanes, as the cost had proved too great." The total amount spent up to this juncture on military aircraft was approximately $10,000. Germany by then had spent nearly $2,000,000 on her air arm.

Such parsimonious policy was still in effect in Britain in the summer of 1909, when Louis Bleriot winged across the Channel from France to England. Britain's comfortable insularity had been forever destroyed, yet neither the War Office nor the Admiralty showed the slightest anxiety. The only government activity in respect to aeronautics then in progress was the Vickers

Company contract to build a rigid airship for the Admiralty. The dirigible was completed in May 1911, two whole years after the firm's tender had been accepted by the navy. Officially designated the R-1, and informally known as the *Mayfly*, it never flew, and that following September irreparably broke its back. As a consequence of this costly fiasco, British airship construction was called to a halt at around the same time that an elderly lieutenant-general —Count Ferdinand von Zeppelin—was putting the finishing touches on Germany's tenth dirigible.

Great Britain has traditionally had a perverse talent for pinching pennies in vital matters, but never has it been more foolishly tightfisted than during the genesis of the British flying corps. Seldom in British history has governmental indifference so closely bordered on the criminal, though few of that nation's historians have expressed even mild wonder at the astounding circumstances in which Britain's air arm was founded—equipped, trained, and, in the main, paid for by private initiative. Lieutenant L. D. L. Gibbs, Captain J. D. B. Fulton, and Captain Bertram Dickson, three officers of the Royal Field Artillery, by buying their own aircraft and paying their own expenses, became the progenitors of military aviation in England. Gibbs had been excited by the Dunne experiments of 1908, and had learned to fly at Chalons in France, where he bought a Henri Farman biplane. Fulton purchased a Bleriot monoplane and learned to fly in his off-duty hours on Salisbury Plain; Dickson's machine was, like that of Gibbs, a Farman double winger.

In 1910, Dickson and Gibbs, in league with a civilian pilot, Robert Loraine, of the British and Colonial Aeroplane Company, petitioned the army for permission to function as aerial scouts in the war games to be held at the end of September. The aviators had a difficult time persuading the authorities to accept their services. The cavalry objected most strenuously to the aircraft which, they said, would frighten their horses. It is not unlikely, since reconnaissance was then the cavalry's special province, that the stated objection was merely a pretext used to hide a real fear of being outdone by the upstart airmen and their newfangled mechanical Pegasuses.

After finally gaining consent, the aviators made a number of aerial reconnaissances whose value was not immediately perceived by the officers in charge of the maneuvers. Perhaps the upper echelon was more appreciative; in any case, the War Office soon afterward declared its intention "to enlarge the scope of the work hitherto carried out at the Balloon School . . . by affording the opportunity for aeroplaning."

Reduced to practicalities, this fine-sounding scheme meant little palpable improvement in policy. All the War Office had really said was that any officer, willing and qualified, could learn to fly on army time instead of his own. Several months earlier, the government had erected a shed at Larkhill, on Salisbury Plain, for the convenience of Charles S. Rolls, a wealthy aerophile who had generously offered to teach soldier-volunteers to fly at his own expense. Rolls, a pioneer of motoring as well as aviation, whose name lives on in Rolls-Royce engines and automobiles, was tragically killed that July while competing in an air meet, and his one-man academy was closed down almost before it commenced operations.

Later that year, after the September maneuvers, when the War Office ruled that army personnel could have leave to take flying lessons, the hangar on Salisbury Plain was reopened. The job of flight instructor now fell to Captain Fulton and a civilian enthusiast, George B. Cockburn. They did much good work at Larkhill, but soon found themselves compromised by a sudden reversal in the War Office program. "The Government," they were informed, "has been advised by the Committee of Imperial Defence that the experiments with aeroplanes . . . should be discontinued, but that advantage should be taken of private enterprise in this branch of aeronautics." If Fulton and Cockburn shook their heads in bewilderment, they had reason enough. Each had almost daily risked his neck alongside his army pupils, both had supplied their own aircraft at no cost to the government save that of fuel; and neither had received extra pay for his services, Captain Fulton collecting only his regular duty pay. If that wasn't private enterprise, what was? And if the government hadn't taken advantage of it, who had? In their roundabout way the War Office bureaucrats were simply trying to say that army pilots would no longer be permitted to attend the flying school except at their personal leisure. Not one of the student flyers, however, quit Larkhill because of this War Office directive, and it changed essentially nothing. It added up to nothing except a bald clarification by the high command of its own irresponsibility.

But the great awakening was not long away. Before 1911 was many weeks old, an armed clash with Germany began to materialize as an unavoidable eventuality. Motivated more by a let's-take-no-chances philosophy than by any positive desire to create a first-class flying force, the War Office, on the last day of February, authorized the creation of an Air Battalion in the Royal Engineers. A month later, on April 1, the new unit came into official being. It was divided into two companies—No. 1, which had lighter-than-air craft, and No. 2, which had airplanes. There were five machines: a Bleriot monoplane, a Wright biplane, a Farman biplane, a De Haviland FE-1, and a bizarre machine designed in France by Louis Paulhan and rather misguidedly procured by the War Office.

The function of the Air Battalion was purely reconnaissance, despite the views of Major H. R. M. Brooke-Popham, the commanding officer of No. 2 Company. The major had for more than a year been telling lecture audiences that he saw no reason why aviators should not shoot at one another with light weapons while in flight. Soon after assuming command of No. 2 Company he put his ideas to the test, had a rifle fired successfully from an airplane, and went so far as to fit a machine gun on the rear cockpit of the unit's Bleriot. An order from battalion headquarters caused him to remove the gun, however, before it could once be tested aloft. The sharply worded injunction further restrained him from carrying any firearm larger than a revolver aboard an aircraft—with the added proviso that it was not to be fired in the air.

At about the time Major Brook-Popham was considering the problems of offensive action in the air, a Franco-German crisis exploded in North Africa, where the French were quietly negotiating their protectorate in Morocco. Germany, seeing the opportunity to extort territorial concessions from France in the Congo, dispatched the gunboat *Panther* to Agadir. Rather than jeopardize their position in Morocco, the French resentfully acceded to German demands. War had been averted by a narrow margin, and all the powers of Europe knew it. Lloyd George had warned Germany in a public speech against such threats to peace. The effect of this, combined with the firm indication of a readiness to support France, lowered the political temperature. But in England, as in France and Germany, public opinion was more jingoistic than ever. As the newspapers ardently extolled the wisdom of safeguarding peace through the wholesale manufacture of war supplies, so the people in each country settled for an arms race. With fresh powder trails being laid in the Balkans, Britain's Committee of Imperial Defence, as part of a general strengthening of the military posture, advised in November 1911, that the government take "measures . . . to secure to this country an efficient aerial service." Its chief recommendation, so long overdue, was that an independent air arm be created; it was to be known as "the Royal Flying Corps and should consist of a Naval Wing, a Military Wing, and a common Central Flying School at Upavon, Wilts." In a memorandum submitted to the committee, Captain Bertram Dickson showed himself an oracle. He said:

"In the case of a European war . . . both sides would be equipped with a large corps of aeroplanes, each trying to obtain information of the other, and to hide its own movements. The efforts which each would exert in order to hinder or prevent the enemy from obtaining information . . . would lead to the inevitable result of a war in the air, for the supremacy of the air, by armed aeroplanes against each other. This fight for the supremacy of the air in future wars will be of the first and greatest importance." [2]

Though Dickson was accorded no serious notice, a royal warrant dated April 13, 1912, formally constituted the Royal Flying Corps. The necessary regulations were promulgated in an army order two days later, and, on May 13, the Air Battalion was absorbed into the R.F.C. to form its nucleus.

The navy, until now very little interested in aviation, immediately opposed the incorporation of its own embryonic air service into a united force which was obviously to be dominated by army personnel. At this time there were only five or six naval officers who had qualified as pilots, all of whom had done so in the privately owned machines of Sir Frances McClean, at virtually

[2] Robertson: *Air Aces of the 1914–1918 War*. The author acknowledges his debt to this invaluable reference work as a prime source of information regarding prewar developments in European military aviation.

no cost to the taxpayers. Still smarting from the R-1 airship failure of 1911, and caught short by the defense committee's plan, traditionalists in the senior service winced at the thought of naval airmen becoming absorbed into an army unit. Actually there was not yet any clearcut definition of command between the War Office and the Admiralty, but the Admiralty's fear of army control was apparently well-grounded. When the R.F.C. was set up, only twenty-two representatives of the naval wing were appointed to the central flying school, as compared to about four times that number from army ranks. When the defense committee picked a navy officer, Captain Godfrey M. Paine, to supervise the school, the Admiralty interpreted it as a transparent gesture of mollification and continued defiantly to establish its own flying school at Eastchurch. And right from the start, sailor-aviators proclaimed themselves to be members not of the Royal Flying Corps but of the Royal Naval Air Service, which officially did not exist. The First Lord of the Admiralty was a relatively young man named Winston Churchill, who regarded it as his bounden duty to protect every last one of the navy's prerogatives. Though he heartily supported an aviation program and soon afterward learned to fly himself, Churchill steadfastly insisted upon divorcing the naval wing from the R.F.C. It took him two years of hard dealing, but finally, on June 23, 1914, the Royal Naval Air Service received official status as a separate entity.

Fortunately, there was in England an abundance of first-rate aeronautical engineering talent on which the air services could rely. His Majesty's Balloon Factory became the Royal Aircraft Factory upon the formation of the R.F.C. in 1912. Until then it had no authority to build heavier-than-air craft and its first airplane, the SE-1, appearing in 1910, was ostensibly a reconstruction of a crashed machine. The second "reconstruction," the BE-1, was produced in 1911; it was a two-seater biplane allegedly concocted from the parts of a Voisin machine that had been sent to Farnborough for repairs. A remarkably trim airplane for its time, the BE-1 was the handiwork of Geoffrey de Havilland, who later managed the Aircraft Manufacturing Company, better known as Airco, and designed such outstanding planes as the DH-4 light bomber. Thomas Sopwith was by now building the forerunners of his splendid combat planes, and Alliott Verdon Roe was on the market with the first examples of a long and illustrious line of Avro aircraft. By 1913, the Avro 504 was being produced in larger quantity than any other British type and it became the standard R.F.C. training machine. Noel Pemberton-Billing's Supermarine Aviation Works—later acquired by the Vickers combine—was now a going concern on the banks of Southampton Water, and the Handley Page factory at Cricklewood had been opened for business by its namesake and founder, Frederick Handley Page. A noted sportsman-pilot, Claude Grahame-White, was also in the commercial race, as were Hugh and Eustace Short. Neither last nor least was Robert Blackburn, who put an all-metal two-seater military monoplane into production as early as 1911, but found the government disinterested. During the war the Blackburn Aeroplane Company specialized in torpedo planes for the navy.

The British designers, almost to a man, favored the biplane over the monoplane, which was not the case in either France or Germany. The monoplane possessed cleaner lines and hence greater speed, but the biplane presented fewer problems from an enginering standpoint. To attain a lift comparable to the biplane's, the monoplane had to have an appreciably wider wingspan. This large expanse of surface required considerable reinforcement, which meant, with materials then available, much added weight; the necessary external bracings, too, created a significant amount of drag and interfered with the air flow. The biplane, with one wing situated above the other and tied in with struts and wires, was structurally more rigid, more stable, and more responsive to the pilot's control. The two wings gave it a larger over-all surface area, enabling it to haul heavier loads than the monoplane.

In 1912, taking up where Major Brooke-Popham had been forced to leave off, the Vickers Company designed an airplane specifically intended to carry a machine gun. Apropos of its purpose, it was labeled the *Gun Bus* and first went on display in the 1913 air show at Farnborough. A pusher biplane of strictly functional design, it had a Maxim .303 machine gun mounted on the nose of its two-cockpit nacelle. This raised little enthusiasm in the War Office. Vickers conducted some firing experiments with the plane but found the belt-fed Maxim too heavy, difficult to handle in the air, and the ammunition clumsy to stow. The firm had been manufacturing this weapon for the British government since 1888—by this time, in fact, it was generally known as the Vickers gun rather than the Maxim—so it was naturally the firm's weapon of choice. Several improved versions of the *Gun Bus* were hopefully brought out by Vickers during 1913 and early 1914, but the model that ultimately became operational—the FB-4, which arrived at the front in February 1915—was armed with the lighter and more manageable drum-fed Lewis gun.

At the same time as the Vickers endeavor a Swiss-born engineer was concerned in Germany with exactly the same problem. Franz Schneider, after having served his apprenticeship with the Nieuport firm in France, became the chief designer of Luft-Verkehrs Gesellschaft (Air Transport Company) in 1912, and aside from creating some excellent airplanes for L.V.G., patented a number of armament devices, including an interrupter gear for a fixed machine gun. Schneider also discovered a method by which an automatic weapon could be fired through the hollow shaft of a revolving airscrew. Still another of his inventions was a ring mounting for a movable gun which could be installed on the observer's cockpit of a two-seater reconnaissance plane. Schneider accomplished all this before the beginning of the war, and his ingenious works were almost completely ignored in higher German military circles. Though he neglected to mention in his diaries the type of machine gun used in his experiments, it was probably the readily available Maxim then being manufactured in Germany under a Vickers license. Later, toward the end of 1914, when the fighting was first beginning among the pilots on the western front, Schneider produced the L.V.G. E-4 monoplane with a ring-mounted Parabellum machine gun for the observer. Of a very advanced design, the machine was not ordered into production because top-echelon military brains assumed that it flew too fast for scouting purposes. But early in 1915, Schneider's flexible ring mounting, together with the 7.92-mm Parabellum gun, became a regulation fixture on German two-seaters.

Essentially a lighter edition of the classic Maxim gun, the Parabellum had been perfected by Karl Heinemann of the Deutsche Waffen und Munitions-fabriken (German Arms and Munitions Factory) in Berlin. A fretted casing supported the recoil of the air-cooled barrel. Coiled around a rotating spool drum, the hundred-cartridge ammunition belt afforded the German gunner a decided advantage in combat, since he had to reload only once to his adversary's twice with the Lewis gun, or four times with the French Hotchkiss. The name *Parabellum*—Latin for "prepare for war"—was derived from the ancient Roman proverb: "If you wish for peace, prepare for war." Among the renowned aces who gained their initial victories with this gun were Manfred von Richthofen, Werner Voss, and Max Immelmann, to name but three. Equal in every respect to the Lewis gun, from which several key features had been pirated, the Parabellum continued in use with the German air service right up to the Armistice. With its generous spool of cartridges, the Parabellum did much to account for German air supremacy for some weeks after its debut.

As winter melted into spring in 1915, fighting in the air was becoming both more frequent and more bloody. The demand for Parabellum guns quickly outran the supply and Germany began looking for an alternative weapon. The Model 08/15 Maxim was again chosen for modification, but this time as a pilot's gun that could be fixed to shoot straight ahead through the propeller arc, for Anthony Fokker had by now introduced his interrupter gear. All that was necessary to adapt the Maxim to the Fokker synchronization system was to cut slots in the water jacket for air cooling and to enclose the webbed ammunition belt to prevent slipstream interference. Since most of these guns bore the proof mark of the arsenal at Spandau, near Berlin, they came to be known as Spandaus rather than Maxims. From 1916 on, all German single-seater combat craft were provided with synchronized, forward-firing Spandau machine guns, while the Parabellum remained the standard observer's weapon —as did the Lewis gun on the Allied side after the belated arrival at the front of synchronized Vickers guns. Thus the Parabellum and the Lewis became the counterparts of one another and were very much akin to each other, which holds true for the Spandau and the Vickers. Other aircraft ordnance faced by Allied pilots were the German Bergmann gun and Austro-Hungary's Schwarzlose, both of which were inferior arms and saw only occasional use above the western front.

It can be seen from Franz Schneider's experience that the prewar attitude of Germany's supreme command toward the development of armed aircraft was no less shortsighted than that of military leaders elsewhere. "A real combat in the air," said the Grosser Generalstab in 1913, "such as journalists and romancers have described, should be considered a myth. The duty of the aviator is to see and not to fight." The German general staff was so adamant in this opinion that it issued an order discouraging the development of fast airplanes, lest they fly too swiftly to permit accurate observation of enemy troops and terrain. Schneider saw fit to ignore this dictate when he designed his very advanced E-4 monoplane, only to find to his distress that the army could be extremely obstinate about its judgments. Other aircraft constructors, too—August Euler as a notable example—met the same frustration after investing time and money in similarly advanced machines. But the order was strictly enforced until the end of 1914, and neither the E-4 nor other worthwhile machines like it entered regular production. Accordingly, in the opening weeks of World War I, German aircraft were mainly in the heavy biplane class, such as the so-called "Flying Bananas" of the L.V.G. and D.F.W. (Deutsche Flugzeugwerke) companies, with a few Taube monoplanes. The Taube, or Dove, was not the product of any particular company; it took its name from its birdlike swept-back wing tips and long, graceful, fan-shaped tail, and was originally designed by the Austrian, Igo Etrich, in 1910. The Taube was very popular in Germany as a sporting plane. Many of them in army service were commandeered from private owners when Germany mobilized for the invasion of France and Belgium. Because the Taube was built in greatest number by the Edmund Rumpler Flugzeugwerke, it was sometimes referred to as a Rumpler monoplane by Allied flyers.

In view of Germany's enviable record of achievement in the realm of technology, the flying machine was strangely late in making an appearance there. Not until November 1909, did a German airplane maintain itself in flight for more than a nervous minute or two. The builder of this plane, Hans Grade, by his own confession had patterned it after a French Antoinette design he saw and admired at an aviation exhibition at Reims. Such a pirating procedure characterized many pioneer aircraft builders in Germany. The French influence persisted through the second year of the war, and some of the finest German service planes were thinly disguised imitations of French machines. The deadly Fokker E-1, for instance, was based on the Morane-Saulnier Type H, and the early scouting monoplanes of the Pfalz Aircraft Works were distinguishable only by their Maltese crosses from Morane-Saulnier Parasols. Among the famous German designers then beginning their careers was Ernst Heinkel, whose autobiography, *Stormy Life,* vividly recalls the backward state of aviation in his homeland in the year 1909:

> The International Flying Exhibition in Frankfort was unbelievably pathetic. . . . Next to small airships and balloons there was a row of German airplanes. There were six-deckers among them, which

looked quite monstrous. There was a half-built Wright plane hanging from the ceiling and, in the corner, a flying machine that Kaiser Wilhelm II's chauffeur Krieger had built. In the whole of Frankfort there was only one German pilot, however, who could really fly with his plane: August Euler. But as his flights were little more than modest hops into the air, the disappointed bystanders called out to him to stop his nonsense.

Aviation's slow start in Germany was in some measure attributable to the phenomenal accomplishments of Count Ferdinand von Zeppelin and his dirigibles. Zeppelin, whom the newspapers were fond of eulogizing as "Germany's man of the century," won his success and the passionate loyalty of an entire nation by his own sheer doggedness in the face of many obstacles. In 1910, when the destiny of the airplane seemed at best problematical, a fleet of Zeppelin dirigibles was already carrying passengers and cargo around Germany on a scheduled basis. These huge aerial merchantmen flew a circuit of the major cities, from Stuttgart to Frankfurt to Cologne, Bremen, Hamburg, Berlin, Munich, and back to Stuttgart, while not a single airplane in Germany could yet be relied upon to fly once around a cabbage patch. Count Zeppelin had completely captured the German imagination, and there was a wide national interest in his ambitious venture. Zeppelin's attainments ultimately became so involved with patriotic vanity that some extremists considered it subversive and un-German to develop heavier-than-air machines. The editor of a leading popular science periodical, for example, looked upon airplanes as "the distasteful preoccupation of dangerously foolish schemers." The future of air travel belonged certainly to airships and not airplanes, and Count Zeppelin's *luftschiffen* symbolized the preeminence of the Reich's technology, whereas winged aircraft were the pitiful fruits of kindergarten science in foreign countries. Though not all the air-minded in Germany were thus oriented, those who were founded their logic on empirical evidence, the *fait accompli,* instead of problematical forecasts of the great future for heavier-than-air machines.

Count Zeppelin, who singlehandedly made such an impact on German aeronautical thinking, had two careers in his long and eventful life, the first as a distinguished cavalry officer. The seeds of his second career were sown in 1863, when he was sent to the United States as military attaché to the Army of the Potomac during the Civil War. Here he saw balloons secured to the ground being used for observation and artillery direction. Though technically a neutral, he participated in several ascents under Confederate fire. Before his return to Germany he joined a mapping expedition to the headwaters of the Mississippi River as a scout-balloonist. It was in the course of this journey, he later said, that the idea for his airships first came to him.

While serving in the Franco-Prussian War of 1870–1871, Zeppelin saw the defenders of Paris launch a series of sixty-six balloons from within the besieged city. All but three or four of the aerostats managed to reach the French provisional capital at Tours with important evacuees and military communiqués aboard. Inspired, perhaps, by the effectiveness of this airlift operation, Zeppelin confided to his diary his tentative plans for a rigid, steerable, lighter-than-air craft. In 1887, he wrote to the King of Württemberg and stated his case for the airship, citing its potential military and economic uses. He mentioned specifically scouting and raiding in warfare and also discussed the possibilities for long-distance transportation and the exploration of uncharted regions in times of peace. Five years after that he approached the Prussian War Ministry with schematic drawings for an immense air-going dreadnaught. A disagreement with the Junker element in the German army forced him in 1894, at fifty-six years of age, to resign his rank. Almost immediately he undertook his own experiments. After four more years of intensive research, Zeppelin formed a public corporation to finance the construction of his first dirigible. Half his funds came from his own pocket; half from the industrial community of his native Württemberg. From the kibitzers, scientists, and laymen alike came only ridicule and disparagement.

The first Zeppelin dirigible took to the air on July 2, 1900, with the proud Graf himself at the helm. Designated as the Zeppelin, it was 420 feet long. Buoyed by nearly half a million cubic feet of hydrogen, it was by far the largest and most elaborate airship that ever had been built. On Lake Constance in southern Germany Zeppelin housed the ship in a floating shed that could be swiveled into the wind and thus prevented the ship from being caught by crosswinds while being handled in and out. On the morning of the maiden flight the lake shore was massed with sightseers; boats of every description, from the meanest shallop to the most opulent of yachts, dotted the water. The expectant multitude buzzed with anticipation until half past seven. Then the dirigible, its great silver body dazzling in the sun, slid slowly from the shed, riding the water on pontoons. At eight o'clock sharp the airship was set free. For a breathless minute, until well underway, it skimmed close to the water. Some among the spectators shouted encouragement, others stared in surprise as the dirigible raised its nose and started to climb. Soon it was 1300 feet high. "From where I stood on the distant shore," a reporter wrote the next day, "it resembled a shimmering arrow caught in motion." But the dirigible climbed no higher. It suddenly lurched and wallowed and slipped off into a shallow glide. The long keel securing the aluminum framework had warped and bent the hull amidships; this had deranged the control surfaces and misaligned the airscrews. The disabled ship balanced itself delicately on the wind and drifted. Twenty minutes after taking off it settled upon the lake near Immenstadt, three and a half miles from its floating home.

Towing the airship back to the hangar and restoring it to flying condition took fourteen weeks and thousands of Reichsmarks. A second test was held on October 17, this time with satisfactory results. Zeppelin piloted his dirigible to an altitude of one thousand feet and steered it in sweeping circles above Lake Constance for an hour and fifteen minutes at an average speed of about twenty miles per hour, then landed back gently on the water. One more successful flight left Zeppelin triumphant in other respects but lacking sufficient funds to bring his invention into practical use. The coffers of his company had been gleaned of every pfennig, and he personally was on the verge of insolvency.

A man of stoic faith and untiring energy, Zeppelin spent the following half decade stumping about Germany in quest of money. Finally, in 1905, his luck changed. The King of Württemberg, long a disciple of Zeppelin, ran a state lottery to raise most of the required capital. The Prussian War Ministry, alerted now to the aerial supremacy of France, where Alberto Santos-Dumont was in his heyday, lent gasbags and gave whatever money was still needed. The Zeppelin 2 flew twice and both times met serious mishap. By this time Count Zeppelin had rallied more support to his cause. Another lottery was held in Württemberg to pay for his third dirigible, which in October 1907, flew a distance of 208 miles nonstop. The War Ministry agreed to purchase the Zeppelin 3 if it could carry out a 430-mile round trip. Knowing the ship was incapable of so long a flight, Zeppelin resorted to shrewd salesmanship, talking the government into buying the ship anyway and letting him use the cash proceeds to build a fourth dirigible with a range of five hundred miles. Soon after its completion in the spring of 1908, this fourth dirigible was torn from its mooring in a rain squall. The craft, driven by a vicious wind, bumped and crunched along the ground until, pinned against a copse of trees, it burst into flames. After fifteen years of hard work and financial loss, Count Zeppelin had nothing.

But Ferdinand von Zeppelin's work had awakened in the German people a fierce pride in a countryman's accomplishments. This sentiment, this *landesstolz,* though the venerable old gentleman could not have been aware of it, had for some time been simmering beneath the national consciousness. The stimulus that brought it percolating to the surface was the untoward destruction of the Zeppelin 4. A spontaneous reaction swept the country. Editorials appeared in every newspaper, asserting that "Zeppelin's success is the Fatherland's success," and poignantly recounting the circumstances of his financial martyrdom. From the nation's bank accounts, salary envelopes, cookie jars, and sugar bowls the money rolled in—$1,500,000 of it. Count Zeppelin gratefully accepted the donations, erected a new factory at Friedrichshafen and, by May 1909, delivered to the German army another dirigible.

At the beginning of the war the Germans were able to field only four of their nineteen military dirigibles and were obliged to use three of Count Zeppelin's commercial craft. Seven serviceable airships were thus available for war duty, the captain of one promptly winning an Iron Cross for directing a submarine attack against a flotilla of British gunboats in the Heligoland Bight.

On the western front four zeppelins confronted a like number of French airships,[3] semirigid vessels of medium size and slow speed, markedly inferior to the silver colossi that escorted the aggressor's vanguard into Belgium and France. The English were even worse off than their ally, for their lighter-than-air fleet practically did not exist. The British army had only two dirigibles of fairly modern build, the navy none at all. The odds, however, were temporarily equalized in the first weeks of fighting, when the French shot down three zeppelins with artillery and, in one case, concentrated volleys of rifle fire. The Germans were foolish enough to use their airships as though the craft, instead of being massive, highly combustible, comparatively slow-moving targets, were impregnable to enemy shot. In subsequent actions the zeppelins rarely descended below ten thousand feet when in range of enemy guns.

In Friedrichshafen Count Zeppelin and his co-workers set themselves the task of manufacturing one dirigible every two weeks. By the end of the war a total of 103 had been produced—forty for the army, sixty-three for the navy. Of these, fifty-one were lost to enemy action, twenty-four to accidental causes, and twenty-one were taken out of commission as unfit for further service. A mere half dozen survived the war unscathed, only to be sabotaged by mutinous sailors at the Nordholz zeppelin station.

Overshadowed by the development of lighter-than-air ships, the airplane received scant attention from German military authorities until early in 1912. It was the effectual employment of flying machines by the French in their 1911 maneuvers that gave the Grosser Generalstab its first inkling of the airplane's potential worth. Had this germ of foresight blossomed into full-flowered enthusiasm at the time it was first planted, Germany could have begun her war as an unrivaled air power; she possessed the technological acumen, the engines, and the productive capacity to forge an invincible armada of airplanes. But here, as in France and England, tradition was the military's golden calf, and the air force was instituted as an incidental part of the Signal Corps.

Though not as popular in Germany as in France, aviation did manage to thrive as a sport. By 1911, there were some dozen flying schools going strong, and two sizable factories, the Albatros and the Aviatik, were producing and selling airplanes at a profitable clip. Many other companies were by now turning out their first machines. Two of the finest reciprocating engines in the world were available—the Daimler and the Mercedes. Army representatives watched demonstrations of these planes with curiosity but with no appreciation of their value in warfare. Because the army was committed to dirigibles, it spent relatively little on heavier-than-air craft. Staff officers saw use for airplanes as only flying observation posts, and rather undependable ones at that. The 1913 war games furnished German pilots with their earliest opportunity to show their abilities under combat conditions, but they failed

[3] Counting only those airships fit for combat operations.

to find two entire divisions that they had been sent to locate. Erich von Ludendorff, probably the most astute of the German generals, whose opinions always had the respectful ear of his colleagues, upon being informed of the inefficacy of aerial reconnaissance, had only contempt for the aviation branch. He would, during World War I, reverse his opinion.

The misconceptions concerning the potential utility of heavier-than-air machines and the haphazard manner in which observers were selected for flight duty—in view of vaunted German military efficiency—are almost incredible. Reconnaissance, as in most other countries, had traditionally been the job of the cavalry, and the airborne observer was naïvely considered to be nothing more than a flying counterpart of the scout on horseback. In theory, this sounded fine, but even the German supreme command overlooked the difference between the horizontal scanning of the cavalryman and the vertical vistas of the airman. No one understood that a flying observer needed special training for what was a brand-new science. The cavalry scout had absolutely no idea of how a supply depot, a munitions dump, a moving column of troops or vehicles, or artillery emplacements appeared from the air. The observers were for the most part volunteers from the cavalry and artillery. Invariably they were officers, while the pilots were not. German officers were required to wear swords or sabers in the field, and were not exempt from this rule when flying; they had to carry their side arms into the cockpits (just as American airmen wore spurs on their boots). Since the observer outranked his pilot and was at all times in command of the plane, the man at the controls was regarded merely as a chauffeur, with no more prestige than a truck driver.

In the majority of German airplanes in 1914, the observer sat in the front cockpit. If it was a biplane, his downward view was blocked by the bottom wing, and his view was further restricted by the mass of wires and struts that held the wings together. If he were in the front seat of the Taube monoplane, his view would be cut off by the generous back sweep of the wing tips. It is hardly surprising that during the opening phase of the war the infantry and artillery commanders attached little credence to intelligence gathered by aerial scouts. Reconnaissance reports of German airmen were notoriously inaccurate, and frequently so misleading as to be worse than worthless. One example: the British Expeditionary Force landed in France during the first week of August, but the German general staff did not learn of the arrival of the British until August 21, when General Alexander von Kluck's rapidly advancing First Army encountered some British outposts. After fifteen consecutive days of unmolested flying over British-occupied territory, not one aerial observer had noticed the enemy's presence.

Nevertheless, the German planes and pilots at the beginning of the war were on the whole equal to those of the Allies. Airplane designers in the three countries were members of a close fraternity, a condition that resulted in exchanges of information and the leasing of patents right up to the summer of 1914. When war broke out, the Halberstadt plant in Germany was af-

filiated with the Bristol Works in England. Oswald Boelcke, bound for greatness in the German flying corps, won his pilot's license in a British-made
Bristol biplane. Gnome engines, French in origin, were being distributed in
England and Germany. The Gnome factory in Germany became the Oberursel
plant and produced rotary engines all through the war. There were more
French airplanes flying in Great Britain than British planes. Armed aircraft
were practically nonexistent, and the aviation squadrons of the warring nations
were potpourris of mismatched machines with little or no effort made toward
standardization.

As of July 1, when the war fever started to mount in earnest, the Germans
had forty-nine sections of six airplanes each, including eighteen home training
units, which, on paper, gave them a force of 294 planes. In actuality the total
number of machines on hand, counting everything that could fly, was only 218.
And more than a hundred of these were reserved for school purposes. France
had twenty-one escadrilles of two-seaters, six to the escadrille, plus four single-
seater units of four planes apiece. Since these figures exclude training craft,
the French had about forty more planes fit for front-line service than the
Germans. The British Royal Flying Corps was officially in possession of 179
machines, less than half of which were capable of crossing the English
Channel under their own power. The Royal Naval Air Service had an additional ninety-three aircraft, about a third of them seaplanes.

These were the aerial strengths of Germany, France, and England when,
on June 28, 1914, the heir to the Austro-Hungarian throne, Archduke Francis
Ferdinand, was assassinated in the streets of Sarajevo. Sarajevo was the capital
of Bosnia, a tiny Balkan nation swallowed up in 1908 by the Austro-Hungarian empire. The Archduke's murderers sought Bosnia's freedom and aimed
for union with the other Slav peoples of southeast Europe. The death of
Ferdinand was blamed on Serbia, one of the sovereign Balkan states. Serbia
received ten humiliating demands from Austria-Hungary, demands chiefly
intended to end Serbian agitation for Bosnian independence. Serbia appealed
to Russia for aid; Russia advised a conciliatory attitude. The Serbians then
agreed to all but one of the terms. Complete acquiescence was actually the
last thing Austria-Hungary desired; it had determined upon a punitive expedition to Belgrade, and had purposely made outrageous demands which it
believed Serbia would not accept. A month after the archduke's funeral Russia's interest in the Balkans led her to prepare for a war she deemed unavoidable. Germany, an ally of Austria-Hungary, warned Russia to halt her
mobilization and to stay out of things. Russia refused. The Berlin government
declared war a few days later.

Russia had an ally in France. A treaty bound the two countries to mutual
assistance in any war against Germany. The Germans therefore demanded that
France define her position in the developing conflict. France tried to appease
the central powers by pulling her soldiers back six miles from the Franco-
German frontier. But Germany had long been seeking any half plausible

excuse for an appeal to arms that would win new *lebensraum* for the Reich. When rumors of French air attacks on German cities reached Berlin, the Kaiser, without bothering to verify the manifestly absurd gossip, cited the alleged raids as causes for war. On August 2, German troops poured into helpless Luxemburg, strategically situated at the junction of France with Germany and Belgium. The Belgians announced themselves neutral and refused to open their borders to the invading army. Denied passage through Belgium, Germany moved to seize it by force, launching her invasion on August 4. The assault on neutral Belgium brought Great Britain into the war on the side of the Allies—France, Russia, and Serbia.

World War I, which soon would engulf almost all the European nations, reach into Africa and Asia Minor, and involve far-off Japan and the United States—the first worldwide war in history—had begun.

CHAPTER IV

✧ *War Sprouts Wings* ✧

THE FOUR YEARS of World War I, in which a majority of civilized nations had a part, saw at least ten million combatants killed and twenty-one million others maimed or debilitated by bullet, shell, bomb, grenade, torpedo, bayonet, poison gas, trench disease, or accident. Another casualty, significant because it made way for a new and previously unknown style of waging war, was Article 25 of the Land War Convention of 1907 held at The Hague. Delegates from forty-four countries attended this conference to draft a set of ground rules for the unscheduled but inevitable fracas some must have felt lay ahead. In Article 25 they piously inserted an embargo against the bombardment of undefended places "by any means whatsoever," but when the conflict did materialize in 1914, it became clear at once that this phrase had no real meaning.

Before a month of war had gone by, Article 25 was broken when, on the night of August 26, a German dirigible dropped eighteen hundred pounds of shrapnel bombs on the besieged Belgian city of Antwerp.

The raiding airship was formerly one of Count Zeppelin's commercial craft, the *Sachsen,* which now flew under the able command of Captain Ernst Lehmann. Two days later the *Sachsen* was joined at its home field in Düsseldorf by the Zeppelin Z-9, fresh from the factory at Friedrichshafen and commanded by a Captain Horn. Together the two dirigibles continued pounding Antwerp. "All told," Captain Lehmann recollected in his postwar memoirs, *The Zeppelins,* "we must have dropped ten thousand pounds of bombs on the fortifications, a bit of military strategy which, if it did no appreciable damage to the enemy, accomplished a greater purpose. For we succeeded in restoring the confidence of the high command in airships; and though only two ships were then available for duty, orders came in thick and fast."

When Lehmann said that only two ships were then in service, his reference was to army dirigibles, of which three had already been shot down by French guns and rifles, and another of which was temporarily laid up for repairs. Five naval zeppelins were still picketing the offshore waters of Germany. The high command's sagging confidence in airships, of course, was the outcome of the triple disaster on the French front, and as Lehmann indicated, it was a short-lived disillusionment—although it did presage the utter distrust of dirigibles two years later. Taking into account that he wrote his book in 1927, almost a decade after the Armistice, the captain must stand guilty of twisting the truth to his own advantage for implying that Antwerp's military installations absorbed the brunt of the raids. At a time when bombs were aimed by the naked eye and hurled by hand, such selective bombardment was impossible. In the first raid alone, twelve civilians were killed and a hospital partially demolished. "Antwerp," reported Reuters of London, "protests against this barbarous attack on the hospital, which was flying the flag of the Hague Convention. Great excitement reigns throughout the town. The bombs exploded with terrific force."

The Antwerp raids, as was to be expected, provoked an excess of apprehension in England. Beneath the frightening headlines the newspapers presented pictures of the aged Count Zeppelin, white-mustachioed and smiling. Here was the nightmare haunter himself, the authentic bogeyman. Would his bomb-laden airships be over London tonight? Most Britons took it for granted that there could be no way of fighting the aerial monsters, no way of repelling them once they did come. Those who knew the real state of British defenses were pessimistic about the effectiveness of a few untried guns and crude airplanes. The fact that three zeppelins had already been brought down by the French army was either unknown to the home-defense planners or was dismissed as phony propaganda. The War Office firmly believed that every zeppelin was protected against fire by an outer layer of nonflammable gas around the hydrogen cells. No one thought a "zep" could be destroyed with ordinary bullets. Even if several drums of machine-gun ammunition were emptied into the body of an airship, it was felt the only result would be a slow leakage of inert gas and maybe some hydrogen, which might—or might not—force the ship down before it could return to base. The conviction was that the only way to destroy a zeppelin quickly and surely was to bomb it. But getting an airplane above a zep and then scoring a hit seemed an improbable task, which indeed it was.

The Royal Naval Air Service was given the job of patrolling the east and south coasts to safeguard maritime traffic from submarines and dirigibles, and also, if possible, to ward off any airborne attack directed against the kingdom itself. Some of the navy planes, more in the hope of sinking submarines than zeppelins, carried a brace of twenty-pound Hale high-explosive bombs, plus two sixteen-pound incendiaries. Most of these planes were further burdened with the weight of pontoons, which greatly reduced their speed and rate of climb. As had been premised, pitting a lumbering seaplane against a high flying airship, when the zeppelins did come early in 1915, proved to be woefully futile. The R.N.A.S. had fifty-two seaplanes and forty-one land-planes stationed at Calshot, Eastchurch, Felixstowe, Fort Grange, Isle of Grain, Killingholme, and Yarmouth. England's only seaplane tender, the H.M.S. *Hermes,* was torpedoed almost immediately after hostilities began, and three Channel steamers—the *Empress,* the *Engadine* and the *Riviera*—were hastily refitted to answer the need. The scouting flights over the Channel and North Sea were by no means safe or pleasant. Inclement weather and choppy water were the worst dangers, and both claimed a toll of men and machines. Commander J. W. Seddon and his observer, Leading Mechanic R. L. Hartley, lost in a fog, became the first airmen in World War I to ditch a plane. Fortunately, perhaps miraculously, their machine remained afloat for eight hours and they were rescued, blue-lipped and soaking wet, by the freighter *Orme.*

Winston Churchill, the First Lord of the Admiralty, sided with the minority of British leaders who calmly discredited the theory that Germany would shortly attempt a cross-Channel invasion. To show the disdain he held for such alarmist thinking, he diplomatically suggested to General Sir David Henderson of the Royal Flying Corps that perhaps a few planes could be relieved of Channel patrol duties and sent to the continent to supplement the small group of overworked army pilots already reconnoitering the enemy. Henderson, graciously conceding that the war was big enough for both the R.N.A.S. and the R.F.C., agreed to Churchill's intelligent proposal. The navy's Eastchurch Squadron was thereupon transferred to French soil, based at Dunkirk, and instructed "to deny all territory within a hundred miles of the city to German zeppelins and airplanes." A veteran aviator, Lieutenant Rumney Samson, was in charge of the squadron and with his men was eager for action. Samson left for Dunkirk with four Sopwith Tabloid airplanes; the rest would arrive in a week or so, he was assured. His other pilots, his fifty mechanics, his armored cars, and a detachment of marines were ferried across the water to establish a makeshift airdrome.

The Eastchurch aviators, the four with aircraft at their disposal, did hardly any flying during their first days in France. A protracted spell of nasty weather kept them grounded most of the time. Since the assigned sector of operations was much too big for four planes to cover anyway, Lieutenant Samson decided to do a bit of ground reconnaissance. He had no adequate maps of the Dunkirk region, but this problem was solved by the fortuitous arrival of seventy-year-old Captain Pierre de Moduit, formerly of the French infantry, who drove up in an expensive limousine with a case of the finest champagne, a dozen cans of *pâté de foie gras,* a bejeweled revolver, and a vivacious young wife, whom Samson mistook as the elderly gentleman's daughter. In a super-lative show of Gallic affability the captain laughingly forgave Samson his *faux pas* and clasped the Englishman's hand in common cause against the enemy. He was a lifelong resident of the district, he said, and boasted of a familiarity with every road in northeastern France. Hearing this, Samson invited his guest along on the scouting expedition. They would take one of the armored cars on which a Vickers machine gun had been mounted and go hunting for Huns. It was a sporting proposition that delighted the septuagenarian, who kissed his wife a loving good-bye and motored off with Samson to search out excitement. About twenty miles from Dunkirk they found what they were seeking. A German staff car with six officers aboard was encountered. Samson, seeing the enemy vehicle was faster, peppered it with the machine gun while his passenger banged away with his fancy pistol. The Germans escaped.

Although an insignificant skirmish, it did have a memorable result. The German officers, presumably unwilling to admit they had been routed by just two men, reported that a full British army was secretly deployed in the Dunkirk-Cassell area. The western flank of the German army in Belgium was therefore bolstered with a division pulled away from the battle for Antwerp, which delayed, at least for a few days, the city's surrender.

Thirty-six hours after shooting up the German staff car, Samson got word of enemy troops approaching Lille to the south. Thirsting for more gunplay, he sped to the supposedly threatened town. The Boches were nowhere near the place, but Samson was mobbed by a populace that was hysterically jubilant on seeing its first British military vehicle. One exuberant Frenchman was so intoxicated with adoration for this brave ally that he flung a wine bottle through the windshield of the car and struck the lieutenant on the jaw.

Samson's communiqués to the Admiralty invariably contained an urgent request for additional men and materiel. Churchill, tunneling through mountains of red tape, somehow managed to scrape together a few more armored cars, several airplanes, and five companies of marines with which to reinforce the Dunkirk beachhead. Samson worked out an appropriate plan of operations. He sent his aircraft out on reconnaissance; when they located a covey of German soldiers, he led his cars to the spot and opened fire. So long as he attacked the enemy's pathfinder patrols—small scouting parties under orders to retreat rather than shoot back—Samson ran into nothing he was not equipped to handle. The first real test came when a large force of Germans was observed moving toward Douai, about twenty miles southwest of Lille. Samson rushed his cars to a bridge over the canal on the eastern edge of the village. He staved off a German victory until the whole French garrison of Douai had time to withdraw. Only when the German artillery opened up and the shellfire grew unbearably hot did he wheel his cars toward the rear. Eight of his men were wounded, a cheap enough price to pay for the salvation of an entire French infantry regiment and a company of horse artillery.

Not many days prior to the fall of Antwerp, Samson established an advance air base within the city. His intention was to retaliate in kind for the nightly zeppelin raids against the Belgians. Four planes flew off from Antwerp to

drop bombs on the dirigible sheds at Düsseldorf and two more to attack
Cologne. As was too often the case, the weather was bad, with poor visibility,
and none of the planes found their targets. Lieutenant L. H. Collett, one of
the pilots, disgustedly told Samson that "looking for the sheds at Düsseldorf
was like going into a dark room to look for a black cat." On October 8, while
Antwerp was actually being evacuated, Samson sent Flight Lieutenant R. L. G.
Marix and Squadron Commander Spenser Grey to have another try. Each
flew a Sopwith Tabloid with a pair of twenty-pound bombs racked beneath
the lower wing. Grey planted both his missiles on the main railroad station
in Cologne, killing three civilians. Marix headed for Düsseldorf and, from an
altitude of six hundred feet, hit the hangar of Captain Horn's newly constructed Zeppelin Z-9. The dirigible erupted in flames. A mechanic, who
happened to be on the roof at the time of the attack, was killed, yet by some
miracle the machine gunners on the towers at each end of the hangar were
not hurt. Wrote Captain Lehmann, whose zeppelin, the *Sachsen,* was housed
nearby: "I drove over to Düsseldorf soon after the raid and was surprised to
find the hangar itself practically undamaged. The Z-9 was a complete wreck.
Only the engines could be used again. Singularly, the [zeppelin's] bombs,
which had been hanging inside the hull, did not explode. Of course they had
no fuses, and when their metal supports melted away in the blowtorch heat
of burning hydrogen, they fell harmlessly to the floor."

Small-arms fire had perforated the Sopwith Tabloid in half a hundred
places, but Marix was pilot enough to coax the machine back to within
fourteen miles of Antwerp before it gave out. From there he pedaled a borrowed bicycle the rest of the way to his camp, which was perhaps an in-
glorious windup to this first successful foray into the German homeland. But
the trade off—one biplane for one zeppelin—made the loss of Antwerp, for
the British if not the Belgians, a slightly less bitter pill to swallow.

The effect in England of the Düsseldorf raid was a relaxation of fear.
People had been haunted by the zeppelin scare for two months now, their
morale ebbing and flowing with the tide of events. August had passed without
the zeps. There were rumors then of a dirigible hiding in the central uplands
and the R.F.C. had ordered a Lieutenant Hucks into the air to chase the
shadow. Hucks made a thorough search and enjoyed the scenery from the
cockpit of his Bleriot but found no airship. After August had gone by free
of attack, the mood of the people began perceptibly to brighten. News from
the front was not good, but at least civilians at home could sleep safely in
their beds. Theories circulated to explain the inactivity of the enemy airship
fleet. Possibly, after all, the weather and distance had beaten them. Some
aeronautical "experts" seriously suggested that the eddies and updrafts of air
from cliffs and hills and tall buildings would preclude the zeppelins from ever
flying over England. Another surmise, which gained credence as General
Kluck slowed down in his push toward Paris, was that the Germans were
utilizing all their available airships as the eyes of the army in France and of

the navy in the North Sea—very much on the defensive against aggressive opening moves by the Royal Navy.

The threat was still to be reckoned with as September came, however, and the government took some precautionary steps. For one thing, the commissioner of metropolitan police, on September 11, issued the first ordinance for the restriction of lighting in London. The actual dimout was not to be enforced until October 1, but the prospect of living in semidarkness—with its disturbing undertones of a breakdown in civilization, a reversion to primeval chaos—again depressed the spirits of Londoners. When most of the street lamps were extinguished on the appointed evening, and the shades drawn in every house, the capital was plunged into the blackness of a cave. It was eerie, unearthly, darker even than had been imagined, and atavistic fears rustled deep in people's souls. At this bleak period came news of the air attack on Düsseldorf's zeppelin sheds. The weight of apprehensiveness began to diminish. The nights continued passing with no warning signals going off, no searchlights probing the sky, no dreaded rumble of engines overhead and no bombs whistling down. By the end of October, many Britons, some of them in the military hierarchy, were predicting that the zeppelins would never come. Among those opposed to this wishful thinking was Winston Churchill; the First Lord believed further that the best way to minimize the danger was to destroy the dirigibles in their own lairs, which Lieutenant Samson had already shown to be a feasible plan. Technically, the R.N.A.S. was a defense force with the given mission of guarding the island itself from attack. Subscribing to the old axiom that the surest defense is a good offense, Churchill authorized the bombing of other airship installations in Germany. Pleased naval aviators lost no precious time in discharging their new responsibility.

Intelligence data indicated that two and possibly more dirigibles were berthed at Friedrichshafen on Lake Constance. An air strike, a masterpiece of meticulous preparation and daring execution, was led by Commander E. F. Briggs against these zeppelin sheds. Selected for the job were four Avro 504 biplanes. The pilots—Briggs, Flight Commander John T. Babington, Sub-Liuetenant R. F. Cannon, and Flight Lieutenant S. V. Sippe—moved their machines to the frontier village of Belfort, which had the closest airfield in France to Lake Constance. So as not to attract the notice of enemy conspirators, who were prevalent in the borderlands, the British planes were dismantled, packed into unmarked lorries, and sent by road to Belfort during the midnight hours. The raid was conceived and planned by Lieutenant Noel Pemberton-Billing, who had quit building airplanes to enlist in the R.N.A.S. Because the raid would be exceptionally dangerous, Pemberton-Billing decided to ascertain beforehand whether the zeps were still nesting at Friedrichshafen. He did this at the risk of being shot as a spy, by donning peasant costume, traveling through neutral Switzerland, and then crossing Lake Constance in a rowboat to the German side. He spent a whole day hiding along the shore and half the following night examining the intended target area. Some forty-eight hours after his departure from Belfort he returned with information that the two zeppelins were still in their hangars beside the lake.

The Avros carried four twenty-pound bombs apiece, a heavier load than that certified safe by the manufacturer. One plane, that piloted by Sub-Lieutenant Cannon, could not take off because of a balky engine. The other three struggled into the air and flew the 125-mile route from Belfort to Mulhouse, across the Rhine gorge and the Black Forest to a spot near Singen, then southeastward to Friedrichshafen. When they arrived over Lake Constance, they descended to within ten feet of the water to avoid detection. About five miles from the target they climbed again to twelve hundred feet. A terse but vivid description of his part in the action is found in Flight Lieutenant Sippe's logbook:

"When half a mile from shed, put machine into dive and came down to seven hundred feet. Observed men lined up to right of shed, number estimated three hundred to five hundred. Dropped one bomb in enclosure to put gunners off aim and when in correct position put two in shed. The fourth bomb failed to release. Made several attempts to get it away, turned, went down to just above surface of lake and made off."

Briggs and Babington inflicted more of the same punishment and left the sheds and adjacent gas works in flames behind them. Babington got back to Belfort with Sippe, but Briggs—his plane crippled with a bullet-pierced fuel line—had to land about fifteen miles outside of Friedrichshafen in a lakeside clearing. Before he could reach the lake, where he hoped to steal a boat and escape to Switzerland, an irate group of civilians grabbed him. They mauled him so badly that German soldiers, when he was finally handed over to them, rushed him to a hospital for first aid. That evening, his head and left arm wrapped in bandages, Briggs was supped and wined by German air officers, who drank toasts to his courage and, British uniform or no, addressed him as "Kamerad der Lufte."

Even while Briggs was being feted by his captors, the Berlin government was preparing a wrathful statement of protest against the raid. Two charges were levied: first, that bombs had been dropped in a "barbaric manner upon innocent civilians" at Friedrichshafen, and second, that Swiss neutrality had been violated by the raiding aircraft. The British Foreign Office, pointing out that uniformed mechanics and zeppelin crewmen had lost their lives in the attack but not any civilians, and quoting extracts from the German press to substantiate this rebuttal, categorically refuted the first charge. The second complaint, which could not be verified one way or the other, was handled with exemplary British aplomb. The British delivered a diplomatic note to the Swiss embassy saying that if the nation's boundaries had been transgressed it was purely unintentional. The note also questioned whether Germany, in view of her blatant aggression against neutral Belgium, might not have disentitled herself from lodging such cynical accusations as this. The

British disclaimer was graciously accepted by the Swiss, after which a peculiar thing happened. The *Berliner Tageblatt*—Berlin's most influential newspaper—printed the whole story complete with the British explanation and Swiss satisfaction with it. "The incident," said the newspaper, "is now considered closed." It could have been that this amazing forbearance was engendered by an unwillingness to continue the embarrassing dialogue about this or that country's neutrality. Or it may have stemmed from the comforting fact that little real damage was done by British bombs, for the smoke and flames seen by the aviators had looked worse than was actually the case. Except for partial destruction of the hydrogen-producing facilities and minor fire damage to the hangars, the German base suffered no impairment that could not be immediately put back in order. Both airships survived the raid intact. As for the gas plant and the sheds, in a week they were restored to functional condition.

When the Admiralty released news of the strike against Friedrichshafen, the British people breathed another sigh of relief. It was beginning to appear as if the zeppelins were going to get more punishment than they dished out. All that was needed to erase the threat permanently were unremitting aerial assaults—bigger, more devastating raids—on the zeppelin lairs in Germany. This theory sounded plausible, and it sufficed as a crutch for British optimism. Then, at ten minutes past four on the afternoon of December 15, the steamship *Ape*, enroute from Hull to Yarmouth, sighted a low-flying dirigible just south of Protector Shoals, heading toward Marblethorpe. Rain was falling and dense shrouds of mist scudded across the water. The barometer had sunk to 29.15 inches. If the zep had come to bomb England she had chosen a bad day. But scarcely was she in sight of land than she abruptly made about and vanished to seaward. What the dirigible was doing there has never been recorded, though probably she had been sent to survey the English coast and found her mission foiled by the foul weather. In any case, she dashed the British hopes for immunity against airborne attack.

World War I, which the Germans had foreseen as a simple six-week academic exercise, was now four and a half months old; and the aviators of the Royal Flying Corps, like their naval brethren, had seen some action and proved their worth. It began for the R.F.C. at Dover on the English Channel a few days after German troops—1,500,000 of them—marched against Belgium and France in accord with a plan devised in 1905 by General Alfred von Schlieffen. The French, meanwhile, adhering to a defensive strategy originated in 1913 by General Joseph Joffre, had arrayed their five armies in Argonne and Lorraine to meet the invader along the rivers Meuse and Moselle. Thus did war announce itself on the continent with the thunder of artillery, the chatter of machine guns, the punctuating crack and whine of rifle fire, and the cries and moans of dying men.

It was much different in Dover, in all of England for that matter, as four squadrons of the R.F.C. prepared to fly to France's aid. If somebody did not know there was a war on and took a stroll from town to the plain at the edge of the white cliffs, he might have thought nothing more grim-purposed than an air pageant was in progress. Along the ditches which bordered the field, to warn the aviators, were planted red pennants. Four large vans were parked in a meadow. Less warlike vehicles could hardly be imagined. Instead of military insignia they bore the names of familiar household wares: Lazenby's Sauce, Bovril Beef Cube, Peak Frean's Biscuits, Stephen's Blue-Black Ink. These vans, plucked from the streets of London, comprised the transport and supply service intended to care for the men and planes that already had begun arriving in twos and threes. According to the R.F.C. manual, each pilot was required to carry with him into the combat zone a spare pair of goggles, field glasses, a tool kit, a canteen of boiled water, a small cooking stove, tinned meat and biscuits, soup cubes, a piece of chocolate, and a loaded revolver. All these items, plus fuel and replacement parts for the planes, were brought to the improvised airdome by the four vans.

By dusk on August 12 there were thirty-seven aircraft on the field ready to go to war, with an additional twenty-six due to arrive in the next two days. The numbers stenciled on their olive-drab fuselages were those of Squadrons Nos. 2, 3, 4, and 5, and it had taken a prodigious job of organization to assemble so many serviceable machines in one place on such brief notice. The first British airplane to land on the continent after the outbreak of hostilities was Royal Aircraft Factory BE-2A No. 347 of Squadron No. 2; flown by Lieutenant H. D. Harvey-Kelly, it departed from Dover at twenty-five past six on the morning of August 13 and touched down near Amiens an hour and fifty-five minutes later. Squadrons Nos. 2, 3, and 4 went to France that day; Squadron No. 5 on August 15. The units had mixed equipment. Squadrons Nos. 2 and 4 were equipped throughout with BE-2's; Squadron No. 3 had Morane-Saulnier Parasol and Bleriot monoplanes and Henri Farman F-20 biplanes; Squadron No. 5 had BE-8's, Avro 504's, and Henri Farmans. The total R.F.C. force consisted of sixty-three flying machines, 105 pilots and observers, 755 mechanics and administrators, and 320 trucks and automobiles.[1]

The airmen of these four squadrons were extraordinary human beings, almost every one. Born of a star-crossed generation and filled with ideals and an appetite for adventure, they met life on its own terms. Lieutenant Harvey-Kelly, lighthearted and imperturbable, brilliantly recommended himself to aviation history until claimed, as were so many, by death. Lieutenant G. W. Mapplebeck, one of the first to be shot down and hidden by the people of Lille—who showed him the printed circulars offering a reward for his arrest—escaped to fly again and die. Famous for the number of crashes he walked away from, Major Charles James Burke, unpopular with his men in Squadron No. 2 because he was a strict disciplinarian, nevertheless won

[1] Robertson: *Air Aces of the 1914–1918 War.*

their admiration and profound respect as a brave and determined pilot. Burke, who had learned to fly while serving with the Royal Irish Regiment, and whose Hibernian brogue was the butt of bad jokes, was killed in 1916 on the opening day of the Arras offensive. Lieutenant Louis A. Strange of Squadron No. 5 did not cross to France until August 16, a day later than his squadron companions. He postponed his departure by complaining of a faulty engine in his Farman biplane. The engine was actually working well enough, however, and he spent most of that night on Dover plain fitting a Lewis gun to a front cockpit mounting of his own devising. Strange, landing in France with the only armed airplane in the R.F.C., had some amazing aerial exploits during the next four years, and, phenomenally, lived to serve in the R.A.F. in World War II. Among the ranks of Squadron No. 3 was Air Mechanic First Class James T. B. McCudden, destined soon to earn his pilot's wings and to go on to become England's fourth-ranking ace with fifty-seven victories to his credit. McCudden's magnificent fighting career came to a curious and tragic anticlimax on July 19, 1918, when the engine of his SE-5 stalled on takeoff and he committed the fatal and—for an aviator of his ability—inexcusable error of trying to get back to the airdrome.

These were some of the young men who flew across the Channel to claim glory and, in most instances, an early grave. They themselves were very nearly the only ones who had any confidence in the usefulness of their machines. They freely acknowledged that the "PBI" (poor bloody infantry) would ultimately win or lose the war, but they insisted they had more to do in France than simply skylark about the countryside and impress the mademoiselles with their uniforms. The letters they mailed home and the thoughts they inscribed in their diaries spoke of the great pride and excitement they felt in being part of a revolutionary new phase of warfare. Even the least imaginative of them sensed that they and their machines would play a vital role in resolving the world conflict. And aviation, through the agency of these British airmen, proved its value swiftly and spectacularly, by an achievement unprecedented in military annals.

The pilots and observers of the Royal Flying Corps took up their assigned task of reconnaissance three days after arriving at the front. From bases near Mons in Belgium, and Amiens in France, they scanned the entire area over which the German legions were advancing and flew as far as Brussels and Louvain. Had it not been for their sharp eyes, the tiny British Expeditionary Force under General Sir John French might have met with immediate catastrophe. On the British commander's right flank the French army was hard pressed and ordered to retreat. In any previous war he would have had to await word of this collapse from comparatively slow cavalry scouts on horseback. But R.F.C. observers were able to report it promptly. More than that, they spotted the enemy First Army led by General Kluck racing either to surround the British force or to annihilate it in the jaws of a crushing pincer attack. As a result of such aerial intelligence, General French managed to withdraw his army without too many casualties. The retreat from Mons, successfully carried out one week after the B.E.F. landed in France, established the airplane scout as a supremely important element of twentieth-century warfare.

Besides the traditional military branches of infantry, cavalry, and artillery, a fourth branch suddenly weighed in the balance of power. Overnight a new dimension had been added to war. Had it not been for the information brought in by aerial reconnaissance, the crucial battle of World War I might have been fought during its initial week. In this battle the British would certainly have been defeated, after which nothing could have stopped the German juggernaut from rolling across France and maybe England as well. This realization, bolstered a couple of months later by the audacious bombing sorties of the Royal Naval Air Service against German zeppelin stations, fostered a tremendous effort on either side of the lines for mastery of the air, which greatly accelerated the pace of aeronautical development.

Germany's flyers did not take long to make their presence painfully evident to the retreating Allies. Early in September, the German infantry penetrated to within twenty-five miles of Paris. Exigencies at the front monopolized the whole of France's air corps; not a single plane could be spared to patrol over the capital. Several afternoons that month, punctually at five o'clock, a lone German aviator, Lieutenant Karl von Hiddessen, flew in above the house-tops. When the big guns on the outlying fortifications heralded his coming, gawking crowds gathered in the parks and on the bridges across the Seine. It was a thrilling tableau they watched. As Hiddessen neared the center of the city, the machine guns mounted on the Eiffel Tower went into action. A storm of lead was hurled up against the solitary flyer who, contemptuously refusing to keep his Taube above bullet range, swooped low over the mass of upturned faces. His purposes was not to drop explosives. His mission was only to prove to the half-bemused, half-enraged Parisians that they could be assaulted from the clouds. The aviator let go from his cockpit a small sandbag containing a note addressed to the people of Paris. The message was always the same. "Surrender!" it demanded. "The Germans are at your gates! Tomorrow you will be ours!" (This note-dropping exploit has been attributed to the famous Max Immelmann, who did not even receive his pilot's certificate until March 1915, six months later.)

Perhaps to demonstrate that Hiddessen's warning was no idle boast, a Lieutenant Dressler in the second week of September dropped the first bombs to land on French soil; they were small four-pounders and exploded harmlessly on the outskirts of Paris, but they worried the French and British, who feared the attacks would be intensified. Dressler, too, piloted a Taube, which informed Allied authorities of the excellence of the German monoplane. The French nicknamed it the "invisible dove," for the fabric on the wings and delta-shaped tail was transparent against a sunlit sky.

In November, the seeds planted by Dressler began to flower. The Germans formed an air unit at Ostend for the sole purpose of bombing. This first all-bomber squadron in history was officially designated as the Brieftauben-Abteilung-Ostende, or Carrier Pigeon Unit, Ostend, which was merely a cover title for its real errand. For some time the squadron's true mission remained a tightly locked secret. Commanded at the outset by Major H. von Gersdorff and equipped largely with Albatros D-2A heavy biplanes, the squadron was entrusted with a German dream. When the German army reached Calais, the Ostend Carrier Pigeons—as the pilots preferred to call themselves—would follow and establish an airdrome there. From that point they would hop across the Channel to bomb England. But the dream never materialized, since the army was unable to secure Calais.

It was not until two months later that the bomber pilots were put into action. On January 28, 1915, they took off to execute a night raid on Dunkirk, the war's first such operation and a sterling success. Several dozen fires were left blazing in the terrorized city and all of Gersdorff's planes returned safely to base. Thereafter the Carrier Pigeons flew regularly, adding French and British airfields to their list of objectives. The unit, its command taken over that spring by a Major Siegert, soon merited the reverence of the Fatherland and the hatred of the Allies for its persistent bombing strikes. Four young aviators who later rose to fame were initiated into the air war as members of the Ostend squadron: Baron Manfred von Richthofen, Ernst Udet, Hermann Goering, and Bruno Loerzer.

England, though she luckily escaped the massive attack planned by the Ostend Carrier Pigeons, and although the dreaded zeppelins had not yet ventured across the North Sea, was twice bombed before the end of 1914. Late in the morning of December 21, a Friedrichshafen FF-29 seaplane—one of the large machines being manufactured for the Imperial navy by Count Zeppelin—veered in from the Channel and dropped a bomb on High Street in Dover. The next day a newspaper in Cologne, under the byline of Dr. George Wagener, printed this short item on a back page:

> At noon today I was at a place on the Belgian coast and witnessed the safe return of naval airman Lieutenant von Prondzynsk, who flew off at 9:30 A.M. toward Dover. He reached Dover and threw down several bombs, one of which may have hit the harbor railroad depot. Between Dover and Calais he observed two rows of torpedo-boat destroyers spaced out from the English to the French coast. . . . With the wind he flew back from Dover in an hour to our position. The bold airman received hearty congratulations for this first trip of a German hydroplane to the English homeland.

Whether the pilot Pronzynsk or the writer Wagener exaggerated the quantity of bombs dropped in the foray cannot be determined. Since no record of the incident exists today in the official German archives (which in good part were destroyed by Allied bombers during the World War of 1939–1945), reliance must be placed with British sources, and these concur unanimously that only one missile fell that day on Dover.

Another German raider visited southern England on Christmas Day. This time it was an Albatros seaplane. At thirty-five minutes past noon it appeared over Sheerness. From there it flew as far west as Gravesend, went inland to Dartford, northwest to Erith; passed over Purfleet and Tilbury, crossed the river again at Shornmead Fort, and dropped two high-explosive bombs near Cliffe Station. Eventually, after scrutinizing the military targets and defense installations around the Thames estuary, the Albatros went out to sea again over Thanet and Minster, having survived interception attempts by R.N.A.S. pilots from the Isle of Grain, who fired rifles and pistols at the intruder.[2] In neither this nor the preceding raid was anyone injured, nor was any real property damage done. The British, in fact, who all this time had been expecting much worse, were more relieved than angered. It was not airplanes but zeppelins—with their larger bomb load—that Britons feared the most. But after the dirigibles had come, done their worst, and then gone, by the third year of war the British population found that heavier-than-air machines were again the greater scourge.

Meanwhile, the French, considering their prewar zest for aviation, had accomplished surprisingly little in the air except to provide interesting targets for their own infantrymen.

The first French air casualty was the dirigible *Montgolfier*, which had been sent aloft from Maubeuge to locate General Kluck's First Army. Despite its smaller size and distinctly different shape, the vessel was mistaken for a hostile zeppelin as it sailed over the French lines. Thousands of trigger-happy *poilus*, weary of sitting and waiting for the German onslaught, gleefully shot the *Montgolfier's* gas envelope to tatters with rifles and machine guns. Thinking they had knocked their fourth zeppelin from the sky, they cheered wildly as the doomed airship writhed and coiled to earth.

The *Montgolfier* was as much the victim of its own inferiority compared to the rigid-framed zeppelin as of the ignorance of French ground forces. On more than one occasion the German infantry blasted away at friendly dirigibles, but owing to the rugged qualities of Count Zeppelin's product and its system of multiple hydrogen cells, no serious harm was ever inflicted. Both sides were also guilty of firing on their own airplanes during the inchoate months of combat, and aviators soon came to appreciate the wisdom of staying beyond bullet range when flying over their infantry in the trenches.

Following the sad loss of the *Montgolfier,* the French had only slightly better fortune with their airplanes. The largest assemblage of planes was in the Côtes de Meuse region between Verdun and Nancy, for it was here they expected the principal German thrust. The main attack, however, was launched across the Belgian border through Maubeuge and Mézières further

[2] Poolman: *Zeppelins Against London.*

to the north. General Joffre, in formulating his defense plan in 1913, had not anticipated the unscrupulous German strategy of sweeping westward through neutral Belgium. Neither had anyone else outside the Kaiser's councils of decision. Although two aviation escadrilles were positioned at Mézières, an interlude of bad weather prevented their flying for five critical days in August, during which the Germans were developing their pattern of attack. (This same period of rain and fog kept Lieutenant Samson and his small band of R.N.A.S. pilots grounded at Dunkirk.) When the weather cleared, the twelve aviator-observer teams at Mézières were told to pinpoint enemy troop concentrations, but the area to be surveyed included the whole of Luxemburg and southwest Belgium, an impossibly large area for so few airplanes to patrol adequately. Seventeen flights went out from Mézières. Of these, only five inspected the vicinity north of Luxemburg where the Germans—taking advantage of fine Belgian railroads—were in reality deploying their forces. It was French procedure to forward reports of aerial observation to the central intelligence section known as the Second Bureau, there to be interpreted and summarized for the high command, and it was on the Second Bureau's estimate that General Joffre relied. Intelligence figured the enemy to have eight army corps and four cavalry divisions in Belgium, which was a gross miscalculation. Actually the German phalanx consisted of sixteen army corps and five divisions of cavalry.

Unlike their British counterparts of the R.F.C., who a few days later saved General French's expeditionary force from possible disaster, the air scouts of France made nonsense of their first wartime assignment. They did worse than simply fail; they brought back altogether misleading information. Of course a portion of the blame must be attributed to faulty interpretation of data by the Second Bureau. Just as airborne observers were inexperienced in spotting troops and equipment on the ground, so were intelligence officers unversed in the art of puzzling out information received. Both would soon improve decidedly.

The Germans inaugurated their campaign against France by spearheading the brunt of their might at the French Fifth Army, commanded by General Laurezac, who was responsible for the forty-mile sector between Maubeuge and Mézières. To the north, strung in a thin line from Condé to Mons, were the four divisions of the British Expeditionary Force. To the south, the French Third and Fourth Armies had already, on the night of August 22, collided with the German Fourth and Fifth Armies. Groping through a murky fog, French riflemen were mowed down by the thousands in the withering crossfire of machine guns. The French were heavily thrown back in fierce battles around Virton-Neufchâteau, but the Germans were too vague as to the situation to exploit their opportunity. The effect, however, was to denude Lanrezac's right flank, and it soon made a fateful difference in the major action to the north, along the Belgian frontier.

The B.E.F. had moved up to Mons on August 22, ready to proceed deeper into Belgium in conjunction with Lanrezac's Fifth Army. On his arrival, though, General French was informed by his aviation scouts that Lanrezac had been attacked and deprived of crossings at the Sambre River. Placed thus in an exposed position, the British commander gamely agreed to stand at Mons to protect Lanrezac's left. But next day Lanrezac ordered his thirteen divisions to withdraw. It was the discreet thing to do in the circumstances, for the German Third Army had suddenly loomed up on his naked right flank near Dinant, and Lanrezac shrewdly perceived this to be the beginning of the enemy's all-out drive on France, which the general staff had been sure would come via Argonne and Lorraine. On August 24, the British, after resisting six German divisions during the day, fell back, having been alerted in the nick of time by aerial reconnaissance to the fact that their right flank had been relinquished to the enemy. The B.E.F. escaped by a whisker, and the great retreat to the Marne was underway. Paced by General Kluck's First Army on the outermost flank, the German horde inexorably pushed back the Allied defense line, which pivoted west and south from Verdun. By September 5, Kluck's elite regiments were bivouacked within a few hours' march of Paris; four other German armies were surging southward along a broad front stretching from Lagny on the west to Châlons-sur-Marne on the east. The following morning General Joffre issued a memorable order of the day:

"At this moment when is about to begin the battle on which depends the salvation of France, the time has passed for looking behind us. Every effort must be made to attack and hurl back the foe. Troops who find themselves unable longer to advance will at any cost hold the positions they have conquered and will die on the spot rather than surrender ground."

Although four years of dreadful slaughter lay ahead, Joffre's order ended the German dream of establishing a pan-Germanic empire in Europe. For the French commander had signaled the start of the battle of the Marne, which would first stem the Germans and then turn them back in a savage counteroffensive. War had never been waged on such a majestic scale. Against 700,000 French and 60,000 British were pitted 900,000 Germans, led by officers who since childhood had been indoctrinated in a death-before-dishonor tradition. As the intensity of the fighting heightened, both sides poured reinforcements into the melee. Men fell like scythed wheat. By November, the Allies had suffered nearly a million casualties, a fantastic figure never to be eclipsed in any three-month period throughout the war. But hedgerow by hedgerow, trench by trench, hill by hill, each wave of charging infantry trampling underfoot the bodies of yesterday's dead, the Allied force recovered territory. The situation map of New Year's Day, 1915, showed the Germans back halfway to the Belgian border. Here the Franco-British advance bogged down, and the trenchline became stabilized. For the rest of World War I the situation would remain essentially unchanged, stalemated, with each side mounting periodic offensives, sacrificing scores of thousands of lives, only to annex a few miles and then be repulsed by the enemy's ferocious counter-attack. In the Somme offensive of 1916, for example, the Allies suffered 750,000 dead and wounded in exchange for fewer than 150 square miles of shell-pocked wasteland, and the Germans lost half a million men before the drive was finally halted. The mightiest armies ever assembled were locked in a gruelling war of attrition. Opposing troops stood in deep trenches, facing each other across a desolate no-man's-land. They dug in to avoid the murderous fire of modern automatic and repeating weapons, and they learned to curse the mud and vermin more than the enemy guns. The earthworks were elaborate, with some observers reporting up to twenty miles of trenches along a front of only five miles.

Aerial reconnaissance naturally assumed an important role in a war that seldom moved and rarely showed its head above ground. The airplane, furthermore, was partly responsible for the military stalemate. Neither side found it possible to deploy consequential numbers of troops without the other's immediate awareness of the move. The element of surprise virtually disappeared from war. The feint and parry of tactical combat was replaced by the bald and brutal frontal assault in which a massive battering ram of attackers rushed against a human wall of defenders. In a contest of this sort it was no wonder that field commanders soon recognized the value of aerial reconnaissance. They saw the imperative need for gathering accurate data about the enemy's daily doings, and they realized that their own intentions had to be kept from the prying eyes of rival aviators, for only then could some small edge be gained on the opposition. It was this factor in particular that catalyzed the desperate race for air supremacy, which led to the development of combat planes and made a science of aircraft armament. The fighter plane was created for the dual job of destroying hostile observation machines and escorting friendly ones into danger zones. And this inevitably meant air-to-air conflict.

In the opening chapter of the war, however, as the Allies receded to the Marne and then clawed their way back half the distance to Belgium, the sheer magnitude of the fighting by infantry and artillery as well as the enormity of the casualties focused the spotlight of world attention exclusively on the ground fighting. The airplane killed or wounded virtually no one. The only aggressive aerial actions were minor ripples in the great mainstream of the war. As yet, the public—and this was true of every belligerent country as well as the United States—had not awakened to the fact that a new and devastating weapon was being forged in the crucible of war.

An interesting commentary on the unawareness of even the German high command of the part being played by the airplane was reflected as late as December 1914, in an address to the Reichstag by Chancellor Theobald von Bethmann-Hollweg. The chancellor, wearing the field-gray uniform of the general staff, reviewed for two hours the whole conduct of the war up to that time. He minutely detailed events on the western front, and he praised the infantry which had captured the "impregnable fortresses" of Liège, Namur, Antwerp, and Maubeuge. The artillery and cavalry came in for their share of encomiums, too. So did the Imperial navy as Bethmann-Hollweg told of its victory at Coronel and paid special honor to the cruisers *Breslau* and *Goven,* and to the *Emden,* "the little ship which has made every sea unsafe for the enemy and before which the fleets of our adversaries tremble." He continued his oration with a reference to the "glorious deeds of our submarines which are today the nemesis of the British navy and the terror of the whole British nation." But never did the speaker mention the Taubes, the Albatroses, or any of the other planes that had been doing earnest if unspectacular work during these frenetic days of trial and error.[3]

Although the duties originally assigned to the air services were for the most part nonbelligerent and in the nature of reporting, the war was not many days old before flyers were active combatants. For the first three weeks or so, the routine of the airborne scout was hardly more dangerous than peacetime flying had been. A typical reconnaissance flight across the lines amounted to a leisurely sight-seeing excursion. As the Germans quickly found out, the only real danger was from the ground. They learned this on August 12, when they suffered their first air casualty, Lieutenant Reinhold Jahnow, who was a victim of French infantry fire. Ten days later, Sergeant-Major D. S. Jillings of the Royal Flying Corps was wounded by German riflemen, though not seriously. And a few days after that, another sergeant—nameless in the public records and likely so at his own request—received a humiliating wound when a bullet from the ground came through the seat of his plane. Many of the British machines were then equipped with metal seats, but not all, as the anonymous sergeant could testify. Immediately after this horrifying incident occurred, almost all the stove lids vanished from R.F.C. field kitchens. Yet, so long as an aviator stayed a prudent distance above the trenches, the risk was small. Encounters aloft between pilots of opposing sides aroused no animosity in either. Habitually they waved a comradely greeting and proceeded along their separate courses without swerving. For the time being, both sides tacitly subscribed to a code forbidding any attempt to harm a fellow flyer, even if he was an enemy. Far below, a million mud-caked men were struggling to exterminate each other, yet in an airplane at five thousand feet, the war was clean and remote and reasonably safe.

The idyll ended on August 25, when some realistic members of No. 2 squadron, Royal Flying Corps, decided the rules could be amended to permit the capture of German aircraft without resort to weapons. Three of the outfit's BE-2's, with Lieutenant Harvey-Kelly at the controls of the lead plane, forced a Taube to land that morning by flying over it and staging mock attacks. This German machine was burned on the ground by its dutiful pilot, but within hours another was driven down in identical fashion near Le Quesnoy and

[3] For this and other portions of the present chapter, the author is indebted to the book by the late Quentin Reynolds, *They Fought for the Sky*.

seized intact. And three days later, Lieutenant Norman Spratt, flying an un-armed Sopwith Tabloid, accomplished the same feat in a solo performance. A new sport was born, which the men of No. 2 Squadron waggishly christ-ened "Hounding the Hun."

Retaliation was not long delayed. Early in September a French reconnais-sance pilot landed at his airdrome with a gaping hole through both wings of his Breguet biplane. He reported that a German pilot had hurled down a brick at him.

Now that the first stone had been cast, an aggressive spirit manifested itself in both camps. A rash of awkward combats were being fought with a won-drous assortment of weapons, the crudest of which were bricks and rocks. Several Frenchmen packed slingshots in their flying jodhpurs in the chimerical hope of hitting any Boches who ventured within rubberband range. Steel darts, called *fléchettes*, became standard ordnance on many Allied planes. Grenades were thrown or dragged through the air on long ropes, the idea being to maneuver them into enemy propellers to be detonated. Grappling hooks were also dangled overboard to shred the wings of enemy machines. Pistols, carbines, muskets, and rifles came into play. One German airman, Lieutenant Georg Paul Neumann, fastened a gramaphone horn to the barrel of a carbine, which added nothing to its effectiveness but gave it the appear-ance of a diabolical new weapon; Allied pilots, on seeing it, fled.

But little damage actually accrued from the great majority of these early gun battles. Firing a hand-held weapon from one moving airplane at another was not conducive to crack marksmanship. More typical of such engagements was that recounted in a German periodical of November 1914:

> Another time he had to fight a protracted duel with a British machine. . . . When the combatants had exhausted all their rifle and revolver ammunition, they blazed away with their Very pistols [flare guns], which made for very poor shooting. After a while, both pilots realized that the only chance of scoring a hit was to get close up, but when they laid their machines alongside, the humor of the situation struck von Leutzer [the German pilot] forcibly, so that he roared with laughter at the sight of two observers solemnly taking deliberate aim, a green light answering a red one. Evidently, the observers were also too tickled to shoot straight, for neither got anywhere near his mark.

Around the middle of September the French and British implemented a policy of air-to-ground attacks against both strategic and tactical objectives, including troop positions, supply caravans, telephone exchanges, freight yards, railroads, and ammunition and poison-gas dumps. Small hand-thrown bombs, which most pilots carried strapped around the waist, and sometimes grenades were hurled down on these targets. Fléchettes were additionally used as an anti-personnel weapon. A French aviator enthusiastically wrote to his family:

What a pleasure to see a convoy on the march! We straddle the
column at a good height . . . so as not to be reached by the bullets
of the infantry, and then the bombs fall! One of these, well placed,
means a dozen of the wretches laid low. The horses scatter, the
ammunition wagons capsize, and then those terrible arrows [fléch-
ettes] follow, hundreds at a time. It is a veritable rain of iron of a
most remarkable and wonderful penetration. Sometimes a horseman and his horse are pierced through and through; men fall like
flies without a sound and without any apparent wound.

The Frenchman's lurid description of the confusion and death, however,
must be regarded with some skepticism. Occasionally bombs dropped upon
infantry and cavalry induced temporary panic, and once in a great while a
raid like the one at Düsseldorf or Friedrichshafen produced telling results,
but on the whole, bombing was nearly worthless as a deterrent to the movement of ground forces. A close survey made by Allied experts revealed the
disquieting fact that out of 141 bombing operations, only three could be said
to have had any telling effect on the enemy.

If bombing wasn't paying dividends, the results of aerial reconnaissance
were at least promising, and in the retreat from Mons, better than that. But
observation was limited to the eyesight of the beholder, and the eye is a
notoriously fallible organ. Deficiencies of human judgment and memory had
to be overcome if the air scout were going to bring back a really true picture
of the enemy's situation. The obvious answer was the camera. There was
already an interest in photography among British airmen and many flying
officers had brought their own cameras and darkroom paraphernalia, but their
work from the air was invariably amateurish and valueless from an intelligence standpoint. The French were ahead of the British in experimenting with
aerial photography; the R.F.C. therefore assigned Major W. G. H. Salmond
to study their equipment and methods. As a result of this investigation, a new
photographic unit was set up. It consisted of Major Salmond, Lieutenant
J. T. C. Moore-Barbazon, and Lieutenant C. D. M. Campbell. These three
were told to cooperate with the Thornton-Pickard Manufacturing Company
in designing an aerial camera that would take pictures that could be readily
processed in the field. In two months, such a camera was being tested. The
observer held it over the side of the banking aircraft by two belts. The film
carriage was geared to a free propeller outside the plane. In the first weeks
of 1915, this camera took pictures of the German-held territory south of
La Bassee Canal. Enlargements showed German emplacements situated at
the exact points where the British planned to attack. Had they not learned
this in time, the British would undoubtedly have lost both the battle and many
lives. Instead they modified the attack and completely succeeded.

On this kind of practical demonstration, the increasingly important role of
the observer and his camera was established. Both sides saw the need for

new and improved two-seater reconnaissance machines. The mortality among planes was high, although very few were destroyed by enemy action. Poor maintenance, unreliable engines, and the fact that most airfields were but hastily converted pastures, often rutted with weed-concealed ditches and animal burrows, all combined to wreck many planes and kill their pilots. By October 31, Germany had lost fifty-two pilots and more than ninety aircraft; in almost every case an accident was the cause. The air services did not yet appreciate the necessity for frequently checking and overhauling their machines. Planes were flown until a structural weakness or a malfunction of the engine precipitated a crash that proper ground care could have prevented.

Toward the end of 1914, the realization dawned on both sides that the best way to prevent enemy observation planes from returning to their bases with useful information was to destroy the machines. There was a lot of confusion about how this would be done. The inexpedience of antiaircraft guns was well known; nor would a really good gun be devised for this purpose throughout the war. The futility of pilots pelting each other with bricks and rocks and the near impossibility of blowing up an adversary with a hand grenade or potting him with a pistol or rifle was by now a matter of fact. The several French airplanes that at this time were armed with machine guns seemed not to have figured in these early combats, or so the French histories imply by failing to cite any such action until October 14, when a Taube monoplane was shot down with a Hotchkiss 8-mm from a Voisin pusher. Why the French were so laggard about using the *mitrailleuse* in the air is not easy to fathom, unless it was because of the prevailing assumption that airplanes were unfit for combat. The British, one of them anyway, were quicker to put a machine gun to aerial use, although the initial results were less than encouraging.

Lieutenant Louis Strange, the fire-eater of No. 5 Squadron R.F.C. who flew his Farman biplane to France with a Lewis gun affixed to the forward cockpit, wasted no time in trying the weapon on the first German plane he saw. On August 22, when most airmen still thought it rather uncouth to shoot at one another, Strange took off from Maubeuge in pursuit of an enemy aircraft. Riding up front as his gunner was Lieutenant L. da C. Penn-Gaskell. The laden Farman could not climb above 3500 feet and the German, 1500 feet higher, escaped as Penn-Gaskell vainly raked the sky with bullets. Strange's commanding officer, Major John F. A. Higgins, rightly concluded that the weight of the gun had prevented the Farman from closing with the Hun. He ordered both the Lewis and its mounting detached from the plane. But matching Strange's ingenuity was his tenacity of purpose, as indicated by this entry in his diary on October 2, 1914: "Fixed a safety strap to the leading edge of top wing so as to enable passenger to stand up and fire all around over top of plane and behind. Took Lieutenant Rabagliati as my passenger on trial trip. Great success! Increases range of fire greatly!"

The aircraft in question was the same Henri Farman. But two weeks afterward, Strange and Rabagliati flew off in an Avro 504. They pursued an

Aviatik two-seater, Rabagliati firing an entire drum of ammunition—forty-seven rounds—without success. Nevertheless, Strange returned to the airdrome a cheerful man. The Avro's performance had scarcely been affected by the extra weight of the gun, and Strange promptly set himself to the task of devising a permanent mounting for the weapon.

The discovery of a more efficient airplane by this determined Briton completely changed the complexion of aerial combat in the fifth month of war. The R.F.C. and the French aviation corps, with Lewis guns fitted to Strange mounts, were soon responsible for many a troubled night's sleep among German air crews who faced scouting missions in the morning. Colonel Lewis' automatic gun had finally won recognition as a superb weapon for winged warfare. Perhaps there were red faces in the United States War Department in February 1915, when *Aeronautics* magazine published a rave notice about the gun:

> With the extraordinary and unforeseen development of fighting in the air, the Lewis automatic gun, which has been adopted by the Royal Flying Service [sic], is peculiarly well-fitted for use on board an airplane by reason of its wonderful lightness and extreme simplicity. . . . One of its main features is that, as against the water-cooling system of every other type of machine gun, it is purely air-cooled. It is exceedingly light, weighing twenty-six and a half pounds, and is gas-operated. Other advantages are: assembly time, thirty seconds only; normal rate of fire, five hundred rounds per minute, singly or in bursts of any number of shots and in any position. The air-cooling is so effective that the gun may be fired continuously without overheating and without changing the barrel. . . .

German flyers, until the end of 1914, were under orders to concentrate on reconnaissance, and were therefore far less aggressive than their Allied antagonists. Probably the Germans did not yet possess a suitable machine gun for aerial use, their chief weapon being the Mauser infantry rifle. When the ring-mounted Parabellum gun entered service early in 1915, it immediately proved superior to the Lewis by virtue of its larger ammunition drum. But the Parabellum and the Lewis had a drawback or two in common. Both were prone to sudden jams and stoppages, which too often occurred at the most crucial moment of a duel. Stowing spare drums of ammunition in a cramped cockpit did not contribute to a gunner's comfort. As a rule, he improvised racks for the drums, or sat on them, or chanced a predicament like that described by the English ace, Major James McCudden, in his posthumously published memoirs:

> Halfway up the loop, I changed my mind and pushed the stick forward, with the result that I transferred my load from my flying to my landing wires. The resultant upward pressure was so great

that all my ammunition drums shot out of my machine over the top wing and into the revolving propeller, which, being a pusher, of course was behind me. . . . There was a mighty scrunch and terrific vibration as three of my four propeller blades disappeared in a cloud of splinters. I at once switched off and removed my gun from my knees, where it had fallen after having been wrenched from its mounting and thrown into the air, owing to the terrific vibration caused by my engine doing 1600 revs per minute with only one propeller blade . . . and I just had wits enough left to pick out a field and make a landing successfully.

The British built quite a number of pusher planes like the one McCudden was flying. It was fairly easy to fit a forward-firing machine gun to a plane of this type. A simple ball-and-socket mounting provided the gunner a good field of fire. But such ungainly machines lacked the nimble performance that befits a combat aircraft. The best of them—the Vickers *Gun Bus,* the FE-2, and the DH-2—were aggravatingly slow and clumsy. Recognizing this fact, Germany invested her confidence in the more efficient tractor planes, with propellers up front. Although they flew circles around the lumbering pushers, their field of fire, limited by the forward airscrew, was restricted to the sides and rear. The deadlier front gun of the pusher offset the greater speed and maneuverability of the tractor plane and, as had happened in the ground fighting below, the battle for the sky had reached a stalemate.

An ironic prank of fate soon upset this parity of power and changed forever the disposition of war in the air.

CHAPTER V

A Gun to Kill With

On THAT DAY IN 1914, when Germany marched gayly to war, a young French aviator found himself stranded, of all places, in Berlin. His name was Roland Garros, and possessing one of those restless natures untrammeled by caution, he ranked among the foremost stunt and competition flyers of his generation. He had entered almost every important air contest in Europe and, as often as not, emerged a victor. He had given aerial exhibitions throughout the United States in 1911. He was the first to fly across the Mediterranean Sea. He had won the Paris-to-Rome and Paris-to-Madrid air races, and the Grand Prix d'Anjou. He was also something of a prodigy in that he was a laudable artist, a talented musician, a singer and dancer of more than modest merit, and a drinker of marvelous capacity. For all that, he was urbane, handsome, and rich.

But on this evening of August 3 he was in trouble. For three weeks Garros had been making exhibition flights over the German capital in his tiny Morane-Saulnier. It was a peerless and thrilling show he put on, and his front-page publicity was dimmed only by the imminence of war. After each triumphant day in the air the glamorous Frenchman was regaled anew by his appreciative audiences. But on this night, surrounded by German officers who had gone wild at the announcement of war, Garros sat glumly and tried to marshal his wits. The wine was good, but he imbibed sparingly. He had to get out of the restaurant, out of Berlin, out of Germany, and back to France. Garros had no intention of sitting out the war in an internment camp, although the Germans would have guarded him with a regiment if they knew what he had in store for them.

A couple of hours went by before he did anything. Then he stood, feigning drunken good fellowship, and staggered giddily to the toilet, much to the amusement of his hosts. When next they saw him again, it would be after he had all but cleared the sky of Germans, for Roland Garros became history's first flying ace and the father of modern aerial combat.

Garros, in his own account of his escape, glossed over the part played by his daring, but the story belongs with the classics of adventure literature. After leaving the toilet through an open window, he hied to the field where his plane was sheltered in a tent, arriving there a little past midnight. Four police sentries were posted night and day with the machine to protect it from souvenir hunters; Garros bribed or talked them into letting him roll the plane out onto the field. The German guards could not have guessed that anyone was crazy enough to attempt what Garros attempted, or skilled enough with an airplane to succeed. In the first place, pilots ordinarily did not fly at night in 1914; with no instruments to provide an artificial horizon, the few who had tried it had left an awful lot of wreckage behind them. In the second place, along with the customary assortment of furrows, stumps, and rocks, the exhibition field was closed in by buildings, trees, and wires, and a belief had grown up that a pilot should have a clear view of such impediments before taking off. Thirdly, as the guards themselves had noted in the preceding three weeks, it took eight men to crank up the Morane-Saulnier—three on either side to hold down the wing, another to swing the propeller, and the pilot to work the priming pump and the ignition switch. The Le Rhone rotary engine that powered the diminutive monoplane had no idling speed. The instant it sparked to life, it was turning over at full throttle, and even six husky men anchoring the wing had trouble restraining the engine's enthusiasm. For all these reasons, then, the policemen acceded to the French aviator's request.

Experienced flyer that he was, Garros always topped the plane's fuel tank immediately upon landing. All he did now inside the tent was stow a couple of extra cans of gasoline in the cockpit for the long flight ahead. Dragging the plane out to his usual starting place, he aimed the nose in the direction least cluttered by obstacles. The night was calm, so wind was not one of his worries. He reached into the cockpit and jiggled a few things. Muttering some appropriate incantations, he went around to the propeller and gingerly pulled it down and away. The engine roared as he dodged the milling blades and threw himself over the leading edge of the wing, which caught him hard in the midriff. Beneath him the plane was bucking, lurching, yawing, gaining speed, threatening to ground loop at any second. Garros hauled himself up on a handful of bracing wires, then literally flung himself into the cockpit. The takeoff was miraculously successful.

Back in Paris he reported for service and was attached forthwith to Escadrille Morane-Saulnier No. 23, a squadron of notables. Besides Garros, the squadron had on its roster such aviation worthies as Adolphe Pegoud, the first pilot ever to loop-the-loop, Eugene Gilbert, Marc Pourpe, Armand Pinsard, and Maxime Lenoir. These men, who had written so many pages of early aviation history in Europe, had for years been preaching to a deaf military department the possibilities of the airplane in war. Now, as members of this select escadrille, they were eager to vindicate their arguments. The army, however, decided they would not qualify as French soldiers until they were subjected to a few weeks of drill on the parade ground and until they were trained in the use of the saber and rehearsed in the minutiae of military discipline. An entire week was devoted to learning how to defend themselves against a cavalry charge. "What they teach us," Pourpe remarked in a letter, "is farcical. We want to fly, and I think the Boches have no horses that tread on air."

The Allied counterpush from the Marne was already in progress when Escadrille M.S. No. 23 was at last turned loose over the front lines. Its job was pure and simple reconnaissance. The sky was still a neutral province, and the airmen in it were mutually regarded as brothers in a happy-go-lucky fraternity, forced by circumstances to serve different masters. Roland Garros was among the irascible minority who scorned this philosophy. At dinner one evening he heard a guest from a neighboring squadron assert that aviators would be foolish to shoot at each other, since merely being in the air was hazard enough. Garros, angrily brandishing a bottle of wine, chased the offender out of the mess tent. As Garros saw them, the Germans were beasts to be shot at, not waved at. His sensibilities had been bruised by the behavior of German troops in Belgium, where atrocities against helpless civilians were then being reported. The beasts were now in his beloved France and, whether they be on the ground or in the air, they had to be eradicated like mad dogs. Garros had a personal grudge to settle also. After his escape from Berlin the German press had branded him a spy and accused him of planning his exhibition tour as a pretext for getting a bird's-eye view of German fortifications.

Garros crossed the path of an enemy plane for the first time on a mid-September morning near Compiègne. It was an Aviatik, slower than his Morane-Saulnier, and he flew up alongside the machine. The German pilot took no evasive action, but with his observer waved a cordial salute. Garros, in order to get in as close as possible without arousing suspicion, waggled his hand in reply. Soon the two machines were wing tip to wing tip. Garros could plainly see the smiles on the German faces as he rested his revolver on the cockpit coaming and squeezed the trigger six times. Though he was not more than forty feet from the enemy, he missed. The Aviatik was still flying along beside him, its pilot too dumbfounded by the Frenchman's breach of etiquette to react. Disgusted, Garros banked away from the Aviatik, shouting vows to do better next time.

After several such futile efforts, he began to realize that he was the victim of an illusion. An airplane, even if it were flying straight and level alongside another, could not be steadied enough to afford predictable shooting with a hand-held weapon. He also noticed that an oncoming plane, seen through the blades of his propeller, presented a relatively stable target, while he himself felt as though he were standing still. But when the oncoming plane cleared the propeller disc, giving him an unobstructed shot, it went flashing by faster than he could draw a bead on it. He was not standing still at all but flying through the air at eighty miles per hour, and his speed, added to the equal speed of the enemy plane, meant he was trying to hit a target moving at 160 miles per hour. Garros thereafter stopped wasting his pistol ammunition, but his desire to kill Germans was as great as ever.

Prior to the war, Garros had rated the Morane-Saulnier monoplane as the "finest flying machine in the world." Now, as 1914 came to an end, he would have paid any price to be piloting one of the two-seater biplanes of another squadron—a Voisin, say, or a Breguet. They were neither as swift nor maneuverable, they were less fun to fly, but they could carry a machine gun on a cockpit mounting, as the Royal Flying Corps had proven through the agency of Lieutenant Strange and his Avro biplane. In January of 1915, at the airfield at Buc, Garros saw the first few French biplanes with Hotchkiss guns experimentally mounted on the top wing so as to fire straight ahead over the propeller arc. Five months later, this arrangement, with Lewis instead of Hotchkiss guns, was standardized on the Nieuport 11, a trim little single-seater biplane aptly called the *Bébé*. But the Baby Nieuport was introduced with a strengthened wing structure to withstand the strain of supporting a rapid-firing weapon. Until the Nieuport 11 appeared, it was begging trouble to operate a gun mounted in this manner, for if the recoil didn't knock the wing entirely off after a few bursts, it did weaken the wing roots and loosen the flying wires. The arrangement also had the handicap of putting the gun above the pilot's reach. At best it would exhaust its ammunition in five or six seconds, and it could not be reloaded until landing. If it misfired and needed a swat or two to start it up again, as it frequently did, well, that was too bad.

But stationing a machine gun on the top wing like this, as Garros quickly discerned, had one big advantage. It permitted a pilot to aim his airplane at an enemy craft seen through the propeller, and this made for surer shooting. Compared to firing a gun on a swivel mount, or one held by hand, it was like scatter-gunning for sitting ducks. Yet Garros was still flying a monoplane. There was no top wing on which to install a gun. A tantalizing vision, that of a German plane framed in the shimmering disc of his propeller, began to haunt him. At twelve hundred revolutions per minute the twin-bladed propeller was practically invisible, and Garros became obsessed with the idea that whatever he could see through, he could shoot through. In the next days he played a dangerous game, flying directly toward enemy observation machines and drawing a bead on them through an imaginary sight on the cowling. By delicately working the stick and rudder pedals, he discovered he could aim his small monoplane with ease and accuracy at a target that seemed relatively stationary.

Garros did some calculating. The propeller revolved twelve hundred times a minute, which meant that one of the wooden blades was passing a given point forty times a second. Were he to fire a single shot through the invisible whirling blades every second, then he had forty chances of blasting off his propeller and disabling his own plane. Even for the reckless Garros the odds looked discouraging, especially when it wasn't a pistol or rifle he intended to fire. He wanted to fire a Hotchkiss gun at ten rounds per second, which multiplied the already impossible odds against him by ten. If this stream of bullets were aimed at the spinning propeller, perhaps the first dozen or so would luckily miss the blades, but certainly the next few would smash the propeller to splinters.

Garros was stymied. Then, on February 8, Armand Pinsard, the man acclaimed by Garros as his best friend, was forced down behind the German lines with a dead engine. With that strange sense of gallantry which still persisted among airmen, the following day a German pilot came low over the airfield at Buc and dropped a note saying that Pinsard was alive, uninjured, and a prisoner of war. Garros, already torn with frustration, at that moment lost whatever patience he had left. Within the hour he stalked into an infantry ordnance shop and tried to requisition a Hotchkiss *mitrailleuse*. The armorers, after hearing his scheme, thought him a candidate for a mental ward. "I have figured it out," he persisted. "If I fire a clip of twenty-five rounds, enough of them will go between the propeller blades to destroy an enemy machine. The gun will be fixed to fire precisely along my line of flight. To hit my target, I need only fly straight at it for the fraction of a minute."

"And you will chop off your own propeller!"

"Yes, but that is nothing. I will glide to a landing. As long as I stay above French territory there is no problem. What is the cost of a propeller when a German plane and its crew have been wiped out?"

One of the armorers stepped forward with a suggestion. He explained that before the war he had been employed by the Hotchkiss Company. He told of Robert Saulnier's experiments with a synchronized machine gun, in which he had participated as a Hotchkiss representative. He remembered that in the initial trial some of the bullets had hung fire and struck the propeller, and that Saulnier had bolted steel plates to the blades to deflect such bullets in subsequent trials. The next day found Garros at Villacoublay, conferring with Robert Saulnier, an old acquaintance. Through Saulnier's intercession, the aviator obtained an indefinite leave from his escadrille and the blessing of his commanding officer, Captain de Vergnette, in his endeavor. Garros returned in March with a spanking new Morane-Saulnier Type N monoplane. Mounted on the fuselage, immediately behind the airscrew, its butt projecting back through the windshield into the cockpit, was a Hotchkiss .303 machine gun. Saulnier bullet deflectors protected the propeller.

The morning of April 1, 1915, after nearly a week of sloppy weather along the front, dawned bright and clear. Traffic in the air was unusually heavy, both sides wishing anxiously to catch up on their reconnaissance. A little to the north of Buc, four German two-seater Albatros planes were flying lazily over the French lines at ten thousand feet. They were unarmed except for the Mauser rifles the observers packed in the rear cockpits. The German flyers were well aware that an occasional French plane might ambush them with a machine gun, but it was not likely to happen at this altitude. Few planes encumbered by the weight of such a gun could yet climb to ten thousand feet. Secure in this knowledge, the observers glued their attention to the enemy trenches below, which from this height were only dark, irregular scrawlings across the land. When they had seen all they wanted to see, and the formation leader was about to give the signal to return, a tiny speck appeared in the distance. As it came close the Germans could see it was a French single-seater. It headed straight at them but they ignored it. It had only one wing. Biplanes could carry machine guns; monoplanes, especially single-seater monoplanes, could not. They watched its approach curiously but without any apprehension, and then a small flower of orange flame blossomed from the snout of a machine gun set right in back of the propeller. Before the Germans could blink in astonishment, one of their pilots was dead, and his plane was careening crazily toward earth. The French plane swerved, and again the bullets came to riddle the fuselage of a second Albatros. It roared down in flames, incinerating its horrified occupants. The remaining two German planes ran for home, the crews pale and unnerved, for today they had seen something never before seen in the air—a gun which spat its bullets between the blades of a revolving propeller.

In four combats within eighteen days Roland Garros shot down five incredulous, unwary German air crews. News of his innovation spread rapidly to every German airfield, and the pilots were soon in a state of near panic. If a French monoplane hove into view, they instantly turned tail and fled. Consternation was felt in the conference rooms of the highest German command. Suppose the entire French and British air forces adopted this fantastic technique? It would be but a matter of weeks until the German air fleet was swept from the sky. And if this happened, Allied troops and artillery would move to new positions unseen and unreported, and thus gain an overwhelming tactical ground advantage.

When the German high command was first informed of this unidentified French aviator shooting a machine gun through a spinning airscrew, the reaction was one of disbelief and derision. Some generals went so far as to impugn the reliability and valor of their own pilots, suggesting that the mere sight of a hostile aircraft "infects them with the hallucinations of hysterical old women." Simple arithmetic proved that a repeating gun could not be fired through a propeller without shattering the blades. Such an arrangement could not work—and yet a rising toll of German airplanes was being reaped by the Frenchman's improbable gun. To resolve this baffling contradiction, the high command appointed a committee of armament engineers to initiate a crash program and develop a similar weapon for German flyers. Before they could get the program started, however, fate intervened. Garros, on April 19, the day after he scored his sixth kill, was forced down by engine failure behind enemy lines. Captured before he could set his plane on fire, Garros suffered the mortification of giving the Germans the very invention on which he had long labored for their destruction.

Twice already had the newspapers of Europe announced falsely that Garros was dead. Once, in the third month of war, it had been a case of mistaken identity, when a Morane-Saulnier piloted by a Captain Reymond had crashed in no-man's-land, between the opposing trenches, and had lain there for hours in the thick of a violent exchange of infantry fire. But Garros' fate this time was witnessed by several of his comrades, and France knew that her proudest champion of the air had indeed fallen.

For weeks no word came as to whether Garros was dead or alive. His captors not only suppressed all news of him but subjected him to many indignities, probably in repayment for his supposed spying activities before the war. He was confined for some months at Magdeburg, but was subsequently transferred to the prison camp outside Cologne. So precious did the Germans consider this celebrated Frenchman, and so apprehensive were they of his ability to make his escape, that they compelled Garros to sign his name in a register every half an hour of the day that he was not under lock and key. This strict scrutiny was unrelaxed for almost three years. In the meantime Lieutenant Marchal, the hero of the longest flight of World War I, was captured and sent to the same compound as Garros. Marchal had flown from the French lines to Berlin, dropped propaganda leaflets into the city, and then onwards to within forty miles of the Russian frontier before exhausting his fuel and falling into enemy grasp. Firebrands both, Garros and Marchal, singly and jointly, tried many times to escape from prison. They finally succeeded together in January 1918. For military reasons the details of their escape were never made public, but somehow they managed to get out of Germany and across the Channel to England. Garros returned to flying duty and found himself up against the brutal law of averages he himself had introduced. Six weeks was the life expectancy of a combat pilot on the western front in 1918. Garros did better. For nine months he roamed the heavens. Then, on the morning of October 5, a Fokker D-7 slid down out of the sun and opened fire with twin synchronized machine guns. If he were lucky, a German bullet killed him instantaneously. If not, he died in pain, for his plane—a tinderbox like all planes of that war—burst into flames and spiraled slowly to the ground.

The ironies of his career are self-evident. He not only had the bitter misfortune of betraying his secret weapon to the enemy; in the denouement he had the worse misfortune to become a victim of just such a weapon. The guns on the Fokker were more sophisticated—mechanically timed to fire through the propeller—but they were the ugly children of Garros' own creation. On that April day in 1915 when he was taken into custody near Ingelmunster, the markings on his plane were recognized as those of the legendary Frenchman with the magical, and murderous, machine gun. The Germans at once shipped the Morane-Saulnier to Berlin for study. To adapt Garros' invention to German use, the authorities summoned Anthony Fokker, the young Dutchman who was just beginning to fulfill his promise as the war's most brilliant aircraft designer. Fokker was selected on the basis of his prototype Eindekker, or monoplane, which in many respects resembled the Morane-Saulnier. Though he had no personal knowledge of combat weapons and had never before examined a machine gun, Fokker agreed to have a look at the system devised by Garros.

What he saw were the triangular steel wedges that had been fitted to the propeller blades to divert the bullets that did hit them. While this protected the airscrew from being shot up, Fokker realized it was a dangerous, almost suicidal device. Even if the metal plates did deflect the bullets, one of the lead slugs would sooner or later bounce back to smash a vital part of the engine, or the pilot. Fokker discarded Garros' invention altogether. He asked to inspect a German machine gun; a Parabellum was brought to him. He thoughtfully dismantled the weapon, studying each piece as he removed it, diagraming the gun's inner workings. He jotted down some hasty calculations. He then said he wanted to take the gun with him to his factory at Schwerin for a couple of days to test an idea.

Schwerin, a quiet lakeside community some two hundred miles northwest of the capital, was four hours away by train. Fokker used every minute of the ride to memorize his diagrams and review his calculations. It was a good thing, he reflected, that his childhood had been spent on the flatlands of Holland. As a boy, exploring the countryside outside of Harlaam, he had often tried pitching stones between the vanes of windmills. Until he discovered the knack, not all his rocks got by the huge wooden blades. It was a simple matter of timing. If he threw just as a vane swung past the vertical, he easily got a rock between it and the next. Now it was a case of getting bullets through the blades of an airplane propeller. The train, clattering on through the night, stopped briefly at Wittenberg and Ludwigslust. When it reached Schwerin, the Dutchman thought he had, if not the whole answer, at least a clue to the answer.

Anthony Herman Gerard Fokker was born in April 1890, the son of a wealthy Dutch tea planter in colonial Java. He was not yet six years old when his father moved the family back to Holland, settling down to a life of quiet comfort in Harlaam, a small city between Amsterdam and the North Sea dikes. "Flying and I grew up together," he later noted in his autobiography, *The Flying Dutchman*. "A few years after that revolutionary invention, I sat as a boy in my father's attic furiously flying a kitchen chair rigged up with Wright controls." The boy had a natural mechanical aptitude. Before he was twelve he had built his own set of electric trains from metal scrap and household utensils. His first big venture as an inventor was a puncture-proof automobile tire. It was rather ingeniously made of spring metal and could not go flat, but the rubber-tire industry nonetheless managed to stay in business. When Fokker was sixteen, he constructed his first airplane in his attic workshop. By the time he was twenty, he had built what he felt to be the fastest, most stable monoplane in the world. He proudly demonstrated it for the military authorities of his own country, and he was curtly informed that Holland was buying planes from experienced firms in France and England, not from young upstarts with no engineering education and with no aviation credentials. He tried to find customers in Russia, France, and England without success. He made a better impression in Germany where, during one of his exhibition flights, he stunned his audience—and collected reams of newspaper publicity—by looping-the-loop. Soon afterward, in 1913, he received an order from the German Signal Corps for ten planes.

Fokker went on from here, building additional machines and his own reputation. He was so preoccupied with the daily problems of running the factory at Schwerin that he never saw the war clouds gathering around him. His ears were attuned to the sound of the Argus engines which powered his little single-seater scouting planes, so he heard neither the bugles of destiny nor the rumble of caissons rolling toward the Belgian frontier. If the dominating powers of Europe were girding for war, it was no affair of a neutral Dutchman, or so he rationalized. But the very day war broke out, Fokker was paid a visit by high military personages and told to increase to the limit his output of airplanes. For a start, the Signal Corps wanted a dozen machines. From that first day of war to the last, Fokker met every challenge the German command put before him. And now in 1915, because a madcap French aviator had fired a gun through a propeller and destroyed six planes, this gifted Dutchman—who resisted every effort by his employers to naturalize him as a citizen of their country—was on the verge of perfecting an invention that would very nearly help to bring about a German victory over the Allies.

After examining Garros' plane in Berlin, while waiting in the *bahnhof* to board his train, Fokker sent a telegram to Schwerin asking three co-workers to meet him upon his arrival there at midnight. Reinhold Platz, a creative welder, had wrought Fokker's first steel-tube fuselage in 1913 and was now his experimental department supervisor. Heinrich Luebbe had barnstormed with Fokker; he was the factory production manager. Bernard de Waal, a boyhood chum, was Fokker's test pilot. Alerted by his telegram, they were dutifully waiting on the station platform when his train pulled in.

During the next forty-eight hours none of them slept. Fokker explained what needed to be done, and they rolled up their sleeves to do it. The Parabellum gun was mounted on an E-1 monoplane, just behind the engine hood and slightly to starboard. The wheels of the plane were securely chocked. Working from his rough sketches, Fokker attached two studs to the propeller shaft, diametrically opposed to each other and in exact alignment with the propeller blades. When the shaft revolved, the studs alternately struck a cam.

The cam operated a pushrod connected by stout wire to the hammer of the machine gun. When the pushrod was actuated—which was each time a propeller blade passed the gun's muzzle—it prevented the hammer from falling against the firing pin. Hence, even if the trigger were depressed, the weapon could shoot only when the blades were not in its line of fire; the airscrew itself governed the efflux of bullets. It took forty-eight hours, almost to the minute, for Fokker and his aides to install, adjust, and test the interrupter gear to their satisfaction. It was not until months later that Anthony Fokker learned that the problem of firing through a propeller had been solved before the war by several different inventors in France, Austria, and Germany. His cam-and-pushrod mechanism, in fact, was virtually identical to that patented in 1912 by Franz Schneider, whose earlier device had been pigeonholed and quickly forgotten.

Fokker towed the gun-equipped monoplane to Berlin, lashing its tailskid to his Peugot touring car. Most of the important staff officers were present at the military field for the demonstration. They looked with disappointment at the propeller; there were no metal wedges protecting the fragile wooden blades as there had been on Garros' plane. "In my confidence," wrote Fokker, "I had not figured on the conservative military mind, which not only has to be shown, but then wishes to be shown all over again, after which it desires a little time to think the whole matter over once more."

First he demonstrated the gun from the ground, starting the engine and shooting at some target butts at the end of the field. He fired three bursts of ten shots each before stopping the engine. The officials gravely examined the propeller, found no flaw in it, but suspected the wily Dutchman had somehow deceived them. Why, they wanted to know, had he triggered only bursts of ten? Was it because the synchronizer would not work properly otherwise? Fokker shrugged his shoulders and proceeded to fire off the remaining seventy bullets on the cartridge belt in a single sustained burst. Then he reloaded and shot a whole band of one hundred bullets. Now the military men were convinced the gun could be operated while the plane was on the ground, but doubted its practicality in the air.

Annoyed at the group's pompous skepticism, Fokker decided to teach them some manners. He directed that some old wings be stacked on the field and told the observers to watch closely to see if he could hit this target from the air. From about nine hundred feet he nosed over, pointed the plane at the piled-up wings and squeezed the trigger. He knew the ground beneath his target was hard rock. The bullets slashed through the cloth wing coverings and ricocheted about the field like angry hornets. The observers scattered in wild confusion, some of them sprinting for shelter in a nearby hangar. "When they took to their heels," said Fokker, "I decided they would never forget that the gun shot from the air as well as it shot from the ground." After he landed, they timidly crept out and viewed the bullet-riddled wings. They examined the propeller blades, which had not even been nicked. Then they consulted among themselves and gave their verdict. Fokker blanched when they told him that the only certain test of the gun was to shoot an airplane down, and that he, although a foreigner and a civilian, should have the honor of demonstrating this proof. In other words, if he expected to receive payment for his synchronizer, he would have to prove its capabilities in actual combat; he would have to go to the front, seek out a French or British aircraft, and destroy it. The German army, since Fokker was by all the rules of war a noncombatant, was prodding him to commit criminal homicide. His protests were useless; the official mind was made up.

He was in German-occupied France within twenty-four hours, at the liaison headquarters of General von Heeringen, near Laon. On the following day, prior to taking off on his onerous mission, the Dutchman was treated to a lunch of cold ham at a plush château where the Crown Prince, commanding the Fifth Army in Heeringen's corps, had taken squatter rights. After this spartan meal, which Fokker was too unnerved to eat, he was chauffeured in the Crown Prince's private motorcar to the flying field. In vain he remonstrated again that he was a neutral, stressing the fact that he would be executed as a spy if forced down and captured behind Allied lines. The Germans had anticipated this argument. They dressed him in the uniform of a German lieutenant, hung an aviator's wings over his breast, and tucked a military identity card in the pocket of his gray wool tunic.

The reluctant warrior flew seven consecutive mornings and evenings without sighting prey. On the eighth day he went prowling in the vicinity of Douai, where he heard there was much aerial activity by the French. Sure enough, while he was ambling along at six thousand feet, he saw a Farman two-seater emerging from a cloud below. Fokker dived at it. The French pilot took no evasive action. Either he was not yet aware of Fokker's presence or he felt no fear of harm. How could he suspect that the German monoplane carried a gun which spewed a stream of bullets through the propeller?

Fokker afterward wrote this account:

> As the distance between us narrowed, the plane grew larger in my sights. My imagination could picture my shots puncturing the gasoline tanks . . . [which] would catch fire. Even if my bullets failed to kill the pilot and observer, the ship would fall down in flames. I had my finger on the trigger. What I imagined recalled my own narrow escapes: the time the gasoline tanks burst; the breaking of the wing at Johannistal when my passenger was killed. I had no personal enmity toward the French. I was flying merely to prove that a certain mechanism I had invented would work. By this time I was near enough to open fire, and the French airmen were watching me curiously, wondering, no doubt, why I was flying up behind them. In another instant, it would be all over for them.

Suddenly, I decided that the whole job could go to hell. It was too much like "cold meat" to suit me. I had no stomach for the whole business, nor any wish to kill Frenchmen for Germans. Let them do their own killing!

Fokker returned directly to Douai airfield and declared that he was done with flying over the front. After a brief argument, it was agreed that he would instruct a regular pilot in the use of the machine gun. Lieutenant Oswald Boelcke, who before dying in an air collision in October 1916, amassed a victory score of forty Allied planes, was chosen as Fokker's pupil. The first news that greeted the Dutchman on his arrival back at Schwerin was that Boelcke, on his third flight, had brought down an enemy aircraft. Boelcke's quick success convinced the German command of the synchronized gun's efficiency. The early distrust by headquarters was replaced with munificent praise of Fokker and his new weapon. Orders were issued to equip as many planes as possible with the interrupter gear.

Lieutenant Max Immelmann, who began duplicating Boelcke's success from the start, was the second pilot to be furnished with a fixed-gun Fokker monoplane. It was an improved model, designated the Fokker E-2, with a hundred-horsepower Oberursel engine in place of the eighty-horsepower Argus. Within three or four weeks, half a dozen E-2's were in service at the front. Immelmann, Boelcke, and the other Fokker pilots—who numbered sixteen by the middle of June—had only to spot an enemy plane and get above or behind it to guarantee the kill. They found that by slightly wobbling the monoplane's nose in circular fashion, they could emit, instead of a straight stream of bullets, a cone of fire, trapping their victim in the center, who, no matter which way he turned to escape, met a curtain of death.

Shooting a slow, defenseless BE-2, Farman, or an obsolete Caudron out of existence was no more difficult or sporting than swatting flies. Before summer the sky was German domain. The German infantry could deploy massively with little fear of detection by Allied air scouts, and, conversely, any significant movement by Allied troops would be seen by undistracted German flyers. It seemed just a matter of time until the Allies, deprived of aerial reconnaissance, would capitulate sensibly. Joyously reading report after report of sky supremacy, the general staff in Berlin was already congratulating itself on winning the war. Much of the credit was openly attributed to Anthony Fokker, who did not want it. This politically indifferent Dutchman had no interest in German conquest; he was concerned only with the design and construction of faster, safer, more maneuverable, and more durable airplanes. His ambitions were never moderated by the realization that French and British airmen were being butchered with his superior planes and his synchronized machine gun.

CHAPTER VI

❦ *Death Flies High* ❧

GERMANY, THANKS TO the inventive wizardry of Anthony Fokker, held mastery of the air and Allied casualties mounted. Some chroniclers of that time and afterward maintained that Holland's neutrality remained inviolate only because the Germans did not wish to offend and lose the services of the Dutch-born designer. While this may have been a consideration, it was not of overriding importance, for there was neither political nor strategic justification for such an invasion. The Dutch, as a people, were solidly in sympathy with the German cause, which obviated the need for any immediate aggression toward Holland. But even if Germany chose to betray this *entente cordiale*, she merely had to wait until Belgium and France and England were subjugated; then she could blockade Dutch shipping and, at her leisure, move in overwhelmingly on the ground. This plan was, in fact, discussed by the Berlin command as a possible final phase of war on the western front, but was never entered definitely on the military agenda.

By some otherworldly logic, British and French armament experts were in no discernible hurry to develop a synchronized machine gun for Allied pilots or even to copy that of the enemy, which was almost daily shooting Allied planes from the sky. For four months the Germans managed to keep the workings of the mechanism a complete secret; pilots using it were forbidden to fly over Allied territory lest the device fall into enemy hands. Their caution was well warranted, although, as things turned out, quite unnecessary. When a Fokker pilot, lost in a fog, set down by mistake on a French field, the German firing gear was thoughtfully inspected, tested, blueprinted, and then—incredibly—locked away to be forgotten. By a means never divulged, several French magazines obtained diagrams of the synchronizer and proceeded to publish them together with detailed analyses of the technical particulars. The editors of these magazines, since they neglected to mention it, were presumably unaware, or else did not recall, that Raymond Saulnier had two years earlier perfected a nearly identical apparatus for the Morane-Saulnier monoplane. The French War Ministry, if its collective memory was refreshed, showed now no greater interest in Saulnier's invention than before. As to how the diagrams became available for publication, they were probably surreptitiously copied by an exasperated official of the War Ministry, who, so fed up with the stolidity of his colleagues, was ready to risk court-martial and professional disgrace in an effort to focus public attention on the desperate need for equipping French airplanes with synchronized guns. But those magazine readers who did see the diagrams were left ignorant of the real significance —in terms of men and machines destroyed—of the enemy's novel weapon system. Themselves uninformed about this matter because of military censorship, the editors could only explain the mechanical operation of the firing gear with no intimation of its revolutionary effect on aerial combat, or of the terrible toll it was extracting from the Allied air forces. Thus, if the diagrams were smuggled into print for the purpose of alerting the people and bringing pressure to bear on the War Ministry to adopt the German synchronizer for use by the French flying corps, the intrigue failed utterly.

Across the Channel in England there was a bit less governmental indifference to the superiority that Fokker had conferred upon Germany. A motion was put forth in Parliament that the War Office endeavor to procure patent licenses from Anthony Fokker, inasmuch as he was a neutral. The War Office, which, to its present sorrow, had spurned the Dutchman's airplanes in 1912, found it necessary to explain that all his worthwhile patents had since then been licensed in Germany and were therefore rather inaccessible. The motion was permanently, and hurriedly, shelved.

In Germany, meanwhile, a new breed of hero had become the people's darling. He was the air fighter, a knight riding a winged charger and jousting with gay abandon in dramatic tournaments high above the clouds. Boelcke and Immelmann personified this romantic image, which the pilots themselves would have conceded was somewhat distorted. Their personal courage was no less than advertised, but their tilts against Allied flyers were handily won with the synchronized gun.

Oswald Boelcke, one of six children born to a university professor in Saxony, came to aviation, as did Immelmann and many others, by way of a cadet corps. In 1912, at the age of twenty-one, he gained a lieutenancy in a communications troop. During a maneuver that year he saw his first military airplane and determined himself to fly—an ambition realized through attendance at the aviation school at Halberstadt, just a few miles from Giebichenstein, the village of his birth. On August 15, 1914, little more than a week after the outbreak of war, he received his pilot's certificate. By early September, he was flying an Albatros two-seater with his brother, Wilhelm, occasionally coming along as his observer. Applying himself diligently to the business of making war, Boelcke was awarded an Iron Cross in October.

That same month, Boelcke learned that his commanding officer intended to transfer Wilhelm to another unit, elsewhere on the front. Complaining jointly to headquarters, the brothers were assured that they would not be separated. But headquarters reneged on its promise. Wilhelm was transferred after all, whereupon Oswald protested so vigorously that he was threatened with being sent to the infantry in the trenches. The squadron physician put him on a three-week convalescence, purportedly because of a severe bronchial infection, although it may really have been to give the disgruntled flyer time in which to smooth his ruffled feathers. This bitter lesson probably explains in part why Boelcke thereafter developed into a stern disciplinarian himself and a very reserved individual.

It was during the first year of the war that he produced the following leaflet, which he called "The Airman's Defense Against Troublesome Questioners":

P L E A S E ! ! !
Do not ask me anything about flying.
You will find the usual queries answered below:

(1)   Sometimes it is dangerous, sometimes it is not.
(2)   Yes, the higher we fly, the colder it is.
(3)   Yes, we notice the fact by freezing when it is colder.
(4)   Flying height, 2000–2500 meters.
(5)   Yes, we can see things at that height, although not so well as at 100 meters.
(6)   We cannot see well through a telescope because it shakes.
(7)   Yes, we have dropped bombs.
(8)   Yes, an old woman was supposed to have been injured, and we put the wind up some transport columns.
(9)   The observer sits in front and can see a hit.
(10)   We cannot talk to each other because the engine makes too much noise.
(11)   We have not got a telephone in the machine, but we are provided with electric light.
(12)   No, we do not live in caves.

This leaflet was distributed to all questioners. Answers (7) and (8) are noteworthy as illustrating both civilian and pilot attitudes toward bombers. They also reveal something of Boelcke's dry sense of humor.

After having flown forty-two operational missions, he was given one of the first armed Albatroses, which featured a ring-mounted Parabellum gun in the aft cockpit. That was in April 1915, the month of Roland Garros' one-man rampage, when few German pilots dared approach a monoplane marked with the French roundel. But Boelcke's aggressiveness, coupled with the consummate skill he exercised in keeping his observer's gun within range of a Morane-Saulnier for half an hour, resulted in the destruction of the enemy machine. This victory brought to the stocky, sullen-faced aviator an Iron Cross First Class and doubtless led to his being selected, four weeks later, to fly the first synchronized gun into battle as a substitute for the civilian "neutral," Anthony Fokker.

During November, after having shot down five of the enemy from the cockpit of his Fokker E-1, Boelcke was ordered to visit Fokker at Schwerin, where he became acquainted with the designer's new E-4 monoplane. Impressed by the big 160-horsepower Oberursel engine, Boelcke introduced the craft into service at the front. It proved a disappointment, however, on account of recurring engine trouble. It failed him, for example, on December 13, when, together with Max Immelmann, he forced a British machine down so low that the kill seemed assured. Boelcke swooped to administer the *coup de grâce;* the Oberursel suddenly began to sputter, the Fokker lost speed and the intended victim escaped. On the morning of January 5, 1916, Boelcke finally did claim a victory with the E-4, but at noon the same day, when ten enemy planes bombed his base at Douai, he was not so fortunate. He was unable to get the temperamental E-4 airborne and so resorted to his old E-1, in which he assisted Lieutenant Ernst Hess in bringing down one of the raiders.

Later that month, both Boelcke and Immelmann, with eight victories apiece, became recipients of Imperial Germany's most coveted military decoration, the Order Pour le Mérite (instituted during the reign of Frederick the Great, when French was the official language of the Prussian court). Boelcke's merit, however, was not only his prowess in the air, for he possessed the priceless knack of imparting to others the hard-won lessons of his own experience. He frequently took it upon himself to evaluate the machines he flew, and his reports usually, though not always, carried considerable weight. His thoroughgoing summary of the E-4 monoplane's deficiencies, which he prepared at Sivry in March 1916, during the cataclysmic battle of Verdun, strongly influenced Anthony Fokker's conception, a year and a half later, of the superlative D-7 fighter. Boelcke, in criticizing the 160-horsepower Oberursel engine, perceived that it was too delicately tuned to continue running smoothly and dependably when subjected to the variations of atmospheric pressure between high and low altitudes. This criticism caused Fokker to revert back to the hundred-horsepower Oberursel on his E-planes, which stayed in production for another four months. The hundred-horsepower engine provided less flying speed, of course, but it was not as dangerously fickle at rarefied altitudes above eight thousand feet. In submitting his appraisal of the Oberursel, Boelcke placed himself among the first to discern the limitations of rotary engines in general. Soon afterwards, aircraft manufacturers on both sides of the war forsook rotary power almost altogether in favor of radial and in-line engines that could better operate with high internal compression ratios and could therefore deliver the kind of speed and performance that aviators were demanding more and more.

Among Boelcke's most valuable contributions to German military aviation were his ideas about unit organization, farsighted ideas that took shape during the struggle for Verdun, in which the German air force, despite its superior equipment, failed at the outset to gain unchallenged control of the sky and thereafter lost the initiative entirely. Boelcke's scheme of reformation was the outcome of some serious blunders. It was by capitalizing on these mistakes that the French wrested away the prerogatives of aerial supremacy, which they exercised mercilessly.

In all its aspects, in the air as on the ground, the defense of Verdun, successful after the longest pitched battle of World War I, shines as a golden highlight in the tapestry of French history. At Verdun, a fortress city situated behind a half-moon of outlying forts, with the gateway to Paris lying open at its back, the French army withstood the utmost manpower and resources of the German war machine. General Erich von Falkenhayn, chief of the German general staff and martial dictator of the central powers, there met disaster and disgrace. There the mettle of Crown Prince Wilhelm was tested and he was found to be a fancy-dress puppet, completely under the domination of Falkenhayn.

For the tremendous offensive against Verdun, the concerted thrust which he promised would end the war in quick and total victory, Falkenhayn had robbed all the other fronts of effective men and materials. Field Marshal Paul von Hindenburg and his crafty chief of staff, General Ludendorff, had formulated a campaign against Russia to put that decrepit giant quickly out of the war and to secure the eastern front. Their plan, charted on a massive scale, might well have succeeded. But the Kaiser, swayed by Falkenhayn and the Crown Prince, decreed that the Russian campaign should be indefinitely postponed and that Hindenburg should send his best regiments to join the forces of the Crown Prince fronting Verdun. Ludendorff promptly quit as chief of staff to Hindenburg and suggested to the field marshal that he should also resign. Grim old warrior that he was, Hindenburg declined to take this action, preferring to remain idle in East Prussia and watch what he predicted would be a useless effort at Verdun. His warning to the general staff was unambiguous, but Falkenhayn coolly ignored the message.

Why did Falkenhayn choose this particular front for his grand offensive?

As early as May 1915, nine months before the attack was undertaken, the great Junker associations of Prussia demanded that Verdun should be captured. Underlying this demand was the fact that the Verdun fortifications guarded a menacing salient projecting into the rich iron fields of the Briey basin. From this region of Lorraine came the ore that supplied more than 70 percent of the steel required for German guns and munitions. Seized at the beginning of the war by the armies of the Crown Prince, the iron fields represented the most valuable piece of French property yet usurped by the invaders. Indispensable to German arms manufacture, the mines of Briey lay only twenty miles from the gun emplacements of Verdun. In the sixteen months between October 1914, and February 1916, the battle line before Verdun had not changed by an inch. The opposing troops were dug in, winter their common foe. Falkenhayn, massing his legions beyond the Meuse valley, confidently hoped to take the city, occupy the French enclave, straighten his forward line, and remove any threat to German interests in Briey. This accomplished, he could then consolidate his forces for the final rush to Paris. A committee of staff officers in Berlin had already been delegated by Falkenhayn to plan his victory parade down the Champs Élysées and through the Arc de Triomphe.

Several weeks prior to the offensive, a large number of Fokker E-planes were concentrated in the Verdun sector, Oswald Boelcke among them. Max Immelmann remained with a smaller group of the monoplane fighters assigned to the British front in Lille. Stationed near Metz, at Sivry, Boelcke and his comrades were charged with the task of holding the air against French reconnaissance planes, since it was imperative that the enemy be deprived of aerial observation in the mobilization area. The Fokker pilots did their job with pitiless efficiency. French losses over the German lines were staggering in late January and the first half of February, and French airmen complained that the Germans were adhering to a cowardly policy in that they fought only behind their own lines.

The Germans knew well what they were doing. Hardly any French air crews braved the protective cordon and lived to tell of it. But exasperation did not end there, for those who did get back were not believed when they reported that the Germans were preparing for an all-out offensive. The French general staff balked at accepting the judgments of a few junior officers who were obviously unfamiliar with one of the axiomatic prescripts of military strategy. Full-scale offensives, according to the textbooks at St. Cyr, simply were not undertaken in January or February, the worst of the winter weather. The observation squadrons redoubled their efforts to obtain proof that would convince the general staff, but they succeeded only in doubling their casualties.

During the second week of February, in near-zero temperatures and wind-driven snow, the German infantry began making feint attacks all up and down the line. As Falkenhayn had guessed, the French command interpreted these hit-and-run assaults as feelers, still anticipating no major thrust until the spring thaw had set in. The French air service, thoroughly demoralized by the distrust of the general staff, ceased trying to penetrate the blockading screen of Fokkers and never ascertained the growing accumulation of strength behind these diversionary sallies.

Preliminary to the main battle, Falkenhayn placed a semicircle of the heaviest guns available—twelve-inch naval cannon and 420-mm siege mortars—around the southwestern perimeter of the Briey mining district. No longer concerned with the problem of avoiding detection, he moved forward the vast forces which he had drained from the east and deployed them along a thirty-mile front. Then, in the frigid predawn murk of February 21, he commenced his drive with a spearhead attack on the village of Haumont, situated near the apex of the great salient enclosing Verdun. The victory here was an easy one, for the French army was caught entirely by surprise.

Falkenhayn based his offensive on new tactics. Having assembled a tremendous mass of artillery, he intended to use these guns to pulverize the French defenses and chew up French counterattacks. In effect, the artillery would secure ground; the infantry, attacking on narrow fronts, would simply occupy it after mopping up whatever enemy troops survived the barrage. As a German staff study stated, "The decision to attack and rapidly seize Verdun is founded on the proven capabilities of heavy and heaviest artillery."

Immediately after the capture of Haumont, Falkenhayn's huge guns were brought to bear on the French fortifications from one end of the line to the other. His next key objective was Fort Douaumont, a strategically located stronghold that the French claimed to be impregnable. For three days and nights the German military chief, probing for a weakness in the French defenses, sent forth one after another of his shock battalions and alternated these assaults with booming fusillades from his howitzer batteries. For three days and nights nothing seemed able to dent the wall of French resistance. The French *mitrailleuses* still chattered, the *poilus* still stood and died. The Germans called upon a new weapon, the flamethrower, to rout the French from their fastness. The Sturmbataillon Rohr, the elite of the elite, the toughest battle-hardened trench busters, tried their hand while carrying small mortars and flamethrowers. They, too, proved mortal. Accordingly, on the night of February 24, Falkenhayn brought the whole might of his siege guns against Fort Douaumont. For nine hours the earth shook. Never before in any war had such intensive and devastating fire been directed against a defensive position. Trenches were obliterated, buildings flattened, battlements shattered, powder stores blown out of existence. Pulped and mangled bodies were strewn everywhere the next morning as the German infantry advanced to take possession of the charred, gutted ruins. A detachment of French riflemen, under orders to fight to the death, tried desperately to restrain an oncoming horde that was barely visible behind rolling yellowish clouds of mustard gas. The rest of the French garrison, those who survived the withering barrage, retreated toward Verdun for a final stand. By nightfall on February 25, not a French soldier was left alive in Fort Douaumont.

Personally superintending the disposition of his troops and artillery, which consisted of fifty-nine army corps and more than two thousand large-bore guns, Falkenhayn had now broken through the outer defenses of Verdun. The tide was flooding against the French. Shells, shells for guns of all caliber, and men, more men, always more men for the defenses around the city, were needed. When German artillery made the French railways useless, another transportation system was hastily improvised, a system that ultimately saved Verdun. It was composed of trucks and motor cars, horse-drawn wagons, pack mules, anything that could haul a few shells or carry a packet of troops. The backbone of this supply system was a large fleet of trucks driven by haggard men whose average daily sleep was three hours, upon whose horizon-blue uniforms the stains of snow and sleet, of dust and mud, were indelibly fixed through the winter, spring, summer, and fall of 1916.

Throughout the long summer Verdun held like a storm-lashed rock. Wave after wave of German infantry in green-gray lines was hurled against the ramparts, parapets, pillboxes, barbed wire, and trenches that surrounded and protected the ancient citadel, while French artillerymen and machine-gunners methodically took their toll. German dead lay where they fell, putrefying in the warm sun until the exposed flesh became the same ghastly hue as the uniforms. No-man's-land around Verdun was a shambles, churned by incessant artillery fire into a naked expanse of craters, pervaded with the nauseating stench of ripe carrion. Troops left long in this inferno appeared to age. Their eyes grew glazed and sunken, their faces drawn.

The French plan was exceedingly uncomplicated. It was to hold out. This they did by standing firm and stoically feeding men into the grinding jaws of death. During that long and tumultuous summer the battle cry of Verdun— "They shall not pass!"—was indited with blood upon the stones of time as a pledge upheld.

German defeat at Verdun, though Falkenhayn would not realize the disturbing truth for another couple of months, became an inevitability in late June, when the British opened a savage offensive against the northernmost German flank. The British forces advanced along the northern bank of the Somme at the same time as the French advanced along the southern bank. The Germans met the Somme drive as best they could, but it cost them the replacements needed for their armies still fighting for Verdun. In consequence, the vigor of their prolonged siege began slowly but perceptibly to wane. As autumn came, the signs of German fatigue and disenchantment were propitious, and the defenders of Verdun struck back. At their head was a general named Henri Pétain, who was to win fame and adulation at Verdun in World War I and hatred and ignominy at Vichy in World War II. Pétain, working in close liaison with General Joffre of the higher command, initiated a series of sudden attacks; driving his forces out of their containment, Pétain exerted a persistant pressure against the enemy on both sides of the Meuse River, which traversed the area. These hard thrusts were followed by a slashing counteroffensive which, on October 24, resulted in the recapture of Fort Douaumont. Nine more days of unremitting battle and the Germans were dislodged from Fort Vaux, their last foothold inside the salient. The evacuation of Fort Vaux marked a finish to their disastrous campaign and also to Falkenhayn's military career. Named as his successor shortly afterward was his severest critic, Field Marshal Paul von Hindenburg.

The kindest thing that might be said of Falkenhayn's commandership was that he limited his losses—which were nonetheless deplorable—to about half those suffered by the French. Before the Verdun battle was ended, nearly 750,000 men were killed or wounded. Two-thirds of these victims were French.

To say the worst of him, Falkenhayn was infected with a congenital short-coming of the German military mind: an arrogant underestimation of his enemy. He viewed Verdun as an unnatural bulge which begged to be squeezed flat. In mounting his offensive, he gambled on catching the French off guard and luring them into a hopeless and exhausting holding action. He was pre-pared to bleed France white and he picked a point of attack "for the retention of which"—in his own words—"the French command would be compelled to throw in every man they have." As the initial gamble paid off, he repeated his first hammer blow again and again, with the avowed aim of sucking more and more French reserves into the trap. The plan worked, except that he neglected to close the trap. Here was attrition with a vengeance, on an unprec-edented scale. It was made possible by Falkenhayn's fearsome array of giant guns, under the cover of which a force of picked troops could be matched with twice or three times as many defenders. If the German army chief failed to pursue his advantage to a victorious conclusion, he set an example in the gruesome art of modern siege warfare which the Allies would copy in turn. Barbed wire, the fragmentation shell, and the machine gun, concentrated at selected points, were the factors that molded the pattern of this negative, internecine strategy for the remainder of World War I.

The airmen of both camps were at once caught up in this vital event. The great battle was not many weeks old when the French flying corps discovered for itself an important role. The service, which had been accepted after sundry misgivings as a substitute for cavalry, in addition to its customary observation duties, now began to function as a tactical adjunct of artillery. Starting in April and continuing through the entire eight months of the siege, every air-plane that could carry bombs went out repeatedly—three, four, even five times a day—to dispense destruction to German troops, gun batteries, rail-heads, and supply columns. Rising to the occasion, and with their enthusiasm heightened by visible daily accomplishments, the French airmen could not be indifferent to the stupendous battle that raged below. The fury of French air-to-ground attacks verged on the fanatical. Although the opposing Fokkers inflicted serious casualties with their synchronized Spandau guns, they were unable to cope with the courageous determination of the French pilots. Statis-tics show that French aviation at Verdun sustained a casualty rate close to 20 percent; for every plane the Fokkers shot down, they missed four. The confidence of German troops was shaken by the constant pounding from above. Messages poured back to headquarters: "We are under aerial bombardment. Where are our aircraft?" "Busy elsewhere" was always the reply. A sardonic oath was coined in the ranks that echoed for many months ahead: "God damn England, France, and Uncle Willy's air force!" (Uncle Willy, of course, was an irreverent reference to Kaiser Wilhelm, whose son and namesake, the Crown Prince, was blasphemed in the diminutive as "Little Willy.") For muttering this imprecation within earshot of their superiors, at least three German soldiers were summarily tried on charges of insubordination and received sentences of from two to four years hard labor.

That spring, German morale was further undermined by the disturbing news that American volunteers, in ever-increasing numbers, were flying for the Allied cause. The creation by the French War Ministry of an Escadrille Americaine in March and that squadron's arrival in mid-April at Luxeuil-les-Bains, opposite the southern flank of Falkenhayn's armies, outraged the Kaiser and his ministers. The German ambassador in Washington, Count Johann von Bernstorff, registering an emphatic protest with the United States government, called attention to the fact that French communiqués frequently contained mention of the American escadrille. Bernstorff argued in his brief that the presence of Americans in Europe as active combatants, in the uniform of a warring power, constituted a "flagrant" breach of neutrality. Legally, the complaint had some validity, but it did not elicit much sympathy. Less than a year had gone by since the German submarine U-20 had sunk the British passenger ship *Lusitania* with 114 Americans aboard. This incident had destroyed almost all pro-German sentiment on the American side of the North Atlantic. The torpedoing of the defenseless Cunard liner, which also took 1198 British lives, had been aggravation enough, but when President Woodrow Wilson sent a note demanding reparation and Germany refused to acknowledge liability, a vociferous part of the American public urged an immediate declaration of war. All this transpired in May and June of 1915, and nearly two years passed before such a declaration was made. Several more links in the chain of circumstances leading to United States participation in the war were forged by the time Count Bernstorff stepped forth to complain of the presence of Americans in the French flying service. The anti-isolationist lobby had grown in size and influence. Its bellicose whoops and howls were more strident than ever. And one of its main sources of gratification was the Escadrille Americaine. The political environment being what it was in 1916, State Department officials reacted to Bernstorff's complaint apathetically and took a lazy six months to smooth over the mere diplomatic superficialities of the situation. Autumn had already settled upon the battlefields of Lorraine when French general headquarters, in response to a request from Washington, promulgated a relevant order. "For diplomatic reasons," it candidly explained, "Escadrille Nieuport No. 124 shall hereafter be known as the Escadrille des Volontaires, and the name Escadrille Americaine, currently in use, must be given up."

But this new designation displeased the American pilots. They thought it colorless and uninspiring. Moreover, it connoted nothing of the proud fact that they were Americans. They asked permission to call themselves instead the Escadrille Lafayette, to commemorate the contributions of that French general and statesman to the American Revolution some 140 years earlier and to symbolize repayment of a debt of honor now that France was fighting for her national survival. Poetic justice was granted, and thus was originated the history-enshrined name of the American squadron that fought under the French flag for nearly two years. But six months before it was known as such, the Escadrille Lafayette was christened in battle and weaned to glory in the grim and ruthlessly violent confrontation at Verdun.

During the Verdun seige Falkenhayn and his generals revealed poor understanding of how best to use their aircraft, either as a defensive or an offensive weapon. The poverty of their air-power concepts was glaringly shown, for example, in their choice of bombing objectives. For their push against Verdun, the Germans had the latest in aerial bombs. However, when it came to dropping these bombs, they invariably chose railway junctions as targets, even though their artillery already precluded the French from utilizing any of the rail lines into the city. This policy was both wasteful and futile. Just one road carried reinforcements and supplies to Verdun. This road—*La Voie Sacree* (The Sacred Way)—was always crammed with vehicles, animal trains, and troop columns. Yet German bombers, obeying explicit orders, completely ignored this ideal target. Had they attacked this vital artery and bombed it until it was impassable, which would have been neither difficult nor exceptionally hazardous, the lifeblood of Verdun would have been choked off and the fortress, as soon as its resources were sufficiently reduced, would have fallen.

German aviation, blundering on all accounts in the protracted siege, eventually lost its mastery of the air, a mastery which had never really been exploited. With the appearance at the front of a new French fighter plane— the tiny Nieuport Type 17—the already ineffectual screen of Fokker interceptors finally collapsed. If blame is to be ascribed, it belongs with the German ground command and not with the willing but overtaxed and misused airmen, whose only foible was a slavish compliance to orders that too frequently were inimical to their own best interests. Unquestioning obedience was expected of them. In keeping with a tradition of rigid military discipline, abject submission to authority was regarded as strength rather than frailty. No army can win a battle, of course, if anarchy displaces central control and destroys the reins of command. But to prohibit discretionary action to airmen, sometimes many miles behind enemy lines, was, as the German generals had yet to learn, both impractical and detrimental. Although the German airmen flew bravely and well, the tactics imposed upon them were wrong.

The organization and employment of German aircraft in the battle of Verdun was in sharp contrast with that of the French. The air space over the front was neatly divided into four sectors, each with its own dawn-to-dusk patrols. A barrier of single-seater scout planes, or as the Germans termed it, a "barrage line" was erected. The idea seemed sensible to Oswald Boelcke. Later he changed his mind.

Comprised of armed Fokkers droning sentrylike up and down the front, this protective screen was suggested to the Germans by the ageless strategy of naval blockade. Used at first to conceal General Falkenhayn's offensive buildup in the Briey basin, the patroling E-planes seemed to succeed for a while. But their strikes were largely against slow and solitary reconnaissance craft, most of which were unarmed except for a pilot's revolver or an observer's rifle. So Boelcke and the Fokker pilots, despite the telling effect of their synchronized Spandau guns, were not actually succeeding quite as laudably as they imagined. They were shooting down, it was true, almost as many of the clumsy Caudrons and Farmans as lumbered across the lines. Moreover, the lucky few enemy observers who did escape apparently saw nothing they were not supposed to see. The Germans jumped to this seemingly logical conclusion when their own air scouts, reconnoitering Verdun and its complex of outlying fortifications through January and early February, reported French unpreparedness for the impending great attack. The French lack of readiness to meet the scheduled assault was prima facie evidence that the "barrage flights" had altogether thwarted French aerial intelligence. But the evidence was deceptive. Falkenhayn's mobilization had been found out, and the French command had indeed been apprised of his aggressive intention. Verdun was forewarned. That the city was not fore-armed was due solely to the incredulity of the French general staff, who had more faith in academic doctrine than in the word of a few inexperienced airmen.

Was it not absurd to think seriously that General Falkenhayn would mount a midwinter offensive? Surely an officer of his stature remembered (as the French could not forget) the historical lesson of Napoleon Bonaparte in Russia.

The air service reports?

Exaggerated.

The stepped-up activity of German reconnaissance planes?

C'est rien. In the spring, and only then, will the offensive come.

Although the blockade was not as impenetrable as events led the Germans to think, it was—during the weeks before the momentous attack—a creditable scheme. If it failed entirely to prevent the French from discovering the build-up of German offensive power, it made them pay a high price for the knowledge. It afforded every advantage to the Fokker pilots. Aside from flying the better combat machines, they were making the French fight under the most adverse conditions possible. German aviators had recognized the prudence of engaging the enemy, whenever feasible, over German-occupied territory. It was safer, in case an emergency landing became necessary, and it was economical in terms of fuel and human vitality, two very essential commodities in waging aerial combat. Doing battle above enemy territory entailed an expenditure of fuel that acutely limited the amount of time an aviator could devote to combative action; often he would have to quit fighting in order to conserve enough fuel for the homeward flight. Also, the long outward trip across the lines tired the pilot the more so in cold weather, and tended to reduce his alertness and skill.

Still another factor which operated on the Germans' behalf, not in the Verdun battle only, but throughout the war, was the prevalence of west winds. A number of World War I flyers refer in their letters, diaries, and memoirs to this circumstance, appreciatively or querulously, depending on which side they served. A Berlin news correspondent wrote in December 1915, after visiting the Fokker pilots stationed at Douai: "A west wind means that while they are locked in contention, our planes and the adversary's are steadily driven over the German lines. If an Allied machine is . . . crippled . . . it must buck the wind all the way home, and is easy prey. The wind is on our team!" Boelcke, because of his gleaming reputation, was probably among the airmen sought out and interviewed, though none was identified in the newspaper article by name. In any case, he was assuredly aware of the wind's favor and undoubtedly took it into account when, just a month or so later, he began patrolling the Verdun line. Since, at Verdun, the obsolescent French two-seaters were sadly inferior in speed, maneuverability, and armament to the Fokker monoplane, a French pilot, once he was set upon, faced the agonizing alternative of fighting to a finish and being killed or of landing and being made a prisoner. The majority, wisely or not, chose death in preference to ignominy and imprisonment.

The extraordinary success of a rejuvenated French aviation force against the "barrage line" of intercepting E-planes that followed, was attributable in large measure to the tactical acumen of a quite remarkable Englishman. He was Major General Hugh Montague Trenchard, who the previous summer—on August 19, 1915—took over leadership of the Royal Flying Corps in France from General Henderson. With dispassionate insight, the official historian of the R.F.C. commented that Henderson had picked Trenchard to take over in his stead because "he knew that in its new chief the flying corps had an officer whose personality must impress itself in the difficult days ahead on a service responsive . . . to the inspiration of its leaders."

As the R.F.C. historian implied, Trenchard, after having headed the Farnborough training center in England and a combat wing in France, was held in affectionate esteem by his fellow air officers. Among officers of the other branches he was not universally adored, but widely respected. Those who found worst fault with him were the old-school thinkers who still regarded airplanes as, to borrow the expression of one such man, "admittedly glamorous but hardly essential to the prosecution of war." To this kind of military neanderthal, Trenchard's outspoken advocacy for ever-greater air power was unwelcome. Known as "Boom" Trenchard because of his stentorian bass voice, the handsome, forty-three-year-old field commander grasped perfectly the part aircraft had to play in warfare and, like his predecessor, he tirelessly appealed for more planes, more pilots from home.

Trenchard replaced Henderson soon after the advent of the Fokker mono-plane, when the R.F.C. was virtually helpless against German technical su-periority. British planes could not equal the Fokker's rapid rate of ascent or its maneuverability in the hands of aces like Boelcke or Max Immelmann, who made sitting targets of the eminently stable but excessively slow and underarmed BE-2 and BE-8 two-seaters, which were the workhorses of the R.F.C. through 1915. Many were shot out of the sky unawares; others were outpaced, outfought, and destroyed piecemeal on reconnaissance and bombing missions beyond the battle line.

Suffering as severely from the pestilence of Fokkers, of course, was the French flying service, and, perforce, its leader, Commandant Major Jean du Peuty, readily put all his knowledge and advice at the disposal of Trenchard.

"They talked and argued over the experiences of the two air services," records the R.F.C. historian. "They came at last to the conclusion that the corps' airplanes could best be protected by what one might call the 'strategic offensive,' that is, by fighting and subduing the enemy airmen away from the airplanes flying in direct cooperation with the army." [1]

Trenchard himself called it "forward action," and believed it to be the only proper way by which to "use and win the air." His theory, which he soon began turning to practice along the British front, was that aircraft had to be used more or less exclusively for air-to-air combat or else for routine commitments on behalf of the army, such as scouting, artillery regulation, and tactical support. Fighter squadrons, in other words, ought to be organized to stop the Fokker from dictating aerial exchanges. Peuty, however, despite the mutual accord cited by the R.F.C. historian, was opposed to any rash attempt to restore the balance by aggressive action, preferring to play a waiting game until the Allies were ready to answer the Fokker in kind. At one point in their conversation, trying to convert the cautious Frenchman to the idea that a determined offense was the surest defense, Trenchard quoted General Ferdinand Foch, who in the battle of the Marne had announced: "My right flank is broken. My left is weakening. The situation is excellent. I shall attack!" Peuty was unmoved. He and Trenchard ended their dialogue for the time being.

Trenchard heard of the attack on Verdun during the night of February 22, 1916, after motoring to his headquarters at St. Omer from Paris in a snowstorm. The news came as no shock to him. Evidence of an imminent German offensive had lately been increasing, and he supposed that the French high command was as prepared as Peuty had appeared only a week before, when they had met for one of their periodic consultations. The two men, notwithstanding their differences of opinion, were by now warm friends and close collaborators. Each respected the other's courage and integrity

[1] Boyle: *Trenchard.* The author has relied heavily on Mr. Boyle's excellent biography of General Trenchard.

without allowing that to interfere with their spirited debates about tactics. Peuty told Trenchard that French air scouts were reporting an enemy buildup along the Verdun front, but he neglected to mention the unhappy fact that the general staff placed no credence in these reports. Trenchard, therefore, having heard only half the story, was taken aback by the unreadiness of the French army at Verdun. When he and Peuty met again, the day after the fall of Fort Douaumont, Trenchard tactfully avoided this whole touchy subject. Instead he renewed his efforts to convince the Frenchman that a policy of "forward action" was now assuredly indicated.

In the six months since he had first voiced his plan for sending up specialized fighter machines, Trenchard had brought about a significant change in the R.F.C. His idea from the beginning had been that aerial supremacy would sooner or later have to be fought for, and the realization that the enemy owned an airborne machine gun vastly superior to anything the Allies were likely to produce in the near future did not deter him. "There can be," he said in a dispatch to Henderson at the War Office, "no standing on the defensive. . . . Survival in three-dimensional warfare depends on maintaining the offensive, whatever the odds or the cost."

He proposed to Henderson that all available armed aircraft—such as they were in 1915—should be concentrated in homogeneous fighter units. Henderson wholeheartedly concurred. He had, in fact, been thinking along the same lines himself. The view of wing commanders in the field, however, was that each squadron should retain a few armed aircraft in its strength to intercept enemy raiders and snoopers as well as to escort defenseless observation and bombing machines through the screen of Fokkers above the German lines. Trenchard and Henderson yielded temporarily to this theory, and the distribution of fighting planes was made accordingly until the spring of 1916, when the scheme of reformation was finally effected.

The Royal Flying Corps, at the time of the Fokker threat, had but one type of operational aircraft specifically designed to carry a machine gun. It was the Vickers FB-5 *Gun Bus,* a pusher biplane carrying a two-man crew. The *Gun Bus* was not a fighter in the strict sense, but rather an armed scout and occasional light bomber. Compared to the Fokker, it was slow and limited to a service ceiling of only nine thousand feet. Nevertheless, it did much good work in France, where the first example arrived in February 1915, and was better able to take care of itself than other Allied planes of that year. The *Gun Bus,* moreover, equipped the first so-called fighter squadron ever formed: Squadron No. 11, which reached France on July 25, 1915, less than a month prior to Trenchard's promotion to the R.F.C. field command. This squadron served as a model of what Trenchard had in mind, and Henderson, in England, authorized the organization and training of other squadrons like No. 11. The development of improved aircraft, capable of dealing with the German E-plane, was also energetically undertaken.

At the front, meanwhile, Trenchard swiftly carried out such technical modifications as could be introduced to lessen the odds. The Lewis gun, for instance, supplanted the observer's rifle in the BE-type biplanes. Every R.F.C. unit kept two or three single-place aircraft on the flight line. Though used as interceptors and escort-fighters, none of them had been originally designed primarily for combat. Most were converted reconnaissance planes made ready for battle by the hasty installation of armament. The best of these was the Bristol Scout, with a Lewis gun mounted on the top wing to shoot over the airscrew or fixed to the fuselage to shoot forward at an oblique angle beyond the airscrew arc. Other of these ersatz fighters included the Martinsyde S-1, which was fairly worthwhile, and the outmoded SE-2 of the Royal Aircraft Factory.

A few of these planes had been fitted with machine guns even before Trenchard invoked his aggressive philosophy. On a July evening in 1915, Captain Lanoe George Hawker became one of the first to emerge from the anonymity which cloaked the early performances of R.F.C. pilots. Hawker took off from Abeele in No. 6 Squadron's Bristol Scout, armed with a Lewis gun on the starboard side of the fuselage. Over the Ypres salient he attacked a German two-seater, which dived steeply to safety. Twenty minutes later he attacked another two-seater over Houthulst forest and put it out of commission with a bullet-shattered engine. Hawker resumed his patrol. Over Hooge, at about eleven thousand feet, he encountered an Albatros observation plane, pounced on it from out of the sun and shot it down in flames. All three of his adversaries were armed with machine guns. For his evening's work, Hawker was awarded the first Victoria Cross to be earned in aerial recounter. Sixteen months later, by which time his name was well known to German airmen, Hawker was killed in single combat with Manfred von Richthofen and became the baron's eleventh victim.

There are too many of his earlier utterances on record to permit the belief that Trenchard formulated his aggressive ideas on the basis of Hawker's inspiring feat. Trenchard's policies antedated by at least a year that evening in July when Hawker went all out after the enemy. But the exploit surely served to reinforce Trenchard's attitude, for Hawker had unequivocally demonstrated that pilots in makeshift fighter planes could destroy enemy observation machines. And as soon as the Trenchard plan of aggressive operations was adopted by the R.F.C., it became evident that these pilots could fight with the Fokker monoplane on terms less disadvantageous than they had feared. Although the results were far from revolutionary, British losses began to decrease, slightly but inspiritingly, and their victories to increase. British airmen again felt they were in a war and not merely a nightmarish game in which they dodged or died.

But the demands on their stamina and courage were tremendous, and Trenchard realized that this was the crucial factor. His tactics would ultimately fail unless the morale of his airmen remained high. His faith in them was revealed by the fact that he gambled so heavily on their dedication to duty. What they thought of him was not important. Trenchard did not yearn for the solaces of popularity; he simply knew his policies were right. It was an attitude that typified him. At one stage of his command, during the autumn of 1915, R.F.C. losses outstripped replacements, and he reduced the number of planes under army control. He did so for the sake of operational efficiency rather than from any squeamishness or slackening of purpose, as was later intimated. He had no patience with what he called "interfering busybodies," and he seldom bothered to answer misinformed criticism.

On occasion, however, Trenchard could be stung into hitting back. Toward the end of 1915, while in London on an official errand, he was sitting one sunlit afternoon in Green Park, enjoying the almost forgotten pleasure of wearing mufti. It was at a time when patriotic women were producing a large harvest of war babies and civilian males wore silver medallions in their button holes to show they were engaged in useful war work and thus immune to public slurs and embarrassment. Trenchard, as he sat musing, perhaps, about the sociological phenomena of wartime, was approached by a sniffy female of uncertain age.

"May I ask you, sir," she inquired, "where's your war badge?"

Trenchard paused for only a breath.

"And may I ask you, madam, where's your war baby?" he barked, and stumped off toward the seclusion of his Berkeley Street flat.[2]

A few weeks later, back in France, he had anything but babies and badges on his mind. The intense slaughter of the Verdun salient had begun, and the French situation was desperate. Fort Douaumont had been taken by the Germans, crisis was piling on crisis, yet Trenchard, in his deliberations with Major Peuty on February 26, could not revise the latter's theories about aviation tactics. Peuty, drawing on his experience as a regimental soldier, contended that French airmen at Verdun were forced to fight defensively. While respecting Trenchard's calculated recklessness in pitting his strength against the enemy's technical superiority, Peuty had no immediate desire to emulate him. The Frenchman regarded the heavy German concentrations as too complex and sinister a threat for incaution in the air, pointing out that an ill-conceived gamble at this juncture could result in irretrievable losses and total impotency against raiding aircraft.

The storm that descended on Verdun continued with unabated violence through the month of March, and it became increasingly clear that the French plan of defense—"They shall not pass!"—was inappropriate to the tussle for air supremacy. Trenchard, astutely aware of Peuty's material shortages, delivered to him as many guns, bullets, and bombsights as could be spared from R.F.C. supply. He sent these goods to Verdun without being asked, at the same time petitioning Henderson in the War Office to replenish his stores. As Peuty had requested, the R.F.C. had taken over almost a hundred extra

[2] Boyle: *op. cit.*

miles of the western front to patrol. Although Trenchard had a short reserve of men and machines, he intensified local pressure on reduced enemy squadrons. In the knowledge that Peuty's battle was also his own, the British air commander did all within his power to help insure success for French aviation at Verdun.

Early in April Peuty wrote to his liaison officer at R.F.C. headquarters:

> I'd like you to thank General Trenchard again for his machine guns. We've had trouble with some which jammed during combats. This seems due less to the tracer bullets he gave us than to the precarious and poor conditions of maintenance at Verdun. I've had one of his Lewis guns fitted to my own aircraft. It proved most useful in an attack with two other Nieuport fighters on two Fokkers and five L.V.G.'s about four miles behind their lines. We had them cold; they were picking their noses in a disgusting fashion. Navarre [one of the early French aces] has shot down four Boche machines in a single day.[3]

Peuty, as this communication indicates, had suddenly learned for himself the truth of Trenchard's earlier assertions that offensive action was the key to aerial superiority. A few days later, he passed more of his observations along to the R.F.C. commander:

"The most characteristic facts about the fighting so far are, first, the new importance of night reconnaissance, and second, the benefits resulting from organizing our fighters into separate groups outside the ordinary army co-operation units. By flying together in threes, our army machines have shown that they can protect themselves, so freeing the real *avions de chasse* for independent offensive action against enemy fighters. . . . In the future, the advantage will go to the side which can carry its striking power the farthest." [4]

All of which coincided exactly with Trenchard's belief and experience. Never had he doubted the courage or competence of French airmen, whose equipment and training were probably better than the British, but he had disapproved of the close control wielded by French ground commanders with no comprehension of air tactics. In this respect the French army had erred almost as egregiously as the German. Peuty was venturing, however, to end this old tradition by progressively creating a new one—as Trenchard had done—in conditions of crisis.

"We are beginning to improve on our new methods," Peuty went on, "though over and over again we have to start from scratch, teaching fresh squadrons that keep arriving. . . . I may say that in my official reports, which are meant to plant a few ideas in the heads of some noble but very old-fashioned gentlemen, I petition for a reorientation of thinking at G.H.Q. I am preparing a detailed summary of my conclusions, which I'll let you have." [5]

[3] Boyle: *op. cit.*
[4] Boyle: *op. cit.*
[5] Boyle: *op. cit.*

This considered document reached St. Omer in mid-April, after Peuty's newly adopted methods had been subjected to severe testing. Trenchard considered it a masterful treatise on air fighting, perhaps because it confirmed so many of his own ideas. As a historical curiosity, it is worth a lengthy excerpt:

> Aircraft can be put in two categories, army machines and combat machines. And these aircraft can be utilized in two distinct ways, either by using the combat machines to protect the army machines, or by letting the latter fend for themselves so that the combat machines can do the real job of fighting.
>
> We have employed both methods, and here are the results. Like the Germans, we began by resorting to the second method, and thanks to offensive zeal we attained a material and moral superiority so marked that the enemy was forced to protect his army machines. . . .
>
> We were proud of this. It made us a little complacent; we surrendered to the demands of our own army corps which wanted close support for their hard-pressed cooperation machines. We thus were coerced into adopting the first method, and were barely able to hold our own with the enemy. The strongest formations of aircraft proved the masters of the situation.
>
> We then resumed the second method—and promptly recouped local air superiority by going after it. There were two main drawbacks. The first was that the corps commanders, misunderstanding what was at stake, protested shrilly at being left in the lurch, despite the fact that their cooperation machines, by flying in formations of three, as instructed, managed to do their work, defend themselves and suffer relatively few casualties in the process. The second drawback has been the . . . nervous strain imposed on our combat pilots, who are carrying the fight nonstop to the enemy's back areas, fighting and dropping their bombs far from their own bases and within constant range of German antiaircraft weapons.
>
> Our losses in the air may be heavy, but . . . our mastery is proving of enormous advantage to the troops on the ground.[6]

Before April passed into May, the French flying service, by the sheer dint of hurling itself without stop at the wall of Fokkers, had wrested the initiative from the Germans. More and more of the once-defenseless Caudrons and Farmans and Voisins, the heavy observation and bomber machines, were mounting Lewis and Hotchkiss guns in the nose of their cockpit nacelles. By flying in formations of three or more, as Peuty stated, they provided enough mutual protection to weather the interceptor attacks. This technique, too, had been perfected beforehand by Trenchard and the R.F.C. Back in late 1915, at the height of the Fokker menace, Trenchard had initiated a new bombing

[6] Boyle: *op. cit.*

policy that violated—and quickly disproved—the long-standing theory that raiders traveling in close formation were more vulnerable to enemy fire than widely spaced or individual machines. Ready as always to risk his reputation —and the lives of his air crews—on the validity of his ideas, he had on more than one occasion assembled what for that time was a large force of about twenty planes and sent them to strike a single objective on each sortie. Although only lightly escorted, the bombers got through almost unscathed, and the effect of their attacks was considerable. Now at Verdun Trenchard was gratified that Peuty had at last stopped temporizing, that he had learned to strike with similar vindictiveness until, by the end of April, the French were dominating the sky. Unmistakably, the experience of the French aviation service in the battle of Verdun demonstrated the value of the strategic offensive.

Strangely enough, someone in the French War Ministry, almost an entire year before the battle of Verdun began, had foreseen the requirement for specialization in the air corps. By March 1915, French aviation had been formed—on paper—ino three task groups: (1) reconnaissance, (2) artillery cooperation, and (3) bombardment. Within a few months, those during which Roland Garros and Oswald Boelcke demonstrated the practicality of airborne machine guns, the French command recognized the fighter escadrille as a fourth classification, albeit a poorly defined one which owed its existence more to wishful dreaming than anything else. Until Peuty wrought the sweeping changes that helped redeem Verdun, the distinctions among the four types of squadrons remained academic, arbitrary, and virtually intangible, with their functions frequently overlapping. The denomination of any given unit indicated more the kind of aircraft it flew than what sort of mission it might be assigned on this or that day. A squadron of Morane-Saulniers, for example, whether equipped with guns or not, was listed on the organization table as a fighter squadron. If a unit flew Farmans or Caudrons, it was ostensibly employed for artillery cooperation. An escadrille of Voisins was nominally a bombing squadron, yet often as not would be utilized for artillery spotting or scouting. Likewise, since they were flying over enemy ground anyway, all French pilots, regardless of their primary missions, were under orders to carry bombs in their machines and drop them on opportune targets. For a time it was considered a mild disgrace for a pilot to return to his airdrome without first having used up his bombs. This policy was abandoned when it became evident that too many airmen, often unable to locate worthwhile targets, simply jettisoned their missiles to be rid of them. To eliminate this wasteful practice, the War Ministry finally ruled that only bombardiers sent to raid specified objectives would be authorized to take along more than four bombs in their planes.

Very early in the war, soon after the Germans, unknown to the Allies, established the first all-bomber unit—the Ostend Carrier Pigeons—in November 1914, France put into action a similar unit consisting of three Voisin escadrilles. Whereas the Carrier Pigeons did not enter action for another couple of months, the French immediately instituted a policy of strategic daylight bombing; later, in the subsequent March, when they recomposed their flying force, they had four Groupes de Bombardment of eighteen Voisins each, sixty-four machines in all, which encouraged them to step up the frequency and intensity of their raids. Several telling blows were struck by the four groups, climaxed on May 26 by a highly successful attack on the poison-gas factory at Ludwigshafen. During this very week, however, Oswald Boelcke laid claim to his initial victim with the new Fokker E-1 monoplane and its synchronized gun.

As the Fokker menace grew in magnitude and fury, the daytime raids by the French became fewer and farther between. In September 1915, when the German monoplanes really became numerous and Allied casualties began mounting at a serious rate, the daylight attacks were altogether terminated. Thereafter, the Voisins bombed only at night. The darkness was a mixed blessing that helped in eluding the swarm of Fokker interceptors, but also made it more difficult for the French raiders to find and hit their targets. Although smaller physical damage was inflicted in the night raids, the psychological impact on the German populace was tremendous. In all the cities of the western Reich any chance for quiet sleep was disrupted by the nagging fear of sudden death from above. If a raid did occur, wholesale panic was often the result. No less staid a personage than Queen Victoria of Sweden, vacationing in Karlsruhe when that city came under attack, was seen running aimlessly about the streets in dishabille.

The steel-framed Voisin, in spite of its sluggish performance, distinguished itself as an estimable piece of machinery. Nominally a bomber, it was more accurately an all-around utility machine, an aerial jack-of-many-trades that also found employment in photoreconnaissance, artillery assistance, and as a transport for priority personnel. The Voisin was a pusher biplane which, because of its versatility and rugged construction, had an abnormally long operational life; with modifications and increased power, the basic prewar design was still in front-line service when the Armistice was signed. The 1915 model—fondly called the "flying bathtub" by its crews (as were pusher types in general)—was driven by a Canton-Unné 140-horsepower engine, took twenty-three minutes to reach 6500 feet, and did a maximum of sixty-five miles per hour. When war was declared, Gabriel Voisin armed four of these planes with Hotchkiss guns at his personal expense; in 1915 the 37-mm Hotchkiss became a standard fixture at its nose. Sitting almost four feet off the ground on its four-wheeled undercarriage, the Voisin had a wingspan of forty-eight feet that gave it steadiness in flight and a robust capacity for carrying big loads. Among the illustrious combat careers launched aboard this plane was that of Charles Nungesser, who emerged from the war as France's third-ranking ace. Other 1915 Voisin pilots were Norman Prince,

Elliot Cowdin, and Raoul Lufbery, members of the vanguard of American volunteers and progenitors of the Lafayette Escadrille.

Toward late autumn and through the winter of 1915–1916, the Fokker monoplane reached its zenith. A measure of its influence can be gauged from the fact that lone British photoreconnaissance craft, flying missions of extreme importance, were accompanied across the line by as many as twelve escorts. The necessity during these comfortless months for uninterrupted aerial reconnaissance and the lack of adequate fighter machines spurred French, as well as British, aircraft designers to feverish activity. Gaston and Réné Caudron evolved a twin-engine tractor plane, the G-4, which they hoped would have better flight characteristics than the pusher types, while at the same time featuring a nose gun. The plane turned out to be a disappointment. It had good climbing ability but was otherwise inadequate. For one thing, the gunner's field of fire was constricted by the shortness of the cockpit nacelle and the close proximity of the engines on either side.

The first twin-engine plane to go to war on the western front, the Caudron G-4 proved an easy victim to German fighter pilots and was hastily withdrawn from service. It was soon followed by a vastly improved design, the G-6, a well streamlined three-seater, propelled by a pair of Le Rhone rotaries (later replaced with Hispano-Suiza in-line engines) and fairly bristling with guns. Alongside other machines of its day, it qualified as a flying fortress. Its crew sat in tandem, the observer in the front cockpit, the pilot behind him, and the gunner amidships in the rearmost cockpit. The observer manned twin Lewis guns that could be swiveled 180 degrees, plus an auxiliary gun that fired downward and forward through a nose hatch. The rear gunner operated two Lewis guns on a ring mount. The G-6, with this armament, was a tough opponent. Escadrille Caudron No. 46, the squadron which saw the plane into action in the spring of 1916, claimed thirty-four German attackers in less than two months. With their five guns manned by the cream of the air-gunnery schools at Cazaux, the big Caudrons were at first used for photo-reconnaissance and bombing. By the end of the war they equipped some forty escadrilles and were in wide employment as escorts. (Several modified versions of the G-6 were produced, giving the design other official designations.) During the development of this sterling airplane, in a test flight at Lyons in December 1915, Gaston Caudron was mortally injured in an accident; his brother, Réné, brought the design to fruition.

With the Caudron G-6, France boasted a heavy biplane that could hold its own against the waylaying Fokkers, but she still had no fighter to outdo the German monoplane. Her best fighting machine—which began superseding the Morane-Saulnier in the summer of 1915—was the Nieuport Baby, the Type 11. It had a fine rate of climb and was every bit as maneuverable as the Fokker, but its high-mounted Lewis gun was decidedly inferior to the enemy's synchronized weapon. Furthermore, the Type 11 had a serious structural weakness; several pilots were killed when the wings of their machines buckled in the air. The fault lay in the single spar of the lower wing, which tended to twist and crack under stress (a defect common to biplanes of the V-strut variety). Early in 1916, a 110-horsepower Le Rhone engine was fitted to the Baby Nieuport and the Type 16 was born. The thirty additional horsepower enhanced the plane's performance, but the larger engine caused it to be nose heavy, so much so that it would fall into a headlong dive with the throttle closed. The best work of the Nieuport Type 16 was attacking ground installations and observation balloons with Le Prieur rockets. Perfected by Lieutenant Y. P. G. Le Prieur of the French naval air service, these projectiles were inserted in launching tubes on the interplane struts, four between the wings on each side, and they were all ignited at once by means of an electrical impulse. Though quite effective, the rockets were soon rendered obsolete by the development of incendiary ammunition.

The French acquired their long-awaited Fokker destroyer in the next Nieuport design, the Type 17, which made its appearance in March at Verdun and thereafter gradually supplanted the Types 11 and 16 in fighter escadrilles. Larger and appreciably more potent than the Baby Nieuport, with speed and aerobatic facility to spare, the Type 17 was truly one of the outstanding aircraft of the middle period of World War I. It decisively vanquished the Fokker E-plane, and many French pilots, as well as Americans of the Lafayette Escadrille, earned everlasting glory at the controls of this sturdy little scout Together with two new British machines that came on the scene in late 1915 and early 1916—namely, the De Havilland DH-2 and the Royal Aircraft Factory FE-2—the Nieuport Type 17 expeditiously undid the German monoplane and established Allied aerial supremacy some three months before the Somme offensive was set in motion.

It remains to be said, however, that even with better airplanes than the Fokker, this turnabout of air supremacy could not have been achieved had the Allies flyers not carried into execution the organizational and tactical theories propounded by General Trenchard. The E-series monoplane, with its radically superior machine gun, promptly upon its introduction won an aerial mastery that was near absolute along the whole front. On the British front, as soon as Trenchard operated his over-all strategy of tactical offense, German supremacy began to dwindle—although no newly designed aircraft had yet been delivered to the R.F.C. in France. By contrast, along the southern half of the line, where Major Peuty was in charge of French aviation, the Germans prolonged their advantage until he followed Trenchard's lead, grouped his fighting planes into specialist units, and exhorted his pilots to hunt and kill the enemy in his own backyard. It becomes clear, then, that Allied victory over the German E-plane was ascribable partly to Trenchard's bold tactical measures. Just as the best-honed tool, misused, is no good tool at all, so the technical improvement of British and French aircraft in this period would not alone have reversed the balance of power, and certainly never to the degree that it was reversed.

None of these harsh realities, meanwhile, had eluded the perceptive mind of Lieutenant Oswald Boelcke, now flying with Field Aviation Section No. 2, attached to the German Fifth Army. The evidences of what was taking place were painfully obvious to this most brilliant German pilot. He himself was daily experiencing the consequences of revived Allied power. Once, for example, on a bright spring morning in the last week of April, while he was patrolling above the Meuse, a French Nieuport that had overtaken him stayed for seemingly endless minutes behind his tail and shot at him. Boelcke climbed, he banked, looped, tried every evasive maneuver he knew, but the Nieuport— a brand-new Type 17—would not be shaken off. The German ace could hear the stuttering report of his antagonist's Lewis gun, the bullets thudding into the frame of his monoplane. He saw them chewing up the fabric covering of the Fokker's starboard wing. Boelcke, well aware of the slimness of his chances for surviving the encounter, seeing that his Fokker could neither outrace nor outstunt the splendid new French pursuit machine, decided to risk everything on one final subterfuge. He waited until the Frenchman fired another burst. Then, in simulation of a plane out of control, he pulled up into a steep climbing turn and stalled off into a spin. As he watched the earth wheeling dizzily toward him, Boelcke, a devout Catholic, prayed. If the opposing pilot were not deceived into thinking the Fokker was doomed, if he followed and continued the chase, then Boelcke would need a miracle to cheat death. The Frenchman, apparently a novice, was indeed fooled by the ruse and thereby lost an opportunity to gain a place in history as Boelcke's conqueror.

When he landed at Sivry and examined the more than ninety bullet holes in his plane, Boelcke knew for sure, as he had suspected for several weeks now, that the day of Fokker domination was over. In typical fashion, he set to work writing two lengthy memoranda addressed to the general staff, one protesting the "wretched" misuse of German air power and outlining redemptive measures of reorganization, the other recommending the rapid development of "modern biplane fighter machines." Boelcke underscored the fact that, since the advent of the Fokker almost a year before, only two other single-seaters had entered German service at the front. These were, he tartly pointed out, the Pfalz E-series fighter and the Siemens-Scheckert D-1, both midwing monoplanes armed with a synchronized gun on the engine cowling, and both almost exact duplicates of the Fokker but rather less reliable in combat.

Because he was Germany's foremost *kampfflieger,* and because he was strenuously supported in his contentions by Captain Rudolf Haehnelt, who was the aviation staff officer of the Fifth Army at Verdun, Boelcke's opinions received respectful attention. To correct the situation, he proposed to reshuffle the entire German air force along much the same lines as Trenchard and Peuty had done in the Allied camp. This, he argued, would permit German airmen to resume fighting on the offensive, as they had formerly done. "The only proper kind of war to wage in the air," he asserted, "is an offensive war. We have remained on the defensive too long." With the right aircraft at their disposal, Boelcke went on, specialized combat units, which he called *Kampfeinsitzerkommando* (Fighting Single-Seater Command), could soon win back the skies for Germany. Captain Haehnelt, after reading his star pilot's report, immediately, and on his own initiative, formed a half dozen small fighter units. Three similar groups were also formed in the area of the Sixth Army by a Major Stempel. The time had come to extend this type of organization along the whole front.

Among those most deeply impressed by Boelcke's thesis was General Erich von Ludendorff, who, since leaving Hindenburg's eastern command, had been transferred to the general staff. Ludendorff, who had favored the idea of an air arm as a separate branch of the army, at this time recommended the establishment of the Deutschen Luftstreitkrafte (German Air Force) in accordance with the tenets laid down by Boelcke. With the Kaiser's approval, the reorganization was effected. Appointed to head the new branch was General Walter von Hoeppner, with Colonel Hermann von der Lieth-Thomsen, who would prove a most praiseworthy administrator, as its chief of staff.

Boelcke, still serving on the "barrage line," was saddened at the end of April when one of the increasingly ubiquitous Nieuports killed his best friend, Lieutenant Karl Notzke (whose replacement, Lieutenant Ernst von Althaus, was destined to become an ace). On the first of May, the mournful Saxon avenged Notzke by destroying a French two-seater. By May 21, his score had risen to eighteen. A day later, he became, by Imperial order, a captain, the first twenty-five-year-old ever to attain that rank in the Royal Prussian army. It was all the more surprising because there was no "von" in Boelcke's name.

Yet another honor befell Boelcke before the end of the month. Colonel Lieth-Thomsen telephoned to inquire whether he would be interested in commanding a fighter squadron in the air force he had done so much toward creating. Boelcke modestly accepted the "kind offer" and was put in charge of Jagdstaffel No. 2. (The German term "Jagdstaffel" approximates the meaning of "pursuit squadron"; the word was quickly abbreviated in everyday usage to "Jasta" or "Staffel.") Boelcke was told he could choose whichever pilots he wished to serve under him. He was by now a national hero, and before he had the opportunity to make his paper command a reality, he was grounded by Imperial decree and forced to make an inspection tour of the southeastern front—Turkey, Bulgaria, and Austria—as much to inspire morale as to oversee the reorganization of air units in those regions. Before leaving France he asked that his itinerary be revised to include Russia also. He wanted to visit as many airfields as possible, for he made up his mind to recruit his pilots for Jasta 2 in the course of his travels. Otherwise he would have had to wait until returning to the western front and waste that much more precious time in getting his unit into action.

Boelcke did one more thing prior to his departure for the east. He wrote a discourse on the techniques of air fighting, based on his own unequaled experience. He did it mainly in order to have a prepared speech to deliver on his tour. When the text was submitted to Lieth-Thomsen for official endorsement, the latter rushed it into print and ordered that every German airman be required to study it until able, when called upon by a superior officer, to repeat it verbatim. These fundamental rules of aerial combat became known as the Boelcke Dicta. They were sound principles, as the test of time indicated. Two decades later in World War II, Nazi Messerschmitt and Focke-Wulf pilots were still putting Boelcke's tactics to practice.

CHAPTER VII

·❧ *A New Field of Honor* ❧·

My FIRST MEETING with a Boche occurred on July 19. I was in a two-seater [Morane-Saulnier] Parasol with [Jean] Guerder, my mechanic-observer, as passenger. I had promised for some time to undertake a pursuit in my airplane, but I had always been ordered on reconnaissances, photographic missions, and that sort of work suited me not at all. . . . It is useful, of course, but monotonous. And besides, it is always set aside for the newcomers to the squadron, and I wanted to show that grit was not the exclusive property of the older men."

This is Corporal Georges Guynemer talking, on the last day of 1915, to his biographer, Jacques Mortane. They are at the airdrome of Escadrille Morane-Saulnier No. 3, at Vauciennes, near Villers-Cotterêts. Guynemer, on his twenty-first birthday, December 24, just a week prior to this interview, had been presented with the Cross of the Légion d'Honneur. It was his second *palme,* for on July 21, 1915, only two days after the day he is describing, Guynemer had been recommended for the Medaille Militaire. The wistful-eyed young aviator, notwithstanding the decorations pinned to the breast of his tunic, has not yet attained the prominence of several contemporaries in the French flying service. He is, however, as Mortane seems cleverly to have divined, destined for aeonian fame. He goes on with his story:

A Boche had been sighted at Coeuvres, and so I took off with Guerder and was soon in pursuit of the enemy. Shortly afterwards we saw him over Pierrefonds, but he saw us at the same instant and fled. As his machine was faster, there was no chance of catching him. Nevertheless, the joy of finding our first adversary made us attempt the most impossible things. From a great distance, a very great distance, we fired at him . . . without any real expectation of hitting him. We chased him as far as the Coucy airfield. where we saw him alight. He must have been well satisfied with his cowardly performance . . . but it displeased us enormously.

There we were with these sad thoughts, when suddenly another black point appeared on the horizon. We sped toward it. As we came closer, it grew in size and was soon plain. It was an Aviatik sailing at about 3200 meters. The German pilot was moving toward the French lines, thinking only of what he might find. He did not guess for a moment that an enemy bent upon his destruction was in his wake. Poor fellow . . .

And we hurried toward that plane which, we thought, really belonged to us. It was not until Soissons was reached that we came up with him, and there the combat took place. During the space of ten minutes, everybody in the city watched the fantastic duel over their heads. I kept about fifteen meters from my Boche, below, back of, and to the left of him. In spite of all his twistings, I managed not to lose touch with him. Guerder fired 115 rounds, but he was having trouble, as his gun jammed repeatedly. Conversely, my companion was hit by one bullet in the hand while another "combed" his hair. He answered with his Hotchkiss, shooting more deliberately than before. At the 115th shot fired by Guerder, I had, I will admit, a very sweet feeling at seeing the enemy pilot slump to the floor of his cockpit, while the "lookout" raised his arms in a gesture of despair and the Aviatik swirled down into the abyss in flames. It fell between the trenches. I hastened to land nearby, and I can vouch that I never felt a keener elation.

Thus began the combat career of Corporal (later Captain) Georges Marie Ludovic Jules Guynemer, the most exalted figure in the annals of French martial aviation. How completely he enthralled the hearts of his countrymen in the turbulent months that followed may be judged from a marble plaque bearing his name in the crypt of the Pantheon in Paris, where the greatest dignitaries of France are interred. "Dead on the field of honor, September 11, 1917," says the inscription on this stone tablet. "A legendary hero fallen in glory from the sky after three years of hard and incessant struggle, he will remain the purest symbol of national ideals for his indomitable tenacity of purpose, his ferocious verve and sublime gallantry. Animated by an invincible faith in victory, he has bequeathed to the French soldier an imperishable heritage which consecrates the spirit of sacrifice and will surely inspire the noblest emulation."

Guynemer does not lie beneath this memorial slab, for no trace was ever found of him or his machine after his death, the Germans eventually stating that his body and the wreckage of his Spad had been obliterated by British shelling. After winning fifty-four victories in the air and twenty-six citations for bravery, after logging more than 660 flying hours and some one hundred combats, and just eight days after his promotion to squadron commander, Guynemer vanished, accepting nothing from his enemies, not even a wooden cross. His last flight began at 08:25 hours, before the early sun could dissipate the autumnal chill of that September night. Lieutenant Benjamen Bozon-Verduraz accompanied him on the sortie. "The morning seemed fraught with maleficence," Bozon-Verduraz later wrote. "Captain Guynemer seemed out of sorts . . . morose. The haze was unusually thick, so that we often lost sight of each other's machine." They crossed the Belgian border, climbing in search of the enemy. At eight thousand feet they broke out of the haze. Guynemer saw a lone two-seater and signaled his companion that he was going to attack. Bozon-Verduraz watched him swing around and maneuver into position for a diving pass. Then the lieutenant spotted a formation of German fighters above. He drew their attention from Guynemer by aiming the nose of his Spad toward their midst and firing. He was too far away to shoot accurately, as he well knew, but close enough so the enemy pilots would turn on him and give chase. Bozon-Verduraz led them off to the north and, after ten or fifteen minutes, lost them in a cloudbank. Circling back to rejoin his commander, he found the sky empty of all aircraft. He eased down into the haze, which was thinner than before, and searched the area thoroughly until he had barely enough fuel left for his return to base. Guynemer never returned.

The disappearance of the great ace was withheld from French press dispatches for more than a week because of the impact it would have on the morale of soldier and civilian alike. The secret was too terrible to conceal for long, however. Newspapers and magazines were already printing rumors and "unconfirmed reports" when the tragic news was officially released in a terse communique from the War Ministry: "Captain Guynemer flew off on patrol at 08:25 hours, September 11, with Lieutenant Bozon-Verduraz and disappeared in the vicinity of Poelcapelle, Belgium, during a combat with a German biplane."

Throughout France the shock and grief were profound. Men wept in the streets and in the trenches. The entire French people joined to keep a mournful vigil, waiting for conclusive word of the missing pilot's fate, hoping against hope that he would somehow reappear, that at worst he had been captured alive. "If a prisoner, he must escape; if dead, he must come back to life," wrote the editor of *L'Illustration*. "They say Guynemer is dead," reflected a writer in *Le Temps*. "Guynemer dead! Bah! Those who believe it don't know him!" In every classroom of every school, prayers were said for the safe deliverance of this hero of heroes, to whom tens of thousands of French children had scrawled letters of gratitude and encouragement; and it could be that the more thoughtful young minds of that luckless generation in France suddenly, for the first time, saw through the falsely glamorous veneer of war. The churches, in the next few weeks, were filled to capacity, and when a special service for Guynemer was announced, even the largest cathedrals could not house the sorrowing multitudes. Politicians, from the highest to the lowest, outdid one another in their attempts to describe the deep anguish caused by Guynemer's absence. "He was," said President Georges Clemenceau, "our pride and our protection. His loss is the most cruel of all those, so numerous, alas, which have been visited upon our ranks. . . . Our revenge will be hard and inexorable. . . . Guynemer was merely a puissant idea in a rather frail body, and I have lived near him with the secret sorrow of knowing that some day the idea would slay the container. . . . He will remain the model hero, a living legend, the greatest in all history."

Considering the immense psychological value to the Germans of Guynemer's demise, it was strange that no claim to have shot him down was forthcoming until four weeks later, in October, when Lieutenant Kurt Wissemann, a Rumpler biplane pilot of Jagdstaffel No. 3, was credited with the kill. According to German sources after the war, Guynemer's Spad crashed in a graveyard outside of Poelcapelle. An army surgeon and two noncommissioned officers allegedly inspected the wreckage and found the pilot dead with a bullet through his brain. Positive identification was made, so the German records assert, by papers recovered from the body. Since the examination was conducted during a heavy barrage of British artillery, the investigators retreated, leaving the corpse sitting in the Spad for later burial. The fact that German propagandists made no fanfare over the event, as they invariably did in cases of other Allied aces being shot down, casts a considerable doubt on the authenticity of their story. The first printed notice of Guynemer's death to appear in any German publication was a discourteous piece in *Die Woche*. In its issue of October 6, this journal devoted to Guynemer a one-paragraph item which claimed, among other slanders, that he attacked "only the weakest opponents" and "if the onset failed, desisted at once, having no stomach for fights of long duration, in the course of which real courage must be displayed." On the same page was a reproduction of Guynemer's flying diploma, a document which could easily have been counterfeited for this purpose. The lateness of the article suggests that the Germans may not have realized that the famed *pilote de guerre* had been shot down until they got hold of some French newspapers, which were full of speculations and eulogistic pronunciations. Lieutenant Wissemann's name, furthermore, was conspicuous by its omission.

Another aspect of the situation has never been clarified. On October 12, a story published in the *Kolnische Zeitung* purported that Wissemann had boasted in a letter to his family of having triumphed over "the celebrated French flyer, Guynemer." "Don't be afraid on my account," he was supposed to have reassured his parents. "I shall never again meet such a dangerous foe." If Wissemann actually wrote this letter, he knew something the German command apparently did not yet know, which he could scarcely have known, in fact, except by clairvoyance. For Wissemann was in turn slain in a duel with Captain Paul René Fonck, another ace among French aces. And it happened on September 30—five or six days before the German authorities showed an awareness that Guynemer was dead, and ten days before Wissemann was assigned the victory in the official German reports. Wissemann was acclaimed posthumously for his dubious victory. Hence, if Guynemer really was shot down in combat, and if Wissemann was in truth his executioner, the latter probably died in his turn without having found out whom he had defeated that misty morning over Poelcapelle. He cannot, then, have written the letter attributed to him by the Cologne newspaper.

Guynemer, whose marvelous élan was motivated by an implacable hatred of the invader, vanished at the height of his career. At the time of his disappearance there was but one other aviator—Baron Manfred von Richthofen, the Red Knight of Germany, with sixty-one victories—who had as yet reached a higher score of victories. Still others, including Captain Fonck, would surpass Guynemer's fifty-three victories, simply because they lived to fight more battles, but none would ever exceed him for dash and daring. Who except this tough little Frenchman freely ventured to attack an enemy plane with his ammunition drums empty, his guns useless? Guynemer not only attempted this astonishing feat, against an armed two-seater, but bluffed the German crew into surrendering! It was fearlessness like this that led him to yet another dazzling exploit, the shooting down of two planes in one minute, and later on the same day, May 25, 1917, the shooting down of two more. It was this pure temerity that explains why he was shot down seven times himself and wounded twice before mysteriously going down forever. It was this utter disregard for danger, together with his fervent patriotism, that caused him to reject the many entreaties from G.H.Q. that he take a rest from operational flying. His health, which had never been good, was very poor in the final weeks of his life, yet he scornfully ignored an urgent plea from the high command, as late as September 7, to refrain from further combat patrols.

Born on Christmas Eve 1894, Georges Guynemer was the bearer of a family military tradition stretching back nine centuries to the Crusades. His father was a St. Cyr graduate who had resigned his commission in 1890 to settle in Compiègne and devote himself to historical research. As a boy, Georges was chronically sick. He may have had tuberculosis, inasmuch as he remained skeletally thin, sallow, and physically delicate throughout his short life. Coddled by his mother and two sisters, his scholastic career at the lycée of Compiègne and then in the Stanislaus Military College was inauspicious. Although bright and imaginative, he was unreliable, disorderly, self-willed, and quarrelsome. With the vague ambition to become a scientist, he was fond of tinkering with mechanical toys and gadgets, and especially delighted in the study of chemistry, on several occasions almost blowing himself up with his test-tube concoctions.

At the age of nineteen, Guynemer tried to enlist in August 1914, but was refused for service because of his health. He volunteered four times again before he succeeded, on November 21, in persuading the authorities to permit him to sign on as an apprentice airplane mechanic. The following day he reported for duty at the Pau airdrome, then commanded by Captain Bernard Thievry. Endowed with magnetic charm, the young recruit was able, with Captain Thievry's help, to talk higher authorities into letting him train as a pilot. On March 10, 1915, he entered his first solo flight in a log book that would trace his aerial experience from that date to July 28, 1916, by which time he had bagged eleven enemy aircraft in 348 flying hours. After two months at flying school, on June 8, 1915, with his corporal's chevrons newly sewn upon his sleeves, he was posted to Escadrille M.S. No. 3 at Vauciennes, where a rarely gifted leader, Captain Felix Brocard, was in command. Six weeks later, bored with tracking back and forth above the front lines on photoreconnaissance, and determined, as he told writer Jacques Mortane, "to show that grit was not the exclusive property of the older men," he won his first combat and his first medal. These "older men" included such notables as Jules Vedrines, Mathieu de la Tour, and Georges Raymond, all future aces and, even at this incipient stage of the war, seasoned battle pilots.

Military aviation, by the spring of 1915, had already begun to shed its swaddling clothes. There was ferment in both camps, the Allied and the German. Little more than a month preceding Guynemer's arrival at Vauciennes, Roland Garros had cut down six surprised enemy, with his machine gun shooting bullets between the blades of his whirling propeller. In June, as Guynemer was acclimating himself to the routine of reconnaissance flying, the Germans began retaliating with their far more efficient synchronized gun in combination with the Fokker monoplane that much resembled the Morane-Saulnier Type-N single-seater, the so-called Morane-Saulnier *Bullet*. Until they learned this monoplane was a Fokker product, French airmen described it in their reports as "the German Morane." If they disparaged it as an obvious copy, they quickly came to respect its fighting qualities, which decisively exceeded those of any coeval Morane-Saulnier. Guynemer, in his initial encounter with a Fokker E-1, was astonished by its agility and fire power. "The enemy . . . fired at least two hundred times, and by a miracle did no more than puncture one of my tires . . . and I did not hesitate, despite the warnings always given us to avoid clouds and haze, to plunge at full speed into an expanse of cumulus and disappear from the eyes of my attacker." After ten minutes of madcap hide and seek, he eluded the Fokker and "made a beeline for Vauciennes, breathing more than one sigh of relief."

Guynemer was happy enough with his assignment to Escadrille M.S. No. 3. Still, had he been granted an option as to which squadron he most preferred joining, he would have chosen Escadrille M.S. No. 26, the outfit in which Garros—now a German captive—had served. To fly with M.S. 26 was then the desire of every young pilot in French aviation. A galaxy of the nation's foremost prewar flyers had been brought together in this unit, and the earliest legends of French heroism in the air had crystalized around their adventures.

First there had been Warrant Officer Armand Pinsard, who received a citation—the first awarded to any French airman—in the third week of the war. The presentation saluted him for having carried out numerous reconnaissances and, specifically, for a single-handed bombing assault on the German general headquarters at Thielt. In November 1914, Pinsard made a forced landing inside enemy territory; he and his observer, a Captain Chaulin, labored feverishly for two hours to restart the engine of their high-winged Parasol monoplane. They managed to get airborne just as a detachment of German infantry approached and opened fire. So hurried was their departure that they had to leave their fur flying coats on the ground, together with Chaulin's rifle and cockpit door. That same month, Pinsard collected his second citation, this for having landed behind enemy lines three times to drop off espionage agents. A quiet, tough career soldier who earned his pilot's brevet in 1912, who later escaped dramatically from German imprisonment after a year of abusive treatment and in 1917 was critically injured in a flying accident, Pinsard survived the war as the eighth-ranking French ace, with twenty-seven victories. Though he subsequently transferred to another squadron, he served with M.S. 26 until February 1915, when he fell into German hands after crashing near Cologne. In distinguishing himself as the first of the French flying heroes of World War I, Pinsard generated great public adulation toward himself, his squadron, and the flying service as a whole. It was he, more than anyone else in those early days of air warfare who awakened the French people's attention to the romantic deeds of a new warrior breed.

But Pinsard did not shoot down any German aircraft until August 1916, three months after his escape from Ingolstadt prison and his transfer to Escadrille Nieuport No. 26 in the Somme sector. It remained for Roland Garros to prove that the air service could effectively dispense death and destruction to the invaders of France. Garros' demonstration added further to the luster of M.S. 26. More than that, it filled many another Morane-Saulnier pilot with a wish to install a forward-firing machine gun behind his propeller, as Garros had done.

Until this time the only planes fitted with guns firing from the nose were the Vickers *Gun Buses* of the Royal Flying Corps and a handful of French Voisins. Being pushers, they had no propellers in front to obstruct the field of fire ahead. But both were clumsy and lethargic performers, poorly suited for air-to-air combat. All other planes equipped with rapid-fire weapons were two-seater tractor types, with guns mounted in the observer's cockpit to shoot to the sides and rear. Some of these could shoot forward as well, but only at an awkwardly high or sideward angle. In any case, fewer than a quarter of the aircraft then operating over the battle lines carried armament any more useful than an ordinary bolt-action rifle. In his eighteen-day killing spree Garros sowed the seed that quickly turned into a full-blown science of air fighting. He did it, first, by setting a determined example, and second, in spite of himself, by having his plane captured and so affording Anthony Fokker an opportunity to examine its firing system and vastly improve upon it by inventing a mechanical synchronizer for German pilots.

Thus did the age of air fighting dawn. There was, in that April and May of 1915, a sudden deluge of requests for automatic weapons in the French flying corps. When Garros fell into German hands and no word of his fate was soon heard, the cry for machine guns grew louder, especially among his comrades in Escadrille M.S. No. 26. First Pinsard and then Garros had failed to return from across the lines. The thirst for revenge was strong. Two members of the squadron who had been flying armed Parasol two-seaters immediately removed their Hotchkiss guns to *Bullet* monoplanes and flew off seeking battle.

Eugene Gilbert, swearing to avenge the missing Garros, declared his intention by painting the name *Le Vengeur* on the fuselage of his newly armed single-seater. Before he had the chance to fire a shot, however, Gilbert lost his way and was imprisoned in neutral Switzerland, where he landed after running out of fuel. Could time be turned around, Gilbert perhaps had his revenge, for in December 1914, his observer had brought down an L.V.G. biplane. It had been only the third French air victory of the war, and the only one Gilbert would ever win. On May 17, 1918, after having escaped Swiss internment and becoming a test pilot at the Morane-Saulnier factory, he crashed to his death.

Maxime Lenoir made good the squadron's vendetta just twelve days after Garros disappeared. Lenoir, with his Hotchkiss gun shooting through the airscrew of his tiny Type-N monoplane, disabled an Albatros B-3 and forced it to land in a French farm meadow. Typical of its period, the "Blaue Maus" (Blue Mouse), as this model Albatros was nicknamed by German flyers, had no wheel brakes. The pilot, wounded in the shoulder and blinded by smoke from the damaged engine, could not keep the plane from ramming a low fence and canting on its nose. He and his dazed observer were taken into custody by an elderly farm hand and held under the muzzle of an antique musket while Lenoir taxied up, saw that everything was under control, and took off again to summon the gendarmes from the nearest town. Lenoir was later to settle accounts with ten additional enemy aircraft before being killed himself.

In May, when the Fokker E-1 made its debut, the demand for machine guns spread through the entire corps of French aviators. With some justification, considering the infirmities of the Morane-Saulnier Type N as an automatic-weapon carrier, the War Ministry declined to furnish this kind of armament to the single-seater monoplane. Although experience more than a year later would show that the Type N could be structurally strengthened to carry a synchronized Vickers gun, the little monoplane could not yet safely absorb the recoil shocks of a rapid-fire weapon. The inherent risks of shooting an unsynchronized gun through a steel-plated propeller further accounted for the War Ministry's reluctance. Experiments were already in progress at Buc airdrome with Hotchkiss and Lewis guns set on the top wings of biplanes so that the line of fire cleared the airscrew arc. Among the planes on which this arrangement was being tried was the prototype of the Nieuport Type 11, for which French designers were predicting great things. And the official French view was that until such time as the Allies developed a synchronizing gear like that of the Fokker, a high-performance biplane with a gun fixed to fire above the propeller would be the most practical solution.

Actually, there was nothing sluggish about the performance of the Type-N *Bullet,* which was comparable if not equal to that of the Fokker E-1. The French monoplane was driven by an eighty-horsepower Gnome or a 110-horsepower Le Rhone rotary engine, both being almost identical to the Oberursel plant of the early Fokker. The Morane-Saulnier was more streamlined than the Fokker by virtue of its large spinner, nicknamed "la casserole," which left only a small annular opening for cooling the engine, so that the spinner was usually discarded in hot weather. The spinner imparted to the plane its bullet shape. With the spinner removed, the resemblance of the *Bullet* to the E-1 was so close—especially in flight—that French troops habitually shot at it from the trenches.

Flying characteristics aside, the Morane-Saulnier was markedly inferior to the Fokker as a fighting machine, because of the latter's synchronized gun. Nevertheless, until late summer, when the Nieuport entered mass production, impatient French fighter pilots had no better airplane in which to face the Fokker. Lacking sanction from the War Ministry and therefore unable to requisition machine guns through legitimate channels, several pilots resorted to begging, borrowing, even stealing and illicitly buying whatever weapons they could from the army. Although aware that the use of deflector plates offered no real safety against shooting off their own propellers—as several pilots discovered to their distress before summer—some fifteen to twenty of them had wangled machine guns for themselves by the end of May. In June, generally with the covert assistance of sympathetic ground personnel, another dozen or so pilots provided their *Bullet* monoplanes with Hotchkiss or, in a few instances, Lewis guns. Many additional Parasol two-seaters were also fitted with swivel-mounted guns.

Escadrille M.S. No. 26 represented, through that troubled summer, the best-armed squadron at the front. After Garros, and then Gilbert and Lenoir, just about all the well-known pilots of M.S. 26 took to the air with machine guns installed behind their propellers; no doubt they used their reputations to secure the necessary guns and ammunition.

Nearly as well armed was Escadrille M.S. No. 3, thanks mainly to the commanding officer, Captain Brocard, who went to exhaustive lengths to obtain proper weapons for his men. Georges Guynemer, in recounting the story of his first victory, which occurred in mid-July, mentioned that his observer was using a Hotchkiss gun. This was not an exceptional case, for nearly all the Parasols in M.S. 3 had by then been so equipped. And several of those to whom Guynemer alluded as the "older men," taking their cue from Garros and his squadron companions in M.S. 26, were by then flying *Bullet* monoplanes with forward-firing machine guns.

Yet, dedicated and courageous as were these pilots, they could not expect to square accounts with the Fokker. The German E-planes were better handled with each passing day and more plentiful. By the end of July they outnumbered the makeshift *Bullet* fighters two to one; by the end of August, almost three to one. It was not the numerical handicap as much as the technical, however, that destroyed French airmen. Adolphe Pegoud, famous before the war as the first man ever to loop an airplane and now flying a Type-N *Bullet* in M.S. 26, complained, for example, of having to duck his head when firing his Hotchkiss. "About every sixth shot," he said, "hits the propeller and bounces back at me. Often I hear it whistle past my ear. Sometimes I fear I am more apt to shoot myself down than I am to shoot down my intended victim." Pegoud went on to describe the vibration caused by the gun's recoil, using adjectives that translate into English as "bone jarring" and "disconcerting." He pointed out also that with a gun able to shoot cleanly through its propeller, the Fokker's superiority was such that a French pilot would have been foolhardy to pick a fight with it on purpose.

Pegoud's words did not govern his actions. Snatching up the cudgel where Garros had been obliged to lay it down, Pegoud hurled himself at the Germans whenever possible. Almost every day, weather permitting, he set out on a long-distance sortie, with a pair of heavy bombs attached to his machine. His list of such raids totaled more than any of his associates at the time of his death, and his method of dropping explosives from low altitudes, so that a hit was better assured, set a pattern that his fellow pilots sought to imitate. In the course of these raids Pegoud participated in several dozen air-to-air combats, and the five of every six bullets that did miss his propeller blades, he used with deadly effect. On July 11, 1915, he brought down his sixth aircraft, a Rumpler Taube, and received the Military Medal. His score tied with that of Garros, Pegoud was hailed as the fiercest air fighter then doing service at the front for any nation. Going after his seventh air victory, on the last morning of August, he attacked a two-seater biplane piloted by a Corporal Kandulski, whose gunner was a Lieutenant Bilitz. In the scrap that ensued, Pegoud was struck by a bullet that severed an artery. Far behind the German lines when wounded, he landed in a fainting condition near Belfort, just within French territory, and died before he could be extricated from the wreckage of his machine. Rather than landing to give himself over to German medical care and prison, he had bled to death.

A splendid military funeral was held for Pegoud on September 3. As the cortege marched slowly toward the cemetery, a formation of German planes circled overhead and strewed flowers upon the somber procession. Among the blossoms were several notes of condolence from enemy aviators who in happier days had been Pegoud's friendly competitors in so many European air events. Soon after his burial, the Legion of Honor was conferred upon this French pioneer pilot of peace and war.

Adolphe Pegoud was probably the first war pilot to be called, in print at least, an ace. This distinction befell him in June 1915, after his fourth victory, when a Paris newspaper panegyrized him as *"l'as de notre aviation."* The term, as applied to military aviators, thus sprang into English and German and every other language of modern civilization, from the French *l'as*—the highest card in a suit. Toward the close of 1915, as French pilots became used to the new art of aerial warfare, they set a standard of five enemy aircraft destroyed in combat as a more exact measure of the ace. But the title originally signified any pilot of exemplary skill and bravery, irrespective of how many kills he had made. In the summer of 1915, when the appellation gained currency in France, only two airmen, Garros and Pegoud, had scores to qualify them as aces in the sense of having shot down five or more aircraft; yet newspapers and magazines were pasting the label on almost every pilot whose courage and endurance exceeded the ordinary.

One such was Corporal Jean Navarre, an army pilot since pre-war days, serving at this time with Escadrille M.S. No. 12 at Villacoublay. Navarre began carving out a reputation for himself early that spring, piloting a Parasol two-seater. The role of the squadron was still strictly one of observation, and although small arms were carried, no serious thought had as yet been given to air fighting except by the far-seeing minority. Then, at about three o'clock on the morning of March 21, a zeppelin was reported over Paris and several M.S. 12 planes were ordered into the air to try to scare off the intruder. Navarre crewed with Lieutenant Réné Chambe (later a fighter pilot himself), who was armed with the usual rifle. As for Navarre, he stowed a kitchen knife alongside his seat and bragged that it was his intention to get close enough to disembowel the monster!

After taking off, he and Chambe prowled the darkness for two uncomfortable hours. In addition to their regular winter dress they wore shaggy bearskin coats, leather breeches, and fur-lined boots, gloves, and headgear; but the biting cold was still painful. Their eyes ached, too, after a while, from the incredible strain of peering into the black nothingness that enwrapped them. They were about to give up the search when dawn rose over the eastern horizon and Navarre saw what looked like a huge airship silhouetted against the dim light. But the apparition, as he raced toward it, disappointingly materialized into a long, spindle-shaped cloud. No zeppelin was met with that morning. The story, however, of this neoteric St. George, wonderfully chasing about the sky after dragons, was published in a Paris journal later that week, and Corporal Navarre suddenly found himself a minor celebrity, one perhaps a bit intoxicated by his first taste of fame.

Navarre, then in his twentieth year, was an incorrigible practical joker who had little respect for the conventions and sacred cows of either the military or civil establishment. Three things he loved—fast planes, fast cars, and fast women—and his off-duty escapades soon won for him as much notoriety as his heroism in the air. A notorious carouser, he prevailed for a time as the *enfant terrible* of the French flying service. Apart from the sky above, his favorite place was the bohemian quarter of Paris. There he was worshiped for his virile good looks, his raffish wit, and his free-handed way with a franc, and he could often be found entertaining a whole bevy of *fleurs de la nuit* in some candlelit café on the slopes of Montmartre. Navarre, in fact, when he flew, always wore a skullcap fashioned from a lady's silk stocking. Many pilots, generally a superstitious lot, carried talismans with them, and articles of feminine apparel were extremely popular for this purpose. Quite a few planes entered battle with a pair of gossamer hose or lace-frilled dainties tied as streamers to the wing struts, and some fair damsel's garter adorned more than one airman's sleeve, hopefully to propitiate whatever dark powers haunted the sky.

At the wheel of an automobile Navarre was well known to the police as a public menace. In Paris alone he was arrested for reckless driving at least a dozen times, though never detained in custody for longer than, say, three or four hours at a time. The police—putting a higher premium on their duty as patriotic Frenchmen than as keepers of the law—had no desire to deprive the aviator of his morning patrol over the German lines, so they merely scolded him, dosed him with black coffee, gave him a comradely pat on the back, perhaps a little pep talk, and bade him au revoir. On a couple of occasions, when Navarre was too deep in his cups for immediate revival, the indulgent gendarmes bothered themselves to the extent of driving him to his squadron at Villacoublay.

Knowingly or otherwise, future authors of aviation fiction would create myriad effigies of Navarre in their hackneyed characterizations of brash young warriors of the sky, paragons of manly rectitude at the controls of an airplane, ready and able always to do or die for the cause, yet who behaved on the ground, in their private lives, as dissolute tosspots and philanderers. These fictional profligates are customarily portrayed as doomed children of fate, whooping it up tonight lest tomorrow night never come, wearing masks of gaiety to conceal their gnawing apprehensions, wining and wenching in an effort to quell their dread of untimely death. Such a one, indeed, was Navarre in real life, the impeccable combat flyer, sublimating his fear in a frenetic round of pleasures. Which is not to say that Navarre was the only roisterer in the French flying corps; far from it. Nor does it say that he was the only model for all the many storybook aviators that have since filled aviation literature (and motion pictures). The flying corps, in fact all the armed forces, not alone of France but her allies and enemies alike, were given to the philosophy of "Eat, drink, and be merry, for tomorrow we die."

World War I, more than any social upheaval before it, dealt a hard blow to orthodox Christian morality. The reasons are self-evident: For the first

time in history armies of millions met in battle, a peculiarly new and terrifying mode of battle, impersonal and monstrously destructive, in which a
few hundred square yards of barren soil were often deemed worth the death
of thousands of men. On the western front oblivion came to multitudes of
soldiers as it comes to a swarm of ants beneath a blind man's shoe. The
atrociousness of such a war, of such indiscriminate slaughter, sorely compromised the old religious ideas that dignified human life and death. Millions
of men who knew not when they might perish, who knew further, many of
them, that they almost certainly *would* be killed, anxiously snatched at every
opportunity of life. And women, either moved by pity or exalted by men's
courage, and desiring to reward heroism with giving (only the hypocrites
called that giving a sacrifice), gave gladly of joy and appeasement. In the
stygian climate of this war the slackening of moral restraint became widely
recognized, tolerated, and even praised.

The increased social free and easiness that occurred during the years from
1914 to 1918 mirrored a convulsive change in the mores of warfare itself.
Symptomatic of this change were the German rape of Belgium's neutrality and
the barbarities perpetrated against the people of that small state. The pro-
miscuous use of toxic gas was a symptom, as were the sneak torpedoings of
unarmed ocean liners and the bombing raids on civilian populations far removed from front-line zones of contention.

World War I was a Prussian war, organized and implemented with Prussian thoroughness, with a single end in view—victory, crushing and complete,
at any cost and by whatever means. To say there was something noble and
sporting about it is to pervert truth with puerile sentimentality. Apart from
the famous Christmas Day incident, when German and Allied troops fra-
ternized between the trenches, and a few isolated instances of chivalry at sea,
the only real spirit of sportsmanship was sometimes manifested in the air.
Even at that, if sky fighting be regarded as a sport, as so many of its champions professed it to be, it was a grisly game played always for the ultimate
stake of human life. If a man was a fighter pilot, his worth was measured by
the number of kills he could claim; the morality of it would not be alien to
the Jivaro Indian, whose social prestige in the Amazon wilderness depends
upon how many shrunken heads grace the doorway of his hut. Yet, in contrast
to the wholesale slaughter of soldiers on the ground, where tens of thousands
sometimes fell in a single day, there was a certain grandeur and cleanness
about doing battle in the limitless corners of the sky. A pilot's skill and
courage weighed materially in the determination of his victory or defeat, and
to that degree at least, he was not some faceless pawn at the mercy of careless death. The war in the air was pretty much a contest between individuals.
It had the romantic trappings of combat in the bygone age of knights errant,
right down to the heraldic tradition of personal color schemes and emblems,
for many of these latter-day paladins, those on the German side in particular,
gaudily decorated their airplanes according to individual taste. The glamour

of all this, appealing to the public fancy, provided a sensational relief from the tedious horror of a land war bogged down in mud, and newspapers and magazines soon began dramatizing the deeds of the better-known air fighters.

Out of it sprang legends of almost superhuman prowess. Many of the tales were apochryphal, of course, although the more imaginative of them could hardly outcolor some actual events. As an example of the patently farfetched prevarications then and since foisted upon unwary and believing readers, there was the story published in a 1915 Paris monthly telling of an unnamed French aviator who exhausted his ammunition supply while trading shots with a German single-seater; instead of turning tail to flee, so it was related, the infuriated Frenchman brought his machine in close above his adversary's, leaped down from his to the other cockpit and, with his bare hands, strangled the Boche. A less outrageous yarn which gained wide circulation in the American press shortly after the war started was that of another unidentified French airman deliberately ramming a zeppelin. While true that several headstrong Gauls did publicly vow to plunge their machines into any German airships that ventured over Paris, none ever made good his pledge. Two members of the French flying corps were, on the other hand, officially cited for crashing intentionally into enemy planes; whether these two really sacrificed themselves on purpose, however, or only accidentally, since neither was around afterward to testify, remains conjectural. And if it be uncharitable to question the motives of dead heroes, it must be said regardless that in the vertiginous frenzy of winged combat, mid-air collisions were not uncommon occurrences.

Delving deeper into the massive body of lore which has grown up around World War I aviation, we find it full of lurid depictions of prearranged duels aloft between opposing champions. For sure, countless single combats were fought in the air, but how many were sequential to formal challenges, as distinguished from circumstantial meetings, has never been documented, and myth has in large part obfuscated verifiable fact. Certainly there were hotspurs who buzzed enemy airdromes and dropped cartels addressed to chosen foemen, daring them to show themselves at an appointed hour and altitude above a mutually familiar landmark, but the recipient of the challenge, for sundry good reasons—not the least of which was a chariness of being lured into ambush—seldom responded to the malicious invitation.

Obviously, for a trained airman to jeopardize himself in such sinister theatricals, particularly if he was a ranking ace, would have been a lamentable squandering of precious, irreplaceable talent; the loss of an airplane was also not to be lightly shrugged off. To defy the foe in the prosecution of duty was one thing, a necessary thing, but to do it sheerly for the sake of personal dignification—to duel for honor or reputation rather than country—to settle individual animosities instead of attending to the larger military need—was something else quite apart. However, rivalries and feuds assuredly did arise between opposing flyers, and, concomitantly, the anarchic nature of fighter-squadron operations rendered any restrictions against private battle virtually impossible to enforce. Hence, although skepticism is indicated, all the numerous anecdotes of hostile trysts in the sky cannot be positively dismissed as false.

Perhaps, too, it is splitting hairs to insist that only an aerial combat formally arranged beforehand qualifies as a duel—a duel, that is, in the narrow chivalric sense of the term—inasmuch as there are many instances on authoritative record of impromptu challenges being given and accepted, and instances galore of combats fought more in the spirit of sporting adventure than in the military interest. Opposing airmen flying daily over the same sector of the front quickly came to recognize one another by the numerical designations and distinctive color schemes of their planes. Thus, in discussing his morning patrol with his fellows, a pilot might have said something like this: "Our old friend 'Skull and Crossbones' was up there today, over near Cambrai road, accompanied by 'Blue Fin' and 'Yellow Wheels.' "

Crossing each other's path as often as they did, it was to be anticipated that sooner or later these constant rivals would clash. A great many incidents can be abstracted from the record to exhibit the enterprise shown by some of the better-known aces. Take as just one example the unalloyed boldness of Captain William Avery ("Billy") Bishop, a Canadian in the R.F.C. who, on June 2, 1917, at dawn, while on a special patrol deep behind the lines, deliberately arrived over a German field where seven aircraft could be seen with their engines running. Bishop's provocative purpose was to test his theory that he would be able to increase his score easily by attacking such machines as they were taking off. Four planes, one after another, attempted to come up and engage him. One after another, he shot down the first three. He later wrote the following account:

> The fourth machine then came up, and I opened fire on him. I was now greatly worried as to how I was to get away, as I was using up all my ammunition. . . . But there was no chance of running from this man—he had me cold—so I turned on him savagely, and, in the course of a short fight, emptied the whole of my last drum at him. Luckily, at the moment I finished my ammunition, he also seemed to have had enough of it, as he turned and flew away. I seized my opportunity, climbed again, and started for home . . . feeling very queer at my stomach. The excitement had been a bit too much. . . . The thrills and exultation I had at first felt had died away, and nothing seemed to matter but this awful feeling of dizziness and the desire to get home and on the ground.

Bishop's triple victory that morning raised his total score to twenty-three enemy aircraft destroyed. During the year and six months still left in the war, while he served with No. 60 Squadron and then was promoted to command No. 85 Squadron with the rank of major, the spectacular Canadian increased his number of victories to seventy-two, which placed him fourth among all the aces of the war, friend and foe included. He emerged second among British aces, and first among those who came from the American continent. (Nine others from Canada—most notably, Major Raymond Collishaw, a naval aviator with sixty victories, and Major William G. Barker, with fifty-three— compiled scores exceeding that of the leading air fighter of the United States, Captain Edward V. Rickenbacker, who accounted for twenty-six aircraft; these nine Canadians, it should be said in fairness, were in action four to five times longer, on the average, than Rickenbacker.)

One of the most decorated pilots of the 1914–1918 war and an Air Marshal in the Royal Canadian Air Force in World War II, Bishop was given the Victoria Cross for his highly successful dawn raid. Others, German as well as Allied, similarly sought battle by presenting themselves above enemy airfields. It happened quite regularly during the early period of aerial warfare that preceded the battle of Verdun, and although pilots found fewer chances later for individual action, it happened occasionally—as in Bishop's case—after Verdun. As for his triple victory, though an eminently splendid feat, it was both equalled and surpassed by other men.

Some pilots, although they found clumsy reconnaissance planes to be easy targets, considered it unsporting to knock down hopelessly inept airmen. Major Bishop himself told of an awkward German two-seater that he and his fellows in No. 60 Squadron called "The Flying Pig." The plane's crew was so incompetent that British airmen refrained from shooting at it, and its safety became of concern to the R.F.C. "It was considered fair sport, however, to frighten it," Bishop made clear. Whenever approached by British aircraft, the Pig began "a series of clumsy turns and ludicrous maneuvers, and would open a frightened fire from ridiculously long ranges. The observer was a very bad shot and never succeeded in hitting any of our machines, so attacking this particular German was always regarded more as a joke than a serious part of warfare."

But fighting in the air was a serious occupation. The pilot who survived six weeks at the front became an old veteran, blessed either with rare ability or luck. At crucial times when the fighting was particularly heavy —in late 1916, for example—the average airman was killed in his initial three weeks of action. Many never lived through their first day. One German pilot, fresh from the replacement pool, presented himself for duty just as enemy planes appeared over the field. Ordered hastily into action, he climbed into a fighter machine and ten minutes later had been shot down and was dead. Though his was probably one of the shortest careers of the air war, many others lasted little longer.

Such an oppressive mortality rate aroused in many pilots, who appeared outwardly gay, a haunting fear of imminent death. The fatalism affected by so many of them was a facade erected to conceal an inner anxiety. The near-suicidal rashness that some of them exhibited was in many cases spurred by a compulsion to avoid any slight suspicion or self-admission of cowardice. While wrestling with their impulse for self-preservation, however, the great majority committed themselves selflessly to a sublime set of values that demanded death before dishonor but was not expressed in words. And so they coped with their fears, repressed them, disguised them, overcompensated for them with acts of raw defiance. As their drinking songs show, they also knew how to laugh at their worst fears. The British airmen had this song:

> Beside a Belgian 'staminet, when the smoke had cleared
>   away,
> Beneath a busted Camel, its former pilot lay;
> His throat was cut by the bracing wires, the tank had
>   hit his head,
> And coughing a shower of dental work, these parting words
>   he said:
>
> Oh, I'm going to a better land, they binge there every
>   night,
> The cocktails grow on bushes, so everyone stays tight,
> They've torn up all the calendars, they've busted all the
>   clocks,
> And little drops of whisky come trickling down the rocks.
>
> The pilot breathed these last few gasps before he passed
>   away:
> I'll tell you how it happened, my flippers didn't stay,
> The motor wouldn't hit at all, the struts were far too
>   few,
> A shot went through the petrol tank and let it all leak
>   through.
>
> Oh, I'm going to a better land, where motors always run,
> Where the eggnog grows on the eggplant, and the pilots
>   grow a bun.
> They've got no Sops, they've got no Spads, they've got no
>   DH-4's,
> And the little frosted juleps are served at all the stores.

Among American pilots assigned to night patrol in Sopwith Camels, a favorite song went like this:

> Oh, mother, hang out your Golden Star,
> Your son's gone up in a Sop.
> The wings are weak, the ship's a freak,
> She's got a worm-eaten prop;
> The motor's junk, your son is drunk,
> He's sure to take a flop.
> Oh, mother, hang out your Golden Star,
> Your son's gone up in a Sop.

Dozens of songs in the same vein were sung by airmen of all the warring nationalities. One, at least, became popular on both sides of the battle line, not only in France but on every front. Translated into many languages, it remains the best-known of the military aviators' ballads. One English version was this:

> The young aviator went Hun hunting,
> And now 'neath the wreckage he lay—he lay,
> To the mechanics there standing around him,
> These last dying words he did say—did say.

> Take the cylinders out of my kidneys,
> The connecting rod out of my brain—my brain.
> From the small of my back take the crankshaft,
> And assemble the engine again—again.

Such songs became part of the legend they were building, a legend that transformed the sky into a new field of battle. Like all legends, though, that created by the first air war distorts fact by focusing attention on the more dramatic events and magnifying them beyond their reality. Fighter pilots, to whom loudest acclaim was given, were pledged to destroy as many opposing aircraft as possible, and many of them went about their work with grim singleness of purpose. The bulk of their victims—and this holds true of the great aces— were slow, poorly armed reconnaissance craft, which made for easier hunting. The ratio of reconnaissance pilots killed, regardless of whether their observers died with them, was significantly higher than that of fighter pilots; yet the courageous perseverance of these humdrum heroes has gone largely unsung. The tasks entrusted to them were of essential importance and bore directly on the management of entire armies, whereas the primary function of fighter squadrons was simply to prevent enemy reconnaissance and was contingent upon the presence of such machines in the air above them. Although bombing operations and artillery spotting were important, too, the first requirement of the air was to watch the enemy and, conversely, to prevent him from reconnoitering one's own positions. The mainspring and underlying consideration of the battle was, therefore, reconnaissance.

In contrast to the familiar glamor of the fighter pilot, the task of reconnaissance crews was prosaic. There was an unentertaining sameness about it, a quiet desperation. Each job was substantially like the next—cross the lines, see or photograph as much as possible, and then try to get back to base again in one piece, all the time attempting to avoid interception in the air. As often as not, the sight of hostile fighters approaching meant disaster. The pilot of a French two-seater described it thus:

> You have the illusion that you are moving along at a respectable
> clip, until a Boche speeds toward you in a Fokker. This accursed
> machine closely resembles our little Morane monoplane, yet it must

be decidely faster, or so you are induced to believe when you are unfortunate enough to be the object of its pilot's angry intention. In this predicament you can heartily sympathize with a cornered animal waiting for the hunter to press the trigger, for you feel naked and helpless, beyond redemption. . . . You sweat. The panic seeps through your pores. You also feel it kicking at your stomach and and strive to confine it down there away from your brain, lest it paralyze you altogether. . . . Everything seems unreal . . . and then you hear the guns hacking and you pray your observer's aim is sharp. All I can do at the controls is stay to a westerly course and summon every trick I know to shun the fusillade of bullets. This is done, if at all, by swerving erratically from side to side, so the Boche does not have a steady target. Also, if I see him banking away to circle around for another attack, I will bank in the opposite direction, as far as I can without losing my heading to the west. In this way we gain an extra few precious moments before he again gets our range. Only as a last shift do I give away altitude, since he can climb like an arrow off a bowstring and enjoys an absolute advantage if I go too low. . . . It is a harrowing, execrable ordeal.

Outrun and outmaneuvered in their heavier machine, the reconnaissance pilot and his observer, when the odds caught up with them, usually perished. When set upon, they turned for home and fought a desperate running battle. With luck, cunning, and excellent marksmanship, they might escape a single assailant—but not very often. Unless the attacker was exceptionally unskilled and spoiled his opportunity, unless his fuel ran low or his ammunition gave out before he could finish his victim, unless friendly fighters happened along to help the observation machine, the latter's survival chances were indeed slender. And when a reconnaissance plane was attacked by more than one machine, as frequently occurred, the contest seldom lasted longer than a frenzied moment or two.

The extreme odds against them disposed some reconnaissance crews to experiment with various schemes they hoped might reduce their vulnerability. At one time or another, the Germans and the French and the British all tested the feasibility of using chemical smoke as a get-away device, the plan being to release a great cloud of the stuff to confound the enemy by hiding the machine from view. For obvious reasons the smoke-screen idea failed.

Many schemes were also tried in fitting extra and ingeniously placed defensive armament, though no weapon arrangement was ever found to offset fully the effect of a fighter plane's stationary, forward-firing machine gun. During the spring and summer of 1915, when the Fokker E-1 was clearing the sky of Allied aircraft, the situation became especially unhealthy for French crews operating the slow, pusher Voisins and Caudrons. Fokker pilots quickly learned they could attack such planes with impunity, so long as they came up behind their prey. The Caudrons and Voisins, only a small number of which were equipped with automatic guns at the time, carried nose guns that could not be fired rearward. Accordingly, as a forlorn gesture of defiance and with little expectation of success, some French observers took to crawling out on the lower wing with a rifle to shoot at a Fokker coming up from the rear.

Later, when the French introduced their Nieuport fighter, it became the turn of German crews flying obsolescent two-seaters—early model Albatroses and Aviatiks and D.F.W.'s—to suffer heavy losses. One man, the rear gunner-observer of an Aviatik, upon seeing his pilot shot dead by an attacking Nieuport, raised his arms to inform his antagonist that the battle was over. He then held up a hand grenade, pulled out its firing pin, dropped it to the floor of his cockpit, and stood saluting the French pilot until the grenade exploded.

Another German, the pilot of an Albatros D-2, landed at the airdrome of Escadrille Nieuport No. 38 and explained to a group of astonished French aviators that he had been waylaid by a trio of fighters that morning. Cut off from the east and unable to make for home, he was chased about until his attackers were forced to let him go, he guessed, for want of fuel. To his own consternation, his own fuel supply then dried up. Speaking perfect French, he suggested to the squadron commander, a Captain Bouche, that it would be a "sporting thing" were the captain to furnish enough fuel to take the Albatros back to German territory. When Captain Bouche turned this proposal down, the imaginative German proposed that a French pilot and an observer be sent up to do battle with the Albatros after it had been refueled. If the German crew came off best, they would be allowed to proceed home unmolested. "Our Captain smiled in a wonderfully gracious manner," recorded a witness to the event, "and said it was impossible to entertain either proposal. He would like to do the sporting thing, but headquarters wanted to inspect the Albatros. So we took them both prisoners and rolled their machine into a vacant hangar."

The nature of observation flying, its defensive character and its often ungainly aircraft, went against aggressive initiative. It was, furthermore, something of a thankless job, seldom rewarded. This was the hunted and not the hunter. The latter might shoot down thirty, forty, fifty, or more of the enemy and earn medals and headlines and public approbation; the number of aces in reconnaissance squadrons could be counted on the fingers of one hand, and even at that, their hard-earned five or six victories seemed small in comparison to the score of a Boelcke or Guynemer. Whereas the single-seater pilot went out to find a fight, the reconnaissance crew had as their main duty to return with their information. Though they complained little, most of them would have preferred the more glamorous duty and were no doubt envious of their brethren in single-seaters. Many of them persistently requested transfers to fighter squadrons. When the outstanding reconnaissance pilot was fortunate enough to have his petition granted, he generally brought to his new task a knowledge and cunning that served him well. Unlike the pursuit pilot who had no experience aboard a slow two-seater, the former reconnaissance pilot thoroughly understood his victim's plight. He could anticipate his thinking and thus effect a swifter victory. That so many renowned aces were ex-reconnaissance men was more than coincidence; only the fittest of them lived to pilot single-seaters in the first place. And in their writings can be found tributes to the crews of the two-seaters as, to quote one of them, "the most deserving and least accredited air heroes."

Because their stories are so much the same—much of it dreary routine, relieved by excitement only when compelled to fly for their lives or fight to their deaths—popular history tends to omit the stories of the heroism of reconnaissance flyers and the importance of their role. Official records must be researched to learn their names and fates.

Since it was relatively easy sport, though necessary work, the shooting down of reconnaissance planes was not held to be as great an accomplishment as shooting down a single-seater scout. The difference was that between bullying to death a disadvantaged enemy and exchanging skill with a worthy opponent in fair and equal combat. Individual combat came closest to the duels of more chivalrous times. There was no melodrama in the war to compare with it, which is the main reason why the aerial duel has been exploited in literature and history to the point where fact merges into myth.

The most sensational of such stories usually tell of ceremonious meetings arranged by formal challenge, according to the classic codes of honor. However, of all the accounts that have been published, three alone have sufficient authentication to abolish doubt. It is also significant that none of these engagements actually took place in keeping with the proper dueling code.

Oswald Boelcke, in June 1916, while at the pinnacle of his career, was challenged to a duel by the French champion, Jean Navarre. Though known to each other by reputation, the two had never come together in the air. Among the several pilots who wrote of the incident afterward was Lieutenant Bennet A. Molter, an American volunteer in the French Flying Corps:

> Following the etiquette of the days of yore, the challenge was written, with the date, hour, and exact location clearly and carefully specified. The rendezvous indicated by Navarre was over the forest of Argonne, which . . . was easy to find and identify from the air. Navarre described the type of his plane [a Nieuport], its individual markings; [he] stated the altitude at which he would fly and wait for Boelcke, so there could be no possibility of mistake or misunderstanding. The challenge, with this information, was sewn in a leather bag, Navarre's card being enclosed, and dropped directly on

a Boche airdrome in such a manner that the Germans could not help seeing it.

At six-thirty on the evening of the day before the date named in the challenge, Navarre engaged three enemy planes in combat and was wounded. Great excitement reigned throughout the French aviation service, for Navarre at that time was the greatest of all French aces. In their concern over Navarre's injuries, and because of their solicitude for his welfare, the proposed duel was forgotten by everybody—save one. That one was Corporal Perouse, of Navarre's escadrille, who had distinguished himself as a soldier in the Chasseurs Alpines but was comparatively new to aviation.

On the morning of the day set for the duel, Perouse, without making known his plans or purpose to anyone, told the chief mechanic of the escadrille that he wanted to try out Navarre's plane. He adjusted his belt of ammunition, armed his machine gun and, when all was ready, flew to the field of another escadrille some ten miles away. Here he waited, smoking incessantly all the while, until thirty minutes before the hour specified in the challenge. Then he took to the air and headed for the forest of Argonne. Remember, he was only a corporal, with less than twenty hours of flight over the enemy's lines to his credit, and he was going to meet the most famous, skillful, and dangerous man in the enemy's flying corps. But not only was the honor of his escadrille in question, the honor of France, as he saw it, was at stake; and he was willing, nay anxious, to defend it and if necessary pay for it with his life.

He reached the point and altitude specified in the challenge and waited, circling round and round, dodging bursting shrapnel from antiaircraft guns. He did not know at what moment or from what direction the enemy might pounce . . . to gain the first great advantage of surprise; perhaps they would try to ambush him with superior numbers . . . to make sure of getting him. He did not know [or] care; too much was at stake to make these questions of any concern to him. So he waited, circling . . . for a full hour—but Boelcke did not appear. If he had met Boelcke, possibly . . . this tale would never have been told. But as it was, there was nothing for him to do but fly back to his escadrille.

Corporal Perouse's prolonged absence in Navarre's plane had meanwhile aroused considerable apprehension at his home field. Upon his return he was greeted by an angry commanding officer who scolded him for his breach of discipline and ordered him confined to quarters, except when flying, for two weeks. Perouse undertook the venture, according to Molter, because "he knew of Navarre's inability to vindicate the challenge and feared the honor of the service might suffer in the eyes of the enemy." As the authority on whose word he based his account, Molter cited Lieutenant Paul Montariol, a pilot of Escadrille Farman No. 44, then stationed at the same airdrome as Escadrille Nieuport No. 67, of which Navarre and Perouse were members. The story was known throughout France, however, having been printed in several contemporary newspapers and magazines. "It should also be reported," Molter concluded, "that two weeks after the incident related, the name of Corporal Perouse was on the list of the missing. But if he met his death, we may be sure he did so fighting; displaying the same spirit of chivalry that prompted him to take the place of his wounded and more famous comrade . . ."

The combat in which Navarre received the wounds which prevented him from keeping his proposed rendezvous with Boelcke, occurred on June 17, 1916, when he was shot down during a battle with a German trio over Argonne. His injuries were severe, and, soon after entering the hospital, on hearing that his brother had been killed at Verdun, his mental health collapsed. By the time he returned to active duty, more than two years had passed. It was just before the Armistice, and Navarre, now a lieutenant, had hardly adjusted himself to the new conditions when hostilities ceased. After the war he flew for a while as a test pilot for the Morane-Saulnier company. Then, on July 10, 1919, he crashed and died. It happened at Villacoublay, where he had been practicing for the Paris Victory Parade in which he planned to steal the show, typically enough, by flying at tree-top level down the Champs Élysées, zooming through the Arc de Triomphe, and then, for his grand finale, executing a series of aerobatic maneuvers above the Étoile.

Navarre, during those chaotic, Fokker-filled months of 1915 and 1916 that witnessed his rise to renown, shot down twelve enemy aircraft. He bagged his first victory on April 1, 1915, when his observer, a Lieutenant Robert, brandishing a rifle in the rear seat of a Morane-Saulnier Parasol, forced an Aviatik to earth after wounding the pilot with one of three rounds fired. As this was only the fourth French air victory of the war, it was loudly hailed in the press. Only a week had gone by since publication of the story telling how Navarre had armed himself with a kitchen knife and flown off to stick it in a zeppelin. Although his sudden notoriety was eclipsed that same April by Roland Garros' startling success with his forward-firing machine gun, Navarre remained a celebrity by virtue of his flamboyant personality and the fact that he averaged a victory a month during the reign of Fokker terror, when Allied victories in the air were decidedly fewer than losses. But Navarre and Garros were not the only pilots of that desperate period to attract the attention of their countrymen. There were some like Garros whose fame preceded them into the war—Pinsard and Pegoud, for example, and Gilbert—and there were other upstart firebrands like Navarre. The inimitable Georges Guynemer at this time rose to prominence. Lieutenant Marcel Viallet, though he piloted a two-seater Caudron, was among the earliest French aces. On a spring morning in 1916, while on a photoreconnaissance mission, Viallet was attacked by three Fokkers, the first of which was in the hands of the great Boelcke himself. Viallet escaped to an emergency landing with his Caudron in flames; a few days later he learned the Germans had listed him as Boelcke's fourteenth victim. Adjutant Réné Dorme, whom the press nicknamed "The Indestructible," who once brought down four Germans in eight hours, and Lieutenant Jean Chaput were others whose names began to make news. An electrical engineer before joining the air corps, Chaput was one of those who in 1915 bitterly resented the technical superiority of the Fokker E-plane. He was wounded and twice shot down by Fokkers, but somehow survived. Unable to outshoot the enemy monoplane, he settled on another method of retaliation. His engineering knowledge convinced him that if he could bite into the fragile rear end of a Fokker with his propeller, the whirling blades would sheer the tail assembly from the plane and leave it helpless. He gave the suicidal idea a try, and the tailless Fokker fell to destruction. But the method proved impractical, since he smashed his own propeller in the process and barely managed to glide to safety. It was, however, the first of sixteen victories and the beginning of prestige for Chaput.

Before the summer of 1916, when the Fokker menace was finally done with, still other French airmen became familiar to headline readers. Captain Alfred Heurtaux, gaining five quick victories that May, and Captain Albert Duellin were among these new heroes. Captain Georges Félix Madon, an army aviator since 1911, who languished in a Swiss internment camp through 1915 and then escaped, was given a Nieuport Baby to fly and promptly distinguished himself as a furious and fearless fighter, specializing in close-range attack; on occasion he chased the enemy right to his own doorstep before delivering a well-placed burst or two of machine-gun fire. A remarkable sharpshooter, Madon was one of the earliest exponents of what came to be known in World War II as "intruder tactics"—that is, attacking enemy aircraft as they neared their home airfield, when their crews, with the end of the sortie in sight, relaxed their vigilance. The Armistice found Madon fourth on the list of French aces. His score was forty-one confirmed kills, but nobody knows how many additional were unconfirmed.

Clearly, then, in that oppressive year of Fokker domination, Navarre had not figured as the only French pilot to attract public attention. But the letter of challenge he addressed to Oswald Boelcke and the mishap that kept him from fulfilling his half of the bargain and assured Corporal Perouse a minor place in the annals of aerial warfare captured the imagination of the French people in 1916 as did few other occurrences that year. That the duel itself never happened afforded French journalists an opportunity to traduce Boelcke and the entire German air service. Boelcke's failure to accept the challenge was made a *cause célèbre*, the reporting of which very nearly exhausted the French vocabulary of journalistic invective. Boelcke, if he ever saw Navarre's challenge, was too much the disciplined soldier, fully aware of his value to German aviation, to let himself be provoked into risking his neck in such wayward histrionics. A man of Boelcke's experience would have been wary of flying into a trap. And a summons to individual combat smelled suspiciously like just that. Indeed, the two remaining air duels known to have taken place both turned out to be traps, and in each case it was the Germans who offered the bait.

In May, 1917, a fast-rising French ace, Lieutenant Charles Nungesser, upon returning from a midday patrol, was shown a slip of paper dropped from a German machine and inviting him to single combat over Douai. He promptly took off to meet the challenge. Not one, but six enemy fighters waited for him, and in the ensuing dogfight he shot down two of them. His victims were Lieutenant Paul Schweizer and Lance-Corporal Ernst Bittorf.

In the only other such "affair of honor" which can be said definitely to have occurred, the challenger was Captain Albert Ball of the Royal Flying Corps. Not yet twenty years old, Ball embodied all the qualities of a truly great air fighter and indeed did become a *rara avis* of war. Beside his singular ability as an aviator, he possessed unshakable faith in the righteousness of the British cause. Though liked and respected by his fellow flyers, Ball was considered something of an eccentric. His philosophy was borrowed from the pages of Kipling, whose poetry he loved to recite, and he had the curious habit of playing the violin at night while he marched in his pajamas around a lighted red flare outside his hut. Prior to leaving on a morning patrol, he always stuffed his pockets with cake, which he ate by the handful while in the air. Of striking appearance, small, nervous, his nose a little snubbed, with piercing brown eyes and long, wavy hair, he delighted in the sensations of aerial combat and once wrote his parents an exultant account of a busy day's work:

> Cheerio dears. . . . Really, I am having too much luck for a boy. I will start straight away, and tell you all. On August 22 [1916], I went up. Met twelve Huns.
>
> No. 1 fight. I attacked and fired two [ammunition] drums, bringing the machine down just outside a village. All crashed up.
>
> No. 2 fight. I attacked and got under machine, putting in two drums. Hun went down in flames.
>
> No. 3 fight. I attacked and put in one drum. Machine went down and crashed on a housetop.
>
> I only got hit eleven times in the plane's [wings], so I returned and got more ammunition. This time luck was not all on the spot. I was met by fourteen Huns, about fifteen miles over their side. My windscreen was hit in four places, mirror broken, the spar of the left [wing] broken, also engine ran out of petrol. But I had a good sport and good luck, but only just, for I was brought down about one mile over our side. . . .
>
> Oh, la, la. Topping, isn't it?

Ball, at the onset of war, had three weeks yet to go before his eighteenth birthday. Despite his youth, he had already established his own brass foundry and electrical repair business in Nottingham, his native town. Enlisting in the Sherwood Foresters, he was gazetted a lieutenant in October 1914. He did not go overseas immediately, and a visit to Hendon airfield so kindled his enthusiasm for aviation that he asked for a transfer to the R.F.C., meanwhile enrolling at flight school for private lessons. Posted at last to the flying corps in January 1916, he joined No. 13 Squadron in France the following month. His normal duties here consisted of reconnaissance and artillery spotting in a BE-2, an airplane he despised. But whenever the chance presented itself, Ball ventured across the lines seeking enemy aircraft—this, be it noted, in a lumbering two-seater, during the worst of the Fokker period. The BE-2 was too stable to evade attack and too slow to run away, and the observer, who sat in the forward cockpit, had his field of fire limited by the maze of struts and wires surrounding him. Plain common sense dictated the type's withdrawal from operations long before this, but the British government had ordered them in quantity, and BE-2's were still being flown into action on the western front as late as April 1917.

Nevertheless, spoiling for a fight, Ball and his observer, Lieutenant S. A. Villiers, often went free-lancing behind the German lines. On at least three of these trips they tried without success to shoot down enemy two-seaters, twice themselves narrowly missing destruction by intercepting Fokkers. This practice gave rise to a hoax which was carried on for some time at Ball's expense. Someone in the squadron sent him a letter which looked official and purported to come from the brigade commander, General J. F. A. Higgins. The letter advised him that if he cared to reconnoiter even deeper into enemy territory, it would be much appreciated by the higher authorities. Such an invitation was irresistible to one as eager as Ball was for action, and the hoaxer soon realized that his mischief could lead to tragic results. At great peril, Ball and Villiers were flying farther and farther behind German lines, bringing back detailed observation reports that the hoaxer made sure never reached the brigade commander. At length somebody decided the game had gone far enough and informed Ball that he had been hoodwinked.

Toward the end of April 1916, Ball got his much-desired opportunity to fly single-seaters, first in a Morane-Saulnier *Bullet,* which he only took up for a few test rides, and then in No. 11 Squadron's Bristol Scout, which was equipped with an experimental machine-gun synchronizer. Ball's initial experience with it was not fortunate. The mechanism had been faultily installed, and when he tried his guns as he crossed the lines, he almost shot away his propeller blades. If he had fired another half dozen rounds, he later calculated, he would have been forced to land behind the German trenches.

Not long afterward, on May 7, Ball moved to Savy airdrome, where, as a member now of No. 11 Squadron, he was entrusted with the squadron's Nieuport Scout. It was pleasing to behold, with its compact build and silvery color, and it remained his favorite weapon to the time of his death. Most of his well-publicized victories were won aboard the Nieuport. After his first trial trip aloft in the new machine, he wrote, "It is T. T. [Terrifically Topping?] So Huns, *look out!*" [1]

No. 11 Squadron, the first complete fighter unit on the western front, had arrived in France during the summer of 1915. It possessed an eager spirit, due in large measure to the precept and example of Major L. W. B. Rees, who had served in it, and whose influence survived. One of only nineteen British airmen to receive the Victoria Cross in World War I, Rees had left a legacy of aggressiveness to the squadron; his main teaching had been that any German machine seen should at once be attacked. To the pilots of this squadron the newcomer seemed out of place, for Ball was rather inarticulate in conversation and they thought him very young. At first they mistook his diffidence for unfriendliness and derisively called him "John." Quiet and inhibited, Ball spent much of his spare time around the hangars, where he watched the mechanics work on the engines and the rigging. He also planted a vegetable garden, where he would dig for hours, rain or shine. When complaints were lodged against the nocturnal noises of his violin, he moved out of the barracks into a tent pitched right next to the flight apron, where, if he wished, he could play his beloved concertos from dusk to dawn without disturbing anyone's sleep. His explanation for this solitary residence, however, was that he preferred camping close to his plane in the event of a sudden scramble into action.

During these first difficult weeks of adjustment some of his seniors saw fit to query his flight reports, for Ball's nonconformity rendered him suspect in their eyes. This, and a good deal of "leg-pulling," helps explain why later Ball never made a claim for anything of which he was not absolutely certain. They chided him for living alone in his tent, which they labeled "Ball's hermitage," as well as for his violin playing. His habit of munching cake as he flew was considered "most queer." He furthermore refused to wear helmet and goggles in the air. At mess one evening, he was asked why. Ball replied apologetically that he liked to feel the wind in his hair. It was not the thing to say at a table of experienced airmen.

Ball accepted the leg-pulling cheerfully. He did not mind being called "John," because, he wrote, they were such a worthy lot that their form of address was not hard to bear. In any case, not many days passed before the nickname was spoken with growing warmth and admiration by those to whom he alluded in his letters home as "the older chaps."

Three weeks to the day after his arrival at Savy, in the course of a morning patrol, he emptied a drum of ammunition into an Albatros D-1 and last saw it falling out of control toward Moyenneville. On the return leg of the flight he forced an L.V.G. two-seater to land behind the German lines. Neither victory could be verified, nor did he claim them. On June 1, he flew over Douai air-

[1] Kiernan: *Captain Albert Ball*. The author gratefully acknowledges his debt to Mr. Kiernan's classic biography, having made free use of it in discussing Captain Ball's career.

drome, inviting combat, and bested—but did not destroy—an Albatros and a Fokker that had teamed up against him. Twenty-four days later he shot down a kite balloon and soon after was awarded the Military Cross. The balloon, which counted for as much as a heavier-than-air machine in the scorebook, was at this time his only confirmed victory; his first positive success over an enemy airplane came on July 2, when he dispatched a Roland C-2 two-seater high above the Mercatel-Arras highway.

From here on, his victories steadily mounted. His style of attack has often been likened to that of Georges Guynemer, his great contemporary in the French aviation corps. To begin with, he preferred to fly alone. His skill was such that when his reputation was made, he was unofficially granted a roving commission. His technique resembled Guynemer's in that it was usually direct, uncomplicated, and sometimes downright impetuous. He generally dispensed with any preliminary preparations. On seeing his prey, whether above or below him, near or distant, he simply shoved the throttle forward and closed to attack it. He seldom started shooting except at the closest possible range. At first he delayed firing because he was a mediocre marksman and knew it, but he quickly discovered that the strategem had an unsettling effect on the enemy. A favorite method of Ball's, not unlike that used by Boelcke on occasion, was to fly head-on toward an enemy in the certainty that if he held his course until a collision appeared inevitable, the German would turn away. As the German swerved, he was vulnerable for perhaps one second, during which Ball hoped to deliver a lethal burst from his machine gun. Near the end of 1916, Ball perfected a dangerous but effective maneuver that few pilots had either the cool nerve or judgment to attempt. He would deliberately permit a German to get on his tail, relying on his sixth sense to tell him just when the German was about to open fire. At that instant, he would snap his Nieuport into a short dive. Before the German could grasp what was happening, Ball was coming up underneath him, pouring bullets into his underside.

In midsummer, during the battle of the Somme, by which time several fighter squadrons had been organized in the R.F.C., Ball took his Nieuport to No. 60 Squadron. It was here he was given his roving commission, which suited him ideally. By the end of September he had thirty confirmed victories and nineteen possibles. The strain was beginning to tell on him, however, and he intimated to his squadron commander, Major R. R. Smith-Barry, that he would like to go home for a while. He feared, he said, that he was losing his composure. As his recent exploits had indicated anything but discomposure, Smith-Barry asked why he thought he needed a rest. Ball answered that it was very simple. When he found himself taking foolhardy risks, he knew his nerves were beginning to affect his judgment. Many pilots, overtired by a long period of combat, recognized the same symptom. The effects of this mental fatigue are described, for example, in the book *War Birds: Diary of an Unknown Aviator*. (The "Unknown Aviator" was Lieutenant John McGavock Grider, who flew and died in 1918 with the American Expeditionary Force;

his diary was anonymously edited for publication by another American ace, Captain Elliott White Springs.) "I have lost all interest in life beyond the next patrol . . ." the diarist noted. "But as soon as I take off, I am all right again. That is, I feel all right, though I know I am too reckless. Last week I actually tried to ram a Hun."

After receiving a temporary transfer from the front, Ball said good-bye to his comrades. On October 4, as winter settled in with much rain, Ball was posted to the Home Establishment as an instructor. While here, on November 18, he was decorated with the Distinguished Service Order by King George V. As a local boy made good, he was feted in February 1917, at a public cere- mony in Nottingham. The mayor delivered a speech in which he recalled the fact that the ace had engaged in more than fifty combats, destroyed ten enemy aircraft, and forced twenty to land in captivity, and that Ball himself had been brought down six times without serious consequence. Apropos of his numerous combats, Ball, blushing with modesty, told the following anecdote:

"I have never met but one German aviator who really had courage. This one gave me the most sporting combat of my career. The duel lasted half an hour. The both of us having exhausted our ammunition, we came side by side to express our mutual admiration. I hope to encounter that adversary again; he was a real sportsman."

Although, with this single exception, his opinion of German aviators was extremely low, and he rarely skipped an opportunity to degrade them in letters home, Ball did not hate them. When his father once wrote him an exhortation to "let the devils have it," he replied: "Yes, I always let them have it all I can, but really I don't think them devils. I only scrap because it is my duty, but I do not think anything evil about the Hun. He is a decent chap with very little *guts,* trying to do his best." In another letter, Ball observed that "nothing makes me feel more rotten than to see them go down." This same remorse was experienced by all those fighting pilots who recorded their inner sensations in combat, by Bishop, Richthofen, Guynemer, Ricken- backer, and dozens of others.

Although he left France at his own request, Ball found his instructional duties irksome and soon applied to return to the front. Five months dragged by before he saw action again. When he did go back to France that following April 1917, it was as a flight commander in No. 56 Squadron. This unit was the first to be equipped with the new SE-5, an aircraft Ball did not at first appreciate. On April 13, therefore, he was given a Nieuport for his personal use, in addition to an SE-5. Ball served in No. 56 Squadron with such out- standing pilots as Captain C. M. Crowe, Captain H. Meintjes, Captain George Bowman, Lieutenant A. P. F. Rhys-Davids, and Major James McCudden, and even they looked upon him with awe. They saw him as a shy, self-conscious youngster, outwardly placid and immune from the doubts and tensions that at times troubled all pilots. They noticed, though, that he slept little, for the sound of his violin gave away his sleeplessness. In the air he performed like a demon. He won a double victory on April 22, sending an Albatros down in flames and forcing a two-seater to land. Other victories followed and soon reconciled him to the SE-5. It was in this plane that Ball apparently challenged two Germans to personal combat.

In the last week of April, during an afternoon patrol, Ball encountered a pair of Albatros fighters. Alone as usual, he opened the attack. The Germans, perhaps out of ammunition, declined battle and flew at full speed for their base. Ball pursued them, firing until he had no more cartridges left. He continued the chase with his revolver in hand, but they made it safely to their field and landed. Ball penciled a message on the paper pad he wore strapped to his right thigh, placed the message inside an empty ammunition drum, and dropped it on the airfield. Above his signature he told his two opponents that he would fly overhead the next day at the same time, and he requested them to be in the air ready to meet him.

The challenged parties, it turned out, had a greater interest in bagging the famous English pilot than in their standing as sportsmen.

When Ball returned the following afternoon, he was pleased to see the two Albatroses circling slowly over the airfield. He picked one and flew straight at it. Before he was close enough to open fire, Ball heard bullets whistling all around him and realized he had flown into a trap. He swerved and counted three uninvited guests lurking to the west, sealing off his retreat. It was five against one, but odds had never previously meant much to Ball, and he probably had no intention of abandoning this fight. Turning his attention again to his two original adversaries, he tried to get near enough to settle accounts with at least one of them. The Germans showed themselves to be wily customers. Aware that they merely had to wait for the chance to close in and finish him off in concert, they evaded his attacks. Ball charged them savagely again and again, shooting at longer range than he liked, but each time he had to cut short his run as a couple of the others slipped in behind him. Finally he used up the last of his ammunition.

Theoretically, Ball should not have remained alive for more than a minute. The Germans now encircled him and took turns diving at him with their guns blazing. Believing that it was all over for him anyway, Ball improvised a plan of escape that was as unorthodox as it was desperate. He suddenly put his machine into a steep descent, pulled up vertically into a sloppy stall, and spun crazily toward earth. Seeing this, the Germans were convinced he had been hit and was falling out of control. With no altitude to spare, Ball recovered from his spin. He glided into a convenient meadow and bounced to a landing. Capturing the notorious Albert Ball alive would be an even brighter feather in their caps, the Germans knew, than killing him. Two of the Albatroses thus alighted nearby while the others flew over the SE-5, wagging their wings in triumph, and then disappeared in the direction of their base to broadcast the news. Ball, slumped over his controls as if wounded, meanwhile kept his engine idling. He waited until the Germans were running toward him, until they were only a few yards away, then slammed the throttle wide open and took off.

Ball returned to his squadron without a scratch. His plane was liberally perforated with bullet holes, which he explained, were received "in a scrap with several dear chaps whose brains have been pickled by all that sauerkraut they devour." He neglected to reveal the circumstances of the meeting, nor did he ever mention the incident again. That Ball had nearly become the victim of his own chivalry toward the enemy remained a secret to his countrymen until the war was past. The story was then uncovered in the memoirs of German pilots who had served with the five airmen who had England's great fighter at their mercy and yet allowed him to escape.

Ball's SE-5 was still being patched in the workshop when, on May 6, he brought down an Albatros single-seater near Sancourt. He did it in true Ball fashion, in his beloved Nieuport. It was his forty-fourth victory, which put him two ahead of Guynemer, whose score he watched as a friendly and deferential rival. Only three days earlier he wrote to his father: "I am feeling very old just now . . . for I am now one in front of the Frenchman." His correspondence that week disclosed a weariness of war. "Won't it be nice," he wrote plaintively to his fiancée on May 5, "when all this beastly killing is over, and we can enjoy ourselves and not hurt anyone? I hate this game, but it is the only thing one can do now." And on the same day, in a letter to his family, he said: "Am indeed looked after by God, but Oh! I do get tired of always living to kill, and am really beginning to feel like a murderer."

A little past noon on May 7, Ball received word that his SE-5 had been repaired. At 5:30 that afternoon he flew off in it and led one of three flights sent in mass formation to patrol the sky between Lens and Cambrai. This was the most dangerous area for Allied pilots then, for it was the center ring of Baron Manfred von Richthofen's "flying circus." But orders had been issued by R.F.C. field headquarters that eighteen British fighters were to be concentrated in the area every morning and evening. The aim was to keep a strong fighting force in the neighborhood of German airfields during their busiest periods of activity. The patrol for this purpose on the evening of May 7 consisted of five Spads of No. 19 Squadron and eleven SE-5's of No. 56—sixteen machines only, as one Spad and one SE-5 turned away early with engine trouble. The two groups were to operate independently of each other.

The SE-5's, with Captains Crowe and Meintjes leading the other two flights, crossed the trenches south of the Bapaume–Cambrai road and then split into three tiers, with Ball on the bottom tier at seven thousand feet. The fading light of evening was punctuated with gathering clouds when, over Bourlon Wood, about three miles west of Cambrai, the squadron encountered a flock of Albatros single-seaters. Uniformly painted red, the Albatroses were from the Richthofen jagdstaffel and were disposed in similar formation to the SE-5's, in three echelons of four machines each. Both the British and Germans knew this was going to be a memorable engagement. They closed immediately.

There was no order in it once the first shots were fired. The pilots, diving, climbing, rolling, twisting, and spinning at well over a hundred miles an hour in the violent maneuvers of a dogfight, lost and found each other again and again in the heavy clouds. For a few minutes there was a teeming melee, then the fight spread for miles as the combatants broke away in twos and threes. The clouds congealed into a dense gloom; it started to rain. Low-level combats had to be broken off because of the poor visibility, and the pilots climbed above the overcast to renew their separate battles at heights between seven and ten thousand feet. The fighting continued sporadically until the sky was black with night. By then, four Germans had gone down. Of the eleven SE-5's, four returned to their airfield. Six others were quickly accounted for. Four had crash landed, their pilots wounded but safe in British care. One, having run out of fuel, had landed at the naval airfield at Auchel. Another, that flown by a recent arrival in the squadron, a Lieutenant Chaworth-Musters, was observed to have broken up under enemy fire. The one man still missing was Albert Ball, last seen diving into a bank of clouds while locked in combat with an expertly handled Albatros.

Nothing of Ball was ever again seen by friendly eye. It was as if the clouds had swallowed him and kept him. For many days mystery and speculation surrounded his disappearance. The newspapers of all Europe headlined the news—"La Chute de l'Aigle"—"Ball est Prisonnier"—"Un As Anglais Disparu." A Spanish journal filled two columns with a recital of his deeds. In Germany, Wolff's news agency flashed the announcement of his death around the world, although at first its identification of Ball was admittedly tentative. *The Times* in London noted on May 18 that there was still no reliable word of his whereabouts, though the last line of its story was in the nature of an obituary: "Beyond doubt his was the most wonderful series of victories yet achieved by a flying man of any nation."

At the end of the month a red Albatros dropped a message on a British airdrome. "R.F.C. Captain Ball," it informed, "was brought down in an air fight on May 7 by a pilot of the same order as himself. He was buried at Annoeullin."

The Berlin *Tageblatt* thereupon proclaimed that Manfred von Richthofen had shot down "England's supreme battle flyer, Captain Ball." A few days after that the German air service claimed that it had been Lothar von Richthofen—Manfred's younger brother and an ace in his own right, surviving the war with forty victories—who defeated Ball. Confusion did not end here, inasmuch as German field headquarters candidly revealed that details of Ball's demise were unknown, adding that he might have been hit by ground fire. The younger Richthofen did claim a victory that evening, but he and witnesses agreed that the victim machine had been a Sopwith, not an SE-5.

The mystery of what actually did cause Ball to crash will probably never be solved.

The true value of Albert Ball cannot be assessed strictly by the number of enemy aircraft he drove down or destroyed, for his contribution to the Allied effort was given as much in terms of spirit as action. Ball emerged as the pioneer fighter pilot of the R.F.C. when that air force finally attained technical and organizational maturity in the battle of the Somme, and his influence served as a lasting inspiration for British airmen. His period as a fighter pilot in 1916 was condensed into a few weeks, and his rise to fame really merited the adjective "phenomenal." He was, in fact, the first R.F.C. pilot to become literally a national idol in England. Known before August, though not widely, as a courageous pilot, by October his eminence as a fighter was recognized everywhere. This is more impressive when it is realized that very few British airmen had until then been mentioned by name in the home press, since R.F.C. policy throughout the war disparaged such publicity. In the French, German, and later the United States air services, any pilot who scored five confirmed victories was automatically called an ace in communiqués. Not so in the R.F.C. Officially, there existed no such thing as a British ace; a man with five or more victories was considered—in theory—no worthier than any other man who gave his utmost, but who, through lack of opportunity or want of skill, failed to collect as many victories. This practice of anonymity was, moreover, generally endorsed by British airmen as a boon to team spirit.

Once the public had a taste of Albert Ball, however, it clamored for more champions, and instructions were sent from the editorial rooms of Fleet Street to hundreds of war reporters in France, asking them in their future dispatches to supply the names of outstanding air fighters. The policy of the R.F.C. was never relaxed in this regard, but it was regularly violated thereafter by the newspapers. And if the flying corps refrained from naming as aces its high-scoring pilots, everyone nevertheless knew who the aces were, and the press and the public used the term freely.

CHAPTER VIII

The Momentous Year

JUNE 28, 1916, WAS a black day for Germany. It marked the end of a man, Max Immelmann, and signaled the end of the era of Fokker domination in the sky. That the man and the era passed away together was fitting, for Immelmann, more than any other German aviator, epitomized the group of aces who flew to success aboard E-series Fokker monoplanes.

Immelmann, by German accounts, fell the victim of a mechanical failure, although British claims attributed his death to the Lewis gun manned by Corporal John Waller at the nose of an FE-2 biplane. According to Franz Immelmann, Max's older brother and biographer, his death was due to a malfunction of the gun synchronizer on his E-plane. It could well have been so; just such a mishap occurred a few weeks prior to his fatal crash. In the earlier instance he shot away both propeller blades and managed an emergency landing. On the day he died, if Franz's post-mortem is correct, the aviator severed one blade and the irregular revs of his engine caused the engine supports to break before he had time to cut the throttle. "He was fortunate," wrote Franz in 1932, "that he was spared witnessing the bitter end [of World War I]. He remained ever a true believer in German ideals, and it was lucky for him that he was not forced to experience the unworthy and unnecessary self-abasement of his compatriots and the inexpressibly wearisome fourteen years of Germany's decline."

The "Eagle of Lille," as Max Immelmann came to be known, was serving with a railway battalion in Berlin-Schönberg at the beginning of the war. Yearning for action at the front, he tried to transfer to the infantry; failing that, he enlisted in the air service in November. Ordered to the Aviation Replacement Section at Johannistal as a flying pupil, he trained in such planes as the Albatros and L.V.G. two-seaters, and the Rumpler Taube. He soloed on January 31, 1915, after fifty-four dual flights, and nine days later passed his preliminary certification test. "All I had to do," he wrote to his family in Brunswick, "was to go up, fly five figure eights, land on the spot where the instructor stood with his red flag, go up again, fly another five figures of eight, and land as before. Finally, I had to climb to at least one hundred meters and land in a glide."

Immelmann carefully detailed the German training regimen in his letters home. Next came the test for his military brevet. For this he was required to make twenty smooth landings, two flights of a half-hour each at five hundred meters, and then a flight of an hour's duration at two thousand meters. Completing the test on February 13, he ascended to 2600 meters, which was a school record. Instead of an hour, he stayed aloft for an hour and twenty minutes. And instead of gliding down from eight hundred meters, he did it from 2200 meters. That day he was moved up to Aviation Replacement Section No. 2, Adlershof, for advanced training, where he survived a minor crash. For his final test he had to do fifteen landings outside the airfield, two flights to Döberitz, and a long cross-country flight. Having completed the requirements, he graduated in mid-March and awaited orders.

At Johannistal and Adlershof, situated just across the road from each other, Immelmann's fellows found him hard to get along with. He was not quarrelsome, but his personality was that of the fastidious introvert. His attitudes toward women were puritanical, and he spent his off-duty hours in the company of his pet dog Tyras, corresponding a minimum of five times a week with his mother, whom he adored, and whom he liked to impress with the glamour and danger of being an aviator. From his letters it is evident that Immelmann lacked a sense of humor, that he was all work and no play. "For us airmen," he wrote, "abstention from alcohol is a basic requisite if we are to earn success without having to complain of overstrained nerves." He avoided tobacco on the same premise. Also he was a strict vegetarian, and he took a good deal of chaffing on this account from his messmates. Worst of all, from the standpoint of social sins at flight school, was the obsessive zeal with which he applied himself to his classroom studies and the supercilious disdain he held for those less dedicated, which included almost everybody. He was by nature a martinet, yet it was Immelmann's mania for doing things exactly right that later qualified him as a top-ranked fighting pilot.

A scientific tactician, Immelmann familiarized himself with every type of French and British aircraft and carefully deduced the best means of attack to be employed against each. He utilized the quick reversement—a short climb in combination with a half-roll—as the surest method of dispatching the British pusher types with guns in their noses, and the maneuver became a part of every fighter pilot's repertoire of tricks. More than half the fifteen victories he tallied before his death were accomplished by this stratagem, and soon the phrase "Immelmann turn" became fixed in the aviation lexicon.

A small man, wiry and well-muscled, he began his active service in the last week of March at Rethel, flying mail and spare parts to the front. In the middle of April, at Vrizy, he worked as an aerial spotter for the 99th Artillery Regiment, using signal lights to regulate fire. In May, he went, like Boelcke, to Aviation Section No. 62, which was then located at Douai and later moved to Pontfaverger. With a Lieutenant Teuben as his observer, he flew an old, unarmed L.V.G. for a while. In this ramshackle biplane he was twice set upon by armed French machines, probably Voisins. Although the L.V.G. was damaged on the second occasion, he reached his base safely with precious reconnaissance data and a few days later received the Iron Cross. It was at this juncture that Lieutenant Boelcke introduced the synchronized gun to his horrified enemies. Immelmann profoundly admired Boelcke; perhaps because of the rare cordiality extended by Immelmann, the two became friends—or more precisely, business associates. Their relationship rested on mutual respect rather than any warm feeling. They passed few of their leisure hours in one another's company, but, when Immelmann took over the next Fokker E-1 delivered to Section No. 62, they often went out together hunting for prey. The parting of their ways came when Boelcke was moved to Metz, leaving Immelmann the unrivaled battle ace in the Lille sector. Here he achieved most of his victories and earned his title as the Eagle of Lille.

Boelcke, returning from his tour of the eastern front to lead Jasta 2 in the final months of his twenty-five years of life, deserted the Fokker in favor of the single-seater Albatros fighter, which could climb both faster and higher. He scored most of his kills in the Albatros, which explains why Immelmann and not Boelcke has been generally remembered as the outstanding exponent of the E-series Fokker. Actually, the entire group of early Fokker pilots was exceptional. Among them, for example, was Lieutenant Ernst Hess, who accumulated seventeen victories in his combat career, first with an Eindekker and then one of the Albatros fighters. There was Lieutenant Walter Hohndorf, killed in a crash in the autumn of 1917, with twelve victories to his credit. And Lieutenant Ernst von Althaus, who lived through the war and continued flying until claimed by a seaplane accident in 1927. And Lieutenant Kurt Wintgens, killed in action in September 1916. And there was Lieutenant Otto Parschau, whose intrepidity and skill won the praise of Boelcke and Immelmann, with whom he frequently flew as a team. Parschau died of wounds in July 1916, having shot down eight Allied aircraft. These Fokker pilots, all except Hess, were conspicuous among the eighty-one German aviators to be rewarded with the Order Pour le Mérite, which was equivalent to Great Britain's Victoria Cross, the Croix de Guerre of France, and the United States' Congressional Medal of Honor.

Men like these, in their pugnacious little monoplanes, dominated the sky until the summer of 1916, for nearly a whole year. Despite this air superiority and the early hopes it created in the German general staff of an impending Allied surrender, Germany did not win the war, nor even Verdun. What the Berlin generals had not contemplated was the sacrificial courage of French and British airmen who, at great cost, persisted in running the gauntlet of Fokkers to maintain visual contact with the enemy. Allied air crews, through the waning months of 1915, anxiously experimented with a variety of armament arrangements, and a collection of very odd machines was designed in an effort to do away with the difficulties of synchronized guns: planes in which the observer stood with his head and shoulders through a hole in the top wing to fire his tripod-mounted machine gun, and the "pulpit planes," with nacelles protruding in front of their tractor airscrews. Considerable improvements were built into the Lewis gun. It was modified and lightened, a spade grip was substituted for the wooden stock, and the fretted radiator enclosing the barrel and gas cylinder was replaced by an aluminum casing. Early in 1916, a double drum containing ninety-seven rounds of ammunition was developed. On the German side the sturdier Spandau gun was adopted to replace the Parabellum as the standard synchronized weapon.

The defeat of the Fokker monoplane, then, was the result of several factors. First, there was the steadfast devotion to duty of Allied airmen. Second, there was the development of complete fighting squadrons by R.F.C. Generals Henderson and Trenchard, which plan was adopted by the French at Verdun. Third was Trenchard's insistence on "forward action," the philosophy that affirmed that air advantage could not be gained without fighting for it, and which was also subscribed to—after some misgivings—by the French. Fourth, and certainly not least important, was the introduction of Allied aircraft that were better able to cope with the Fokker.

Until the opening weeks of 1916, when four squadrons equipped with Royal Aircraft Factory FE-2 pushers landed in France, Squadron No. 11—equipped with the Vickers FB-5 *Gun Bus*—remained the sole all-fighter unit of the Royal Flying Corps. The FE-2, which looked so much like the *Gun Bus*, was found capable of dealing with the Fokker—defensively at least. According to British histories Corporal Waller, when he allegedly shot down Max Immelmann, was in the forward cockpit of an FE-2 piloted by Lieutenant George S. McCubbin of No. 25 Squadron. Informally known as the "Fee" by its crews, the earlier model FE-2 carried a Lewis gun on a bracket in front of the observer's cockpit; later a second Lewis was fitted on a telescoping pillar mounting to fire backward over the top wing. The observer, without a parachute, had to stand with only his feet inside his cockpit to do this. Both guns had leather pouches to catch the ejected cartridges, which otherwise would have sailed back into the pusher propeller. The FE-2's were thoroughly outclassed by the new Albatros fighters that appeared that summer, but they were not withdrawn from service till more than a year later. When attacked, their crews learned to form a defensive circle and thus protect the blind spot under their tails. The Fees could put up a stiff resistance. In combat with them Manfred von Richthofen was badly wounded, and Lieutenant Karl Schaefer, an ace with thirty victories, was killed.

To supplement their fighter strength, the British, at General Trenchard's pleading, purchased a few Nieuport Type 11's in the autumn of 1915. The qualities of the little French machine were readily appreciated by R.F.C. pilots, though it fell short of being a Fokker nemesis, as the later Nieuport Type 17 became in the following spring. At the end of the year the De Havilland DH-2 was hopefully sent to the front to help withstand the Fokker onslaught. It proved better than the Baby Nieuport and a real match for the enemy monoplane—which amazed everybody on both sides, Geoffrey de Havilland included. The DH-2 was another pusher biplane, the only single-seater of its species then in the air. The plane was notoriously tricky to fly, with ultrasensitive controls and a propensity to stall off and spin if carelessly handled in turn and climb maneuvers. The rotary Gnome Monosoupape engine presented an even worse danger; two veteran pilots were killed when the cylinders exploded and severed the tail booms of their machines. Mostly, however, the pilots who manned the DH-2 complained of its poor protection against wind and temperature. James McCudden, who flew the type for a while in 1916, wrote of one winter patrol: "I didn't care whether I was shot down or not, I was so utterly frozen."

The DH-2, when the supply caught up with the demand, did ultimately play a big part in checking the Fokker E-plane, with the result that the Allies had short-term air superiority at the start of the Somme offensive on July 1, 1916. In one action that day a DH-2 pilot won the Victoria Cross. He was Major L. W. B. Rees, who had established a reputation as a determined fighter in No. 11 Squadron and was now in command of No. 32. Rees singlehandedly accosted a formation of ten German two-seaters. Although wounded early in the engagement, he forced down two and dispersed the remainder.

The unanticipated success of the DH-2 led to the hurried development of a similar pusher-propelled scout by the Royal Aircraft Factory that spring; this was the FE-8, a single-seater version of the FE-2. The FE-8 made its debut at the front in August, just in time to be soundly thrashed by the Albatros D-2, the new German fighter that quickly brought to a close the summer interlude of Allied supremacy. For good measure the Germans also unveiled their Halberstadt and Pfalz D-class fighters, not quite as fearsome as the Albatros, but sturdy and maneuverable and more than a match for Allied machines.

It was, then, the DH-2 and the Nieuport Type 17 that finally overcame the long-reigning Fokker monoplane. Among those few in Germany who had foreseen this event long before it happened was Anthony Fokker himself, who in November 1915, upon testing the high-powered E-4, was well aware that the design could not be further refined. Work was accordingly started on two biplanes, the Fokkers D-1 and D-2, both of which went into service at about the same time as the Nieuport 17. Neither of the Dutchman's new machines really showed much promise; in some ways they were inferior to the monoplane they were meant to supersede. Oswald Boelcke condemned them both as being too stable for high-speed aerobatics. Naïve about such distinctions and mesmerized by the Fokker name, Berlin ordered the planes into production and wagered extravagant hope on their success. The price of ignoring Boelcke's advice was paid in blood, for the new Fokkers were completely outclassed by the improved Nieuports and the British DH-2's as well. Only a small number of these Fokkers saw action, and almost all of them were shot down as soon as they encountered opposition from any of the new Allied scouts. The scepter of air superiority had now passed from German to Allied hands, and after nearly a year of having things pretty much its own way, the German air command was filled with consternation. The pressing need for a single-seater to deal with the new Allied fighters resulted in a desperate decision to build copies of the French Nieuport. Just when the situation seemed darkest, however, providence intervened in the form of another new biplane, the Albatros D-1, brought out with little fanfare by that firm in August. Not only would this machine—or rather its descendants, the D-2 and D-3—spell finish to Allied superiority; it would retain the German advantage through most of another year.

Of very advanced design, the Albatros D-plane had a fuselage of semi-monocoque construction that was covered with plywood instead of fabric for reinforced strength. Its profile was sleek as a shark, and in combat it was as savagely efficient. Its engine, the liquid-cooled, straight six-cylinder, 160-horsepower Mercedes, was among the truly great engines produced during the war and was perhaps better than the Rolls-Royce and Hispano-Suiza of the Allied side. The men who flew the D-1 had but a single criticism, that the top wing obscured their view. The Albatros company therefore lowered the wing closer to the fuselage, and this minor modification transformed the D-1 into the D-2. Not the least of its assets were its synchronized twin Spandau machine guns.

First flown in a squadron on Sunday, September 17, by Captain Boelcke and the select pilots of Jasta 2, the Albatros immediately showed itself to be a spectacular fighting machine. The performance of the plane was further enhanced by the fact that the men in Jasta 2 were entirely inexperienced as pursuit pilots. Chosen by Boelcke during his tour of eastern fronts, they had assembled in August at Lagnicourt to be tutored by their famous leader. Boelcke, recalled to France after the Somme offensive, had found diamonds in the rough. Among them was Manfred von Richthofen, the future Red Knight of Germany, whom Boelcke had plucked from a two-seater squadron in a quiet sector along the Russian front. Also there were Lieutenants Ernst Bohme, Max von Muller, Hans Immelmann (a cousin of the great Max Immelmann), and Sergeant-Major Leopold Reimann, all of whom afterward made honorable names for themselves, Muller winning the Order Pour le Mérite.

During the first half of September, using an Albatros D-1 as his personal aircraft, Boelcke was the only fighting member of the squadron. The youngsters he had gathered around him were impatient for action, but he knew it would have been suicidal for them to attempt combat against veteran foemen until they had familiarized themselves with their new machines and thoroughly rehearsed the tactics he had worked out for them. For almost three weeks the eager pilots of Boelcke's unit could only watch the feats of their mentor. They expected him, as Richthofen wrote, "to eat an Englishman every day for breakfast." Daily at dawn he took off, seeking prey. When he returned and joined his students at the mess table each morning, they waited anxiously to hear his report. Boelcke made a little ritual of it, saying nothing until the question came: "Any luck today?"

"Look at my chin," Boelcke would reply, "and tell me if it's black."

"Black as coal!"

"Well, then, that's all right," said Boelcke, and the reverent group knew that he had added to his growing total of victories. The grime on his chin—the only portion of his face not covered by goggles and helmet—was powder from his machine guns, and when Boelcke used his guns, he almost always bagged game. On September 16, at 5:45 A.M., over Havrincourt Wood, he shot down Captain George Cruikshank of the R.F.C. with one short burst. Cruikshank, himself an ace with five kills, was not taken unawares. The two of them jockeyed for twenty minutes to obtain favorable positions, and Cruikshank had fired several times before Boelcke touched his trigger. The German did as he lectured his pupils to do, holding his fire until the range was close and the enemy machine squarely framed within his gunsight. Upon returning to base he preached the lesson once more to his attentive brood and announced that on the following morning they would have the chance to put all he had taught them to practical use. Graduation day had come for the apprentice air fighters at Oswald Boelcke's unique school.

Sunday, September 17, dawned bright. The crisp clarity of the air testified to the nearness of autumn. The rising sun still sat on the horizon as the aspiring warriors of Jasta 2 flew off behind their leader in their brand new Albatros D-2 biplanes. While flying from Lagnicourt to the front, Boelcke spied two formations of British aircraft—eight BE-2's on a bombing mission with six FE-2's in escort. The British formations were bound for Marcoing station, an important rail depot located deep behind the lines. Seeing that the enemy planes were still on their outward journey, Boelcke knew there was no need to rush into the attack. He heeded another of his own rubrics—secure any possible advantage before attacking. To afford his group the benefit of height, so they could pounce from above when the moment came, he climbed. Then he circled until the Jasta was positioned between the sun and the enemy machines, thus insuring that the British gunners would suffer the solar glare in their eyes as they tried to aim their weapons. Now he kept his flock in tight formation and patiently stalked his quarry. A pall of smoke shrouded Marcoing station after the BE-2's had dropped their bombs. Wary as they were, the British airmen cast frequent glances earthward to ascertain what kind of punishment they had inflicted on the depot. Noting their distraction, Boelcke chose his moment to strike.

At his signal the Jasta dived, each man picking a target. Silhouetted against the bead of Boelcke's gunsight was an FE-2 in center formation. Closing fast, he opened fire, spraying the nacelle and engine with bullets. He got off two quick bursts before hurtling past his prey. Pulling back the control stick, he leveled the Albatros out of its descent and zoomed upward again in a steep climbing turn. Now he approached his target from behind and below, where the British gunner could not shoot for fear of hitting the tail of his own machine. When he was within seventy-five yards the German ace let go a sustained burst. A wisp of whitish-blue smoke trailed from the FE-2's engine. The plane faltered and slowed into a winding glide, crippled but still in the pilot's control. The gunner was crumpled in his cockpit, dead or wounded. Boelcke did not enjoy killing his opponents and often voiced regret that his victories involved their deaths. He was better pleased when he could bring them down alive and entertain them at his mess. Instead of finishing off the defenseless FE-2, he removed his finger from the trigger and followed the plane down far enough to be convinced it would not manage to limp back to Allied territory. He was about to rejoin the battle upstairs when he noticed that the disabled plane was heading straight for a German observation balloon, as if to ram it. A thick concentration of ground fire was already directed on the plane. Cursing the Britisher's suicidal defiance and at the same time admiring his courage, Boelcke saw the FE-2 suddenly disintegrate amid the maelstrom of bursting shells.

Richthofen elected also to attack one of the FE-2's. Remembering Boelcke's admonition not to fire except at close range, he almost collided with the British machine before shooting at it. The British pilot, Lieutenant L. B. F. Morris, and the observer, Lieutenant Thomas Rees, were both experienced airmen and they promptly took appropriate defensive measures. Rees, standing on his cockpit seat, fired back over the top wing, while Morris banked the machine from side to side whenever Richthofen was in the FE-2's blind spot.

With too many bullets passing his way for comfort, Richthofen resorted to an artful ruse. He broke off the fight, dived into a cloud and, hidden from his adversaries' view, doubled back for another try. Again he approached the FE-2 from under its tail. Evidently Rees and Morris missed seeing him, for they attempted no evasive action. Richthofen commenced shooting from fifty yards. There was no return fire; both occupants of the FE-2 were hit and the engine disabled. As the exultant novice swerved aside, he saw the propeller of the enemy plane stop. He watched fascinated as the stricken FE-2 nosed over and went down. Morris, mortally wounded, summoned the strength and presence of mind to control the descent and to land on the edge of a small German auxiliary airfield. Richthofen followed, landing nearby, almost wrecking his Albatros in his eagerness to inspect his prize. He sprinted to the FE-2 as others came running and driving up from the far side of the field. Rees was already dead, a neat red hole in his scalp and another in his neck; Morris, still breathing as they laid him on a stretcher, died on the way to the hospital. Baron Manfred von Richthofen had indisputable proof for his first victory claim—two dead British airmen and the slightly bent airframe of their machine.

There was loud rejoicing in the officers' mess of Jasta 2 that evening. Not only Boelcke and Richthofen but Bohme and Reimann had scored. Seven other German planes had joined in the fray, and all together six FE-2's and two BE-2's had been destroyed. After three dismal months of Allied domination, a new combat machine had shown itself capable of weighting the scales again in Germany's favor; it was simply a matter of mass-producing Albatroses and filling the sky with them. News of the event boosted the morale of German flyers everywhere. But that night the men of Jasta 2 had particular cause to feel gratified, and Captain Boelcke was delighted by the sharp performance of his student body in its graduation exercise.

Beer tankards, in the armies of many nations, are customary as presentation pieces. Boelcke awarded one to each of his officers upon the achievement of their initial victories, and the toasts which were drank on these occasions became a traditional ceremony in the German air service. Richthofen, with a sportsman's regard for trophies, decided to go one better than tradition and present himself with a miniature loving cup for this and each of his successive victories. He ordered the first cup of his special set that night by mail from a jeweler in Berlin, describing the kind he wanted in explicit detail—"small, plain, five centimeters tall and three centimeters across the top diameter, with sloping sides to a base smaller than the top, the whole to be done of sterling silver with dull gold plating inside." He instructed the jeweler to engrave on the cup the inscription "1. Vickers 2. 17.9.16."

The numbers and the word indicated that the cup commemorated his first victory, that the type of aircraft shot down was a Vickers, a two-seater, and that the combat had taken place on the seventeenth day of the ninth month of 1916. Richthofen, who made the same mistake on several subsequent trophies, wrongly identified the FE-2 as a Vickers *Gun Bus*. Few German airmen seemed able to differentiate among the various British pushers, all of which were commonly designated to be Vickers one- or two-seaters, as the case may have been.

Richthofen's morbid collection of metalware increased rapidly. On the sixth day after Lieutenants Morris and Rees were slain, he posted another note to Berlin. "One more cup, please," it read in effect, "just like the last ordered. Engrave it as follows: '2. Martinsyde 1. 23.9.16.'" And a week after that he destroyed another FE-2, and the happy jeweler in Berlin removed from his shelf another silver cup on which to etch a brief necrology.

While awaiting the arrival of his third trophy, the fast-rising prodigy of Jasta 2 registered the victory with his mother in a letter to the family estate in Schweidnitz. "On September 30," he wrote, "I brought down my third Britisher. His plane burned as it fell to the ground. One's heart beats faster when the enemy whose face one has just seen, goes down enveloped in flame from an altitude of twelve thousand feet. Naturally, nothing was left of the pilot or his plane when they crashed. I salvaged a small fitting as a remembrance. From my second Britisher I have kept the machine gun, the breech-lock of which has been jammed by a bullet . . ."

In the large house at Schweidnitz there was for many years after the war a Richthofen museum. Superintended by his mother, it became a patriotic shrine. Here were displayed the multifarious souvenirs and trophies sent home by the German ace: machine guns, pistols, flare guns, propellers, wing struts, cartridge drums, ammunition belts, serial numbers and insignia cut from the fabric of planes he shot down. Also on exhibit were sixty silver loving cups, representing three-fourths of his total of eighty victories. After inscribing the last cup with the obituary of Richthofen's sixtieth victim, the jeweler had to decline further orders. He had exhausted his silver supply and could get no more. The aviator's final twenty victories were thus memorialized only in the official records and by the graves of those he felled.

In the flush of his first three kills, however, still tingling with pride to be flying under the leadership of Boelcke, his admired master, Richthofen continued pursuing his game without stint. Victories four and five were his by October 16, and his sixth came to him on October 25, a fact which he mentioned casually to his mother: "The weather is rather poor here now, but even so I brought down my sixth Britisher yesterday." He closed this letter with a significant observation, a clue to his ambition. "Formerly," he said, "a pilot was decorated with the Order Pour le Mérite after he had brought down his eighth plane. Now they have eschewed that practice, although it becomes always more difficult to shoot one down. During the last four weeks . . . we have lost five planes out of ten."

The very day Richthofen penned these words, Oswald Boelcke lost his life. Men died every day in the air, so that it was accepted as a sad matter of routine, but that Boelcke could fall seemed impossible. Promoted to captain at age twenty-five, a holder of every feasible decoration, with an as yet unequaled record of forty enemy aircraft destroyed, the squadron leader was thought to be invincible. In battle he may have been, but even this nonpareil was vulnerable to the vagaries of fate. Flying alongside Lieutenant Bohme on October 26, the two of them in pursuit of a British single-seater, they both were compelled to bank abruptly when another British machine, chased by Richthofen, intersected their flight paths. In that quick movement their planes touched, Bohme's undercarriage causing a rent in Boelcke's wing. The ruptured wing was ripped away by the rushing air, and Boelcke careened helplessly to his death. Some histories say that Bohme, blaming himself for the tragedy, had to be restrained from suicide that night.

Richthofen, though profoundly saddened by the passing of his respected leader, was ready as ever to fly and fight. On November 3, the day of Boelcke's funeral, he found time to patrol before attending the church service; spotting a lone FE-2, he dived on it with both his Spandaus spewing bullets. The FE-2, its wings and fuselage holed like a colander, fell east of Lens. Richthofen then returned to the airdrome, donned his dress uniform and drove to the cathedral in Cambrai. As Boelcke's star protégé, he was appointed to stand at the head of the sealed casket with a tray of the dead hero's medals. Boelcke was honored by friend and foe alike. Among the many flowers and tributes were two laurel wreaths, one dropped by the Royal Flying Corps, the other brought in person to the cathedral by a quartet of invited British air officers from the prisoner-of-war camp at Osnabruk. By Imperial decree that day, Jasta 2 was renamed Jasta Boelcke; until the end of the war, though its deeds were less publicized than those of the squadrons that later flew under Richthofen's aegis, the Boelcke Squadron remained an elite unit in which German aviators felt privileged to serve. That evening after the funeral Richthofen retired to his quarters and wrote to Berlin for his seventh trophy cup.

The thunderclap of that fateful October 26 faded away, and the war continued unabated, leaving little time for mourning. The air advantage provided by the Albatros D-2, and by the even better D-3, which arrived at the front in January 1917, was never as clearly incontestable as that previously enjoyed by the Germans with their Fokker monoplane. Soon after the Albatros entered service, the odds were somewhat equalized by the belated appearance on Allied planes of machine-gun synchronizers. Instead of one standard device, however, there were five disparate types, all of which operated on the basic Fokker principle. Aside from this common parentage, about all they shared alike was linkage to a Vickers .303-caliber gun. The Vickers was employed because, as a fixed weapon, it was superior to the Lewis in several respects. It was more easily operated by an interrupter gear, had a higher rate of fire, and being belt fed, did not require reloading after every ninety-seven rounds. But the gun was not entirely trouble free at the outset. The rate of fire was very slow with the engine throttle back; also, a double feed often caused a jam when the expended end of the cartridge belt coiled under the gun and re-entered the breech. More serious was the drastic shortage of Allied synchronizers and their lack of uniformity. Worse yet, none of the five mechanisms could be used with more than a single gun, whereas the enemy Albatros, Halberstadt, and Pfalz fighter planes were armed with twin guns, affording twice the firepower. This distressing situation was not to be improved by the Allies until May 1917, when a vastly more sophisticated synchronization system made its debut aboard the redoubtable Sopwith Camel. Known as the "C.C. gear," the new synchronizer was developed by George Constantinesco, a Roumanian-born designer of rock drills, and R.F.C. Major George C. Colley. Hydraulically operated, the C.C. gear did away with the complicated linkage of mechanical interrupters. With its firing impulse transmitted by oil pressure, the gun continued shooting its full quota of bullets per minute regardless of engine speed. The C.C. gear could be handily installed in any airplane, furthermore, and made to fire two Vickers guns simultaneously.

Through the last quarter of 1916, therefore, and the first five months of 1917, up until the introduction of the C.C. gear on the Sopwith Camel and the Spad, Germany retained a perspicuous advantage in the air. Making the most of it were the young fighters of Jasta Boelcke. After Boelcke's death Lieutenant Stephan Kirmaier assumed Jasta command, and the fact that his men could claim twenty-five victories in the subsequent month, November, bespoke his qualification as successor to the dead ace. But Kirmaier, too, died before the month was out, falling prey to the gunner of an FE-2. There was gloomy silence in the mess that night and much headshaking. Then, a day later, the sadness of Kirmaier's death was dissipated by the jubilation that greeted a splendid triumph. In a thrilling half-hour duel, Richthofen shot down Major Lanoe G. Hawker, the courageous opponent whom the Germans had paid the compliment of characterizing as the English Boelcke. It was the second coup for Richthofen in less than a week. On November 20, he had achieved the "double event" by bagging his ninth and tenth British machines on the same day.

The next commander of Jasta Boelcke was Captain Franz Walz, who arrived at the airfield on November 29. Perhaps it was a wise decision to choose an officer from another squadron; the deaths of Boelcke and Kirmaier, occurring so close together, caused the men to suspect that a jinx had befallen them and that a similar fate awaited anyone who led them. Foolish superstition perhaps, but it might nevertheless have prevented one of their own number from doing justice to the office of leader. Walz led the squadron for seven months without even scratching himself shaving, then resigned his command, complaining of nervous fatigue, to fill an instructor's post in the homeland. During his period of leadership the group of young German aviators ripened to expertness. Names such as Otto Bernet, Adolf von Tutschek, and Werner Voss attained prominence, as did that preeminently of Manfred von Richthofen. The long battle of the Somme drew to its conclusion, and with December came bad weather, which reduced their activities; but they still contrived to enter another ten victims in their squadron book that month, to bring the year's total up to eighty-six. The new year did not begin too auspiciously. Only three victories were scored in January to offset the deaths of Hans Immelmann and Sergeant Karl Ostrop. An even worse blow that month was the departure of their best pilot, Richthofen.

The German high command had by now thoroughly comprehended the principle of the Jagdstaffel. Its selected bands of marauding pilots, men who could shoot as well as they could fly, were henceforth to be transferred to any sector of the front where the enemy's machines were at the moment especially troublesome. Thus the Germans could gain at least a temporary edge that would enable their own slower two-seaters to carry on reconnaissance jobs in comparative peace. If one Jasta did not suffice, then two would be sent into the area, or three, until finally the enemy was wiped out or obliged to stay on the ground. More Jagdstaffels were therefore decreed, and as each of the new units was formed, its members invariably clamored to have a Boelcke man as their leader. And so the high command took Richthofen away from his companions and put him in charge of Jasta 11. Captain Walz was left to wonder who would be taken next.

But in the ensuing three months the Boelcke unit glutted itself with kills: fourteen in February, fifteen in March, twenty-one in April. Jasta Boelcke lost only three of its own pilots. The legacy left to the Boelcke Squadron by its founder and namesake was being proudly perpetuated, and if Richthofen was now a competitor, were not Bernet and Tutschek and Voss piling up scores that he would have to strive hard to beat? One day in April the squadron wrote six victories in its book, Lieutenant Bernet himself accounting for five of them. That was a record, so they thought, which not even Richthofen could equal. Yet, before the end of May, Richthofen shot down a Spad, an FE-2, two BE-2's and a Nieuport, all in a single day. A spirited rivalry had grown up between Jasta Boelcke and Jasta 11 to see which could acquire the greater number of victories. In effect it was Jasta Boelcke versus the Jasta 11 leader alone, for Richthofen, doing combat in his all-red machine, downed ten victims in March; in April he claimed twenty-one, as many as the whole Boelcke outfit combined!

During these months of ascendancy for German aviation, Lieutenant Werner Voss, his Albatros ostentatiously decorated with hearts and swastikas, emerged as a figure of extraordinary skill and daring. A glutton for victories, there was nothing he would not do to add to his score. Richthofen, before leaving Jasta Boelcke to take over his own command, had recognized the unusual talent of nineteen-year-old Voss. The two became friends and once went on a brief furlough together to visit Voss' parents in Krefeld. There, in the modest house at 75 Blumenstrasse, near the flourishing dye factory that Werner expected someday to inherit, Herr and Frau Voss could not contain the excitement they felt at having their eldest son bring home the German ace of aces as his guest. Yet there were rumors—rumors that persisted long after both men were killed and the war ended—that the baron was jealous of Voss' ability and considered the young *kampfflieger* a threat to his position among German fighter pilots. When Richthofen was given command of Jasta 11, he had the up-and-coming aces Emil Schaeffer and Karl Allmenroder transferred too. That he didn't take Voss along probably gave rise to the rumors. Actually, however, Voss preferred to stay with Jasta Boelcke, where he would have a better opportunity, he knew, to add to his mounting score. With the baron as his flight leader, Voss had been prevented from flying alone or departing from organized attacks with the entire formation. Voss fought best when he could select his own method of combat and not be encumbered with his flying mates. He was an individualist, one of those rare and fearless pilots who flew solo patrols in addition to the required sorties with his squadron. He never hesitated to attack any number of Allied planes he chanced upon during these lone excursions over the front, and more often than otherwise he shot down at least one victim.

By April 1, Voss had twenty-three victories, just nine less than Richthofen. On that morning he flew his Albatros to the Jasta 11 airfield on a liaison mission. The baron warmly welcomed his old friend, whom he had not seen since transferring out of Jasta Boelcke. Their conference concerned a plan to coordinate temporarily the operations of the two squadrons. After their talk, Richthofen offered to accompany Voss on his return flight, suggesting that they take a roundabout route over the front lines. Along the way they spotted a small formation of Sopwith two-seaters below them. Richthofen swooped to attack the rearmost machine, which had lagged well behind the others. Voss did not dare to assist in the kill. To do so, he felt, since the Sopwith looked like cold meat, would insult his superior in rank and victories. Richthofen hit the enemy observer on his first pass. He poured long bursts of fire into the undefended plane on subsequent passes, but each time he failed to send it falling. At last the Sopwith's fuel tank was punctured, and the British pilot, Lieutenant P. Warren, glided to a landing with his engine stopped.

Voss was surprised at the apparent difficulty Richthofen had in disposing of the helpless two-seater. Now, for the first time, he gained a sure confidence in his ability to surpass the baron's score. Many experts on both sides, then and later, wrote that Voss was the better combat flyer, fighting as he did with instinct rather than a preconceived plan. Voss improvised while he fought, whereas Richthofen occasionally found himself at a loss if his tactics needed sudden revision in the heat of a fight.

A good-looking youth with dark hair, smiling blue eyes, and a medium build, Voss had come to aviation from the cavalry, the Second Westphalian Hussar Regiment, with which he had seen action at the beginning of the war on the eastern front. During the battle of Verdun he flew as an observer, becoming a pilot on May 28, just in time to fly an Aviatik in the battle of the Somme. The happiest moment of his military career came on November 21, when he was transferred as a fighter pilot to the celebrated Boelcke Squadron. Here he piled up victories until May 20, 1917. The high command then finally took notice of Voss' record and posted him to Jasta 5 as leader He scored six additional victories by June 4, raising his total to thirty-four enemy aircraft destroyed.

Soon afterward, on June 26, Richthofen was given command of Geschwader No. 1, which was formed by consolidating Jastas 4, 6, 10, and 11 under a single chief. This battle group became the first German "flying circus," so called because its component squadrons constantly migrated along the front to areas where they were most needed, and when a squadron moved, it did indeed resemble a traveling circus troupe, with truck convoys or railroad cars loaded with personnel, equipment, and aircraft in all stages of dismantlement.

Geschwader No. 1 quickly developed into one of the most feared and formidable fighter-plane organizations in the history of military aviation. It was imperative that the squadron leaders be men of tremendous competence if the group was to function properly. Richthofen, who was an excellent judge of character and ability, therefore selected his men with great care. In July, when Lieutenant Ernst von Althaus was relieved of his command of Jasta 10 to become a combat instructor, the baron appointed Voss to take over that squadron. The aircraft then being used were Pfalz and Albatros single-seaters, and those of Jasta 10 were uniformly trademarked with red noses. On occasion, Voss flew an all-silver Pfalz D-3 with a red spinner and body stripes. By August 16, Richthofen led the race for victories with fifty-eight; Voss was still in the runner-up position with thirty-seven kills to his credit.

Like the French ace, Guynemer, Voss was a fighter and not an administrator. The worry and responsibility, the interminable paperwork entailed in running a squadron irritated the twenty-year-old flight commander, and the strain of leadership began to show. His closest associates noticed a marked aging in Voss' face and in his manner during that troubled summer of 1917.

The seesaw contest for air supremacy, essentially a technological contest, was now again being won by the Allies. German success had reached its peak in April, when British casualties were so high that it has been remembered in England as "Bloody April." Beginning in May with the appearance of improved aircraft—SE-5's, Sopwith Camels, Spads, and Nieuports armed with twin synchronized guns—the Allied air forces regained the initiative, which was securely theirs by July. The British had been hurt not solely because of the muddle and delay in producing first-class machines, but also because of their implacable determination to maintain the offensive no matter what the price. Every pilot of the R.F.C. was aware of the fact that to practice the doctrine of attack day in and day out meant heavy losses, especially against an enemy as clever and uncompromising as, for example, Werner Voss, Manfred von Richthofen, and their Jagdstaffels. But these losses were accepted without flinching. The mood of British airmen during this season of crisis has been aptly described as "grim and gay," the first quality being displayed in the air, the second in the mess. However many empty chairs there might have been, the spirit of cheer was never allowed to depart from the board.

The high incidence of British casualties through that winter and early spring can be attributed in part to another factor—namely, a shortage of experienced flyers. In November and December of 1916, the R.F.C. undertook to replenish its ranks, so sadly thinned in the four bitter months of the Somme struggle which had cost the lives of nearly nine hundred British airmen. General Trenchard had asked for a revitalized air force consisting of 106 active, and ninety-five reserve, squadrons. To his amazement, his request was seconded by the powerful voice of the army commander-in-chief, General Sir Douglas Haig, who had not before exhibited any concrete interest in aviation.

Though his request was granted, Trenchard found achieving it to be quite another proposition. By the early months of 1917, little new manpower was available apart from youngsters leaving school in England. The R.F.C. accordingly sought to recruit volunteers from the army, which was understandably reluctant to let them go. In desperation, finally, the War Office ordered regimental commanders to make an appeal to their men on behalf of the flying corps. Upon receipt of this directive, the majority of officers, unwilling to promote the depletion of their own regiments, obeyed its letter but not its spirit. Many left the appeal to their sergeant majors, who were shrewd enough to sense that the fewer the volunteers, the happier would be their superiors. One infantryman, who did transfer, preserved for posterity the "appeal" delivered by his sergeant major. It amounted to a bald invitation to oblivion. "If any of you wants to go to 'eaven quick," the sergeant major bellowed, "now's your chance. They're askin' for volunteers to learn to fly and become officers in the ruddy R.F.C. If any of you feels 'is old age isn't worth waitin' 'round for, step two paces forward out of ranks and I'll take the bloomin' idiot's name. But don't forget, it's a 'ell of a long way to fall—and you falls only once!"

With such encouragement as this to prod them, hundreds of young soldiers showed their preference for dying in the air instead of in the mud. As a sop to complaining army commanders, the War Office permitted them to keep a string on these volunteers. Those who consented to take flight training would remain listed on regimental rosters and only be temporarily attached to the R.F.C., with the understanding that if they did not prove acceptable for air service, they would be returned to their regiments. Too often, however, those who failed at flying school did it the hard way and were unable to rejoin their regiments, being either dead or crippled.

Spring was not many weeks along when an influx of volunteers began arriving from Canada. By arrangement with Washington the Canadians had trained in flying schools opened in Texas. When the United States declared war on Germany in April, the number of trainees from north of the border trebled and quadrupled, but several dozen had already won their wings at Texas airfields prior to that time. Among their instructors was Vernon Castle, the Canadian-born dancer who, with his wife Irene, had been the rage of Broadway musical comedy before his enlistment. Castle taught the rudiments of airmanship aboard a Curtiss JN-4 Jenny. There were frequent accidents at the field and a distressing mortality rate among student pilots, primarily because they occupied the forward cockpit and the instructor sat behind, where the danger of being crushed by the engine in a crash was less. With the safety of his charges uppermost in his mind, Castle reversed the seating order and placed himself in the front cockpit. More to save face than by desire, his fellow instructors followed suit and it soon became authorized procedure for them to take the "suicide seat." Many of them were thereafter killed in consequence of a learner's clumsiness or panic. First to meet such a death, when a student froze at the controls and dived full-speed into the prairie, was Vernon Castle.

The arrival of these Texas-trained Canadians was greeted as a godsend by the straitened R.F.C. leadership. In England it had always been an exasperatingly long process to turn raw recruits into qualified pilots, for the training schedule was usually foiled by bad weather in all but the summer months. The Canadians, on the other hand, after intensive, uninterrupted weeks of Texas schooling, were thoroughly trained in acrobatic flying and gunnery. They needed only a few familiarization flights in one or another of the latest fighter planes and a couple of weeks of instruction in formation flying and tactics, after which they were ready for front-line service. Their presence in France was felt very quickly.

Meanwhile, British reconnaissance crews, who always suffered worst in periods of enemy superiority, were hearing reports of a new two-seater which was being tested in England. It finally appeared early in 1917 in time to join the fighting above Arras. It was the Bristol F-2B, and at first sight a disappointment to its hopefully expectant crews. Apart from its long, circular-cowled nose and two-hundred-horsepower Rolls-Royce engine, the machine looked uncomfortably the same as previous planes of its class. The men of No. 48 Squadron, who received the first six examples sent to France, had anticipated something radically new, and their pessimism seemed woefully justified as soon as they flew the two-seaters into battle. Behind their squadron leader, Captain W. Leefe Robinson, they were unfortunate to meet Manfred von Richthofen and four of his colleagues in Albatros D-3 scouts. There ensued a short and decisive scrap. Four of the Bristols were brought down; the other two scarcely managed to hobble home. Captain Robinson landed his bullet-riddled plane in German territory and spent the rest of the war in captivity. He was no small prize, being the pilot who first shot down a zeppelin over London and a holder of the Victoria Cross.

In his action report that evening, Richthofen dismissed the new British machine with contempt. It was a pushover for the Albatros, he said, and his opinion was quickly made known to all German pilots. Richthofen had unwittingly passed a sentence of death on dozens of his fellow airmen, who for a long time treated the Bristol lightly and had to pay the price. For the "Brisfit" or "Biff," as it was later nicknamed, soon showed itself to be a much deadlier aircraft than either side had at first thought. After that first calamitous encounter the plane began acquitting itself as one of the finest all-purpose fighting machines of the war, since it combined the best qualities of the one- and two-seater by virtue of its ruggedness, its long-distance flying ability, and its surprising speed and maneuverability. Captain Robinson had made the mistake of sallying forth before he or his men had an appreciation of the flight behavior or potential of the Bristol. Unaware of the plane's versatility, they flew it as they were accustomed to flying other two-seaters, staying in defensive formation while the observers tried to hold off the assailing

Albatroses. Actually, as British reconnaissance pilots soon discovered to their immense pleasure, the Bristol was most effective in combat when flown in similar style to a single-seater. This was particularly true of the models that went to the front late that spring; in addition to a brace of ring-mounted Lewis guns for the observer, these models featured for the pilot a Vickers gun synchronized to fire through the airscrew with a C.C. gear. Racks were also provided for light fragmentation bombs and three twenty-pound Cooper bombs to be utilized in ground attack and contact patrolling. By October 1918, more than seventeen hundred F-2B's—the later models with oval-shaped cowls and Sunbeam Arab powerplants—were used successfully for high-speed reconnaissance, tactical bombing, escort fighting, and offensive scouting.

As an example of the Bristol's marvelous capabilities, Captain B. E. Baker, leading a flight of No. 48 Squadron on a photography mission in August 1917, reached an altitude of 22,000 feet, while the rest of the patrol got up to between 19,000 and 21,000 feet. During this rarely precedented ascent, four of the six aneroids broke. The pugnacity of the Bristol can be summed up by the fact that Captain Andrew E. McKeever, a Canadian posted to No. 11 Squadron in May—when the Vickers *Gun Buses* of that unit were being replaced with the new machines—scored the majority of his thirty victories while piloting an F-2B. On one occasion in October, he was set upon by nine Albatroses. Not a man to temporize, he flew through the enemy formation twice, shot down two in flames and a third out of control. His successes were shared by his observer, Sergeant L. F. Powell, and the dauntless Canadian became by far the greatest two-seater ace of the war. He died on Christmas Day 1919, of injuries incurred in an automobile accident in the United States.

The Bristol F-2B, despite its many merits, was not all tea and crumpets. For one thing, it was a demanding aircraft to fly. A few Sopwith Triplanes and Sopwith Pups, single-seaters donated by the Royal Naval Air Service, had preceded it into action with the R.F.C. These were easy to handle, and the men first given the Bristols assumed the new machines—being two-seaters— would be even more tractable than the two Sopwith types. The Bristol was not that accommodating. It had to be wheedled and wooed before it allowed you to take liberties. But once you had learned its ways, and so long as you kept your wits about you, you had a dependable and responsive machine that was a creditable match for German fighters. That is to say, it was better able to fend for itself than any other two-seater to enter service on either side. It cannot be said without argument, however, as some aviation historians have implied or asserted, that the F-2B was as efficient a fighting machine as the single-seaters of the post-1916 period. Its maximum speed at ten thousand feet was 105 miles per hour, which equaled or surpassed that of coeval German fighter craft, but its maneuverability—while remarkable for its size and weight —was less sprightly than that of opposing single-seaters. Though its speed enabled it to outdistance most enemy interceptors, and its rear guns provided a sting in its tail, the Bristol was at a distinct disadvantage in close-range dogfights where aerobatic agility often meant the difference between success and failure. It needed more room for a turn, for example, and was clumsier to loop or roll. These handicaps could be diminished by an adroit pilot and sharpshooting observer, as Captain McKeever and Sergeant Powell certainly demonstrated, but the Bristol was not the complete answer for renewed Allied air supremacy that spring. Although the F-2B was an answer to every reconnaissance pilot's prayers, it was not a thoroughbred fighter—nor could it be with its forty-foot wingspan, its 2800-pound gross weight, and its two-man crew—and it did not come into good supply until summer, by which time the initiative had already been resumed by the R.F.C.

Another two-seater, one with a checkered reputation, came into wide use that spring and summer. It was the Royal Aircraft Factory RE-8, which had gone to France for operational trials as early as June 1916, and immediately acquired a bad name. These prototypes were very prone to spin, and their top wings, built in three sections and rigged with both stagger and dihedral, were found to be unsafe. When the first RE-8 squadron, No. 52, arrived in France in November 1916, a series of accidents so adversely affected the unit's morale that re-equipment with older BE-2's took place, and several more months elapsed before the RE-8 was put back into service with modifications in its design. Though the improved model evoked little enthusiasm, it was ruled acceptable; and by September 1917, sixteen squadrons were flying RE-8's on the western front.

Awkward and outdated, tricky to land and slow in maneuver, the RE-8 carried out the bulk of British artillery spotting and photoreconnaissance in the last eighteen months of war. It mounted a Vickers gun, operated by the pilot and geared to fire through the propeller, on the port side of the fuselage and twin Lewis guns for the observer in the rear cockpit. The frame was wood with a fabric covering, and the fuselage, sloping upward toward the tail, combined with the raked engine and a large air scoop to give a curious broken-backed appearance to the plane. Usually an easy mark for enemy fighters, it occasionally triumphed. On August 21, 1917, Lieutenant Eduard von Dostler, a ranking German ace with twenty-six victories and the commanding officer of Jasta 6 in the Richthofen Geschwader, was killed by an RE-8 gunner. And in the following June Lieutenants R. C. Armstrong and F. J. Mart of No. 3 Squadron, Australian Flying Corps, shepherded an undamaged Halberstadt back to their field at Flesselles. Early dislike for the RE-8 changed gradually to tolerance and ultimately to affection; it became the "Harry Tate," taking the name of a London music-hall comedian. All told, more than four thousand RE-8's were manufactured through the latter half of World War I.

The year 1917, which began so bleakly for Allied airmen, will long remain important in history. During that year the United States renounced its traditional policy against entangling alliances and joined in an overseas war, thus irreversibly tying together the destinies of America and Europe. In Russia there was a national revolution which has not since permitted the international community to regain political balance. War propaganda—some true, most of it false—poured oil on the fires of emotion. But not the best of fiction writers could overstate the real enormity of slaughter. And the war that year grew bigger, and even fiercer. For example, British artillery in France increased from fifteen hundred pieces of all calibers on January 1, 1915, to more than five thousand pieces on New Year's Day 1917.

With the fighting at Verdun and along the Somme finally and mercifully ended, and with European battlegrounds in the paralyzing grip of winter, the year began with foreboding silence. It was "all quiet on the western front." It was for both sides a respite in which to lick their wounds and think out strategy for the coming spring. The French and British planned ambitious campaigns. They anticipated important, even decisive gains, basing this optimism on the enemy's attenuated reserve strength. Wearied and decimated in the gruesome battles of 1916, the German army found its need for replacements thwarted by the exactions of a multifront war. The Allies, with their greater reservoir of manpower, were better off in this respect. Berlin therefore decided to assume a defensive posture in the west.

General Robert-Georges Nivelle, who succeeded Marshal Joffre as the French field chief, convinced his government that a full-scale offensive—"a mighty blow of a gigantic fist" as it was termed—should be directed against the so-called Noyon bulge. This was the huge salient that extended at its closest proximity to within about sixty miles of Paris, the same giant pocket the Allies had been trying to reduce since the battle of the Marne. Nivelle began massing his forces, but the Germans made the first move. Commencing in late February and proceeding through March and the first week of April, they conducted a staged withdrawal from the Noyon bulge and redeployed along a series of well-fortified positions, known by the Germans as the Siegfried line and by the Allies as the Hindenburg line. A masterpiece of timing and logistics for which General Ludendorff could take credit, the withdrawal represented the greatest movement on the western front in thirty-three months of warfare. It was an astute strategic adjustment. Although it cost him some thirty miles of ground, Ludendorff managed to consolidate his strength. The new defensive line was shorter than the old. It could be held with thirteen fewer divisions, a vital consideration in light of the urgent need for reserves. The retirement also gave the Germans more time to prepare for the impending assault. As they abandoned the salient they had so long occupied, they scorched the earth behind them, demolishing roads and railways, razing villages, farms, and woodlands, poisoning wells. Wrote a French journalist who toured the region: "No grass grows, no birds sing, nothing is to be seen but charred ruins and shattered trees. . . . The Boches have desolated the countryside." As the Germans intended, the Allied advance across this blackened waste was slowed by the many engineering works required along the way.

The horrific campaigns of 1917 were begun on April 9, Easter morning, by the British, their attack aimed at Arras and the northwestern extremity of the Hindenburg line. Until April 24, along a fifteen-mile front, aided by heavy concentrations of artillery fire and using new mustard-gas projectors, General Sir Edmund Allenby's Third Army and a corps of Canadians pressed forward against stiff enemy resistance. The dominating heights of Vimy ridge were stormed repeatedly by the Canadians. The steep glacis was soon carpeted with bodies, but the ridge was seized and secured, which would have been an achievement of consequence a year later. Because it was so expensive, however, Arras in 1917 was at best a limited victory. British and Canadian casualties numbered more than 84,000. Paying that grim price, an advance of two to four miles was accomplished, some 18,000 Germans and 230 guns were captured, and 57,000 enemy troops were killed or wounded.

The "mighty blow" of General Nivelle, his "gigantic fist" consisting of fifty-four divisions, was unleashed on April 16, while the cannon were still roaring at Arras to the north. The French moved out along a fifty-mile front which stretched between Soissons and Rheims. Encompassing the 650-foot eminence of the Chemin des Dames, and the Craonne plateau, crisscrossed with gullies and ravines, the area had been converted into a natural fortress by the Germans. Nivelle's grand attack petered out on the first day, but this strutting general—who had often publicly boasted that his campaign would crack the German defenses "as a mallet smashes a walnut"—kept driving his troops to their own massacre. Ultimately they captured the commanding terrain feature, the Chemin des Dames, and pushed a few shallow dents into the German lines. The price was appalling. When the battle was over in late May, French losses exceeded 120,000 men. Nivelle—who lives in history as an example of the untoward influence of the persuasive military personality on politicians naïve in the art of warfare—was sacked. Marshal Henri Philippe Pétain, the "Saviour of Verdun," became the army's new head.

Nivelle's brand of leadership, climaxed by the bloody debacle at Aisne, had aftereffects which obligated Marshal Pétain to put aside temporarily the prosecution of the war against Germany. No sooner had he assumed command than the French army was convulsed by mass mutiny. Perhaps nobody but Pétain could have put the pieces back together again. His rapport with the *poilu* was broad and deep. He was known as the soldiers' friend and enjoyed their trust. Pétain spared nothing of himself in dealing with the emergency. During his first month in command he personally visited ninety-odd divisions, listening to the complaints of the men, inspiring the officers, and arranging for more leave and better food and recreation. By mid-July the danger of rebellion had passed. With a semblance of discipline restored, France went on—as best she could—with the war.

But Pétain found it necessary to husband his vitiated forces. He needed time to nurse them back to full recovery. He therefore informed the British that they would have to fight on through the remainder of 1917 with little

French assistance. This was woeful news. Although America had come into the war, and her khaki legions would soon arrive in ever-increasing shiploads, the strategic situation, which had been so favorable to the Allies in January, was now reversed. Other problems beside that of French morale had arisen. The revolutionary regime in Russia had capitulated, affording Germany hundreds of thousands of additional troops for movement from the eastern to the western theater. A disastrous spring campaign had left Italy badly in want of help. And the French army, because of the lingering disaffection in its ranks, could man only the dormant sectors of the long line from the Alps to the north coast.

Having no alternative, the British shouldered the awful burden thrust upon them. General Haig had for months been contemplating a major offensive in Flanders to recapture the Belgian channel ports. Now he had further reason for such an offensive, for it would draw enemy forces away from the weakened French front. Twice already the scene of military carnage, the Ypres salient— prounced "Wipers" by the British tommies who fought there—was again selected as the site for a great battle.

The third battle of Ypres developed into one of the harshest ordeals of the war. The British drive opened on July 31, in a steady drenching downpour. Artillery, all through the month, had pounded the German positions. Warned by this bombardment, the Germans had formed new reserves and bolstered their lines. More important was the weather that summer, which was abnormally wet and had transformed the Flanders plain into a wide morass of liquid mud. The advance stalled almost immediately in the waist-deep mire. Caissons sank to their wheel hubs and were useless. Men staggered wearily over duckboard tracks, the wounded falling into the shell holes alongside, many of them drowning before being found by stretcher bearers. Horses and mules by the thousands bogged and perished in the vast welter of fluid clay. Weapons caked and would not fire; even food was tainted with the taste of mud. There was no possibility that Haig's offensive could gain the Channel ports, but for three grueling, horror-filled months the British kept attacking in the rain and muck, and dying wholesale. The heroic Canadians at last captured Passchendale ridge, a key point, in November, and that was the only bright spot in a dismal picture. The ill-starred campaign came up short of its main objectives. The third battle of Ypres was another futile bloodbath, the British losing nearly 380,000 men as against half that many German casualties.

Pétain, meanwhile, had chanced two small offensives, more to restore confidence among his troops than to win territory. Carefully planned and strictly limited in scope, both were minor triumphs. During the third week of August twelve French divisions seized the surrounding heights of Verdun, sustaining negligible losses while taking ten thousand prisoners. Near Malmaison on the Aisne, Pétain's Tenth Army launched a drive on October 23; by November 2, with the help of tanks, surprise, and smooth coordination between all arms, the Soissons salient had been eliminated, and all the high terrain of the area was in French hands.

There was more good news that November in France. A man of furious energy and unshakeable courage, who fiercely hated the Germans and knew how to spur his countrymen to greater efforts and further sacrifice, replaced the adynamic Paul Painlevé as premier. He was Georges Clemenceau—"The Tiger"—and his sworn determination to crush his country's ancient enemy, together with Pétain's victories at Verdun and Malmaison, emphasized the fact that France had risen again in its stalwart strength.

November also witnessed another British campaign. From November 20 to December 7, the British drove toward Cambrai, employing new and revolutionary tactics. Its technology and usage perfected, the tank was at last used in mass rather than in penny packets. The ground before Cambrai was well drained and solid. At Cambrai the tank came of age, and 324 of them started the surprise assault against a section of the Hindenburg line. Like monstrous beetles they waddled across no-man's-land, closely followed by infantry. The tanks were covered by smoke, and carried their own trench-bridging equipment—huge bundles of fascines, or brush. By evening the British had pierced all except the rear line of enemy resistance, punching a deep—but irregular—bulge in the Hindenburg line toward Cambrai. About 180 tanks were out of action, but only 65 due to German fire. Unfortunately, Haig did not have sufficient reserves in tanks or men to exploit the advantage. After heavy fighting for Bourlon Wood, a sudden German counterattack won back a large part of the British gains. Nevertheless, Cambrai showed that mechanized armor, properly used, could break the stalemate of trench warfare.

The year closed on a dour note for the Allies, but 1917 also brought a bright gleam of hope. Although a revolution in Russia had overthrown the Czar and removed Russia from the war, the United States, with all its abundant resources, was now in the lists against Germany. Major General John J. ("Black Jack") Pershing had been in France with his staff since June. Soon thereafter, elements of the First U. S. Infantry Division plus a regiment of marines came as the vanguard of the American Expeditionary Force. Then the doughboys began arriving at the rate of fifty thousand per month (a number that would increase sharply in 1918). On October 23, units of the First Infantry moved into the front line near Nancy; in November, three American soldiers were killed in action. Soon, very soon, hordes of fresh and eager Americans would stream into the trenches to bolster the flagging French and British.

As yet, with the exception of the Lafayette Escadrille and a few volunteers with the Royal Flying Corps, there were no American airmen at the front. But they were being trained in France and England as well as in the United States. The First Aero Squadron, A.E.F., reached France on September 3, and other squadrons arrived that fall and winter. But there were unforeseen delays, frustrating and disheartening postponements. Instead of weeks, it required months to organize, school, and equip the American units to the point where they could function as a combat force. Another factor that somewhat deferred the appearance of American units at the front was a variance of opinion between Allied headquarters and General Pershing as to the disposition of A.E.F. ground and air personnel. The Allies wanted to utilize American detachments exclusively as replacements for their own battered and over-spent armies; Pershing, on the other hand, insisted on a separate army responsible for a specific sector of the front. He did, however, agree that A.E.F. units could serve temporarily as integral parts of certain French and British divisions until such time as they could be reunited under his command. This was accomplished, though not till August 1918, just two months prior to the Armistice.

If the Allied flying corps received no material succor from the United States Air Service in 1917, they did get a substantial morale boost. While the reaction to America's war commitment was never as ecstatic as American histories have often portrayed it to have been, there was a tangible leavening of spirits among Allied airmen generally. The blowhard promises of American politicians and industrialists to "darken the skies of Europe" with airplanes were implicitly believed, and this faith engendered in battle-weary French and British aviation squadrons a renascence of optimism, as did the presence of A.E.F. pilot-trainees. Contributing further to this effect was the corresponding dejection which the American declaration of war induced on the German side. Back in April—that "Bloody April" in which the R.F.C. suffered German air superiority at such terrible cost during the first stages of the Arras campaign—the news of America's declaration of war was a peg on which British flyers hung their hopes for the future. To that extent, at least, did the entrance of the United States into the conflict benefit Allied aviation that eventful year.

As for the revolutionary regime in Russia quitting the war, this had little direct bearing on French and British pilots in the west. The Russian resignation came like a kick in the groin for Allied ground forces, for it meant that nearly a million German troops, released from fighting on the eastern front, would soon take up positions along the western line. But only indirectly, only insofar as they could be affected by the comprehensive strategic situation, were the flying services of France and Great Britain adversely affected by the Russian surrender. The balance of air strength would not be more than minutely altered.

The war in the east had never entailed much air activity. The Russians, always hard up for airplanes, had no choice but to concede German mastery in the sky. In February 1917, the month preceding the accession of the Kerensky government, the Russian air service possessed 1039 planes. Scarcely a third of these were up-to-date combat craft. The best part of Czar Nicholas' aviation force at the front was divided into four groups of either three or four squadrons each, fewer than two hundred machines sparsely scattered over a very wide area. The Germans did not need or care to spare men and machines for operations on anything like the same scale as those on the western front; they sustained a flying force in Russia just large enough to assure a firm upper hand. Lacking both the equipment and the incentive to contend evenly with the Germans, Russian pilots generally shied away from air battle. Corporal (later Captain) Bert Hall, one of the original members of the Lafayette Escadrille, who was sent from France to Russia in January 1917, to assist in rehabilitating the Imperial Air Service, made mention in his diary of the lassitude of Russian aviators. "They fly," Hall observed, "about six hours per month and rest the remainder of the time."

Although several aircraft factories had been established before the war in Russia, and Russian army aviation got its start in 1911, the industry did not prosper there in a way comparable with other great powers. Wartime production totaled only about 4700 machines, most of them foreign types built under contract. The one notable Russian designer of that time was Igor I. Sikorsky, who during the 1917 Bolshevik putsch immigrated via France and England to the United States. As an American citizen in World War II, after a highly successful career designing and manufacturing commercial and military airplanes, the most memorable of which were his flying amphibians of the 1930s and the prototypes of the famous Republic P-47 *Thunderbolt* fighter which Allied pilots flew against the Luftwaffe from 1942 to 1945, Sikorsky perfected the first really practical helicopter. As a young prodigy in his motherland, he received from Czar Nicholas a gold watch in 1913 for his services to aviation. The timepiece was paltry compensation for what he achieved that year. To everyone's amazement he had created the world's first four-engine aircraft, called the *Russian Knight,* and then an even larger version with a top wing spanning 105 feet, the *Ilya Mourometz,* named after a mythical folk hero. This second plane set an international record on February 12, 1914, by climbing to 6500 feet with sixteen passengers and a dog, and flying over Moscow for five hours at an average speed of sixty-two miles an hour. Seventy-three of these giants were constructed as bombers before 1917, and they were the pride of the Imperial Air Service. With no fewer than forty struts between its expansive wings, the *Ilya Mourometz* was normally armed with two Maxim guns, a carbine, and 1120 pounds of bombs. Its massive fuselage had glass nose panels and windows and provided completely enclosed accommodations for its crew—pilot, co-pilot, bombardier, and air mechanic. Sikorsky also designed a small fighter plane, the S-16, virtually the only fighter craft of Russian creation to enter even limited production.

Excepting the Russo-Baltic Wagon Works, where the Sikorsky designs were built, all the Russian aircraft firms of any importance were engaged entirely in the licensed manufacture of French machines. The V. A. Lebedeff concern in Petrograd, where Aviatik and Albatros biplanes had been built previous to the war, was supplying Morane-Saulniers, Deperdussins, Farmans, and Voisins. The Dux Company in Moscow not only made Farmans and Morane-Saulniers but Nieuport Scouts, as did the Petrograd plant of S. S. Shchetinin and Company. The Russian-built Nieuports, having undergone various design "improvements" at the instance of aviation headquarters at Kiev, were less than useful. They had a nasty habit of suddenly diving into the ground. When, after a number of serious accidents, War Office inspectors finally got around to examining some of the wreckage, they discovered that the angle of incidence of the wings had been reduced by almost a half.[1]

The finest combat machines available to Russian pilots were either captured from the Germans or imported, primarily from France but also from England. The French sent many types, the best of which were the Nieuports and a few Spads. The British, in 1916 and early 1917, delivered 251 planes, including such types as the BE-2, the Sopwith 1½-Strutter and the Vickers FB-19 (a single-seater, very pretty to look at but thought not good enough for service on the western front). Russia also purchased from the United States some single-engine flying boats produced by the Curtiss Company, which had been transacting business with the Imperial government since 1911.

The organizational structure for the supply of equipment and stores to the Russian armed forces in World War I was bedeviled by graft, corrupt officials, political intrigue, and plain inefficiency. Furthermore, nearly all imported materiel had to enter the country through Murmansk and Archangel, from whence it was transported south by rail. Along several stretches there was no more than a single-track road, quite inadequate to meet the heavy traffic demand. When a British expeditionary force landed at these northern seaports in the summer of 1918, one of the first acts of the aviation contingent was to assemble the Nieuports and Sopwiths they found still reposing in waterfront warehouses and freight yards.

Taking into account all that Russian pilots were up against, it is small wonder there were only eighteen Russian aces in World War I—and only three with better than a dozen victories.

The foremost battle pilot in the service of the Czar was Captain Alexander Alexandrovich Kazakov, officially credited with the destruction of seventeen German aircraft. He was both taller, six feet in height, and older, in his middle twenties and balding, than most of his fellow airmen. With his lean face, his wide mustache, and piercing steel-blue eyes, Kazakov presented an austere and imperious countenance. He was, however, in the words of a man who served with him, "quiet, modest . . . unassuming . . . almost naïve." He did not like killing, and he attended, whenever possible, the funerals of his fallen adversaries. He was religious and always carried an icon of St. Nicholas on the instrument board of his plane. He had been a cavalry officer at the onset of the war and remained a keen horseman, usually managing to take his horses with him when his air unit moved.

Kazakov received his pilot's certificate in February 1915, at Sevastopol, where he conceived the idea of bringing down enemy machines by means of

[1] Robertson: *Air Aces of the 1914–1918 War.*

a weighted grapnel suspended on a long cable. With this contraption—or rather in spite of it—he achieved his initial victory on March 18, close by the village of Guzov. Kazakov had gone aloft to intercept an Albatros two-seater which was directing German artillery fire. As the enemy plane made for the lines, Kazakov began to unreel his iron hook, but the winch jammed before he could get more than a few yards of cable off the spool. Soldiers of both sides watched from the trenches below as the German observer opened fire with a rifle. Kazakov dived on the biplane and rammed it with his under-carriage. The Albatros fell like a dead bird while the jubilant Russian glided to a crash-landing behind his lines. After that, his tactics for attacking two-seaters were more orthodox.

On August 20, 1915, Kazakov was given command of an *otryad,* or squadron. Later, in 1917, he was put in charge of the newly formed No. 1 Fighter Group, comprising four squadrons. This unit became known as the "Death's Head" group since its aircraft—mostly Morane-Saulnier monoplanes and French Nieuports—were uniformly painted with a skull and crossbones on their rudders.

Near the end of the year, after the October Revolution, the Imperial Air Service broke up. Discipline vanished, and officers had to flee from the threatened violence of their subordinates. Most sought refuge with French and British forces on the eastern front. On March 3, 1918, the Soviet government signed the peace treaty of Brest Litovsk with Germany. By then the Allies had definitely set themselves against the Reds, and intervention began in partnership with White Guard counterrevolutionaries, who had maintained a provisional government in Siberia. British troops arrived to occupy Baku, Batum, and the oil fields of Transcaucasia. Captain Kazakov, meanwhile, with thirty-four other Russian pilots, was sent that summer by Sir John Hill, leader of the British military mission in Moscow, to join the expeditionary force which had landed at Archangel, Murmansk, and Bakeritza. Given the rank of major and placed in command of the Salvo-British, or No. 1 Squadron, Kazakov led his unit brilliantly through the next twelve months, flying first a Nieuport Type 17 and then a Sopwith Camel. He shot down, it has been estimated, fifteen "Bolos" (as Bolshevik aircraft were called by the British).

Kazakov's death was needless and unbefitting. It came soon after he heard that the British intended to recall their expeditionary force from Russia, which news seemed to disturb him traumatically. His comrades noted that he began acting edgy and morose. Five days later, on the evening of April 3, 1919, he ordered that his plane be readied for flight. His behavior was more peculiar than ever. When the engine was started, he did not advance the throttle gradually but instead slammed it full on. The engine stopped, and he was visibly angered. When the engine had been restarted and the chocks yanked from the wheels, the machine took off. Kazakov did not try to gain altitude, but kept the craft at twenty feet until he gathered maximum speed. Then, abruptly, he pulled up in a steep climb and started to loop. The little plane stalled halfway through the maneuver and dived vertically into the ground. Kazakov was killed instantly. He apparently made no effort to save himself.

Second on the list of Russian aces, with thirteen victories, was Lieutenant Commander Alexander P. Seversky of the Imperial Naval Air Service. In 1915, having just received his commission, Seversky was posted to the Second Bombing Squadron, based on Oesel Island in the Baltic Sea. On July 2, during the course of his first night misssion, his two-seater seaplane was shot down in the Gulf of Riga. The force of the crash caused a bomb to explode in the cockpit, killing the observer and blowing off Seversky's right leg. This might well have been the end of his flying career, but in fact it had hardly begun. After his convalescence and a term as an inspector of aircraft production, he returned at his own request to active duty. After one magnificent exploit, in which he shot down two Germans and saved a damaged Russian plane from a formation of enemy fighters, Seversky was awarded the very rare Order of the Gold Sword of St. George. The Kerensky government, in September 1917, appointed him vice-chairman of the Russian Naval Air Mission to the United States. Following the October Revolution, he remained in America to serve as a test pilot, to design aircraft and, among other things, to write the best-selling book, *Victory Through Air Power,* in 1942. He founded the Seversky Aero Corporation in 1922, before becoming a naturalized American citizen.

CHAPTER IX

·❧ Squadrons Elite ❧·

GERMAN AVIATION, AS IT had in 1916 at Verdun and the Somme, failed again in 1917 at the most critical junctures. Events at Arras in some respects paralleled happenings a year earlier on the western front. When the Allies set in motion their summer push along the Somme in 1916, fighter pilots equipped with De Havilland DH-2's and Type-17 Nieuports promptly exposed the long-reigning Fokker E-plane as an obsolescent machine whose only merit was fire power. In numbers, the British and French air forces possessed a three-to-one advantage. In organization, having already abandoned the practice of parceling out planes to small army-controlled units, they began flocking their warbirds under the wing of the highest command echelon. In employment, they were firmly committed to offensive action.

Preparation for the eastward drive along the Somme stressed the air weapon. For example, cooperation between the artillery and flying corps was sharpened by dividing the battle area among the available observation craft and gun batteries. Radio call letters were used for the first time to distinguish each zone; improved tuning devices facilitated the reception of wireless signals when dozens of aircraft were transmitting at once. From the outset, Allied cannoneers had everything their own way. While aerial observers located targets, bombers persistently raided the German rear, tying the German air force to a defensive war. The shelling itself disrupted communication between German infantry and artillery. Throughout the first three months of the Somme fighting —until the formidable D-type fighters came forth in sufficient numbers to offset the Allied advantage—the German infantry had only token support from its artillery, which was blinded by a lack of observers aloft. The Kaiser's troops were likewise deprived of tactical air cover, just as they were at Verdun, and in their bitterness they began reporting any and all planes as "Allied," regardless of markings. The result of this was that German aviators were frequently fired upon, occasionally with fatal effect, by German antiaircraft gunners.

In August, when the discredited General Falkenhayn handed in his resignation as supreme western commander, his successor, General Ludendorff, did much toward rectifying the costly aviation mistakes that had been made in the battles of Verdun and the Somme, both of which still raged. Ludendorff ordered a concentration of planes in the north, drawing many from Verdun, where the Germans had been maintaining constant pressure in the hope of sapping Allied strength from the Somme. By mid-October more than six hundred German aircraft—largely first-class machines—were being flown in missions along the Somme; the entire output of Albatros D-2 single-seaters, furthermore, was being funneled into the Somme sector, as was that of the almost-as-good Halberstadt and Pfalz D-planes. Though still outnumbered, German airmen now had the better combat craft and began to strike back. Following the Allied lead in formation flying, massing their strength in coordination with army ground action, they improved their methods both tactically and strategically, all of which endowed them with truly fearsome superiority. By the end of October, the British commander complained of 75 percent losses in fighter and reconnaissance machines. The Germans, paced by Jasta 2, the notorious Boelcke Squadron, knocked down 311 Allied planes between September and December, losing but thirty-nine themselves. Only bad winter weather spared the Allied air forces from more of the same terrible punishment through December and January. But the die had been cast for the subsequent spring, and when the weather mellowed in February 1917, the ordeal began anew for British and French airmen. It would reach its culmination in "Bloody April," in the hotly contested sky over Arras.

On April 7, just two days before the British attack on Arras, Squadron No. 56 of the Royal Flying Corps, arrived on the western front and proceded to Vert Galand airdrome, some six miles from Doullens on the road to Amiens. Among the pilots in the squadron was Captain Albert Ball, the leading British ace, now a flight commander, happy to be back at the front after seven months of monotony as a combat instructor in England. After leaving France in October 1916, Ball said during an interview with a reporter in Nottingham: "To bring down a lot of Huns, you have to be patient and practically live in the air. There are not many of them about and you have to be quick and seize your chances or the bird will have flown away. Sometimes you will make ten flights in a day and never get a fight."

It did not take long for Ball and his illustrious comrades in No. 56 to find that conditions at the front had changed. From the time Ball left France in the previous autumn, the German air service had retained the whip hand. German flyers had acquired the habit of the offensive, though not to the extent they might have, and had been savagely exploiting the advantages of their superior machines. By the time No. 56 Squadron set up housekeeping at Vert Galand, the Germans were at the peak of their effort, thoroughly at home in their aircraft, and although outnumbered as at almost every period of the war, ready to pay a heroic price to stay in control of the sky. It was a more crucial situation than Ball had known in the autumn, a different war entirely.

Now the fighting was not in the German back areas but over the lines and on the British side of the trenches. The Germans exerted their strongest effort in the region of Cambrai and Douai, on the Arras front, where in March they gained tremendously in confidence for having noted that there were still, even after the winter doldrums, no British machines able to give them real competition. The picture, however, was not so rosy as they thought. Conserving its best flying stock for the forthcoming battle of Arras, the R.F.C. appeared weaker than was actually the case. Newly developed aircraft—the SE-5 fighter with its synchronized twin Vickers guns, the big but nimble and superbly armed F-2B Bristol fighter, as well as the De Havilland DH-4— were purposely being held in abeyance for the impending Arras campaign. Suspended at the same time was the production of such older types as the Sopwith two-seaters, planes with an enviable history, which were dangerous to attack even when they were outdated, mainly because they seemed to attract determined crews. The pusher types, too, including the Vickers *Gun Bus*, the DH-2, the FE-2 and FE-8, their venerable service as fighters ended, were written off, except for night bombing. Through that torturous spring British reconnaissance and artillery-spotting planes took the brunt of the beating as usual. But their vital work on behalf of the army continued, although the best fighter craft could not yet be used for protection. These things help to account for the heavy casualties suffered through February, March, and April—but there was also Manfred von Richthofen.

In the story of military aviation, 1917 must be recorded as the year of Richthofen. Between January 4, when he shot down a Sopwith 1½-Strutter on the Somme, and November 30, when he killed R.F.C. Captain P. T. Townsend in an SE-5 near Moevres, the Red Knight bagged forty-eight British aircraft and increased his running total of victories to sixty-three. In April alone, during the siege of Arras, he dispatched twenty-one enemy planes from the sky, as many as were claimed that month by all the members combined of his former squadron, Jasta Boelcke, who were no tyros in the air-fighting department. Now the leading ace of the war, the commanding officer of Jasta 11, and soon to become ringmaster of his own "flying circus," the twenty-five-year-old nobleman was in the full flush of success, at the height of his combat career.

Rittmeister Manfred, Freiherr von Richthofen was, of course, the enemy pilot most talked about in R.F.C. messes along the front. Here he was colloquially known as "the Baron," "the jolly old Baron," and "the dear old Baron," almost always with that cordial regard traditionally voiced by proper Englishmen for a worthy opponent, whether in war or in sport. If ungrudging admiration be accorded an enemy, that of the R.F.C. was not misplaced in Richthofen. Of the eighty planes brought down by the baron before his death in April 1918, all were British. Precisely 130 pilots and observers were his victims, eighty-three of whom were killed and accounted for, with eleven missing and presumed dead. Just as Max Immelmann and Oswald Boelcke had inspired the whole German air force to greater efforts and a fuller confidence, so Richthofen gave added courage where it was never a scarce commodity, among the rank and file of German airmen. His presence in action was probably of more importance to German morale than that of any pilot ever was to the R.F.C. He knew, furthermore, how to exploit his prestige and did so to the utmost degree. But it is a question whether he did so as a national paradigm or as a selfish individualist.

Some of Richthofen's traits were undeniably unattractive. His preoccupation with souvenirs and trophies and his yearning for medals and promotions reveal an appetite for personal fame and glory. In battle he was not a gracious winner; shooting down the enemy and getting credit for the victory, doing so as expeditiously and safely as possible, were all that seemed to matter to Richthofen through most of his career. He was never a man to gamble against odds. His reluctance to take risks grew in direct proportion to his experience at the front and the radiance of his image. Always mindful of the tactics inculcated by the lamented Boelcke, Richthofen would ride the higher air at the head of his formation and seek hostile machines. He seldom fought alone. When a dogfight was on, his usual procedure was to remain above until his chance came to dive at some unfortunate straggler on the fringe of the melee or at any other opponent who happened to be at a disadvantage. Then Richthofen would descend like a hawk upon the selected victim. "Everything in the air beneath me," he once boasted, "is lost." His pilots were all crack specialists who did no other work but hunt for Allied machines to destroy. They were not used even for escort duty, save when they furtively accompanied a decoy plane of the kind that British, French, and, later, American airmen learned to treat with much wariness. An unfrightened, lumbering old German two-seater in the offing and down low, or a couple of them, imparted to Allied pilots a distinct warning of possible danger lurking in the sun or the clouds above. This alluring trap was a favorite gambit of Richthofen and the adroit pilots in his charge.

Almost every airman had now and then some bowels of mercy for an opponent hopelessly outclassed. Such compassion was alien to Richthofen's philosophy of warfare. In his autobiography, published shortly before his death, the baron wrote of one fight against a British two-seater in the course of which he perceived the enemy pilot to be wounded and the plane to be showing signs of catching fire. The German ace, in a rare mood of kindness, maneuvered so as to compel his adversary to land in the German lines. This humane consideration was, however, not usual with the Red Knight, who was out to beat records and gain title as the foremost German battle flyer. His avarice for victories was well known and often discussed with no little acerbity among the pilots he led. Though never to his face, they complained that he robbed them of their just recognition. Certainly, the large account of victories with which he was credited by his government would have required pruning in the case of a British aviator in the R.F.C. Richthofen's official score of eighty planes shot down was widely declared to include some sent to earth by his squadron in combined attack, where the destruction of a victim was the work of several machines. On at least two or three occasions, moreover, he was seen to administer the finishing stroke to a plane already crippled by one of his subordinates in a fair fight.

All the bad that can be said of him has here been said, and the portrait must be balanced. Richthofen's unique and demanding role in the war goes a long way toward excusing his less endearing qualities as an air fighter. That he was a merciless warrior does not even need an apology, for his job was not to spare the enemy but to kill him, and any other conception of a soldier's duty in battle is cheap nonsense. If a soldier has too many compunctions about killing, he may in his procrastination be killed. Richthofen, therefore, perhaps felt constrained to set an example of brutal, pitiless action against the enemy. Since he was the peerless example of the German air hero, it was important for him to pile up an impressive victory score, as the high command repeatedly exhorted him to do. Being an asset of incalculable value to the German cause, his well-being was a matter of prime concern, more so to the government and people of Germany than to himself. General Ludendorff appraised Richthofen's worth to be that of three divisions of infantry. It was really more, for the loss of Richthofen was the loss of a symbol of German invincibility.

He was, then, a man in the middle, pressed on the one hand always to win more victories, and, on the other hand, to avoid harm to himself. He was a ropedancer endlessly urged on to new and more wonderful feats by a taskmaster who at the same time begged him please not to fall and hurt himself. For a fighter pilot to seek an ever-greater number of victories and yet not expose himself to danger were mutually exclusive endeavors. And these factors must be mixed in the pigments used to paint a picture of the man, to dim the bright hues of legend and bring forward the colors of truth. His effort to satisfy the contradictory demands on him explains, probably better than any other analysis of Richthofen, why he behaved the way he did.

Born in Breslau on May 2, 1892, Manfred von Richthofen descended from a stock of Prussian junkers that acquired its baronage far back in the seventeenth century. His paternal forebears were landowners, squires of the county seats who managed their estates with thrift and efficiency and found their fun in hunting and riding. On his mother's side, in the family of Schickfuss, it was the same. Conservatives to the bone, it was their aim to work hard, respect order, and to amuse themselves in the saddle and on the game trail. Old Uncle Alexander Schickfuss, after shooting the fur and feathers off all species of Silesian fauna, became somewhat renowned as a huntsman in the wilds of Africa and Asia. Richthofen's father, a career officer in a Uhlan regiment, bedecked the walls of his Schweidnitz home with four hundred deer heads and stuffed birds, all brought down by his gun. He served through the war as a major of reserve, but died a short while after the Armistice.

From this line of modern primitives came the future Nimrod of the air. Conformity, reputed to be the forte of his country, was not bred into him. He was essentially an individual. The spirit of the hunter, the stalker, was strong within him, and with it ran a pride in conquest, the natural outgrowth of vital competitive and combative senses. Even as a small boy, the hunt was his life and the trophy his goal. Before he was big enough to stay on his feet against the recoil of a shotgun, he was caught in the act of shooting tame geese on the family pond. Richthofen was like his father and, no doubt, like all his ancestors in the matter of trophies. He believed it incumbent upon the hunter to show the prey he ran to earth. For him the war in the air was the highest expression of his ingrained urge to hunt. He fought, not with hate, but with an awareness of duty and a love of fighting. It was his joy, his sport, his passion. He had the courage to kill and be killed, and the war was his hunting license. On leave from killing at the front, he hunted deer, elk, boar, and birds, and brought their heads to the manor house at Schweidnitz. He was brave and knew it, gloried in it, flaunted it with his challenge to the world of his enemies. Wounded and decorated, he became the guest of kings and queens. The youth of a nation made him its idol, cheered him, followed him on the street. Girls by the thousands worshipped his photograph and filled his mail with letters by the sackful. There was one he wanted to make his wife, but not his widow. He knew he was going to be killed. Death visited every air squadron much too regularly for him to believe otherwise. Under the date of June 22, 1916, he wrote to his mother: "What did you say about Immelmann's death? In time, death comes to each of us here."

In the escutcheon of the Richthofen family there was a motto which read: "Clear like an unshaded crystal remained the splendor of the name." To no member of the clan was this more apt than to the illustrious Manfred. He was the eldest son, followed by Lothar, who was also to become an ace. Another brother, Bolko, too young to serve in the war, was born in 1903. According to Prussian custom, the senior entered the cadet corps. This was followed with a lieutenancy in Uhlan Regiment No. 1, with which unit he rode into action early in the war, first on the eastern front and then on the western, in Alsace. Richthofen was quick to discern that the glad days of cavalry were over, and at his own request, he was transferred into the infantry, where he hoped to see more fighting. When, in April 1915, he received instructions to prepare himself for quartermaster duty many miles removed from the front lines, he wrote to the commanding general of his division. It was concise and rudely candid. "My dear Excellency," he wrote, "I have not gone to war to collect cheese and eggs, but for another purpose." The rest of the letter was an official application for his transfer to aviation.

His sarcastic request gained him his wish, and it is not recorded that his departure was accompanied by any great sorrow on the part of his superiors. In any case, he went in May to Cologne for training as an aerial observer, thence to a reconnaissance unit in Russia. His next move brought him back again to the west as a member of Germany's first and still very hush-hush bomber squadron, the so-called Ostend Carrier Pigeons. But Richthofen was dissatisfied here with the extended intervals of inactivity, as well as the big twin-engine aircraft coming into service as bombers—which he deprecated as "apple barges"—and he asked to return to reconnaissance flying. This plea, too, was granted, and soon afterwards, with his pilot, a Lieutenant Osteroth, he succeeded in downing a Farman. Since it fell into the French lines, however, no verification of the victory was forthcoming, which irritated him. Nevertheless, Richthofen then knew what he wanted. The huntsman's lust in him had been aroused. And just a few days later, on October 1, to give added impetus to his desires, he met for the first time Oswald Boelcke.

Boelcke was already well known for having shot down four hostile aircraft, a feat then still generally regarded as phenomenal. Richthofen posed the obvious question. "How," he asked, "do you manage to shoot them down?"

"It's elementary," Boelcke replied. "I fly close to my man, aim carefully, fire, and then, of course, down he falls."

Richthofen reflected that he employed somewhat the same technique, but his opponents did not seem to go down so readily. Thinking it over, he concluded that the difference lay not as much with the aviator as with the plane he flew. Boelcke had the benefit of a new, light Fokker monoplane and a synchronized machine gun, while he worked a ring-mounted weapon aboard a torpid two-seater biplane. He resolved to become a pilot and indeed, after twenty-five training flights, he went up solo for the first time. He did well until the landing, when, failing to slow enough in his approach, he crashed. More weeks of training and examination followed; then, on the day after Christmas, he received the reward he craved, his pilot's certificate. It appears, though, that his instructors did not have sufficient confidence in his ability to send him to the front. He chafed under the delay. On January 11, 1916, he wrote to his mother: "Since spending the New Year's holiday at Schwerin [where he toured the Fokker plant], I have not flown once. It rains incessantly here, and I seem to be making no progress. I should love to be at the front right now. I think there is a lot going on there."

During spells of fair weather in January and February he undertook practice flights around Germany, landing at Breslau and Luben, and once at his home in Schwidnitz. Another excursion brought him back to Schwerin, ostensibly to improve his knowledge of aircraft engines, but more probably to solicit the influence of Anthony Fokker and thereby secure an assignment to the front as an E-plane pilot. If such was his scheme, it availed him nothing. In March, upon being posted to an air station opposite the besieged bastion of Verdun, he was piloting an Albatros two-seater. Richthofen's penchant for combat could not be stifled, however. He wanted a fight in the air, with himself operating both the flying controls and the machine gun. Accordingly, as the French were doing with their Nieuports, he mounted a gun on the top wing of his Albatros to fire upward and straight ahead over the propeller. At this stage of the war it was almost unheard of for more than one machine gun to be carried. Other pilots ridiculed the idea, and his observer might well have considered it as poaching upon his preserve, but Richthofen anxiously sought an early opportunity to test its practicality.

The chance came on April 26, when Richthofen and his observer sighted a Nieuport machine wearing French colors. The two watched the enemy plane for some time and then flew toward it, although Richthofen was not yet clear in his mind as to how he should make his attack. The problem was solved for him as the Frenchman swerved to fly away, exposing himself to attack from behind. This maneuver would have been safe had the German plane been equipped only with a rear machine gun, and it is probable that the Nieuport pilot did not notice the unusual mounting of the forward gun on the Albatros.

Richthofen closed to within sixty yards of the Nieuport. So great had been his disappointments as a pilot that he had small expectation of bagging his prey, but he did want to reap the profits of practice. Aiming at the tail of the craft directly in front of him, he fired a burst of shots. The Nieuport answered by zooming upward and sideslipping on one wing. Richthofen was then surprised to see the French plane cartwheeling down through the air. Both he and his observer thought the French pilot was not really in trouble. They thought he was trying to trick them, to lure them down into a disadvantageous position by pretending to be falling out of control. Like most German airmen they were rather contemptuous of, and sometimes bewildered by what they regarded as "antics" on the part of Allied aviators. Whereas the French and British taught and encouraged aerobatics in their training programs, the Germans still held the view in 1916 that "stunts" were of no practical value. But this particular Frenchman was not shamming. He was dead or dying. His Nieuport never righted itself. It crashed into the forest behind Fort Douaumont, and Richthofen's observer clapped him on the shoulder to congratulate him upon his victory.

At almost the very same locale that day a Fokker pilot destroyed another French aircraft, a two-seater, and the daily German war communique that evening stated: "Two hostile flying machines have been shot down in aerial fighting above Fleury, south and west of Douaumont." After his breakfast the next morning, Richthofen gloated in a letter to his mother: "In haste—

some happy news. Look at the communique of yesterday. . . . One of these planes was dropped by my gun. . . ." He had won nameless acknowledgment, but for the second time was thwarted by the army rule that ignored, insofar as an airman's record was concerned, any planes brought down behind enemy lines. His pride in achievement was great, but he felt a certain pique in being again denied what he considered his just due of credit for the kill.

The opportunity came for a few uneventful flights in a Fokker monoplane, then he was posted back to the Russian front on two-seaters again, which disgruntled him sorely. But the trip east led directly to the turning point of his career. There, shortly afterwards, at Kovel, he was interviewed by Oswald Boelcke during the latter's inspection tour of the eastern theater. The battle of the Somme had begun in France, and air supremacy had passed to the Allied side, with painful repercussions for German ground forces. Commanding the German First Army in the embattled river valley, General Karl von Bülow described the situation with an insight into the effects of tactical aviation which few of his contemporary officers seemed to have. "The state of affairs," he reported, "has been aggravated by the enemy's superiority in the air. . . . Not only do enemy flyers direct artillery fire, unmolested, but by day and by night they harass our infantry with bombs and machine guns. . . . Although losses thus caused have been small, their occurrence has had a decided lowering effect on troop morale. . . ." A German prisoner taken at Delville wood had scratched in his diary: "During the day, one hardly dares to be seen in the trenches, owing to the English airplanes. They fly so low that it it a wonder they do not pull us out of the trenches. Nothing is to been seen of our German hero airmen."

Neither the broad view of the general nor the worm's-eye view of the trench soldier was exaggerated. British aircraft made continual reconnaissances and bombing and strafing sorties; they spotted for heavy artillery massed along the entire twenty-five-mile front. In vain the Fokkers tried to check them. German pilots found themselves suddenly powerless against the DH-2 and the Nieuport. They lacked the physical means to repel the British air offensive, and the inspiration, too. Max Immelmann was dead, and Oswald Boelcke was absent from the western front by Imperial decree. Boelcke, then sojourning in Bulgaria, was therefore hurriedly recalled to organize and command a new kind of fighter-plane squadron—a Jagdstaffel—such as he himself had envisioned and proposed four months earlier at Verdun. Given a free hand to select his men, he returned via the Russian front, visiting airfields along the route to muster suitable talent.

Upon hearing that Boelcke was to make a stopover at Kovel, Richthofen could not conceal his excitement. Boelcke, when he arrived, wearing the star of the Order Pour le Mérite, took temporary quarters in a railroad carriage. Outside this a long queue of hopeful pilots formed up; Richthofen, fidgeting with nervousness, stood near its head. His heart beat faster as he was ushered in for his audience with the nonesuch of German aviation. To Richthofen's great relief, Boelcke remembered his face and recalled their previous meeting. The interview, as Richthofen later recounted it, was brief and informal.

"Would you like to go with me to the Somme and see some real fighting?" Boelcke inquired.

Richthofen answered, "Ja!"—a bit too eargerly, he feared.

"Then you shall," said Boelcke.

Three days afterward, the future Red Knight was speeding across Germany on a train, bound for that valley of blood, the Somme basin. "From now on," he later observed, "began the finest time of my life."

So commenced his rise to everlasting fame. It has been said that when Boelcke was once asked who among his protégés would be his successor, he pointed to Richthofen. Whether this is true or not, Boelcke was a capable fisher of men, and Manfred von Richthofen soon proved his best catch.

After bagging his first confirmed kill on September 17, 1916, shooting down R.F.C. Lieutenants Rees and Morris in their FE-2 in the course of that initial outing of Jasta 2, Richthofen piled success upon success. By November 9, he had eight victories. On November 23, the distinguished Major Hawker fell to the baron's guns, his eleventh victim. When he had run his score to sixteen, he was appointed to command Jasta 11 and awarded the Order Pour le Mérite two days later. His luck held, even after his eighteenth victorious combat, when the upper wing of his Albatros D-3 splintered in the air and he miraculously escaped injury in a crash that jarred the plane completely to pieces. His impact upon his enemies was felt acutely on March 9, 1917, when he led a quartet of Albatroses against nine FE-8's of R.F.C. Squadron No. 40. While Richthofen disposed of a DH-2 that had evidently been attracted to the fight, his men picked off four of the "Fees" and left the rest of the German air arm nothing to claim that day except an antiquated Morane-Saulnier Parasol, one of those it was the misfortune of R.F.C. Squadron No. 3 to be still flying. His luck was magical. Toward the end of March he was shot down in an action against fifteen British aircraft and once more walked away unscathed from a crash landing. By April 2, he had thirty-three silver trophies in his private collection, each representing a British machine blasted from the sky.

Richthofen, young, dauntless, with sharp eyes and nerves so far unimpaired, was at his zenith. He was fully addicted now to the visceral joys of the aerial hunt, and April 1917 was the month of his greatest personal glory. His twenty-one victories that month averaged out to one for every day he flew, a record unequaled by any other pilot of World War I. At the head of his fighting unit, he flew the heavens like a rapacious hawk in search of "fresh meat," as he often referred to his victims. He produced results and demanded ever-increased "production" from the members of his Jasta. He kept detailed accounts of their flights and combats and grew intolerant of those who failed to reap their share of the grisly harvest.

Dealing death in the air in such magnitude was beyond the experience, knowledge, and imagination of Germany's war lords. It became the boast at supreme headquarters that Richthofen's presence on any new sector was sufficient to cause extensive Allied troop movements, which was, of course, wishful hyperbole. But Richthofen was definitely and conspicuously a prime mover in the conflict aloft. Paced by Richthofen, the German air service during that "Bloody April" above the Arras front, inflicted upon the R.F.C. its worst casualty rate of any thirty-day period of the war. Emboldened by Richthofen, German airmen fought with impassioned fervor and pushed the line of air battle from their rear areas to the enemy's front yard. They gained an aerial superiority which Germany would never enjoy again before the Armistice. Between March 31 and May 11, the Germans claimed to have destroyed four British planes for each of their own planes lost, a total of 120 victories as compared to thirty defeats. Yet it appears that they understated British losses, for the official dossier of the R.F.C. reveals that, in the month of April alone, 151 British aircraft were counted missing.

The decision of the War Office in London to withhold the general introduction of new aircraft at the front until the Arras campaign had been opened was to a large degree responsible for the egregious death toll among British flyers, who were grossly outclassed in their obsolescent pusher-type machines. But in spite of this handicap, the British, with characteristic tenacity, refused to change their offensive policy and continued pressing the fight. It made a difference. Whereas, during the interval of Allied superiority at the Somme in 1916, the German air force had been reduced to virtual impotence, the turning of the tables did not bring the same results at Arras in 1917. Although the severity of British losses broke all existing records, R.F.C. pilots were not allowed—nor did they show any inclination—to deviate from the standing order to "carry on" as usual. There were still plenty of last year's machines to fly, and never a lack of young Englishmen eager to escape the filth, tedium, and horror of the trenches and to fight it out in the clouds. They took off daily in their winged crates to encounter almost certain death. It was, as one reporter wrote, "like sending forth butterflies to sting wasps."

Among the emerging grandees in Jasta 11 at this time was Lothar von Richthofen, Manfred's brother, who joined the unit in March directly from flight school. Prior to his pilot's training, he had served as a dragoon in the heavy cavalry, and then, for five months, as an observer in the air force. Manfred, who had originally prevailed upon him to enter the aviation branch and pulled strings to have him assigned to Jasta 11, painstakingly tutored him in the ways and means of aerial combat. For a fortnight after his arrival at the Douai airdrome Lothar was pledged to practice locally, sharpening his marksmanship, familiarizing himself with his machine and with the district geography. Then, like a fledgling bird of prey being guided on its first foraging trip by its doting mother, he was taken on an offensive patrol by Manfred, who bade him to watch the method of attack, but to stay clear if a fight developed. This prohibition, however, went against Lothar's impetuous nature. On his third patrol with his brother, when a target presented itself, Lothar gave chase. Manfred, alarmed at first to see his ward part company, felt a glow of pride as Lothar skillfully pursued his quarry—and shot it down.

If anything, Lothar was even more determined to achieve victory credits than was his already famous brother. Manfred himself insinuated as much when he wrote of the younger Richthofen as a "shooter," while likening himself again to a "hunter." These terms, by his definition, described two disparate types of fighter pilots. Manfred was the sort who carefully chose his opportunities, weighing all the factors before committing himself to the attack. And once he had achieved a kill, his goading instinct was for the moment appeased; not for fifteen minutes or so would he feel the urge for renewed aggression. Lothar was distinguishable in Manfred's mind as the "shooter," the impulsive and perhaps somewhat trigger-happy charger who rushed after the foe at every sighting and was insatiable in his quest.

Just as they approached combat differently, so their tactics differed once the battle began. Soon after they started patrolling together, Manfred was horrified the first time he saw Lothar's Albatros flip over on its back and plunge, spinning earthward, with a British machine close behind. As he watched, the Albatros righted itself and banked into a favorable position from which to fusillade the plane that had tailed it down. It was a ruse which Lothar used often again. He was an exponent of aerobatics—one of relatively few on the German side—and Manfred was not.

The variance in their attitudes and techniques led now and then to minor rifts in their relationship, as, for example, on the occasion of Lothar scoring his second and third victories in a squadron tangle with a formation of British raiders. Hounding an enemy machine, Lothar put a burst of shots into its fuel tank and saw it blossom into fire and smoke. Without waiting to ascertain whether or not the stricken machine would go down before it reached the British lines, he immediately switched his attention to another British craft nearby, killed its pilot, and followed it down until he saw it crash alongside a German infantry bunker. After landing, Lothar tweakingly asked Manfred, "How many did you get?" Manfred replied, "One." And Lothar retorted, "I got two!" Manfred was visibly annoyed at his brother's conceit. He therefore challenged Lothar's claim, ordering him up to the lines to secure confirmation. Dejected, Lothar returned with verification for only one victory. His claim for two was subsequently allowed, however, since both the British planes were seen to have crashed by other members of the flight. At Manfred's bidding, they had purposely delayed filing their reports to cure Lothar of his cockiness.

The Richthofen brothers—Manfred, the cool, methodical executioner, and Lothar, the flashy and precipitant go-getter—being brothers, were fundamentally birds of a feather after all. They both relished the thrills of sky battle and the abundant prestige it brought to its champions. Both were animated by personal ambition, certainly more than by any abstract idealism, and this, too, caused a slight but persistent friction to develop between them. Its basis was *jalousie de metier*, and it subtly manifested itself when Lothar showed that he was a remarkable adept at shooting down enemy aircraft, as witness his attainment of twenty victories in his first five weeks of operational flying. Lothar made no secret of his aspiration to outshine his brother, and Manfred admittedly saw in Lothar a potential rival for the plaudits which belonged to Germany's ranking ace. They never discussed the competition between them except in ostensible jest, though each must have sensed that the other's smile was perhaps artificial. Manfred's feeling in this was plainly ambivalent. On the one hand, he felt a big brother's pride and feared for Lothar's safety; on the other hand, despite family ties, he begrudged Lothar's mercurial success. The same emotional dichotomy affected Lothar. Such, at least, was the case with both of them if the writings of several of their contemporaries in the German air service are to be believed.

Manfred's disquiet, moreover, was not entirely unwarranted. Considering that Lothar started his pilot's career a year later and was grounded three times with serious wounds, that he thus participated in decidedly fewer combats, and that he enjoyed none of the tactical prerogatives that Manfred enjoyed as leader—such as staying high above a fight and plucking easy victims—the younger Richthofen did exceptionally well in scoring his forty victories. It is likely that his headlong zeal for action stemmed from the realization that he needed to get things done in a hurry if he expected ever to emulate Manfred. Had circumstances been kinder, he would undoubtedly have approached much nearer the eighty-victory mark set by his brother. Lothar was that good a fighter pilot.

In this regard, it should be noted also that Manfred, some months afterward, regretfully observed that he, too, contrary to his huntsman's conscience, but citing the exigencies of war as his justification, had turned into a "shooter" like Lothar. Yet facts do not support his contention and rather contradict it. Since instead of becoming more reckless, as his statement would imply, he grew increasingly cautious and calculating, his reasons for embracing such a notion and revising his image are hard to fathom. Could it be that he did not really believe what he was saying after all, but said it in an attempt to confute those who belittled him as being too unadventurous? Although this criticism—which was indeed heard from many rank-and-file pilots at the front —contained more than a grain of truth, it was unenlightened and redolent with envy, and it overlooked the obligations he had to heed as the standard-bearer of German aviation.

During that hectic April at Arras, flying with Jasta 11 under the watchful eye of his brother, Lothar von Richthofen participated in more combat action than most other airmen had seen in far longer service. On the last day of the month a new German policy was implemented in the air, which became painfully evident to British aviators who met a massed formation of about twenty machines sweeping over the battle area. Made up entirely of D-class fighter craft, the formation comprised flights from Jastas 3, 4, 11, and 33. Because the red Albatroses of Jasta 11 were most readily identified, the formation was promptly dubbed "Richthofen's circus" by the Royal Flying Corps. The same epithet, two months later, would be permanently applied to Jagdgeschwader No. 1, the chase group commanded by Manfred von Richthofen until his death in April 1918. The formation encountered by the R.F.C. on this day, however, was only a temporary grouping sent up to test the efficacy of the Jagdgeschwader plan. Although the participating pilots, from four separate Jastas, had never previously flown together as a unit, they met with moderate success in a series of meetings with enemy SE-5's, FE-2's, and Sopwith Triplanes. The resultant losses were six British to five German. Manfred von Richthofen, who departed the next day for a six-week vacation, which included audiences with the Emperor and Empress, argued that better results could be anticipated once proper tactics had been evolved for the group formation and the flights had been fully rehearsed in teamwork.

In his report of that day's activities, the baron amply praised the Sopwith Triplane, which he had heard about but never before seen. A three-winged single-seater of the Royal Naval Air Service, its Vickers gun synchronized with the new hydraulically operated Constantinesco-Colley (C.C.) gear, the so-called Tripe Hound went into service on the western front with three naval squadrons in support of the hard-pressed R.F.C. The first triplane to enter combat, it completely outclassed the hitherto very successful Albatros D-3, as well as the Halberstadt and Pfalz D-planes, having more speed and a tighter turning radius, though only half the firepower. Naval Squadrons Nos. 1, 8, and 10 made their presence felt during the air crises in April, May, and June. Flight B of No. 10, known as the Black Flight, accounted for eighty-seven German aircraft before July. The pilots were Canadians all, foremost among them Flight Commander Raymond Collishaw, and their machines bore the names *Black Death, Black Maria,, Black Roger, Black Prince,* and *Black Sheep*. The description "Black Flight" referred to these names, not to the color of the planes, which was olive drab.

Introduced immediately after the Sopwith Triplane was the more conventional-looking Sopwith Camel biplane, a yet more deadly fighter, and the last operational three-wingers were duly exchanged for Camels in November 1917 by the R.N.A.S. In light of the fact that only 150 were built, it is surprising how much they influenced the trend of design. A host of triplanes and—presumably in the conviction that if three wings were good, four would be better—quadruplanes were constructed by the leading German and Austro-Hungarian aircraft manufacturers in efforts to match the performance of the extraordinary "Tripe Hound." Albatros, D.F.W., and L.V.G. were among the companies to build experimental triplanes, but Fokker and Pfalz were the only ones to perfect three-wing designs promising enough for service production. The more memorable was the Fokker Dreidekker, or DR-1, which arrived at the front near the end of August, was flown by several German aces, including Manfred von Richthofen and Werner Voss, and remained in production until May 1918, when the splendid Fokker D-7 made its appearance. Well over three hundred DR-1 triplanes were turned out by the Fokker works before the design was scrapped.

Manfred von Richthofen left Douai airdrome on May 1 to begin his long and well-earned holiday from war. Having been summoned to an audience with the Kaiser at general headquarters in Cologne, he flew there directly as a passenger in a D.F.W. two-seater which was piloted by the technical officer of Jasta 11, Lieutenant Krefft. Coming straight from the front in an airplane that had little room for luggage, he wore an ordinary field-gray uniform under his leather flying suit that contrasted sharply with the immaculately dressed staff officers. The next morning he was presented to the Kaiser after progressing through interviews with Field Marshal Hindenburg, the chief of general staff, and General Ludendorff. During their talks with Richthofen, Ludendorff discussed effective ways of killing the enemy, whereas Hindenburg digressed upon the average number of shots necessary to kill a bison. Kaiser Wilhelm II had evidently been briefed about his famous visitor, for Richthofen was congratulated for his fifty-second victory and also his twenty-fifth birthday, which happened to be on May 2. There followed a birthday gift from the Kaiser—a bust of his royal self. Formalities were by no means over. That evening the aging Hindenburg, who nevertheless outlived Richthofen by almost two decades, had arranged an elegant dinner in his honor. And for the next day, the Empress had expressed a wish to meet him, which entailed a flight to fashionable Bad Homburg, where she was in residence. From then until his return to the front on June 14, Richthofen spent most of his time tramping the Black Forest and various private preserves in search of animal instead of human game.

From May 1, the day on which Richthofen flew off from Douai with the prospect of a long leave ahead of him, there was instead of an all-red Albatros at the head of Jasta 11, a red Albatros with yellow ailerons and elevators. Although the planes of the squadron were uniformly red, only that of the elder Richthofen was without any patch of distinguishing color on its wings, fuselage or empennage. Yellow was Lothar von Richthofen's trademark, chosen because it was the ceremonial hue of the dragoon regiment in which he had formerly served. Manfred, the dutiful if apprehensive big brother, had entrusted command of his squadron to Lothar prior to his departure, no doubt with an emphatic warning not to do anything rash. Events conspired immediately to try Lothar's ability as a surrogate commander. The trial, severe as it was, did not find him wanting.

The advent of new and superior aircraft moved the R.F.C. in May to intensify its usual offensive policy. Equipped more and more with SE-5's, Bristol fighters, De Havilland DH-4's, and updated Nieuports, with naval aviators on the scene in their Sopwith Triplanes—and with the Sopwith Camels now beginning to trickle to the front—the British air service was determined to avenge the massacre of "Bloody April" and to seize, once and for all, a thorough mastery in the sky. As a consequence, there was considerable activity for the next few weeks in which Jasta 11 played so prominent a part that Douai and its environs became the locus of increased aerial activity by the R.F.C. It was during this fierce and constant fighting that the brilliant British ace, Captain Ball, while leading a flight of No. 56 Squadron on May 7, was mysteriously shot down. Due to the bad weather and the poor visibility that day, which made it impracticable to fly in full formation, Lothar von Richthofen had wisely split his unit into three independent sections, or *Ketten*. This explains why there was no great clash of formations that evening, but a series of skirmishes and single combats in and out of the clouds.

If victory scores are discounted as a criterion of excellence, Ball, with his forty-four victories, was probably, as we have seen, the greatest of British air fighters in World War I. Although comparisons may be odious, he was much the counterpart of Oswald Boelcke. He did much to originate and adapt the tactics and techniques of air fighting in the R.F.C. of that period, just as Boelcke had done for German aviation, and early stalwarts like Jean Navarre and George Guynemer for French aviation. Albert Ball brought to combat an individual touch. He fought with ingenuity, skill, and absolute courage. He believed in closing with his adversaries, even to the extent of imperiling his own beloved Nieuport. It has always been the custom to measure the worth of a fighter pilot by the number of victories he gained, without regard to time or circumstance. Such an assessment is necessarily invalid, as are most oversimplifications. Ball and his gallant contemporaries, friend and foe alike, must be assessed against the fact that fighting techniques were still then largely empirical. With no one to teach them very much about their precarious vocation, Ball and Boelcke and the other pioneer aces were innovators whose probative experiments in action paved the way for others who, in 1917 and 1918, had a fund of ready advice and experience on which to draw. These later pilots, furthermore, though their courage and skill were no less genuine than those of their predecessors, flew better planes, with better armament, against more plentiful targets. Whereas Ball complained of a shortage of enemy machines in 1916, combats were commonplace by 1917. Thus, it is the comparison between the early and the later ace, the estimate which relies solely upon their respective victory scores, which is not merely odious but misleading. And it becomes an interesting, if perhaps futile, speculation to wonder what a Roland Garros, say, or a Jean Navarre might have accomplished with one of the more sophisticated aircraft of the later period of the war, and, conversely, how well a Richthofen would have done aboard, for example, an E-type Fokker monoplane.

The riddles surrounding Albert Ball's death remain unanswered. Although dubious theory held that he was shot down by Lothar von Richthofen, Lothar himself put in a claim for a Sopwith Triplane, presumably of No. 8 Squadron, R.N.A.S., which unit by chance skirted the vicinity of the action that evening. Lieutenant Wilhelm Allmenroder, of Jasta 11, stated that he unmistakably saw Lothar close behind an enemy biplane, firing at it as he tailed it down into the evening mist. Allmenroder's report noted that no other planes were about, and that the British machine seemed to be diving out of control when it and Lothar's Albatros disappeared into the lower darkness. Lothar afterward insisted that he had engaged a triplane, not a biplane, and had indeed shot somebody down. But he could not give a coherent account of the action. On his way back to Douai after nightfall, he lost his bearings and strayed across the British lines, still flying very low. Near Vimy ridge he was hit by ground fire and wounded in the hip. Bleeding profusely, he was racked with nausea and felt his consciousness ebbing away. Somehow he made it back to the German side and managed an emergency landing before he blacked out. To the vacationing Manfred von Richthofen there came a telegram informing him of his brother's misfortune.

Assured that Lothar would recover, Manfred continued shooting capercallie on the state hunting preserve in the Schwarzwald near Freiburg, unmindful of the fact that conditions at the front were fast changing from what they had been when he left only a week before. The beginning of June found him still hunting wild life, though now it was bison on the estate of the prince of Pless. Pitting his wits and rifle against these horned monarchs of the forest, which at that time existed in Europe only at Pless and on the lands of the late Czar Nicholas II at Bialowicza, elated him. Richthofen, with his own hands, assisted in the work of skinning a trophy-size bull he had brought down. He personally hacked off the enormous head, and after having it properly mounted, placed it on the wall over his bed in Schwidnitz, where it served to disturb the repose of a maiden aunt who occupied the room upon her visits to the ace's mother.

Richthofen's sport was cut short by some more bad news from the front. The struggle in the air had become a struggle indeed. The lopsided advantage enjoyed by German airmen through "Bloody April" no longer prevailed. The benefit of superior equipment, which had to a major degree been responsible for Richthofen's record bag of victories that month, had evaporated. The new British aircraft had at last reached the front in sufficient quantity to disconcert a German air force that, having had things its own way for so many months, had tended to grow complacent at the upper command level, if not among the pilots and gunners who could never permit themselves, no matter what the odds, to be overconfident.

Because of this complacency at the top, little developmental work had been initiated by German aircraft manufacturers in the nine or ten months since the introduction of the Albatros, Pfalz, and Halberstadt D-series machines. In May and June, therefore, upon the resurgence of Allied strength in the air, there began a frenzied race to make up for time lost. The Albatros company modified its D-3 design, then hurriedly modified the modification and placed in production the faster, more rugged D-5. Pfalz and Halberstadt similarly improved their D-planes. A forward-looking gentleman whose name and ideas would attract great vogue after the war, Professor Hugo Junkers, was busy perfecting an all-metal single-seater monoplane, a squarish but clean-lined affair that appeared as a two-gun interceptor in October 1917, and from then on flew in small numbers at the front. Designated the Junkers J-7—and in two subsequent versions, the J-8 and J-9—and nicknamed the *Blechesel*, or Tin Donkey, the plane had a then unique structure consisting of corrugated aluminum sheeting riveted to a tubular frame.

Aware that the air command was in a buying mood for fighter machines rather than the heavy reconnaissance craft it had been supplying, the Rumpler factory jumped into the race with a well-streamlined little biplane single-seater with a plywood fuselage. Though capable of attaining a very high ceiling, the Rumpler D-1 could not maintain height when carrying out combat maneuvers; in addition, because of its complicated construction, it was a difficult type to mass-produce and to service in the field. Nevertheless, it saw limited service throughout the balance of the war and was liked by those who piloted it.

Anthony Fokker, meanwhile, was figuratively chained to his drawing board, drafting the blueprints for his DR-1 triplane. At the Pfalz plant in Spayer-am-Rhein chief designer Ernst Eversbusch was also laboring over the plans of that firm's triplane, which like Fokker's would be designated the DR-1, although the two machines neither looked nor performed alike. Exactly ten of the Pfalz triplanes were built, of which only four or five saw combat. On the other hand, more than three hundred of the Fokker version were rushed to front-line airfields and proved to be commendable fighting machines. The first triplane from the Fokker factory went to Werner Voss on August 28; the second was flown by Manfred von Richthofen himself, who took delivery of his machine on September 1. The rabbit-quick maneuverability of the Fokker DR-1 compensated for its lack of speed at high altitude, and for two months the pilots of Jagdgeschwader No. 1—the Richthofen circus—ably demonstrated its capabilities. But like its paradigm, the Sopwith Triplane, the DR-1 had a shortlived popularity—shorter, in fact, than the Sopwith's. In late October, two flying officers, Lieutenant Heinrich Gontermann, an ace with thirty-nine victories, and a Lieutenant Pastor, were fatally injured when their triple-deckers crumpled in the air. The type was withdrawn from operations. Although reissued with strengthened wings in December, it never recovered from this setback and was not supplied to many units.

Richthofen, at Pless, received the order canceling his extended leave on the afternoon of June 10. The situation at the front, during the preceding week, had become critical. Jasta 11, however, still stationed at Douai in the now dormant Arras sector, was meeting with less opposition, for the main Allied effort was concentrated farther to the north, around Ypres, where the

British had started their drive for the Belgian Channel ports in the morning darkness of June 7. The great explosion set off that morning by sappers of the Royal Engineers under the German positions on Messines Ridge was felt like a small earthquake as far away as London. To prepare for the Ypres campaign, many units of the Royal Flying Corps had been transferred from Arras, so that German airmen in the north were outnumbered approximately two to one. Richthofen was recalled to the front both to provide a lift to morale and to play a starring role in the new scheme of forming certain squadrons into unified battle groups.

Richthofen flew a circuitous route back to Douai. First there was some business at Adlershof in relation to the forthcoming Albatros D-5 airplane. From Adlershof he went to Krefeld to attend the funeral of an old friend and thirty-victory ace, Lieutenant Karl Schaefer, who had fallen under the guns of Lieutenant Rhys-Davids of R.F.C. Squadron No. 56. Perhaps he was especially aggrieved by Schaefer's death, for the latter had once saved brother Lothar's life. Lothar, writing after his narrow escape, had told of how another Albatros had picked an enemy chaser off his tail. "It was Schaefer, thank God. . . . I would have laid any wager that within the next half minute I would be shot to the ground. . . . Instead of me, my adversary fell flaming to his death. Schaefer accompanied me back to the airdrome and I bought him the best bottle of champagne in the mess. Good that one could at least do that."

From Krefeld, after a short visit with Schaefer's family, the baron proceeded as instructed to supreme headquarters at Bad Kreuznach, there to be decorated with the Cross of Valor by King Ferdinand of Bulgaria, and, more importantly, to confer on the subject of organizing and commanding Jagdgeschwader No. 1. With due deliberation it was decided that this undertaking should be scheduled for the end of June in order to afford Richthofen a couple of weeks in which to get back into the swing of things at the front.

He arrived at Douai on June 14, the day Lieutenant Karl Allmenroder (brother of the aforementioned Wilhelm Allmenroder) received the Order Pour le Mérite, the fourth member of Jasta 11 to win that coveted award. When Lothar von Richthofen was wounded and put out of action on May 7, during Manfred's absence, command of Jasta 11 had devolved upon Allmenroder, who was extremely well regarded by the elder Richthofen. But things were not the same. The old order was changing and the Red Knight, a conservative at heart, was not altogether happy with the new. Yet another of the old guard passed away three days later when a Lieutenant Zeumer, with whom Richthofen had flown in 1915 on the Russian front, was killed in a dogfight. Richthofen suspected that Zeumer had purposely lost the encounter. He knew in any case that Zeumer died as he would have wished, in combat, and thereby cheated a death from natural causes by only three or four months, for Zeumer had a tubercular condition that was entering its terminal phase. A medical examination, in fact, which would certainly have put him in the hospital, had been scheduled for the morning after his last patrol. Killed that week, too, was yet another of Richthofen's old comrades, one of the few noncommissioned pilot-officers still in the German air service, Sergeant-Major Sebastian Festner, with twelve victories to his credit.

Having returned to active duty, Richthofen realized that he was more than ever the cynosure of many eyes, that it was squarely up to him to show that his long hiatus had not dulled his skill. In four days he was back in form. Leading his squadron in an Albatros D-3, he attacked an artillery-spotting RE-8, and firing at point-blank range, shot it down. He saw both occupants of the British machine slumped in their seats, apparently dead. Driven by the wind, the RE-8 fluttered lazily toward the earth in uncontrolled circles and crashed in a farmyard, where the wreckage burned.

With the Ypres battle raging to the north, the British retained relatively few planes in the quiescent Arras sector. Here the Germans for once enjoyed a marked numerical advantage. Although they carried out frequent ground-strafing attacks with virtual impunity, wreaking heavy punishment on the enemy infantry, the German fighter pilots—including the eager experts of Jasta 11—found few opportunities to increase their personal victory scores. They tried every method they knew to bait their opponents into combat, but without success. The unwonted hesitancy of R.F.C. airmen was pardonable; they had the desire but lacked the strength. Weak as was British aviation at Arras that June, it was soon further depleted in consequence of events back home. Fourteen German bombers, on June 13, raided London in broad daylight, causing loss of life and a good deal of property damage. A public outcry compelled the War Office to withdraw No. 56 Squadron to Kent and No. 66 Squadron to Calais for home-defense duties. This left the R.F.C. in Arras with only a single fighter squadron, No. 19, whose obsolescent Spad S-7's were equipped with the troublesome and unreliable 150-horsepower version of the Hispano-Suiza engine. Since they were so grossly outnumbered and outclassed in the matter of machines, the pilots of No. 19 Squadron quite sanely repressed their combative urges.

Starved for targets in the air around Douai, Richthofen obtained permission to guide offensive patrols northward into the Ypres region. Soon afterward, preliminary to the founding of Jagdgeschwader No.1, Jasta 11 was moved to a new base at Marke, Belgium, in close proximity to the British line at Ypres. Piloting a factory-fresh Albatros D-5 that was painted a vivid crimson, the baron won his fifty-fourth victory in the fading twilight of June 23.

With Jasta 11 transplanted to Belgium, in the thick of the Ypres battle, and with two victories to indicate that Richthofen had lost none of his old virtuosity, the much-discussed regrouping of squadrons could at last be effected upon receipt of headquarters authorization. The provisional go-ahead for the creation of Jagdgeschwader No. 1 came in a series of communications over the military telegraph, and the new unit—forty-eight aircraft strong—initially ventured against the enemy at dawn, June 25. Richthofen and Karl Allmenroder, who often flew wing to wing these days, shot down a two-seater apiece near Le Bizet. And on the next morning Richthofen scored again, cutting an RE-8 into chunks of falling debris with repeated bursts of fire. That day, June 26, the official charter for the Richthofen circus arrived at Marke in the form of a telegram from the chief of staff of the army. The text read: "Jagdgeschwader No. 1 incorporates Jastas Nos. 4, 6, 10, and 11 (Stop) The Geschwader is a self-contained unit (Stop) Duty is to attain and maintain air supremacy in sectors of the front as directed (End of Message)." The final sentence was particularly significant. Therein was revealed the intention to deploy the multi-squadron group whenever and wherever changing conditions dictated. J.G. 1—to use the military abbreviation—was to be shunted from place to place as the need arose. Like Oswald Boelcke's old unit at Metz, it was given ample transport and personnel so that it would possess rapid mobility. This, plus the fact that the planes of the four squadrons were painted all the colors of the rainbow, made the "circus" label appropriate indeed. In somber contrast, the flying machines of the R.F.C. were generally either a functional olive-green or camouflaged by the addition of irregular brown-and-buff parquetry.

J.G. 1 was centered in Flanders, around the city of Courtrai. At Marke, Richthofen had his headquarters, together with Jasta 11; at Cuene was Jasta 4; at Bissegem, Jasta 6; at Heule, Jasta 10. Richthofen selected his subordinate commanders with care. Jasta 4 was in custody of Lieutenant Kurt von Doering, who, with the comparatively low score of three victories, nevertheless had a distinguished career to warrant his privileged position. Lieutenant Eduard von Dostler, a Bavarian career soldier who had proven his ability as a fighter pilot in Jasta 34 by getting almost twenty victories in quick succession, was transferred to the head of Jasta 6 at Richthofen's request. Dostler was killed, after raising his battle score to twenty-six and winning the Order Pour le Mérite, on August 19 by the gunner of an RE-8 biplane. Jasta 10 boasted a leader of note in the person of Lieutenant Ernst von Althaus, the veteran who had earned the Order Pour le Mérite back in the salad days of Boelcke, Immelmann, and the Fokker E-plane. He, too, was picked by Richthofen on the basis of meritorious service.

Jasta 11 was placed in the young but capable hands of Lieutenant Kurt Wolff, who just two months earlier had received the Order Pour le Mérite. Two months later, in mid-September, he crashed to his death after having achieved the not inconsiderable score of thirty-three victories. Richthofen possibly would have named Allmenroder to resume command of the squadron if this very able pilot had not been slain the day after the official birth of J.G. 1. He fell in combat on June 27, the victim of a long-range shot by the gunner of a British two-seater. His Albatros at first glided down, but the glide became a dive that ended in a crash between the lines in front of Ypres. The following night a German infantry patrol retrieved his body, and Allmenroder was laid to rest in his hometown of Solingen-Wald. He had been devoted to his leader. Shortly before he fell, he wrote in a letter to his sister: "You beg me to take leave, but the situation at the front is similar to that last spring at Arras. I would find no ease with you. Richthofen and I fly always together, one looking after the other. We have many newcomers in the outfit and I am among the few remaining old dependables. You can understand why he would prefer me to stay, and at the moment I do not wish to go." Allmenroder had thirty enemy planes to his credit when he went down.

The efficacy of J.G. 1 at Ypres and elsewhere during the months that followed was moderately good, and the amalgamation of squadrons became a standard feature of German air strategy. Temporary groupings were occasionally formed to coincide as an operational expedient with major ground offensives; such a formation was called a Jagdgruppe. Twelve of these temporary unions were formed at various times and were in existence for varying periods: one, Jagdgruppe No. 8, became a permanent unit on being redesignated Jagdgeschwader No. 4. As shown by the numerical designation of this newborn fighter team, Jagdegeschwaders No. 2 and 3 had meanwhile been organized. J.G. 2 was at first commanded by Captain Rudolf Berthold, a forty-four-victory ace known as the "Iron Knight," who after being severely wounded was replaced by Lieutenant Oskar von Boenigk, another expert with twenty-seven victories at the close of the war. J.G. 3 was competently led by Captain Bruno Loerzer, who finished the war alive with forty-one kills. Among the squadrons contained in J.G. 3 was the elite Jasta Boelcke.

Whereas the Jagdgeschwader was invariably composed of four squadrons, the transitory Jagdgruppe might include from two to four squadrons. Examples were Jagdgruppe No. 9 which comprised Jastas 3, 37, 54, and 56 under Lieutenant Franz Schleiff, and Jagdgruppe No. 10 under Lieutenant Ritter von Greim, which had but two component squadrons—Jastas 6 and 34. There was also much shuffling of the squadrons which made up any one Jagdgruppe.

As with the Jagdgeschwader, the purpose of the Jagdgruppe was to secure local ascendancy, if only for a few crucial days. When enough squadrons were centralized in any area, of course, the plan worked. In the case of the Richthofen circus, success was never as great as sensational press reports of that time induced many people to conclude. If someone less newsworthy had been leading J.G. 1, and if the group had numbered fewer personalities—for Richthofen assiduously stocked his troupe with the finest talent to be had— a clearer perspective would have been possible in viewing the potency of J. G. 1 in particular, and German aviation as a whole, during the final sixteen months of the war. Because the spotlight was trained so exclusively on the Red Knight and his band of aces, the rest of the German air force of that period has been largely relegated to the dim and seldom-explored recesses of history's stage. What can be said with certainty is that the consolidation of Jastas into combat groups kept Germany in the war as an air power. With fewer planes available to them than to their opponents, German pilots, by concentrating their resources and by a grim exercise of will, managed to make a real contest of it right down to the last bullet fired. Fighting the balance of the war in arrears, they steadily dropped further behind the Allies in the quantity, although not necessarily the quality, of their aerial equipment.

The Royal Flying Corps, in accordance with its policy that did not recognize such a thing as an ace, differed from the Germans, and the French as well, in repudiating the practice of congregating the best fighter pilots into elite units. The British alone of all the combatants did nothing officially to publicize the triumphs of individual airmen, although citations for decorations, mentions in dispatches, and, ultimately, the newspapers gave some indications of personal intiative and success. Still, the British authorities never bowed to persistent demands for information concerning exceptional air fighters. Since, technically speaking, it had no aces, the R.F.C. could have no ace squadrons.

Whether this policy was right or wrong will always remain a vexed question. In favor of the British philosophy is the fact that for every ace there were ten, twenty, or even thirty pilots whose accomplishments were less spectacular but whose actions were no less valuable. It was natural that the flying services should produce their heroes, yet nobody can irrefutably assert that the contributions of this gifted minority were in the sum worth more than men like Captain J. E. Doyle, R.F.C., who was not an ace but who wrote: "Before long . . . I came to realize that a flight commander's job was a whole-time one incompatible with such pastimes [as solo patrols]." Of his feelings after seeing a member of his flight shot down, Doyle had this to say: "I knew in that instant that I should have spent all my spare time with my flight, discussing and putting them wise to every wile of the enemy, and taking the novices for constant instructional flips over the lines. After that day I never flew by myself except by order on special mission. I realized that it was a far better thing to concentrate on turning my flight into as efficient a fighting unit as possible than to go out in search of individual laurels."

Yet, second to none as patrol leaders were such individualists as Major James McCudden, who did service in six squadrons at various times at the front, and Major Edward Mannock, who flew little more than a year in combat and compiled a victory score of at least seventy-three, a record that stands highest on the list of British aces in World War I.

There were few men still living in 1918 who could, as Major McCudden did, have written an autobiography titled *Five Years in the Royal Flying Corps.* Having enlisted in the Royal Engineers as a bugler in 1910, he moved over to aviation in 1913 and became a First Class Air Mechanic with No. 3 Squadron. He was serving in that capacity when war broke out, and he arrived in France with the first British air contingent to cross the Channel. McCudden participated in the nomadic existence of the R.F.C. during those early months of the war by attending the squadron's Bleriots and Farmans under arduous field conditions. He was thus one of a handful of airmen who served through most of the war with the flying corps, one of a handful who in 1918 had first-person recollections of the formative days of military aeronautics—already become a distant era.

Perhaps there were a dozen aviators still flying who could remember back to early days when such primitive biplanes as the Farman, because of the many struts and bracing wires surrounding the cockpit, were called "bird cages." McCudden was among this small veteran band who had witnessed the frenetic evolution of "bird cages" into battle planes. Before his death on July 9, 1918, McCudden won fifty-seven aerial combats, a score that qualified him as fourth best in the R.F.C. No enemy killed him. After being promoted to major and receiving the command of No. 60 Squadron, he was taking off from Auxi-le-Château airdrome to join his new unit when the engine of his SE-5 failed. McCudden made the fatal mistake of trying to turn downwind for a dead-stick landing on the airfield he had just left. He himself, twice an instructor during his long service, had lectured students against this suicidal procedure. What alien impulse caused him to crash cannot be known. A moment's panic, perhaps, for which he—like so many airmen—paid with his life. It was in his case a curious and tragic anticlimax to a magnificent service career.

McCudden, who earned his pilot's brevet in the spring of 1916, soared to the peak of his greatness while serving as a patrol leader with No. 56 Squadron, which he joined in mid-August 1917, immediately after that unit returned to the front subsequent to several comparatively dull weeks of home-defense duty along the Kentish coast. McCudden then had seven victories to his name. When he left the squadron seven months later for an instructional tour in England, he had all his fifty-seven victories.

No one flew harder or with more resolve than this little red-blond Irishman, one of the few pilots who had risen from the ranks. His delicately lined face and soft blue eyes belied his deadly purpose and flawless skill. During his lengthy apprenticeship with the R.F.C. he learned everything there was to learn about an engine, a machine gun, and an airplane. He always flew an SE-5, which he rated the best among Allied fighter craft. A technician to his finger tips, McCudden could not accept a plane as it came from the factory. Before chancing combat in a new machine, he would test it thoroughly and improve it. To begin with, he got rid of every ounce of superfluous weight. Then he improved the engine by installing special high-compression pistons. The increased power-to-weight ratio added ten miles per hour to his speed. "I've done so many things to my plane," he wrote to his brother, "that I can fly it up to twenty thousand feet easily. I take a lot of interest in my engine, my guns and the plane itself, and keep making adjustments to get more speed and higher altitude."

Though never consumed by blind hatred of the enemy, McCudden was the kind who could look back upon a victorious engagement and exclaim, as he did in the pages of his book, "By Jove, that's the stuff to give the Hun!" He did not exult in killing but only in acquitting his task well. He thought of his job as a trade to be worked at like any other in the pursuance of greater proficiency. While his admiration for the headlong attacks of an Albert Ball was touched with awe, it was not his way of doing things. His tactics were completely cerebral. To dash recklessly into the midst of a formation of German planes was to him an act of needless folly. To do a proper job, he felt, one's emotions had to be firmly overruled by cool logic. But he was human and his calm detachment was now and then disturbed by the gruesome. Once, for example, he sent a burst of bullets into an Albatros. A trickle of flame appeared, and the enemy machine started to go down. McCudden followed it. The flames spread until they enveloped the whole fuselage and began licking away the wing fabric. Suddenly, McCudden saw the doomed pilot writhing in agony, his body a wind-whipped torch. McCudden had trouble sleeping that night, yet the next morning recovered his composure and confided to a companion at breakfast that a war pilot had to forget such incidents if he was "to do his work effectively." Squeamishness was a luxury the combat flyer could ill afford. "After all," he said, "we are nothing but hired assassins."

Although their fighting styles differed, McCudden, like the late Captain Ball, often took off voluntarily on solo missions. On these he shot down a goodly number of his victims, frequently stalking them for many miles before pouncing at the most advantageous moment. He also liked to coax his machine up to twenty thousand feet and wait patiently for an unsuspecting two-seater to pass below. No Rumpler or L.V.G., which normally carried on reconnaissance from seventeen thousand feet, ever expected any British fighter to attack from above. The only warning they had was the jibbering report of machine-gun fire from the diving SE-5. Unlike Ball and the majority of other high-scoring aces, McCudden seldom tried to close in on his target. He was a sure marksman, among the most accurate shots in the air. With only a single short burst he once shot down a German almost a quarter of a mile away. Because of the special attention he paid to his guns and synchronizing gear, he had far fewer stoppages than usual, even at the high altitudes he ranged, where icing was a problem. Rarely did his plane come home scarred by bullet holes; when it did, he was disgusted. As a careful, skilled craftsman, McCudden figured he had no excuse for letting an enemy get near enough to hit him. Although he admired gallantry, he advised against it and consciously restrained his own sporting instinct. He took no unnecessary risks. What in another man might be interpreted as excessive caution was recognized in McCudden for what it was—the mark of a canny professional who knew that war was a more serious business than soccer or rugby. He knew, too, that the rules had changed since the days of mailed armor and lances. "The best way to get a Hun," he told pilots who asked his counsel, "is to find him before he sees you." Those who adhered to his doctrine lived much longer as a generality than those who tried to emulate Albert Ball.

In No. 56 Squadron McCudden's command was B Flight, the same patrol

team formerly led by Ball. No. 56, through the latter phase of the battle of
Arras and the remainder of 1917, was probably the nearest thing the R.F.C.
ever had to an elite squadron. Its complement of officers was studded with
aces, not as the result of any planning but rather by providential circumstance. The best of them were in B Flight: McCudden and the five Lieutenants
Rhys-Davids, R. A. Mayberry, C. A. Lewis, G. H. Bowman, and R. T. C.
Hoidge. "There was a wonderful spirit in this squadron," McCudden wrote,
"which was entirely different from any squadron with which I had yet come
in contact." He further noted that the "wonderful, offensive spirit" of Albert
Ball "was preserved by the squadron, and in Rhys-Davids we had a second
Ball, for neither knew the word fear, and it was largely the splendid example
they set that made the squadron do extraordinarily well at a time when, taken
collectively, the German morale was at its very zenith." The time alluded to
here by McCudden was "Bloody April." He also mentioned that his assignment to No. 56 had been no accident, explaining that he had made up his
mind to become a member of that unit "under any pretenses whatever."

The men he led in B Flight had all flown in company with Ball a few
months earlier, which meant they were fully battle-tempered before McCudden
took over as their commander. Each knew his job and possessed the courage
and ability to do it more than satisfactorily. Rhys-Davids, prior to his death
in October that year, claimed twenty-two German aircraft. Bowman and Mayberry respectively claimed thirty-two and twenty-five victories in their brilliant
careers. Hoidge's toll of enemy planes ultimately amounted to twenty-seven.
Lewis finished with eight. Thus, if McCudden's score were thrown in, these
half dozen flying furies accounted for 171 German machines.

Richthofen's Jagdgeschwader was directly opposed now to No. 56 Squadron
in the Ypres arena, and there were daily fights against these superb flyers.
Jasta 10 suffered heavy losses in early September, and Richthofen, who coun-
tenanced no excuses from his subordinate leaders, summoned his old comrade
Werner Voss to replace Lieutenant Althaus at the head of that squadron. Voss
was the first German ace to appreciate the maneuverability of the Fokker
triplane as a distinct advantage over the speed of the then-standard Albatros
and Pfalz D-types. He had been flying the three-winger only a few days when
he assumed command of Jasta 10, and the combination of an expert pilot and
a smart-handling plane soon proved hard to beat. The machine became Voss'
main interest in life. He coddled it as he would a treasured pet. He was
obsessed with it. He had it painted silver-blue all over except for the red
cowling, which was a squadron marking. On the front of the cowling, utilizing
the appropriately placed air intakes as eyes and a nose, he whimsically painted
a mustachioed face that some said was a caricature of the Kaiser. True or not,
it gave a clue to the aviator's sense of humor.

On September 3, five days after the machine was delivered to him, Voss
scored his initial victory in the triplane by shooting down a Sopwith. In the
next three weeks he brought down nine more Allied machines, getting the last

of these on the dawn patrol of Sunday, September 23. His total then stood at forty-eight enemy planes destroyed, all in the relatively short span of fourteen months. He was only thirteen victories behind the Red Knight, and the gap was closing. The prospect of overtaking Richthofen in the race for scoring honors cheered him. After landing that Sunday morning and climbing out of his triplane, he was wreathed in smiles. His brothers, Lieutenant Otto Voss and Corporal Max Voss, both of them in the infantry, were at the airfield to visit him, and he told them that he remembered never having felt a warmer glow of self-confidence. The three attended chapel together, then chatted over a leisurely lunch. They spent a couple of hours wandering about the base, Werner proudly showing off his squadron's equipment. A snapshot was taken of them standing at the nose of Werner's Pfalz D-3, parked in a hanger since the delivery of his triplane. The brothers enjoyed a farewell schnapps in the officer's mess, after which Otto and Max returned to their units. Neither suspected that he would never again see Werner alive.

Late that afternoon, Voss took off alone in his tiny silver-blue chaser and lightheartedly headed for the front in search of his forty-ninth victim. Passing over the smoldering rubble that had once been the town of Ypres, flying at seventeen thousand feet, he sighted below him six Bristol two-seaters escorted by a like number of SE-5 fighters. Undeterred by the twelve-to-one odds against him, he singled out the rearmost SE-5 as his target and went into the attack. As he dived he spotted two flights of RE-8 observation craft and two flights of Sopwith Camels off to the southwest, too low and too far away to interfere. Voss opened fire. His chosen adversary, caught by surprise, peeled off from formation in a steep spiraling descent. Voss continued shooting, then became aware of yet more planes—behind him! A quick glance backward revealed six SE-5's roaring down at him. Voss broke off his attack to concentrate on the rapidly approaching biplanes, which were those of B Flight, No. 56 Squadron, R.F.C., led by Captain James McCudden. What ensued was one of the epic sky battles of World War I.

"We were just on the point of engaging six Albatros Scouts away to our right," McCudden wrote of the event, "when we saw ahead of us . . . an SE-5 half spinning down . . . pursued by a silvery blue German triplane at very close range. The SE-5 certainly looked very unhappy, so we changed our minds about attacking the six V-strutters [Albatroses], and went to the rescue of the unfortunate SE-5. The Hun triplane was practically underneath our formation now, and so down we dived at a colossal speed. I went to the right, Rhys-Davids to the left, and we got behind the triplane together."

Escape from this cross fire seemed impossible for Voss. If he tried to dive away, he would be jumped by the Sopwith Camels below. And the upward route was sealed off by the Bristols and SE-5's he had just dived past. The air was crowded in every direction with enemy machines. Voss improvised an evasive maneuver that completely confounded his assailants.

"The German pilot," wrote McCudden, who did not learn the identity of the man in the triplane until after the battle, "turned in a most disconcertingly quick manner, not a climbing or an Immelmann turn, but a sort of half-flat spin. By now the German triplane was in the middle of our formation, and its handling was wonderful to behold. The pilot seemed to be firing at all of us simultaneously, and although I got behind for a second time, I could hardly stay there for a second. His movements were so quick and uncertain that none of us could hold him in sight at all for any decisive time."

The six machines of B Flight, joined by the SE-5 he had originally singled out, now surrounded Voss. The remaining British single-seaters, SE-5's and Sopwiths, seventeen of them, and the six Bristols circling above and below, guarded the avenues of escape. The two flights of RE-8's stood farther off to witness the spectacle. It was something to see; Voss, cornered, fighting with the ferocity and cunning of a crazed demon. The Fokker incredibly twisted away from pass after pass, spreading the British planes over many miles of sky, balking every attempt to shoot it down. Whenever an SE-5 got on his tail, Voss flipped away in another unconventional maneuver to attack others in the pursuing pack.

McCudden reported the rest:

> I now got a good opportunity, as he was coming towards me nose on, and slightly underneath, and apparently had not seen me. I dropped my nose, got him well in my sight, and pressed both triggers. As soon as I fired, up came his nose at me, and I heard clack-clack-clack-clack, as his bullets passed close to me and through my wings. I distinctly noticed the red-yellow flashes from his parallel Spandau guns. As he flashed by me, I caught a glimpse of a black head in the triplane with no hat on at all.
>
> By this time, a red-nosed Albatros had arrived and was apparently doing its best to guard the triplane's tail, and it was well handled, too. The formation of six Albatroses which we were going to attack at first stayed above us and were prevented from diving on us by the arrival of a formation of Spads, whose leader apparently appreciated our position and kept the six Albatroses otherwise engaged.
>
> The triplane was still circling round in the midst of seven SE-5's, who were all firing at it as opportunity offered, and at one time I noted the triplane in the apex of a cone of tracer bullets from at least five machines simultaneously, and each machine had two guns.

Most pilots, fastened in the converging fire of ten machine guns, would have been hashed to death, but Voss managed to maneuver out of the trap each time. More than that, he broke through the ring of pursuers and had a slight chance to flee for safety; instead he returned to the fight with even increased determination. The fearless youngster pelted every one of his adversaries' planes with machine-gun bullets. His own plane was riddled, but still in flying condition with no loss of control. The uneven combat raged for several more minutes before the spellbound spectators. "By now," observed McCudden, "the fighting was very low, and the red-nosed Albatros had gone down and out, but the triplane still remained. I had temporarily lost sight of the triplane whilst changing a drum of ammunition, and when I next saw him he was very low, still being engaged by an SE-5 . . . the pilot being Rhys-Davids. I noticed that the triplane's movements were very erratic, and then I saw him go into a fairly steep dive . . . and . . . hit the ground and disappear into a thousand fragments, for it seemed to me that it literally went to powder."

Rhys-Davids, in this last fitful scene of the drama, emptied his upward-firing, top-wing-mounted Lewis gun into the madly maneuvering Fokker. He repeated this action, each time exhausting a full cannister of cartridges. Finally in a favorable position to use his synchronized Vickers gun, he flailed the triplane's cockpit with bullets. The Fokker suddenly stopped its elusive evolutions and slid into a gentle glide to the west. The Englishman reloaded and shot again at Voss, who presumably was wounded and definitely was disoriented, or else he would have chosen an eastward descent toward German-occupied land. At a height of five or six hundred feet the silver-blue Fokker stalled, then fell to earth on the Allied side of the line. It was five minutes past six on that Sunday evening, and Werner Voss, twenty years old, the second leading German ace, was dead.

McCudden wrote: "It was now quite late, so we flew home to the airdrome, and as long as I live I shall never forget my admiration for that German pilot who singlehanded fought seven of us for ten minutes, and also put some bullets through all of our machines. His flying was wonderful, his courage magnificent, and in my opinion he is the bravest German airman whom it has been my privilege to fight."

Later, in the No. 56 Squadron mess, the main topic at dinner was the marvelous combat waged by the as yet unknown German. "We all conjectured that [he] must be one of the enemy's best," McCudden recalled in his book, "and we debated as to whether it was Richthofen or Voss." A wire from headquarters the next morning said that the dead aviator had been found wearing the Boelcke collar and the Order Pour le Mérite and was in fact the illustrious Lieutenant Voss. "Rhys-Davids came in for a shower of congratulations and no one," so McCudden wrote, "deserved them better, but as the boy himself said to me, 'Oh, if I could only have brought him down alive,' and his remark was in agreement with my thoughts."

Not long after Voss had been killed, a batch of decorations arrived for the men of No. 56 Squadron. Ball received a posthumous Victoria Cross, Rhys-Davids received the Distinguished Service Order, Bowman received a bar to his Military Cross, as did McCudden. The presentation ceremony was followed with merriment in the squadron mess. Food and drink were both good and plentiful, the band was in fine fettle, and many invited guests partook of the conviviality. Rhys-Davids was the special hero of the occasion. Everyone present concurred with McCudden's conviction that the mantle of Albert Ball had fallen on the shoulders of the modest young Etonian who had shot down Voss. The opinion was that Rhys-Davids, if he lived, would go on to be among the greatest air fighters the world would ever know. He was, however, a confirmed practitioner of Ball's incautious combat methods and had just a month more of life left to him.

Those who were acquainted with Rhys-Davids described him in their writings as "generous and warm-hearted," a "gracious, quiet-spoken chap" who was "easy to win . . . affection and friendship." That he was incapable of meanness, petty guile, or dislike even for the enemies he fought every day, was demonstrated when, at the climax of the celebration, McCudden called upon him to make a speech. Rhys-Davids at first declined, but the clamor grew so insistent that the flustered pilot had to rise to his feet and say something. He stood there for a moment and then, a hush having settled into the hall, he raised his glass and proposed a toast to Manfred von Richthofen. They were, he explained, fighting against men of exceptional valor who merited a gesture of esteem, singularly so the notorious baron, the most deserving foeman of all.

They drank the toast enthusiastically, except for one fellow. He remained seated and bitterly muttered, "I won't drink a toast to that son-of-a-bitch."

The sullen dissenter was Captain Edward Mannock, a pal of McCudden's, attending the party as a guest from No. 40 Squadron, stationed nearby. Mannock's refusal to drink to Richthofen surprised nobody who knew him, for he loathed all Germans and everything German with almost pathological intensity and made no secret of it. Destined to become the leading British ace, Mannock was an unusual character in other respects. He was of Irish extraction like McCudden, and, like McCudden, he had come up the hard way. The son of a soldier, Mannock was born in Aldershot on May 24, 1887. His early life had been restricted by the limitations of his father's pay as a corporal. A straitened childhood turned for the worse when Corporal Mannock left the army and deserted his wife and five children, who were left destitute. Edward, then twelve, a sensitive, retiring, intellectually curious youngster who read every book he could lay his hands on, thoroughly appreciated the efforts of his mother, his older brother, and his sister to keep the household intact. Edward had to quit school to help out. His body supported by a pair of thin, twiglike legs, his face wearing a lugubrious expression seldom crossed by a smile, he delivered groceries, became a barber's assistant at fifteen, served with the army ambulance corps, and finally was hired by the telephone company as a lineman, a job he liked. The company moved him to Wellingborough, where he boarded with a childless couple named Eyles, and to elderly Jim Eyles he transferred all the affection he would ordinarily have given to his father. The warm personality of Jim Eyles probably was the influence that saved the boy from becoming a social misfit; the abandonment by his father and the poverty of his growing-up years cut emotional scars into him that may well have remained festering wounds had it not been for the kindness of Mr. and Mrs. Eyles. To them he was "Pat," though the flying corps would always know him as "Mick" Mannock.

A thoughtful young man whose outlook was deeply colored by his background, Mannock developed an abiding interest in politics. Shortly after his twentieth birthday he became an active member of the local Labour Party, which, as he saw it, fostered the cause of the underdog in the British economy. He disapproved of many things—wealth, sham, social position, immorality, and finally the Germans and their concept of *Kultur*. He frequently lectured on behalf of the Labour Party and revealed himself to be an articulate critic of the government and the laissez-faire evils of big industry. But he was a staunch patriot who never let his political views obscure his loyalty to the Crown. At this time he was a teetotaler and a fairly regular churchgoer, although he professed to have no particular religion. Having spent portions of his boyhood in Ireland, India, and South Africa as an army child, he seemed to have trouble putting down roots. His restless spirit prompted him in January 1914 to take employment abroad, and the beginning of the war found him working as a district inspector with a British telephone company in Constantinople.

When Turkey threw in her lot with Germany, he was interned and put to hard labor. He tried several times to escape and was severely punished for being so rash. Thrown into a cell, he tried to eat the bread and water but vomited repeatedly and came down with fever. He lost weight and broke out in septic sores. His health, which was never robust, steadily deteriorated until at last the Turks decided to repatriate Mannock if only for the reason that he was a physical wreck, more trouble to keep alive than his captors considered worthwhile.

On his return to England in April 1915, after a few weeks of recuperation, he rejoined his old ambulance unit in the Royal Army Medical Corps. His hatred for the enemy was becoming increasingly intense. He could not bear the idea of some day being ordered to care for a wounded German and so requested a transfer. They put him in the Royal Engineers, where in April 1916, he received his commission as a lieutenant. At about this period his imagination was kindled by reports of the achievements of Albert Ball in the skies of France. Mannock was already disenchanted with his duty in the engineers. He devoutly believed that the only way to beat Germany was for each and every Allied soldier to exterminate as many Germans as possible. Combat, and especially aerial combat, would give a man a chance to do this. Mannock applied for a transfer to the R.F.C.

He was then twenty-nine, rather old for active flying. And he looked closer to forty, a tall, lean, hard-bitten fellow, with clear-blue eyes, a steady gaze, a grim sadness fixed upon his face, and few words to waste. When he showed up for his medical examination he was wearing Wellington boots and spurs, and carried a riding whip. A doctor inquired why an engineer was so equipped. Mannock dryly responded that he was in disguise. He had no time for small talk. He was in deadly earnest about the war and wanted to come to grips with the enemy.

One of the minor mysteries of the war is how Mannock contrived to pass so rigorous a medical test as that for pilot recruits in the R.F.C. Among other infirmities, he had a congenital defect of sight—probably astigmatism—affecting his left eye. Both eyes of every candidate were required to be perfect. It has been presumed that the medical officer in a forgetful moment uncovered the sight chart for a few brief seconds, and in this space of time Mannock's good eye registered and absorbed the necessary data. If true, this peculiar ability of his to pick out and memorize objects in a twinkling was one of the chief powers which helped him to shape his talents as an air fighter and leader.

His transfer to the R.F.C. came through in August, whereupon he went to Hendon to learn to fly. He had no difficulty handling a plane aloft but was poor at landing. In this respect he had much in common with other aces. It is curious to reflect that many of the best air fighters of World War I were wretched pilots in the airfield sense of the word. Complete masters of their machines in the air, they were often lacking in the ability to land smoothly; Richthofen and Voss were no exceptions to the rule.

On February 1, 1917, Mannock was commissioned a flying officer and posted to Joyce Green Reserve Squadron, where he realized that he was just beginning to learn something about flying. Here it was that Mannock and McCudden came together, the latter serving as an instructor of advanced combat techniques. "I was allotted a Bristol Scout for my work," McCudden related, "but as it was not ready yet, I used a DH-2, which I 'spun' regularly to the great consternation of the pupils there, who regarded the machine as a super death trap, not knowing that in its day it was one of the best machines in the R.F.C." Mannock was one of the lucky pupils assigned to McCudden, who was greatly impressed with Mannock's seriousness of purpose if not his flying skill. They became good friends and were almost brotherly in their feelings toward one another. Mannock's other friend was Captain Meredith Thomas, who shared quarters with him.

Afterwards, Thomas wrote about Mannock:

> One particular incident regarding his training I well remember. That was his first solo flight on a DH-2, when he was told, as all were told in those days, "Don't turn below two thousand; if you do, you will spin and kill yourself."
>
> Mick proved this wrong early one Sunday morning in March, when he accidentally got into a spin at about one thousand feet over the munitions factory—then just across the creek on the edge of the airfield—and came out extremely near the ground and the munitions factory, and landed successfully in a small field which

was too small to fly out from. He was accused of spinning intentionally, and after a rather unpleasant scene in the mess and later in the CO's office, was threatened with being turned down.

We were great friends at Joyce Green and had many both amusing and serious talks when waiting in the cold on a fuel drum—at one period for a whole three weeks—for a flight, but I cannot recall anything definite beyond our mutual disgust because of the manner in which the staff threatened the pupils, many of whom had seen pretty severe war service before transferring or being seconded to the R.F.C., while the staff had seen very, very little, and in some cases, none.

My first impression of Mick was: he was very reserved, inclined toward a strong temper, but very patient and somewhat difficult to arouse. On short acquaintance he became a very good conversationalist and was fond of discussions or arguments. He was prepared to be generous to everyone in thought and deed, but had strong likes and dislikes. He was inclined to be almost too serious-minded.[1]

Mannock arrived at the front in the first week of "Bloody April" as a replacement to No. 40 Squadron. The assignment was to his liking. No. 40 was a tried and proved outfit, equipped with Nieuports and right in the middle of the pitched battle for the air above Arras. It numbered among its pilots such resolute warriors as Captain W. A. Bond, Flight Lieutenant C. R. MacKenzie, Captain W. MacLanachan, Captain F. Godfrey, Captain G. E. McElroy, Captain Cecil A. Lewis—to cite only those who were, or would become, aces—and a fine commanding officer, Major Robert Loraine, who in peacetime had been a very talented actor.

Because he was a newcomer and therefore automatically treated with suspicion, and because his austere appearance and his reticence were mistaken as signs of unfriendliness, Mannock was not readily admitted into squadron camaraderie. His first day was marred by an incident that upset his fellow officers but did not even cause him to frown. Upon going to dinner that night he found only one empty chair in the mess. Supposing it to be meant for him, he sat down. The room fell silent. Mannock uncomfortably noticed everyone staring at him. He looked back wonderingly from face to face.

"Well," he asked politely, "have I done something sinful?"

"You're sitting in Pell's seat," he was gruffly informed.

"Sorry," said Mannock, getting up from the table and scanning the room for another chair.

"You might as well stay there," one of the pilots said. "There's no place else. And Pell, poor chap, didn't come back today."

Mannock nodded coolly and sat down again. Nobody thought he would,

---

[1] Jones: *King of Air Fighters*.

but this reluctance among pilots to occupy the chair of a fallen comrade did not affect Mannock. He was a hard-boiled pragmatist to whom a chair was a chair, no matter who had sat in it. He spurned sentimentality and superstition, or, more precisely, was completely impervious to them. A fatalist, he accepted with no visible qualm the possibility—the high probability—of being killed. He remembered not only the lessons but the fighting philosophy of James McCudden, whom he sometimes called "Mac." Raw boldness and fiery impetuosity, he felt, were inimical to a combat pilot's best interests; the man who won was he who had mastered his emotions as well as the flying and shooting skills. McCudden had told him, and he firmly believed, that an intelligent pilot must alloy his fervor with sound, reliable judgment. Mannock knew this to be the sanest approach to aerial fighting, and at first it interfered with his effectiveness. His natural impulse, detesting Germans as he did, was to rush pell-mell at the enemy, his guns blazing, and kill or be killed. He repressed this urge so strongly that he overcompensated for it with too much caution. During his first weeks with the squadron, in fact, some of his mates impugned his courage, for he had yet to get close enough to a German plane to open fire.

Captain G. L. Lloyd, known as "Zulu" Lloyd because of his African upbringing, a veteran aviator of No. 60 Squadron, joined No. 40 about this time and befriended the saturnine Irishman. He took every opportunity to defend Mannock and went so far as to predict that he would, once he had a victory or two under his belt, become an excellent air fighter. Mannock, insisted Lloyd, simply required time to get the hang of things.

Acutely aware of what they were saying about him, Mannock finally opened his scoring with an enemy observation balloon destroyed late in the afternoon of May 7. Enroute to the airdrome he was elated by his feat, confident it would remove the stigma from his reputation. But no one in the squadron paid the slightest attention that evening to the fact that Mannock had scored. By the time he got back from patrol and made his report, it was dark outside. The funereal atmosphere in the mess hall told him that something was amiss. His questioning look was answered with the news, passed along the grapevine from No. 56 Squadron, that Albert Ball had not returned from a fight with the Richthofen Jasta. Mannock, it has been said, wept.

It is noteworthy that in one of his infrequent letters to his mother, written a few days after his initial victory, Mannock neglected to mention the fact that he had shot down a German balloon:

> I haven't heard from you in reply to my last letter, so I suppose that it has gone astray. . . . You will see from the address above that we are prohibited from giving the name of the place at which we are stationed, but I can say that we are in the actual thick of it, and I go across the lines every day (sometimes three times) when the weather is not prohibitive. The battlefields wear an awful aspect

as seen from above—covered with shell holes and craters, which remind me of pictures of what the earth looked like at the very beginning of things. It's extraordinary how anything can live through such a bombardment. . . . I fly a machine of my own, and I can tell you it's very lonely up in the clouds all by one's self, with the antiaircraft shells coughing and barking all around one, and big guns on the ground flashing and spitting continuously. I've been over the German towns, but the Huns clear off almost invariably when they spot us coming. . . . Now I don't want you to send me anything, as there is plenty of everything here—tobacco, food, music, sports . . . but no girls, so don't waste what little cash you have in needless expense. I'm all right here. There are lots of interesting things I should like to tell you, but the censor forbids, so I'll leave them to your imagination.[2]

Before this letter arrived at its destination, Mick Mannock had a narrow escape from death. Carrying out some routine firing and diving exercises near the airfield, he bore down from two thousand feet and tested his guns over a dummy target area. He had fired only the first few rounds when he heard a loud snapping noise and saw the right bottom wing tear away from the fuselage. He somehow managed to land, but the Nieuport piled up. The ground crew rushed over to see if they could drag Mannock, or his remains, out of the debris. To their amazement, they saw him strolling off in another direction. They caught up to him. Mannock looked very strict and stern, picking the chief rigger in the group and scolding him for allowing defective wing struts to be fitted. It was Mannock's idea of a joke. Everyone knew that the fault lay more with the French factory than with the well-trained and conscientious R.F.C. riggers.

Those in the squadron who maintained that Mannock might have a yellow streak soon happily ate their words. As "Zulu" Lloyd had foretold, a profound transformation came over the unsmiling Irishman once he had drawn German blood. Not that he began immediately to accumulate additional victories. Another full month was to elapse before an enemy plane, a two-seater, would fall to his guns. But in the interim he manifested unmistakable symptoms of waking up to the harsh realities of life and death in the air. Mannock, who was not a natural flyer, had reacted to the criticism of his squadron mates by arguing, with a vehemence typical of the self-justifying delinquent, that "good flying never killed a Hun yet." It was, as he was doubtless acutely aware, a lame excuse for his foibles. It was, furthermore, a transparent rationalization, since, because of his bad eye, he was not a good shot either.

Mannock, through May and June, no longer tried accommodating his punctured ego; instead he applied himself assiduously to the task of improving both his piloting and gunnery skills. Rather than sit brooding around the

[2] Jones: *op. cit.*

airfield, he was in the air at every opportunity, as he strove to be at one with his aircraft and to learn to compensate with his shooting for his virtually unilocular vision. The difficulty of trying to hit something with one eye nearly blind was in determining the proper range, and Mannock nicely overcame this difficulty. He persevered and his perseverance paid off. On July 12, he shot down a two-seater, and on the next day another. His Military Cross was awarded on July 22. A promotion to captain was his before the end of the month, and with it the job of flight commander.

A letter mailed on the last day of July to his closest confidant, his former landlord in Wellingborough, Jim Eyles, affords a glimpse of Mannock just after he acquired these hard-earned honors. "Got the M.C., old boy, and made captain on probation," and that was all he said about it. "Had some more luck," he went on, changing the subject, "only bad this time. Busted two buses in the past three days. Engines broke in midair. Got down all right. Some pilot! The C.O. congratulated me. Hurt myself a little bit on the second occasion, but not much. . . . One day last week I had five bouts of my own and fired off 470 rounds of ammunition. . . . Lost some fellows during the last week. One was hit by Archie [antiaircraft] direct. Went down in a spin from seven thousand feet. . . . Thanks for the French quotation. As you say, there is a good time coming."

As his successes became more numerous, Mannock grew increasingly enthusiastic in his work and increasingly bitter in his hatred of the Hun. As a patrol leader he had few peers—perhaps none—in any of the combatant air forces. When he was leading a patrol, he was a team man to the marrow of his bones. His actions were always carefully planned, his formation was never surprised, and his supreme unselfishness more than a few times gave credit for one of his victories to another. He had a special knack for nurturing green pilots through their first trying weeks. His own tribulations as a novice endowed him with a sympathetic understanding of their problems. Often, after hitting an enemy plane, he would veer off to permit one of his new men to finish it off, and later he would insist that his bullets had missed and that the novice should get the credit for the kill. Once, in writing to Jim Eyles, he mentioned the fact that he had forty-one victories. "If I have any luck," he said, "I think I may beat old Mac. Then I shall try to oust old Richthofen." It was the only reference in any of his correspondence to his total of enemy planes shot down, and it was evidently intended merely as a playful poke at his pal McCudden. The fact is, according to those R.F.C. flyers who left reminiscences of their service with Mannock, he never really knew or cared exactly how many Germans he had shot down. He certainly had more than the seventy-three officially attributed to him, and possibly as many as ninety or a hundred.

Regardless of his actual score, which will never be reckoned, it was not nearly high enough to satisfy the urge that was in him. Mannock, it seemed, had the war persisted another twenty years with him still in the thick of it, could never do away with enough Germans to appease his rage. When a comrade died, he was unashamed to weep, but his tears were not of grief alone; they were also tears of frustrated wrath because he could never kill enough of what he once called "German vermin" to balance accounts for the death of even one countryman.

In December, in the fighting around Cambrai, No. 40 Squadron was somewhat belatedly re-equipped with SE-5's. The change from rotary Le Rhones to water-cooled, stationary Hispano-Suiza engines required some getting used to, and during the transition there was a loud lamentation in the squadron for the familiar old Nieuports. Only Mannock, who had always felt—contrary to most—that the Nieuport was a little too slow, fell in love at first try with the SE-5, reveling in its superior performance and shooting down two enemy planes by the end of the month. The others took a while longer to feel at home on their new mounts, but at last came around to Mannock's way of thinking. The Irishman, however, was not there to hear his opinions vindicated. He had returned to England on January 2, 1918, to be rested, officially with twenty-three victories behind him, but more probably with forty or thereabouts.

Made restless by the inactivity in England, Mannock went back to France at the close of March as a flight commander with the newly formed No. 74 Squadron. Among his comrades here was Captain Ira "Taffy" Jones, who, once having broken the ice with a victory on May 7, 1918, scored forty kills in the six remaining months of the war. Pinned to the instrument panel of Jones' SE-5 was a square of cardboard on which was scrawled the slogan: "He must fall. Remember Ball." Jones lived to fly and fight in World War II, and in 1934 his excellent biography of Mick Mannock was published, aptly titled *King of the Air Fighters*.

In three combat-fraught months with the "Tiger Squadron," as No. 74 came to be called, Mannock added thirty-six to his official tally but is known definitely to have shot down at least four others for which he did not bother to obtain confirmation. It was while flying with No. 74 that he was bitten suddenly with an obsessive dread of being burned alive. Always now, just before taking off on a combat mission, he would check his pistol to assure himself that it was loaded and in well-oiled working order. If anyone asked why, he matter-of-factly explained that he intended to put a bullet through his brain if his machine caught fire. "They'll never burn me," he vowed. But he burned many of them with no sign of compunction and rather with undisguised glee. He kept a diary. In it he penned this entry and several others in a similar vein: "I sent one of them to hell in flames today . . . I wish Kaiser Bill could have seen him sizzle."

Upgraded to the rank of major on June 18, the sullen Irishman left No. 74 to go on leave prior to assuming command of No. 85 Squadron in early July. Most of this leave he spent with McCudden, whose death on July 9 came as a terrible shock to him. Despite the knowledge that McCudden had died in an accident, Mannock swore vengeance and led his squadron with even greater fury and determination. Little more time, however, was left him.

It was fitting that Mannock's last combat was fought with the purpose in mind of giving a victory to a new hand. A German two-seater, probably an L.V.G., set upon first and disabled by Mannock, was polished off by Lieutenant Donald C. Inglis, a recent arrival at the front. There can be no better witness to what happened on that bright summery morning of July 26, 1918, than Inglis himself.

> My instructions were to sit on Mick's tail, and that he would waggle his wings if he wanted me closer. I soon found that I didn't have much chance of looking around, as Mick would waggle and the only thing I could do was to watch his tail and stick tight, as he was flying along the lines at about thirty to fifty feet up and not straight for more than thirty consecutive seconds, first up on one wing, then the other. Suddenly, he turned toward home, full out and climbing. A Hun, thought I, but I'm damned if I could find one; then a quick turn and a dive, and there was Mick shooting up a two-seater. He must have pegged the observer, as when he pulled up and I came in underneath him I didn't see the Hun shooting. I flushed the Hun's fuel tank and just missed ramming his tail as I came up, when the Hun's nose dropped. Falling in behind Mick again we did a couple of circles around the burning wreck and then made for home. I saw Mick start to kick his rudder and realized we were fairly low, then I saw a flame come out of the side of his machine; it grew bigger and bigger. Mick was no longer kicking his rudder; his nose dropped slightly and he went into a slow right-hand turn around about twice, and hit the ground in a burst of flame. I circled at about twenty feet but could not see him, and as things were getting pretty hot, made for home and managed to reach our outposts with a punctured fuel tank. Poor Mick. All I could say when I got into the trenches was that the bloody bastards had shot my major down in flames.

Thus Mannock perished as he feared he would, enveloped in flames. The random bullet of an unknown German infantryman presumably struck a vital part of his machine. Perhaps another bullet, discharged from his own revolver by his own hand, or maybe the impact of the crash spared him the pain of dying by fire. Nothing of him remained to be committed to the grave, and this too may have been a mercy, for Mannock in life would have fulminated angrily at the prospect of being interred after death by the enemy he so starkly despised.

A minor army of British airmen thereafter dedicated themselves to taking revenge for Mannock. The most successful of them was Taffy Jones, his former companion in No. 74 Squadron, who between that tragic July 26 and the November Armistice brought down twenty German aircraft and pronounced each a monument to Mannock's memory. One historian has asserted that Jones revised the slogan in his cockpit to read "Remember Mannock and Ball," though substantiating testimony elsewhere seems lacking. Whatever the case, Jones—who became "Grandpa Tiger" to the pilots of No. 74—was inspired to marvelous ferocity by the uncompromising example of Mannock, as were so many others, and Mannock's name was linked forever with Albert Ball's as a proud watchword for British air fighters.

Their combat techniques were different, Mannock's and Ball's, as were their sentiments toward the war and the Germans, but they shared qualities in common: magnificent courage, a high sense of duty, a feeling of responsibility for their brothers in battle. Each, too, had an aversion to publicity. Each held a modest view of his own importance and wholeheartedly endorsed the British policy that discouraged recognition by the press of individual pilots. At a time when famous pilots were being extravagantly lionized, Mannock and Ball shied from it like poison. Ball, however, to his pained annoyance, failed in spite of his best efforts to keep his name out of the public eye. Mannock, on the other hand, being older and more worldly, and also forewarned by Ball's earlier experience, succeeded almost too well in wearing his anonymity. Brilliant as he was as a fighting pilot, he was little known in England at the time of his death. His name appears almost as an afterthought in the six-volume official history *The War in the Air,* and even the award of his Victoria Cross was not announced until July 18, 1919, a whole year after his death. Though all of this accorded well with what Mannock himself would have wished, posterity must remember him in the concluding words of the citation for his Victoria Cross:

"This highly distinguished officer, during the whole of his career . . . was an outstanding example of fearless courage, remarkable skill, devotion to duty and self-sacrifice, which has never been surpassed."

CHAPTER X

Les Cigognes

W HEN THE QUESTION is asked, as it eternally will be asked, "Who was the greatest air fighter in World War I?"—an unequivocal answer is impossible. As with any qualitative analysis, specific criteria must be laid down before a judgment should be attempted. That overworked and often abused adjective—"greatest"—needs in this case to be scrupulously defined. It must be allowed beforehand, for example, that the pilot with the largest sum of victories was not necessarily the most valuable or even the most skilled airman in his cause. Too many factors require consideration. How long did he serve at the front? In what capacities? At which period of the war? Flying what types of aircraft against what kind of opposition? If a pilot's worth were to be judged strictly on the basis of score, Manfred von Richthofen, with eighty confirmed victories, would be the greatest, and any additional discussion rendered pointless. Since, then, a high victory score does not by itself measure the air fighter's merit in full dimension, other considerations need to be weighed.

It does not seem arbitrary to say that the single most important qualification for greatness was leadership. Nor does it seem necessary to reiterate that a brilliant battle pilot did not always make a good leader. Some outstanding individuals like Billy Bishop, Georges Guynemer, and Werner Voss—to name but three—simply did not possess the temperament to lead. These men fought emotionally from the heart, relying on superlative flying ability and marksmanship to dispatch their enemies. Usually they waited in the sky until a hostile formation appeared below and then, exploiting speed and surprise, dropped hawklike upon their prey. Such tactics could only be used by individualists, since even a small group of attackers had difficulty staying together in such swift maneuvers. Lone hunters—with the glaring exception of James McCudden, who nicely accommodated himself to either situation—commonly found their styles seriously hampered when they flew as patrol leaders.

The greatest air fighter evidenced a lofty sense of duty, was unselfish about his personal claims, and placed the safety and morale of the men he led above all else except getting the job done. He studied the ever-changing developments in his field and exerted every effort to pass along his knowledge to others. If he was granted authority and freedom of action, he made the most of it, not merely by venturing on solo forays but by improving the team performance of his entire flight or squadron or wing. As an exemplar, yes, but also as a mentor he inspired his pilots. And his character as well as his deeds in this way affected the pattern of aerial warfare.

Employing these standards of greatness, and giving due weight now to the number of victories won in battle, three men—Albert Ball, James McCudden, and Mick Mannock—emerge indisputably as the foremost British air fighters. Ball, a daring innovator and the first really high-scoring British ace, cannot be put on a par with either McCudden or Mannock as a patrol leader; he was, metaphorically speaking, a one-man band rather than the conductor of an orchestra. This leaves Mannock and McCudden. Counting only his officially corroborated victories, Mannock's score of seventy-three was more than McCudden's fifty-seven, and there can be little doubt that Mannock was the more gifted leader and teacher. True, his motivations sprang from a reservoir of unregenerate hatred for the enemy; he fought with a totally negative attitude. But he learned to cool his angry urges with a rational, businesslike approach to the nasty work at hand. He stopped at nothing to promote the welfare and effectiveness of each and every pilot in his command, and nobody knows how many victories Mannock presented to beginners in order to instill them with pride and confidence.

On the German side, two names leap to the fore—Boelcke and Richthofen. The theorist and deviser, Oswald Boelcke set an enviable example, and his teachings were still valid long after his death. Without detracting from his tremendous contribution, it must be remembered, however, that he served at a time when German air power was in the ascendancy and that he was killed before aerial conflict grew as widespread and fierce as it did during the second half of the war. For these reasons, his achievements—his achievements in actual combat, at least—were eventually overshadowed by those of his star protégé, Richthofen.

Which then, Mannock or Richthofen, was the greater? Their personal scores, as indicated in the official records, were separated by only a small margin. Both excelled as leaders and dealt wholesale havoc in battle. Richthofen was respected by his subordinates; Mannock was revered. The British ace served two tours in France, thirteen months in all, while Richthofen fought first as an observer and then for more than two years as a pilot. Although Jagdgeschwader No. 1, the Richthofen circus, was for many critical months the fighting spearhead of the German air service, the Red Knight as a rule operated over his own ground. Mannock's command was the smaller, but he regularly sortied over German territory. His and Richthofen's combat roles were diametrically different, the one offensive, the other largely defensive. Mannock's function was to flush, stalk, and kill; Richthofen's was to intercept, engage, and kill. The dangers of attacking the enemy behind his own lines were, of course, maximal. A single bullet in a vulnerable part of one's machine meant, at the best, an unpleasant sojourn in prison camp until the war ended. But because in Mannock's heyday the British air service outnumbered the German, chances were against his being continually jumped by superior enemy forces. Patrolling and fighting offensively, Mannock could furthermore utilize the inherent faculties of his fighter planes—speed and sudden attack—to the fullest advantage.

So it was Richthofen who contended with the worse difficulties. The criticism often leveled against him, that since most of his victims fell behind German lines he was an overly cautious fighter, is a *non sequitur* insulting by its implications to his memory. He was not so much cautious as judicious. That he seldom trespassed over British-held territory was the result of circumstances beyond his control. Throughout much of the war on the western front the German army was on the defensive, and the aviation units deployed behind that army were used in an ancilliary defensive capacity. Richthofen did not govern grand strategy. He was a junior officer whose basic obligation was to inflict the maximum number of casualties upon the Allies while keeping his own losses to a minimum. In this he succeeded admirably. Faced with a stronger enemy and committed to the defense, the tactics fashioned by the shrewd, pitiless, highly elusive Red Knight were perfectly suited to the adverse conditions under which he fought. As proof there is the fact that when, a few weeks after Richthofen's death, another leader, Lieutenant Hermann Goering, adopted a more aggressive policy, Jagdgeschwader No. 1 was punished by being temporarily withdrawn from action. Any humbug about sportsmanship and chivalry in the air was repudiated by Richthofen, as it was by Mannock, and properly so. Both were uncompromising realists. Each, upon impartial scrutiny, had unendearing qualities, perhaps Richthofen more than Mannock, but war is no popularity contest, and their personality traits had no direct bearing whatever upon their claims to greatness. All that matters is which one of them did the better job for his respective country. And when everything has been considered, it was Richthofen.

In being ranked a notch above Mannock, Richthofen must also, by the process of elimination, be hailed as the finest combat pilot of the war as a whole, inasmuch as Mannock in turn has to be rated above any of his French or American counterparts. His score was slightly bettered by the top French ace, Captain Réné Paul Fonck, with seventy-five victories, who served through three years of action and claimed to have been hit only once by an adversary's bullet. It should be appreciated, however, that from the onset of the British drive along the Somme in 1916, the Germans viewed Great Britain and not

France as the power they would have to defeat in the air, and for the remainder of the war their crack squadrons were deployed against the Royal Flying Corps. Hence, of all the Allied aviation forces, the British met the stiffest opposition. Mannock fought against the German elite whereas Fonck did not, and Mannock for this deserves the brighter mark in history. Fonck, a disagreeable, unmagnanimous man, was little called upon as a leader, moreover, which further detracts from his claim to fame.

As for America, she simply did not produce a pilot whose record compared with that of any of the European super-aces. Although numerous volunteers had for long flown with Allied squadrons, the first units of the United States Air Service were not in action until the spring of 1918, just eight months before the Armistice. Neither among those American aviators who preceded their nation in fighting against Germany nor among those who came later in General Pershing's expeditionary force was there one whose accomplishments rivaled Mannock's or Fonck's. The top scorer of the Lafayette Escadrille, Major Raoul Lufbery, a naturalized American born in France and reared in Connecticut, had seventeen victories when he died in combat. Captain Eddie Rickenbacker of the regular air service, who shot down more enemy machines than any of his compatriots and showed himself to be a very able patrol leader, downed twenty-six aircraft between April and November 1918. He had the ability, perhaps, but not time enough in which to compile as imposing a record as some of his illustrious British and French colleagues, or his German antagonists.

The fact that British flyers, from mid-1916, were confronted with the cream of German air fighters did not mean the French were having a frolic. French aviation, though it suffered no equivalent of "Bloody April," painfully felt the fist of German air superiority during those desperate early months of 1917, and the casualty toll was sufficiently distressful to stir public indignation.

There was, on March 14, a heated session in the Chamber of Deputies that heard one fuming legislator declare that "France is proceeding on the surmise that any ramshackle plane is satisfactory if it provides a Frenchman the opportunity of dying gloriously." The applause was deafening. Within days a brief but sensational scandal ensued as a consequence of disclosures about aircraft manufacturers bribing well-known air heroes—with lavish favors if not cash—for the purpose of securing testimonials on behalf of newly designed machines. The recommendation of an eminent pilot, as the manufacturers learned early in the war, all but assured a machine's good reputation. Similar charges were lodged on several occasions in Germany against that nation's aircraft firms, especially the Fokker concern, and there, as in France, the charges were not entirely false. They were exaggerated, however. In neither country was the sin as widespread or pernicious as the accusers imputed. Bribe or no bribe, and friendship notwithstanding, an inferior plane was suicidal to fly in combat and no pilot in his right mind would stamp it with his approval. When the planes of two competing companies were just about equal in performance, then a manufacturer's largess could undoubtedly buy preferential treatment for his product. So long as the plane was up to specification, where was the real harm? The real harm rested, of course, in the demoralizing effects of exposure by the press, as the French experience demonstrated. Although no punitive measures were taken against the alleged offenders, the few names mentioned were nationally respected ones, and the reaction of the French people was typically mixed and typically piquant. Editorial comment ranged all the way from a figurative shoulder shrug and a *"c'est la guerre"* to righteous anger and the curiously somber glee of French cynicism.

A hurricane of declamatory denunciations in the French legislature drove the Minister of War, General Louis H. G. Lyautey, to accept the role of scapegoat and resign. With him went the undistinguished and administratively inept General Guillemin, his aviation adviser. An ardent proponent of modernized air power and a masterful organizer, a civilian career official who got things done, Daniel Vincent was appointed to the new post of under secretary of military aeronautics and was given, among other chores, the responsibility for creating a department which would combine the army and navy flying forces under its own unified, independent command. Slashing through mountains of red tape and ignoring the anguished reaction of generals and admirals, he completed the merger by August. But it was actually a showpiece, and cooperation between the two branches might be described as similar to that between the army and navy wings of the R.F.C. in 1912.

Vincent did more, meanwhile, than simply work for the consolidation of the two aviation branches. A more useful fruit of his deft management was that the air establishment became no longer a political football, and this in itself decidedly improved the *esprit de corps* of pilots daily challenging enemy superiority at the front. A step he took in response to the public clamor for internal reform was to diminish the influence wielded over the high command by prestigious airmen in the field, who were totally unauthorized to meddle in the shaping of headquarters policy. Doing this, Vincent boldly grabbed a touchy problem by the forelock. The more prominent French aviators had grown accustomed to having their whims indulged. Pampered and petted, they lived luxuriously by comparison to the wretched *poilu* in his mucky, filthy, verminous burrow. Whereas the night was filled with terrors for the trench-dwelling infantryman, the flyer could usually look forward to a warm meal, hot water for bathing and shaving, a clean uniform, vintage wine and fine brandy, good fellowship, entertainment at the airdrome two or three evenings a week, and perhaps a motor trip to a nearby town for a flirt with the mademoiselles. The airmen had, too, that dream of the infantry's dreams, a heated barracks and a snug bed in which to sleep every night. He enjoyed these amenities and others besides. There was no practical reason why he should not have had such comforts and privileges; so long as they did not interfere with the performance of his duties, it would have been unthinkably stupid to deny them. These vital young men, who in all probability were about to die for their country, deserved whatever pleasures could be afforded. The airmen of every combatant nation lived as well as conditions permitted, which for officers at war was very well indeed. But no others had been coddled like the French—the celebrated French aces in particular—by a lenient, doting high command.

Ungloving a hand of stern authority at the new Air Ministry in Paris, Daniel Vincent promptly instituted a program of necessary reforms. Standing no nonsense from prima-donna temperaments, he recast the whole texture of command practices. He had no objection to his pilots living comfortably nor to granting them slack rein in their leisure hours, yet he insisted that military discipline be restored. Where his recent predecessors had run the air force rather like intimidated parents beset by a mob of spoiled brats, Vincent brandished the firm hand of a benevolent, considerate, but absolute rector.

Favoritism, of which a large portion had been doled out to leading aces, was no longer tolerated. For the anonymous majority of French airmen, whose deeds were less conspicuous than those of their renowned confreres, but whose devotion to duty was no less sincere, Vincent's prescriptions came as a welcome and refreshing change. Morale at the front took another sharp upswing. It did, as Vincent guessed it would, even in those recherché escadrilles composed preponderantly of aces, though it took a little longer.

What began as simmering enmity between Vincent and his flying elite in a short while mellowed into mutual esteem and a harmonious working relationship. Several factors brought about this reconciliation. For one thing, German superiority started to wane in May and declined further during that spring and summer, and this easing of tension naturally spurred a collateral rise in French spirit. Not without justification, it also redounded to Vincent's credit and enhanced his popularity. Both at the front and in the Air Ministry there was an improvement in the psychological climate, a dispersal of the clouds of mistrust. But there were other more subtle reasons for this emendatory rapport which did credit both to the under secretary and to the probity of the French aces when put to test.

The aces at first disliked Vincent because he threatened their prerogatives. Instead of an air force operating on the inconstant and inequitable basis of personal influence, with a small clique of select pilots having the best of it, the new air chief managed things strictly by the book. Requests for policy decisions and favors now had to pass up through the chain of command. Such requests were treated in accordance with the operational picture and the common good, never on the basis of partiality. The advice of knowledgeable pilots was still solicited and weighed, but no longer accorded the status of holy dogma. The salutary effect of all this, which the disgruntled aces gradually came to appreciate and approve, was a more efficient organization on all levels. Vincent worked marvels in bettering the lot of all, the high and the lowly. He expedited the introduction of new combat machines—updated Spads and Nieuports—which materially helped reverse the tide against German airmen, and this above everything earned him the gratitude and loyalty of pilots at the front. In return for what he gave them—a close-knit and well-equipped fighting team with a reinvigorated sense of purpose—the noblesse of the French flying corps soon gladly relinquished their claims for special privilege.

The most jealously guarded privilege the aces had enjoyed was that of choosing who would be allowed to serve in their crack squadrons. Until Vincent inaugurated his new order, a pilot had to attain considerable prominence before being honored with an invitation to join one of the all-star escadrilles. Vincent, however, ruled that replacements would henceforth be attached to these units only as needed and that they would be ordinary replacements from the regular reserve pool, many of whom had never even flown within range of enemy guns. This ruling was the main source of friction between the aces and the man they first regarded as, quoting one incensed squadron officer, "a tyrannical dilettante whose esoteric schemes will . . . ruin the air force." But Vincent knew that this self-perpetuating caste system was primarily to blame for much that was wrong with the air force. Putting an end to it automatically undercut the ace's influence and strengthened the moral fiber of the service as a whole. It took nerve to abrogate the prejudicial advantages of prestige and thus to incur the animosity of France's best pilots. Vincent, in fact, did not reject the possibility of a mutiny.

Nothing so disastrous happened, but there were loud complaints and bitter mutterings and pessimistic forecasts that the undeniable efficacy of the elite squadrons would be smothered by mediocrity. When the first new replacements arrived in these squadrons after Vincent's controversial ruling, they were mostly untried youngsters directly out of flying school, and they were not welcomed by the veteran aces. But an unexpected phenomenon occurred which in the next few weeks calmed ruffled tempers. It was seen that the efficiency level of the squadrons did not go down to that of the new men, but rather that the proficiency of the new men rapidly came up to squadron levels. Pilots who had not been attached to these units because they lacked fame were, many of them, becoming famous because they served in these prize squadrons. Flying alongside the pacemakers of French combat aviation, the newcomers kept pace. Those who did not were soon dead, wounded, captured, or transferred to less dangerous stations.

Although the French early embraced the practice of dubbing a pilot an ace and mentioning him by name in an official communiqué upon the occasion of his fifth confirmed victory, the original intention had not been to collect these adepts into elite units. There was, however, a trend in this direction from the very beginning of the war. Prior to the battle of Verdun, before the establishment of homogeneous fighter squadrons, the most famous French flying unit was Escadrille Morane-Saulnier No. 26. Its notoriety was due to the number of eminent prewar aviators who had come together in its ranks—Roland Garros, Armand Pinsard, Eugene Gilbert, and the rest—and to their pioneering feats in waging war in the sky. Another unique squadron, one organized in the summer of 1915, was Escadrille Nieuport No. 77, informally called the Escadrille des Sportifs (Squadron of Sportsmen) due to the number of sports personalities included on its pilot roster. Its brightest light was Lieutenant Maurice Boyau, the international soccer star who at the time of his death, September 16, 1918, had thirty-five victories to his credit, an achievement that placed him fifth on the list of French aces. Lieutenant Gilbert Sardier, also a well-known athlete, and Lieutenant Georges Boillot, a well-known racing driver—Sardier with fifteen German aircraft shot down and Boillot with five—were others who distinguished themselves in this outfit. With two escadrilles of such picturesque and specialized character already in existence, a broad precedent had been set for the formation of elite squadrons composed largely of aces. Such units came into being in 1916 at Verdun and during the battle of the Somme. Their creation, once there were thoroughbred fighter squadrons participating in full-scale aerial warfare, was all but unavoidable. Contrary to the impression left by most historians, the French system of ace units was the natural product of evolutionary process and not the result of any previous planning. The system developed entirely out of circumstances. Only after it had been several months in de facto operation was it consciously adopted and implemented as a way of life in the flying corps.

When the Germans hurled their shattering might against Verdun, the French air service was and had been paralyzed for weeks by enemy superiority. The army defending the fortress city, deprived of air intelligence, fought blindly. A relatively small force of Fokker monoplanes led by Oswald Boelcke had successfully denied use of the sky to French observation planes. Major Peuty, the man in charge of French aviation in the Verdun sector, with his back against the wall, finally acceded to the advice of General Trenchard, whose "strategic offensive" had since the previous autumn enabled the R.F.C. to work effectively against the Fokker threat. Following Trenchard's precept, Peuty concentrated his Nieuport Type 11 fighter machines into homeogeneous units to be sent en masse to clear a path for reconnaissance and artillery-spotting machines. Six *escadrilles du chasse* were thus formed and placed under the field command of Captain Tricornot de Rose, an aging veteran who in March 1911, had received the first military brevet in French aviation. As each squadron became operational in its new role, it was ordered to fly as a unit and "to seek the enemy, engage and destroy him." This, inasmuch as Trenchard had not quite yet integrated British single-seater machines into completely pure and separate pursuit squadrons, was the earliest use of all-fighter units under a single tactical command and the first organization of formation flying on a large scale.

The six escadrilles under Captain Rose's resourceful administration were all in action by the end of March. Among them was the Lafayette Escadrille, newly formed of American volunteers and officially designated Escadrille Nieuport No. 124. Another noteworthy unit was Escadrille Nieuport No. 65, which included among its number a fast-rising young ace named Charles

Nungesser. Still another was Escadrille Nieuport No. 3, commanded by Captain Felix Brocard. Formerly a Morane-Saulnier squadron, this escadrille became the first to serve provisionally as a single-seater fighter squadron in September 1915, when it was re-equipped throughout with brand-new Nieuport biplanes, much to the gratification of its most promising pilot, Lieutenant Georges Guynemer. Because it arrived at Verdun already equipped and ready to go, Escadrille N. 3 was the first to tackle the German air service in the endeavor to overcome the Fokker monoplane and seize control of the sky. At this juncture the escadrille adopted the stork, pictured gracefully in flight, as its battle insignia. Two stories have been told explaining the choice of the stork device. The bird was the heraldic symbol of Alsace, which the French wished to regain on winning the war. The other explanation is simpler, more logical, and probably nearer the truth: the stork is considered a good-luck harbinger in most of Europe. Whichever the case, this great-winged bird would soon become the symbol of an entire league of French aces.

Much was learned at Verdun, many valuable lessons. Fighter formations kept the Fokkers busy so that observation and artillery-spotting planes could once again fulfill their imperative functions. Pleased by the success of this strategy, the French began assembling another battle group at Cachy airdrome in prepartion for the Somme offensive, scheduled for late June. Although the main assault was to be mounted by the British Fourth Army, the French Sixth was assigned to lend support.

The new air group was placed in the capable hands of Captain Brocard, who also continued as commanding officer of Escadrille N. 3. Brocard was selected because Captain Rose, after providing a splendid account of himself, had been killed at Verdun. Consisting of six—and later eight—escadrilles, the group was attached to Sixth Army headquarters. Instructions were to patrol in large formations, virtually around the clock, to maintain aerial supremacy. Together with the R.F.C., the French made easy work of the German air service that summer above the Somme. The strategy twice proven, it was decided after a series of top-level conferences in September and October to organize permanent fighter groups, each to comprise four single-seater escadrilles (although later, in 1917 and 1918, five or six units came to be incorporated in some of these French multisquadron teams). In November, at Cachy, Groupe de Chasse No. 12 was put together of Escadrilles N. 3, N. 26, N. 73, and N. 103. At its head was Captain Brocard, whose command of Escadrille N. 3 devolved upon the famous ace, Lieutenant Alfred Heurtaux. The stork emblem was chosen to represent the entire group, each of the component squadrons depicting the bird in a different attitude of flight to distinguish among them. This was the origin of the combat group that attained imperishable glory as *"Les Cigognes,"* or "The Storks," a fraternity of aerial warriors whose exploits against the hated invaders cheered and nourished the French people through two oppressive, harrowing years of a war more devastating and bestial than humanity had ever before imagined possible.

The prodigious accomplishments of Groupe de Chasse No. 12, although history seems to have glossed over the fact, derived in no slight degree from the inspiration and forceful personality of its first leader, Captain Brocard. Even before Verdun, Brocard had transformed Escadrille N. 3 into one of the first fighter squadrons deserving of that description. And even before that, while his squadron was still flying Morane-Saulniers and doing reconnaissance work as Escadrille M.S. 3, he had encouraged his pilots to arm their planes with machine guns, to stop waving and start shooting at the Germans.

Felix Brocard, twenty-nine years old when he assumed command of M.S. 3 in April 1915, had learned to fly long before the war broke upon France. Aside from showing himself to be a pilot of rare enterprise and reliability in the opening months of conflict, he displayed exceptional leadership qualities and demonstrated a firm grasp on the principles of combat aviation at a time when few military brains had yet awakened to the potentialities of the flying machine. Excepting Roland Garros, Jean Navarre, and three or four others, the early French aces were the pupils of Brocard. Among them was Guynemer, the "winged sword of France," who later wrote: "On June 8, 1915, I reached M.S. 3, established then at Vauciennes. It was commanded by our master of all things, Captain Brocard. . . . To him I was an amusing boy. He took pleasure in giving me all the advice I wanted. And there was much of this!"

Brocard, probably more than anyone else, was the architect of the French system of collecting aces into elite squadrons. He began mustering skilled pilots from other escadrilles into his own during that autumn of 1915, after M.S. 3 had been re-equipped with Baby Nieuports, redesignated N. 3 and ordered to show what a homogeneous fighter-plane squadron could really do. Desperately wanting to convince the top brass of the usefulness of pursuit aviation and the wisdom of creating additional Nieuport squadrons, Brocard had no qualms about pirating talent from the variegated and largely impotent squadrons then in French service; he desired the best available personnel to man his tiny machines. Of the ten flyers in his escadrille, he replaced half with hand-picked individuals taken from other units. However, since there was little activity at the front that autumn, Escadrille N. 3 achieved nothing like spectacular success, which fact goes a long way toward explaining why Major Peuty, until faced with impending catastrophe at Verdun, so stubbornly resisted General Trenchard's advice to organize French Nieuport pilots into offensive patrol teams.

During the battles of Verdun and the Somme in 1916, Brocard, now with an entire combat group in his charge, stepped up his search for aviators of star quality. A superior pilot or an infallible sharpshooter was not infrequently met in those exacting days of war, yet a combination of the two skills in one slim lad of twenty or thereabouts was unusual enough to attract more than casual attention. Add to these qualifications the characteristics of courage, initiative, judgment, and intuition, all developed to the keenest degree, and the human product became so remarkable that he towered above his fellows. Such exceptional men caught no one's eye quicker than Brocard's. And once Brocard deemed them worthy of joining a Stork squadron, and they had expressed their willingness—which ordinarily was done with unbounded enthusiasm—the group commander would not rest until the necessary transfer had been made. Nevertheless, although the great ambition of most French airmen was membership in the Storks, there were some, a few aces, who politely declined Brocard's tempting invitation. Nungesser, who wound up his battle career with forty-five victories, remained by preference in Escadrille N. 65, which left Brocard's command when he formed his second group for the Somme offensive. Captain George Madon, the fourth-ranking French ace with forty-one victories, stayed with Escadrille Spa. 38. Lieutenant Michel Coiffard with thirty-four victories, and Lieutenant Jean Bourjade with a score of twenty-eight, were other top aces who did not serve in the Storks, as were Lieutenants Gabriel Guerin and Pierre Marinovitch, each with twenty-three conquests. There were those, too, of the *Escadrille des Sportifs,* and finally the pilots of Escadrille Spa. 90, called *Les Coqs* because of the crowing-cock insignia on their planes. This squadron—having in its number such stalwarts as Lieutenant Marc Ambrogi, Adjutant Maurice Bizot, Adjutant Charles Mace, and Adjutant Jean Pezon—was in the forefront of the French air campaign through much of the last two years of war, winning a reputation second only to that of the Stork group.

But Brocard, at Verdun and after, succeeded in gathering many estimable air fighters into his troupe. Around a nucleus of accomplished aces in Escadrille N. 3, he built a cohort of champions, four squadrons of the *crème de la crème.* Among the first to transfer to the Storks were the Captains Alfred Heurtaux and Albert Deullin and Lieutenant Réne Dorme, the three of them joining Escadrille N. 3, which Heurtaux would soon lead.

Heurtaux was a most colorful figure who had already achieved the singular feat of bringing down an enemy machine with just one bullet. He often amused himself in the midst of battle by winking, smirking, thumbing his nose, and sticking his tongue out at his encircling enemy. This open contempt for them increased their hatred, he explained, and tempted them to shake their fists at him in reply, to lose their caution to blind fury, which exposed them to his coolly calculated attack. His disdain for danger and his positive confidence in his plane and armament were powerful factors in his continuous success.

Between Heurtaux and Dorme, during the terrible hecatomb that was Verdun in the spring of 1916, an exciting rivalry developed as their scores increased side by side. Heurtaux had the higher tally when, in a single week, Dorme shot down eight Germans and leaped ahead. This lead he retained for a year, until May 25, 1917, the day he fell with his flaming Spad to destruction. In company with Captain Deullin, he engaged in a combat and lost. Three days later, Captain Brocard described in glowing terms the wonderful fighter Dorme had been, and how well liked. His nickname, "Père" Dorme, which he stenciled on the fuselage of his plane, was hardly due to his age— he was only twenty-seven when he died—but rather to his fatherly benevolence and serene countenance. He was a stickler for perfection in flying; it was his boast that he could recover from a spin with an accuracy of a quarter turn, and this accuracy was translated into an insistence on leaving nothing to chance when making preparations for a flight. Before taking off, he habitually walked slowly around his airplane checking every bolt, rivet, and cotter pin.

If we remember that French aviators had fewer opportunities than the British for bagging a kill and that their scores were generally lower, Dorme's score of twenty-three was ample testimony to his ability. Only eight of his countrymen did better, and his friendly rival, Heurtaux, who survived the war a twenty-one-victory ace, never did overtake him. (It must be said for Heurtaux, however, that he was three times out of action with serious wounds.) Perhaps the finest epitaph accorded Dorme was written by another squadron comrade who met the same fate less than three months later, George Guynemer. Of Dorme, Guynemer said: "His uprightness, his kindness and honest warmth made him beloved of us all. Endowed with steel-like strength and tireless energy, he was gentleness itself."

Escadrille N. 3, which in early 1917 was re-equipped with Spads and officially renamed Escadrille Spa. 3, of all the Stork squadrons was by far the most damaging to German life and limb. First to bear the stork emblem in battle, this squadron, from the time it spearheaded the French counterthrust in Verdun skies until the final stacking of arms, fought with a savage verve and deadly efficiency that raised it above any other unit in the French flying corps. Its deeds became epic legends, its extraordinary pilots proverbial heroes. So effulgently did it outshine its companion Stork squadrons that many historians have been guilty of referring to the Cigognes not as a group but as just this one squadron. Guynemer alone brought down twenty-one enemy planes in actions above Verdun and the Somme, raising his total score at the end of 1916 to twenty-nine confirmed victories. On the French front that frightful year, the five leading bêtes noires of the German airman were Guynemer, Heurtaux, Dorme, Deullin, and Lieutenant Mathieu de la Tour, all of them members of Escadrille N. 3. It has been written, perhaps apocryphally, that the German air command put a price on the heads of these five Frenchmen. If this dubious story is factual, the German motive would be easy to understand.

Sparked by this quintet of skilled combat men, Escadrille N. 3 loosed many painful blows on the enemy air service. The squadron, on September 14, 1916, received a unit citation in these words: "Under the command of Captain Brocard, [Escadrille N. 3] has shown a drive and devotion to duty without equal in the operations over Verdun and the Somme, having taken part from March 19 to August 19, 1916, in 338 aerial combats, shooting down thirty-six aircraft and three balloons, and forcing thirty-six other badly damaged aircraft to land." Captain Brocard dedicated this accolade to Guynemer by writing at the foot of it—"To Lieutenant Guynemer, my oldest pilot and my most brilliant Stork." The very next week, Guynemer justified the encomium by bringing down three black-crossed machines in one day, September 23, and was himself sent crash landing from ten thousand feet without injury.

The man who did most, along with Brocard, in shaping this squadron was Alfred Heurtaux, who also had the longest tenure as its commanding officer. Under his leadership was built Escadrille N. 3's reputation for ruthless determination, exceptional marksmanship, and murderous effect in battle. A cadet at St. Cyr when war broke out, Heurtaux was immediately commissioned a second lieutenant in the Ninth Hussars. Within a few days his regiment was deployed in the Vosges, skirmishing with advance parties of the enemy army. Heurtaux commenced his distinguished military career earning one citation after the other. His courage and resourcefulness were demonstrated on the evening of August 23, 1914, for example, when he saved an artillery battery from being overrun by the enemy. The battery was being deserted by a unit of French infantry under withering attack as Heurtaux, leading a reconnaissance party, happened upon the scene. Finding the infantry commander helplessly wounded, Heutaux took charge of the situation and ordered his cavalrymen into the abandoned trenches, thereby affording time for the threatened guns to be moved to safety. The advancing main German line was less than a hundred yards away when Heurtaux and his troops remounted their saddles and continued on their way.

September saw the regiment moved to the Somme, and October to the Ypres-Nieuport line, where it sustained heavy casualties. This did not suit Heurtaux in the least, and when applications were invited for transfer into the air service, he eagerly volunteered. Unwilling though his colonel was to lose an officer already holding three citations, Heurtaux's persistence brought the hoped-for transfer and he reported in November to Escadrille M.S. 26 for training as an observer. Training, such as it then was, consisted of a few ascents as a passenger aboard the unit's Voisin, after which he was considered competent to serve as a crew member in one of the new Morane-Saulnier Parasol two-seaters. After a succession of crashes, he decided it was advisable to handle the controls himself when he flew rather than remain at the mercy of some very accident-prone pilots. Flight instruction and a year of outstanding work as an aviator in Escadrille M.S. 38 preceded his entrance—at the request of Captain Brocard—into the Storks. In his first month with Escadrille N. 3, Heurtaux won five victories. By the close of the Somme campaign, fourteen German planes had fallen prey to his guns.

Flying daily over the Somme valley, high above the ceaseless volley and thunder of cannon, Heurtaux, Dorme, and Guynemer often patrolled as a threesome. On August 7, they discovered a new function for their already overworked combat machines. Leaving the field before daybreak, each having stowed extra belts of ammunition in his plane, the daring trio descended low over a German bivouac located behind the third line of trenches. Hedge-hopping just a few feet off the ground, they appeared suddenly over the startled camp. Reveille had just sounded below, and the Germans were drowsily standing roll-call. The sight of the French planes caused them to break ranks in panic. As Heurtaux later described the scene as it looked from his cockpit, "the Boches ran wildly in all directions like a swarm of fear-crazed ants." The exultant Frenchmen weaved back and forth above this bedlam, each in turn swooping and strafing. A steady hail of bullets raked the confusion of gray-clad bodies. German machine guns were brought to bear on the zooming Nieuports, but the three pilots quickly scattered the gunners and continued their rout. Only after the Germans had found refuge in their dugouts—all but the sprawling dead and wounded—and there was nothing more to shoot at, did the Frenchmen give up the attack.

Their thirst for enemy blood unslaked, their ammunition not yet exhausted, they turned eastward along a road clogged with army trucks and riddled the vehicles with bullets. Then, seeing a distant train of coaches loaded with troops, they dashed over to meet it. They flew so low that they could glimpse each other's planes through the windows of the railroad cars. They fusilladed the entire length of the train, killing both the engineer and stoker in the loco-motive. Before returning to the airdrome, they sprayed the coaches with the last of their ammunition. "It was," Heurtaux noted, "a stimulating business we did today."

During July and August, while the Somme campaign was in progress, the older Nieuport with a Lewis gun on the upper wing was exchanged for the newer type with a synchronized Vickers. In September, however, came the first two Spad single-seaters shipped to the front, which were tried out by Heurtaux and Guynemer. Despite some misgivings about the in-line engines, both men were rapidly converted to the merits of the new machines, and five months later, in February 1917, at Luneville on the Lorraine front, the entire Cigognes group was outfitted with Spad S-7's. With these planes, Escadrille Spa. 3 shot down more than two hundred of the enemy in the subsequent six months, a record never equalled by any squadron throughout World War I.

Soon after Heurtaux received his Spad in September, he accomplished a rather incredible double victory. A German squadron had been making things unpleasant for French two-seaters in the sector patrolled by Escadrille N. 3, and the Storks were ordered to remedy the situation. Heurtaux led flight after flight into the region south of Bapaume, almost every time encountering a quintet of orange-painted Albatroses, only to be stood off in combat. Exasperated, the escadrille leader ventured out by himself on September 18. Upon catching sight of the sharklike Albatroses overhead, Heurtaux flew his Spad around in small circles. The Germans, each after the other, dived to the attack. Again and again the Spad was hit in the wings, until at last all five German pilots had used up their ammunition. It was now Heurtaux's turn. Opening fire, he shot two of them down in flames before abandoning the chase in order to conserve enough fuel for his return journey. Five days later, Guynemer —who had christened his Spad the "Vieux Charles" and inscribed the name on its fuselage—dealt with another pair of the orange Albatroses, and the fifth was never again seen.

Heurtaux, in resorting to his desperate ruse and using himself as his own decoy, became the first pilot ever to score with a Spad S-7, a machine destined for great works. Not many days previous to this encounter, he had won the last victory he would get in a suddenly obsolescent Nieuport. In that action he had dived alone to attack a flight of seven Albatros D-2 single-seaters, passing across the lines in V formation toward Cachy. Choosing the enemy leader, who he figured was best protected in mid-formation, Heurtaux expended only five rounds before his target blossomed smoke and dived into the ground. His victim, it was afterward ascertained, was the well-known German ace, a recipient of the Order Pour le Mérite, formerly among the fiercest champions of the Fokker monoplane, Lieutenant Kurt Wintgens.

Heurtaux, twenty-four years old on May 20, 1917, his broad oval face bottomed with a squarely resolute chin and inset with dark eyes that peered intently from beneath jutting brows, who vied with his friend Dorme to see which would exact the higher price from the enemy, who led Escadrille Spa. 3 to its matchless rank in French aviation, was unable to spend that birthday in the air. After getting his fifteenth and sixteenth kills over Mangus Wood in the final week of December 1916, Heurtaux took a brief leave in order to recuperate from wounds received in battle. As if to celebrate his return to the front on January 24, 1917, that day brought him another double victory— a two-seater over Parvillers in the morning, and in the afternoon an Albatros D-2 over Rocquigny. Shortly after dawn the next day, he conquered again, and his twentieth confirmed victory was recorded on February 6. At the end of March the Cigognes group was sent from Luneville to Bonnemaison, a vest-pocket field on the Aisne River, to participate in the offensive of the Chemins des Dames. Here ensued a bloody interlude in the fortunes of Escadrille Spa. 3.

The last week of April, four pilots were lost. Heurtaux replied with a victory on May 4, ambushing an Albatros two-seater over Fismes. It spun straight into the ground from twelve thousand feet, and the observer miraculously walked away from the wreckage with a sprained ankle and a scratched nose. Heurtaux would never shoot another foeman from the sky, for the following day he emerged from a cloud directly in the path of two German single-seaters. A bullet in the arm caused him to lose control of his Spad. Fortunately, the plane put itself into a shallow, circling glide and did not spin or dive, affording Heurtaux time in which to recover his wits, straighten out, and return to his own airfield. In the hospital sixteen days later, on his birthday, there was a special supper served to his guests. Among the diners was the German observer who had recently been his opponent.

Captain Albert Auger was given interim command of Spa. 3 pending Heurtaux's return. The son of a French general and an accomplished poet and artist, Auger had a love for flying and sometimes waxed ecstatically in verse over the exhilerations of "reaching for God's vast blue vestment, the sky." This romantic bent did not impair his fighting zeal one bit. Before entering the aviation branch, Auger gained several citations as an infantryman for exemplary conduct in battle. Cool and audacious, he became noted for repeated narrow escapes after vicious assaults on enemy air formations. Known for his generosity and lack of self-appreciation, he was grievously mourned when, on July 28, he was fatally hit during an hour-long tussle with four enemy machines. Less than a week before his death he wrote his mother that he feared the terrific strain under which he had been living had so injured his health that he "could not hold on till the war is won." Over Auger's coffin Captain Heurtaux, attending the funeral with his splintered arm in a sling, spoke a short, and typically French, oration.

For the next nine days, until Heurtaux was able to resume command on August 7, Guynemer had custodianship of Spa. 3. During Heurtaux's absence many pilots had been lost from the squadron, among them his close friend, Réné Dorme. In the month of May, on the Aisne, forty-seven French fighter pilots were put out of action, killed or wounded. Anxious after his three-month absence to pick up the threads of his run of victories, Heurtaux found himself sorely frustrated in August by a scarcity of enemy aircraft. The Storks were now stationed at Berques, near Dunkirk, on the Flanders plain; German aviation was almost wholly preoccupied at Ypres with the Royal Flying Corps. On September 3, not expecting to encounter any opposition, Heurtaux was testing a new Spad S-13 near his own airfield. It was his initial trip in the plane, which was not yet battle ready, having arrived at Berques only the previous afternoon. At twenty thousand feet, to his mingled surprise and gratification, he espied a two-seater lumbering below, its wings marked with the Maltese cross. He promptly dived to the attack, but his shots missed, due, as he believed, to a faulty adjustment of the sights. Turning about for another pass, this time neither of his guns fired; something had gone wrong with the synchronizing mechanism. As Heurtaux swerved from the two-seater, the German gunner triggered a few quick bursts at close range. Bullets slashed through the Spad's fuselage. Heurtaux rolled into a spin to avoid pursuit, but even as he whirled earthward he felt a succession of shocks and saw his uniform reddening with blood on his right thigh. He managed a landing within the British lines. Rescued and rushed to a hospital, his leg had been pierced by a couple of incendiary bullets (which, though outlawed by international covenant, were used by both sides). Heurtaux survived because of a blessing in disguise. An artery and vein had been severed, but the burning phosphorous which coated the bullets had cauterized the wounds and prevented him from bleeding to death. He was not, however, fit to fly in combat again.

Once more Guynemer, now with fifty-two victories to his credit, filled the shoes of a squadron commander. But these shoes pinched; he was temperamentally unsuited to the job and knew it. In the "Vieux Charles," on September 6, he scored his valedictory kill. Five days after that, in his eighth day of command, the youngest and most venerated French hero of the war flew off toward the Belgian village of Poelcapelle, never more to be seen. As some of his squadron mates observed, among them Lieutenant Bozon-Verduraz, the man who accompanied him on that ill-fated patrol, Guynemer had not been his former self since shouldering the burdens of leadership. Perhaps, as they theorized, he was too far out of sorts to fly safely against the enemy. The price of his perturbation was a delayed reflex, a moment's confusion, an instant's hesitation, which for the combat aviator was often a prelude to death. After three days went by with no word of Guynemer's fate, Captain Georges Raymond was named as the new unit commander.

The other Stork squadrons, meanwhile, though they compiled proud records in comparison to most escadrilles, were but shadows of Spa. 3. Numerous citations were awarded to all the Cigognes squadrons in recognition of works well done. Escadrille Spa. 26 received this one shortly after the Armistice:

> An escadrille in which the qualities of aggressive initiative have never failed.
>
> Distinguished in Belgium in 1914, and giving in 1915 a living impetus to the birth of pursuit aviation, following the example of Lieutenant Garros, brilliantly carried along by Captain [Xavier] de Sevin, it continued to give battle upon all fronts with equal success.
>
> It has inflicted heavy losses on its adversaries, obtaining fifty-one victories and disabling seventy enemy aircraft.

Fifty-one verified victories and seventy probables, an unimpressive score compared to that of Spa. 3, was nevertheless better than many of the great bulk of non-Stork squadrons could show.

The leading ace of Spa. 26 was that hardy veteran with his twenty-seven kills, Captain Armand Pinsard, who alone accounted for more than half the escadrille's confirmed victories. Pinsard, who had flown in the squadron before his capture by the Germans in February 1915, escaped from the maximum-security prison at Ingolstadt and was reinstated in his old unit—now equipped with Nieuports—at Cachy during the Somme struggle. Flying since 1912, a pioneer in French military aviation, Pinsard at last dispatched his first enemy plane on August 23, 1916, his own machine receiving eight bullet holes in the exchange. He had the honor, a couple of months later, of being asked to fly the squadron's first Spad single-seater, the new model S-7. Although accustomed to the more maneuverable rotary-engined Nieuports— and Morane-Saulniers before that—Pinsard quickly familiarized himself with the Hispano-Suiza powerplant and was full of enthusiasm for the rugged Spad airframe. His appraisal of the new plane was submitted in writing. "The engine and chassis . . ." he said in summation, "are a combination which should contribute enormously to the success of French pilots." Giving substance to his words, he increased his victory log rapidly in the weeks that followed. By June 5, 1917, he had already destroyed sixteen German aircraft. In the succeeding year, between July 8 and August 29, 1918, after twice being laid up with injuries, he shot down seven kite balloons. He added four victims to his total before the Armistice, finishing his hectic battle career as the eighth-ranking French ace.

Second in Spa. 26 only to Pinsard, insofar as score was concerned, was Captain Xavier de Sevin, who came to the Storks from Escadrille N. 12 in May 1917, with six victories already his. Five months before this, Captain (then Lieutenant) Sevin had won prominence for a most valuable reconnaissance mission. In atrocious weather conditions, on a sleety December day with a cloud ceiling of no more than five hundred feet, he had spied enemy reserves massing along the Verdun line, where the French army was regaining the ground lost at the beginning of the year. Sevin's report enabled the Allied command to forestall a major counterattack. Not content merely with bringing back this urgently needed information, Sevin also carried out an audacious low-level machine-gun attack on a large concentration of German troops, scattering them in disorder.

Sevin served in the Cigognes with Spa. 26 on the Aisne front and then, later in 1917, in Flanders during the Ypres drive. In the final eleven months of the war he saw action on the Oise, the Marne, and in the hard-fought Ardennes campaign. Participating thus in the battles of St. Mihiel and Château-Thierry, and doing combat over the front during the last great German offensive, he blasted another half-dozen of the enemy to destruction and increased his total bag of victories to twelve. He was, at the close of hostilities, the very highly regarded commanding officer of Spa. 26. He stepped into this job in the spring of 1918, replacing Captain Mathieu de la Tour, whom Captain Brocard a year earlier had transferred from Spa. 3 to the head of Spa. 26. After winning nine victories in a long and creditable career, Captain de la Tour was shot down and hospitalized with serious wounds, his military service finished.

A colorful character in Spa. 26, who met a tragic end, was Lieutenant H. Noel de Rochemont, the possessor of a finely pointed and rather macabre sense of humor. It was his special joke to dive at an isolated enemy position as though to strafe it, only instead to drop a provocative message promising that if the recipient would meet him in Paris that night, a woman of extreme beauty—described in explicit anatomical detail by Rochemont—would be the prize. Sometimes he returned to the same position day after day, dropping more missives, telling the Germans that the passionate young lady was very disappointed at their continued absence, enclosing snapshots of her wearing nothing but a shameless smile. The psychological impact of Rochement's "mail," as he termed it, was potent on these misery-laden trench rats. They knew, of course, that he was taunting them, but in their deprivation they could not easily remain impassive to his prurient descriptions of the fictional femme and how she would minister to their desires. The photographs he supplied were especially delectable, and Rochement's visits were soon being eagerly anticipated. Six or seven "postal deliveries" were usually sufficient to quiet their suspicions and bring the Germans out of their holes, dancing and waving friendly hellos, when next he appeared overhead. Rochemont then gleefully mowed them down with his twin machine guns and laughed all the way home.

A grim jester, Rochemont aptly displayed on the fuselage of his plane a broadly grinning skull. Equally as cunning and pitiless in air-to-air battle, he revealed himself to be something more than a mere jester, taking seven victories in the seven months between March and September 1916. But then, on September 15, both his legs horribly mangled by Spandau bullets, he crashed behind the German lines and within a couple of hours died on a surgery table while doctors were amputating his crushed limbs. Rochemont cannot technically be included as a Stork, since he died shortly before Spa. 26 became permanently attached to the Cigognes group. He was by any measure an imaginative and proficient pilot, however, whom the Storks would doubtless have been happy to count among their number in subsequent campaigns.

Of the four original Stork squadrons, Spa. 73, though it fought with courage and resolve, became the laggard in accumulating victories. Captain Brocard, hoping to sharpen the squadron's performance, finally placed the unit under the command of a seasoned ace, Lieutenant Deullin, who along with his transfer from Escadrille Spa. 3 received his promotion to captain. This was on February 22, 1917, by which time he had claimed eleven victims in several dozen combats aloft.

Albert Deullin was laconic and retiring by nature, a savant of classical literature, a brilliant scholar in his younger days, when he attended universities in Germany and England as well as his native France. Immediately upon the start of war he enlisted in the cavalry and took an active part in the futile but gallant defense of Lorraine. He spent the winter of 1914–1915 in the trenches. The idea of flying obsessed him, and the following spring found him training as a pilot, qualifying for his brevet in June. The following month he was posted at his first operational unit, Escadrille Farman No. 62, where he carried out the usual tasks of artillery regulation, photography, scouting, and bombing. His work here was valuable enough to merit a citation in February 1916, and this, together with his own beseeching petitions to Major Peuty and Captain Tricornot de Rose at Verdun, secured him a transfer to fighter planes —not only fighter planes, but the famous Escadrille N. 3. Since Deullin had not yet had an aerial victory, Captain Brocard, then still commanding the escadrille, greeted him coldly. But it was not long before Deullin showed his mettle, sending a German two-seater down in flames near Verdun on March 31. He did not win the victory unscathed, however; he suffered a bullet-smashed arm which consigned him to inactive duty until May, when he rejoined the squadron at Cachy, this time enjoying a warm welcome. Deullin thereafter made the best possible use of his stork-emblazoned Nieuport, shooting down an additional nine German machines by the end of the year. His eleventh conquest was made in a new Spad S-7 on February 10, 1917, twelve days before he assumed leadership of Spa. 73, with Brocard's injunction to improve this squadron's standing.

Spa. 73 did improve after being placed in Deullin's stewardship, but Deullin himself remained its only outstanding ace. In March, while Luneville was the Stork base of operations, he acquired his twelfth victory; in April, over the Chemins des Dames in the Aisne valley, he scored his thirteenth and fourteenth. One after another, in Flanders and at Soissons, he fought in the great battles of 1917, striving not for personal éclat, nor to cultivate a crop of self-concerned individualists, but to enhance the team performance of the squadron. Deullin thoroughly approved of the egalitarian policies instituted that summer by Daniel Vincent, whereas Brocard never fully subscribed to them. This difference in perspective prevented Deullin and Brocard from ever working in close harmony. They each liked and respected the other, but their divergent views upset their relationship. Although his motives may have stemmed from another source, when Captain Brocard was relieved of the Stork command and moved up to headquarters in early 1918, he transferred Spa. 73 out of the Cigognes and into Groupe de Chasse No. 19, naming Deullin to command that group. It was a promotion for Deullin, of course, but some interpreted it also as an obtuse manifestation of Brocard's disfavor. Deullin went on through the final stages of the war to raise his total of confirmed victories to twenty.

The removal of Spa. 73 from the Storks left a vacancy which Escadrille Spa. 67 was assigned to fill. Captain Brocard, retaining his proprietary interest in the group though no longer commanding it, himself selected this squadron to replace Spa. 73. The reasoning behind his choice seems simple to reconstruct. Spa. 67 had a commendable service record dating back to the Morane-Saulnier era; furthermore, it was a free-lance unit as yet unattached to any permanent combat group, which obviated many complications in ordering its reassignment. Spa. 67—or N. 67, as it was then designated—had done much good work at Verdun in 1916. There, between February and the middle of May, until he was wounded and hospitalized for the rest of the war, Lieutenant Jean Navarre had led the squadron's retaliation against the German air force and won eleven of his twelve victories. Lieutenant Marcel Viallet, later that year on the Somme, downed nine enemy machines. And seven kills were made by Lieutenant Georges Flachaire that year at Verdun and after.

When Spa. 67 was incorporated into the Cigognes in 1918, its victories numbered twenty-two. In the eight months it flew with the Storks, the squadron increased its total kills with another twenty-two victories. Lieutenant Pierre Pendaries, a seven-victory ace, scored four times during this period. During this period, too, Lieutenant Jean Derode accounted for six German aircraft, and Adjutant Edmond Pillon got the last two of his eight victories. The last man to see Guynemer alive, Lieutenant Bozon-Verduraz, coming to the squadron in April from Spa. 3, scored his fourth and fifth victories that month and was officially declared an ace. The renowned Captain Fonck, taking temporary command of the escadrille for a few days, achieved his thirty-fourth and thirty-fifth victories on April 12, both within fifteen minutes. Although Fonck was technically still a member of Spa. 103, these two kills were listed to the credit of Spa. 67.

Because he served a year and a half with Groupe de Chasse No. 12 and became its leading ace, the story of Captain Réné Paul Fonck reveals much also about the triumphs and tribulations of Spa. 103 in particular and the Stork contingent as a whole during the final phase of the war. Not only was he the top-scoring French fighter pilot, but also the highest-scoring Allied pilot. He was born at Saulcy-sur-Meurthe in the squat brown foothills of the Vosges mountains. There was nothing in the beginning to mark him as different. The son of an ordinary family in a commonplace small town, when the war broke out he was but one of millions of French youths stirred by the prospect of martial adventure. He was twenty when called up as a conscript on August 22, 1914, and transported to the classification center at Dijon. This was a hastily erected tent camp situated alongside an airfield on the outskirts of the city. Fonck had read a lot about balloons and airplanes as a boy, and here, to his fascination, he found himself among the flying machines and airmen he had long admired. His impulsive request for acceptance into the aviation branch was summarily refused, however, and the disillusioned recruit was posted to an engineer battalion for training. What followed were the sorriest five months of his career—building bridges on the Moselle, digging trenches, repairing roads, installing latrines, and the rest of it. But through it all, once every week, he entered a written plea for transfer to the flying corps.

Fonck had already despaired of ever getting out of the engineers when, in February 1915, he received an order to pack his things and report to St. Cyr for aviation training. This took the form of eighteen days of lectures on the theory of aerodynamics, followed by a further spell of blackboard instruction at Lyon. Finally, on April 1, he went to Le Crotoy, here to learn the mysteries of actually taking a machine into the air and keeping it there.

The first few days at Le Crotoy were devoted to taxiing and bouncing up and down aboard the flightless "rollers" or "penguins"—standard monoplanes with clipped wings to prevent them from getting more than five or six feet off the grass. On these the pupil mastered the art of controlling a machine at all stages up to that of becoming airborne. Fonck, after demonstrating his ability to steer a straight course on the ground at any prescribed throttle setting, then received dual instruction on a forty-five-horsepower Caudron, from which he graduated to the sixty-horsepower version. Within a fortnight he passed his emergency-landing test and his altitude test. Next he completed a cross-country flight to St. Cyr, where he passed his written examination and was awarded his brevet together with a pair of silver-brocade wings to sew upon the left sleeve of his royal-blue tunic.

Now a qualified pilot with a school record that was almost perfect, he arrived at the front in mid-June as a replacement in Escadrille Caudron No. 47. At Corcieux in the Vosges he was in his native district, and it was fitting that he would score here a year later the first of his seventy-five confirmed victories. Flying an underpowered Caudron G-3 two-seater, however, his initial encounter with the enemy bore no fruit. It happened while he was returning from a reconnaissance over the Colmar region; meeting a German two-seater on a similar mission, he could do nothing but fume at his own negligence in not carrying a rifle. He vowed never again to fly unarmed. Less than a week later, on July 2, he came upon another German plane over Munster and this time attacked, using his carbine, firing several shots. His opponent promptly fled, so that Fonck considered himself to have won at least a moral victory.

Toward the end of that summer there began a period of feverish activity, with incessant reconnaissance patrols and bombing sorties, many at very low level and at night. Fonck now distinguished himself as a cool pilot who did not blench under stress. He was cited in the dispatches after two months of front-line duty for having buzzed the German trenches in a badly crippled plane, while braving a storm of bullets and shrapnel in order to bring his observer back safely with valuable intelligence regarding the disposition of enemy artillery. A few days after that, the squadron now stationed in Champagne, near the village of Cuperly, Fonck returned to base with a thrilling tale of a disconnected fuel hose, a quick landing behind the German lines before his gasoline ran out, a hurried repair, and a takeoff under fire, with a troop of German cavalry galloping toward him full speed. None of his amused comrades believed him, but he insisted his story was true. The very next morning a chance shot from the ground punctured his fuel tank. He managed to stay aloft just long enough to crash-land near a French outpost, within range of enemy riflemen. Bullets whined and kicked dirt about him as he unshipped the camera and photographed the damaged Caudron. This time he had proof of what he told his squadron mates.

Autumn saw the escadrille moved to the Oise sector at Estrées-Saint-Denis, where, on November 27, 1915, he received his second citation, this in recognition of consistent good work as an artillery spotter. It was about this time that Fonck began affecting airs about himself which then and throughout his life—he died in 1953 in Paris—alienated many who would otherwise have cherished his acquaintanceship. Fonck became an intolerable braggart; worse than that, his self-applauding stories often exceeded the limits of credibility. Fonck, for example, by the end of the war had made claim to 127 victories; while he might have scored a few more than the seventy-five officially verified and credited to him, he could not conceivably have shot down the gross number of German aircraft that he said he did. Never, though, did he withdraw a victory claim, not even when later investigation proved conclusively that he was in error.

Fonck had a consuming appetite for fame, and yet, curiously, although his traits were those of a man unable to earn glory and so constrained to steal it, he was certainly no mere jackdaw in peacock's feathers. It cannot be questioned that he was a singularly gifted battle flyer, possessed of courage and skill to spare. Of all his contemporaries, friend and foe alike, only one—Manfred von Richthofen—reaped a richer bounty of victories by official reckoning. Fonck won the coveted Croix de Guerre, the Medaille Militaire, the Légion d'Honneur, twenty-eight other citations from the French government, and a basketful of tributes from all the Allied countries. These added up to enough honor for a squadron, but not enough to gratify Fonck's insatiable hunger. Even if it meant claiming near-miraculous achievements, he had to be the greatest. And, compelled by his yearning, he made such claims. On many occasions he stated that his plane had never been struck by a German bullet in air-to-air combat. Afterward he recanted and said, yes, he had once been hit in the wing by one bullet. One bullet, no more! His boast has been almost universally accepted as unvarnished fact. It can never be disproved and may after all be true, but for even the finest aviator, the absolute paragon, to have participated in as many aerial clashes as did Fonck and be hit just once strains the most childish credulity.

Through 1916, Fonck's reputation grew as a mettlesome airman. But so did his other reputation, that as a poseur. To French flyers at the front he became notorious as a fabricator of improbable adventures, hair-raising escapes, and fabulous victories. And this was only one strike against his popularity. There was also his personality, or lack of it. He was a poor mixer, awkwardly quiet, and morose. His sense of humor was venomously barbed. Apart from talking about his own exploits, he seldom contributed to the conversation in the mess. He spent long hours alone, did not drink, and had the uncongenial habit of taking a nap after every patrol, thus excluding himself from the animated bull session which always followed a flight over the lines. Then, too, he started and finished each day with calisthenics, a solemn ritual which his carelessly conditioned comrades found highly entertaining to watch. Amusing also, they thought, was his almost foppish fastidiousness. Crisply handsome, a pencil-line mustache adorning his thin face, Fonck was always immaculately garbed and groomed. He wore his dress uniform, cleaned and neatly pressed, at all times except when airborne. Wearing it around the airfield in off-duty hours, when informality was the rule, was one more affectation that subjected him to sarcastic jibes and snickers.

So it becomes plain why Fonck, despite having shot down more Germans than any other Allied pilot, failed to emerge as the ideal of the French flying corps. His ego craved exaltation; this exaltation eluded him, ironically, because his stupendous egotism detracted from his truly marvelous accomplishments. Had he simply let his actions speak for themselves, he would have realized his ambition. But as it was, Georges Guynemer, unaffected by success, humane, winsome, generous, self-effacing, always a sympathetic friend, became the hero's hero. Fonck, this complex of unendearing qualities, was icily clinical in his approach to aerial combat; he seldom if ever made mistakes. Guynemer, whose eagerness sometimes got the better of his judgment, betrayed human frailties which added warm touches to his image. Men could identify with him, and so he became the sentimental favorite. He could never have written, as Fonck did, such a statement as, for instance, "I put my bullets into the target as if I placed them there by hand." Fonck was indeed an impeccable virtuoso in the sky, but back at the airdrome he strutted and brayed like a pompous ass.

On March 1, 1916, returning from a reconnaissance with a certain Adjutant Jaunaut as his observer, Fonck professed to have attacked an enemy two-seater that dived vertically into the ground. It happened too far behind the German lines to be confirmed. Fonck nevertheless turned in a vaguely worded victory chit, neglecting to mention that Jaunaut—who may be supposed to have done the shooting—had been riding in the rear seat. The claim was disallowed for lack of corroborating evidence, but Fonck entered the "victory" in his log, numbering it the first on *his* list of 127.

Near the end of May, a pilot-sergeant named Noel, flying alongside Fonck, received a direct hit from an antiaircraft shell. Fonck landed close to the wreckage and retrieved the sergeant's body. It was a brave and gracious thing to do, much appreciated by the men of Escadrille C. 47—until Fonck proceeded to cheapen the deed by telling of it again and again, embellishing it each time with new details of his own daring. Significantly, perhaps, although he had been the sole witness to Sergeant Noel's death, Fonck was not asked to speak at the funeral. A month later he narrowly missed a similar fate himself, for a shell tore through his starboard wing, cracking a spar and removing two ribs on the way.

During that long, hard summer, Fonck continued giving a good account of himself in action, as he flew the perilous reconnaissance patrols, artillery-spotting missions, and bombing raids that brought death to so many and glory to so few. Verdun had taught the French the value of aerial bombardment and now their two-seater squadrons were developing naturally in that direction, Escadrille C. 47 among them. French designers were providing improved machines to supplant the clumsy, primitive crates of 1915. In July, the single-engine Caudron G-3 was replaced by the twin-engine G-4. At the nose of his new plane Fonck mounted a machine gun to fire forward through the clear space between the two propellers. Back in the Vosges again, on August 6, flying with a Lieutenant Thiberge over Roye, he was ambushed by two Fokkers. Apparently startled to find this Caudron armed with a machine gun, the Germans scurried eastward after a harmless exchange. Though he had no realistic hope of catching them, Fonck set out to give chase, then noticed behind him a string of antiaircraft bursts, indicating the presence of more enemy planes. Turning to follow the line of black puffballs, he came across

two Rumplers about 150 feet apart, heading toward Montdidier. Fonck attacked. No sooner did he commence firing than one of the Rumplers sheered
off into a steep descent. The German pilot, diving like that and allowing Fonck
to get on his tail, had obviously panicked. So had the German gunner, who
was firing wildly in all directions. The antiaircraft batteries ceased their barrage, leaving Fonck free to pursue his advantage. This he did, until, to his utter
amazement, the Rumpler landed. Fonck put down, too, nearby. Their revolvers drawn and cocked, he and Thiberge gingerly approached the sitting
two-seater, expecting some kind of desperate trick. Instead they found both
German crewmen waiting passively to give themselves up. In his book, *Mes
Combats,* Fonck noted that in all his experience this was the single case in
which unwounded Germans with an undamaged aircraft voluntarily surrendered.[1]

There was no uncertainty about this victory, and the elation he felt in
attaining it convinced Fonck that he could never again be happy as a reconnaissance flyer. His ache to be a fighter pilot was so acute that he sought
combat now whenever he could in his inappropriate Caudron. In October,
on the Somme, he alleged that he had shot down an Aviatik that was directing
enemy artillery. There were several French planes in the area at the time he
specified, but none had seen the combat he described. Due to the chaos then
reigning at the front, any other means of verification was impossible and the
claim was nullified. Fonck, in his log, however, counted it as victory number
three.

Escadrille C. 47 was moved in March, 1917, to the Aisne, near Fismes.
This was the terrible spring, a period of savage aerial fighting up and down
the entire line, a season of manifold horrors that culminated in "Bloody April"
for the British. While the Royal Flying Corps was being decimated by a
superior force of Albatroses, Pfalzes, and Halberstadts, single-seaters swifter
and more heavily armed than anything else at the front, French airmen were
faring little better, though spared the brunt of enemy fury. That month of
March, Fonck, piloting the same old Caudron, was surprised along with
another Caudron by five Albatros fighters. The odds were great against the
French two-seaters, but the German challenge was accepted. Repeatedly
shaking off and evading his attackers, Fonck handled his hefty machine as if
it were a chaser. Seeing the other Caudron in trouble, he dived beneath the
three Albatroses that were circling it, leveled off, and held his plane on the
verge of a stall to afford his observer a perfect shot. The chatter of a Lewis
gun, the shriek and hollow bang of an engine blowing to pieces, smoke and
falling debris, an instant's disbelief, and then glowing satisfaction aboard the
victorious Caudron—these quickly-unfolding events marked the end of one
Albatros and its luckless pilot.

But the score was soon evened. The other Caudron, already streaking the

[1] Robertson: *Air Aces of the 1914–1918
War.*

sky with wisps of hot smoke, was pinioned in the cross-fire of all four remaining Albatroses. It lurched and reeled down toward the French lines and crashed only yards behind the trenches. Its pilot, a Sergeant Raux, was severely burned, his observer killed. The German fighters now turned to deal with Fonck. They climbed, regrouped, and dived at him in single file. Then, inexplicably, they veered off without shooting and disappeared in the direction of their own lines.

This second confirmed victory and the wonderful manner in which it was won brought Fonck's name to the attention of the authorities. His prayers answered, he was released from Caudrons and recommended for transfer to a pursuit unit. After training in single-seaters for a month at Plessis-Belleville, completing the conversion course with honors, he was assigned to a Spad in Escadrille Spa. 103 at Bonnemaison, where he reported on April 15, 1917. Gladdened and a bit dazzled by his good fortune, though certainly not bothered by self-doubt, Fonck found himself a member of the Storks, the most august guild of battle aces in French aviation. Like all initiates to the group, he was welcomed in person by its commanding officer, Captain Brocard, who briefed him on routine, explained what would be expected of him, imparted words of encouragement, and conducted him on a tour of the base.

The four squadrons at Bonnemaison shared a common mess, and there, that evening, Fonck was introduced to Stork nobility. He met Guynemer, Heurtaux, Dorme, Deullin, Pinsard, and all the living legends of Groupe de Chasse No. 12. In company like this, Réné Fonck was a nonentity, but he had behind him about five hundred hours of Caudron time over the lines and four citations, including one from the British. He was confident, unawed, and only a little less presumptuous than before. He envied these celebrities more than he admired them. If he put them on pedestals, he figured it would not be long before he would be up there with them.

Fonck's first patrol with Spa. 103, a three-plane sortie on April 28, resulted in a short brush with a flight of Albatroses. There were no fatalities on either side. On May 3, after only a week in the Storks, Fonck reverted to the pattern that had been his in Caudron days. Accompanied by another Spad, he was in the air to familiarize himself with the locale. But Fonck lost his escort and reported back alone with a lengthy account of an encounter with a German two-seater above Berry-au-Bac. "I fired twenty rounds," he affirmed. "Victim spun out of fight and crashed.'" Telephone checks with balloon stations and observation posts provided no confirmation of any aerial combat that morning in the vicinity of Berry-au-Bac. The claim was invalidated.

A couple of days later, on May 5, Fonck was flying over Laon with three squadron mates. A formation of five Fokker D-2's attacked them, and a dog-fight ensued, a wild melee with everyone maneuvering frantically and firing at anything that flashed by their gunsights and looked hostile. One of the German planes was shot down. Fonck, when he got back to the field, claimed that he had been the victor. The others submitted reports stating that a Fokker

had been destroyed, but that it was impossible to say when it was hit or by
whom. When such reports were handed in, the question of who would get
credit was usually settled by cutting a deck of cards. Fonck, however, insisted
the kill had been his alone and refused to gamble for what he argued already
belonged to him. Rather than quibble, the others withdrew their stakes in the
victory and let him keep it.

That same week Fonck surprised a Rumpler two-seater at eighteen thousand feet and shot it down. It fell in French territory, crashing into an army
field kitchen, injuring several cooks and KP's, and setting fire to a truck and
some tents. That Fonck had won a victory was clearly established. Though
he counted it his seventh, it was officially his fifth. On May 21, before going
on the furlough awarded to a man who had just become an ace, he turned in
another victory claim that could not be confirmed.

The next four months were critical, oppressive, and costly for the French
air service. As in the spring, losses that summer were heavy and morale was
low. French airdromes in advance areas were raided nightly, robbing pilots of
necessary sleep, fraying their nerves, rendering them more susceptible to the
contagious and ever-present terror of imminent extinction. Reconnaissance
and bombing escadrilles were being drubbed by massive formations of enemy
interceptors. Fighter squadrons, encountering superior numbers of superior
machines, suffered drastic setbacks, and many aces—some among them of
considerable renown—were slain or wounded or taken prisoner. During that
spring and summer, hundreds of French airmen perished in obscurity, the
public hardly noticing until the statistical sum of their deaths reached horrifying proportions. But the aces, when they fell, were effusively, even extravagantly, mourned. More grief attended the passing of Dorme, for example,
than accumulated from several score casualties in non-Stork squadrons. All
France groaned when Heurtaux was shot down and hospitalized—sobbed
when Auger, his shortlived deputy, was killed—wailed when Heurtaux was
wounded again, this time seriously enough to preclude him from further flight
duty. There was a nationwide gasp at the news that Deullin was shot down in
July, then a huge sigh of relief when it was disclosed that his injuries were
slight. And in September, when the incomparable Guynemer vanished forever, a great nation inconsolably beat its breast. At the time of Guynemer's
martyrdom, however, after four months of parliamentary debate, investigations, bureaucratic ping-pong, and stormy deliberations between civilian and
military authorities, steps had been taken to restore French prestige in the air
—solid, sensible steps. In August the Air Ministry was created, its chief the
competent Daniel Vincent. By uniting the army and navy flying services,
Vincent immediately effectuated a more practical utilization of available equipment and manpower. His reformation of the command apparatus, together
with his discountenance of special privilege, bolstered morale at the front.
His demands for accelerating the development and production of improved

aircraft immensely profited the situation, and as that dismal summer ended, the crisis began to ease off.

If it was a rough go for the flying corps generally that summer, it was a personal disaster for Fonck. He got one confirmed victory on June 12, and then faded into a two-month eclipse. Since the Germans were hunting in sizable packs, solo patrols were discouraged and Captain d'Harcourt, commanding Spa. 103, ordered more flights at full strength. Fonck, complaining that he felt hamstrung in the midst of a formation, became impoverished for victories. He filed four claims between June 12 and August 2, but each in turn was rejected as unconfirmable and unlikely. In each case he had won his purported victory after becoming separated from the squadron and going his own way. His autobiography, written after the war, contained what might be interpreted as an unwitting confession that he had not always strayed from formation by accident. "I preferred to fly alone," he asserted. "Thus I was able to have more adventures comfortably because I did not have to worry about comrades less experienced than myself getting into bad positions. It was when alone that I performed those little coups of audacity which amused me."

But still, claustrophobic complaints aside, Fonck began in August to give demonstrations of flawless ability on those occasions he did not go off marauding by himself. On August 9, ten thousand feet over Dixmude, Spa. 103 encountered an armada of thirty-two Fokkers and Albatroses that was attacking a flight of French bombers. Two Sopwith 1½-Strutters, their gunners already dead, looked like easy meat. Three Fokkers were diving to the kill when Fonck intervened. A single touch of the trigger sent one Fokker plummeting in flames. The other two turned on him, but he quickly disposed of another while the third fled. The battle over as abruptly as it began, Fonck joined the rest of the squadron enroute home. His joy at winning a double victory was soon bitterness.

This time, perhaps, he was cheated of his rightful due, for only one victim was credited to him in spite of supporting testimony by another pilot to having seen both Fokkers destroyed. It was not clear why the claim was disallowed. The man who upheld Fonck's brief, Lieutenant Claude Haegelen, was himself a practiced combatant whose deposition could not have been triflingly dismissed. Scrupulous in his own claims, he ran up a total of twenty-three victories by the end of the war, twelve of them against observation balloons. Only Fonck, of all the aces in Spa. 103, brought down more enemy aircraft.

By his own arithmetic, of course, Fonck did get a twin kill that day, and if robbed of full official credit, he still acquired something quite as important —a friend. After this incident, Fonck and Haegelen, with their disparate temperaments, seemed drawn together like the opposite poles of a magnet. Fonck by now must have been starved for a sympathetic comrade. He and Haegelen hailed from the same neighborhood in the east of France, and Haegelen had vouched for his double victory; here were two bases on which to build a friendship. Fonck cultivated Haegelen's good will, and Haegelen, who must have possessed the understanding and charity of a saint, freely indulged him. Theirs was a strained association, but Haegelen remained Fonck's only intimate in the service and his principal defender. "He is not a tactful man," Haegelen once wrote of him. "He is a tiresome braggart and even a boor, but in the air—and this is what really matters when we are struggling for national survival—this man Fonck is a slashing rapier, a steel blade tempered with unblemished courage and priceless skill. Up there he is transformed. If any of us is in difficulty with a Boche, or a whole flock of Boches, Fonck rushes to our aid. But afterwards he cannot forget how he rescued you, nor let you forget. He can almost make you wish he hadn't helped you in the first place."

In September, twelve gloomy days after Georges Guynemer failed to return, Captain Brocard chanced to meet Fonck in front of the hangars and informed him that all hope for Guynemer had been abandoned. The Storks in these twelve days had made a crusade of avenging their lost favorite. Fonck had claimed six victories, three of which were confirmed, but with his customary lack of grace, he antagonized his colleagues more than he pleased them. On this day, September 23, after hearing Brocard's sad news, Fonck immediately had his Spad rolled out and took off. Within minutes he saw a German two-seater intent on reconnaissance; diving on it from out of the sun, he delayed his fire until almost colliding with the enemy plane. A short burst hit the pilot and the plane went into a loop, ejecting the gunner, still alive, at the apex of its arc. Fonck had to maneuver sharply to avoid the falling body which passed within feet of his wing tip. The two-seater, a mass of burning rubble, plunged into the ground.

As he often did, Fonck then proceeded to mar his own deeds. Guynemer had invented a distinctive sky signature, a method peculiarly his, by which he announced a victory. When he returned after downing an enemy, he circled the Stork airfield before landing and rapidly opened and closed his throttle, producing a cadence that sounded like: *"J'en ai un!"*—"I have one of them!" After his victory on September 23, Fonck announced it as Guynemer had always announced his. No doubt he thought it an engaging way in which to dedicate the victory to Guynemer's memory, but the Stork veterans resented it as an affront to that hallowed memory. Fonck, suspected of trying to insinuate himself as the missing hero's successor, was roundly reproached that evening in the mess. Even Haegelen rebuked him. An outsider looking in might well have deduced that Fonck had been caught defacing Guynemer's headstone. And in effect, as far as the Storks could see in their anger, he had.

Since he omitted reference to the incident in his book, Fonck's reaction to this fuss can only be inferred. His inner poise seemingly was unruffled, encased as it was in armor-plated pride, and he probably thought himself wrongly accused, which indeed he may have been. Judging from what transpired in subsequent weeks, he was anything but chastened.

During the Storks' last day on the Flanders front, September 30, Fonck accosted a Rumpler two-seater at twelve thousand feet, attacking it from beneath its tail and hitting both pilot and gunner with a single burst. The stricken machine flipped over on its back, one wing came off, and the bodies of the crew were thrown out. From papers found on the pilot's corpse, he was identified as Lieutenant Kurt Wissemann. The name meant nothing for the time being; Wissemann was decently laid to rest as just another hapless enemy. Six days later, however, almost a month after Guynemer's disappearance, this same Lieutenant Wissemann was posthumously cited by the Germans for having shot down the great French ace.

That was Fonck's fifteenth certified victory and the turning point of his life. He was acclaimed then and therafter as the avenger of Guynemer. Sought out and interviewed by a host of newspaper and magazine writers, there was no reticence in him when talking of his own exploits. He told one interviewer of his "humble jubilation" at becoming the "tool of retribution" and shooting down the "murderer of my good friend Guynemer."

Fonck, jubilant as he said, was scarcely humble. Disregarding the official tally, he declared himself the winner of thirty combats, an inflated figure that was widely publicized. Guynemer had fifty-three victories at the time of his death; accordingly, Fonck's claim of thirty lifted him to the position of heir apparent. But why didn't the journalists bother to verify the easily ascertainable facts? Or, supposing they did go to this bother, why was Fonck not unmasked?

The press normally tends to exaggerate on the rosy side in wartime, enhancing the truth to make it palatable and reassuring for an anxious citizenry. In this case, the printed accounts neglected to point out that Fonck's assertions were poorly substantiated. It is further likely that the French Air Ministry, through politic silence if not active complicity, deliberately contributed to Fonck's aggrandizement. Having lately taken over in the face of severe criticism of the flying corps, the ministry perhaps felt it needed a new hero to carry on in Guynemer's stead and thereby divert people's minds from recent French reverses in the air. If such was the government's intention, Fonck looked like the best bet for casting in this exalted role. He was pretentious, he did not have the winning personality of Guynemer, but the public neither knew nor cared about that. Fonck's assets, on the other hand, were considerable from headquarters' point of view. He was a phenomenal air fighter. He belonged to the Cigognes. He had shot down Guynemer's slayer. Over and above these qualifications, he was ascetic in his tastes and habits, a spartan. It was improbable that Fonck would ever embarrass the service by getting himself involved in some scandalous escapade with wine or women. He preached against the evils of drink and was firmly engaged to his hometown sweetheart; in fact he married her before the end of the year.

There was another conspicuous candidate for succession to Guynemer. He was Lieutenant Charles Nungesser of Escadrille Spa. 65. In the first week of October, when Fonck shot down Wissemann, Nungesser's official score stood at thirty victories. This was twice the number of confirmed kills that Fonck had and precisely the number to which Fonck pretended—a curious coincidence. By proper scorekeeping methods, Nungesser was the leading French ace still alive and doing flight duty. There were reasons, though, why Nungesser was not chosen to inherit the nimbus of Guynemer's glory—not as much of it, anyway, as was apportioned to Fonck.

Total fearlessness was at once Nungesser's greatest asset and his greatest fault as an air fighter. Feats of stamina, strength, and courage were his *raison d'être*. As a boy, he lived in Paris until he was ten, and then moved to Valenciennes with his mother when his parents separated. He was passionately interested in sports, taking part in soccer, track, bicycling, motorcycling, swimming, and boxing. His earliest ambition was to become a racing driver or an aviator. He made evident in the war that he was prepared to run the most incredible risks provided there was some chance for success in what he had undertaken. "A strong heart does not fear death," he liked to say, "even in its most terrible aspect." It was no idle philosophy. Nungesser finished the war with almost as many wounds as victories. His more serious injuries included a fractured skull, brain concussion, seven separate jaw fractures, a shattered palate, a smashed right arm, and an atrophied left leg. Following a crash on takeoff in January 1916, in which he broke both his legs, he was unable to walk without a cane.

Nungesser was a tall, husky lad of sixteen when, in the winter of 1908, he quit the technical school he was attending and began adventuring. His mother bought him a ticket to Rio de Janeiro, where he intended to look up an uncle. His grandiose plan was to find work, save his money, and go into business building automobiles and airplanes. He made progress toward both goals. Four years of trying to contact his uncle brought him to Buenos Aires, where a wealthy Argentinean hired him to maintain and drive racing cars. A fortuitous meeting with a fellow Frenchman, a barnstorming exhibition flyer, gave Nungesser the opportunity to learn to fly. He was earning his living as a demonstration pilot for a local manufacturing shop when at last he located his uncle and joined him on his sugar plantation, deep in the bush. While here he began constructing his own plane, but it was not to be completed. In the summer of 1914, Nungesser had a presentiment; abandoning everything in South America, he embarked for France.

Eight weeks or so before the guns of war sounded, Nungesser volunteered for the infant French aviation service. The recruiting officer shook his head. At twenty-two, the blond and sparsely bearded Nungesser appeared an adolescent. Army aviation, he was told, was for older, more mature men. Offended and glum, he enlisted in the crack Second Hussars and became a cavalryman. The war was barely a month old when he earned his first decoration. It was the Medaille Militaire, and the sheer bravado he showed in winning it was of the rarest order. The action occurred during the retreat to the Marne. Nungesser's cavalry squadron found itself hemmed in, cut off from help, and rapidly running low in rations and ammunition. He offered to lead a patrol in an effort to find an escape route. But the patrol, after a few abortive attempts, was unable to break through the ring of German riflemen. Figuring that one man had a better chance than several, Nungesser infiltrated through the enemy line and made a lone reconnaissance. Reaching the Laon-Coucy road, he met two weary stragglers. A rumbling noise sent them to cover in a ditch. The noise grew louder and resolved itself into a Mors touring car bearing the black-and-white pennant of the Imperial German Staff Corps. Nungesser organized an impromptu ambush. The sudden report of three rifles saw two German officers slump dead in their seats. The driver, superficially wounded, made the mistake of stopping. Nungesser and his confederates leaped from the ditch and rushed the automobile, killing the driver and three more officers at point-blank range. Then, in a furious dash, while fired on by both sides, Nungesser drove to the safety of the French lines. As he himself stated, the Germans were shooting at French uniforms and the French at the German car. Besides receiving his medal, he was permitted to keep the Mors as a gift from his commanding general. Capitalizing on the general's good graces, he asked for—and was granted—a transfer to aviation.

On March 2, 1915, just five days before Guynemer arrived there for flight training, Nungesser departed from Avord airdrome as a breveted pilot and commenced upon a battle career unsurpassed for madcap adventure and misadventure. Based at St. Pol, near Dunkirk, with his first operational unit, Escadrille Voisin No. 106, he spent that spring flying a two-seater on reconnaissance and returning time after time with his plane gashed and shattered by bullets and shell bursts, much to the disgust of his mechanic, a put-upon individual named Pochon, who was obliged to spend most of his evenings patching up the damage. On April 26, Nungesser had the temerity to attack an Albatros which carried a Parabellum gun in its rear cockpit. His own observer was armed with a carbine. When the Albatros refused to accept combat, Nungesser angrily chased it toward the German lines. What he failed to realize was that he was being sucked into a trap. The German pilot was not running away; he was leading Nungesser over an antiaircraft battery. By the time Nungesser awoke to this fact, his plane was shredded by shrapnel, its engine sputtering a few last spasms of life. Staying aloft almost by will power alone, he managed a dead-stick landing on the French side of the lines and walked away from the wreckage with his dazed observer.

Being shot down taught him nothing of the folly of trying to use a dray horse as a cavalry charger. Roland Garros that very month had shown how airplanes could fight as well as scout, and Garros' electrifying success no doubt reinforced Nungesser's belligerency. Nungesser ignored the fact that whereas Garros had been flying a nimble little Morane-Saulnier and had fitted it with a stationary forward-firing machine gun, he, Nungesser, was laboring through the air in an ungainly two-seater with only a rifle for armament. Several times in the next few weeks he attempted to engage the enemy, only to have his aggressiveness unanswered. Spoiling for a fight on the afternoon of May 11, he simulated a distressed aircraft in an endeavor to entice a pair of Albatroses into close range, but his opponents seemed disinterested and once again he was foiled. The following day he attacked an Aviatik without result, and on May 16, an L.V.G. likewise frustrated his purpose.

When Nungesser finally did shoot down his first German, he did so in his usual spectacular manner. The squadron had been moved to a field near Nancy. It was in the process of being re-equipped when he was named as standby pilot one evening. Nungesser was a great man with the ladies; sitting around a deserted airfield all night was not his idea of fun, especially when the bars in Nancy were inhabited by so many pretty and patriotic mademoiselles. To relieve his boredom, he wandered around the hangars and became intrigued by a brand-new Voisin that had just been delivered. His own plane was typically battered, with dozens of patches sewn over bullet holes. Toward dawn, suddenly, he was bitten by an irresistible urge to give the new plane a tryout. Taking the duty gunner along, he flew off with the firm intention of bringing down an enemy machine. The new Voisin bore a swivel-mounted Hotchkiss at the bow of its cockpit nacelle, which convinced Nungesser that victory depended only on finding a suitable target.

Half an hour later, the airdrome alert sounded. Five hostile aircraft had been detected approaching Nancy. The standby pilot was ordered to intercept, but Nungesser was nowhere to be found. As the squadron commander pondered what action to take, the telephone rang and an excited voice informed him that one of his planes had downed a German raider. Bewildered, he initiated a search of the hangars and discovered the new Voisin missing. Just at this unpropitious moment, Nungesser alighted. For leaving his post he was sentenced to eight days arrest. Asked if he thought his punishment unfair, Nungesser replied that any pilot who had shot down an Albatros with a Voisin deserved the Croix de Guerre. The Albatros was exhibited in Nancy for several days afterward, and the grateful townspeople made Nungesser's confinement to quarters easy to endure by sending him presents of food and wine. His commanding officer showed there were no hard feelings by awarding him the Croix de Guerre. Even more to his liking, Nungesser also received a transfer to single-seaters.

In November, having completed his training on Nieuports, he was assigned to Escadrille N. 65 which was then being formed at his old base near Nancy. On his first day here he painted on his plane the emblem by which he would be known for the rest of his military career: a large black heart enclosing a skull and crossbones beneath a coffin flanked by two lighted candles. That done, he took off and performed a dazzling thirty minutes of low-level aerobatics over the center of Nancy, creating such a disturbance that the civil authorities telephoned his commanding officer and protested. The latter, waiting on the tarmac for Nungesser's return, greeted him with the caustic observation that he ought to impress the enemy and not the French population with his flying. The carefree pilot thought about that and decided it was a reasonable request. He refueled his Nieuport and flew off again, this time to buzz in over the nearest German airdrome and repeat his stunt performance, again at low altitude. Upon arriving back at base, he reported to the squadron commander that orders had been carried out. The result was another eight days of simple arrest.

But forty-eight hours later, on November 28, Nungesser scored his second victory by shooting down one of a pair of Albatroses he encountered over the Moselle. This earned him remission of the remaining six days of his punishment, another mention in dispatches, and the Légion d'Honneur. During the winter lull at the front, on January 29, 1916, he piled up his machine on takeoff and went to the hospital for an extended stay; it was this, the worst of his numerous crashes, that left him with a partially paralyzed leg.

In April, flying over the Verdun inferno, he shot down a balloon and two L.V.G.'s, one of which he photographed as it fell. The end of that month found him convalescing from a bullet wound. In mid-May he rejoined his unit at Bar-le-Duc. Victories followed, and for virtually every victory a narrow escape from death.

Nungesser was infected with a surfeit of rash courage, so much that it seemed to crowd out every vestige of his instinct for self-preservation. Launching into battle at every opportunity, relying on naked audacity to see him through, he seldom emerged from a combat except by the skin of his teeth. His Nieuport became a crazy quilt of patches. Once he came back with twenty-eight bullets lodged in the wing frames; on another occasion he was forced to land with forty holes in the cowling alone. His wounds and injuries succeeded one another at a rate that would have unnerved a less temerarious man. And yet, between intervals in the hospital, almost always flying with some portion of his body bandaged or splinted, he continued to score. By New Year's Day 1917, he had twenty-one confirmed victories to his credit. He could not celebrate the holiday, however, as he was in traction after having his improperly knitted fractures broken by bone surgeons and reset. After his release from medical supervision in March, headquarters implored him to rest, and he agreed to this on condition that he be allowed a roving commission to fly whenever he felt up to it. That agreed, he was given a special Nieuport, fitted with a Clerget engine. He flew the plane to St. Pol for a couple of relaxing weeks at the seashore, so he said, but he went patrolling early every morning.

While "resting" at St. Pol, Nungesser reopened his scorebook on May 1, 1917, and attacked a formation of six German naval planes over the Strait of Dover. He sent one down into the water and caused another to pancake on the beach near Dunkirk. Returning to his squadron, he got four additional kills in the next two weeks, and then achieved a victory left unrecorded in his total—one, indeed, he far preferred never to have won. Taking off after a forced landing between the lines, he was set upon by a British single-seater which drilled some fifteen machine-gun slugs into his Nieuport. Nungesser attempted to break away, but his assailant stayed on his tail, firing, giving Nungesser the idea that it might be a German at the controls of a captured aircraft; the Germans were known to have resorted to this ruse before. He frantically pointed to his French markings, but the pursuer kept firing at him. Although Nungesser would rather not have risked harming an Englishman, even if it meant letting an enemy escape, he was unable to outspeed the British plane and so had no option but to come about and defend himself. He vanquished his antagonist in a brief fight and watched him tumble wing over wing to earth. Hoping desperately that his victim was a German masquerading in friendly colors, he landed beside the wreckage. To his sickened horror, he found the dead man to be in fact a British pilot, presumably a novice who had misread the Nieuport's bizarre escutcheon as a black cross. As soon as possible afterwards, Nungesser had broad bands of red, white, and blue painted across his upper wing as an additional recognition feature.

Meanwhile, the distinctive insignia emblazoned on the flanks of his plane, inasmuch as it was by now familiar to the Germans, was responsible for another extraordinary event that same day. It was upon returning from his tragic mix-up with the Englishman that Nungesser received a challenge to single combat. Dropped on the airfield from a lone Albatros during his absence, the note of defiance was scrawled in French and addressed, "To my worthy opponent, Monsieur Skull and Crossbones." Upset as he was after shooting down an ally, Nungesser reacted sullenly to the sinister invitation. Four o'clock was the time appointed for the duel; it was now but a little past noon. He fidgeted around the mess hall for an hour, listening impatiently to the warnings of his comrades against accepting the challenge, then spent another hour carefully checking his aircraft and guns. At half-past two he took off, still smoldering with a guilt that could only be assuaged by spilling German blood. On the way to meet his challenger, he detoured over an enemy airfield and strafed it—a thoughtless act that consumed precious fuel and ammunition better reserved for the coming fight. Arriving fifteen minutes early at the locale specified in the German note, he was immediately attacked by six Albatroses diving from cloud cover. Nungesser automatically banked into a gradual descent and gathered speed for a wide loop. At the top of the loop he rolled into an Immelmann turn. The maneuver brought him up behind the Albatroses, which were unable to recover until they had plummeted past him. The battle was short and vicious. Nungesser, firing an uninterrupted stream of bullets, emptying a whole canister of cartridges, dispatched two adversaries on his initial sweep. Then, his fuel supply running low and with only one load left for his guns, he disengaged himself and departed full throttle for home. To his relieved surprise, the four remaining Albatroses let him go unmolested.

On August 16, his thirtieth victim crashed in the Houthulst forest, but

Nungesser was now being taxed to the limit of his endurance. He could walk only with great difficulty and often had to be carried to and from his machine. The torment in his left leg steadily worsened until, on September 12, he set forth on a flight to Paris for a long-overdue leave. No sooner, though, had he gained cruising altitude than a Halberstadt single-seater attacked him. A combat ensued, with the two contestants so evenly mached that neither was able to get a clear shot at the other. Near fainting with fatigue after half an hour of strenuous aerobatics, his ailing leg numbed by the painful exertions of kicking the rudder pedal, Nungesser regretfully decided to quit the bout and try to make it into Le Touquet airdrome, fearing the burst from behind which he was certain would come. The Halberstadt did an amazing thing. Instead of taking advantage of Nungesser's obvious plight, it trailed him in toward the French field, touched down some fifteen yards behind the Nieuport, taxied alongside—whereupon the German pilot waved in salute—and promptly took off again. Nungesser wanted to go up for another round with his chivalrous opponent but was too tired. He said afterward that he felt humiliated.

Landing later that day at Issy, he learned that Guynemer was missing since the previous morning and that he himself was now the leading French ace. But Nungesser refused to acknowledge the fact, saying that so long as his score remained below Guynemer's fifty-three, he could not accept the title. Nungesser's diffidence, contrasted with Réné Fonck's arrogant grandstand play, reveals further why the latter became generally affirmed as the new figurehead of French aviation.

That the Air Ministry saw fit to keep quiet when Fonck hoodwinked the press into believing he had thirty victories, twice the official tabulation, might again be ascribed to the fact that Nungesser, though he could have boasted of thirty bona fide victories, was not exactly the kind of hero headquarters wanted. As a man, Nungesser was by far the more popular at headquarters. He was roguish and witty, a ribald raconteur with few equals, a good companion for a riotous night on the town. He was good fellowship personified, and the desk officers in Paris esteemed him for his waggish, rollicking bonhomie.

Fonck was by comparison a priggish bore, a stodgy misfit in the boisterous, uninhibited society of soldiers in wartime. But he was a businesslike air fighter, an exceptionally talented pilot and marksman, courageous as he had to be while chary of needless and improvident risks. He flew and fought as the textbook advised, cautiously, weighing consequences, economizing his fuel and ammunition, never facing unfavorable odds without good reason. In his off-duty hours, furthermore, he was as decorous and sober as a churchwarden, a pillar of respectability. If Air Ministry officers were hypocritical in choosing —or, more accurately, in remaining silent and permitting newspapers and magazines to choose—Fonck over Nungesser as the flying corps' new standard bearer, theirs was the hypocrisy of practical politics. Nungesser's wild behavior, his rowdy episodes and daredevil clowning, his ungovernable rashness in combat, all weighed against him. His barroom high jinks and amatory antics might any day have ensnared him in scandal, a liability the Air Ministry did not want to incur. There was also the likelihood, what with his past record of injuries and his incorrigible disregard of danger, that Nungesser would not long remain in active service, that he would be killed or permanently wounded. Headquarters was understandably unwilling to endorse him as Guynemer's successor, for he possessed defects of prudent wisdom that the Air Ministry was trying to breed out of its pilot trainees. Fonck therefore became the idol of French aviation, and if he took his position too cockishly, he nevertheless went on to prove that nobody had more right to it.

In the remaining weeks of 1917, following his lucky victory over Lieutenant Wissemann on September 30, Fonck claimed to have shot down nine additional enemy planes and received official credit for four, which brought his confirmed score to nineteen. A few days before Christmas, the winter lull having settled upon the front, he applied for an extended leave, went home to marry his fiancée, and spent an idyllic honeymoon on the Mediterranean coast. He returned to his escadrille on January 18, 1918. The very next morning, in the course of two separate dogfights on the same patrol, he bagged an Albatros and a Fokker (which he always spelled "Focker"), thus winning his first authenticated double victory. He got one more confirmed kill above the old Verdun battleground, where he shot down a large machine of uncertain manufacture, probably an experimental type, on February 5, after which the Cigognes group moved into Champagne again.

According to the official ledger, Fonck, Deullin, and Madon were all now on the same score, with only Nungesser ahead of them. The knowledge that Nungesser was still technically the leading French ace rankled Fonck. Viewing Nungesser as a rival and keenly sensitive to the dagger-sharp criticism of other pilots for having had so many of his claims discounted, Fonck became more obsessed than ever with a determination to amass victories. His worst detractors could not help but admire him as he continued and even accelerated his tremendous scoring pace. The end of March found him with thirty-two confirmed victories, including four double kills. This tied him with Nungesser, whose luck of late had not been good.

After his prolonged health cure in Paris during the previous autumn, Nungesser, still on doctor's orders to avoid physical strain, was assigned to carry out combat indoctrination of new pilots in N. 65. Flying with a different one each day, he kept in the background while his pupils engaged in actual battle but was always ready to intercede if a fight seemed to be going the wrong way. One night, while enroute to Paris by car with his mechanic, who was at the wheel, Nungesser was involved in a serious accident that killed Pochon and again broke his own jaw. Going back into action on December 31, he scored several victories too deep in German territory for confirmation. He did not add to his official total until March 12, when his thirty-first victim fell near Craonne. By March 29, Fonck, with thirty-two victories, had gained first place on the list of aces. Nungesser equaled this the next day. Fonck replied with his thirty-third kill and intense rivalry between them persisted, first one and then the other leading until Fonck ultimately clinched a decisive margin. Hence, when Nungesser downed his fortieth enemy plane on July 16, Fonck had already reached the forty-five mark.

Nungesser, after yet another sojourn in the hospital, resumed scoring on August 14, destroying two balloons on each of two patrols. Wounded again on the following afternoon, he nevertheless increased his sum to forty-five, which victory brought him his fifteenth mention in dispatches. With that score he finished the war, during which he acquired, among myriad honors, the American Distinguished Service Cross, the British Military Cross, a Croix de Guerre from France, Belgium, and Portugal, and the Serbian Cross of Karageorgevitch.

Through that spring and summer, Fonck's victories regularly came in multiples. His most memorable day was May 9. For some time he had been promising himself that he would answer his many critics in the flying corps by performing a dazzling *coup de maître*—shooting down five machines in a single day. As he stood on the airfield that May afternoon and watched the slowly clearing fog, he little thought that within a few hours he would achieve his ambition and even surpass it. The hour was late, almost four o'clock, before the fog lifted sufficiently for him to take off with two other Spads. Climbing rapidly toward the lines, they soon encountered a German reconnaissance two-seater escorted by a pair of fighters. Diving on them, Fonck attacked the first head-on and killed the pilot instantly; then a swift reversement, another touch of the trigger, and the second enemy fighter erupted in flames and corkscrewed to earth. Fonck saw the third member of the enemy trio, perhaps thinking himself overlooked, racing for refuge. His machine disintegrated in the air after another burst from Fonck's guns. In forty-five seconds Fonck had wiped out a formation of three. The wreckage of all three was later found near Grivesnes, strewn about an area less than a mile square.

Hardly had the Spads landed than the wires were humming with the news, but Fonck was airborne again by half-past five. At twenty minutes after six, he spotted a lone two-seater over Montdidier. Judging course and distance, he entered a cloud to come out again directly under the enemy plane, where its crew could not see him. They died without knowing what happened. A formation of four Fokkers and five Albatroses then came upon the scene. Fonck hesitated before risking an attack. The desire to get his five kills overruled his innate caution, however, and he picked off the rearmost Fokker. He now had his five victories and wanted to head back to base, but found himself being hotly pursued by eight fighters. When the leader of the German formation tried to cut him off and turn him eastward, Fonck managed a quick burst that yielded victory number six. His way clear, he sped back to the French lines, leaving behind two telltale columns of smoke. By eight o'clock that evening, his sextuple victory was officially verified.

Fonck always spoke of it as an unparalleled achievement, although three British pilots—Captain William G. Claxton, Captain H. W. Woollett, and Captain J. L. Trollope—also accomplished this remarkable feat. Trollope had done it a month and a half before Fonck; Claxton and Woollett a short time afterward. But Fonck did earn the unique distinction of repeating his coup. In September, he again accounted for six confirmed victories in one day! And, were it not for a machine-gun stoppage, he might well have shot down eight that day, as his awe-struck squadron mates in Spa. 103 unanimously attested.

Fonck, in the final months of the war, dispelled any doubts that may have lingered about his supremacy in the French flying corps, when he scored half a dozen more double victories and three triples. Attaining his fifty-fifth confirmed kill before the end of July, he bypassed the record of the previous champion, Guynemer. In the latter two weeks of that month, Fonck wrote twelve victories into the official scorebook, averaging a conquest for every day he flew. In an epic ten seconds on August 14, attacking a three-plane enemy formation, he gave each a short burst and dispatched the lot. They crashed almost on top of each other near the town of Roye. His last recorded victory, though not the last he claimed, was won ten days before the Armistice. Catching sight of a German two-seater whose crew was preoccupied in dropping propaganda leaflets, Fonck sent it smashing into the ground amid a great shower of fluttering paper.

An outstanding point about Fonck's success in aerial combat was his extreme thrift with ammunition. That, combined with his aversion to unnecessary peril, made him a formidable adversary. He went to thorough lengths to analyze the tactics of his opposition, working out detailed schemes of attack to be employed in almost every conceivable set of circumstances. He devoted hours to mastering the art of deflection shooting, of gauging the lead distance required to hit a moving target, so that his prospective victim, once selected, was as good as doomed. In many instances, five or six rounds sufficed to knock down his prey, so unerring was his aim. His boast—"I put my bullets into the target as if I placed them there by hand"—was not empty. His other boast, however, that he had been the victor of 127 combats, rings as hollow as a kettle drum. By authoritative computation, at the cessation of hostilities Spa. 103 was accredited with 104 definite victories and sixty-one probables. Fonck thus alleged that he alone had destroyed more enemy aircraft than were known with certainty to have been destroyed by his entire unit. Beyond question he did bring down more than the seventy-five planes officially allowed him, but not even his virtuosity could have reaped 127 kills, nor anything approximating that number. Nevertheless, the seventy-three victories he did score in Spa. 103—remembering that two were won in Escadrille C. 47—comprised almost three-quarters of the squadron's definitely confirmed kills.

Fonck never lost his overbearing vanity. The press eventually saw through him. His splendid triumphs were hailed in print, but his swelling conceit soon became perceptible to the public. Perhaps, if Réné Fonck had appreciated the wisdom of modesty and let his actions speak for themselves, he would have replaced Guynemer—or at least shared a place with him—in the hearts of his countrymen. Fonck was duly praised for his brilliant deeds, he was enshrined as the top-ranking ace of France, but Georges Guynemer is still remembered and venerated as the incarnation of French *esprit* in that first air war.

CHAPTER XI

A Vanguard of Eagles

WITH THE DEVELOPMENT of *pur sang* fighter squadrons immediately preceding and during the battle of Verdun, the several functions of pursuit aviation soon became permanently fixed in the scheme of things at the front. The special province of these squadrons was to police the air. Their chief duty was to patrol an assigned sector and to harry the enemy by attacking whenever possible, thereby keeping out hostile reconnaissance and bombing machines. It was also their job to protect planes of their own side that were engaged in reconnaissance, the regulation of artillery fire, or bombardment.

But, in addition, the fighter pilot was still required to act as a scout. While flying a sortie, he was supposed to note the number and types of enemy aircraft he encountered and where and when these were seen. He kept his eyes peeled for new enemy batteries, any activity on roads behind opposing trenches, and the presence of military trains in railway depots. He was expected to do all this in the turmoil of actual combat, when the air was latticed with streamers of smoke from machine-gun tracer bullets and aircraft were darting and wheeling for position in a confused intermingling of tricolor cockades and black crosses. Fighter planes did not become generally known as such, in fact, until midway through the Verdun holocaust. And even after that, a single-seater was still usually called a scout plane.

It was at this critical juncture of World War I, the battle of Verdun, the maturation point of pursuit aviation, that a squadron of American volunteers entered the lists as flyers for France. There were seven original members in the Lafayette Escadrille—or, as the group was at first designated, the Escadrille Americaine. For those who understood the demands on these seven, their exploits staggered the imagination. Later recruits to the squadron, who were fresh from the grueling regimen of French flight training, worried whether they could measure up to the standards set by these early volunteers. Listening to the reports of veteran pilots during his first days with the escadrille, Sergeant James Norman Hall heard "accounts of exciting combats, of victories and narrow escapes, which sounded like impossible fictions." Hall was a writer as well as an aviator, and he noticed that these astonishing accounts "were told simply, briefly, as part of the day's work, by men who no longer thought of their adventures as being either very remarkable or very interesting." What, he wondered, ever could seem remarkable to them in the future, when the war was over?

The casual mien of case-hardened pilots persuaded Hall to believe with others that aerial warfare was fostering "a new type of mind," a peculiar mentality that evolved directly from the ordeal aloft. Those who fought in the sky were typically neither insensitive nor morbid. The more reflective of them candidly admitted that personal courage was a variable and unpredictable property, that there were times when they were utterly fearless and other times when only a sense of shame kept them going in the midst of danger. Fear was a disease to dread; survival and sanity hinged on one's ability to withstand its fever. Even the most reckless airman now and then fretted over the possibility that in the event death was not sudden but slow, he might succumb to terror and die like a coward.

Imagination, fear's servant, was a curse. Novice pilots often wrote "last letters" before departing on patrol; they climbed into their machines convinced they would certainly perish within the next hour. But the veterans, reassured by their own durability, took a healthy interest in their work and spoke nonchalantly about their chances of falling in flames. Fatalism, or a deep religious conviction that answered the same purpose, was their spiritual armor, their antidote to fear. They believed, as one said, that "if some bozo writes your name on a bullet, it will get you." "If I thought I could somehow alter the course of destiny, or inveigh against God's plan for me," another philosophized, "I would go absolutely nutty. We are feathers on the winds of fate, so hope for the best and wait for the worst."

The great majority of pilots felt a strong dislike for the slaughter that was part of their duty. Most of them expressed a disinclination to take advantage of the defenseless position into which their superior skill or luck had forced some unfortunate foe. "War on the earth may be reasonable and natural, but in the air it seems the most senseless folly," Hall opined. "How is an airman, who has just learned a new meaning for the joy of life, to reconcile himself to the insane business of killing a fellow aviator who may have just learned it, too?"

But, coerced as they were by brutal necessity, they accustomed themselves to killing. Hall himself achieved fame for his daring in combat. Born and raised in Iowa, he was touring England at the beginning of the war and enlisted in the British army. He served with the Royal Fusiliers until October 1916, when he entered the French flying corps. In the following June he joined his countrymen in the Lafayette Escadrille. After eight months of front-line service for France, he was transferred in February 1918, to the United States Air Service—as were most Americans in the French flying corps—and commissioned a captain. A flight leader in the U.S. 94th Pursuit Squadron, in May he was shot down near Pagny-sur-Moselle and spent the rest of the war in various German hospitals and prison camps. Hall destroyed four enemy planes before falling into captivity and won six citations and three medals, including the Croix de Guerre with five palms.

In the same way the airman reconciled himself to killing, so he learned stoicism about the deaths of friends and squadron mates. United in a common adventure, sharing the same hardships and dangers day after day, the pilots of a squadron lived and worked in close fraternity. The bond between them was tight, but the nature of their job made it mandatory to stay clearheaded and to seal their hearts against emotions that might befuddle their fighting perception; thus, in spite of their closeness, their interdependence and loyalty, bitter experience inured them to the harsh facts of death. It taught them to maintain an almost callous indifference to the loss of a friend. Anger, a rage for revenge, was the normal reaction that had to be spiked; too often fury contaminated good judgment. This need to insulate one's sensibilities, to keep one's blood cool in such heated circumstances, was for many of them, as they affirmed, the toughest test they faced.

The Lafayette Escadrille was called upon to face this test as often as any unit, and more often than some. Four of its original seven members were killed within a year; a dozen others who afterward joined the squadron fell in combat before the United States Air Service became an operational reality at the front. The long priority of their service, as well as their immense prestige, made the volunteer pilots models for emulation. As the first Americans to become experienced combatants in the sky, they helped to shape the flying and fighting techniques that later had to be assimilated and mastered by A.E.F. pilots. Having been weaned to battle above Verdun, the escadrille figured prominently in the transition of pursuit aviation from a misapprehended and misapplied science to a potent tool of twentieth-century mechanized warfare. During the escadrille's first year, air fighting gradually ceased to be an improvisation and developed into an art of maneuver, with established patterns of offensive and defensive tactics. Team play and numerical weight assumed greater importance than individual prowess. Previously a solo fighter, the pursuit pilot now had to curb his appetite for lone errantry and fly as one of a well-disciplined pack. There were still some colorful freebooters prowling the sky, as there would be in diminishing number right up until the end of the war, but the heyday of the solitary hunter was rapidly dusking in 1916, almost as soon as it had dawned. Fighting in the air came to be more and more a matter of keeping formations intact under all conditions. Except for a handful of adroit specialists with roving commissions, pilots who were grandstand players or who found it difficult to follow their leaders' instructions exactly did not as a rule last long against enemy formations.

In considering the historical significance of the Lafayette Escadrille, it becomes evident that the outstanding accomplishment of the volunteers was their influence on American public opinion at a time when the United States was neutral and under some pressure to remain so. The neutrality of the United States was at once the major obstacle confronting the founders of the escadrille and their most forceful argument used in urging the French to permit foreign enlistments in the flying corps. At first the French rejected the scheme on two grounds. One was the need for constant vigilance against spies posing as neutrals. Unhappily, a German agent had already wormed into French aviation by means of a forged American passport; before he was caught and summarily executed, he had worked untold mischief. In the second place, there was no real need for volunteer aviators; there existed in France a superabundance, rather than a shortage, of flying personnel. Thousands of French youths were clamoring to be admitted to this new and romantic branch of the service. But the French authorities, as always, were shrewd diplomats. They wanted American support desperately. Aware that sympathy in the United States lay largely with the Allied cause, they realized that the presence of a band of young Americans in French planes, who fought spectacularly in the sky, would arouse widespread interest and further stimulate pro-Allied sentiment at home. For this reason mainly, the French relented.

Although Norman Prince, a wealthy socialite of Pride's Crossing, Massachusetts, has generally been credited with conceiving the idea behind the Lafayette Escadrille, it is impossible to attribute its inception to any individual person. The appearance of the unit was the result of steadfast effort by many individuals who refused for more than a year, despite official rebukes and heartbreaking discouragements, to forsake the idea. In the summer of 1914, before the war had even begun, but when it loomed as an inevitability, there stirred the first manifestations of the spirit that would culminate in the creation of the Lafayette Escadrille. One of the earliest determinate steps was taken that August 3, when Kiffin and Paul Rockwell of Asheville, North Carolina, wrote to the French consulate in New Orleans, tendering their service in case war actually broke out. They did not wait for a reply. Learning that immediate passage was available, they sailed for France four days later.

That same week in Paris, an appeal to serve was circulated among American residents and tourists. Prominent among its signers was William Thaw, a wealthy playboy from Pittsburgh who had earned some notoriety as a hydroplane pilot and who, while an undergraduate at Yale, had flown a Curtiss flying boat from Connecticut to Atlantic City nonstop. Thaw had learned to fly at the Curtiss school in 1913 and had come to France with his brother, Alexander, to market an automatic stabilizer invented by the latter. He tried to enlist as a military pilot but was turned down because of his nationality.

Undismayed, he joined a group of Americans awaiting acceptance into the Foreign Legion, the only French unit in which aliens could serve. The group, which had been organizing and drilling in Paris, was inducted into the legion on August 21. Besides Thaw it included the Rockwell brothers; Robert Soubiran of New York, a race-car driver; Bert Hall, a Missouri boy who had become an international tramp, famous for his tall stories and his penchant for marrying; Victor Chapman, a New Yorker studying architecture at the Beaux Arts following his graduation from Harvard; and James Bach, a mechanical engineer who had been born, and spent most of his life, in Paris.

Others like them soon rallied to the Allied cause. James Norman Hall, across the Channel, enlisted in the British army. Didier Masson traveled all the way from Los Angeles to shoulder a rifle in the regular French infantry. How he contrived to get into the regulars is not known, unless he used his name and fluency in the language to pass himself off as a French national. He had learned to fly in France in 1909, had barnstormed about the United States as an exhibition pilot, and had done some military scouting as a mercenary—a one-man air force—for the Mexican Government in 1913. Masson arrived in France aboard the same ship as William E. Dugan, Jr. Originally from Rochester, New York, Dugan had left an executive office with the United Fruit Company in Central America to deliver himself into the Foreign Legion. Another who would later wear French wings after serving as a legionaire was Paul Pavelka, a seaman who had worked his way across the ocean with a shipload of horses.

Bert Hall, in his book *One Man's War*, wrote of his experiences:

> Our first glimpse of the Legion was something of a shock—the mixture of colors and races, the many languages, the rough-looking customers. Some of us wondered if we had been right smart in going over to the Invalidies that day and signing up for the duration. But we were in by that time and there was no getting out now.
>
> It didn't take the officers long to put us through our training period at Toulouse. We marched a bit, shot a bit and did some bayonet practice. The gun I was carrying was known as a reformed rifle. The lands and the rifling inside the bore were almost worn away, but it was a good old gun and my marksmanship with that blunderbuss got me a promotion "poco pronto"; that is, I became a first-class soldier (which in some ways compares with the first-class private in the United States army, except in pay).
>
> After four days in Toulouse we were issued our regulation costumes—blue jackets, red breeches, blue sash, red kepi, and the short black leggings (we called them multiers). Besides this, we carried a shovel, a pick, a rifle, a canteen, 125 rounds of ammunition, a knapsack containing our emergency rations (which we had

already eaten), a gamel (messpan), and a blanket. And was that
a load!

These Americans in the Foreign Legion, though they tried to stay together,
were divided into small groups and assigned to separate regiments. Completing their training in eight weeks, they marched with their units 165
kilometers to the front and entered the trenches on the night of October 17
at Verzenay, about twenty kilometers southeast of the besieged city of Rheims.
There was a short stay here, during which they underwent their first shelling,
then a trek to relieve a division at Craonelle. They hiked fifty-six kilometers in
nineteen hours, on empty stomachs, not being fed until they reached their
destination. Bert Hall's description of sights and experiences along the way
is graphic:

> Once we encountered a German cavalryman hiding in a chimney.
> His left arm had been shot off and he had plastered it over with
> mud. Strange to say, the stump of his arm was healing quite nicely.
> He said he was afraid to come out and allow himself to be cap-
> tured, as he had been told that the French would kill their pris-
> oners. . . . Our route took us through the city of Rheims. The
> cathedral hadn't been damaged very much up to that time, but the
> city showed signs of war, and the smaller places through which we
> passed were terribly shot up. What I don't understand is how some
> of those French people ever located their property after their vil-
> lages were so entirely destroyed, every landmark being gone. . . .
> In some places, the fronts of buildings were blown away and the
> entire household was open to the view of passersby. In other places
> everything had been burned. In several villages our men found
> placards telling of the German invasion and setting forth the de-
> mands of the German army—so many francs, so much flour, so
> much sugar, so much tobacco, so many dozen eggs, etc. And the
> bodies, swelling under the sun! And the spiked helmets! And the
> smashed equipment! And the endless line of ambulances coming
> back from the front with their cargoes of suffering and death!

As the legionnaires approached the Aisne canal system, several companies,
Hall's included, were combined into a "sacrifice battalion" and ordered forward to contact the enemy. Before they had advanced far ahead of the main
body, however, a German plane appeared overhead and began circling. Hall
wrote of the attack,

> Almost at once the 77's were bursting over us . . . and many of
> our best men went down before we could find cover. We were in
> open country at the time, mostly sugar-beet fields. I remember well
> because I had uprooted one of the beets and was eating slices of it.

Every time a shell came near, we would duck—lie down or in some way protect ourselves from the dispersion of the shrapnel. It was interesting to watch some of the fellows. They would put their heads under the beet leaves, leaving their backsides high in the air. I was reminded of the legend about the ostrich.

It was ten o'clock that night when they wearily flopped into the trenches at Craonelle. Here they found the sanctuary of muskrats. "The mud was knee-deep," Hall discovered. "Our uniforms were sodden with perspiration and rain and mud. Bill Thaw produced a canteen containing about a water-glass of wine. . . . He divided it with me. Dear old Bill, he was a good soldier, and a generous devil, too."

They were in the thick of it now, muddied to their knees, cold, hungry, exhausted, awakened to the sordid realities of war, living more like animals than men, still full of spirit but neither so gay nor cocksure as a few weeks ago in Paris. Their manifold miseries and dangers were shared by all the. many Americans who went into action then and later with the Foreign Legion, that polyglot cohort that more dramatic historians have characterized as "the legion of the damned."

Like almost everyone else in France the American volunteers were confident the war would be over quickly, by the end of 1914 without a doubt. "The big engagement is now in progress about Dixmude," Victor Chapman wrote home in the first week of November. "The news is good but nothing decisive. The only result I could wish for is that the Germans should be driven out of France before the cold weather sets in." If this German push toward the Marne could be halted—this "final German effort," as Chapman referred to it elsewhere in his letter—then the fighting would probably be over by Christmas; joyous carols could once more be sung to peace on earth, goodwill toward men. Of course they learned otherwise, and to remind them of their misspent optimism, they had the infernal tribulations of life in the trenches.

"Oh, it was a jolly life, those trenches!" exclaimed Bert Hall. "I wish I could get it down on paper exactly the way it was, but I'm afraid I can't. There was something besides the facts—something more than the mud and the blood and the grave-digging, and shell-shocked days and nights—something ghastly—something unbelievable."

The facts in themselves were bad enough. For the munificent sum of twenty-five centimes a day, the equivalent of an American nickel, the legionaire endured the frozen winter darkness, the lack of sanitation, the reek of decaying waste, the steady diet of cold rations, the intermittent rain of crashing shells that exploded with the din and force of Jehovah's wrathful thunder, and the specter of death lurking beyond every next tick of the clock. And there was always the vermin, as Hall testifies.

In the trenches we spent our time reading, talking and sleeping when possible. Also killing totos. . . . The totos were our most popular sport, at first. That's the French name for them, and some people call them seam-squirrels, or cooties, or nits. I think the totos must be of German descent, as each one carries an Iron Cross on its back. They get to be pretty good-sized if permitted to thrive. We had nothing to kill them with, so in a few days we had some good big ones. We used to have names for them, such as Gyp the Blood, for they were always bent on murdering someone by degrees. I had one I called Lefty Louie because he limped; he had a bad left leg. We were also bothered by rats. When we first saw a rat, we used to feed him, but we soon found that we had made a mistake. Almost overnight they were with us by the thousands. They would eat your shoes and run all over you at night. Between the rats and the totos, there was little sleep to be had.[1]

Each regiment of the Legion spent four days in the front line of trenches, six days in the reserve line, four days in a rear-area rest camp, then returned to the forward ditch again. Patrols crept out nightly into no-man's-land, sometimes encountering enemy patrols in pitch blackness. Opposing squads soon learned to fight it out with knives, bayonets, and bare hands, or to ignore one another altogether; the sound of a shot from the opaque void between the trenches usually drew rifle and machine-gun fire from both sides, thereby trapping the patrols in the middle. The constant artillery barrage took its toll in the earthworks, but casualties became especially heavy during offensive operations, when bayonet charges were mounted against concentrated machine-gun fire. For the infantry, it would be this way throughout the war.

They had not yet been at the front a month when William Thaw began talking with James Bach, Bert Hall, and the Rockwell brothers about the prospect of forming an all-American unit of volunteer aviators. The same notion was also being discussed on the other side of the Atlantic, in Marblehead, Massachusetts, by a couple of student pilots at the Burgess School of Aviation. One was Norman Prince, who had begun flight training at his own expense in order to go to France and offer himself as an airman. Prince independently hatched the idea in October and talked it over many times with Frazier Curtis, a well-born Bostonian attending the Burgess school in the hope of afterward gaining admittance into the Royal Naval Air Service. Prince tried to persuade Curtis that he should go to France instead of England, but Curtis, inasmuch as he could not speak French, clung to his preference for the British service. He embarked for London on Christmas Day 1914, promising to proceed from there to France if his endeavor to enlist in the R.N.A.S. proved unsuccessful. Refused in England—ostensibly on account of

---

[1] Hall: *En l'Air!*

his citizenship, but perhaps in fact because of his age, for Curtis was in his early forties—he went to Paris in February 1915, joining Prince and the others in their efforts to interest the authorities in the organization of a corps of American flyers.

The pilgrimage to France, meanwhile, continued. Brimming with idealism and hankering after excitement, the volunteers streamed across the Atlantic from every corner of the United States. They arrived by the hundreds to offer their lives for a cause that was, or still seemed, far removed from the affairs of their own country. Although their actions were officially frowned upon at home, they felt they were repaying a debt to France for her aid more than a century before in the American Revolution. "To the valor and devotion of . . . Frenchmen we owe our very existence as an independent nation," noted A. Piatt Andrew, a founder and administrator of the Field Service of the American Ambulance, writing in October 1916, "and nothing that Americans have done for France during these last hard years of trial can be thought of— without embarrassment—in relation with what Frenchmen did for us in those unforgettable years of our peril from 1777 to 1781." Established in the opening days of the war with a gift of ten Ford trucks whose bodies were improvised from packing crates, the American Ambulance rapidly evolved into a large-scale operation of mercy, attracting a greater number of volunteers than any other service unit, more than four hundred drivers and medical aides, of whom twenty-eight were cited for bravery under fire and awarded the Croix de Guerre. Quite a few of the American vanguard who subsequently entered French aviation had their baptism at the battle front as ambulanciers, among them Elliot Cowdin, James McConnell, Dudley Hill, Robert Rockwell, Clyde Balsley, Chouteau Johnson, and Larry Rumsey.

The first American to fly for France, the first actually to fly for any belligerent power in World War I, was an unsavory character, an obscure exhibition pilot named Hild, who by some mysterious means became an army aviator immediately following the outbreak of hostilities. After a short period of training, Hild deserted, returned to the United States, granted interviews to newspapers in which he claimed to have flown at the front, and passed many remarks insulting to France. Making matters worse, he was often seen in the company of German military attachés in Washington. Hild's behavior naturally aroused the French government to suspect other volunteer aviators, and these suspicions became stronger when, right after Hilde's desertion, French counterintelligence caught the enemy saboteur whose fake American passport had helped him gain entrance into the flying corps.

In light of these untoward events, plus the fact that the aviation branch never lacked native-born recruits, the number of Americans who inveigled their way into the French air arm in 1915—months before the creation of the Escadrille Americaine—is surprising. James Bach, Bert Hall, and William Thaw were the first to crash the gate that had been slammed shut against aliens who would serve in the flying corps. In December 1914, while their regiment was on rest behind the lines, these three visited a nearby airfield where they talked to an old acquaintance of Thaw's—Lieutenant Felix Brocard, then the senior pilot of Escadrille Deperdussin No. 6, the same man who would later command the famous Stork combat group. They requested Brocard's assistance in obtaining transfers to aviation. Impressed by the earnestness with which the Americans argued their case, Brocard agreed to use his considerable influence on their behalf.

Ironically, Bach and Hall, neither of whom had ever previously sat in an airplane (although Hall once or twice told an improbable tale of having flown in Turkey during the 1912 Balkan War), were transferred within a few days, while Thaw, a registered pilot, did not receive orders. When he was next in a rest area with his regiment, it was farther from the airfield than before, but Thaw, who hated walking under any conditions, trudged thirty-two kilometers through deep snow to see Brocard again. A week after that he was transferred from the Foreign Legion directly into Escadrille D. 6. With only on-the-job training to prepare him, Thaw began as an observer on Deperdussin monoplanes. He soon tired of sitting in the passenger's seat, however, and convinced the authorities of his ability to qualify as a military aviator. He was sent to St. Cyr as an *élève-pilote* and in March 1915, after an exceptionally short schooling, was breveted to fly a Caudron G-2. Because Bach and Hall would continue in training until midsummer, Thaw became the first American to fly at the front in World War I.

Upon winning his wings and while awaiting assignment to an active squadron, Thaw went to spend a few days with Bach and Hall at Pau, where they were receiving dual instruction on Voisins. Here he met three other Americans, new arrivals at the school, Norman Prince, Frazier Curtis, and Elliot Cowdin. To his surprise, Thaw heard from Prince that permission—tacit consent, at least—had already been secured from the War Ministry for the formation of an all-American squadron and that he, Thaw, had been named to serve in that squadron. Thaw, thinking it over, was not enthusiastic. By his own testimony he now turned lukewarm toward the idea, for he had completed his training and was about to return to the front, this time as a fully fledged aviator. He was still at Pau when orders came instructing him to remain there as a utility pilot until his five compatriots could be breveted and formed into a squadron as planned. Thaw knew that it would be several months before his fellow volunteers would graduate as pilots; Bach and Hall were showing themselves to be slow learners, each having crashed twice already, and the others were just beginning to acquire the knack of taxiing a flightless practice machine across the field. He therefore went to the War Ministry and asked to be sent to the front at once, figuring to join the other volunteers later, when and if the Escadrille Americaine should become a reality. The request was granted and in the last week of March he reported for duty with Escadrille Caudron No. 42, operating from Nancy and afterward from Lunéville. He was made a sergeant on May 18, and in the same month was cited once in divisional and twice in army orders. Then and for the next three months or so, Thaw was the only American in service above the battle lines.

Prince, together with Curtis and Cowdin, had enlisted early in March. It had taken much wheedling and diplomatic string pulling, but they accomplished much more than merely getting themselves into the uniforms of French airmen. Despite protest from various government quarters, they cleared the way for other of their countrymen who wished to get into the flying corps. And Prince, helped in no small measure by Curtis, had succeeded in his prime objective, exacting from the War Ministry a promise—not in so many words, but strongly implied—that Americans would be allowed eventually to fly as a body.

Arriving in France aboard the *Rochambeau* on January 30, Prince immediately set himself to the task of creating French interest in his project. Curtis, after being turned down by the R.N.A.S., joined him in Paris four days later. Using a suite of rooms at the Hotel Palais d'Orsay as their base of operations, they worked day and night, exploiting every avenue of influence available to them. There were many rebuffs and discouragements. They were hopeful, for example, when they received a dinner invitation from Jacques and Paul de Lesseps, ranking officials of the Paris Air Guard who favored their proposal. Until the wee hours of morning they and the Lesseps brothers explored the situation from every angle. A letter offering the service of a squadron of American flyers was drawn up and addressed to the Minister of War, Alexandre Millerand. The letter availed nothing except a polite "Thank you, but . . ."

A breakthrough was finally achieved in mid-February when, at a soiree in the home of an American expatriate, they met Elliot Cowdin. Hearing their scheme, Cowdin immediately caught their enthusiasm. Cowdin, who was a member of a patrician New York family and was serving now as a driver in the American Ambulance, introduced them to John Jay Chapman, Victor Chapman's father, whom he knew from stateside. The elder Chapman in turn introduced them to Robert Bliss and Robert Chanler, prominent members of the American colony in Paris. These two believed profoundly in Prince's idea, that it was both feasible and constructive. In this they were in a minority, for most American residents in the capital, adopting a pious attitude toward United States neutrality, deemed it not only impossible but plainly unwise to organize a squadron of volunteer airmen. Prince found in Bliss and Chanler helpful and industrious advocates who gave practical support by arranging for introductions and interviews with well-placed representatives of the French military and civilian establishments. The most fruitful of these meetings was that with a sympathetic and cooperative Frenchman, Jarousse de Sillac, who had important connections in the government. Sillac, on February 20, wrote a hortative plea, nicely honed in its selling point, to his friend in the War Ministry, Colonel Bouttieaux:

I beg to transmit to you, herewith attached, the names of six young men, citizens of the United States of America, who desire to enlist in the French air service—an offer which has been declined by the Minister of War. Permit me to call your attention to this matter and to emphasize its vital nature. It appears to me that there might be distinct advantages in the creation of an American escadrille. The United States would be proud . . . that certain of her young men, acting as did Lafayette, would come to fight for France and civilization. The resulting sentiment . . . could have but one effect, to turn the Americans in the direction of the Allies. . . . If you approve these considerations, I am confident that it will be possible to accept these young men and to authorize their enlistment in such a manner that they may be grouped under the control of a French chief. In doing this, you will contribute to the happiness of these six Americans.

To which Bouttieaux replied in a letter dated February 24: "I think that your candidates will be welcomed. They should contract an engagement in the French army for the duration of the war, and should agree to fly only the aircraft issued to them by the French command."

The six to whom Sillac alluded were Prince, Curtis, Cowdin, Thaw, Bach, and Hall. Prince had learned through the grapevine that the latter three had already gained access into the aviation corps. Because French squadrons at that time had a flying complement of six, Prince feared that unless he could submit six names his scheme stood no chance of being approved; accordingly, he advised Sillac to include Thaw, Bach, and Hall as likely candidates for the proposed Escadrille Americaine. During the week following the receipt of Colonel Bouttieaux's letter, Prince, Curtis, and Cowdin signed their enlistment papers and were sent to Pau to begin their flight training. They were joined here by Bach and Hall, who had commenced training at Buc and were transferred at Prince's request. It was not long after this that Thaw made his visit to Pau, heard all that had transpired, and then departed impatiently for Escadrille C. 42 on the Lorraine front.

Meanwhile, another American in Paris, Dr. Edmund L. Gros (later a lieutenant-colonel in the United States Air Service), then one of the heads of the American Ambulance, had been thinking, quite independently, of the possibility of forming a unit of American volunteer airmen. In the Foreign Legion, Americans had already distinguished themselves as combatants, and among the ambulance workers were dozens of young men eager for a more direct participation in the fighting. It occurred to Gros that here was splendid material which might indeed be used to better purpose in the French flying corps. To recruit would-be pilots, he instituted a canvass of ambulance men in late May. This activity brought him in touch with Frazier Curtis, who was recuperating from injuries sustained that spring in a series of training accidents and was using part of his sick leave to muster additional volunteers for flying service.

Curtis was doing his missionary work at the ambulance station at Neuilly, early in July, when he learned that Gros was busily engaged in the same endeavor. From that Paris suburb he contacted Gros by mail. He wrote:

> I went to the American Ambulance today to see if I could find any drivers who wanted to enlist in French aviation. . . . Men of flying experience would be preferred, but those of apparent aptitude (knowledge of French, gas engines, etc.) will be acceptable. I am told that you are keen on getting up a big corps, so we ought to be able to work together. . . . I am here on sick-leave, three accidents having left me pretty well jarred up. I expect to go to the seaside for a good rest in a day or two, but am very anxious to see you first.

Meeting Curtis shortly after this, and through him Jarousse de Sillac, Gros discussed with them his ideas and the three found themselves in hearty accord both as to their goal and the means of attaining it. The plan now was not simply to form a single squadron but an entire corps of volunteers, which they tentatively christened the Franco-American Flying Corps and which would have the Escadrille Americaine as its nucleus. Their campaign mapped out, Curtis left for a needed vacation on the Riviera, his injuries serious enough— as he soon found out—to prevent him from returning to military service. Obliged to accept his release from the army, he stayed a little while longer in Paris and then sailed for home. Though he never finished his training, the valuable pioneer work he did in his half year in France went far toward ensuring the future success of the American volunteer movement in French aviation.

With Curtis out of the picture, it devolved upon Gros and Sillac to carry on negotiations with the French authorities, to capture the interest of influential Americans, and to keep the project moving toward realization. But a stunning setback awaited them. After all the hard work, the elaborate planning, the blandishments and arm-twisting, the high hopes that had been built up, Gros and Sillac were dismayed to discover that the War Ministry had absolutely no intention of enfranchising an American escadrille. Whereas additional volunteers were being admitted into the flying corps in small numbers, several besides the original six having enlisted in the intervening months since March, nothing like a concrete promise that they would be permitted to serve as a unit had yet in fact been conceded by the French. The letter written in February by Sillac? The seemingly favorable reply from Colonel Bouttieaux? The former had mentioned the creation of an American squadron; the latter had omitted any reference whatever to such a squadron being formed. Gros and Sillac were told that a false inference had been drawn from Bouttieaux's letter, that they had been laboring all this time under a regrettable misapprehension. They were told furthermore that the War Ministry had always been and was still averse to grouping Americans at the front.

Vexed by this stinging disappointment but undeterred in their determination, Gros and Sillac organized an action committee composed of backers from the American community and other partisan Frenchmen like Sillac himself. A marathon of meetings was convened in the handsome town house on the Avenue de Bois de Boulogne where Gros resided. The product of these meetings was an ever-increasing pressure on the War Ministry. The efforts of the committee quickly bore fruit. General Hirschauer, the chief of military aeronautics, that July accepted an invitation to dine with the promoters of the escadrille and was persuaded of the practicability and benefits of such a plan. To everyone's relief and satisfaction, he agreed to give an order for the formation of an American squadron. It was the first firm step toward actual attainment of a great vision. However, what with the many details remaining to be settled, and the proverbial slowness of military business procedures, another nine months elapsed before the Escadrille Americaine entered existence. Not until April 1916, did the dream finally become a reality.

At the front, meanwhile, Thaw was no longer the sole volunteer on operational flight duty. Cowdin, in April, and then Prince, in May, were breveted, both of them being posted to Escadrille Voisin No. 108, a bombing squadron. In August James Bach and Bert Hall went together into Escadrille Morane-Saulnier No. 38, where they flew two-seater monoplanes, and Bach soon afterward won the woeful distinction of becoming the first American airman to be captured by the enemy.

His unlucky day was September 23, 1915, when he was sent on a special mission with another pilot of M.S. 38, a Sergeant Mangeot, their errand being to land two French soldiers, demolition experts dressed in civilian clothes, behind the German lines near Mézières. The two soldiers carried with them a large quantity of explosives with which they were to destroy a section of railroad between Mézières and Hirson. After gathering information about the disposition of enemy troops, they were to try to make their way back across the lines as best they could.

What brought Bach to grief was his own gallantry. The landing site chosen by the two soldiers was a rough clearing overgrown with tall weeds and studded with bushes and saplings. Bach and Mangeot set their machines down without mishap and saw their passengers off safely toward the railroad. Then Bach put on full gas and was airborne, heading for the French lines. Looking back, he saw that Mangeot's plane had capsized on the ground. He landed again and picked up the French pilot, who was unhurt, but in taking off the second time, one wing of Bach's Morane-Saulnier struck a tree. The machine caromed sideways into a dense grove at the edge of the clearing. Neither man suffered worse than superficial cuts and abrasions, Mangeot surviving his second crash within the space of a few minutes. Late that afternoon, walking homeward through a neighboring wood, they were seized by German sentries.

Imprisoned at Laon and subjected to more than a month of relentless interrogation, during which they confessed nothing, Bach and Mangeot were court-
martialed as "spy carriers." Owing largely to the efforts of a German lawyer,
they were found innocent and spared the death penalty. Bach spent more than
three years in various prisoner-of-war camps. By right of seniority he became
the "Herr Direktor" of the Amerikanischer-Kriegsgefangenen Club. His eligibility for that office was no fault of his own, however. He made several attempts to escape, but was recaptured each time.

The small flock of early American warbirds was also joined in May by
Didier Masson, already an experienced military flyer when he arrived in
Europe, having formerly served as the entire aviation force of President
Alvaro Obregon's army during the 1913 unrest in Mexico. There, piloting a
Curtiss airplane of forgotten description, Masson had often singlehandedly
attacked the entire navy of his chief's implacable foe, rebel General Victoriano
Huerta. It had been an even contest, for the Huerta navy, in the matter of
equipment, was in a class with the Obregon air force. A single decrepit gunboat with engines barely able to furnish headway, manned by a motley crew
of beachcombers and sailors of fortune, kept the sea lanes open, after a
fashion, for the Huerta gunrunners. Masson's premier appearance above this
antique battletub caused quite a commotion. All he could do, though, was
drop a load of tin cans that had been filled with powder and tied up with
pieces of wire. He hurled down hundreds of these missiles in repeated raids
on the gunboat, but never, so far as he could determine, with any appreciable
effect.

No wonder, then, Masson resigned his Mexican commission and, at the
outbreak of the other great war in 1914, hastened to France to offer his experience as a soldier-aviator. After five wearisome months in the regular
infantry, he finally got himself into the French flying corps in February 1915.
Because he was a member of the Aero Club de France, having learned to fly
six years previously under its auspices, Masson was classified as an advanced
trainee. Breveted on May 10, he went to the front to pilot two-seaters in
Escadrille Caudron No. 18, and embarked thence upon his long and distinguished French service.

May was the month, too, in which the daring, enigmatic, and much-
admired Raoul Lufbery began his pilot training. Destined to shine as the
brightest star of the Lafayette Escadrille, Lufbery's career at the controls of
a military aircraft was but one more chapter in a life crammed with excitement.

He was born in France of French parents in March 1885. His mother died
a year later and he was placed by his father in the care of a family in the
Auvergne Mountains. In 1890, his father remarried and emigrated to the
United States, settling in Wallingford, Connecticut, but Raoul was left with
his grandmother in Blois. He never saw his father again, although he went
to work in a chocolate factory when he was fourteen and sent most of three
years' wages to Connecticut. Soon after his seventeenth birthday, bored with

working and attending school, young Lufbery set out to see the world. During the next four years he journeyed throughout France, Algiers, Tunis, Egypt, Turkey, and the Balkans, taking any odd jobs he could find to pay his expenses. From Hamburg, Germany, where he worked for three months to earn the price of his fare, he voyaged to America to visit his father. But the elder Lufbery, doing business as a dealer in rare stamps and unaware of his son's impending arrival, had just sailed for Europe in quest of specimens for his collection. Raoul, cooling his heels for a year and a half, waited restlessly in Connecticut, and then, his father having not yet returned, he resumed his travels. He went to Cuba, from there to New Orleans, and on eventually to San Francisco. Hired as a hotel clerk, he hoped to save enough money to buy passage across the Pacific, but his earnings were discouragingly meager. Seeking a shortcut, he enlisted in the United States army and managed to get himself shipped to the Philippines, where he remained for more than two years, his time in the army enabling him to become an American citizen. When his period of enlistment had expired, he moved on to Japan and after that to China. Insatiably curious, always eager for fresh adventure, he rambled about China for months, working part of the time for the Chinese customs service. Then his wanderlust brought him to India—and a crossroads in his hitherto aimlessly nomadic life.

While seeing the sights of Calcutta on a steamy September morning in 1912, Lufbery found himself suddenly engulfed by a crowd of onrushing natives. True to his bent, he let himself be swept along in this river of humanity to a field outside the city. There, to his fascinated joy, he saw a flying machine. Nearby, a distraught European was shouting French maledictions and gesticulating wildly at a gang of coolie laborers who were erecting a tent hangar. Lufbery strode over and offered to superintend the job, a suggestion gratefully accepted. The man introduced himself. He was Marc Pourpe, itinerant French aviator, touring the Orient and staging exhibition flights in a Bleriot monoplane that had seen more than a little wear and tear.

This incident marked the beginning of Lufbery's long and intimate association with Pourpe and of his own occupation with airplanes that was to continue until his death in aerial combat six years later. By a fateful coincidence, Pourpe's *mécanicien* fell ill that week and decided to return to France. Lufbery replaced him and under Pourpe's tutelage became a very adept mechanic. A strong bond of comradeship was instantly cemented between the aviator and his newfound assistant. "Their friendship," observed the editor of the magazine *La Guerre Aerienne,* writing Lufbery's obituary in 1918, "was a veritable cult."

Both of them young and venturesome and unburdened by responsibility, they spent more than a year traveling together through the ancient civilizations of Asia and putting on air shows wherever they stopped. In some places they were looked upon as gods, in others as imposters. Once, in China, the natives, feeling their reputation as master kite builders threatened, constructed out of bamboo and rice paper an exact, full-size replica of the Bleriot. It flew beautifully but lacked one essential feature. It had no engine. It would not "sing." To compensate for this deficiency, they attached a box of bees. The insects made a splendid buzz, as anybody standing close by could hear. But high in the air, much to the chagrin of the Chinese, the bees could not compete with the musical box on the foreign devils' man-kite.

Proceeding from the Far East to Egypt, Pourpe undertook a long-distance flight from Cairo to Khartoum and return, for which he received much publicity. Lufbery preceded or followed him on every stage of the trip, traveling by Nile steamer and dhow, on donkey and camel, by train, and sometimes on foot. The flight a rousing success, they went directly to Paris and purchased a Morane-Saulnier monoplane that they wanted modified at the factory to fit their special requirements. The summer of 1914, the last season of peace that either of them would know, found them awaiting delivery of this new machine, happily anticipating another extensive tour of the Orient. But war was declared and their plans had to be canceled. Pourpe at once enlisted in army aviation. Also in order to serve, Lufbery, technically an American, was obliged to join the Foreign Legion. Within a couple of weeks, however, through Pourpe's intercession, Lufbery was shifted into the flying corps and accompanied the aviator to the front as his mechanic.

On the second day of December, while doing reconnaissance behind enemy lines, Pourpe was killed. Lufbery's grief, inconsolable at first, gradually became transfused with an angry longing to avenge his friend's death. To that purpose, in January 1915, he asked permission to fly. There was the usual official procrastination, four months of it, because of his American citizenship, but his petition was finally granted in May. He was sent to the aviation school at Chartres. Training on Farmans, he received his brevet at the end of July. After that, switching to Voisins, he completed a ten-week course in bombardment and was posted to Escadrille Voisin No. 106. As a member of this squadron, participating almost daily in bombing missions, he served until the following spring, when the Escadrille Americaine came into being. Desiring to throw in his lot with his adopted countrymen, Lufbery then obtained a transfer to pursuit aviation and went to the depot at Le Plessis-Belleville to qualify on Nieuport single-seaters.

Thus, at the close of 1915, with Bach repining in a German prison camp and Curtis incapacitated by the injuries he incurred at Pau, there were six American airmen on active service: Thaw, Hall, Prince, Cowdin, Masson, and Lufbery. But the ingression of volunteers into the French flying corps had not ended there. Seven others were already nearing their graduation from flight school. Those still in training were Victor Chapman and Dudley Hill, accepted for air service in August; Kiffin Rockwell, Chouteau Johnson, Clyde Balsley, and Larry Rumsey, accepted in September; and James McConnell, accepted in October. Paul Rockwell, Kiffin's brother, had been badly wounded

in the shoulder while skirmishing as a Foreign Legionnaire. Unable to wield
the heavy load required of an infantryman, he was relegated to a desk in the
propaganda section of army field headquarters. Later, upon creation of the
Escadrille Americaine, he was asked by its members to act as their unit
historian and public relations officer, which he did gladly. Kiffin himself had
sustained a thigh wound during a bayonet charge at Vimy Ridge. He effected
his transfer to aviation—at Thaw's instigation and with his help—while
convalescing.

More than five months had now elapsed since General Hirschauer consented to authorize the formation of an American squadron; with six volunteers breveted and another seven about to finish training, there was ample
personnel to warrant the establishment of such a squadron—and yet, as 1915
waned away, no definite steps were being made toward the grouping of
Americans at the front.

The committee organized by Dr. Gros and Jarousse de Sillac had not for a
moment eased its pressure on the War Ministry. Dozens of letters had been
exchanged, numerous conferences had been held, proposals and counter-
proposals had bounced back and forth like balls in a tennis match, all to no
avail. The main obstacle was Hirschauer's bureaucratic hebetude, his stubborn, almost phobic, aversion to nailing down final decisions. Gros and Sillac
found him maddening to deal with. He vacillated. He temporized. He dawdled
over details, real and imaginary. He quibbled incessantly. He hemmed and
he hawed, mercurially revising his ideas at the slightest pretext, pinning
arbitrary provisos to everything he said, dodging a firm commitment to any
course of progress. By his inconstancy and multifarious elusions he snarled
the negotiations in a great labyrinthian thicket of sticky red tape. And, as the
end of the year approached, the advent of the Escadrille Americaine seemed
no closer at hand than it had seemed on that long-past day in July when
Hirschauer pledged his cooperation.

Another complication arose. Thaw, Cowdin, and Prince became involved
in a contretemps that nearly put the projected escadrille out of business before
it was started. The three of them were given a month's leave in December
to visit the United States, an event that attracted a vast amount of public
attention there. There was a wide appeal in the thought of these young so-
cialites having seen action as flyers over the western front. They afforded
thrilling copy for a nation athirst for first-person news of the war, and newspapers throughout the country devoted entire columns to reporting their
exploits abroad. Especially interested were the German secret-service agents
who trailed them wherever they went, and the German ambassador in Washington, who made a demand that they should be interned, charging that their
presence as active combatants garbed in the uniform of a foreign power constituted a breach of American neutrality. The protest had some legal strength.
It was upheld, in fact, by some scupulously impartial editorial writers, but

they were the minority. Anti-German sentiment had been running high since the sinking of the *Lusitania* eight months earlier, and the majority opinion strongly favored letting the three return to France. While State Department officials writhed on the horns of this diplomatic dilemma, the visiting airmen went ahead and solved it for them, much to the relief of everyone concerned, except the disgruntled Germans.

Caught in this curious international controversy—Thaw spending his leave in Pittsburgh, Cowdin in New York City, and Prince in Massachusetts—the three were now being tracked by sleuthhounds of the American and French, as well as the German, secret services. Exchanging coded messages shortly before the expiration of their leave, the worried trio devised a stratagem for sneaking out of the country.

Cowdin first of all arranged with sympathetic port authorities for himself and his two co-conspirators to be permitted, when the time came, to board a French liner that was scheduled to sail a few days later. He notified Thaw and Prince when these arrangements were set. It was then up to each of them to shake off their shadows and get to the pier just prior to the ship's departure. On the crucial day Cowdin led a retinue of bewildered undercover agents on as breathless a chase about Manhattan Island as has ever been seen in a movie thriller. Thaw and Prince, each relying on his own resources, succeeded equally as well. The three of them were at sea, bound for the war zone, before anyone knew they had gone.

In the meantime, in France, the so-called Franco-American Committee, the lobby headed by Gros and Sillac, had reached an impasse in its dealings with the recalcitrant General Hirschauer. Its efforts were now being directed toward Réné Besnard, the civilian sub-secretary of military aeronautics, who all along had tacitly endorsed the project. Besnard lacked the power to take any straightforward action. Although he liked the idea, he was apparently unwilling to risk the disapproval of his superiors by openly working for the creation of an American squadron. But he did confide his goodwill to Gros and Sillac, and they hoped through him to influence the Minister of War, Millerand. Consequently, on January 24, 1916, Gros sent Besnard a letter that was astutely couched in a flattering overstatement of the latter's authority to get things done:

> The members of the Franco-American Committee wish to express
> to you their sincere thanks for the approval you have given to their
> plan, which encourages them to continue their efforts. . . . I would
> be grateful if you could obtain through General Headquarters the
> grouping of American pilots in the same squadron. This has often
> been promised us, and it is of the utmost importance that such a
> squadron be constituted. Most of the pilots are already familiar with
> the Nieuport airplane, and would be proud to have the honor of

being assigned to a fighting squadron equipped with Nieuports. Among those who are already breveted, and of whom several have already distinguished themselves, permit me to recall to you the names of the following, who could be grouped immediately: Lieutenant Thaw; Sergeants Cowdin, Prince and Masson; Pilots Hall, Balsley, Chapman, Rockwell, Rumsey and Johnson. Captain [Georges] Thenault, commandant of Escadrille Caudron No. 42, has already made a request to be commanding officer of the American squadron, and the Committee would be grateful for your approval of his assignment. In addition to the fully trained pilots, there are a few American volunteers, particularly qualified to become flyers, who have submitted requests to be transferred to aviation . . .

We would be happy if, in the interests . . . of the Franco-American Flying Corps, you would be kind enough to take measures to transfer these young men to aviation as expeditiously as possible.

That Gros failed to mention Raoul Lufbery is explained by the fact that Lufbery as yet had had no dealings with the American volunteer movement and furthermore was probably altogether unaware of its existence. He had come to the flying corps by a unique and circuitous route, and his presence at the front was certainly unknown at this time either to the Franco-American Committee or to any of the other pilot-volunteers. As might be suspected from his background, Lufbery was taken more readily as a Frenchman than an American. His least favorite conversational topic, moreover, was himself and his personal history, colorful as that was. Because of his reticence, he became known among the flying fraternity as an "inscrutable chap." Hence, naturally enough, it occurred to no one at this time, not even his closest comrades in Escadrille V. 106, that Lufbery was anything but French. Not until hearing of the formation of the Escadrille Americaine and deciding that he would like to serve in this unit did he see any good reason for revealing his true nationality.

Gros, had he known of Lufbery's eligibility, would most certainly have included him in the letter to Bresnard as a prospect for the American squadron. Another veteran aviator was another selling point, and Gros needed all the selling points he could muster. Consider in this connection his recourse to bald exaggeration, saying that "most of the pilots are already familiar with the Nieuport airplane." The truth of things was that only two, Masson and Cowdin, had so far flown Nieuports. Both exceptionally skilled airmen, they were selected to train on the little biplane as soon as it was perfected as a combat machine. Before the end of September 1915, Masson was posted to Escadrille M.S. 68, and Cowdin to M.S. 38. They were among the first in these units to fly Nieuports, which gradually thereafter replaced the various

Morane-Saulnier monoplanes. By the same token, they were the first Americans who could be called pursuit pilots in the purest sense of that term.

During the month of February 1916, Colonel V. F. A. Regnier was made director of aeronautics, and no time was wasted in winning him to the cause of the American volunteers. On March 3, Gros and his collaborators sent to the new director a forceful plea for action:

> Following our letter of January 24, addressed to M. Réné Besnard, and of which a copy is enclosed, allow us respectfully to call your attention to the situation of the Americans enlisted in the French army. M. Millerand, General Hirschauer and M. Bresnard, after careful study of the question, decided that the American pilots should be united in one squadron. General Headquarters also took this view, and it was furthermore decided that Americans should fly the Nieuport fighting planes. Notwithstanding this . . . only four have been grouped at Le Plessis-Belleville. [Rockwell, Johnson, Balsley, and Hill were stationed here together in the Paris Air Guard.] The others are scattered, and most of them have not been assigned to Nieuports. . . . The Franco-American Committee, which has taken upon itself the task of choosing volunteers from the United States . . . would be very grateful if you could find it possible to carry out the decisions taken after careful reflection by your predecessors.

Regnier's reply was both courteous and satisfactory. He said that he had already broached the subject of an American squadron with general headquarters and had been assured that such a squadron was soon to be formed. He also stated that each and every American student-pilot who showed himself capable of flying the Nieuport would be trained on that aircraft. The signal passages of Regnier's letter, announcing that the protracted efforts of the Franco-American Committee had at last been rewarded with success, were these:

> Responding to your letter of March 3 . . . I have the honor to communicate to you the following information. I had already considered the question of an American squadron and, as early as February 20, I asked the Commander-in-Chief [Millerand] to advise me of his intentions in this matter. General Headquarters has just replied, informing me that an American squadron will be organized of the pilots whose names follow: William Thaw, Elliot Cowdin, Kiffen Rockwell, Norman Prince, Charles C. [Chouteau] Johnson, Clyde Balsley, Victor Chapman, Lawrence Rumsey and James R. McConnell . . . I have every reason to believe that the squadron will be established rapidly . . . and I will keep you posted as to what is being done in this matter.

Why now, after so many months of demur, did the French decide suddenly to comply with American requests? No doubt the battle of Verdun and the exigent condition of French aviation at the front had much to do with it. That frenzied battle was now in its third week, and its serious implications were frighteningly manifest in the size and ferocity of the German attack. The air commander at Verdun, Major Peuty, aware of the need for as many homogeneous fighter squadrons as could be developed, was entreating general headquarters for such a force. Experienced airmen were all at once at a premium. Among those available were the American volunteers. Here they were, begging to be grouped as a Nieuport squadron, and there in the besieged citadel at Verdun, screaming for Nieuport squadrons, was Peuty. No longer was there any plausible excuse for putting off the Americans. If they so dearly wanted to fly Nieuports in their own escadrille, let them. They could be hurriedly trained on the single-seater machines and then thrown into the critical Verdun sector, while at the same time fulfilling General Hirschauer's original promise.

In the last week of March the pilots named in Regnier's letter—some of whom were in service with front-line units, some with the Paris Air Guard, and the rest with the Réserve Générale Aeronautique—were assembled at Le Plessis-Belleville, the sprawling aviation depot located a short distance north of Paris. Enthusiastically they began an intensive program that included flight instruction on the Nieuport, gunnery, combat procedures and tactics. Oddly enough, although he had been piloting a Nieuport at the front for the past six months, Elliot Cowdin was required to undergo the full course of instruction like anyone else. Didier Masson, the only other volunteer hitherto breveted on the Nieuport, was inexplicably left out of Regnier's personnel list and was not among the trainees at Le Plessis-Belleville. That he stayed at the front by preference is a safe assumption. His attachment to the Franco-American Committee having at best been tenuous, Masson was not deeply committed to the creation of an exclusively American squadron. The idea of taking time out to duplicate his previous training would not have appealed to Didier Masson, who was by nature an individualist.

In less than four weeks the American contingent was ready. The order formulating the Escadrille Americaine—officially designated as Escadrille Nieuport No. 124—was promulgated on April 17, and that evening, at Ciro's restaurant in Paris, a dinner was held to celebrate the grand event. Present were all the volunteers who had trained at Le Plessis-Belleville, several of their French *moniteurs* and mechanics, Gros, Sillac, and others of the Franco-American Committee, and Paul Rockwell, on this night inducted as an honorary member of the squadron and asked to function as its historian and publicity representative. Prince, Chapman, McConnell, and Kiffin Rockwell left the same evening for Luxeuil-les-Bains, where the unit was to begin active service. They were joined a couple of days later by Thaw, Cowdin, and Bert Hall.

Jimmy McConnell wrote of the squadron's arrival:

> On our arrival at Luxeuil, we were met by Captain Georges
> Thenault, the French commander of the Escadrille Americaine . . .
> and motored to the aviation field in one of the staff cars assigned
> to us. I enjoyed that ride. Lolling back against the soft leather
> cushions, I remember how in my apprenticeship days at Pau I had
> walked six miles for my laundry.
>
> The equipment awaiting us at the field was even more impressive
> than our automobile. Everything was brand new, from the fifteen
> Fiat trucks to the office, *magasin,* and rest tents. And the men at-
> tached to the escadrille! At first sight they seemed to outnumber the
> Nicaraguan army—mechanicians, chauffers, armorers, motorcy-
> clists, telephonists, wireless operators, Red Cross stretcher-bearers,
> clerks! Afterward I learned they totaled seventy-odd, and that all
> of them were glad to be connected with the American escadrille.

The pilots were installed in a handsome villa adjoining the famous hot
baths of Luxeuil. With their French officers, Captain Thenault and Lieutenant
Alfred de Laage de Meux, they messed at the finest hotel in town, or rather
dined like epicures. A pair of automobiles, gray landaulets with brass headlamps, were always on hand to transport them in style to and from the airfield. What really impressed them, though, were the Oriental servants who
cleaned their rooms and attended to their needs. Thousands of laborers had
been imported from French Indo-China to work for the army, excavating
earthworks, clearing land, caring for livestock, laying railway tracks, repairing
roads, digging graves, constructing all kinds of military facilities, airfields included. The sight of them cutting grass, tamping earth, and filling ruts and
pot-holes on runways was familiar to French flyers. The more fortunate of
these workers became white-jacketed domestics in officers' quarters.
McConnell noted:

> I began to wonder whether I was a soldier or a summer resorter
> . . . I thought of the luxury we were enjoying, our comfortable
> beds, baths and motor cars, and then I recalled the ancient custom
> of giving a man selected for the sacrifice a royal time of it before
> the appointed day.
>
> To acquaint us with the few places where a safe landing was
> possible, we were motored through the Vosges mountains and on
> into Alsace. It was a delightful opportunity to see the glorious
> countryside, and we appreciated it the more because we knew its
> charm would be lost when we surveyed it from the sky. From the
> air the ground affords no scenic effects. The ravishing beauty of the
> Val d'Ajol, the steep mountainsides bristling with a solid mass of
> giant pines, the glittering cascades tumbling down through fairy-

like avenues of verdure, the roaring, tossing torrent at the foot of
the slope—all this loveliness, seen from an airplane at twelve thousand feet, fades into flat splotches of green traced with a tiny rib-
bon of silver.

The Americans were sent to Luxeuil, a relatively quiet region at the
southern extreme of the line, barely at all within the battle zone, to become
a fully equipped escadrille. For the next two weeks they practiced as best
they could in the three Baby Nieuports that had been allotted to them
for the purpose. They took turns in flying these obsolescent machines until
delivery was completed, on May 14, of their regular operational machines,
the latest Nieuport Type 17's.

No one was yet permitted to venture near the enemy positions unless
Thenault went along as guardian angel. He would take up the new pilots, a
pair at a time, and skirt the German lines in order to condition his wards to
the terrors of antiaircraft fire. While the rumble of one's engine usually
drowned the noise of the explosions, the flash of bursting shells and the
attendant puffs of smoke—black, white, or sulphurous yellow, depending on
the kind of powder used—could disconcert an uninitiated pilot when the
lethal blossoms began to dot the air above, below, all around him. Some
pilots never accustomed themselves to it, their composure progressively de-
teriorating under the daily strain. Although antiaircraft fire was notoriously
inaccurate in World War I, it did have its value as a psychological weapon,
many pilots testifying to its abrasive effect on their nerves. The gunners opposite Luxeuil were better shots than most. Thaw's machine was struck at
thirteen thousand feet during the escadrille's initial sortie. Hits at that range
were uncommon. According to Thenault's flight report, however, the enemy
gunners had the squadron too precisely bracketed for this to be dismissed as
just a lucky shot.

Except for Thaw's plane receiving some minor shrapnel holes, and everybody getting separated for a while in a local overcast, the squadron's maiden
patrol was without notable incident. At five in the morning Thenault pointed
out on his map the route they were to follow. Punctually at six o'clock they
took off and almost at once lost visual contact with each other. Even on a
clear day the diminutive Nieuports were mere specks against the broad pan-
orama below and limitless expanse above. On this morning the lower air
was thick with haze, and higher up, great towering islands of cumulus were
gathering into a tightly-packed ceiling. The tiny machines bored upward,
first through dingy curtains of vapor and then into the damp, dense interior
of the clouds. Each plane, during its groping ascent, was a small world alone.
McConnell wrote:

> Forging up above the mist into sunlight, at seven thousand feet,
> I lost the others altogether. Even when they are not closely joined,
> the clouds seen from immediately above, appear as a solid bank of

white. The spaces between are indistinguishable. It is like being in
an Arctic ice field. To the south I made out the Alps. Their glittering peaks protruded up through the white sea about me like majestic icebergs. Not a single plane was visible anywhere, and I was
growing very uncertain about my position. My splendid isolation
had become oppressive when, one by one, the others began popping
up above the cloud level, and I had company again.

The squadron regrouped in a *V* formation and headed eastward. Soon the
clouds had dropped behind them and the fertile plain of Alsace could be seen
stretching to the Rhine. Near Dannemarie they saw the German trenches,
brown graffito scrawls meandering across the patchwork of farmlands newly
planted for the spring. Then the antiaircraft opened up at them, filling the air
with flowers of smoke and jagged metal splinters. Thaw felt his Nieuport shud-
der as a cluster of flak tore through its wings, but he had no trouble regaining control. At Thenault's signal, the squadron climbed to sixteen thousand
feet. At this elevation the danger of being hit by ground fire was minimal,
but it was difficult to breathe in the rarified atmosphere, and it was so
bitingly cold that the men shivered in their fur-lined flying suits. Not until
several miles had been put between them and the antiaircraft batteries did
they descend to a more hospitable altitude.

Having crossed the lines, they fixed upon a northerly course. Each of
them repressed a surge of emotion as they passed over Mulhouse and into
Germany proper. They kept their port wings at a right angle to the Rhine and
continued on this bearing for about half an hour. A ninety-degree turn
brought them to where the threading trenches intersected the Hartmanns-
willerkopf and they saw little spurts of smoke that marked a downpour of
Allied shells slamming into the enemy fortifications. Now they were over
French territory again, on a homeward bearing, each man engrossed in his
private thoughts, all of them disappointed by the uneventfulness of this, their
baptismal mission.

During their tenancy at Luxeuil they would become increasingly restless
for battle. Hardly more exciting than the routine hops they had flown in their
training days, this first excursion across the frontier typified their subsequent
sorties from Luxeuil. McConnell, writing of this first patrol, said: "We had
been keeping an eye out for German machines since leaving our lines, but
none had appeared. It wasn't surprising, for we were too many."

Actually, there were very few German aircraft that far south of Verdun,
as every fighter plane the Germans could spare was then being utilized in
the desperate siege. The Kaiser's air force had been systematically culled and
pared to token strength in other sectors, and the standing order to his pilots
in such areas was to avoid combat except in self-defense or unless specifically
directed to intercept Allied bombers. Attacks of volition were tolerated only
against opponents hopelessly outnumbered.

History's first military airplane, the Wright Model A, with Orville Wright at the controls, undergoes tests at Fort Myer in 1909. *(U.S. Signal Corps)*

Bid tendered by the Wright brothers to build an airplane for the Signal Corps at a cost of $25,000. *(Smithsonian Institution)*

Form No. 2.

Signal Corp United States Army.

ADVERTISEMENT AND PROPOSAL FOR SUPPLIES OR SERVICES.

WAR DEPARTMENT,
Office of the Chief Signal Officer,
WASHINGTON, December   190

To the Public:

ARTICLES REQUIRED.

Heavier-than-air flying machine, in accordance with specification No. 486, dated December 23, 1907   25,000

To be delivered at Fort Myer, Va., where trial tests will be made.

E. Russel,
Major, Signal Corps, U. S. A.

We do hereby agree to furnish within 200 days, securely packed for shipment, delivered f. o. b. Fort Myer, Va. the articles as above shown at the prices affixed thereto by us, subject to all the conditions of the above advertisement.

(Signature)   Wright Brothers
(Address)   Dayton, Ohio

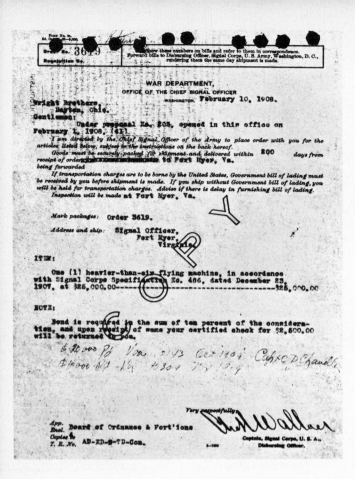

Signal Corps purchase order placed with the Wrights on February 10, 1908, for "one (1) heavier-than-air flying machine." *(Smithsonian Institution)*

OPPOSITE, TOP—The wide-winged Curtiss JN-4 "Jenny" served as the standard trainer at army flight schools in the United States. *(U.S. Signal Corps)*

OPPOSITE, BOTTOM — British-designed DH-4, powered by the Liberty engine, was the only warplane built in America that saw action at the front. Pilots nicknamed it the "flaming coffin." *(U.S. Army Air Forces)*

Scoring almost simultaneous victories on April 14, 1918, Lieutenants Douglas Campbell (*left*) and Alan Winslow became the first U.S.-trained airmen to shoot down enemy planes. Campbell went on to become the first official ace of the United States Air Service. *(U.S. Signal Corps)*

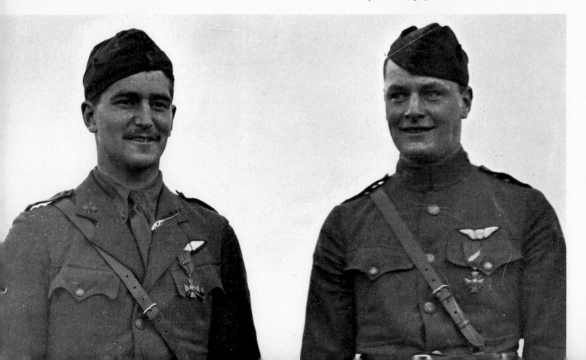

Workmen of the Packard Motor Company prepare Liberty engines for final tests in early 1918. (*U.S. National Archives*)

German engine-fitter at the Albatros factory installs a 160-horsepower Mercedes unit in a D-3 biplane. (*U.S. Air Force*)

Anthony Fokker in 1916, just after designing his deadly triplane.

Captain Oswald Boelcke, credited with forty victories before his death in October 1916, perfected the techniques of squadron teamwork in the German air force. *(Library of Congress)*

Cockpit and synchronized machine gun of the Fokker E-1. The first operational fighter with a device enabling a pilot to fire between the propeller blades, the E-1 had a greater effect on aerial combat than any other plane of World War I.

Oberleutnant Immelmann †
(letzte Aufnahme)

610
Postkartenvertrieb W. Sanke
BERLIN N 37

"The Eagle of Lille," Lieutenant Max Immelmann. This postcard portrait of the bemedaled air hero sold by the millions throughout Germany during the war years. (*U.S. Army Air Forces*)

OPPOSITE, TOP—Kaiser Wilhelm II (*fourth from left*) visits a frontline airdrome near Verdun in 1916. (*U.S. War Dept. General Staff*)

OPPOSITE, BOTTOM—German anti-aircraft battery on the Somme, 1917. (*U.S. War Dept. General Staff*)

Grim officers and men view the wreckage of Immelmann's plane at the site of his fatal crash. (*U.S. Air Force*)

Solitary Nieuport patrolling the no-man's-land at Verdun.

British Sopwith with Lewis gun mounted on top wing and telescopic sight. Compass and tachometer are visible in cockpit. *(U.S. Air Force)*

Georges Guynemer's Nieuport bearing the stork insignia of Escadrille N.3. (*Library of Congress*)

Ring-mounted Parabellum gun in rear cockpit of a German two-seater. (*U.S. War Dept. General Staff*)

Shown here *(left)* early in his flying career, the frail Guynemer became France's most beloved ace.

The Morane-Saulnier Parasol single-seater as it appeared in 1917. Though sleek for its time, it was decidedly inferior to contemporary Nieuport designs. *(U.S. Army Air Forces)*

In terms of enemy aircraft destroyed, the British Sopwith Camel was the most successful fighter of the war. *(U.S. Army Air Forces)*

Two-seater FE-2, known as the Fee to the British airmen who flew them through 1917 and 1918, did much good work as a reconnaissance plane, light bomber, and occasional fighter. *(U.S. Army Air Forces)*

Fast, strong, and easy to fly, the British SE-5 was recognized by both friend and foe as a formidable fighting machine. *(U.S. Army Air Forces)*

Albatros two-seater was photographed from immediately above by a British aviator during a dogfight. *(U.S. Air Force)*

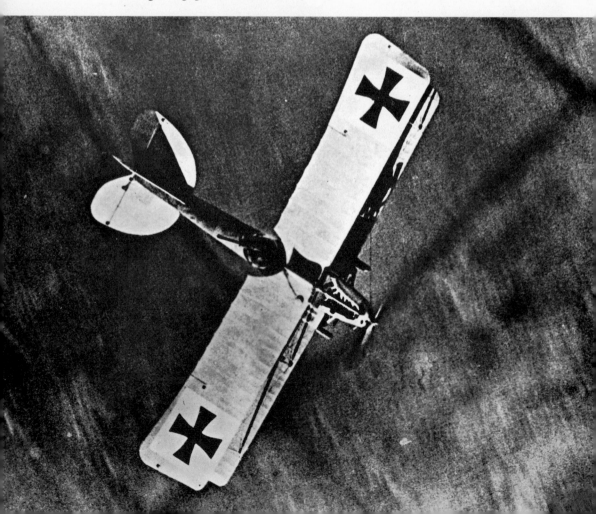

Trailing smoke as it plummets earthward, a French plane is claimed by a German defender *(arrow)* over the lines at Verdun. *(U.S. Air Force)*

Albatroses of the Richthofen Circus stand on the flight line, ready to take off at a moment's notice. *(U.S. Air Force)*

The ace of aces, Baron Manfred von Richthofen *(foreground)*, and pilots of Jagdgeschwader No. 2 stand for inspection at Douai in March 1917. The following month, "Bloody April," was the most successful of the group's history. *(U.S. Air Force)*

At the height of his career, Richthofen *(left)* talks things over with one of his squadron commanders, Lieutenant Hans Klein, just prior to the great German offensive of March 1918. *(U.S. War Dept. General Staff)*

England's second-ranking ace, with seventy-two victories, Major William (Billy) Bishop is seated in the Nieuport Scout he flew in early 1917 as a member of No. 60 Squadron R.F.C. *(Library of Congress)*

Impelled by his hatred of the enemy and undeterred by any cares for his own survival, Major Edward (Mick) Mannock shot down seventy-three German aircraft, to qualify as the highest-scoring pilot of the R.F.C.

Wearing the stork badge of the Cigognes, the elite battle group of French aviation, Sergeant (later Captain) Albert Duellin distinguished himself at Verdun and in the battle of the Somme, and scored a total of twenty victories. *(U.S. War Dept. General Staff)*

His tunic encrusted with medals, Lieutenant Charles Nungesser poses for portrait after claiming his forty-fifth victory in August 1918 *(USIA)*

Nowhere along the western front was there a more tranquil tract of sky than above Luxeuil and its surrounding country. But for an occasional enemy two-seater, always at immense height, always unescorted and never too far from the sanctuary of its own lines, the restive American escadrille saw nothing in the air to shoot at. These German reconnaissance planes, on glimpsing anything that vaguely resembled a Nieuport, promptly fled. Sometimes they made for the Swiss border and violated that nation's neutrality in the sure knowledge that their pursuers would not dare attack. Once over Swiss soil and carrying more fuel than any Nieuport that persisted in the chase, the two-seaters could leisurely proceed eastward until their way was clear and then make for home. As a rule, however, when these Germans were in danger from would-be attackers, they dived to very low altitude and scurried back to the east behind a covering barrage of antiaircraft fire. Their topside camouflage was excellent, consisting of parti-colored lozenges that blended almost invisibly with the ground below. Giving chase, the Americans invariably lost sight of their quarry in that startled moment when their attention was distracted by the first few bursts of antiaircraft fire.

But there was one German pilot who, despite his orders to the contrary, refused to flee so ignominiously. For his vain defiance, his and his gunner's lives became forfeit. The victory, won by Kiffin Rockwell on his fifth day of active service at the front, was the first to be entered in the scorebook of the American squadron.

Rockwell was flying alone when, over Thann, he detected the enemy aircraft, a wide-winged L.V.G., emerging from a cloud about a thousand feet overhead. He started to climb, only to see the German machine roll into a steep diving turn toward home. Anticipating another futile pursuit, Rockwell leveled off and took after the two-seater. Near the village of Uffhulz, the German did the unexpected. Sick, apparently, of always shirking battle, he abruptly throttled back as though to let the Nieuport overtake him. Rockwell, now approximately six hundred feet higher than his adversary and a half-mile or so behind him, nosed downward in a gently sloping descent. His path would bring him under the L.V.G. and enable him to attack its blind spot. The enemy gunner spewed bullets at the approaching Nieuport; Rockwell did not swerve. Reaching a point beneath the L.V.G., he pulled up smartly and steered for its belly. A few deft rudder and elevator adjustments brought the cross hairs of his gunsight squarely against the big plane's fuselage, just behind the wing roots.

He closed to within thirty yards, which gave him time for a single short burst. Speeding past the L.V.G., he executed a graceful chandelle and came about for another swipe. No more shooting was necessary. Rockwell saw the German pilot crumpled sideways in his seat, dead or unconscious. The gunner, unharmed, was sitting stock still, his hands clamped to the cockpit coaming. He was transfixed with fear, his mouth hanging open, his eyes bulging as the doomed plane veered into a vertical power dive and splashed against the earth near a German artillery emplacement on the outskirts of Uffhulz. By queer coincidence, his victim fell near the spot where Rockwell himself was to lose his life four months later.

Confirmation of the victory preceded him back to the airfield. "An observation post telephoned the news before Rockwell's return," McConnell wrote, "and he had a great welcome. All Luxeuil smiled upon him—particularly the girls. But he couldn't stay to enjoy his popularity. The escadrille was ordered to the Verdun sector."

CHAPTER XII

⟨ *The Lafayette Flying Corps* ⟩

THE AMERICAN pilot-volunteers knew their hour of trial was upon them when they were suddenly transferred to the Verdun sector. "While in a way we were sorry to leave Luxeuil"—quoting James McConnell—"we naturally didn't regret the chance to take part in the world's greatest battle." On the eve of their departure, they suffered a mild foretaste of what lay ahead. Some German planes materialized suddenly in the night murk and bombed the field, killing six of the squadron's ground personnel. Chapman, Rockwell, and Thaw, the standby pilots, went up to engage the raiders but could not find them in the darkness. Yet the bombing caused little excitement compared with going to Verdun. As Bert Hall scribbled in his diary: "We'll get even with the boches over Verdun. Up that way there's a real war going on."

They left Luxeuil on May 20, two days after Rockwell had drawn first blood for the escadrille. As soon as the pilots were off in their Nieuports, the trucks and tractors, hauling the rest of the men and equipment, set out in convoy. By air it was a bit more than an hour's trip to the new operations site, a medium-sized field outside Bar-le-Duc, about eighteen miles south-south-west of Verdun.

After landing, the pilots stowed their machines in the hangars and went to inspect their sleeping quarters. A commodious villa halfway between the town and the airdrome had been assigned to them, and comforts were as plentiful as at Luxeuil. But if any of them still thought lightly of his prospects, he was soon divested of such illusions. Even at Bar-le-Duc, twenty miles from the actual battle, they could sense their proximity to a vast military event. The smoke-shrouded sky, the recurrent peal of cannon, the acrid scent of burnt gunpowder, the roads clogged with troops and matériel, and the distressing number of ambulances, all brought an acute realization of a titanic battle in progress.

At mess that evening, Captain Thenault gave a solemn lecture regarding the situation at Verdun. On a large wall map he indicated the major landmarks and features of the sector, the trench lines and artillery positions, the locations of other aviation fields. Within a twenty-mile radius of Verdun, such fields abounded. Thenault explained that the American squadron had been placed on a rotating timetable with the other Nieuport units, each of which had its prescribed flying hours, so there was always an *escadrille de chasse* over the lines. In addition to these scheduled patrols, hunting forays would be made across the German trenches. Thenault made much of the fact that the Americans would be serving with the elite units of the French flying corps, veteran squadrons of renowned aces—Guynemer, Heurtaux, Dorme, Deullin, and their compeers. To further inspire his charges, Thenault read an aviso from the Franco-American Committee in Paris. It said that cash prizes would be awarded for decorations and citations. Fifteen hundred francs would go to any pilot winning the Légion d'Honneur. The Medaille Militaire was worth a thousand francs; the Croix de Guerre, five hundred francs. For a citation in dispatches the bounty was two hundred francs. Then, adjourning the dining-room briefing, Thenault distributed navigation charts to the pilots, which they were to study until bedtime; there would be no opportunity for orientation flights, he needlessly told them, since the outfit would take off early tomorrow morning on its initial sortie from Bar-le-Duc.

This first contact patrol, like almost all they subsequently flew at the Verdun front, occasioned a vicious combat over the enemy trenches. Although the Germans now seldom intruded above French territory, unless on a nocturnal bombing jaunt, their defense against Allied aircraft was stiff, merciless, and well coordinated. The Americans had been warned to expect savage opposition, but even the most alarming of these cautionary sermons had understated the case. The wonder of it was that nobody of the squadron was killed that day. None returned to base without a telltale rash of bullet scars on his plane. Bert Hall's machine was the worst damaged, its fabric slashed and tattered in a dozen places, some of the holes so large that his mechanic, Corporal Leon Barracq, could poke his head through them to examine the frame of the fuselage for cracked braces and longerons.

"It came near being my last sortie," Hall conceded, "and all because I misunderstood the signals." Thenault's absolute order was not to attack except on his cue. But when the squadron had crossed the German lines and was over the city of Étain, Hall spied a formation of hostile planes passing below.

At the same moment he saw Thenault dive as if to attack. Choosing one of the Germans for his own private little fight, Hall also dived, thinking the entire squadron was with him. Thenault descended only a short distance, however, then pulled up again. Hall continued diving, unaware that he was alone until it was too late. Later he gave the following account:

There was nothing for me to do but take my medicine. The sky seemed full of German planes. I got a good burst into the one I had originally picked out and he turned away with his motor limping badly. I didn't have time to see what happened to him after that . . . I was being engaged by five enemies at once. They peppered me and made me like it. I used up all my ammunition and did all the stunts I could think of to keep from presenting a target to the broadsides they were driving at me. We twisted and turned and dived and slipped and acrobated around madly. Several times I was so close to my antagonists that I could see their faces quite plainly. Finally, I turned over on my back and went down in a spin, as if I had been hit. Two of them followed me. The fight started at twelve thousand feet. When my altimeter registered fifteen hundred feet, I noticed that the Germans had given me up as a goner.

In an instant, I took advantage of this situation and, leveling off my plane, I started for home with every ounce of speed I had. My lead was very slight, but they had relaxed their vigilance just long enough. I hedgehopped all the way back to Bar-le-Duc, and when I arrived, Leon, my mechanic, was almost in tears. My plane was full of holes. Leon had to work all night to repair my little Nieuport. Leon was an excellent mechanic.

While Hall was having his troubles below, the main body of the squadron was beset by a snarling swarm of Fokkers. The melee lasted about ten minutes; then, his fuel running low, Thenault disengaged and headed for home, the rest of the squadron following suit. Five or six Fokkers—the new D-type biplanes that had just entered service—tried to stay on the tails of the retreating Nieuports, but only as far as the French lines. Although neither side scored a victory, the Americans, outnumbered and inexperienced, clearly got the worst of it. In the feverish days that followed, they would suffer more punishment. But they would dish out some of their own, too.

Before they were fairly well settled at Bar-le-Duc, Raoul Lufbery reported for duty with the squadron. He came fresh from single-seater training at Le Plessis-Belleville, where learning to handle a Nieuport had not been easy for him. Strange though it seems in light of his subsequent success as a *pilote de chasse,* Lufbery was at first rated by his instructors as inept for pursuit flying and better fitted to remain a *pilote de bombardment* in the unit with which he had been serving, Escadrille V. 106. Ruining several planes in sloppy landings, for a while he appeared incapable of ever putting a Nieuport down smoothly on an airfield. But he was resolved to avenge the death of his old friend Marc Pourpe, and so he persevered, overcame his clumsiness, passed the qualification tests, and joined the American squadron, ultimately, on May 24.

His new comrades looked upon his arrival as a lucky omen, for that same day saw Bert Hall shoot down a German observation craft. And the very next morning, firing a well-aimed salvo from his Vickers gun, William Thaw transformed a Fokker D-2 biplane into a falling cresset of flame. Two victories were won within eighteen hours of Lufbery's arrival, so that "Luf" was greeted like a messenger of blessings. Hardest struck by this notion was Hall. After bagging his first kill, upon returning to Bar-le-Duc and climbing out of his cockpit, Hall was met by the soft-spoken newcomer who introduced himself saying that he had arrived just an hour before. The time of Lufbery's arrival coincided closely with that of Hall's victory. Inordinately superstitious, a man who bedaubed his plane with tiny dollar signs to buy off the Fates, Hall attached some mystical significance to these events. That night, mixing a couple of gallons of potable cheer in a water bucket, he threw a little party to celebrate. "I was the bartender extraordinaire," he penned in his diary, quite obviously pleased with himself, "the non-drinking bartender who concocted the best cocktail in all of France. . . . Raoul Lufbery joined us today . . . [and] I had my first luck against the Heinies. We took Luf in with open arms. He looks lucky, and the boys love him."

Auguries and portents notwithstanding, any luck that Lufbery may have brought to Bar-le-Duc was shortlived. Thaw did indeed finish off a Fokker that next morning, but later the same day, far to the enemy's rear, a fierce combat ended none too agreeably for the Americans. Thaw was wounded in the shoulder and elbow, and an explosive bullet detonating against Rockwell's windshield tore several gashes in his face. Despite the blood that seeped under his goggles and blinded him, Rockwell managed to reach a French airdrome and land. Thaw, bleeding effusively from a severed artery, struggling to keep control of his plane, pancaked to earth almost on top of a trench, landing with such impact that his undercarriage collapsed. Dazed and too weak to walk, he was borne by some poilus to a field dressing station, whence he was sent to Paris for further treatment. Rockwell was less seriously hurt. A few slivers of glass were removed from his cheeks and forehead, his deeper lacerations were sutured, and after one day's rest in bed he was permitted to resume flying.

A week later, Victor Chapman was wounded. Considering his insatiable craving for battle and the zeal with which he attacked, it was a miracle he had not been hit before. Chapman never missed a chance to fly, accumulating more flying time than anyone else in the squadron. He fought against any odds, on one occasion against fifteen enemy planes. By the end of May, his Nieuport was a sieve of patched-up holes. Chapman's nerve, in McConnell's estimation, was "almost superhuman," and his devotion to the French cause "sublime." The day he was wounded he singlehandedly attacked four German machines. Swooping down from behind, one of them, a Fokker, riddled his Nieuport. A bullet creased his scalp, momentarily stunning him, but Chapman regained his wits in time to escape the trap and fired several shots to show he was still alive. Holding a broken control rod in one hand

and navigating his plane with the other, he made a landing at an airfield near Vatlincourt. Here his wound was dressed, his plane repaired, and he immediately took to the air again in search of more action. He would take no rest. With a bandaged head, he continued to fly and fight daily for the next three weeks—until his death.

Chapman was reconciled to the probability that he would be killed. "Of course, I shall never come out of this alive," he confided to an uncle in a letter written during his last week. That fact accepted, he seemed obsessed by the desire to shoot down at least one German before the end. "Once," according to his mechanic, Corporal Louis Bley, "they were mending his machine gun, but seeing his companions fly off, he ran to his Nieuport, jumped in and went up without his combination—that is, in his ordinary clothes—above the enemies' lines." Bley told of another day when Chapman came in after an explosive bullet had pierced his fuselage and blew apart the turnbuckle of a wing wire. "This same bullet entered his left sleeve and passed through, grazing the flesh and slightly burning the skin. The afternoon of the same day, after another sortie, he returned with a bullet through the aluminum bonnet of the engine." Bley also related that Chapman, in order to render his plane less visible, often amused himself by scratching off the green paint with a ten-centime coin. "I, his mechanician," Bley wrote, "painted the fuselage a pale gray. The paint was not dry the next day when Chapman learned that the Boches were over Verdun, and was off all the same with the paint wet. I didn't like this, and told him he had better wait. He refused, and said, 'Who cares for paint! If I bring down my Boche, that's as good as a new coat of paint.' " [1]

Although he expected to die, Chapman took pains to convince his parents that the life he was leading contained no extra element of danger. His correspondence to them was buoyant and reassuring. On the day he was wounded, he neglected to mention the fact in a letter to his father. As always, he filled his pages with vivid, often rhapsodic descriptions of his aerial patrols, which he made sound more like fanciful knightly errands than the grim forays they were.

On June 1, his head aching from the damage of that afternoon, he wrote:

> This flying is much too romantic to be real modern warfare with all its horrors. There is something so unreal and fairylike about it which ought to be told and described by poets, as Jason's voyage was, or that Greek chap who wandered about the Gulf of Corinth and had giants try to put him in beds that were too small for him, etc.
>
> Yesterday afternoon it was bright, but full of those very thick fuzzy clouds like imaginary froth of gods or genii. We all went out.

[1] Chapman: *Victor Chapman's Letters from France.*

All but I and the Captain got lost and turned back, so we two
flitted about over mountains of fleecy snow, full of shadow and
mist. The sight of him reminded me of the story of the last fly on
a polar expedition as I followed his black silhouette. I went down
to a field near the front and flew again at five o'clock. Then it was
marvelous. At three thousand meters, one floated secure on a
purple sea of mist. Up through it, here and there, voluminous
clouds resembling those thick water plants that grow in ponds; and
far over this ocean, other white rounded ones just protruding, like
strands on some distant mainland. Deep below me I could just
distinguish enough of the land now and again to know my whereabouts—the winding Meuse in its green flood banks or that smoldering Etna, Fort Douaumont. But off to the north, hovering and
curveting over one of the bleached coral strands, like seagulls—not
Nieuports surely! They were the modern harpies: the German
machines for the chase. In the still gray mist below, now and again
I caught sight of a Farman or Caudron sweeping over the corner
of the lines to see some battery fire. But as I peered down, a livid
white object moved under me going south, with the tail of a skate.
"There is my fish and my prey," I thought as I pointed downward
after the German reglage machine, "but prudence first." So I
searched in the water-plant clouds. Yes, sure enough, the venomous
creatures are there, as dark specks resembling the larvae one sees
in brackish water—three of them moving the same way. Those are
the Fokkers. I did not want to have them fall on my neck when I
dived on the fat greasy boche!

This morning we all started off at three, and, not having made
concise enough arrangements, got separated in the morning mist.
I found Prince, however, and we went to Douaumont where we
found two German reglage machines unprotected and fell on them.
A skirmish, a spitting of guns, and we drew away. It had been
badly executed, that maneuver! But ho! another boche heading for
Verdun. Taking the direction stick in between my knees, I tussled
and fought with the mitrailleuse and finally charged the rouleau,
all the while eyeing my boche and moving across Vaux towards
Etain. I had no altitude with which to overtake him, but a little
more speed. So I got behind his tail and spit until he dived into his
own territory. Having lost Prince, I made a tour to the Argonne
and on the way back saw another fat boche. "No protection in
sight." I swooped, swerved to the right, to the left, almost lost
him, but then came up under his lee keel by the stern. (It's the one
position they cannot shoot from.) I seemed a dory alongside a
schooner. I pulled up my nose to let him have it. Crr—Crr—Crr—
a cartridge jammed in the barrel. He jumped like a frog and fled

down to his grounds. Later in the morning I made another stroll along the lines. Met a flock of Nieuports, and saw across the way a squad of white-winged L.V.G. How like a game of prisoner's base it all is! I scurry out in company, and they run away. They come into my territory and I, being alone, take to my heels. They did come after me once, too! . . . but I had height so they could but leer up at me with their dead-white wings and black crosses like sharks, and they returned to their own domain.

This afternoon we left together, it being our turn for the lines at 12:30. The roly-poly cotton wool clouds were thick again. Popping in and out of them, I ran upon some puffs such as one sees when the artillery has been shooting at airplanes. . . . Yesterday I had fruitlessly chased about such puffs to find the avions. More smoke balls! There above me, like a black beetle, was the boche! But well above me, and heading for his lines. For twenty minutes I followed that plane ever in front of me, and inch by inch, almost imperceptibly, I gained in height and distance. He veered off to give me a broadside; I ducked away behind his tail; he turned off again; I repeated, but I did not have enough extra speed to maneuver close to him, though I temporarily cut off his retreat. After three passages-at-arms, he got away. Then, like a jackass, I went on to Verdun and found no one. On my return what tales were told! The boches had come over Bar-le-Duc and plentifully shelled it; two of our pilots had their reservoirs pierced and one had not returned. The town, the station, the aviation field all shelled—forty killed, including ten school children. . . . Yes, this is what comes of getting notoriety. There were disgusting notices about us in the papers two days ago—even yesterday. I am ashamed to be seen in town today if our presence here has again caused death and destruction to innocent people. It would seem so . . .

A couple of days prior to Chapman's being wounded, the squadron gained two additional members, Chouteau Johnson and Clyde Balsley, who had been on the air guard over Paris. They came to Bar-le-Duc on May 29. Three weeks later—June 18, to be exact—Balsley was shot down in his first real dogfight. Until that day he had been flying back of the French lines, learning the country and getting "air sight." Except for a couple of long-range exchanges with the enemy, he had encountered no opposition. So he was on his initial combat mission when he took off with Thenault, Prince, and Rockwell to escort a trio of artillery spotting machines. They were on the German side of the lines, at about twelve thousand feet, when they met a large enemy patrol, and the battle became general at once.

Balsley dived on an Aviatik whose pilot didn't see him. Opening fire, his gun popped just once and jammed. While he tried to clear his weapon, the

Aviatik and a second enemy plane chased him, firing briskly. Balsley was struck in the hip by an explosive bullet that made a dreadful wound. It was a good thing he was high off the gound, for his right leg was useless, the sciatic nerve torn apart. He tried to work the rudder bar by grasping his leg in his hands, but this did no good. Finally, he landed in a field of wild wheat, behind the French secondary line, his Nieuport turning over and throwing him out. Dragging himself along for a few yards, he lay there, not knowing whether he was in French or German territory. Artillery began searching for his machine. The pain was excruciating, but Balsley did not let himself lose consciousness until he was found by some soldiers. Seeing their French uniforms, he gasped a "thank God" and fainted. His rescuers carried him to the shelter of a nearby fort, and later he was moved to an evacuation hospital at Vatlincourt, behind Verdun, where doctors at first despaired of his life. Ten fragments of the explosive bullet were removed from his stomach alone, and many more from his groin, hip, and leg. He underwent seven operations in the following months. Not until the autumn of 1917, a year and a half after being wounded, was he well enough recovered to return to America. Although permanently crippled, he offered his services to his country, was commissioned a captain, and did valuable administrative work in the Pursuit Division, United States Air Service, at Washington.

Five days after Balsley's misfortune, tragedy visited the squadron again, this time in its worst guise. The date was June 23, and it marked Victor Chapman's last flight. Before leaving, he packed some oranges in his plane to take to Balsley, who liked to suck them to relieve the parching thirst caused by the surgery on his stomach. The fine details of Chapman's death were never ascertained. Kiffin Rockwell, in a letter to the deceased flyers mother, told all that anyone knew of what happened:

> The morning weather was good, and he went out at the regular hour with the rest. There were no enemy planes over the lines, so the sortie was uneventful. He came in, and at lunch fixed up a basket of oranges which he said he would take to Balsley. We went up to the field, and Captain Thenault, Prince and Lufbery got ready to go out on patrol. Victor put the oranges in his machine and said he would follow the others over the lines for a little trip and then go and land at the hospital. The Captain, Prince and Lufbery started first. On arriving at the lines, they saw the first two German machines, which they dived on. When they arrived in the midst of them, they found that two or three other German machines had arrived also. As the odds were against them, they did not fight long, but immediately started back to our lines and without seeing Victor. When they came back, we thought that Victor was at the hospital. But later in the afternoon, a pilot of a Farman and his passenger sent in a report. The report was that they saw a fourth

Nieuport arriving with all speed who dived in the midst of the Germans, that two Germans dived toward their field, and that the Nieuport fell through the air, no longer controlled by its pilot. In a fight, it is practically impossible to tell what the other machines do, as everything happens so fast, and all one can see is the beginning and then, in a few seconds, the end. That fourth Nieuport was Victor, and, owing to the fact that the engine was going full speed when the machine fell, I think that he was killed instantly.

He died the most glorious death, and at the most glorious time of life to die, especially for him, with his ideals. I have never once regretted it for him, as I know he was willing and satisfied to give his life that way if it was necessary, and that he had no fear of death. . . . Yet he is not dead; he lives forever in every place he has ever been, and in everyone who knew him, and in future generations little points of his character will be passed along. He is alive every day in this escadrille and has a tremendous influence on all our actions. . . . You must not feel sorry, but must feel proud and happy.[2]

The squadron's first fatality, Chapman, was also the first American airman to die in World War I. A wave of profound emotion swept the French people, whose political and military leaders were inspired to rare eloquence in their numerous tributes.

Soon after Chapman's death the nature of battle changed in the sky above Verdun. The grand offensive that the Allies unleashed along the Somme in July, as was intended, drained German strength from the Verdun sector. In order to contain the British drive, the Germans were compelled to shift considerable forces—including their best air units—to the new battle area. For the remainder of their stay at Bar-le-Duc, therefore, the American pilots faced opposition that, though every bit as earnest as before, was neither as skilled nor adequate in force. This change did not come about overnight, of course, but happened gradually as more and more German squadrons were pulled out of the Verdun sector. The hunting consequently improved for the American escadrille. Bert Hall got his second kill on July 23, and four days after that, Lieutenant de Laage de Meux bagged a two-seater. On the last day of the month, Lufbery opened a four-victory spree that included a double score on August 4. Hall conquered again on August 28, and then, on September 9, Prince and Rockwell shot down one each.

Among the German airmen who left the Verdun sector in early July was the celebrated Oswald Boeicke. A few days prior to his departure the great ace had a brief scrape with the Escadrille Americaine, as this extract from his diary recounts:

[2] Rockwell: *War Letters of Kiffin Yates Rockwell.*

I was ready to move on June 30. Imagine my bad luck, and on the very day I was destined to make my exit from the local stage . . . I had gone up twice in the morning and was loafing around the field when I suddenly heard the sound of machine guns and saw a Nieuport attacking one of our biplanes. The German landed safely. "The devil is loose at the front," he told me, all out of breath. "There are six Americans out there. I plainly saw the flag on the fuselage. They are very aggressive and fly far to our side of the lines."

I didn't imagine things were quite so grim and decided to go up and give the Americans a welcome. They were probably expecting it; politeness demanded it. When I met them, they were flying back and forth above the Meuse, close together. I approached one and said hello with my machine gun. He seemed to be a beginner; at any rate, I had no difficulty getting within a hundred yards of him and keeping him well under fire. As he was somewhat at a loss, I was justified in thinking that I could bring him down. But luck foiled me. My machine had just been overhauled at the factory, and after firing about seventy shots, the gun jammed. While I was trying to remedy the trouble, the other five Americans attacked me. Since I had no defense, I preferred to withdraw, at which the whole swarm was after me. I maneuvered by tilting my machine to the left and letting it drop. A few hundred yards and I righted it. But they still followed. I repeated the maneuver and flew back to camp, little pleased though unharmed. I last saw the Americans resuming their patrol along the front. My rotten luck had angered me and, upon reaching the airdrome, I got into my second machine and went off again. I was hardly fifteen hundred yards high when, with a loud explosion, my engine broke apart and I had to land in a meadow.

The records of the Escadrille Americaine reveal the identity of the pilot whom Boelcke attacked as Elliot Cowdin. Cowdin did not learn the name of his antagonist until the following year, when Boelcke's diary was posthumously published in Germany and found its way into France.

This memorable combat was among the last in which Cowdin participated. A month later, in August, he was forced to retire from active service because of ill health. Hospitalized for six weeks, he was then attached as a liaison officer to the Royal Flying Corps headquarters in Paris. In January 1917, he was released from the French service and returned to America. The end of the war found him with major's rank in the United States Air Service and an adviser to the Board of Aircraft Production.

By mid-September 1916, when orders came to quit Bar-le-Duc after four months of fighting above the battlefields and gruesome midden piles of Verdun, the Escadrille Americaine could count twelve victories to its credit. Twelve was also the number of airmen in the escadrille at this juncture. Besides Captain Thenault and Lieutenant de Laage de Meux, their French officers, the following Americans were on active duty with the unit when its operations at Bar-le-Duc were ended: Lieutenant Thaw, who had returned to the front before his wounded arm was entirely healed; Adjutants Prince, Hall, Lufbery, and Masson; Sergeants Rockwell, Hill, Rumsey, Johnson, and Pavelka. Didier Masson had joined the contingent in June, arriving just in time to mourn the death of Chapman, and Paul Pavelka had come in August. As for Sergeant McConnell, he was temporarily laid up with a sprained back, the result of a landing accident.

From Bar-le-Duc, with its potpourri of memories, the squadron was ordered to Le Bourget, the great Paris aviation center. Told to leave their planes behind for the unit that was to replace them, the pilots boarded the Paris express with all the joviality of college men off on a holiday. High spirits were warranted, for they were to have a week's leave in the capital. Where they would go after that, they did not know, but presumed it would be the Somme. As it turned out, a wrong guess.

Although her streets and boulevards were no longer brightly lit, a strict blackout having been enforced since the Germans began bombing the city, Paris still smiled gaily for men on leave. Delicious food, drink, and beautiful girls abounded; and the man in uniform, especially if he wore a badge of wings, was showered with hospitality and welcome.

The escadrille was joined that week in Paris by an additional recruit, Robert Rockwell, who had completed his flight training at Pau and had been held several months in the reserve. An Ohioan, born and bred in Cincinnati, he was not related to Kiffin and Paul Rockwell. After a year of voluntary work as a medical assistant, he had enlisted in the aviation section in February 1916, under the sponsorship of the Franco-American Committee. During his career with the American squadron he experienced some nasty punishment at the hands of enemy patrols. Once, for example, on May 6, 1917, in the course of a solitary patrol, he encountered a formation of seven German single-seaters coming into the sun. Thinking that his advantageous position would offset the odds, he attacked the rearmost plane. Before he could pick it off, the other six turned in unison and pounced upon him. He escaped by some freak of chance and limped into the airdrome half an hour later, his tires punctured, his aileron controls scarcely operable, the braces of his landing gear badly cut, and his wings pierced in many places. In another combat his engine failed at a critical moment, leaving him no alternative but to dive through a flock of hostile fighters. Halfway through the dive the radiator of his lubricating system burst, soaking him with thick castor oil that coated his windshield and obscured his vision, so that he was at the mercy of the pursuing Germans. He dived for thousands of feet, and the enemy, thinking him dead, finally abandoned the chase. Rockwell pulled out of his dive at very low altitude and raced home, contour flying all the way.

Despite many nerve-racking adventures of this kind, he kept his grip on himself through more than two years at the front. Much of his spare time he devoted to answering adulatory letters from unkown female correspondents in America. All the men in the squadron received such fan mail, mostly from adolescent girls and moonstruck matrons. When a photograph was requested, Rockwell would send a shamelessly idealized portrait of himself and then ignore further notes, letting his distant admirers pine away in hopeless longing —a punishment, he said, for their "unwomanly boldness." In the last eight months of the war, holding a captaincy in the United States Air Service, Rockwell distinguished himself as a flight commander in the 103rd Pursuit Squadron, assuming over-all charge of the unit soon after the Armistice.

Besides Rockwell the Escadrille Americaine acquired another "member" during that carefree week in Paris—an amiable lion cub named Whiskey. The only animal domiciled with the squadron to date had been Captain Thenault's police dog, Fram. Inasmuch as almost every aviation unit boasted its menagerie of assorted pets, the Americans seized the opportunity to adopt a unique mascot. Seeing the baby lion advertised for sale in a newspaper, they bought the winsome whelp for 125 francs. A fuzzy, bright-eyed male who nodded off in blissful contentment the moment he had someone's finger to suck, the cat went everywhere about the city with his keepers. "Whiskey," according to McConnell, "had a good view of Paris during the few days he was there. Like most lions in captivity, he became acquainted with bars, but the sort Whiskey saw were not for purposes of confinement." Some months later, the pilots deciding that Whiskey wanted a sweetheart, a young lioness was procured. Her name, of course, was Soda. And from then on, wherever the squadron was stationed, Whiskey and Soda resided together in a spacious pen behind the hangars, the pride of the escadrille and the envy of other squadrons.

Their Paris vacation at an end, the pilots learned to their surprise and disappointment that they were being sent, not to the Somme after all, but to their former base at Luxeuil-les-Bains. Arriving there, however, they hardly recognized the place. Billets now lined the field, and many additional hangars had been erected. Antiaircraft batteries, manned by British gunners, were in concrete emplacements around the perimeter of the camp, and a recently paved apron was crowded with British planes.

There were thirty-six of these huge, awkward-looking biplanes, their upper wings spanning eighty-five feet, their slender fuselages forty-eight feet in length, each with an enormous vertical fin at the stern. Eight pairs of struts bolstered the astonishingly wide wings, plus two outboard king posts and a large quantity of bracing wire. Beneath the box-shaped nose was an intricate four-wheeled undercarriage. Each of the planes, despite its large dimensions, was driven by a single 285-horsepower Rolls-Royce engine and carried a pilot and bomb-aimer in tandem cockpits situated far forward in the spindly, slabsided fuselage. Armament consisted of a single Lewis gun in the aft cockpit and eight sixty-five-pound bombs slung along the bottom of the lower wing. This was the Short Bomber, a product of the Short Brothers factory in Kent. The machines belonged to the Third Wing, Royal Naval Air Service, a major force totaling more than a thousand officers and men, of whom only a tenth actually flew, and which had moved to Luxeuil in midsummer. Apart from the British, who as yet—in more than six weeks—had not begun local operations, there were two French Nieuport squadrons based on the field, the Escadrille Americaine making it three.

Because of a delay in getting their new planes, the Americans had little to do for a few days but lounge about the hotel where they were quartered, visit the British in their barracks at the field, or go walking. Thaw spent his mornings fishing in nearby mountain streams, returning once with a three-foot trout, and Lufbery one afternoon picked two baskets of mushrooms. Writing of this tranquil interlude, McConnell suggested that "it was about as much like war as a Bryan lecture." The sarcastic allusion here to William Jennings Bryan mirrored the deep resentment that the volunteers in France harbored toward the isolationist faction at home. Bryan, a chief spokesman for nonintervention, had resigned in a huff from President Wilson's Cabinet in June 1915, to protest the government's policy in dealing with the *Lusitania* incident. Previously, as Secretary of State, he had proposed to the European belligerents that they conclude a truce and let the United States arbitrate their differences. His implausible "peace plan" having failed and his resignation from the Cabinet accepted, the famed orator went stumping through the country to deliver speeches—his detractors called them harangues—in favor of continued neutrality, which viewpoint naturally did not find favor with the vanguard of volunteers already fighting and dying abroad, as much for the honor and interests of their motherland, they were convinced, as for the cause of France and the United Kingdom.

The squadron had been idle at Luxeuil for five days when the first two of their new planes arrived. Few additional planes came after that, so the unit was never at full flying strength during its second short stay at Luxeuil. The pilots drew lots for the machines, Kiffin Rockwell and Raoul Lufbery winning possession of the first arrivals.

They embarked upon their initial patrol on September 23, early in the morning. Losing one another in the air, each flew on by himself, which was now a dangerous thing to do in the Alsace sector. As during their previous time at Luxeuil, there was little ground fighting in the region, but enemy air activity had increased markedly. Due to the size of the combined French and British aviation force at Luxeuil, and the threat its presence implied, the Germans had to keep a strong force in opposition. Allied estimates placed some forty to sixty Fokkers at the Colmar and Habsheim installations alone. Nettled by the ominous concentration of enemy bombers and chasers and expecting a massive raid at any time, the Germans resorted to their old formula of defense, that of "line" patrols up and down the local frontier.

They furthermore maintained a constant surveillance of Luxeuil and its auxiliary airfields, particularly those at Fontaine, where two squadrons of R.N.A.S. Sopwiths were encamped, and at Corcieux, which housed an escadrille each of Farmans and Breguets. The German observation planes, always protected by single-seater escorts, probed deep into French territory. It was their special trick to send a plodding two-seater ahead to invite attack; then, should a Nieuport dive after it, a covey of Fokkers would suddenly speed down from high concealment, cut off the Frenchman's retreat, and methodically dispatch him. A Nieuport pilot stood small chance if caught in the trap.

Kiffin Rockwell, on his first flight since leaving Verdun, discovered this awful fact too late. Heading east toward the lines, hugging a trace of gossamer cloud, he spotted an enemy reconaissance craft about a thousand feet below him and rushed to the attack. According to the commandant of a nearby village garrison who witnessed the combat through field glasses, Rockwell approached so close to the two-seater that a collision seemed unavoidable. The German gunner opened rapid fire when Rockwell started his descent. Out of nowhere three Fokkers dropped on the Nieuport's tail, their Spandau guns chorusing in its wake. But Rockwell ignored his attackers. He plunged through the hail of bullets and only when very close did he commence shooting. For a second it appeared as if the two-seater were hit, so the commandant said in his report, but then he saw the Nieuport bank sharply and pivot into a perpendicular dive, shedding its wings as it hurtled down "like a stone." It crashed in a small clearing, a few hundred yards behind the trenches and less than a mile from the spot where Rockwell, four months earlier, had slain his first enemy.

German artillery promptly began lobbing shells at the wrecked Nieuport. Careless of the bursting shrapnel, some French gunners from a nearby battery dashed out and recovered Rockwell's remains. There was a hideous wound in his breast where an explosive bullet had torn through. A doctor, examining the body, testified that if it had been an ordinary bullet, Rockwell would have had a fifty-fifty chance of survival. As it happened, he was killed the instant the unlawful missile exploded.

Lufbery that morning narrowly escaped a similar fate. He, too, engaged a two-seater, but before he was able to get within fair range, a pair of Fokkers swooped down from behind and blasted his plane full of holes. Exhausting his ammunition, he landed at Fontaine. There he heard of Rockwell's death and was told that two other French machines had been knocked down within the hour. Ordering his Nieuport to be refueled and re-armed, Lufbery took off to avenge his comrade. He crisscrossed the lines for almost an hour, then made a wide detour to the German base at Habsheim, but all to no avail. He saw not a single enemy plane during his angry hunt.

The night before he was killed, while the squadron was gathered in the hotel dining room, drinking and passing time with some civilian guests from the village, Rockwell had remarked that if he were shot down he would like to be buried where he fell. It was impractical, however, to place him in a grave so near the trenches. His body was draped in a French flag and brought back to Luxeuil, and his funeral was worthy of a field marshal. Among those who attended was his brother, Paul, who had fought by his side in the Foreign Legion. Pilots from every camp in the vicinity flew over to render homage to the American. Virtually every officer and enlisted man of the local French aviation force marched behind the bier. And the British airmen, followed by a detail of five hundred of their support troops, joined the solemn cortege. As the slow-moving procession of blue- and khaki-clad mourners passed from the church to the cemetery, airplanes circled low overhead and dropped a profusion of red, white, and blue flowers.

Rockwell's death spurred the squadron to greater exertions. The few who had planes sought relentlessly after the enemy. Prince shot one down on October 10, just two weeks after Rockwell was buried. Lufbery, the most successful pilot of the escadrille, would venture over a German airfield to rake it with machine-gun fire and to dare the Fokkers to come up and fight with him. While Prince was out in search of a combat one afternoon, he ran into a crowd of enemy machines that Lufbery had aroused. They converged on him, catching him unprepared, and for several terrifying minutes held him in a murderous pattern of bullets, one of which detonated against the leading edge of a lower wing and shattered it. Another cleaved an upright between the wings. That the weakened wing did not collapse was inexplicable, but Prince succeeded in nursing his plane back from Mulhouse, where the battle occurred, to the home field at Luxeuil.

Later that same day Lufbery once again missed death by the scantiest margin. Over the lines on a twilight patrol, he encountered a German with whom he had a fighting acquaintance. The two were evenly matched, feinting and dodging, neither getting a clear shot at the other, and all the while drifting farther into the German lines. They were nearing Habsheim when Lufbery glanced back and saw antiaircraft bursts dotting the western horizon. A German machine was over French ground, and it was Lufbery's duty to drive it off. Wagging his wings, he bade his adversary farewell. The enemy did the same, at which Lufbery sped away to intercept the other German. Along the way, however, he was surprised by a Fokker which he had not noticed hovering above his flight path. Before he could escape, three bullets punctured his engine, two passed through the fur-lined flying suit he wore, one richocheted off his hard leather helmet, another ripped apart one of his flying boots; his Nieuport was liberally holed from cowling to tail, and its elevator fin was competely shot away. That Lufbery, the unpromising student at Le Plessis-Belleville, had developed into an exceptional aviator was amply demonstrated; very few men could have safely maneuvered so badly damaged a Nieuport to earth as he did. The plane was so thoroughly riddled that the chief mechanic, taking a cursory look at it, decided without hesitation that it was beyond repair and ordered it to be stripped of usable parts and then scrapped. Fortunately, Lufbery was over French territory, or his forced landing would surely have resulted in his being made a prisoner.

The uncertain wait at Luxeuil came to an end on October 12. Late that afternoon the great armada of aircraft that had been aggregated in the Vosges district by the Allied command—a fleet comprising more than a hundred bombers and fighter planes—raided the Mauser Works at Oberndorf, a sprawling complex of factories producing rifles, bayonets, ammunition, shell casings, automatic weapons, and other battle utensils for the German army. Cloaked in utmost secrecy, the raid had been in the planning stage since early summer, and at the front everyone knew that a large-scale operation was in preparation for the new British and French squadrons in the area. The riddle of the target was solved only when the pilots were briefed immediately before zero hour.

The British group at Fontaine, in their single-seater Sopwiths, which carried four small bombs apiece, went off first as pathfinders. Next the French Farmans and Breguets departed from Corcieux. Then, from Luxeuil, the Short Bombers, laden with tons of bombs, taxied off two abreast and arranged themselves in formation for the long trip. The combat machines, which were to convoy the bombers as far as the Rhine, swiftly climbed and circled above their charges. Bert Hall commented on the raid in his autobiography:

> I shall never be able to forget the proportions of the raid—the tremendous flock of bombing planes and the various patrols of protecting ships. Now if you fly from Colmar, slightly north of east for ninety-five kilometers, you will come to the town of Oberndorf, and Colmar is seventy-eight kilometers as the crow flies from Luxeuil; therefore, the flight was 173 kilometers each way, provided the planes stayed on the course exactly, which everyone knew could never and would never happen. The Nieuports could not stay in the air all this time. They carried gasoline and oil enough for about two and one-half hours of flying, so it happened that the protection ships had to go part of the way and then come back for gasoline, leaving the bombers to their own devices, which included the tender mercies of the German attacking planes.

But Hall had no direct participation in the raid. Only four pilots of the Escadrille Americaine were assigned to escort duty: Lufbery, Prince, Masson, and Laage de Meux. The rest of the squadron, those who had planes, flew to Luneville to assist an escadrille of light bombers, a unit new to the front, in putting on a show intended to divert some of the enemy fighter force away from the main bombing formation. Together with the light bombers and another pursuit squadron, the Americans flew along a section of the front between the forest of Parroy and the town of Blamont and struck targets of opportunity. Two German reconnaissance planes were destroyed by the multisquadron patrol, although neither victim fell to the American pilots. Hall described the patrol as follows:

> We did, however, shoot up the troops on the ground, and on the way back from our last sortie, we finished off a Boche balloon. . . . We also attracted a great many German planes and in that way we helped the cause of the bombers to no small degree. Our ground-strafing was almost as interesting as the balloon-jumping that served as a climax to the day. Once I spied a company of heavy artillery-men, moving some rather long slim guns into place. A terrific bar-rage of antiaircraft and machine-gun fire came from the ground, but . . . the patrol tipped over and each man fired at the scurrying artillerymen as long as he could without crashing into the ground. We covered the countryside with bumped-off German artillerymen. The last I saw of that outfit was their horses galloping off over the hills. Poor frightened things—I have always been glad we didn't happen to hit any of them.
>
> It was on our last go-round that I spied some extra activity near the little village of Ignsy. I tipped over and shot a few bursts at what was moving on the ground, when all of a sudden, I realized that there was a semi-deflated observation balloon nestling on the ground, waiting to be put away for the night. What a thrill that was! We had been hedge-hopping for most of the afternoon; other-wise, I should never have had this piece of good fortune. By pulling a quick virage and zooming a bit, I was presently in position to do the neatest piece of execution I have ever done. Several sharp-eyed comrades of mine realized what was happening and immediately joined the sport.
>
> On the ground, the balloon crew must have been working like fiends to get their prize out of my reach, but they had started too late. I pushed over from about two hundred meters and withheld my fire until the last fifty meters of the dive. . . . The season of the year and the lateness of the day had no doubt made the outer skin of the balloon a little moist and it took the bullets longer to do their work. One of the French pilots afterwards said that he thought the balloon caught fire from something we had ignited on the ground alongside the hydrogen condensers. . . . There was a bright glow of flames and then a long column of beautifully tinted fire shot sky-ward. The inside of the column was bluish, much like the flame of a Bunsen burner. About that time, something happened on the ground. It must have been the explosion of the reserve gas tanks. We didn't stay around long after that, and how those German gun-ners did wave us goodbye with about half a million dollars' worth of good shells, every one of which missed us by a safe distance. I

didn't put in for a confirmation; I let the French pilots do that . . .
I had enough scores already.

As a fruitful consequence of this diversionary action, the Germans were
caught off balance by the raid at Oberndorf and had fewer than usual of their
fighting machines in a position to meet the Allied bombers. But the bombers
were still attacked—savagely—and six of them shot down. Conversely, two
Germans were dispatched by the planes they attacked, and before the operation was over, the four escort pilots of the Escadrille Americaine had each
accounted for a victory. On the outbound flight, Laage de Meux bagged a
Fokker as it was harrying another French machine, and Didier Masson did
likewise. Later, when the bombing expedition was on the way home, Lufbery
sent a Fokker to earth, and Prince picked off an Aviatik two-seater that was
valiantly being used as a fighter in a desperate attempt to retaliate against
the raiders.

Among the largest strategic air raids of the entire war, the strike at Oberndorf proved an unqualified success. Greater damage was inflicted, and fewer
casualties incurred, than had been anticipated by the most optimistic estimates. First to reach the target, the Sopwiths of the R.N.A.S. dropped low
over the Mauser Works, released their bombs, and headed back to Fontaine
without incident, all of them returning except one, whose pilot lost his bearings because of a faulty compass and strayed into Switzerland, where he was
forced to land by a shortage of fuel. When the Farmans and Breguets approached the factory compound, they found the rifle workshop, the main
objective, already ablaze. They unloaded their missiles on the building for
good measure and left behind them a seething mass of flame. The Short
Bombers, arriving in their turn and seeing the rifle workshop well on fire,
dropped their explosive cargoes on the adjacent factories. The immense conflagration was visible for miles around, and for miles around the earth intermittently shuddered as the flames touched off store after store of powder and
ammunition. Eerily silhouetted in the fiery suffusion was a gigantic pillar of
smoke. What he saw in the aftermath, a German newspaperman likened to
"the very central furnace of hell itself."

The Nieuports, having meanwhile doubled back to Luxeuil for more fuel,
went up again toward the Rhine to clear the air of any German lying in wait
for the returning fleet of bombers. It was on this sortie that Prince shot down
his Aviatik. Lufbery scored only minutes later, attacking a trio of Fokkers;
he downed one and dispersed the other two. This being his fifth confirmed
kill, he was mentioned by name in the communiqués that night and officially
recognized as an ace—the first American ace.

To guard the rearmost echelons of returning bombers, the Nieuports continued patrolling until sunset. A solid wall of cloud slid up from the western
horizon, and daylight faded rapidly. Alone in darkness, each man faced the
ticklish problem of locating a field and getting into it by means of his instru-

ments and whatever visual reference he might hope to see in the gloom. Slower-moving machines, with their inherent stability and low angle of glide, could be set down after dark with relative ease, but to grope for the ground in a Nieuport was to court disaster.

Shortly after nightfall Lufbery made for Corcieux, whose landing area he saw dimly lined with kerosene lanterns. Lowering toward the field and watching his airspeed indicator but ignoring his altimeter, which was unreliable at such low heights, he glided in above the field, eased back his control stick, decelerated the plane and lifted its nose to the correct landing attitude. Still too high when he cut his throttle, he slammed down upon the turf and bounced violently into the air again. Quickly recovering, he settled the plane on its wheels and tailskid and rolled to a halt. Taxiing off to a hangar, he was accorded a warm greeting from some Farman pilots whom he had escorted toward Oberndorf earlier in the day.

Just minutes later, as his hosts were showing Lufbery to the mess, they heard another Nieuport circling in the overhead blackness, its pilot inspecting the field preparatory to landing. It went twice around, then flew off and came about for the final approach, gliding lower all the time. The drone of its engine was suddenly stopped by a horrendous, jolting crash. Lufbery sprinted across the field ahead of the others. First to reach the crumpled wreckage, his heart sank. The mangled Nieuport, resting upside down, was Norman Prince's. It had struck a high-tension cable that was stretched above the trees on the edge of the airdrome. The cable had fouled the Nieuport's undercarriage, snapping the plane forward into the ground. The plane hit nose first and went careening across the grass, tumbling over and over. Flung from the cockpit, his safety belt tearing loose on impact, Prince's legs were both broken, and he suffered internal injuries. In spite of the terrific shock and his intense pain, he did not lose consciousness. Retaining his composure and even his sense of humor, he gave orders to the men who had run out to pick him up, and soon afterward, having been told the cause of his mishap, he heard another plane circling to land and joked about the favor he had done for the incoming pilot. "If that fellow gets down all right," he whispered to Lufbery, "he'll have me to thank for taking that damn wire out of his way."

On the ambulance ride to the hospital at Gérardmer, with Lufbery in attendance, Prince sang songs loudly to keep up his spirits. Following a preliminary medical examination, he was assured that his injuries were not grave, but the next morning Prince declined into a coma, never to awaken. A blood clot had formed on his brain. As he lay uncomprehending on his bed, he was visited by a delegation of his fellow aviators from Luxeuil; Captain Thenault, in a sad little ceremony, promoted him to second lieutenant and decorated him with the Légion d'Honneur. He already held the Medaille Militaire and Croix de Guerre. On October 15, Prince died. He was buried at Luxeuil with full military honors, the grandeur of his funeral matching that, only three weeks earlier, of Kiffin Rockwell.

The Escadrille Americaine had been deployed in Alsace to participate in the Oberndorf raid and for no other purpose. Accordingly, six days after the raid, the unit received orders to leave for Cachy airdrome on the Somme front. On the eve of their departure, the Americans were guests of the British pilots at a farewell banquet. Among many toasts of mutual regard, the British proposed one "to the Yanks, our guardian angels," expressing their keen appreciation of the fact that four men of the American squadron had wiped out four Germans while escorting the bombers most of the way to and from Oberndorf.

From Luxeuil that next morning, those with planes flew directly to Cachy, the rest of the squadron traveling by rail. This latter group, passing through Paris, was reinforced by three more volunteers who had recently completed their flight training. Frederick Prince, Jr., who ten months earlier had come over from Massachusetts to serve as a pilot with his brother Norman; Willis Haviland, a Chicago lad who had transferred to the flying corps from the ambulance service; and one of the earliest American recruits to the French Foreign Legion, Robert Soubiran.

Much to their discomfort, before the pilots were snugly established in their new post, the autumn weather turned prematurely cold. Having been accommodated in deluxe villas and hotel rooms during their tours of duty at Luxeuil and Bar-le-Duc, they had grown accustomed to waging war in high style. They were totally unprepared for the rugged living conditions that awaited them at the airfield in Cachy Woods. Instead of a cozy villa or hotel, they were quartered in a crude portable barracks, an elongated barn that was hastily erected in a sea of ankle-deep mud, nine miles from the nearest town. The structure barely afforded shelter. Rain and chill wind penetrated every chink and joint of the thin walls and roof. Until blankets were supplied some nine or ten days after their arrival, the pilots had to curl up to sleep in their heavy flying clothes. Without their own kitchen facilities, they were fed in the various messes of the other seven escadrilles that occupied the base.

During this difficult adjustment period, on days when there was no wind or rain, a dense fog—for which the Somme basin is famous—hung like a pall over the airfield and dampened the men's morale as well as their clothing and everything else they touched. The cantonment, but for the planes and motor vehicles parked in view, reminded the Americans of a rising boom town in the Yukon back during the gold-rush era. Connected by a network of wooden duckwalks, all the buildings were clustered along one side of the field, interspersed with assorted tents. The large canvas hangars were surrounded by the storage tents of their respective escadrilles. Clapboard barracks for the pilots and maintenance crews stood close by, the unit command tents situated between them. Farther back were the latrine sheds. To service the entire camp there was a first-aid shack, a poorly stocked commissary, a bathhouse, and the power plant that generated electric light. And in one oversize tent was the community bar, the profits from which were donated to the Red Cross.

Since the weather was against it, and because most of them still had no planes, the Americans were precluded from flying for more than a week following their arrival at Cachy. They used this time to put their dreary quarters in order. Masson, who was elected *chef de popote,* together with Thaw obtained permission to go to Paris in one of the squadron's light trucks. There, with the help of Dr. Gros and the Franco-American Committee, a stove and cooking utensils, along with sundry other necessaries, were purchased and taken back to the field. All hands went to work and life was soon made bearable. "In fact," McConnell noted, "I was surprised to find our lodgings as good as they were when I rejoined the escadrille a couple of weeks after its arrival in the Somme. Outside of the cold, mud, and dampness, it wasn't so bad. The barracks had been partitioned off into little rooms, leaving a large space for a dining hall. The stove was set up there, and all animate life from the lion cub to the pilots centered around it."

The squadron's move to the Somme had come just seven months after its original muster at Le Plessis-Belleville. Since that time its member pilots had fought 157 combats and scored sixteen confirmed victories, Lufbery alone accounting for nearly a third of the enemy planes shot down. The volunteers—most of them—were seasoned veterans now, the possessors of a commendable battle record, and yet Cachy was a whole new experience for them.

Never before had they shared a field with so many *escadrilles de chasse,* nor had they ever been stationed in such intimate proximity to no-man's-land. They sensed the war more acutely here than at Luxeuil or Bar-le-Duc; it swirled around them, intruding into their consciousness at all hours of the day and night. They heard a "symphony of war notes," as McConnell termed it, but they witnessed the awesome spectacle, too, and felt its reverberations as the "big show" unfolded in the distance. When there was activity in the trenches, the concussion of heavy artillery shook the ground beneath their feet, rattled the barracks windows, made the furniture dance, and sometimes shattered the chinaware. From their doorstep they could see a line of observation balloons, and beyond the balloons, airplanes darting like swallows amid the flash and smoke of antiaircraft fire. The bark of machine guns echoed across the field and was accompanied now and then by the hollow whistling sound of a fast plane diving to the attack. Occasionally, a stricken plane could be seen falling, its downward progress marked by a thin black streak against the sky.

Cachy, nearer to the front lines than any other aviation camp in the sector, was a prime target for enemy raiders. The Germans preferred to drop their bombs at night, and they came often, so that dusk-to-dawn standby duty at Cachy was a taut, expectant vigil. Two pilots from each squadron on the base, sixteen men in all, were placed on watch nightly, ready to scramble into the air at any slight suspicion of attack. These nocturnal attempts at interception, however, proved woefully ineffectual; none of the German raiders was ever shot down, whereas French casualties incurred in night accidents averaged more than one fatality a week.

The manifold dangers of night flying outweighed any potential benefit. One of the American volunteers, Paul Pavelka, had a bad time of it, for example, when engine trouble caused him to lag behind the rest of the flight. In the minute or two it took him to get the engine running smoothly again, he lost sight of the formation and found himself completely lost. For what seemed an eternity he flew around aimlessly in the darkness in the hope of glimpsing some familiar perspective below, his desperation mounting. The needle of his fuel gauge was leaning far to the left and declining rapidly toward zero, when he noticed a pinpoint of light at ground level, swinging to and fro. He cautiously glided lower and saw the boundary of a small airdrome, a field completely strange to him. Someone, hearing him and guessing his plight, was waving a lantern to attract his attention.

The field was possibly German, but that was academic to a pilot whose fuel tank would run dry at any second. Pavelka, after making his landing, was greatly relieved to hear French voices raised in greeting. He also heard the safety catches of several rifles being relocked, for the men who had led him safely to earth had not known whether he was friend or foe. Pavelka had come down at Martainville, forty kilometers from his home field in Cachy Woods.

By the end of the first week of November, the Escadrille Americaine was fully equipped again with Nieuports, including several of the latest Type 27's. Ready and eager to resume operations, the unit was attached to the newly formed Groupe de Chasse No. 13, commanded by the eminently capable, if finicky and somewhat splenetic, Major Phillipe Fequant. Incorporated in the group were Escadrilles N. 15, N. 65, N. 84, and the American squadron, N. 124. (Three months later, Escadrille N. 88 would be added to the lineup.) The American squadron remained a part of this fighting combine throughout the rest of its time in the French flying corps, until the United States Air Service absorbed the unit intact and redesignated it the 103rd Pursuit Squadron.

The other four squadrons then based at Cachy were the celebrated Storks of Groupe de Chasse No. 12, with whom the American volunteers had been briefly teamed at Bar-le-Duc. The brightest star in this galaxy, Georges Guynemer, was now flying the first Spad single-seater. This machine, the Type 7, ruggedly constructed, highly maneuverable, its top speed exceeding 120 miles per hour, outclassed every other fighter concurrently in use by either side. When, in late November, a Spad was allocated to the American squadron, Captain Thenault, exercising his prerogatives as commanding officer, reserved it to himself. The much-desired Spads were gradually thereafter dispensed to other members of the squadron, but the Type-17 and Type-27

Nieuports continued in service for several more months, and formations of mixed aircraft were not uncommon during the winter of 1916–1917.

It was here at Cachy, on November 16, only a few days after entering operations above the Somme, that the volunteers were surprised and disturbed to receive from French general headquarters the directive ordering the name of their squadron changed. For six months now the German ambassador in Washington, Count Bernstorff, had been acrimoniously protesting the frequent reference to the Escadrille Americaine in French communiqués. Bernstorff argued that the United States government, by its silence in this matter, was tacitly consenting to the presence of American airmen at the front and thereby violating the laws of neutrality. Ultimately, after months of delay, the Department of State saw fit to act and therefore asked the French authorities to refrain from labeling Escadrille N. 124 as an American unit. Rightly or wrongly, but understandably, the volunteers regarded this as a galling rebuke from their own government and an ignominious surrender to German bluster. In America the pro-Allied press was of the same mind, especially those editors advocating United States involvement in the war, who seized upon the incident and used it as a weapon with which to stimulate more pro-Allied sympathy.

"For diplomatic reasons," decreed French headquarters, the Escadrille Americaine would thenceforth be called the Escadrille des Volontaires. Feeling this title to be too colorless, the squadron members appealed to Dr. Gros, who conferred with a Captain Bertaud of the War Ministry. Finally, on December 6, at Gros' suggestion, it was agreed that the squadron would be known as the Escadrille Lafayette—and so it has best been known ever since.

The question of a new name resolved to their satisfaction, the flyers adopted an insignia for their planes: the head of an Indian chief, depicted in aquiline profile and adorned with a majestic, eagle-feathered war bonnet. The portrait was of no particular Indian but was copied, with minor artistic license, from the trademark of the Savage Arms Company that appeared on some ammunition boxes in the squadron's magazine tent.

Patrolling on any kind of regular schedule was possible only until the last week of November, when winter rain and fog settled over the region again. Sloppy weather prevailed almost without interruption. Through all of December and the first half of January, there were hardly a dozen days clear enough for flying. During this entire period Lufbery was the sole member of the Escadrille Lafayette to score a victory; he shot down a two-seater on the morning of December 27. At almost the same moment, quite near the place where Lufbery's victim fell, Guynemer blasted his twenty-fifth enemy machine from the sky. He wrote of it in his diary: "December 27, 1916. Hunting. Attacked a Walfisch from ten meters. Each of us fired fifteen rounds. The Boche cut two of my cables, but he crashed to earth south of La Maisonette." (By "Walfisch," borrowing the German word for "whale," the French aviator meant, of course, a large aircraft.)

In mid-January, when the weather finally cleared for a spell, a severe frost gripped the battlegrounds of northern France. Infantry operations came to a virtual standstill. In the air, although both sides maintained daily patrols, flights were essentially defensive ones intended to ward off enemy reconnaissance. Encounters between opposing fighters were thus infrequent and, for the most part, desultory skirmishes. The low incidence of combats might also be explained by the freezing temperatures that made flying a misery and chilled many a pilot's ardor for doing battle. The planes of that time, moreover, were prone to cold-weather disorders. Particularly troublesome were the Hispano-Suiza powerplants of the Type-7 Spads, engines that, because of excessive vibration, were none too dependable to begin with. The main difficulty now, in this season of bitter cold, was that the engines lacked radiator shutters and so could not warm up to optimum internal operating temperature, which drastically reduced their efficiency. Later-model Spads came equipped with vastly improved Hispano-Suizas, and with properly insulated cooling systems, but the men flying Spads in the winter of 1916–1917 were compelled to fit makeshift vanes to their engine radiators and pray for the best. Not only the Spad, of course, but all types of aircraft suffered chronic winter ailments, creating problems for the mechanics who tended them and dangers for the men who piloted them. If nothing else went wrong, there was always the prospect of skidding out of control or puncturing a tire when landing on a field slicked with ice and ridged with frozen snow.

On January 24, 1917, Lufbery again brought down an enemy machine, his seventh. He attained the victory during the squadron's last patrol from Cachy, for the next day was canopied with dark clouds and lashed by new snow, and on the day after that, along with the rest of Groupe de Chasse No. 13, the unit moved to Ravenel, near St. Just, which would be its base of operations until early April. While at Cachy, mainly because it had been kept down by weather for so much time, the squadron had not met with a single casualty. There had been a turnover of personnel, however.

Before the Americans were two weeks at Cachy, Bert Hall—under curious and shadowy circumstances—transferred to one of the Stork squadrons, Escadrille N. 103. The consensus of historical opinion has always been that Hall, on account of his boorish ways, his petty grudges, and tiresome bragging, became so unpopular with the other pilots that they exiled him from the squadron. None who were in a position to know the full story ever divulged it. Nowhere in the entire body of the many pilots' writings, the official unit history included, is there an explanation for Hall's sudden departure from the squadron. A discreet and perhaps charitable conspiracy of silence obviously prevailed in compliance with a finely pointed code of etiquette. In circumspect fashion Hall himself provided the most pregnant clue to what had occurred. Revealing no other details, he noted in his diary on October 29, 1916: "Had orders to transfer from N. 124 to N. 103 today. Moved with as little excitement as possible. I hate goodbyes. . . . Captain d'Harcourt made quite a lot of my coming into N. 103. They had a little party—extra food and all that.

I think the [Escadrille Americaine] is glad to get rid of me. I don't blame 'em."

Hall may have been hard to live with, and he may have been ostracized for some unprepossessing frailties, but he deserved no man's contempt in either case. From between the lines of his memoirs, he emerges as a rather pathetic rascal. There seems to have been nothing more reproachful at the root of his perversity than an overgrown inferiority complex. Hall was exceptionally short, skinny, somewhat bandy-legged, his wizened countenance vaguely remindful of a dried-up lemon. Swagger and strut though he might, even in his resplendent blue uniform he did not look the sort of chap he yearned to be, the kind of blade he called a "gay-dog hero." Patent in his writings is a craving for loud applause. His underlying sense of inadequacy could only have been heightened by his association with his fellow volunteers, every one of whom was better endowed than he with social grace. They were wellborn, many of them, well bred, well educated, and all of them were debonair and self-assured. He tried to fit in but lacked the polish and finesse.

A homely little curmudgeon whose childhood had been blighted by poverty, whose schooling had been curtailed by the need to work and help support his family, who had run away in his teens and slummed around Europe, Hall was the unhappy product of his own past. Among other things, he cheated at cards and dice and was caught at it, and once he forged another pilot's name to a bar bill. In urbane society he was a misfit. In the air, although he exhibited courage and skill, his performance was marred by the manifestations of his afflicted ego. Selfish for acclaim, he was reputed to have hogged targets and to sometimes attack a plane that a squadron companion had already damaged and was near finishing off, thereby disrupting the other man's attack and permitting the enemy machine to get away. Poaching victories, of course, would have made a pariah of any pilot, and it may have been the main reason for Hall's ejection from the squadron.

Given a new Spad to fly in Escadrille N. 103, Hall bagged his fourth German machine on November 23. Upon returning from this patrol and reporting his success, he was congratulated by Captain d'Harcourt, who exclaimed, "Vive le Spad!" Hall's response was faithful to form. "Non," he retorted. "Vive Bert Hall!" Less than a month later the boastful American was transferred out of the Storks and sent to Russia on a "diplomatic aviation mission."

"I am supposed to help the Russians pep up their flying," he wrote, "and also to report back to Paris what is going on." Until mid-March 1917, Hall toured the eastern front as a technical adviser to the Czar's air force. With the onset of the Revolution, however, the abdication of Nicholas II, and the mutinous ferment in the Imperial army, Hall departed aboard the trans-Siberian railroad for Vladivostok. From there he went by way of Shanghai to Japan and booked passage to San Francisco. Arriving in July, he found the United States mobilizing feverishly for its part in the war. "Never have I been asked so many questions," he penned in his diary. "The Americans haven't the remotest idea of what the war is about—not the remotest! And as far as aviation is concerned, the average public is a dud."

In October he was summoned to Washington to testify before the Senate Committee on Aviation and the Council of National Defense, which included among its members the distinguished inventors Thomas A. Edison and Hudson Maxim (Sir Hiram Maxim's brother) and the Secretary of the Interior, Franklin Lane. Hall wrote of his interrogation:

> A senator whose name I shall not mention but whose voice is loud and whose brains are soft asked me the dumbest questions. . . . He first asked me how many airplanes it would take to lick the Germans. As there was no logical answer to this bloomer, he asked another. "Lieutenant Hall," he said, "if the United States Signal Corps should dispatch five hundred American-made airplanes to France next month, I mean, fly them to France under their own power, would it not be possible for this superb fleet to carry enough bombs to reduce the German strongholds to a smouldering mass of ruins?" I said, "Senator, what kind of airplanes would they be?" "Oh," he said, "that's unimportant . . ." and he took up a sheet of paper with a lot of typewritten information on it. "Suppose [the senator continued] they would be standard biplanes, or the [Curtiss] JN-4 army tractors, or any good stout planes—any good ones that could carry two or three men each and the necessary cold steel."
>
> Of course I wanted to laugh . . . it was too ridiculous for words. I stuttered around a bit and tried to be as diplomatic as possible, but the senator did not want diplomacy. He wanted to be put in his place and finally I did it. I told him as calmly as possible that the idea of flying the Atlantic was sheer insanity and if five hundred planes were rolled out of the hangars tomorrow morning, there wouldn't be five hundred trained pilots in the entire western hemisphere who could fly them. So the senator left in a huff and the committee members who remained had a good laugh.

Soon after this Hall requested release from the French service in order to enlist in American aviation. His request granted, he then failed to honor his bargain, joining neither the United States armed forces nor any other. To this day, therefore, the French military records list him as a deserter.

Hall's peccadilloes and peculations did not end there. After the war he went to China and was commissioned by Sun Yat-sen's Nationalist government to instruct Chinese airmen. It was also his duty to procure planes and equipment for the Nationalist air force. On one occasion, the Chinese authorities entrusted him with $34,000 for a consignment of aircraft armament that never arrived. Brought up on charges of embezzlement, Hall was convicted by a United States consular tribunal and sentenced to two and a half years in McNeil Island penitentiary. For the two decades following his prison term,

Hall lived in obscurity. When he was killed in an automobile accident near Castalia, Ohio, in December 1948, few newspapers bothered to print obituaries about the picaresque character who had ranged the sky with the first contingent of American battle pilots in World War I.

Back in that dismal autumn of 1916, during the Escadrille Lafayette's assignment to Cachy airdrome, two other aviators besides Hall took leave of the squadron. Lawrence Rumsey, suffering ill health, after a period in the hospital was given a medical discharge. The second to go, Paul Pavelka, responded to a plea for volunteers to serve on the Salonika front. Nine months later, having flown numerous missions there, Pavelka died of injuries received in a fall from horseback. The squadron became poorer by yet another man in February 1917, immediately after the move from Cachy to Ravenel, when Frederick Prince left the outfit to become an instructor at Pau.

Counting the outcast Hall, four men left the escadrille between the last week of October and the first week of February. On the other hand, seven new pilots joined the unit in that time. Among them was the zealous and sad-fated Edmond Genet, namesake and direct descendant of the notorious Citizen Genet, whom the Revolutionary government of France sent as ambassador to the United States in 1792, and whose indiscretions led to his recall. The Citizen never returned to France, but settled in Albany and married the daughter of Governor De Witt Clinton. It was their great-great-grandson who joined the Lafayette Escadrille at Cachy, after serving a year in the trenches with the Foreign Legion.

A shy, blond youth, born November 9, 1896, at Ossining, New York, Genet decided at an early age to make the navy his career. Unable to pass the entrance exams at Annapolis, he enlisted as an ordinary seaman. When war broke out in Europe, he wanted to fight as a volunteer in French uniform, but could not secure his release from the Navy. After weeks of brooding, he went AWOL and sailed for France in January 1915, to enlist in the Foreign Legion. Transferring to aviation in the spring of the following year, he trained for six months before commencing active duty on the Somme. In a letter to his mother, he recorded his impressions:

> This is the most dangerous branch of the service but it's the best as far as [the] future is concerned, and if anything does happen to me, you all surely can feel better satisfied with the end than if I was sent to pieces by a shell or put out by a bullet in the infantry, where there are seventy-five out of a hundred possibilities of your never hearing of it. The glory is well worth the loss. I'd rather die as an aviator over the enemy's lines than find a nameless, shallow grave in the infantry, and I'm certain you'd all feel better satisfied, too.

In his fourth month with the escadrille Genet died as he said he preferred dying, the victim of enemy antiaircraft fire. He was the first American killed

after the United States declared war against Germany. With a ceremony
impressive in its simplicity, he was buried at the little military cemetery at
Ham in the midst of the season's last snow storm. Shortly after the Armistice,
the Secretary of the Navy cleared Genet's name of the technical charge of
desertion.

The other six who joined the squadron around the same time as Genet, all
of them from either the Foreign Legion or the American Ambulance, were
Walter Lovell, Harold Willis, Stephen Bigelow, Edward Hinkle, Edwin Parsons, and Kenneth Marr, an Alaskan prospector who had brought over a
string of huskies for ambulance service in the snowy reaches of the Vosges
mountains.

Hinkle was in his middle forties, well past the prescribed age limit for
candidates in the French flying corps. His health, moreover, was less than
good. He was nevertheless accepted, completed his training, and actually flew
a few operational patrols before sickness forced him out of service. The
arrival of seven new pilots within so brief a time, an unpromising aspirant
like Hinkle among them, attests to the ease with which American volunteers
could now get into French aviation. One of these seven, Edwin Parsons, in
his book, *The Great Adventure,* had this to say:

> Practically unknown to each other, one by one we volunteered
> in the Foreign Legion for the duration of the war, and, after medi-
> cal inspection and several days at Legion headquarters at Dijon,
> were transferred immediately to the primary training schools, with-
> out the necessity of trench service. We were a heterogeneous crew,
> in all degrees of physical condition, mentality and education. But
> the French neither asked nor apparently cared where or how much
> we had gone to school and paid scant attention to physical handi-
> caps. Their greatest and practically only requirement was that we
> should have that intangible something called guts.

Parsons, to illustrate how lenient the French had suddenly become in their
requirements for prospective pilots, described the medical tests he underwent
at the induction center:

> But the most difficult part of my tests were yet to come. Stand-
> ing me off at ten paces in front of an eye chart whose letters looked
> as large as the Corticelli sign in Times Square, he [the examiner]
> commanded me to read.
> "The second line," he'd say, "the third letter. I see there a B.
> What do you see?"
> Sure enough, it was a B, and I'd say so.
> "Bon!" he'd explode enthusiastically.
> Then we'd do some more . . . silly exercises, he calling the letters
> as I checked up on him. He was right every time. He never tried

to cross me by calling the wrong letter. He wasn't taking any chances I'd be wrong, and his "Bon!" grew bigger and better with every answer.

Then we passed to the color charts, where we repeated the same delightful procedure.

"I see red. What do you see?"

"Red, Major."

But why go on? In two shakes of a lamb's tail, it was all over.

He gave me a friendly pat on the bare back that sent me staggering across the room and, signing his name to my papers with an official flourish, he congratulated me on being a perfect physical specimen and said that as far as he was concerned, I could go out and get myself killed at any time "Pour la France."

Parsons, who destroyed eight enemy machines before the war's end, was one of the American volunteers to whom the French pilots referred as a "chic type" and meant it as a sincere compliment. Dashing and handsome in his dress uniform, he seemed born to distinction. "Seeing him on leave," wrote James Norman Hall, "one might easily have thought him an *aviateur des boulevards,* who had never been nearer to the front than Paris." His leave spent, Parsons would return to the airdrome, don his well-worn flying clothes and a pair of sabots, and could always be seen, ten minutes before takeoff hour, clopping briskly out to the flight line. In combat his steady nerve and diligent perseverance were exemplary. He remained with the Lafayette Escadrille until early 1918, when the unit was taken over by the United States Air Service. Seeing the chaotic condition of American aviation at that juncture and profiting from the experience of other volunteers who were being transferred—losing weeks and even months of flying time in the process—Parsons elected to stay with the French and joined the famous Stork squadron in which Guynemer had flown, Escadrille Spa. 3. Parsons finished the war a lieutenant, decorated with the Medaille Militaire, the Belgian as well as the French Croix de Guerre (with eight palms), and the Belgian Croix de Leopold. Two decades later, during the inceptive stages of World War II, he tried forming another Lafayette Escadrille to go again to the aid of a French people threatened for the third time in less than a century by the Germans. The project fell through, and Parsons enlisted instead in the United States navy, in which he reached the rank of rear admiral before his retirement.

Parsons, Hinkle, and the others who entered the American squadron in the 1916–1917 winter, soon found themselves involved in a full-charged struggle for supremacy between Allied and German airmen. The latter at first were in the firm ascendancy, thanks to their D-series combat machines—Pfalzes, Halberstadts, and especially Albatroses—which were in more plentiful supply than any comparable French machines, such as the Nieuport Type 24 or the Spad Type 7. For its part, the Royal Flying Corps was anxiously awaiting introduction of the SE-5, the remarkable Bristol two-seater fighter, and the Sopwith Camel; meanwhile they made do primarily with outmoded pushers and obsolescent Nieuports and Sopwiths.

This, then, was the spring that culminated in "Bloody April," a violent season of frightful losses in the Allied air forces. Whereas British and French airmen did seize the initiative by summer, they accomplished it only at tremendous human cost. The British suffered worse by far, but the French casualty rate nevertheless reached its highest point of the war. Indeed, so many casualties were sustained that General Lyautey, the Minister of War, and his staff of aviation heads gingerly resigned amid the resultant furor of public indignation and political censure—whereupon the efficacious reformer, Daniel Vincent, assumed the post of air chief.

The Germans had attained their aerial dominance, or rather resumed it, early in the fall of 1916, following the interval of Allied superiority during that summer. Coincident with this enemy resurgence and in response to it, the French further liberalized their already loose requirements for pilot-trainees. As a result of this relaxed policy, the doors were opened wider to American volunteers. For them to get into the French flying corps became easier than it had been at the time just prior to the Somme offensive, when Parsons, Hinkle, and the rest of their group were admitted to flight school. Hence, the number of Americans wearing wings for France took a sharp upswing that autumn. Where only seventeen volunteers had been taken into the flying corps up until the end of 1915, fifty-eight American enlistments were passed by the close of 1916, and eighty-four by April 1917, when the United States entered the hostilities against Germany. And then, between that April and August of 1917, during Daniel Vincent's initial three months in office—mainly because the United States had renounced neutrality, but also because Vincent actively encouraged the American presence in French aviation—the number of American enlistments swiftly doubled and very nearly trebled. It shot up to 212 by August 4, on which date the last of such enlistments—that of a New York City youth, scarcely eighteen years old, named Ellison Boggs—was allowed, and the number would have continued multiplying at an accelerated pace had not United States authorities asked the French to refrain from accepting any more Americans into their armed forces. It should be noted incidentally, for the sake of statistical accuracy, that a grand total of 268 volunteers were actually enrolled in French aviation during the first three years of the war, but that fifty-six of them were discharged before earning their brevets for reasons of health, ineptitude, or misconduct. Roughly another fifteen were killed or seriously injured in training accidents; these, since they became casualties in the course of duty, are counted among the 212 generally considered to have done flying service. The failure rate was thus little more than 20 percent, which for those days was quite low.

Of the almost two hundred Americans who flew combatively for France in World War I, forty-eight served at some time or other in the Lafayette

Escadrille. The rest, approximately three-quarters of the entire volunteer force, were scattered throughout the regular French flying corps. But for a few who specifically requested assignment to bomber or reconnaissance units, they were integrated within fighter squadrons, including some of the best such squadrons at the front. Like their countrymen in the Lafayette Escadrille, they piloted single-seater battle planes, Nieuports or Spads, and they did themselves and their nationality proud. By the end of hostilities the volunteer group as an entity had laid claim to 199 official victories—and this figure excludes at least twenty-five unquestionable kills that for various reasons failed to be confirmed by the French or American authorities. Significantly enough, these volunteers—all but thirty-four of whom eventually transferred into the United States Air Service or, in a few cases, the United States Naval Air Service— obtained the great majority of their victories while flying with the French. As against their fine record of enemy aircraft destroyed, sixty-four of them lost their lives while on operational duty, nineteen were gravely wounded in action, and sixteen fell into German captivity.

The American aviation volunteer, whether serving in the Escadrille Lafayette or some other squadron, regarded himself fundamentally as a member of an air force within an air force. Despite signing a contract that obliged him to obey French commands, and prepared though he was to die if necessary in French uniform, he felt he was really—in a practical as well as an altruistic sense—furthering the best interests of his own country. The typical volunteer insisted that his identity as an American be neither obscured nor diminished in importance. As a result, he firmly asserted that he belonged not to the French flying corps as such but rather to the Franco-American flying corps that Dr. Gros and his recruiting committee in Paris had propounded and ultimately brought into existence.

The cliquish bent of these American airmen and their double loyalties might understandably have disquieted the French command, but from the War Ministry down through the strata of military leadership the French remained tactfully noncommittal on this subject. Such sentiments on the part of foreign volunteers must surely have been anticipated, and their belief that they were doing service for their homeland as much as for France could only have increased their combat efficiency. These considerations then, plus the fact that the term "Franco-American flying corps" was occasionally employed in communications emanating from all the levels of authority, make it probable that no strenuous objections were raised against the volunteers' viewpoint.

Implicitly, therefore, on a sort of quasi-official basis at least, the Franco-American flying corps, with the Lafayette Escadrille as its heart, was recognized to be a separate, if subordinate, body. It was, except for the all-volunteer squadron, so thoroughly interfused with the parent air force as to have no visible cohesion, no outward shape or substance of its own. Formless, lacking any independent volition, it did, nevertheless, exist. It existed not merely on committee letterheads, nor simply in the minds of its promoters and personnel, but as a dynamic element in the Allied war effort. Knitting the volunteers closer together in common purpose, providing a focus for their mission, reinforcing the inspirational conviction that theirs was a sacrifice not only for France but also, in the final analysis, for the United States, the Franco-American flying corps—or, as it was formally redesignated in 1917 and is best remembered, the Lafayette Flying Corps—loomed as a factor of definite influence. By the courage, skill, and devotion of its member pilots its presence was made painfully evident to the Germans and gave them notice that American sensibilities had been outraged by Germany's aggression—that it was only a matter of time before the full weight of the United States would be thrown behind the cause of democracy.

Not surprisingly, by virtue of its franchise as an exclusively American combat team, Escadrille N. 124 figured as the cynosure of the volunteer air force. Unique, colorful, and effective, the squadron was constantly in the eye of the press and the public, the deeds of its champions receiving loud acclaim. The rest of the volunteers—the majority—widely spread and thus lost to conspicuous view, enjoyed comparatively little personal notoriety. The splendid achievements of several worthies went unremarked in contemporary news reports, so that their names remained generally unknown for some while. The most deserving of them, in fact, died unsung. The fame that finally did attend them was posthumous.

One such was Sergeant Frank Baylies, of New Bedford, Massachusetts, who embarked for France in January 1916, to join the ambulance service. Fourteen months later, yearning for real action, he enlisted as a pilot-trainee. In the entire Lafayette Flying Corps only Lufbery shot down more enemy machines than Baylies, who shot down twelve—and did it in a much briefer career.

Husky, ruggedly handsome, his square-jawed face adorned with a bristly, straw-colored mustache, Baylies was an extrovert by nature and was unmeasured in his enthusiasm for everything he tackled in life. At the controls of an airplane he was not blasé to danger but awake to its heady sensations, almost addicted to them. Where Lufbery combined a cool caution with his mastery in shooting and combat tactics, Baylies' success lay in his readiness to take chances and his superlative airmanship. The French pilots of the Stork elite, who watched and tutored him, declared that he possessed the qualities of the greatest aces—the unerring aim, the skill in maneuver, that indefinable sixth sense for outguessing the enemy. His irrepressible *joie de coeur*, however, seemed often to displace his instinct for self-preservation. Once, for example, during one of his first few solo hops as a student at Avord, he scared the wits out of his fellow students and his instructors when they saw him execute a *vrille* in an ancient Bleriot monoplane. He explained afterward that he did it on impulse, sheerly for the fun of it. An unparalleled stunt that a pilot of longer experience would never have attempted unless he wished to commit suicide, it gave rise to Baylies' reputation as a rashly intrepid, yet singularly gifted, pilot.

Upon receiving his brevet in autumn 1917, Baylies was delighted at being assigned to Escadrille Spa. 3, the hallowed squadron of Dorme, Heurteaux, Deullin, and Guynemer. The newly fledged volunteer was immediately acknowledged to be an aviator of exceptional flair. His French comrades predicted a brilliant career for him, and he was not slow in confirming their expectations. The Storks, always patrolling the most heated sectors of the western front, were usually pitted against first-class opposition, and in a succession of desperate clashes with such formidable Jastas as—to use their sobriquets—the "Rednoses," the "Checkerboards," and the "Tangos," Baylies soon distinguished himself as one of the prodigies of an *escadrille d'élite*. His tactics were faultless. He was a dead shot, and he seldom quit a fight until his enemy was hurtling earthward, dead in his cockpit or enveloped in flames.

Baylies, in his anxiety to make sure of a victory, once descended almost to the ground, less than a quarter mile to the rear of the German trenches. His victim crashed, but before he could regain altitude, his own plane was raked by infantry fire and its engine put out of action. With propeller stopped, he glided to a landing between the French and German lines, only a few yards from the latter. Unhitching his seat belt the instant his wheels touched down, he leaped from the still moving Spad, dodged a couple of Germans who tried to grapple him, sprinted to a French advance post, and escaped through a storm of enemy bullets.

Toward the end, Baylies was considered invincible. In attacking, he held his fire until at point-blank range, when his initial burst was usually lethal. According to a writer who was acquainted with Baylies at the front: "His modesty was always charming; no amount of success could turn his head or alter his simple statement that his victories were due to luck. In a crowd he did not often speak seriously, but his close friends knew that beneath his jovial manner ran a vein of thoughtfulness and genuine idealism; it was not for pure love of adventure that he worked so honorably as an ambulance driver, joined the aviation corps, and made at last the greatest sacrifice."

Baylies was killed late in the afternoon sunshine of June 17, 1918, during some heavy fighting along the west flank of the Marne salient, between Crévecoeur and Lassigny. The exact circumstances have never been ascertained. One Stork pilot reported that Baylies' Spad caught fire and went down after being attacked by four monoplanes. But German records show no monoplanes in combat units at this time, although the Fokker E-5—a parasol type—was then undergoing tests and two months later, in August, officially entered operations. Another, more plausible, account of Baylies' death was furnished by Adjutant Reginald Sinclaire, an American flying with Escadrille Spa. 68, who happened to be in the vicinity. He and a squadron companion sighted an enemy patrol deep within German territory, and Sinclaire, as he turned to attack, saw a trio of Spads still further in, pursuing a small pack of Fokker triplanes. He noticed that the French machines bore Stork insignia. When his combat broke off, Sinclaire glimpsed a distant machine, which he feared was a Spad, falling in flames. It was undoubtedly Baylies. Though he died in relative obscurity, Baylies' name later became linked with Lufbery's, everlastingly so, as a transcendent hero of the American aviation vanguard.

The name of a third volunteer also belatedly achieved celebrity. An equally inspiring figure, whose career closely duplicated that of Baylies, was Sergeant David E. Putnam, the number-three ace of the Lafayette Legion. Reared in Brookline, Massachusetts, a tall, athletic, serious-minded youth of twenty, fresh from his sophomore semester at Harvard, Putnam hurried to France in the spring of 1917, right after the United States had declared war, and enlisted as an airman. At Avord, where he took the slow Bleriot training, and then at Pau, his instructors were impressed as much by his sense of purpose as by his above-average flying skill. Putnam's life now held but one goal: to get into the thick of battle, preferably as a member of the Escadrille Lafayette. His impatient desire to finish his training made him always the first to arrive at the practice field and the last to leave it. And on days when bad weather prevented him from flying, Putnam's good humor deteriorated into gloom and irritability.

On December 12, after graduating from flight school with top class honors, Putnam was profoundly disappointed to learn that he was being ordered to Escadrille N. 156 instead of the Escadrille Lafayette. His dedication and headlong aggression seemed undamped by this disappointment, however, and were quickly appreciated by his squadron mates. "Our sector was a very quiet one," a comrade wrote of him at this period. "German planes were scarce, and if we wanted a fight we had to go a long way hunting behind the lines. This was especially forbidden by our commandant; you know how cautious the French are in giving young pilots permission to do any *chasse libre*. When we were fortunate enough to get this permission, you could rely on Putnam to stretch the privilege to the limit. I speak from experience, remembering that it was he who led me into my first scrap, when we were twenty-five kilometers in German territory."

That following spring, the squadron exchanged its Nieuports for Morane-Saulnier A-1 monoplanes, a vastly improved development by this manufacturing firm of its circa-1915 Parasol designs. Harnessed to a 160-horsepower Gnome Monosoupape engine that propelled it at speeds exceeding 125 miles per hour, its high wing slightly backswept, its twin machine guns mounted side by side on the cowling and hydraulically synchronized with the airscrew, the A-1 Parasol was the smallest, trickiest, and among the fastest of all World War I fighter machines. In handling this little hornet, Putnam's artistry reached a perfection that astonished even the oldest veterans of the squadron. On one occasion, while hunting by himself over the lines, Putnam attacked a formation of eighteen German single-seaters, shot down the enemy leader, and got clean away. His diminutive chaser, swift and agile as a hawk, almost invisible against the sky, became the terror of the local German airmen.

Putnam was transferred in early summer to Escadrille Spa. 38, a unit of long and outstanding service, now commanded by one of France's foremost aces, Captain Georges Madon. It was here that the American attained the peak of his effectiveness, for Madon took a special interest in him and taught him many valuable lessons. Putnam, retaining a style of his own, soon surpassed the promise that Madon perceived in him. His greatest feat was performed on June 5, 1918, above the Marne, when he dispatched five German planes in as many minutes. Because of some procedural technicalities, only one of these victories was entered in the official ledger, but there can be no doubt about the other four, as several eyewitnesses saw them go down. Even though he had been deprived of credit for these four kills, Putnam was officially a six-victory ace when, on June 8, he was commissioned a first lieutenant in the United States Air Service and given command of the 134th Pursuit Squadron. In the few weeks left to him before his death, he brought down five additional Germans, and his conduct of the squadron evoked warm praise from both his superiors and subordinates. Unlike many squadron leaders, he never allowed his administrative work to interfere with the regularity of his flights and combats.

Only as a unit commander did Putnam attract any attention from the press. Until then, like most volunteers serving outside the vaunted Escadrille Lafayette, his luster had been hidden behind the cloak of anonymity. By the day of his death, September 13, 1918, he had acquired a modest éclat, however, to which he was completely indifferent. The end came when he and another pilot were challenged by eight Fokkers. Putnam promptly shot one down, but as he maneuvered to engage a second, a pair of enemy planes slipped behind him and let go a withering, sustained crossfire. The top wing of Putnam's Spad disintegrated. The Spad nosed over into a vertical dive, and the pressure of gathering velocity then tore the bottom wings from their roots. Putnam, when extricated from the wreckage by German soldiers, was found with two bullets in his head and several more in his chest and arms. He had probably been killed instantaneously.

"It was," wrote a compatriot, perhaps a bit wistfully, "a splendid death in the midst of battle, certainly the ending he would have chosen for himself." For his service with the French, Putnam had been awarded the Croix de Guerre, the Medaille Militaire, and the Légion d'Honneur; after his transfer to American aviation, General Pershing conferred upon him the Distinguished Service Cross, as well as proposing him for the Congressional Medal of Honor.

In contradistinction to Baylies and Putnam, Lufbery did not die with fame owing to him. He had become a popular hero and, of course, he knew it. The newspapers and magazines in France and America were full of his scintillating exploits. Mothers in both countries named their newborn babes after him. Parisian chefs brought forth such culinary treats as Aubergines

Lufbery and Faisan Lufbery. Scores of adoring young ladies addressed passionate proposals to him by mail. Recognized and hailed wherever he went in public, mobbed by admirers on the streets and in hotels and bars, feted at all sorts of civil functions, a Frenchman by birth and an American by naturalization, he was the toast of two continents. James Norman Hall observed:

> Seldom was there a *prise d'armes* at the airdrome that Lufbery was not among the pilots to be decorated. How we unheroic and unknown airmen envied him the greetings he had from such men as Guynemer, Fonck, Nungesser and others who had achieved greatly: "Tiens, Luf! Comment ça va, mon vieux!" He never boasted or took credit to himself. He counted his success as three-fourths luck, and was always surprised that so much of it should come his way. When foolish people tried to flatter him, he used to say to us after they had gone: "Well, you know, it's funny what things people will say to a man's face. I wonder if they think we like it?" He had to take a lot of it whether he liked it or not, but it had no unfortunate effect on him. He was always the same old "Luf."

The facts, however, contradict Hall's assertion that Lufbery was unaffected by success. As time passed and his renown increased, Lufbery seemed to develop an ever-stronger antipathy toward being fussed over. Fewer and further apart were his public appearances. Reporters found him less willing to grant interviews and more evasive in the answers he did give. Before the close of 1917, Lufbery began to live almost as a monk, only rarely leaving the sanctum of the airdrome for an evening in town. Although affable as ever in the company of aviators, and never rude to anyone, he avoided civilians as much as possible and spent more and more of his leisure alone. Solitude seemed to hold some needed consolation for him. His favorite off-duty recreation was picking wild mushrooms. On rainy days when there was no flying, he would disappear into the woods on lonely *reconnaissances des champignons,* often returning with a supply plentiful enough for the entire squadron. He also devoted many of his spare hours to romping with Whiskey and Soda, the lion mascots. Both cats were partial to him, especially Whiskey, who followed him around the airdrome like a faithful pet.

In January 1918, Lufbery received his major's commission in the United States Air Service, but his new employers at first showed incredibly poor judgment in their use of his talents. The American authorities sent him to the aviation center at Issoudun, gave him a rolltop desk, paper and pencil, and absolutely nothing to do. There he sat, day after day, whittling his pencil or scratching doodles in a notebook and wondering what the hell he was doing shut up in an office. He neither understood nor cared anything about the routine of preparing reports and keeping inventories and indents. His place was at the front, guiding a patrol into action. At Issoudun, surrounded by officers who had only the vaguest conception of what was involved in managing an air force under actual combat conditions, Lufbery was a pathetically helpless creature out of his element.

Relief came when he was sent with the 94th Pursuit Squadron to Villeneuve-les-Vertus in the Champagne sector, close by the Marne. But no fighting could be done because, although most of the pilots had planes, they had no armament. During a month of waiting for the rest of their equipment, Lufbery rehearsed the men in their combat tactics. Sometimes he led them as far as the lines, where they gazed longingly across no-man's-land and saw patrols of enemy aircraft that they could not attack. On the way back from one of these sterile excursions Lufbery landed at the airdrome of the Lafayette Escadrille, there to visit some of his former wing mates. "Well," he glumly told them, "it's nearly a year since the United States declared war, and what do you suppose the 94th is doing? Waiting for machine guns! Six hundred million dollars appropriated for the United States Air Service, and we're loafing around behind the lines because we can't get enough guns to equip a dozen planes!" [3]

Finally, in mid-March, a weapons shipment reached the squadron. It consisted of just six Vickers guns, so that only three of the squadron's Nieuports could be fully armed. In these three planes, shortly past daybreak on March 19, Major Lufbery and Lieutenants Douglas Campbell and Edward Rickenbacker undertook the first flight over enemy lines to be made in the war by pilots of the United States Air Service. The patrol, though uneventful, was at least a beginning, a source of encouragement for America's flying doughboys—whom one French journalist had dubbed the "impatient virgins."

Not until April 10 did the 94th Pursuit Squadron get into operations as a whole unit. The squadron was now stationed at Toul, and only four days later, right above the base, Lieutenants Campbell and Alan Winslow, shooting down a German apiece in one-two order, scored the first United States Air Service victories of the war. For the time being, however, the region around Toul was quiet. Except for the spectacular Campbell-Winslow success, the squadron's first two weeks of service were practically devoid of shooting. Lufbery took out patrols daily and satisfied his old penchant for lone hunting, but always without result. Few enemy aircraft were abroad, and those that were refused to give battle. But the honeymoon was shortlived. Toward the end of the month action in the sky suddenly grew hectic. Rickenbacker, demonstrating the mettle that would take him to the head of the list of American aces, had his initial victory on April 29, when he blasted an Albatros single-seater from the sky over Pont-à-Mousson.

The sky around Toul began to echo increasingly with the clack and chatter of machine guns as the tempo quickened. Lufbery scored a pair of victories, his sixteenth and seventeenth. Campbell joined the scoring race and, by the

[3] Hall and Nordhoff: *The Lafayette Flying Corps*. The author has relied heavily on this classic work and gratefully acknowledges his debt.

end of May, he and Rickenbacker had each shot down the five planes necessary to qualify them as aces. But Lufbery was no longer present to congratulate them. Since May 19, Lufbery had been dead.

The German airman who sent Lufbery to his grave remains nameless in history. Whoever he was, he presumably never learned the identity of his victim; he might even have been unaware that he had made a kill, for the German archives nowhere mention the combat in which Lufbery met his end. Perhaps the victor, although he must have seen the Nieuport start to burn, did not have time in which to view the ensuing crash. Since the action occurred well behind the French lines and confirmation was impossible, he may simply have neglected the incident in his action report. Inasmuch as he was the gunner of a fast-retreating photoreconnaissance plane, such might well have been the case. Killed in the bright sunshine of a warm spring morning, Lufbery's vengeful zeal for battle led him to his tragic fate.

It was shortly before ten o'clock when a lone German reconnaissance plane was spotted coming across the lines and an alert was received at the American airfield. As the plane passed over Mont Mihiel, flying at considerable altitude, an antiaircraft battery began shooting at it. The plane was directly above the airfield when it was hit. Seeing it fall off into a loose spiral and thinking it a goner, the antiaircraft gunners ceased firing. But the German pilot, only seconds before crashing, regained control and headed back toward home, laboriously climbing as he went. Lufbery, watching from the airfield, decided to go up and finish off the crippled enemy plane. His own Nieuport was hangared for repairs, but there was another Nieuport standing on the field. He asked if it was fueled and armed and ready for flight. When a mechanic nodded affirmatively, Lufbery jumped into the seat and was quickly airborne.

The German was about seven miles from the field when Lufbery overtook him and, at about two thousand feet of altitude, fired several short bursts. His guns then apparently jammed, for he turned away and circled for a few minutes. While thousands of troops watched from the ground, he cleared the jam and came back at the enemy machine again from behind. The German gunner let go one frenzied burst and Lufbery's machine exploded into flames.

The Nieuport never swerved as it came down at full speed in a shallow descent. While it was still two or three hundred feet up in the air, Lufbery leaped from his cockpit. His body landed amid the flowers of a peasant woman's garden in a little village on the outskirts of Nancy. There was a small canal nearby, and the theory arose that Lufbery, seeing a slight chance, had jumped in the hope of falling into the water. His squadron mates, when they heard the bad news, drove to the village. "We arrived at the scene less than thirty minutes after he had fallen," Rickenbacker wrote. "Already, loving hands had removed his body to the town hall, and there we found it, the charred figure entirely covered with flowers from nearby gardens."

There is sad irony in the fact that Lufbery, Baylies, and Putnam, of the eleven Lafayette aviators who became aces, were the only ones not to survive the war. The other eight—Lieutenant Paul F. Baer, nine victories; Lieutenant Thomas G. Cassady, nine victories; Captain G. de Freest Larner, eight victories; Lieutenant Edwin C. Parsons, eight victories; Major Charles J. Biddle, seven victories; Captain William Ponder, seven victories; Adjutant James A. Connelly, Jr., six victories; and Lieutenant Colonel (which rank he assumed one day after the Armistice) William Thaw, five victories—lived to see their gallant efforts rewarded in the collapse and capitulation of the German army.

Through 1917, based first at Ravenel and then consecutively at Ham, Chaudun, Saint-Pol-sur-Mer, Senard, and again at Chaudun, the volunteer squadron hurled itself against the enemy without stint, paying out brave men's lives for its telling successes. Flying at the forefront of every French advance, covering the rear of every French withdrawal, the squadron that year fought hundreds of air-to-air combats. In tactical support of the infantry, it prosecuted dozens of air-to-ground strafing attacks. Its planes comprised part of the fighter escort for several massive bombing strikes beyond the German border. The squadron was at the peak of effectiveness when, in early December 1917, it was ordered to La Noblette, a small airfield lying north of Châlons-sur-Marne, in the Champagne sector, where enemy preparations seemed to herald an impending offensive. Here, even as it continued in day-to-day operations, the squadron became disbanded.

Ever since the United States entered the war, there had been talk of transferring Lafayette aviators into American service, but the United States army had done nothing tangible toward effecting the changeover. Finally, at La Noblette, the pilots of Escadrille Spa. 124 were advised by their executive committee in Paris to secure their release from French service so they could be duly commissioned as American officers. All in the squadron but Parsons went along with the plan and requested discharges. Their requests were promptly processed by the French, but—due to inefficient handling on the part of the American authorities—the commissions did not come through until February 18, 1918, after a delay of some two months. Thus, the American pilots of the Escadrille Lafayette, from the time of their French discharge until the paper work was at last completed, had technically been flying and fighting as civilians.

Its complement of aviators forming the nucleus of the 103rd Pursuit Squadron of the United States Air Service, the Escadrille Lafayette ceased to function on that February 18. The Spads and the Indian-head insignia also passed to American jurisdiction. French pilots were assigned to replace the departing volunteers in Spa. 124, which retained its official designation but was christened with a new *nom de guerre*. The squadron continued in operations as the Escadrille Jeanne d'Arc, and it accounted for twenty-six more official victories before the truce, nine of which were scored by Captain Paul V. d'Argueff, an ace of fifteen victories at the end of hostilities.

The rest of the Lafayette Flying Corps, those pilots scattered through other French squadrons, were transferred slowly during the winter and spring. Some remained for several weeks or months on detached duty with their former units, others were sent as instructors to the American training fields at Tours and Issoudun, until they could be posted to regular squadrons at the front. Volunteer pilots who had not yet completed their training in French aviation schools were taken over by the American service as soon as they were breveted. By June 1, 1918, nearly all who had applied for transfer had received their American commissions.

CHAPTER XIII

·⚜ *Monsters in the Sky* ⚜·

ON JULY 2, 1900, when he got his first airship into the air, Count Ferdinand von Zeppelin conveniently ushered in the new century with a German miracle. The hydrogen-buoyed dirigible, liberated that morning from its floating shed on Lake Constance, rose to an altitude of thirteen hundred feet before its aluminum skeleton warped out of alignment and rendered its steering mechanism useless, leaving the huge craft to drift helplessly to a watery landing three and a half miles from its takeoff point. If not entirely successful, neither was this maiden flight a total failure. The mere fact that so large a vessel could sail aloft was impressive, and the thousands of onlookers who witnessed the event—from boats on the lake and from the shore— sensed an epoch being born before their eyes.

Three months thereafter, in its second and third ascents, the refurbished Luftschiff Zeppelin 1 (LZ-1) flew well enough to vindicate the hopes of its sixty-two-year-old inventor. No longer was he quite so universally ridiculed as the "mad count." His success, he had always said, would be the Fatherland's success, and now he had mastered the aerial realm. Here, in the shape of a long, silver, rigid-framed, cylindrical gas envelope, actually surmounting the wind, was a promising symbol of German excellence. Fervently, Zeppelin addressed himself to the task of bringing this promise to full fruition.

The count planned a larger, stronger, faster airship. No sooner did he begin preparing blueprints for the projected LZ-2, however, than his company ran short of funds. His backers felt they had not seen, in three short, cautious trials, enough evidence to justify their further investment. But Zeppelin persevered with almost obsessive obstinacy. The next four years he spent fruitlessly searching for necessary capital. Finally, he persuaded the Union of German Engineers to endorse his theories, and the blessing of experts gave interested parties the confidence which one lone visionary had been unable to impart. The Prussian government granted him fifty thousand marks; a public lottery in his home state of Württemberg raised another 124,000 marks; sympathetic industrialists provided materials, engines and gas fillers free of charge. To this Zeppelin added four hundred thousand marks of his own—practically all that remained of his personal fortune after almost two decades of costly experiments—and produced his second dirigible.

LZ-2, completed in 1905, flew but twice before disaster overtook it in January of the following year. Nearly destitute and in a fit of discouragement, the aged count one day announced: "I shall build no more airships." But only a few days later he met Dr. Hugo Eckener, the man who would become his partner, his chief engineer, confidant, publicist, and biographer. Blond, bearded, talented Eckener, a doctor of economics and a journalist, who thirty-odd years afterward would be dubbed a professor by Adolf Hitler and awarded a gold medal by the Royal Aeronautical Society of Great Britain for his contributions to aerostatic science, did not know exactly what to make of Zeppelin at their first meeting. "The old gentleman," he wrote, "was wearing meticulously correct morning clothes, with silk hat and yellow gloves, the courtly and distinguished aristocrat of all times." Zeppelin's appearance and dignity commanded Eckener's respect, but when the count discussed the future of giant airships, Eckener suspected he might be listening to the prattle of a "stubborn old fool . . . in his dotage."

Unable to take leave of the count without seeming rude, Eckener politely listened to the old man's ideas and gradually fell under their spell. Before the afternoon was over, Eckener had become thoroughly infected with the other's obsession for providing the Fatherland with a fleet of mammoth lighter-than-air cruisers. More than that, he made himself responsible for building Zeppelin into an object of national hero-worship. The German people, admiring his dogged determination, had already taken Zeppelin to their hearts, and Eckener's publicity campaign fired their imaginations to the point of subscribing enough money for a third dirigible. Of further improved design, the LZ-3, completed in October 1906, outperformed any other airship in existence by negotiating a 208-mile flight nonstop. The German War Ministry, where Zeppelin's ideas had always been brusquely dismissed as too fantastic, now began to view him in a warmer light.

As early as 1886, when his airships were only crude paper sketches, Zeppelin had hinted at the military applications to which they might someday be put. "With a favorable wind," he jotted in his notebook, "dirigibles could be used for intercommunications between our colonies in Central Africa, and for provisioning troops in the field." This was the pith of his earliest appeals for government grants to help finance his invention. But the War Ministry ignored him. For the next twenty years, until the LZ-3 demonstrated the potential utility of colossal-sized, rigid airships, the military dogmatically refused to look at the count's plans and models. The general staff, in fact, issued an order expressly forbidding officers, even in their off-duty hours, from participating in his experiments. "He is," said a German general in 1906, "an ex-army crackpot who fabricates clumsy monsters which, like the hulking reptiles of antediluvian antiquity, are doomed by their size to extinction." And Kaiser Wilhelm II that year called him, "Of all Swabians, the greatest donkey."

More than a century had now passed since free balloons were first employed in battle by the French army; more than forty years had elapsed since tethered balloons were employed by Union forces in the American Civil War; thirty-five years had gone by since balloons helped Parisians in the Franco-Prussian War. By this late date the feasibility of using powered ballons for reconnaissance was evident to every army; it was simply the hugeness, the stupendous size of Count Zeppelin's product that caused military brains to boggle with skepticism. The German army was indeed concerned with lighter-than-air craft. Developments had been going ahead secretly for some time, with no less a personage than the Kaiser himself a patron of aeronautics. The emperor, in July 1906, had established Motorluftschiffen-Studien-Gesellschaft —the Society for the Study of Motor Airships—the purpose of which was stated by its first president on the day of its founding: "As soon as some definite success is obtained by the efforts of the society, the acquired results will be sent to the military authorities and put at their disposal to use as they see fit."

By summer 1907, two nonrigid types were ready for flight testing, both of modest dimension in comparison to the Zeppelin type. One was the creation of a Major Gross, commander of a balloon battalion near Berlin; the other of Major August von Parseval of the Bavarian army, a skillful designer who later would accrue minor success producing semi-rigid military airships. The Gross and Parseval dirigibles took to the air together that July, watched by the Kaiser. Tailored to War Ministry specifications, the two craft were of medium size, uncomplicated by any interior framework in order that they might be readily deflated and packed aboard a carriage for transport. To the army, a small dirigible that could be handily moved from place to place seemed far more desirable than a large rigid type. If a rigid dirigible had to alight in the open, there were mooring problems; if it returned to a distant hangar after each mission, its service range would thereby be reduced. Emptying the gas envelope in the field made the small ones preferable because a large craft would require too much hydrogen if it had to be refilled for each flight. Portability, the one feature denied a rigid Zeppelin-type vessel, especially appealed to militiary men who liked equipment that could take its place in the line of march.

What the army experts wanted, then, was pretty much a motorized captive balloon, and that was what Gross and Parseval had each produced. The two craft flew fairly well, the Parseval better than the more flaccid Gross. Merely seeing them lift off the ground elated the Kaiser, although the designers were somewhat disappointed at what they saw. It was just three months after this that the latest Zeppelin dirigible so thoroughly eclipsed the performance of any other lighter-than-air ship so far developed. The War Ministry, hearing that the LZ-3 had covered 208 miles in sustained flight, finally had to confess that perhaps the count was not crazy after all. Before October was out, the army sent a team of observers to evaluate the LZ-3's military potential.

In Great Britain, meanwhile, where aviation was still in its barest infancy, a solitary voice told the British public what was going on at Friedrichshafen. Harry Harper, the first British air correspondent, writing for the London *Daily Mail,* furnished a day-by-day commentary on Count Zeppelin's progress. In mid-October he reported:

> In anticipation of an early official ascent which will in all probability be followed by its transfer to the German Imperial government, Count Zeppelin's airship is being tightly guarded against intruders and investigators.
>
> Out upon the glassy surface of Lake Constance the giant craft lies hidden in the floating corrugated-iron shed. Count Zeppelin's crew are at work inside, making various changes suggested by the successful trials. When they have finished, Count Zeppelin is confident that he will be able to sail for an unbroken period of twenty-four hours.
>
> German military experts were exultant over the Count's recent achievements, and are bringing their utmost influence to bear to induce the government to purchase the ship without waiting for further experiments.
>
> Count Zeppelin's maneuvers with his airship during the past week have been most remarkable, and have convinced everyone that his ship is the most efficient at present in existence.[1]

To the knowledgeable reader, Harper's reports were loaded with portent. There was reason enough already to suspect the territorial ambitions of Imperial Germany. The Kaiser lately had often boasted of the great fleet of warships he was building. What purpose was there for such an armada if not to defy British sea power, the one big obstacle to German expansion? "Our future lies upon the water," the Kaiser had said. His army was the strongest in the world, and he had publicly vowed to raise his navy to the same level. Privately he liked to affect the bogus title of "Admiral of the Atlantic." And that October, when the German emperor's visit to King Edward in England was headline news, it occurred to some of Harry Harper's readers that this vaunted domination of land and sea might also include the sky.

The German army bought the LZ-3, and ordered a second airship. The latter, the LZ-4, was completed in June 1908, and destroyed by fire two

[1] Poolman: *Zeppelins Against London.*

months later. In the course of a twenty-four hour flight it was forced down by engine trouble. Before it could be repaired, a sudden storm tore the dirigible from its moorings, whereupon it exploded into flames and was quickly reduced to a mass of twisted, smoking debris. Among the crowd of spectators was David Lloyd George, then the British Chancellor of the Exchequer, touring Germany. He wrote of the spectacle in a letter:

> I was deeply impressed by a scene I witnessed at Stuttgart. On our arrival we learned that a "Zeppelin" was about to make an exhibition flight. We went along to the field where the giant airship was moored, to find that by a last minute accident it had crashed and been wrecked. Of course, we were deeply disappointed, but disappointment was a totally inadequate word for the agony of grief and dismay which swept over the massed Germans who witnessed the catastrophe. There was no loss of life to account for it. Hopes and ambitions far wider than those concerned with a scientific and mechanical success appeared to have shared the wreck of the dirigible. Then the crowd swung into the chanting of *Deutschland uber Alles* with a fanatic fervor of patriotism. What spearpoint of Imperial advance did this airship portend?

The tragic end of the LZ-4 caused nationwide lament. The German people, scarcely realizing it, had come to interpret the airships as symbols of their exalted Kultur. Determined to allow him to continue—and thus bring credit to Germany—they donated more than six million marks to a "Zeppelin Fund," money enough to finance a spacious new lakeside factory at Friedrichshafen. Suddenly aware of the count's enormous popularity, the Kaiser decided to capitalize on it. In November he was at Lake Constance to witness a flight by the government-owned LZ-3. Zeppelin took the Kaiser in a white motorboat to the floating shed, the party including several important staff officers from Berlin. The Kaiser, muffled in a heavy greatcoat, watched from below while an admiral and a general went up for a ride aboard the airship. The flight was smooth and uneventful, and Zeppelin's passengers were favorably impressed, complaining only of the need to shout above the engine and transmission noises when they wanted to be heard.

Decorating Count Zeppelin with the Order of the Black Eagle after the LZ-3 had landed, the Kaiser spouted a sonorous encomium:

> In my name and in the name of the German nation, I heartily congratulate your Excellency on this magnificent accomplishment which you so wonderfully have displayed before me today. Our Fatherland can be proud to possess such a son . . . who through his inventiveness has delivered us to a new milestone in the advancement of the human race. It is not too much to say that we

have today lived through a great moment in the evolution of human culture. I thank God, with all Germans, that He has deemed our people worthy of you. May it be permitted to each of us, as it has to you, to be able to say in the twilight of our lives, that we have served our dear Fatherland so beneficially. As a token of my admiration . . . I bestow upon you herewith my high Order of the Black Eagle.[2]

The Kaiser, who not long before had sneered at him as a donkey, embraced the startled count three times and shouted: "His Excellency, Count Zeppelin! Conqueror of the air! Hail!"

With the emperor's warm approval, the government made him another generous grant with which to pursue his experiments. But the count, through the ensuing two years, suffered further setbacks. The LZ-3, after thirty months in army service, was wrecked in April 1910, and the next ship built—the LZ-5—was consumed by fire that September, after having flown in the Imperial war games. Due to these continual mishaps, attributable mainly to incompetence on the part of military crews, the War Office announced it would buy no more "zeppelins," as they were by now called. Actually, the announcement was the outcome of a steady deterioration in Zeppelin's relationship with the War Office. There had always been a sizable body of officers who lacked faith in his airships. Subsequent to the purchase of the LZ-3, this group had increased rather than diminished in number and influence, and the arguments raised against Zeppelin's ideas sounded both reasonable and cogent. Major Gross, chief agitator for the anti-Zeppelin faction, tellingly summed up these arguments in a lecture before the Society for the Study of Motor Airships. Speaking in January 1909, Gross pointed out that of the four zeppelins produced up to that time, two had been wrecked, one (the LZ-1) had been disassembled after an unsatisfactory career, and the remaining vessel (the LZ-3), now a year in army commission, had yet to demonstrate its military usefulness. He further pointed out that zeppelin flights had been made, for the most part, over water. Two ships had come to rest on land, and both had met calamity. (It was not until March 16, 1909, two months after Gross' speech, that a zeppelin chanced a prearranged landing on the ground.) "Certainly," the major concluded, "the acquisition of the LZ-3 was folly. We have gained nothing more than a costly, overly large, unwieldy airship of dubious value, whose performance is no better than that of smaller dirigibles."

Gross left his closing statement unqualified when, in fairness, he should have explained that he was referring to the LZ-3's performance in field maneuvers. It was undeniable that the zeppelin had been outshone by the smaller, nonrigid types in tactical exercises—although only because the ship had been misused by the army command. Like all the count's dirigibles, the LZ-3 had

---

[2] Dudley: *Monsters of the Purple Twilight.*

not been designed for tactical employment. What the military authorities failed to understand was that Count Zeppelin never intended his airships for tactical, or short-range, reconnaissance. A cavalryman by background, the count believed that horsemen needed no assistance in reconnoitering an enemy's forward positions. But he knew from personal experience that the work of the cavalry in the enemy's rear was less than adequate. Here, he reasoned, a dirigible could be of service.

This was a radical departure from traditional concepts. Military aeronautics had always been confined to tactical reconnaissance. As scornfully as any cavalry officer, Zeppelin considered this a waste of time, a duplication of effort. Why build small motorized balloons when it was deep within hostile territory, not along the immediate battle front, that aerial scouts were needed? Their ability to fly would enable them to avoid the hindrances that hampered the movements of saddle troops. Their bird's-eye view would afford them a complete picture which earth-bound horsemen could rarely obtain. Their speed would make up-to-the-minute strategic intelligence possible. However, to undertake this kind of reconnaissance, an airship would have to be capable of attaining tremendous altitudes and staying airborne for at least twenty-four hours. This was the reason for the large capacity of Zeppelin's designs. But the War Ministry, blind to his purpose, insisted on judging the LZ-3 on its ability to maneuver in a limited space, which the smaller types, particularly the Parseval, could do much better. This misapplication of the LZ-3, plus the fact that it required a larger ground crew than the other craft, explains why so much doubt was cast upon its usefulness.

The army's failure to grasp Zeppelin's precept provides a key to the history of the German military dirigible fleet from 1909 until after the beginning of the war. Army intransigence at first caused the zeppelins to be frowned upon. Then the success of the type aroused such public sentiment that the authorities were forced to revise their opinions. Finally, although it accepted zeppelins as the mainstay of the lighter-than-air fleet, the army made no assessment of their potential for long-range scouting. When the war came, the Marne campaign, for example, presented several opportunities where a successful strategic reconnaissance might have affected the outcome. But Zeppelin's original scheme remained only an old man's dream.

By throwing the count's airship into direct competition with the small non-rigids, the army stirred up strong controversy. The supporters of the various types disparaged and unmercifully calumniated their rivals. Major Gross, in another of his lectures, plainly insinuated that Count Zeppelin had pirated his ideas from the labors of an earlier experimenter named David Schwarz. The count's seconds paid a visit to Gross and only a command from the Kaiser averted a duel. Nicholas Basenrach, a member of the Motorluftschiff-Studien-Gesellschaft who sold one of his designs to the War Ministry in 1909, wryly quipped that "if you do not swear by the rigid or non-rigid systems, but are inclined to favor the semi-rigid system, you are not simply a stupid fellow or an imbecile, but a filthy scoundrel." [3]

The army's on-again, off-again romance with lighter-than-air ships was at its hottest in early 1908, following government purchase of the LZ-3 and the Parseval and Gross models. Without distinguishing as to type, General Helmuth von Moltke, chief of the general staff, that January recommended to the War Ministry the acquisition of fifteen military dirigibles. By the middle of 1910, six were in service with the army—the LZ-3 and LZ-5, a Gross, a Basenrach, and two Parsevals. By the end of 1910, the two zeppelins were wrecked and the others, in that year's Imperial war games, had made sorry showings. Already on the downswing, army interest in aeronautics waned lower than ever, as evidenced by a communication, dated March 3, 1911, from Moltke to the War Ministry:

> In my memorandum . . . [of] January 13, 1908, I said that the number of airships required by the Supreme Command was fifteen. Meanwhile, the airship trials and the Kaiser maneuvers of 1909 and 1910, as well as the memorandum of the Inspector-General of Military Transport . . . of December 28, 1910, have shown that the achievements of airships have belied the assumptions on which the above estimate was based. Moreover, the artillery experiments at Rugenwaldermunde in 1910 have revealed the inordinate dangers which airships risk from howitzers and antiaircraft guns, even when flying at considerable height. . . . Lastly, the progress of aviation has led to the utilization of airplanes as another possible means of reconnoitering from aloft.
>
> All these developments have prompted me to examine the question of whether the original demand for fifteen airships is still advisable. . . .
>
> Since it cannot be said with certainty that we shall overcome the present defects in our airships, and to what extent airplanes will, either in conjunction with or in substitution for airships, take over the business of reconnaissance, I have become convinced that the Supreme Command should be satisfied . . . with establishing a fleet of nine airships for the army until we are in possession of reliable data as to the relative merits of airships and airplanes as employed in the field. [4]

Inasmuch as airplanes did ultimately supersede dirigibles as scouting machines, Moltke's verdict later stood as a testament to his prophetic acumen. It did, that is, in the eyes of those historians who were apologists for the German army and chose to overlook the fact that Moltke would again reverse

[3] Cuneo: *Winged Mars.* The author here gratefully acknowledges his debt to this source.   [4] Cuneo: *op. cit.*

his thinking in this matter less than two years afterward. Be that as it may, his ruminations clearly indicate how little the general staff appreciated the potentialities of airships as long-range reconnaissance craft. Here was a suggestion that the zeppelin be replaced by an airplane whose flight duration record in Germany in 1911 was three hours and six minutes! Zeppelins by this time had already undertaken flights lasting more than twenty-four hours! That the army was prepared to gamble on the airplane is commendable as a sign of foresightedness, but that the chief of the general staff should declare himself disenchanted with an airship capable of remaining aloft an entire day, shows how insensible was the high command to the need for strategic reconnaissance.

Count Zeppelin was never in the good graces of the Prussians who ruled the War Ministry, and their prejudiced refusal to acknowledge that the other dirigibles were not in a class with the rigids was heavily responsible for the government's failure to purchase any additional zeppelins until mid-1913. Also to blame, probably more to blame, was their utter misuse of the two zeppelins they had procured. Merely seeking a means of tactical scouting as a substitute for captive balloons or as an adjunct to the cavalry, the military authorities missed the fact that zeppelins were intended by their creator for a different role, a special function. Comparing them to smaller dirigibles, nonrigid types designed strictly in conformance to army dictates, was no comparison at all. A separate set of criteria was necessary for a valid appraisal of the zeppelin's true military worth.

Long before General Moltke's decision to curtail the quota of army airships, Count Zeppelin and his supporters had seen the handwriting on the wall. Noting the drop in official interest after the 1909 war games, the count formed a subsidiary company, Deutsche Luftschiffahrt Aktien-Gesellschaft—commonly known from its initials as Delag. Although to see his invention become a vital part of the German war machine remained the count's fondest desire, the new concern was incorporated as a commercial transport company. He founded this first airline in order to widen the market for his products, since he was not allowed to sell them abroad, and would have considered this unpatriotic in any case.

By the onset of World War I, a fleet of Delag zeppelins was carrying passengers and light cargo all over Germany, departing on schedule from hangars at Baden-Baden, Potsdam, Düsseldorf, Johannisthal (which field serviced Berlin), Gotha, Hamburg, Leipzig, and Dresden. Scarcely a German man, woman, or child had not seen the *Viktoria Luise,* the *Hansa,* or the *Sachsen,* or, before them, the *Deutschland* or the *Schwaben,* sliding through the boundless skies with effortless grace and imposing grandeur. Almost forty thousand citizens had actually booked passage aboard the zeppelins; in combination, these great-proportioned vessels, bearing emotive names instead of stark numerals, had traveled upwards of a hundred thousand miles without a single human fatality (although the first Delag airship, the *Deutschland,* crashed and burned on one of its trial trips, and the *Schwaben,* after a triumphant year's service, likewise became a victim of fire).

Beginning with the *Schwaben* in 1911, marked improvement was built into the huge aerial transports. Long aware of the principal reasons for zeppelin accidents, the count and his right-hand man, Dr. Eckener, took whatever remedial steps they could in designing the *Schwaben.* A major fault with previous models had been that the engines were not powerful enough. The *Schwaben* had the advantage of engines newly developed by the gifted Wilhelm Maybach, units which for their time featured an exceptionally efficient power-to-weight ratio. Equipped with three of these driving plants, totaling 450 horsepower, the *Schwaben* cruised at the then-astonishing speed of forty-five miles per hour. Another difficulty with earlier zeppelins had been their extreme unwieldiness on the ground. Eckener solved this problem by erecting a new hangar for the *Schwaben* at Baden-Baden, situating it in line with the prevailing winds. The absence of crosswinds thus simplified ground handling, and similar hangars were quickly installed at zeppelin ports elsewhere. There were, of course, vulnerabilities inherent in lighter-than-air craft that could not be corrected. The flammability of hydrogen, for instance, was a constant danger which zeppelin crews—and passengers—had to live with. (Helium, inert and therefore uncombustible, was and still is a practical monopoly of the United States government.) Airships, moreover, were sorely dependent on favorable weather conditions for their safety, and meteorology was at best an ill-contrived science prior to World War I.

When the *Schwaben* entered commercial service in June 1911, nature obviated the need for accurate weather reports by presenting the ship with three months of almost continual sunshine and gentle breezes. Again and again the gleaming dirigible, sailing through the summer blue, accomplished one successful journey after another. The count's star had been fast fading, but, thanks to this sterling Delag flagship, faith was restored and the nation once again went Zeppelin-mad. Even when fate eventually claimed the ship, which caught fire from static electricity on June 28, 1912, the disaster could not dim its magnificent record. In its one triumphant year of plying from city to city, the *Schwaben* completed 218 circuits, carrying an aggregate of 2380 persons in her commodious salon cabin.

The ruin of the *Schwaben* was further minimized by the fact that Delag had christened a new dirigible in February, the *Viktoria Luise,* and introduced a second that July, the *Hansa.* Joined by the *Sachsen* in May 1913, they carried on where the *Schwaben* had left off. Their aerial voyages were not marred by any mishap. It became stylish to have ridden in a zeppelin, the mighty size of which made the airplane appear puny. As the aged inventor had wishfully imagined, the thousands of people who flew in his dirigibles, and the hundreds of thousands who watched them soar so majestically overhead, acclaimed the zeppelin as the symbol of German supremacy in the sky.

Sensitive as always to popular opinion, though still contending publicly that giant airships had no important place in warfare, the high command began to evidence a changed tenor in its official conclaves and internal correspondence. Symptomatically, during the summer of 1912, Delag was secretly informed that its air crews would thenceforth be military reservists and participate in periodic drills with both the navy and army. In November General Moltke wrote a memorandum advocating that the army buy "twenty airships of the largest model." In the next month he recommended that only zeppelins and other comparable rigids be procured, and that construction of all nonrigid and semi-rigid types be halted. No explanation for this turnabout of policy was forthcoming. However, Moltke's own writings leave little doubt that he had been caught up in the craze engendered by the stunning success of the *Schwaben.* Also significant is that Moltke formulated these decisions shortly after taking a trip aboard a Delag airship. Although his description of the flight contains no allusion to the military aspects of such a dirigible, he was obviously deeply impressed by the experience.

The War Ministry, acting immediately on Moltke's say, had one more slap for Count Zeppelin's face. A dirigible was hastily purchased for the army in December 1912—not a zeppelin but a Schutte-Lanz, which rival company had been operating for a year and had produced this one ship. The old count, on hearing of his competitor's sale, was livid with rage. His angry mood persisted for several weeks, until an army procurement officer placed an order for a zeppelin. That one, and six more—including three for the navy—were to be sold to the military before the outbreak of the war.

In fairness to the War Ministry, its purchase of the Schutte-Lanz was a sound decision. A large rigid, more streamlined than the slightly larger zeppelins, the SL-1—as it was designated—had many innovational features that enhanced its appearance as well as its performance. The framework was formed of triangular girders of laminated aspen wood rather than the aluminum rings and longerons used by Zeppelin's company. This was an attempt to increase the elasticity of the frame, the Schutte-Lanz engineers believing that one reason why the zeppelins crashed was that their interior structures were too inflexible. An outer frame of latticed wood gave the hull its circular shape and supported the gas envelope. The choice of materials and method of construction reflected the fact that the Schutte-Lanz technical staff was composed of nautical engineers and shipbuilders who brought to the aeronautical field their special brand of theoretical and practical knowledge. As it later turned out, for reasons never specified, they abandoned the wooden framework in subsequent models and resorted to metal girders and beams. These naval architects, however, brought to their dirigible enough good ideas to revolutionize the design of all future airships. The engines, for example, instead of driving the propellers through shafting, drove them direct, and were slung out from the hull in power cars. The tail assembly was beautifully simplified by attaching the control surfaces to the trailing edges of the fixed fins, thus overcoming the complexities and inefficiencies which characterized the boxlike arrangement employed on contemporary zeppelins. The keel, further-more, was placed within the hull's contour instead of outside. These, together with the SL-1's internal gangways, enclosed gondolas and other features, were later adopted by other rigids, including the zeppelin.

The first Schutte-Lanz airship flew so satisfactorily that the German gov-ernment awarded contracts for several more. Between February 1914—when the SL-2 made its debut—and the end of the war, the company manufactured twenty-one dirigibles, some of which played an active part in the great airship raids over England during 1915 and 1916. After the Armistice, Schutte-Lanz ceased production, although it maintained an office in New York City as late as 1930. Curiously enough, the particulars of this company's existence seem to have been neglected by aeronautical annalists despite its manifold contribu-tions to aerostatic technology, not to mention the important role it assumed in the German war effort. The story of the Schutte-Lanz dirigible has doubtless been forgotten because it was so thoroughly overshadowed by the dramatic history of the zeppelin, and because its development began at a time when the imminence of war lowered a curtain of censorship around all military events. Schutte-Lanz, as a matter of fact, remained a name little known to the layman, even in Germany, throughout the war years; the type was commonly called by the generic term, "zeppelin." A result of this confusion has been that the debt owed by future airships to the Schutte-Lanz design has seldom properly been acknowledged.

General Moltke's recommendations notwithstanding, and in the spring of 1913 he requested that only zeppelins be purchased for the army, the War Ministry persisted in buying other dirigibles, including several semi-rigid varieties, with the limited funds at its disposal. About a half-dozen types, including zeppelins, were flown in army and navy maneuvers in the eighteen months preceding World War I. Dr. Eckener, for one, blamed this dispersion of funds for the embarrassing fact that no zeppelin at the outbreak of hostili-ties had sufficient speed, climb, and lifting capacity to render it effective in front-line operations. Eckener's argument boils down merely to an apologia, however, since the sum expended on these various other types would hardly have financed any far-reaching experiments by Zeppelin's company. In his claim, furthermore, Eckener disregarded the benefits of competition, a clear-cut justification for the War Ministry's refusal to consent to a Zeppelin monoply. The so-called "super zeppelins" that emerged from Friedrichshafen in the latter part of 1915 owed much to the engineering genius of Schutte-Lanz, a rival concern.

Any critical investigation of the pre-World War I evolution of military aeronautics in Germany—or any other nation—reveals how paltry was the importance attached to the need to perfect an air weapon. With a few notable exceptions, high military leaders held obstinately to the belief that nothing use-ful would come of airships and airplanes. Aircraft were unwelcome and em-ployed as sparingly as possible by ground commanders whose practical knowledge of aeronautics would not have filled a thimble. Even among the proponents of air power, the ideas governing the role of flying machines rested chiefly on untried hypotheses, some of which were hilariously harebrained in retrospect. There was, then, in all nations a gap between theory and actual practice. In the case of Germany, however, a casual examination of the mere plans would result in a distorted picture of that nation's prewar attitudes and accomplishments. Historians have sometimes done this without noting the curious discrepancy between their inferences and the rudimental character of the German air force at the beginning of the war. Hence, any discussion of the then-prevailing theories is misleading unless it is qualified by a careful consideration of actual practice.

In Germany, more so than in other countries, a proliferation of literature, official and otherwise, was published on the highly speculative subject of wartime aeronautics. From 1890 to 1914, for example, there appeared a series of service manuals for German balloon detachments. Significantly enough, no basic textual changes were made between that issued in October 1903, and the one in circulation when war broke out. This was a period in which captive balloons—known as *drachen,* or kites, in the German soldier's argot—were losing grace among top military advisers. That the manuals lacked revision spoke of a stagnation that in turn reflected this slackening interest.

A balloon detachment was expected to discern the deployment or approach of an enemy force; aside from the usual organizational notes and a lengthy exegesis on balloon handling and maintenance, the manuals provided little other useful information. Artillery spotting was considered only as it pertained to classic fortress warfare. Succeeding editions altogether omitted reference to the airplane as a potential menace to balloon-borne observers. Nowhere was the word "parachute" to be found, although during the war a balloonist was apt to fall more heavily unless he unhesitatingly jumped overboard at his first glimpse of oncoming enemy planes. The army ballooning manuals skipped, too, any discussion of defensive measures. During the ensuing hostilities, it was not long after airplanes began carrying armament that balloon detachments were ringing their positions with antiaircraft guns. These were ranged to confront attacking aircraft with an all but impenetrable wall of fire, so that shooting down one of the fat, sausage-shaped *drachen* became a difficult and harrowing feat. The few pilots who specialized in this task won the profound respect of their fellow airmen, although the unenlightened public, thinking it easy to destroy so large and stationary and combustible a target, did not always appreciate the rare courage and skill involved.

As his handbook said, even as late as November 1914, a German balloonist-observer could seldom see an object more than four and a half miles distant. It was discovered soon in World War I, however, that this visual limitation was due in part to the shameful fact that inferior field glasses were being used; when better ones were allocated, the observer's visual range increased—nearly doubled—to eight miles. Another drawback was found to be the small size of the pre-1915 aerostats, which caused them to buck and sway excessively in the wind, so that holding one's eyes to a pair of binoculars was no simple trick. These undersized *drachen* sometimes bounced so violently that their passengers could endure but a few minutes before a bad case of nausea or vertigo incapacitated them. Such balloons, for this reason, could not be flown at any great height. A larger, higher-flying type, introduced early in 1915, augmented the observer's range of vision by an additional two to four miles, at the same time making his condition a more comfortable one.

Here were obvious faults that easily could have been rectified long before the advent of war, except that nobody in authority seemed concerned. The disinterest in military aeronautics was manifest, and the official manuals, taken at face value, have misled researchers into believing that the German command was more greatly concerned with aerial reconnaissance than it was.

Similarly, in 1913, the general staff produced a secret paper entitled *Aircraft in the Service of the Army,* and a reading of this slim volume reveals again how very far apart theory and practice lay from each other in the genesis years of German air power. A work of remarkable perspicacity, the lack of attention it received from military hierarchs later became notorious. According to the tenets of its anonymous author, dirigibles were to function as strategic—that is, long-distance—reconnaissance craft, especially for the purpose of detecting the movements of major armies. Dirigibles were also to execute bombing raids against rear targets, such as troop encampments, railheads, supply depots, bridges, and important logistical routes. The principles of bombing operations were examined at length. A concluding paragraph anticipated that the continuing improvement of airplanes would eventually permit them to assist in these tasks and "perhaps by 1920, to supplant dirigibles entirely as weapons of attack."

The mention of strategic reconnaissance seems to contradict the assertion that the army failed to comprehend Count Zeppelin's plans in that connection. Such statements were not unusual. The German Field Service Regulations of 1908 acknowledge that "dirigible balloons are eminently useful for strategic reconnaissance." The sincerity of these statements can be judged by the fact that army authorities forced the only ship designed for that errand into competition with airships intended purely for tactical scouting, and did so under conditions favorable to the latter. And in 1911, the chief of the general staff was wondering if airplanes, which then averaged about forty miles of flying range, could replace airships capable of cruising all day long at better than thirty miles per hour.

Indeed, it is impossible to uncover any substantial proof that the general staff really believed what it preached about lighter-than-air craft being used for long-distance reconnoitering. Consequent to the poor results obtained in the 1909 and 1910 Imperial war games—for which fiascos the army more than the airships must be indicted—none of the giant rigids found military employment again until 1913, and a review of that year's maneuvers has disclosed only a perfunctory mention that two zeppelins had taken part. At that time, as during the first weeks of World War I, a staff officer was required to go along on every flight. These officers, making general nuisances of themselves, were inadequately trained for the job and often requested dirigible commanders to attempt impossible tasks. Their presence was a gesture to the regulations, but their actions betrayed the casual character of the gesture.

Events during the first days of the war erase any lingering doubt as to whether the general staff entertained any serious intention of utilizing airships for strategic reconnaissance. Then—when antiaircraft defenses, particularly in back areas, were practically nonexistent—the zeppelins had a golden opportunity to prove the thesis of their inventor. From all evidences, however, the German staff had drawn up no plans for instituting such deeply probing reconnaissances. A startling revelation is that when hostilities seemed imminent, and an eager zeppelin commander asked leave to prepare his ship for long-distance flying, permission was curtly refused.

Not until August 7, 1914, during the second week of war, was a dirigible sent to reconnoiter on the western front. This was after the crucial period of initial deployments; the greatest opportunities for strategic reconnaissance had already been lost. Even the mission of August 7 was in the nature of tactical scouting, as were all dirigible reconnaissances that followed during the invasion of Belgium and France. Analysis of operations in the opening stages of the war thus clearly refutes any notion that the German army meant to use its aerial spies except for localized observation of the enemy. Theory, as enunciated this time in the 1913 treatise, *Airships in the Service of the Army,* once again bore no faint resemblance to practice.

The same book's emphasis on bombing has reinforced the popular concept that zeppelins were viewed with warm military favor as raiders. Beyond question, the general staff esteemed this activity more than strategic reconnaissance. The first assignment it gave a zeppelin was to bomb Liège on August 6, 1914. Yet the ineptitude with which the raid was planned and executed indicates how little the high command understood about airships.

Bombing had been widely discussed in German military circles, but final opinion had always tended to underrate its importance. An official source shows that bombing trials prior to the war had been conducted with just one zeppelin and that the results were less than conclusive. In the second month of World War I, the only "bombs" available to Captain Ernst Lehmann, the most famous of zeppelin commanders, were artillery shells to which bits of horse blanket had been tied to make them strike nose on.

The crudeness of these measures exposes the fallacy of thinking that the German army had prepared its lighter-than-air force to perpetrate bombing raids. The onset of hostilities actually came before the dirigibles were properly accoutered for warfare. Captain Lehmann afforded an insight to this state of affairs when he wrote: "War! We had never seriously considered war. . . . We had no idea what was to be done with us, for there was no provision for zeppelins in the General Staff's schema. Although zeppelins had already been flown in maneuvers, their military worth was deemed trivial." In the same vein, a naval airship commander, Lieutenant Treusch von Buttlar Brandenfels, had this to get off his chest: "In peacetime the military dirigible was allotted a quite subordinate role. . . . Had Germany devoted a little more energy to the development of zeppelins in peacetime, they would have scored far more telling successes at the very beginning of the war than those which stand to their credit. Zeppelins would then have been what the English tremulously surmised them to be."

While the German authorities were pessimistic about, or indifferent to, airships as instruments of battle, no hint of official skepticism was allowed to leak out to the public. Such a disclosure would have drastically undermined civilian pride in the nation's armed might. Disconcerting questions were liable to be raised about the quality of the army's airplanes, inferior as they were to comparable French machines. The populace had come to the firm conviction that the zeppelin assured the Fatherland of incontestable dominion in the sky. Just the size of the ships spelled power and strength; a serene voyage on the *Viktoria Luise,* say, or the *Hansa,* or the *Sachsen,* would convince any doubting Hans or Fritz of the zeppelin's infinite superiority to an airplane. When it is remembered how even foreigners were impressed by the sight of a zeppelin, the glowing faith of the German people can be fathomed and recognized as a vital morale factor.

Outside Germany, in the outlying countries of Europe, belief in the prowess of the zeppelin was implicit. The achievements of German dirigible builders, Count Zeppelin foremost among them, were regarded as ominous for the future. The French and English cast worried eyes at the silver-skinned leviathans that flew the German sky, and the psychological effect was potent, magnifying the threat beyond reasonable proportion.

Many a historian has alleged that German policy makers had some glimmering of the zeppelin's value as a "big stick" in their international dealings. "The size and famed attainments of the zeppelin seized upon the imagination," expounded one such author, "and the Germans had thought that the huge craft would spread terror among their foes. . . . A campaign of suggestion, carried on through the press of the world long before the war, was diligently followed up after the outbreak of hostilities. Marvelous accounts were given of zeppelin armadas that could cruise for thousands of miles with a formidable crew of men and enough explosives to wipe out whole cities. It was intimated that Germany had dozens of these airships." Assertions like this, abundant in the historiography of World War I, are difficult to substantiate; obviously, no German then believed or at least would admit that the vaunted prepotency of the zeppelin was sheer propaganda and that the stupendous dirigibles were but paper tigers.

Fright stories did indeed flood European newspapers and magazines, but proving them the handiwork of German agents or sympathizers is an impossibility. It is more plausible, anyhow, considering the insatiable human appetite for lurid reading matter and the surfeit of writers eager to answer the demand, to assume that native talent concocted most of this penny-dreadful copy with no ulterior motives in mind. The simpler explanation is usually the true one, which again supposes that German intrigue had nothing to do with the profusion of zeppelin-scare articles in the foreign press. While some of the stories did, of course, emanate from Germany, they never—as far as can be ascertained—sprang from official quarters. London trembled in 1912, for example, when Reuters released the text of a speech delivered in Kiel by a retired German naval captain turned professional lecturer, a man named Pustau, whose provocative conjectures apparently lacked any official sanction. "Let us imagine a war with England," Pustau proposed, "which from time immemorial has had an unwarlike population. If we could only succeed in tossing some bombs on their docks, they would speak with us in quite different terms. With airships we have, in certain circumstances, the means of carrying the war to the British Isles." He asked his listeners to envision the terror with which England would hear the beating of the zeppelins' airscrews. "It is true," he went on, "that Great Britain has several airplanes stationed along its south coast, but they cannot maneuver at night, and can, therefore, afford no protection against airships." [5]

Even had the German government instigated all the zeppelin-scare propaganda that inundated Europe in the years prior to World War I, the reaction could not have been more to its advantage. The rash of reports from countries around or near Germany bears witness to the hysteria generated by these published depictions. An entire French village succumbed to panic one night when local pranksters released a homemade fire balloon and ran through the streets shouting "Zeppelin!" But in most instances, as might be expected, investigation revealed the ethereal interlopers to be cloud formations in the moonlight or some such other natural phenomena misinterpreted and distorted by overstimulated imaginations. In 1913, as it does every eighth year, the planet Venus passed through a phase of exceptional magnitude. It was so abnormally bright that many people did not recognize it as a familiar astral fixture; millions in Europe, and even in Asia, mistook it for an alien airship. The inhabitants of a remote Russian settlement actually unloaded their rifles at it.

Acutely prone to these threats was France, an air-minded country with a long tradition of military ballooning, the very birthplace and chief cultivation ground of aeronautics. Frenchmen, the brothers Jacques and Joseph Montgolfier, back in 1783 had contrived the first successful aerostat, a hot-air type. Made of paper-lined linen and lifted aloft by the heat of a fire of straw and chopped wood, the gorgeously-hued vessel rose to fifteen hundred feet in a public demonstration at Versailles, bearing a sheep, a duck and a rooster as its first passengers. Among the dignitaries who witnessed the ascent was the

[5] Dudley: *op. cit.*

American ambassador to the royal court, Benjamin Franklin. When the balloon had risen into the sky and appeared no bigger than an orange, Franklin was asked: "Of what use is it?" He nimbly evaded a prediction by asking in turn: "Of what use is a newborn babe?"

Immediately upon the heels of the Montgolfiers' triumph, in August of the same year, Professor Jacques Charles, a French physicist, stole the show by fabricating the first spherical lute-string bag of silk and inflating it with an as yet little known gaseous element called hydrogen; except as curiosities, hot-air balloons became quickly obsolete. Three months later, in November, J. de Rozier made several captive ascents, and then with his intrepid friend, the Marquis d'Arlandes, he flew a hydrogen balloon over Paris to become the first men in history to sail the sky. Reaching a height of three thousand feet, they covered five miles in twenty minutes.

It was only in the next year, 1784, that the idea of a dirigible occurred to French experimenters—namely, two brothers named Robert—who attempted to control a seven-hour flight in a melon-shaped hydrogen balloon with a crew of six using silken "oars." The question of propulsion was obviously of paramount importance, and in the ensuing century, until the perfection of internal-combustion engines, all manner of schemes were tried and abandoned by, principally, French aeronauts. In 1852, Henri Giffard built a spindle-shaped gasbag that responded feebly to the rudder while flying into a gentle headwind. More successful was the government-subsidized *La France,* which, in 1884, rose, circled a field, and returned to its departure point; however, its engines were too weak to be practical. When the government in disappointment deserted aeronautics, private individuals carried on. Especially famous was Alberto Santos-Dumont, the colorful Brazilian emigrant who had adopted Paris as his home. With his nonrigid airships, fourteen in number, which he built and flew between 1897 and 1904, Santos-Dumont enchanted the Parisians. His splendid flights stirred mild military interest in England, if not in other countries. But Santos-Dumont, who went on to design and race airplanes, was to be remembered as the "father of sport flying." He was not concerned with military aeronautics. When the military potentialities of his sport had become apparent, he had already retired from the air.

The French were the first to use a balloon in war, when they used one for observation at the battle of Fleurus in 1784. Napoleon formed the first balloon company and took it along with him on his ill-starred expedition into Egypt. Three generations later, balloons played a major role in saving Paris from the prolonged siege of Bismarck's armies. And soon after that war, France employed its aerial observers in several colonial campaigns in Africa.[6]

Hence, at the close of the nineteenth century and for the next seven or

[6] The British also made use of kite balloons in South Africa during the Boer War.

eight years, until the German zeppelins began to make good, France stood first among nations as a practised exponent of military aeronautics. For a while it seemed as though no other country would overtake this lead. Count Zeppelin still figured as just another experimenter in 1902, when a splendid new dirigible—built by the Lebaudy brothers, Paul and Pierre, from plans prepared by the engineer Henri Julliot—was unveiled. When Colonel Charles Renard, one of the designers of the old *La France,* saw this ship plowing through a stiff headwind, he exclaimed: "Aerial navigation is no longer a Utopia!" [7] Over the following three years, the ship—called simply the *Lebaudy,* but also known as the *Jaune* from its yellow envelope—flew often and well. In 1905, the government evinced interest. Flights were carried out under military supervision; even the Minister of War went aloft. Finally, in December, when a crisis burst forth in Morocco, the ship was offered gratis to the republic. France accepted, and the *Lebaudy* became the world's first military dirigible.

In the remaining prewar years the French commissioned eleven more Army dirigibles. According to a timetable drawn up in February 1910, a fleet of twenty ships—together with the required sheds and accessories—was to be in service by the summer of 1914. That the War Ministry never fulfilled this intention was due largely to the enthusiasm that attended the ever-improving performance of airplanes in French field maneuvers of that period. From then on, airships would be relegated a back seat to airplanes—and airplanes, until the fourth month or so of World War I, would occupy a back seat to almost everything else in the French military arsenal.

Only the purchase of fifteen rigids between the beginning of 1912 and August 1914, kept Germany ahead. On the other hand, French military heads were somewhat more broad-minded in their theories. They divided their motorized balloons into three functional classes: the *vedettes* for artillery cooperation and local reconnaissance, the *éclaireurs* for medium-range reconnaissance, and the *croiseurs* for deep reconnaissance. The lack of *croiseurs*—cruisers—was an acknowledged defect in the French aerial fleet. There were demands that it be remedied. Public officials made many promises, and some pains were taken in an unavailing attempt to build a rigid after zeppelin lines. What resulted was a gigantic grotesquerie, about as airworthy as a white elephant.

No dirigible comparable to a zeppelin was available for active French service when the war broke out. Regarding this fact, a German historian in later years noted: "Although the idea would have been distasteful to him, had Count Zeppelin been a Frenchman, he would have been a much happier person. The French people would have been happier too, and dirigible technology would have been in a far more advanced state than it was in the opening days of World War I."

[7] Cuneo: *op cit.*

When France went to war, only four airships of the ten on the army list were in condition for service at the front.[8] And these, with their small size and low engine power, were of doubtful utility. All of them nonrigids or semi-rigids, as a group they appeared designed to present as much air resistance as possible. From 1910 through the remaining interlude of peace, it was widely complained in France that the army's efforts in the area of dirigibles were none too energetic. Not only were the promised airships not appearing, but if a service craft was decommissioned, no replacement was forthcoming. A nation alert to the rapidly evolving progress of aeronautics, with their long history of attainment in that field, the French people were understandably alarmed at the specter of zeppelin attack during the unsettled years preceding the war.

Although less air minded than the French, the English were every bit as prone to epidemics of zeppelin fever. The more thoughtful in England did not need Bleriot's trans-Channel flight in 1909 to remind them that man's ability to ride the air jeopardized the protection so long afforded by their insularity and their peerless navy. It was well in advance of any real German success with lighter-than-air ships that the popular prints in England began to discuss the looming danger posed by foreign aircraft, zeppelins in particular. A grand invasion from the sky was conjured into view to emphasize with frightening contrast the pitiful condition of British military aeronautics.

At the time Count Zeppelin was arousing official German interest with his third dirigible, the British War Office released an elucidation of its attitude vis-à-vis aeronautics: "The policy of the Government with regard to all branches of aerial navigation is based on a desire to keep in touch with the movement rather than to hasten its development. It is felt that we stand to gain nothing by forcing a means of warfare which tends to reduce the value of our insular position and the protection of our sea power."

It was not until 1890 that aeronautics achieved any official status in the British army, a balloon section then being attached to the Royal Engineers. Near the end of that decade, in the Boer War, three balloon companies were sent into operations. The home press reported enthusiastically about "the flying eyes of our brave campaigners in South Africa," but the opinion of military professionals was less high. Hindering the balloonists, first, was the mountainous terrain that obstructed their line of vision; second was the prevalence of high winds that made them too sick to fulfill their assigned tasks. The poor view this gave the War Office of aeronautics became confirmed later by post-war economies. In 1902, when an officer returned from France with a report on Santos-Dumont's dirigibles and recommended trials with similar aircraft, he was informed that the budget for balloons was being halved.

Later, however, funds were specifically released for the construction of a

[8] Two ships, *La Patrie* and the *République,*
had been destroyed in accidents.

dirigible, and by a great feat of initiative the British army managed to complete a small nonrigid dirigible that was named the *Nulli Secundus.* It came far short of its name, however, and made only three brief flights before being dismantled. The end of the *Nulli Secundus* was loudly bemoaned by the press, who headlined its passing alongside the news that the German army had just purchased its first zeppelin, the much-publicized LZ-3. The subsequent outcry moved His Majesty's government to appoint a committee to consider this unprecedented threat to national security. After weeks of dragged-out deliberation the committee advised that the menace was sufficient to warrant construction of another military balloon to undergo tests and thereby enable the authorities to determine more definitely the appropriate countermeasures. In the following spring, the army air section brought forth a diminutive nonrigid, aptly called the *Baby.* It compared to a zeppelin as a prune to a watermelon. A disappointment, it was rebuilt twice, first as *Dirigible IIa* and then as the *Beta.* Under the latter name it was moderately successful. Another small dirigible, known formally as the *Gamma* but nicknamed the "Yellow Peril" by the men who risked their necks flying it, appeared shortly afterward. It was not too good a ship.

Despairing of ever getting a decent airship of domestic manufacture, the Admiralty ordered a large nonrigid from a French constructor, Clement-Bayard. The transaction received extensive publicity, the *Daily Mail* financing a hangar for the ship. When delivery was delayed for over a year, the enthusiasm began to change into suspicion. And when the much-heralded vessel arrived, its poor quality occasioned an investigation. It was discovered that the Clement-Bayard factory had sent over a dirigible that the French government had refused to accept. Nevertheless, seeing a chance to drive a bargain, the War Office bought it at half price. As is often the case with cut-rate merchandise, it proved useless and was dismantled, never to be flown again.

Another newspaper, the *Morning Post,* in the meantime had organized a public subscription with the object of buying a Lebaudy semi-rigid from France and presenting it to the War Office, which for its part agreed to erect a proper shed. Upon its arrival in October 1910, while being put into its hangar, the dirigible fouled the roof, and its envelope was badly torn. Investigation disclosed that the Lebaudy factory, without telling anybody, had increased the ship's dimensions. The roof of the shed was raised and the dirigible repaired—but on its maiden voyage at Farnborough it hit a house and was irretrievably damaged.

By November 1913, the Military Wing of the Royal Flying Corps possessed four airships—the *Beta, Gamma, Delta,* and *Eta*—all of a kind, being small nonrigid types of limited flight endurance. The best dirigible in England at the time was a Parseval semi-rigid that the Admiralty had purchased from that German designer. That November, the four army ships were transferred to the Royal navy with the army's blessing.

In 1910, soon after the Clement-Bayard and Lebaudy dirigibles were realized to be useless duds, a British science journal shocked its readers with the revelation that "a mysterious aerial cruiser, laden with twelve tons of high explosives, has flown the North Sea, circled over London and returned to Germany. This new dreadnought of the German navy was aloft ninety-six hours, maintaining a speed of thirty-eight miles per hour, this even in the face of a storm-pressure of almost eight meters." [9] The citizens of Sheerness, a quiet fishing community on the mouth of the Thames, created a sensation when they claimed to have spotted a dirigible over the estuary—headed for London —on the night of October 14, 1912. Reports in the last three months of that year alone placed spectral zeppelins over Dover, Portsmouth, Liverpool, once again over Sheerness, and on two separate occasions over Cardiff. In response to public clamor Parliament passed an Aerial Navigation Act empowering the Secretary of State for Home Affairs to restrict the flight of aircraft over prescribed localities. As a further step, the War Office, smartly aware that vulnerable points were fully exposed to aerial attack, provided quick-firing fixed and mobile guns to British shore defenses, and the Royal navy put into production semi-automatics for light cruisers and destroyers. As a temporary expedient for dealing with zeppelins, it was decided to install two six-inch guns apiece at the Chattenden and Lodge Hill gunpowder magazines, "in a position to open fire without delay."

Some voices tried to calm the nation's fears. In speeches and interviews and official bulletins, government spokesmen repeatedly belittled the danger, the chief of aeronautics at the War Office saying, for example, "We are not yet convinced that either airplanes or airships will be of any utility in war." "Such cares as these," soothed a rhetorician of the House of Lords, leaning on a trite simile, "should be shaken off as dew drops from the lion's mane." Early in 1913, the First Lord of the Admiralty, Winston Churchill, who was a firm proponent of increased air power, pointed out in the House of Commons that only in the preceding twelve months had Germany begun to reap the fruits of years of expense in the construction of airships, and that "up to a very recent period, it was doubtful whether any worthwhile military results would be achieved." The press discounted his sober view, which was amazingly near the truth, and the citizenry continued to be bombarded by a mass of articles portraying the zeppelin's ability to wreak destruction on the kingdom. The substance of such articles may be gleaned from a small sampling of their titles: "The Airship Menace," "The Peril of the Air," "Foreign Airships as Nocturnal Visitors," "The Black Shadow of the Airship." [10] It was the stuff of nightmares.

Looking back from the middle period of the war, a British journalist observed: "During the last five years, the pet bogy of England has been an invasion by air. Newspapers gave frequent prominence to stories of strange

[9] Dudley: *op. cit.*   [10] Cuneo: *op. cit.*

midnight visitors who came in ghostly flying machines. First they were seen in Scotland along the coast, then throughout the British Isles. The nerves of the nation were pitched to believe almost anything that had to do with a host of zeppelins or monster airplanes that would drop death from the sky and level England's might. Germany knew this," he erroneously but forgivably concluded, "and fostered the feeling."[11]

When the actual career of army and navy dirigibles—especially the zeppelins—is dispassionately examined, it is astonishing how they buttressed domestic morale and terrified the prospective enemy. The wholesale wreckage and sorry accomplishments of German airships in the opening weeks of belligerency tell an eloquent story of ignorance, mismangement, and neglect, the roots of which can perhaps be traced back to the general staff's failure to comprehend why Count Zeppelin had contrived such large flying craft. The hollowness of his triumph over rival airship builders must be noted. Although his ships became the accepted military type, and quite a number were bought, their role in German war plans remained ill considered and confused. As a result, the zeppelin design did not progress rapidly enough along martial lines, and when the fighting started, the ships were in no state for effectual participation. More than that, neither the army nor navy knew how to employ them properly. Yet—despite the many mishaps and retarded development, even though the dirigibles had flunked in field maneuvers and thrown but a handful of practice bombs, notwithstanding the rescripts of the Hague convention which ostensibly safeguarded civilians from aerial assailment—the vast pneumatic dragons cast mordant dread into the hearts of the non-German peoples. The deep psychological impact made by the comparatively few air raids of World War I becomes accessible to later-day understanding only when the grip of the untried weapon on the European mentality of that era is fully grasped. In later years, the Third Reich would brandish its Luftwaffe as a minatory blackjack, but the nations of the world would then have ample reason to fear the thunder of German engines overhead. By contrast, there was little basis for the pre-1914 apprehension of zeppelins. But the Allied countries were too much haunted by the grim visage of bomb-glutted aerial demons to perceive the frail foundation of Germany's lighter-than-air force at the inception of hostilities.

The German people were no less deluded, though by a different contagion. Lulled into a false sense of invincibility, expecting miracles of their highly touted dirigible fleet, they were bound for bitter disillusionment. German writers, like their colleagues everywhere else in Europe, poured forth myriad fantasies of great armadas of sky monsters emerging from the cavernous night and hurling down devastation upon enemy cities, seldom specified by name but usually bearing a marked resemblance to Paris or London, even

[11] Cuneo: *op. cit.*

New York! For the war-oriented subjects of the Kaiser, it was delicious, intoxicating imagery. Purposely kept in the dark as to the government's cheap estimate of the zeppelin's military worth, they earnestly believed that Germany possessed—quoting a Berlin newspaper item of June 1914—the "ultimate weapon." They did not learn until far later in the war that in the first weeks of battle only four of the nineteen big dirigibles in military service were in condition to fly at the front—and that three of these four were shot down within days of their appearance over the French lines.

As the world approached war, however, the position was much different from that presented by newspapers to fevered imaginations. In reality Count Zeppelin, with his cast-iron will, and Dr. Eckener, with his flair for commercial showmanship, had yet to persuade the military clique that giant airships would have a vital role to play in warfare. Confident the War Ministry's mind would be changed by a dramatic demonstration of such an airship's faculty for long-distance travel, they announced plans for a flight to the North Pole. Just days later, however, on Sunday, June 28, 1914, a Serbian student assassinated the heir to the Austrian throne, the Archduke Francis Ferdinand, and the troubled surface of European peace was shattered. On July 28, Austria declared war on Serbia, and her ally, Germany, made accelerated preparations for fighting at Austria's side.

Before many more days passed, the captains of the *Sachsen,* the *Hansa,* and the *Viktoria Luise,* rather much to their surprise, received urgent telegrams from the War Ministry ordering them to keep their airships grounded. Army engineers were soon fitting tiny radio nacelles and machine guns and bomb racks to the three dirigibles. Each of the hulls, to furnish extra lifting capacity so that bombs could be carried, was lengthened by twenty-five feet. Black military numerals were painted on the undersides and vertical fins. Thus, invoking the national emergency as its excuse, the War Ministry, after years of procrastination and neglect, now hurriedly confiscated the count's commercial fleet.

An ordinary man might have thought himself cruelly used by the government, but the irrepressible count was only pleased that three more of his dirigibles were wanted, and needed, by the Fatherland. That they would fly in defense of Germany was enough. His joy undoubtedly stemmed from an altruistic love of country, although he must have realized that lucrative military contracts were in the offing. Not only was he building dirigibles now, but also hydroplanes for the Imperial navy.

Immediately after Germany announced her belligerency, Dr. Eckener shuttered the Delag main office in Hamburg and went to the naval airship division at Kiel to volunteer himself as a dirigible commander. According to Eckener, he was told "you must put out of your head any notion that you are going into battle. Your life is too valuable to us for training zeppelin crews. We have too few airship captains as it is."

And that septuagenarian idol of the German masses, Count Zeppelin, wherever he went in public, was greeted with the refrain which every loyal man, woman and child sang:

> Zeppelin, flieg,
> Hilf uns im Krieg,
> Fliege nach England,
> England wird abgebrannt,
> Zeppelin, flieg.

CHAPTER XIV

"Gott Strafe England!"

A MONG THE FEW men of military stature in the world who had the discernment to perceive the war potential inherent in the clumsy, fragile, undependable contraptions that were airships and airplanes in the first decade of the new century was General Giulio Douhet of Italy. At a time when aeronauts and aviators stood as much chance of falling from the air as flying through it, Douhet had already projected his mind's eye into the future and seen the regrettable culmination of their strivings. He saw a vision of air power as it might appear in machine-age warfare.

In 1909, while commanding Italy's aeronautical battalion, an embryonic unit consisting of a flimsy dirigible and a motley collection of outworn balloons, Douhet began writing an essay published two years later under the matter-of-fact title *Rules for the Use of Aircraft in War*. He was among the first to state that modern technology would transform war into an unlimited struggle between whole nations and that it could no longer be merely the traditional battles between trained combatants. In an epoch of aerial aggression, the Italian predicted, civilians would come under direct attack. General staffs everywhere, he noted, tended exclusively toward looking backward and trying to diagram the next war purely on the basis of how the last was resolved, without taking into account any new factors or equipment. Pinning his faith more to airplanes than airships, Douhet asserted that these were already a reality to be reckoned with.

Here was a wealth of shrewd foresight to which scarcely anyone in the Italian, or any other, government accorded serious consideration. Douhet was gratuitously dismissed as another raving theorist. Had one European nation acted decisively on his prospectus, that nation would have entered World War I with a tremendous initial advantage. But none did, obviously.

The sequential moves of conventional warfare as then taught in all military classrooms, from West Point, St. Cyr, and Sandhurst to the German War College, were basically these: (1) advance until the objective is secured, until stopped by enemy action, or until circumstances dictate that the advance be halted; (2) regroup, concentrating main strength at pivotal positions along the front; (3) attack again at the propitious moment, or if attacked first, stand off the enemy and counterattack if and when feasible. From this classic— and here oversimplified—strategy, Douhet deduced that an essential function of the air corps would be to weaken key defensive points in an opposing line by bombing. But there would be other targets—rear bases, routes of supply, networks of communication, sources of production, and civilian populations—behind the front that should also be hit. The very foundation of an enemy's combat capability should be wiped out. The air corps, said Douhet, should never be merely a tactical tool of either the army or the navy but must act as a separate, independent striking force. His final conclusion was that since aircraft would inevitably be used to ward off assailing aircraft, a full-blown clash in the sky would perforce develop.

For proposing that urban centers be bombed, Douhet's critics labeled him a barbarian. He reminded them that in every European country virtually all factories producing armaments were located in the midst of cities. A stony realist, he suggested that no such thing as a gentleman's war had ever been waged except in puerile story books and prettified, perfumed histories. Chivalry in armed conflict, he maintained, was a mawkish fiction, "a fantasy of fools and innocent children." An intellectually honest man, Douhet felt that war was a rape of reason—in his words, "a criminal insanity that should be terminated as quickly as possible, by whatever available means, for the sake of every suffering soul involved."

For his candor, Douhet lost almost all his friends in the Italian military community. The generals and admirals seemed to take his outspoken opinions as personal affronts, for they showered him with vituperation. They sarcastically pointed out that airmen would be useless for seizing and holding ground, and that victory resulted only when enemy territory was physically occupied. You win a war, Douhet rebutted, when you compel the other side to submit to your will. Recalling Napoleon's debacle in Russia a hundred years earlier, he argued that inserting troops into a land was not necessarily the same thing as conquering it. He then explained that if the air force can create intolerable conditions—panic, hunger, immobility, industrial collapse—a hostile power must concede defeat regardless of the status of its armies in the field. Once that happens, the details of occupation can be arranged without further bloodshed.

His detractors mocked Douhet's "theory of frightfulness." Nevertheless, progressive military thinkers would adopt it in principle before the end of World War I as a precept of grand strategy. And in World War II, aviation having reached its maturity, the grim auguries of General Douhet would come very close to a terrible actuality.

The astute Italian was a man ahead of his time, and like many prophets before him, he was condemned. His ideas were not state secrets but were widely published in the press, and his *Rules for the Use of Aircraft in War* was stocked on bookstore shelves. His unpalatable yet realistic and militarily sound theories and his insistence upon frequently and tactlessly criticizing decisions of his superior officers led to his court-martial (a fate that another crusader for air power, General William Mitchell, was to share for similar reasons in the United States in 1925). Douhet was adjudged guilty of insubordination and sentenced to a year's imprisonment. Walls could not still his fervency, however. Now he devoted almost every wakeful hour to writing articles and pamphlets, and exchanging correspondence with some of the few converts he had made.

There was at least one partisan of Douhet's in France, although nobody in authority paid much attention to him either. He was Captain Ferdinand Ferber, an early disciple of Santos-Dumont, Bleriot, and the Wright brothers. Whether Ferber had any direct contact with Douhet is doubtful, but he certainly studied the Italian's gospel and preached it. In 1911, he was interviewed by a reporter for a French aviation magazine, *L'Aerophile*. After hearing Ferber's predictions about the coming importance of aircraft in warfare, the puzzled reporter asked how a combat could actually be fought between two airplanes. Ferber answered:

> The contest will unfold in much the same way as all fights between birds have ever taken place. For instance, a hawk, when it wants to grapple a raven, first pursues it. The raven, finding itself overhauled, ascends in spirals, and the hawk starts to climb in a parallel line, seeking its chance to pounce. If the raven rises higher than the hawk, it escapes; if it cannot, its recourse is to plummet, although during the descent it is liable to be hemmed in by the hawk. Every time the hawk darts upon the raven, the latter will try, with a clever sideslip, to avoid the fatal impact. If the hawk has been dodged, there is a respite, for the hawk overshoots its mark and loses an elevation which must laboriously be regained. Should the race for altitude be resumed, the contest is no longer in doubt. The raven, weaker and slower of wing, will ultimately be impaled by the pursuer's talons. Given enough time, the hardier, fleeter bird will almost invariably vanquish its prey. In a like manner, but with guns and grenades instead of beak and claw, will men in flying machines do battle.

To its credit, the magazine did not disparage Ferber's vision as an absurdity. Its editor, after mentioning that similar ideas had been put forward in Italy, commented:

> Until the day arrives when bigger and faster airplanes have been

perfected, until machines capable of hurling large quantities of explosives are built, Captain Ferber's surmise must remain more or less hypothetical. Were a war to begin tomorrow, the Zeppelin dirigibles of Germany and our own Lebaudy types might be tentatively employed as aerial battleships. It would seem, however, that they are too cumbersome and unreliable to be of much expedience as armed raiders. . . . We concur with Captain Ferber when he says that aeronautical technology will improve at an ever more rapid pace. The great nations should beware of the ugly potentialities he warns us against.

Sooner than anyone expected, the gruesome forecasts of Douhet and Ferber began to come true. A war did begin in the figurative if not the literal tomorrow, and gradually, as the struggle grew more bitter, there came the realization that modern battle had no room for such niceties as chivalry, decency, or respect for contracts and international agreements. By 1916, both sides had to a clear degree adopted the philosophy of Giulio Douhet. To the extent permitted by the means at their disposal, the Allies and central powers alike—whenever it suited their respective purpose—unleashed "frightfulness" upon each other's homelands. If German offenses against civilian populations heavily outnumbered those committed by England and France, it was largely because the Germans were better equipped for the job. Furthermore, the record of German atrocities was magnified and given wide circulation as part of a calculated Allied propaganda effort to arouse sympathy among the neutral nations, the United States in particular.

It is incontrovertible, of course, that Germany began fracturing the tacit rules of so-called civilized warfare sooner in the game than did the Allied countries. When it was all over and a peace treaty was being negotiated at Versailles, a member of the German delegation was overheard by Georges Clemenceau to muse, "I wonder what history will say of this deplorable war?" The French Premier, the individual most responsible for the degradation of Germany in that 1919 compact, tartly retorted, "History will never say that Belgium invaded Germany." Nor will history ever deny that Germany from the beginning treated civilians as military targets.

The doctrine of unconditional warfare was demonstrated most dramatically by the zeppelin raids on England, an eventuality that both sides had for years been anticipating and speculating over. But German lighter-than-air operations did not enjoy an auspicious start. In early August, within the space of forty-eight hours, three zeppelins were destroyed on their initial war missions. First to go down was the LZ-6, which was bombing some forts around Liège. A dense overcast kept the LZ-6 at low altitude; repeatedly hit by ground fire, it lost so much hydrogen that it fell before reaching its base again at Cologne. Next morning the LZ-7 ventured from Baden-Baden to reconnoiter in the Vosges. Cruising at a height of only half a mile, the 520-foot-long zeppelin was surprised by a sudden volley from below, where a large body of French troops was hidden in a woods. A storm of bullets and exploding shrapnel drove the stricken vessel off to crash near Saint-Quirin in Lorraine. That same day the LZ-8, outward bound from Trier, was subjected to heavy fire by over-zealous German troops. It was only a few hundred feet up when, apparently unawares, it came over the enemy trenches. At that range the huge zeppelin presented a target impossible to miss. Its helm controls were shot away, and its gas cells holed like a sieve. Helpless, absorbing terrible punishment as it went, the LZ-8 finally drifted lower toward Badonvillers forest and wrecked itself. The crew spilled out of the gondolas and tried to cremate the vast carcass that sprawled and sagged across the pine tops, but at that instant a squadron of French cavalry, sabers flailing, rode down at them. Covering their retreat with rifles, the crew escaped and—eleven hours later—reached their own lines.

The one remaining army zeppelin fit for service, the recently commissioned LZ-9, had meanwhile bombed Liège—or attempted to. Damage to the ancient city was negligible, few missiles striking within its boundaries. The bombs, which were simple nose-weighted artillery shells of the makeshift variety, could not be relied upon to fall straight or to explode on impact. According to Captain Horn, the LZ-9's commander, more than half the bombs thrown down at Liège were duds.

Due to its drastic zeppelin losses at the front, the German army cautiously kept the LZ-9 hangared for the ensuing three weeks. Due also to these losses, the army and not the navy took over the *Sachsen, Viktoria Luise,* and *Hansa,* the three commercial ships commandeered from Delag, although the crews remained naval reservists. Then, on August 26, occurred the incident that shocked a naïve world and brought to a brisk ferment the long-simmering British dread of German dirigibles. Antwerp—already badly damaged by an unremitting artillery siege—was bombed from the air. Twelve civilians were killed, many more injured, and part of a hospital demolished. More raids were prosecuted against the beleaguered Belgian city. Six nights in a row, the LZ-9, commanded by Captain Horn, and the *Sachsen,* commanded by Captain Lehmann, attacked Antwerp with newly developed shrapnel and incendiary bombs. And after each successive raid, the English pored over their morning newspapers and shuddered.

Early in September, while the army's dirigible force was still licking its wounds and gloating over its raids on Antwerp, the aeronautical lead in Germany was assumed by the navy. Captain Peter Strasser, since mid-1913 the zealous and competent head of the navy's airship division, had resolved to create an aggressively effective fleet of zeppelins. An experienced mariner of the air who had been trained on the *Hansa,* Strasser possessed the implacable, driving personality needed to convince his seniors that his ideas were right. His greatest ambition was to fly against the British Isles, and he found a staunch ally in his old friend, Dr. Hugo Eckener. Through their joint efforts, a standing order for a minimum of two ships a month was placed with the Zeppelin works. To satisfy the demand, supplementary production shops were annexed to the Friedrichshafen plant, and a branch factory raised in Potsdam. At the same time, additional airship bases were established throughout western and northern Germany, those already in use being enlarged and sweepingly improved. Strasser insisted that reliability should be the overriding quality to aim for in the construction of new vessels. Modifications were accordingly worked out by Count Zeppelin, who had ceased pathetically haunting the corridors of the War Ministry asking for a job on active service and met regularly with Strasser and Eckener in conferences lasting late into the night; because one was seldom seen without the other two, they became known around naval headquarters as "the Holy Trinity." [1]

It was decided to keep down the size of the zeppelins in the interest of easier ground handling, but the design was tidied up externally and its interior framework refined in minor respects. With good results, new engines were installed. These were heavy-duty Maybachs, recently introduced six-cylinder units unsurpassed for dependability. Since the craft would have to cope with nasty turns of weather while en route to England across the North Sea, Strasser had them all equipped with extra-powerful radios capable of transmitting and receiving messages over a three-hundred-mile range so that meteorological data could be exchanged constantly with base—and some abortive experiments were made with crude wireless homing devices. Completed under Eckener's supervision, a chain of weather stations extended along the coast from Ostend to Königsberg by the end of October.

The concerted buildup of naval zeppelin strength was avidly watched by the German public already feeling the pinch of a British sea blockade and agitating for stern reprisal. "Gott strafe England!" had become a national slogan. It appeared everywhere in Germany, printed in jagged, shouting red letters on kiosks, lamp poles, fences, and the walls of buildings. Patriotic grandmothers embroidered it upon flowered samplers and pillow covers. Youngsters recited it in their classrooms at the beginning of each daily school session. Bending to popular sentiment, the Kaiser issued a proclamation in which he forthrightly sanctioned air raids on England, and his anxious subjects waited impatiently for the spectacle of London, Liverpool, and Manchester being razed and gutted by bomb-kindled torrents of flame. Grand Admiral Alfred von Tirpitz, chief of the Imperial navy, had some premature qualms and misgivings. He wrote to his wife from headquarters in November:

> The English are in terror of our zeppelins, perhaps with sufficient cause. I contend here, wherever I go, for the standpoint of "an eye for an eye," but I am not in favor of the evil policy which is lately gaining vogue. I mean the policy of "frightfulness." The indiscriminate dropping of bombs is wrong; they are repulsive when

[1] Dudley: *Monsters of the Purple Twilight.*

they kill and maim children and old women, and one can too soon
grow callous to such wanton cruelty. We should not be so oppor-
tunistic as to stoop to our baser instincts. If an airship fleet were to
set fire to London in thirty places, then the repulsiveness would be
lost sight of in the immensity of the effect.[2]

In December, five months after entering the war with but a single operative
zeppelin, the German navy had a pack of five poised to strike. The army,
however, still shaken by its August losses, declined to cooperate with a navy
proposal for consolidating the two forces in order to launch an immediate
aerial offensive against the enemy kingdom. Further delaying action came from
the Kaiser's inability to make up his mind whether or not to include London
among the places to be attacked. Tirpitz's immediate subordinates, the Admirals Bachmann and Pohl, shared none of his humane compunctions. Bachmann handed up a memorandum saying that "we should leave no means untried to crush England, and successful raids on the enemy capital, in view of
the nervousness of the British people, would pave a shortcut to this end."
Pohl presented a memorandum, too. London, he argued, was a defended city
in the sense of The Hague convention's definition and bristled with targets of
great military consequence. "Our airships would take every precaution to
avoid damage to historical sites and private property," he avowed. "The effects
of such a raid . . . would be far-reaching upon the enemy's morale and
matériel." Tirpitz reluctantly but dutifully passed along these memoranda to
the Emperor. After two weeks of silence on the matter Wilhelm II summoned
his admirals to hear his decision. He reiterated his intention to bomb England
and gave the necessary go-ahead order, but with the stipulation that targets
be "scrupulously limited to docks, shipyards, armories and other prime military objectives." Some admirals were less pleased when His Imperial Highness
added that London proper was to be spared.

Recognizing the thin edge of the wedge, the advocates of terrorist measures
against the British homeland were temporarily contented. A beginning could
be made and swiftly expanded upon until a scheme they had surreptitiously
plotted could be effected, a plan for burning London to the ground. Master-
minded by Strasser and suborned by Bachmann and Pohl, the scenario called
for an armada of at least a dozen zeppelins, each carrying three hundred incendiary bombs, to attack the British capital in unison. A secret poll of aeronautical experts, including Count Zeppelin, Dr. Eckener, and some veteran
airship commanders, indicated that so devastating a raid would be technically
feasible once the necessary materials had been accumulated. Neither the Kaiser
nor Tirpitz was as yet informed of the project, although the latter probably
heard of it within a short time.

For a start, meanwhile, the navy readied three zeppelins for an opening
foray against the British Isles. Two of these, the L-3 and L-4, commanded

---

[2] Dudley: *op. cit.*

respectively by Captain Johann Fritze and Captain Magnus von Platen Hallermund, were based at Fuhlsbuttel; the third, Captain Treusch von Buttlar's L-6,
was hangared at the navy's new airship headquarters at Nordholz. Each of the
three sister ships had a hydrogen capacity of 950,000 cubic feet and could
remain airborne for thirty hours at a normal speed of forty-six miles per hour.
Their ceiling was nine thousand feet. With all regulation equipment aboard,
they could each carry between five and six hundred pounds of bombs. Some
of this paraphernalia was safely dispensable, however, and the skippers usually managed to leave quite a bit behind in order to carry more bombs.

Takeoff was postponed for nearly a week because of bad weather, but on
the morning of January 19, 1915, the raiders embarked for the east coast of
England. After rendezvousing with the L-3 and L-4 halfway across the North
Sea, Captain Buttlar had to turn back with engine trouble. Captains Fritze and
Platen proceeded on course. At quarter to seven that evening, while pedaling
along Ingham beach in Norfolk, a bicyclist saw, as he said, "two bright stars
moving apparently thirty yards apart." What he sighted were the running lights
of the approaching zeppelins. Veering northward and skirting the shoreline,
the two craft diverged at eight o'clock, the L-3 heading inland via the Haisboro
lightship, the L-4 continuing coastwise in the direction of Bacton. The first
zeppelin incursion of England had commenced.

Once landfall had been put behind them, uncertain of their navigation and
chilled to the bone in their unenclosed gondolas, Fritze and Platen cursed the
weather they encountered. It was a typical winter's night in Norfolk—a cold
porridge of fog interspersed with sleet, rain, and snow. Now and then they
would find a break in the oppressive cloud and drop their bombs randomly
at whatever cluster of lights they chanced to see below. Fritze released nine
twenty-pounders on Yarmouth, killing two persons, injuring three, damaging
a few cottages, and sinking a barge in the river. The rest of his bombs fell
harmlessly about the surrounding countryside.

Platen did greater mischief. Groping along a course from Bacton to Cromer,
to Beeston, to Thornham, to Brancaster, to Hunstanton, to Snettisham, he
scattered his lightweight missiles as he went. It was only by coincidence that
a radio-monitoring post at Hunstanton—specially tuned to zeppelin wave-
lengths—was narrowly missed. Flying southward along the wide bay known
as the Wash, Platen saw the lights of King's Lynn and made for them. He
lowered toward the town and let go his remaining bombs, among which,
according to his report, were four 110-pounders. Two men and two women
were killed, another fourteen adults and three children injured. Homes and
shops were hit, as well as the generating house of the Docks and Railways
Company. Platen noted in his log that he was fiercely shelled by antiaircraft
guns and followed by searchlights over King's Lynn, which town he thought
was either Hull or Grimsby on the mouth of the Humber, some sixty miles
farther to the north.

Chronicling Platen's experience, an official German naval historian sug-

gested that "by thus opening hostilities, the place in question has only itself
to thank that the airship took defensive action and dropped seven 110-pound
high-explosive bombs." But the guns were figments of Platen's heated imagination, and the searchlights merely the glare of street lamps refracted in the
foggy drizzle. The officers and men of the L-3 and L-4 were decorated with
Iron Crosses, which they did not have long to show off; both zeppelins three
weeks later were blown down in a storm near the Jutland coast, the survivors
being rescued and interned by Danish fishermen.

Berlin characterized the raid as "attacks on some fortified places," and the
German press acclaimed the national genius that had at last spelled a finish
to England's insularity. "The moat has been bridged!" brayed a Munich
headline. "Our glorious airships," boasted a jubilant editor in Hamburg, "will
persevere in their attacks on the enemy asylum, and every bomb will be an
arrow piercing the coward's gut. . . . Our aerial avengers will smash the island
citadel." Vowed the Cologne *Gazette,* "We shall never allow these splendid
weapons to grow rusty."

As a lot, the British newspapers reacted with aplomb and almost incredible
restraint. Although denouncing the raid as a blatant violation of The Hague
agreement and duly castigating the Germans as, among other unflattering
things, "despicable brutes and savages," "craven wretches," and "contemptible
Huns and Vandals," there was discernible in many editorials an unconscious
sigh of relief. The long and woeful wait was ended; the zeppelins had come,
and it was not as bad in reality as had been feared. The toll of casualties was
nothing to shrug off blithely, of course, but neither was it cause for runaway
hysteria. "The hateful airships will bring death to a few of us," a sage hand
wrote in the *Morning Post,* "but it will take something else to herald our doom
as a nation. You may rest assured that England and her sturdy allies will win
this war in spite of the hulky bags of gas the modern-day Teutons regard as
their salvation, when they have none. The depraved and atavistic scoundrels
might as well put their reliance in Wotan's legendary thunderbolts." What
most annoyed British journalists was that the L-4's attack seemed deliberately
aimed at King George V and Queen Mary, who, until that morning, had been
spending Christmastide at Sandringham House, only a few miles removed from
King's Lynn.

Press reaction in the United States was significant insofar as the future
trend of events was concerned. Practically every major daily in the country
accused the Germans of flagrant brutality. The New York *Herald,* for example, asked: "Is it the madness of despair or just plain everyday madness
that has prompted the Germans to select for attack peaceful and defenseless
resorts on the east coast of England? What can Germany hope to profit by
these ruthless attacks on undefended places? Certainly not the good opinion
of the peoples of neutral nations." In Milwaukee, with its many families of
German extraction, the *Free Press* ran this extravagant headline: "Zeppelins

Bombard Sandringham as King George and the Queen Flee. Panic Grips Capital as Foe Steers Course for London."

In Norfolk, during and after the raid, an atmosphere of unreality pervaded the entire happening. People could not quite accept the evidence of their senses when they heard the throb of engines in the dismal sky and glimpsed the glinting silver flanks of the monster above, boring through draperies of damp mist, eerily illumed in the pale nimbus that overhung the village—and then the startling flash and quake and din of detonating bombs. They plainly saw the heads of the German crew as the L-4's control car almost fouled the schoolhouse spire in Thornham. And the next morning, while driving to King's Lynn, a district member of Parliament, Halcombe Ingleby, stopped at Snettisham, seeing there in front of the church a group of townsfolk discussing the raid. The vicar appealed to Ingleby to confirm whether the attack had been perpetrated by an airplane or an airship. The vicar said it had been a huge biplane, and that he had seen it loose a bomb. Two bystanders claimed also to have seen the culprit. "All I can say," declared one, a woman, "is it was the largest sausage I ever saw in my life." The other described it as looking "like a church steeple sideways." A spate of spy stories circulated in the aftermath, breathless witnesses swearing to an impossible number of suspicious vehicles signaling to the zeppelins—a "dark, closed motor carriage, an Austin or maybe a Daimler, with a green light on top," a "car with a fiery beacon," a "motorcar with two powerful headlamps blinking on and off," a darkened automobile with four occupants wearing "strangely muffled headgear." [3]

The German naval command hailed the raid as an encouraging success and gave Strasser a virtual carte blanche with which to conduct repeated sorties. Step by step, from then on through the spring and summer, Strasser and his team worked up toward the major effort: the all-out assault on London.

In the first week of February the Kaiser, under considerable pressure from his naval advisers, assented to bombing any military targets in the capital that lay east of Tower Bridge. It was for London the L-3 and L-4 were bound when they crashed off Jutland. On February 28, the L-8 tried to make it from Düsseldorf, but strong headwinds necessitated landing at an army dirigible field in Belgium. With a Captain Beelitz its master, the L-8 sat through an interval of squally weather and then, on March 5, made a second attempt. This time it ran into a gale out of the unchartable west and was blown back over Calais, where French coastal artillery shot it down. A British reporter saw the dirigible destroyed and sent home this word-picture:

> The zep's bow heaved suddenly upward. . . . The long cylindrical envelope went all red inside, glowing like an immense Chinese lantern. I saw three crewmen fall or leap from the after nacelle. There was a vast blossom of liquid flame and a deafening concus-

[3] Poolman: *Zeppelins Against London.*

sion as, with much the force of a volcano, the great aerial cruiser erupted amidships. Its hull was snapped in two. . . . Two writhing masses of twisted metal and burning fabric slithered gently down to the white-capped sea, spurting geysers of steam upon meeting the cold water. Some few of the French cannoneers cheered aloud, but most watched in rapt silence, hardly believing what they saw.

Perturbed over Strasser's sway with the Kaiser's naval chiefs, his persuasive powers having gained him the first real blow against England, and jealous of his initial if alloyed success, the army's airship section roused itself into activity. Early losses were recouped before the middle of winter with a batch of new and far better dirigibles, and bases had been established in Belgium and occupied France, affording a relatively short haul to England. On March 17, undertaking the army's first cross-Channel jab at the enemy, Captain Lehmann flew one of the new zeppelins, the Z-12, from Maubeuge, his destination the east side of London.

"She was a modern raider built for war," he wrote of the Z-12, to which he and his crew were transferred from the *Sachsen* in January. An example of a new line of dirigibles, its design was advanced even in comparison to concurrent naval airships. With a capacity load of twelve tons, the Z-12 could maintain headway of fifty-six miles per hour, representing a decided increase over the *Sachsen's* top speed. Instead of open control cars, there were enclosed cabins, connected by a companionway inside the hull.

No sooner had he familiarized himself with the ship than the enterprising Lehmann began testing a scheme for concealing the Z-12 above the clouds while still being able to see his target on the ground. "Our idea," he wrote, "was to produce a small observation car which might be lowered a half mile or more beneath the zeppelin." It was not his invention but that of a Cologne inventor by the name of Hagen, who contacted him to say that such an apparatus was ready for immediate trial. Hagen brought with him a hand winch spooled with a thousand feet of wire, installed it in the Z-12's bomb compartment amidships, and suspended an old butter cask from the end of the wire. To prevent it from whirligigging in the slipstream, the cask was furnished with a crude stabilizing vane. It also had a telephone hooked up to the wheelhouse. Eight weeks before his March 17 probe against England, Lehmann first tried this device. "As I was lowered some five hundred feet below, there came a series of shocks caused by the jerks and stops of the creaking old hand winch. There I hung exactly as if I had been in a bucket in a well. I kept a wary eye on the wire, which looked none too strong . . . but it held."

By the day of his intended raid on London, Lehmann had provided himself with an electric winch and 2700 feet of plaited steel cable with an insulated telephone line running through the core. The observation car now was no converted butter barrel but a streamlined capsule with a functional stabilizer. Full of optimism, he set out from Maubeuge in mid-afternoon. Aided by a lively tailwind, he made faster time than he anticipated, so that he had to lie away from the Kentish coast until well after nightfall. At ten o'clock he moved inland and promptly ran into fog. "I took the kite up as high as I thought wise, but at six thousand feet the soup was as thick as ever. We wandered around a while, hoping to find the Thames. Then I flew as low as I dared, but it was no good." Lehmann returned to base without having seen London or much else of England. Unlike many of his colleagues, he refused to throw bombs helter-skelter at invisible targets.

Lehmann, although attached to the army, was a naval officer and a zeppelin commander since the early days of Delag. He was a personal friend of long-standing to both Strasser and Eckener. That he enjoyed their fullest confidence is revealed by the fact that Strasser consulted him in regard to the hushed-up plan for desolating London. "The plan," related Lehmann, "was drafted . . . without any official authority. The idea was to equip from twelve to twenty zeppelins and drill their crews to function as a coordinated task force. Each ship would carry about three hundred fire bombs. They would attack simultaneously at night. Hence, as many as six thousand bombs would be rained upon the metropolis at once. . . . When asked for my technical opinion, morality aside, I agreed it was definitely workable."

In view of their friendship, it was natural for Lehmann to tell the airship director of his experiments with the sub-cloud car. He did so at the first convenient opportunity, a couple of evenings after his futile sally against London, when he received a bid to join Strasser and Eckener for dinner in the Nordholz officer's club. Strasser requested that he be given a ride in the dangling lookout car, which was done within the week. His enthusiasm for it was boundless; he ordered that all existing and future dirigibles in his command be fitted with similar appliances and put himself in charge of further developing and testing them. He seemed to revel in riding in the observation cars, and he worked in close conjunction with Zeppelin engineers on a series of improved designs.

A year later, in April 1916, during a trial run in one of them, Strasser was almost killed. The airship having attained sufficient height, he climbed into the tiny pod and gave the signal to lower away. The stout cable was a half mile long. However, about three hundred feet down, as the winch slowly but steadily paid out cable, the stabilizing fin of the car became entangled with the zeppelin's radio antenna—a weighted wire hanging free from the aft gondola. It caught the car and tilted it upside down. The cable, meanwhile, continued unraveling from the winch and was bellying in a slack loop below Strasser, who saved himself from being tipped out only by clinging to the sides of the car. Suddenly the antenna gave way, sending the car and its passenger plunging until brought up at the end of the cable with a violent, sickening jolt. Miraculously, Strasser survived with nothing more serious than assorted cuts and bruises.

Throughout the opening months of 1915, German army airship crews, concentrating on targets in France and the British-held corner of Belgium, struck at Nancy, Calais, Cassel, Saint-Omer, Hazebrouck, Poperinge, Compiègne, and—in a telling raid on March 20, in which a munitions factory was destroyed—Paris. Since radio communication was dangerous so near the front, a network of searchlight beacons was set up across occupied territory as an aid to nighttime navigation. Upon hearing an airship in their vicinity, the attendants would flash their code names and quickly douse the light. This was often the only way a zeppelin commander could reckon his whereabouts. The landmarks discernible at night were few and generally hard to identify, and astronomical observations were difficult even on clear nights, the hull of the airship obstructing any panoramic view of the stars. Then and during the rest of the war, more dirigibles would be lost as a result of accidents and wayward meanderings than would be brought down by enemy guns.

With the coming of April, a new zeppelin, the L-9, was delivered to the navy at Nordholz. It was commanded by Lieutenant Heinrich Mathy, a freshman skipper whose eagerness for action marked him high in Strasser's esteem. The aeronautics chief entrusted a reconnaissance mission to Mathy on the evening of April 14, delegating him to pinpoint likely objectives along the northeast coast of England between the Humber and Tyne rivers. Mathy did as instructed, but at the completion of his scouting run, he staged an impromptu foray on Tyneside, inflicting slight damage although fatally injuring a mother and child. The following night, three more seasoned skyfarers, the Captains Boecker and Buttlar in the L-5 and L-6, and a Lieutenant Peterson in the L-7, took off together to raid Humber port facilities. Strasser himself went along in Peterson's ship for observation.

The heaviest attack was made by the L-5 as it strewed bombs on Henham Hall, Southwold, and Lowestoft, well to the south of the prescribed target area. All three commanders reported being caught in searchlights and receiving hits; in fact, there were no searchlights and just three pom-pom shells were fired, all of which returned to explode on the ground, plus a furious rifle volley from a battalion of Sussex Cyclists. The only zeppelin hit was Buttlar's L-6, a punctured gas cell impeding its flight back to Nordholz. Arriving home several hours behind the other two raiders, Buttlar found Strasser sadly writing up an official obituary for the overdue L-6.

These early naval zeppelin models, restricted in size and based in Germany, did not quite have the range of London. The army on the other hand, operating with some faster ships from newly built sheds in Belgium, could reach the British capital with reasonable ease. Lehmann wanted to try again, but a successsion of troubles with the Z-12's engines called for extensive repairs. It therefore became the honor of Captain Erich Linnarz, veteran commander of the LZ-38, stationed at Brussels, to accomplish the first aerial assailment of London.

Linnarz tried several times, unsuccessfully, before he finally reached London. On April 29, in his initial venture across the Channel, he was thwarted by fog, barely attaining the enemy coast. In the early morning darkness of May 11, he got as far as Southend and dumped some incendiaries close to the anchored hulk of the *Royal Edward,* an old steam frigate that housed German prisoners of war, although he had no way of knowing this. He also showered missiles on Southend itself, causing three civilian casualties and setting a lumberyard on fire. In addition, he dropped a large cardboard placard on which he had scrawled in red crayon: "You English. We have come and will come again. Kill or cure. German." Seven nights later found him over Kent, where he scattered ineffectual bombs before heading seaward. At dawn Lieutenant R. H. Mulock of the Royal Naval Air Service, while patrolling in his eighty-mile-an-hour Avro 504 single-seater, spotted the LZ-38 cruising serenely at two thousand feet over Armentières. Mulock began shooting with his Lewis gun, which jammed. By the time he cleared the stoppage, the zeppelin had vanished.

Linnarz twice again raided the Thames estuary. On May 26, in a second assault on Southend, he was met by gunfire and planes, which he eluded, leaving behind three dead and three injured. A local R.N.A.S. searchlight caught the LZ-38 in its beam, the first time a zeppelin or any invading aircraft had ever been illuminated over British soil. This was considered no mean feat, each member of the searchlight crew being presented with a silver badge.

On the last night in May, Linnarz succeeded in finding London. Departing from the new zeppelin base near Brussels, he intersected the Belgian coast between the lighthouses of Ostend and Zeebrugge. Linnarz knew that a straight westerly course from these twin beacons would bring him eventually to the outer mouth of the Thames. As the meteorologists had promised him, the thirty-five-year-old airship commander, a former infantry officer and instructor at the Charlottenburg military academy, found perfect weather asea. Visibility was excellent, a full moon due to reach its zenith at about half-past eleven, which was his estimated time of arrival over the sleeping British capital. Shortly before ten o'clock Linnarz slowed the zeppelin to a hover off the bottom lip of the Thames estuary to check his compass bearings, then headed toward the North Foreland.

The LZ-38 handled beautifully. Penciliform, 536 feet in length, its cotton fabric envelope painted metallic gray, a large black cross emblazoned under its sharp-pointed nose, the ship was always described by Linnarz in terms of loving admiration. "My pretty baby," he once called it. Packed within the hull were eighteen bladders of hydrogen, rendered leakproof by an overlay of goldbeater's skin. According to an avouchment by the Zeppelin company, any two of these drum-shaped cells could be pierced by enemy shot without seriously impeding the dirigible's performance. Since the gas was lightly compressed, it would not readily escape in any case. Powered by four heavy-duty Maybachs, the LZ-38—in common with other post-1914 zeppelin models— possessed one more vital advantage. Although even the slowest airplane could overtake it in level flight, it could handily evade any winged foe by discharging its water ballast and, its nose aimed skyward, gaining altitude at a rate surpassing a thousand feet per minute. Thus it could virtually leap beyond the reach of existing planes, even to such rarefied heights as twenty-three thousand feet. The LZ-38's maximum bomb-load comprised almost nine hundred pounds, which Linnarz chose to utilize with five 110-pounders and about four dozen seven-pound incendiaries. For protection against aerial attack the ship was armed with five machine guns, a pair in each gondola, plus another one in a turret atop the hull, which was a completely new feature. Crewing the ship, besides Linnarz, were three officers and sixteen men.

Studying the moonlit prospect below, Linnarz saw the trace of white surf that delineated the shoreline. He smiled tensely at the helmsman and gave him a revised heading. Turning further northward, the zeppelin heeled gently to starboard. As it brushed by the foreland near Margate, the town blacked out but distinguishable in the pallid lunar glow, Linnarz ordered all hands a cup of broth from the aluminum pot on the electric stove. The hot drink was welcome. Despite the double suits of underwear, the heavy sweaters, flannel scarves, leather jackets, wool-pile hats, and fur-lined boots they wore, the crewmen were cold in the unheated cabin. And now, Linnarz ordering the lights extinguished as the ship made landfall, they found themselves in an isolated little world of throbbing engines, wanly glimmering dials and gauges, whispered orders, and squeaking struts and wires.

Coming inland near Shoeburyness, Linnarz swung his ship to the west again. Unseen from the ground, he passed over Brentwood, staying well away from the Thames, and then angled southward. As the LZ-38 approached the northeastern districts of London, an expectant hush settled into the cabin. Speaking in a hoarse whisper, Linnarz ordered the man at the elevator wheel to take the ship higher. "We are at seven thousand feet," was how he later described this first air raid on a great metropolis. "At full speed we steer for their capital city, the jewel of their civilization. I am standing at my command station, every fiber of my body taut." He switches on the necessary lamps; they provide a muted greenish light. The moment has arrived.

"Let go!" I cry. The first bomb has been hurled at London! We wait with bated breath, listening. We lean over the side, watching. What a damned long interval between release and impact, the bomb falling those thousands of feet. "It's a dud," someone mutters, voicing the anxiety of us all—and then the quick flash, the faintly audible thud of the explosion, a chorus of hurrahs in the cabin. Already we have frightened them below. Away goes the second, an incendiary bomb, thrown out by hand, a pin being removed to activate its percussion cap. Suddenly the searchlights come alive, right, left and all about us, stabbing the night, reaching after us like the legs of gigantic spiders. Soon the gleaming hull of the airships lies athwart two dazzling rays of light and others are converging toward us. . . . It is difficult to explain how we manage to survive the shrieking tempest of shells and shrapnel, for according to the chronometer we have spent a good hour in the unabating barrage. . . . When London is far behind us, we can still recognize it plainly, a gorgeous arch of firelight flickering in the sky above the city, and the searchlight beams still playing back and forth, crossing and re-crossing each other, more than sixty of them still searching for the bird that has flown. Silence closes in around us, and the landscape beneath, bathed a yellowish green by the moon, seems barren of all life.[4]

On districts from Shoreditch to Leytonstone, the LZ-38 had sown its death seeds, then to turn homeward unscathed. Although in his official report Linnarz said solemnly that he had attacked only London docks and military establishments, it was impossible in the darkness, from seven thousand feet, with the crude bombsight at his disposal—merely a cross-haired telescope fixed to swivel on a calibrated fulcrum—even to approximate where his bombs would hit. Actually, they killed seven persons, injured thirty-five more, and did about a hundred thousand dollars' worth of damage to houses and business premises. Londoners, however, did not panic.

On the afternoon preceding the raid, Winston Churchill was at Hendon airfield, looking over a new Sopwith naval biplane. The pilot, Lieutenant Ben Travers, showed Churchill the rifle he had been issued for shooting down zeppelins, saying confidentially, "It's got incendiary bullets, sir." The First Lord of the Admiralty smiled and nodded as though that made the big dif-ference. Zeppelins had been much on his mind lately, and he knew too well that the rifle and the underpowered Sopwith epitomized the utter inadequacy of England's defenses against aerial attack. The Sopwith did not even get air-borne until the LZ-38 had emptied its bomb bay and made off—and then the plane crashed with a stalled engine. Travers was found staggering in the darkness, knocked half silly. His gunner, Lieutenant Douglas Barnes, lay in the wreckage, dead.

Captain Linnarz became an overnight celebrity in Germany, he and each member of his crew receiving the Iron Cross. The raid on London temporarily satisfied the popular demand for retaliation against the British public on ac-count of the "hunger blockade." The German press effervesced with fustian praise of the exploit. The Leipzig *Neueste Nachrichten* declaimed:

England no longer an island! London, the heart which pumps lifeblood into the arteries of the degenerate huckster nation, has been mauled and mutilated with bombs by brave German fighting men in German airships. . . . At last, the long yearned-for punish-

[4] Dudley: *op. cit.*

ment has befallen England, this people of liars, cynics and hypocrites, a punishment for the countless sins of ages past. It is neither
blind hatred nor raging anger that inspires our airship heroes, but a
religious humility at being chosen the instrument of God's wrath.
In that moment when they saw London being consumed in smoke
and flame, just as Sodom was burned by fire from heaven to requite
the wickedness of its people, they lived through a thousand lives
of an immeasurable joy which all who remain at home must envy.[5]

Among the most envious of Linnarz and his army crew was the Imperial
navy. Strasser was livid with jealousy; upon hearing the news, he paced his
office for hours, wringing his hands behind his back. That very next night—
by no sheer coincidence—a Captain Hirsch in Zeppelin L-10 from Nordholz
tried to emulate Linnarz's feat but succeeded only in bombing Sittingbourne
and Gravesend, which he thought was Harwich, with poor results.

A lone aircraft, a Short S-81 seaplane piloted by Flight Leader W. P. de
Courcy Ireland of the R.N.A.S., was sent up to intercept the L-10. Ireland
realistically expected no success, and he had none, although simply lifting his
particular plane off the water in the dark was a creditable performance. Not
the greatest flying machine in the annals of naval aviation, the S-81 was
optimistically called a Gun Carrier; however, the semi-automatic Vickers gun
with which it was experimentally armed in 1913 had proved too cumbersome
and had long since been scrapped. With its clumsy pontoons, its graceless
configuration, and its inadequate powerplant, the two-seater could only carry
the pilot, its rear cockpit remaining always vacant. It also had a disconcerting
tendency to sling oil in the pilot's face at the most critical moments in the air.
This, in fact, was one of the rare occasions when Ireland, flying with a pair
of sixteen-pound Hale bombs on his lap, managed a decent takeoff. He saw
nothing of the L-10; even had he spotted the zeppelin, he was mystified as to
what he could do about it. Merely getting back to base alive was triumph
enough.

After the initial raid on Norfolk in January, the few guns dotted about
eastern England and the few available R.N.A.S. planes allotted to the air
defense—which operated from coastal stations and from airdromes around
the periphery of cities—did what they could to interfere with the ever more
enterprising zeppelins. As for the "wall of coastal batteries" which worried
Linnarz, it did not exist except as a series of isolated emplacements, interspersed with long stretches of unguarded shoreline. Immediately following the
London raid the ground defenses of the capital and its easterly approaches
were increased, and some second-grade corvettes and light cruisers based on
the Humber were fitted with antiaircraft guns with which to shoot at any
zeppelins seen coursing over the North Sea en route to or from England. The

[5] Poolman: op. cit.

guns then in use, however, especially when fired from heaving decks at sea, were of very limited performance.

The airmen of the R.N.A.S., in their lumbering, unstable, and deficiently armed machines, found the hitherto untried business of night flying difficult and treacherous. Through the summer of 1915, nocturnal patrols were continually flown, since enemy dirigibles were reported lurking in the offshore mists. Bacton and Great Yarmouth afforded the only bases fully equipped, although auxiliary fields were established up and down the coast for emergency landings. With the stamina and talents of the men strained and the capabilities of their frail machines overtaxed, the pilots were frequently killed in crashes or simply disappeared in the all-pervading blackness. Seldom did they even sight a zeppelin. The few times they did see one, the pilots were almost always unable to attack, for the airship commanders had learned to stay at altitudes that provided virtual impunity.

A subject of constant debate in the pilots' mess concerned the best part of a dirigible's anatomy at which to aim when ramming it, this being considered the surest method of attack. It was believed that the only other way for an airplane to destroy an airship was to bomb it. A curious misconception was prevalent as to the defensive strength of the German dirigibles. It was thought that each zeppelin was protected against fire by a layer of nonflammable, inert gas. Aside from however many bombs they could carry without overburdening their planes, the pilots' antizeppelin weapons consisted of a rifle fitted to launch grenades, a shotgun firing chain shot, or a Very pistol with two rounds of rocket ammunition—such ordnance being rated as hardly better than useless. Another device was exhaustively tested, the Rankin dart, a somewhat fantastic brainchild of the naval engineer, Commander Frederick Rankin. This was a hollow tin cylinder, the size of a candle, one end a needle-form steel head and the other a lid through which was inserted a spindle coupled with a barb-shaped vane. The tube was loaded with incendiary composition, this to be kindled by a friction match attached to the spindle. When it struck a zeppelin, the dart was supposed to pierce the envelope, whereupon the barb would grab hold and yank the match along a strip of emery board, thus setting off the chemical charge and igniting the cloth integument of the zeppelin. Since to fling the dart with any remote hope of accuracy a pilot would have to fly perilously close to a dirigible, the quaintly diabolical gadget never got past the experimental stage.

Many traditionalists in the British navy winced at the thought of the senior service being called upon to play nursemaid to civilians, but Winston Churchill was running things, and he had a staunch right arm in the person of Lord John Fisher, the earnestly respected and well-liked ex-chief of the Admiralty whom Churchill had reclaimed from retirement at the age of seventy-four. Choosing Lord Fisher as his second in command was a wise move by Churchill. He knew himself to be an incisive thinker, a born decision

maker, loquacious and ingratiating when he wished to be, but he was relatively young and a bit too petulant in spite of himself, which detracted from
the image of authority he sought. More than that, he was brashly intolerant
of the usually slow administrative processes, the myriad details and red tape
of bureaucratic routine, and there were those who complained that he cared
too little for the regular way of doing things. Where Churchill was criticized,
everyone admired Lord Fisher. Years before the war he had warned that for
England's safety the German fleet should be "Copenhagened" (destroyed, as
Admiral Horatio Nelson had destroyed the Danish fleet at Copenhagen in
1801). He had much the same disarming warmth and glib humor as
Churchill, yet also the wealth of experience, the calm judgment and diplomacy
that Churchill then lacked, these shortcomings obscuring his true budding
greatness.

Unhappily, their association was not longlived. Later that spring, a difference of opinion between them over the ill-fated Dardanelles campaign resulted
in disharmony at the Admiralty. Arthur Balfour was appointed First Lord,
and Churchill resigned in the autumn to command the Sixth Royal Scots
Fusiliers in Belgium. But while accord lasted, they made a rather wonderful
and formidable team, Churchill and Fisher, the swashbuckling newcomer and
the temperate, wise old owl. They functioned almost as a unity, each com-
plementing the other, their personalities meshing as two pieces of a jigsaw
puzzle. Churchill preferred to work late at night, whereas Fisher was at his
desk in the very early morning, sometimes before daybreak. He would arrive
in his office to find the ink barely dry on dozens of Churchill memoranda;
he would depart punctually an hour before teatime and leave a sheaf of notes
for Churchill, each initialed with the bold cursive "F" familiar to old-timers
in the Admiralty. If Fisher agreed with Churchill that it was necessary to
divert ships and planes for the unaccustomed duty of warding off zeppelins,
not even the most hidebound traditionalists dared protest too vigorously. And
so a handful of naval aircraft, such as they were, and a squadron of tired
surface vessels joined the home defense.

On Sunday, June 6, less than a week after his sensational venture against
London, Captain Linnarz set out again to raid the British capital. This time
the LZ-38 was not alone, for somewhere over Bruges, shortly before dusk, it
rendezvoused with two sister zeppelins, the LZ-37 and the LZ-39. The "tree
frogs"—as the meteorological experts were called, scampering up tall poles as
they did to make their observations—had forecast that a low fog would
materialize at sea after nightfall. That Sunday had been unseasonably hot and
muggy across northern Europe, the thermometer zooming up to ninety degrees
around noon, but toward evening a brisk cold front advanced from the west
and caused a rapid condensation in the heavy, humid atmosphere. In London
they had sweltered all day; now they shivered in the sudden cold snap and

cursed the vagaries of spring weather. Forgetting the impending coal shortage of which they had been warned, they lit stoves and fireplaces against the chill. In his pulpit that afternoon the Bishop of London worked a comforting bromide into his sermon. "When the people of London speak of the danger of zeppelin raids," he declaimed, "they should thank God that they are allowed to have a bit of danger. We do not want to leave all the danger to the boys in the firing line." Such platitudes were of less cheer on a cold night, however, than a crackling good fire in the hearth.

Reaching the twin lights at Ostend and Steenbrugge, and making due west between them to fix their bearing on the Thames, the German airmen could see the predicted mist curling inshore across the strand below and wreathing the dunes with slithering filaments of wispy vapor, reminding Linnarz, he said, of muslin palls. As the three zeppelins proceeded farther to seaward, the mist coagulated about them and reduced their visibility almost to nil. They were cautiously cruising above the Strait of Dover when their wireless receivers began rhythmically clacking. Base was radioing instructions to them: "Terminal weather unsuitable. Cancel primary mission. At your discretion, strike alternate target." Their original intention frustrated, they turned southwestward on a course to Calais, to disgorge their bombs over an important rail junction behind the British front. Shortly after midnight, the wraithlike trio headed over the sea again for home.

At about ten o'clock that night a barrister named Russel Clarke, an amateur radio enthusiast living on the Norfolk coast, picked up some unfamiliar signals on his homemade shortwave receiver. Guessing it might be the Hun, he telephoned the Admiralty, where the mysterious dots and dashes were promptly tuned in and monitored. Not until half an hour later did the navy's expensive listening station at Hunstanton, with its sophisticated equipment and government-trained operators, ring up the Admiralty to report the enemy transmissions. The movements of the zeppelins were plotted there in Whitehall and then relayed direct to Wing Commander Arthur Longmore, the R.N.A.S. officer in charge at Dunkirk. The plan was to catch the zeppelins off guard, at relatively low altitude, as they descended toward their base.

The navy then had eleven aircraft assigned to Dunkirk operations: five Avros, a Bristol, one Vickers, two Farmans, and two Morane-Saulnier Parasols. Longmore, who later served as an air chief marshal in World War II, had brought his little flying group from Dover to Dunkirk in February, part of its assignment being to contend with the Belgium-based zeppelins. In his thirties himself, his pilots were much younger and generally a temerarious lot. Just four days before this, dressed in an extraordinary assortment of naval tunics, they were photographed smiling beside their planes. Now, at quarter to one in the morning, Monday, June 7, Longmore was notified that the three zeppelins were nearing attack range. He sent off Lieutenants Alexander Warneford and John Rose in the Morane-Saulniers to intercept in the vicinity of Ghent, and Lieutenants John P. Wilson and John S. Mills in their weight-carrying Farmans to bomb the dirigible sheds on the outskirts of Brussels, in Évère. Longmore's hope was to catch one or more in the air, or failing that, to hit them on the ground after they landed.

Flying wing to wing, Warneford and Rose had not gone far when the latter encountered trouble. The lamp on his instrument panel went out and he made a forced landing in a flax field near Cassel, unhurt but with his machine resting upside down above him. Alone now, Warneford sped on toward his quarry in his little monoplane. It was scarcely a week old, its elegant if somewhat unwarlike red-and-gray paint still smelling factory-sweet. Warneford had improvised a rack beneath the fuselage so that he could release his bombs by pulling a cable that protruded up through the cockpit floor. Prior to take-off he had loaded six twenty-pounders into the rack.

About ten minutes after seeing Rose's distress sign and losing sight of him in the mist, Warneford entered the range of two German antiaircraft guns known as Archibald and Cuthbert. Guarding the zeppelin lanes, they were high-velocity cannon, hurling shrapnel shells as high as 22,000 feet. But in the foggy darkness, firing at the sound of his engine, their aim was nowhere near him. The Morane-Saulnier's engine was so noisy that Warneford had no hope of hearing the zeppelins, which, in any case, often drifted with throttles shut down. He had to rely on sighting his prey, and the odds on a night such as this were heavily against that kind of luck. He was thinking this glum thought when, a few miles west of Ostend, to his incredulous delight, he saw the LZ-37 nosing downward across the coast. He kept the long, smooth, slender gray shape in view for most of the forty-five minutes he spent overtaking it. A gusty headwind had set in, dismembering the thick tendrils of fog into sparsely scattered pockets. Above, silhouetted by a crescent moon, patches of cloud were pasted to the indigo firmament like cardboard cutouts. As he closed the gap to about a quarter mile, Warneford could see the LZ-37 joggle in the wind while lowering toward its lair at Gontrode.

Warneford's presence was detected by the topside gunner, who opened fire without waiting for the command to do so. The LZ-37's master officer, Lieutenant Rudolf von der Haegen, began whistling frantically through the speaking tube, demanding to know why there was shooting. The answer came back: "Airplane, three hundred meters astern." The gun above the hull and the two mounted in the rear gondola, all capable of being swept through a wide arc, obliged Warneford to keep his distance. Aware of the zeppelin's vastly superior rate of climb, he was careful to avoid any move that might provoke it into a sudden leap skyward. He dropped back, staying just beyond effective range of the German machine guns, which soon ceased their lethal chattering.

A nerve-wracking game of patience ensued, Warneford warily stalking the zeppelin and awaiting his chance, and Haegen hoping to lure him within shot of the German ground batteries. The monotonous drone of engines was all that could be heard as the desperate contest continued. For forty minutes it remained a standoff. Then, for a reason that will never be ascertained, Haegen put down his bow and began to flee for Gontrode.

Here was Warneford's break. A straight and level course would bring him over the downward slanting dirigible, now plainly visible ahead, the sheen of moonlight playing upon its silvered skin. Reaching a point eight to nine hundred feet directly above it, and cutting his motive power, he glided toward the LZ-37 in a tight descending spiral. "I volplaned to within 150 feet of the monster," he wrote, "and released six bombs. The sixth struck the envelope of the ship fair and square in the middle. There was an awful explosion. . . ."

Warneford saw the LZ-37 engulfed in a tremendous ball of orange flame. The sonic shock tossed his little Morane-Saulnier more than two hundred feet higher in the air, flipping it upside down. Dazed for a moment, he recovered control and circled the fire-lit arena, watching with fascination the monster dying below him, "its pieces ablaze, strange and terrible torches . . . hundreds of them floating lazily to earth. I later learned that the glow could be seen as far away as the front-line trenches."

A fiery comet, the forward section of the zeppelin plunged three thousand feet into a dormitory of the Convent of St. Elizabeth in Mont-Saint-Amand, a suburb of Ghent. The gondola tore loose, crashing through the roof. The building caught fire. Two nuns and two orphan children were killed and many others injured. The LZ-37's sole survivor was the coxswain, a man named Roemer, who was thrown unconscious from the gondola onto a bed which only seconds before had been occupied by a sleeping nun. He was courageously rescued by the sisters. Quoted in a postwar magazine article, he described his ordeal thus:

> I felt a hit. The ship lurched and began to quake, and my helm spun wildly. It found no more resistance, a sign that our steering system had become useless. The gondola was swaying so violently that I lost my footing. I went skidding across the deck. My head glanced against a metal upright and I was momentarily stunned. By the time my wits returned, there was nobody in the gondola but me. Everyone else had either jumped or had been pitched overboard. . . . The whole ship above me was a roaring, hissing inferno. Instinctively, I pressed myself flat to the deck and began clawing at the rails, trying to elude the tongues of flame licking down at me. The heat was unbearable. I was being roasted alive. I wondered how long it would take to fall three thousand feet. It seemed an eternity in hell. I knew the end was close at hand, but I actually welcomed the oncoming collision as preferable to the slow torture of incineration. At last the gondola slammed into something. I was

vaguely aware of the crash. I felt myself somersaulting through the air just before I blacked out. When I regained consciousness, I was in the hospital, swaddled from head to toe in bandages. The pain was excruciating. The flesh of my arms, legs and torso was frightfully singed. I still carry the hideous scars. They remind me daily to praise Christ for my deliverance.

The lurid effusion of light that filled the sky above Mont-Saint-Amand was seen by Warneford's squadron mates, Lieutenants Wilson and Mills, as they arrived over the big zeppelin shed at Évère, thirty miles southeast of Mont-Saint-Amand. In their sluggish Farmans they had been scouring the airship routes all this time in the hope of ambushing the LZ-38 at low altitude. Having seen nothing of their prey, they had barely enough petrol left to bomb the shed and get back to Dunkirk. A pleasant surprise greeted them as they came over the target—the LZ-38 had already put in and was just being handled into the shed. As he maneuvered for his bombing run, Wilson was caught by searchlights. Thinking fast, he pointed his flashlight at the ground and blinked it on and off as if signaling that he meant to land. Those below obligingly withheld their fire, affording him plenty of time for carefully aiming and dropping his explosives. He was followed by Mills, who let go his load before the stupified German gunners had sufficiently recovered their composure to start shooting. The pair of them got clean away, leaving in their wake an alp of rampant flame. The shed and the LZ-38 were both reduced to ruin, Linnarz and his crew escaping by the merest margin.

Wilson and Mills were back at Dunkirk several hours before Warneford showed up—minus his plane. Warneford had found it necessary to set down behind enemy lines to mend a leaky fuel hose coupling that no doubt had been knocked loose by the jarring blast of the bomb-stricken LZ-37. Makeshift repairs were the best he could do, and when he took off again, his engine kept sputtering, threatening to give out at any instant. Preoccupied with this problem, he strayed off course. In the deceptive half-light between darkness and dawn, he was then unable to find a clue to his whereabouts. He headed for the coast, where map reading was simplified by the well-defined contour of the beach and its unmistakable landmarks. He met the sea at Cap Griz Nez, having flown thirty-five miles too far west of Dunkirk. Just then, as he banked his plane toward base, his engine quit. He came down on a wide flat which the ebbing tide had left exposed.

Despite a rough landing—the wet sand impeding his wheels, causing the undercarriage to collapse—Warneford was unhurt. When he did get back to his squadron, it was almost noon and a fine, sunny morning, and he was met with great cheers from his fellow pilots. Wilson and Mills, having detoured on their return flight to investigate the great glow of fire over Mont Saint-Amand, had brought back word of Warneford's success as well as their own. Commander Longmore had already notified Whitehall, where no time was wasted in informing the press of these glad tidings. Thirty-six hours later, Warneford received a communication from Buckingham Palace: "I most heartily congratulate you upon your splendid achievement of yesterday, in which you singlehanded destroyed an enemy airship. I have much pleasure in conferring upon you the Victoria Cross for this gallant act. George. R.I."

Warneford's thrilling story graced front pages everywhere in the Allied world, relieving the dreary grimness of the other war news. He was the "zeppelin destroyer," the first aviator ever to conquer a dirigible in air-to-air combat. France, which had also been in the grips of a zeppelin phobia, instated him as a knight of the Legion d'Honneur. His picture began to appear on postcards and cigarette cards a couple of weeks later, but by a cruel fate Warneford was cheated of the chance ever to see these popular tributes.

A few days after his epic victory, Warneford was sent to Paris by Commander Longmore to take delivery of a Farman biplane on behalf of the R.N.A.S. Paris was Elysium for a triumphant hero, and Warneford was heaped with its heady delectations. He was the lion of the town, and he loved it. Elinor Glyn, the well-known novelist, notorious for her amorous escapades, appointed herself his escort. He was mobbed, she wrote, by "beautiful, expensively gowned women in silver-fox capes, where both the beau monde and demi-monde congregate." Backstage at the Folies Bergère, a *danseuse* garlanded him with flowers. The Ritz refused payment for his luxurious suite and arranged a fancy dinner banquet in his honor. Called upon to propose a toast, Warneford did so in his faltering handbook French: "Vive la France! Vivent les Allies et à bas les Boches!" In a short speech, he revealed that he had no plans to go home on leave. He was unaware of it, but a gala welcome was in fact being prepared for him in London; his furlough papers, drawn up at the Admiralty's behest, were already awaiting him on Longmore's desk.

After three hectic days and nights Warneford wearily reported to the aviation depot to test-fly the Farman he had been assigned to ferry to Dunkirk. Accompanying him was the American correspondent Henry Needham, whom Warneford had promised to take for a ride. Longmore had admonished him to remember that a Farman was not a Morane-Saulnier and to handle the bigger, clumsier machine with restraint. He had risen only seven hundred feet and was still climbing hard when he attempted a steep crosswind turn. The Farman stalled off into a rapid spin before Warneford could muster his muddled senses. Neither pilot nor passenger had bothered to strap himself in, and both were thrown out and killed. Warneford's body made a dent twelve inches deep in a green cornfield; the Cross of the Legion of Honor, which he had worn since it was awarded to him, was driven through his jacket into his rib cage.

The loss of the LZ-37 and LZ-38 put a stop, temporarily at least, to the German army's zeppelin raids, and Strasser, still building a naval air fleet for his projected destruction of London, had done little more than probe the British home defenses. Strasser permitted only men of the highest caliber to serve aboard his airships. Volunteers all, they had to evidence, Strasser specified:

> A keen love of flying, a deep devotion to duty, will power, self-control, and the mental alertness to form proper decisions quickly; good eyesight, physical dexterity, and sound general health, especially heart and nerves; no tendency to dizziness or seasickness; a well-coordinated sense of direction; an appreciation of the basic principles of warfare; an understanding of tactical and strategical conditions; familiarity with the science of ballistics and a practical skill at gunnery; the ability to operate an aerial camera and interpret the resultant photographs; a working knowledge of internal-combustion engines, meteorology, telephony, wireless telegraphy, signaling lamps, and the use of carrier pigeons.[6]

Strasser prized his crewmen as the elite of the German navy—not without justification—and he frequently lectured them on their "sacred obligation, the demolishment of London." He exhorted them that they must be prepared to "make the supreme sacrifice for the Fatherland, which is the crowning glory for any loyal son of Germany." He gave them periodic pep talks that usually consisted in part of a derogatory appraisal of army zeppelin procedures. Seldom, for example, did he neglect to point out that army crews brought along parachutes instead of additional bombs, implying this to be cowardly. "A crew of twenty-three taking parachutes weighing thirty pounds each," he troubled to compute aloud, "amounts to 690 pounds, which is a considerable quantity of ammunition to leave behind." Parachutes were verboten on naval zeppelins, and Strasser was proud to be the author of the ruling. He never discussed, however, the vials of poison distributed to his crews as a means, the instructions said, "of instant, merciful death in the event you are trapped by fire and no other escape is available."

Strasser had the kind of men he needed, but not yet the dirigibles. Through June and July, therefore, he carried out no more raids against England but rehearsed his crews intensively and acquired nine new zeppelins of improved design, the first of which was the L-11. These ships were the equal of the army's in every respect. With 1,126,000 cubic feet of gas capacity and a gross lift of 36.4 tons, including extra machine guns and an increased bomb load, their static ceiling surpassed thirteen thousand feet. Four Maybach engines produced an airspeed of sixty-one miles per hour. Strasser also acquired a

[6] Dudley: *op. cit.* The author's debt to Mr. Dudley's enthralling book is gratefully acknowledged.

couple of the Schutte-Lanz type which—perhaps in consequence of his close personal ties with Dr. Eckener and Count Zeppelin—he disparaged as the decidedly inferior make and utilized mainly for coastal patrol.

August 9, 1915, was the date Strasser set for his first major blow against London. The indefatigable airship leader went along himself on the raid aboard the L-11, which was commanded by the veteran Captain Buttlar. It and three sister vessels were to give their attention to London, while the L-19 and L-10—older models of shorter range—were to strike optional targets along the northeast coast, preferably in the industrial centers of the Humber and Tyne.

Fastidiously planned and initiated with exuberant optimism, the ambitious venture wound up an abysmal fiasco. As for the L-9 and L-10, they did nothing better than scare a few dozen families who had rented isolated vacation cottages here and there on the Norfolk seaside. None of the raiders bound for London got near the city. The L-13, Captain Mathy's new ship, had to make about with engine trouble before England was even sighted. The remaining trio became separated and thoroughly confused. The unseasoned skipper of the L-14, one Lieutenant Wenke, loosed his bomb cargo harmlessly over some Kentish grassland. Buttlar wandered too far north in search of Harwich, the naval base there having been picked by Strasser as the alternate objective. Buttlar, attacking Lowestoft in mistake for Harwich, accomplished no material damage. Captain Peterson, in the L-12, likewise thought he had located Harwich when it was really Dover, far away to the south. Hit by antiaircraft fire, he scattered his missiles aimlessly—or rather jettisoned them in order to preserve altitude. He tried to reach Belgium, his ship crippled, bleeding hydrogen as it went. A few miles off Zeebrugge, the L-12 splashed gently into the sea.

Meanwhile, one of the R.N.A.S. pilots at Dunkirk, Lieutenant J. R. Smyth-Pigott, had taken to the air in his Avro to assail the L-12 with the two twenty-pound Hale bombs and six hand-grenades he contrived to stow in his cramped cockpit. Shortly after eight o'clock in the morning, he found the zeppelin awash, resembling more than anything else an overgrown whale dozing in the summer sun. Racing toward the stranded dirigible, a German torpedo boat opened fire at the British plane, as did the nearby Ostend batteries. Smyth-Pigott, seeing the L-12 was already a goner, elected to return straight to base with the news. Moments after he departed the scene, three other planes of the Dunkirk squadron happened to arrive and attempted to sink the prostrate leviathan. In the attempt, Lieutenant D. K. Johnston was shot down dead; his two wing mates, their ammunition spent in futility, had no choice but to head for home. By a remarkable providence, not a single casualty had been suffered aboard the L-12. It was towed by the torpedo boat to Ostend and subsequently dismantled for salvage.

Twice again that month, Strasser was foiled in determined efforts to blast London. Wenke, on August 17, came close to success when he managed to reach the easternmost part of the city and dropped sixty bombs. He claimed in his action report to have caused "the collapse of buildings and the outburst of flames from great fires . . . between Blackfriars and London bridge." Strasser read the report and was impressed that here was a promising young airship commander, but Wenke had either deliberately lied to enhance his own reputation or else had mistaken some local reservoirs for the Thames. Whichever the case, except for a pumping station at one of the storage basins, nothing of importance was hit—nor anybody killed or injured—by Wenke's bombardment.

If Wenke did falsify his report, it availed him nothing tangible in the meager few days of life that were left to him. Hardly three weeks later, on September 3, while bringing the L-10 down to its berth at Nordholz after substituting for that ship's regular skipper on a routine reconnaissance, Wenke and the entire crew perished in a mysterious explosion. The L-10 blew itself to smithereens as Strasser stood watching from the officer's club terrace. The disaster remained disturbingly unaccountable until Strasser pieced together an explanation. In its flight the zeppelin had been exposed to the hot sun for several hours, and Strasser recalled how, just before its descent, it had risen slightly. Some hydrogen had apparently been released to ease the excess pressure of the heat-expanded gas. Strasser had noticed a small tuft of cumulus near the zeppelin. The cloud must have been charged with electricity, he surmised, which had touched off the explosive gas and air mixture. To prevent the repetition of such an accident, Strasser cautioned his commanders not to discharge hydrogen in the vicinity of clouds. He also told them to switch off the radio and all other unessential electrical appliances as a routine landing procedure. A few months before this Strasser had made it mandatory for his crews to wear rubber-soled boots. This, too, had been an insurance against fire, since Strasser realized that the nails in ordinary footwear might strike a detonating spark against the metal decks or framework of a ship.

The zeppelin raids against England were stepped up in September by the German army and navy alike. Envious of the praise that the rival service was reaping in the press and sensible of the public demand for intensifying the attacks on London and other British cities, the army got back into the action on September 7, when the LZ-77 and LZ-74, a matched pair of newly commissioned ships commanded respectively by Captain Horn and a Captain George, together with the Schutte-Lanz SL-2, commanded by a Captain Wobeser, flew north to south across London and emptied their bomb bays with astonishing ineffectiveness. The total damage was a ladies' dress shop on Fenchurch Street. The SL-2 spilled the last of its load on the Isle of Dogs before retiring to crash on arrival at the Berchem-Sainte-Agatha sheds in Belgium.

The next afternoon, fearing again for the navy's precedence in airship operations, Strasser hurriedly sent three zeppelins to strike London. Only Captain Mathy in the L-13 reached the capital. Raining down fifteen high-explosive and fifty-odd incendiary bombs, he left a swath of awful destruction in his wake. Besides flawing Cleopatra's Needle with shrapnel scars, Mathy caused thirty-five civilians to die, another thirty-seven to be seriously injured, and he reduced to ashes and rubble more than $2,500,000 worth of property— about one-fourth the aggregate damage suffered by the city during the entirety of World War I!

Heinrich Mathy, already a minor hero in Germany, became the focal figure of impassioned national acclaim upon news of his latest success, the greatest yet achieved on a zeppelin sortie. A Mannheimer by birth, thirty-two years of age, brown-eyed, lean and ramrod straight, an inch or two taller than the norm, his short-beaked naval cap squared smartly on his close-cropped head, Mathy had received his commission in 1902. He had volunteered for lighter-than-air ships a year before the war and had cut his teeth aboard the erstwhile L-1 and L-2. He already had more than a hundred aerial voyages behind him when he first set out against England. Admired by his superiors, adored by the men who served under him, Mathy was an exemplary dirigible captain, iron nerved, resourceful, calculating, and ready to risk all when the stakes warranted. He was praised often and warmly by Count Zeppelin himself.

On the morning of September 9, upon his return to Nordholz after his telling assault on London, Mathy appended a disturbing note to his otherwise cheerful report to Strasser. "In future, with clear skies and a bright moon," he advised, "zeppelins will be able to stay only a short while above London, and it will be difficult to single out special targets." [7] He rested his conclusion on the discovery that London's defenses had been substantially stiffened, more so and sooner than German intelligence had foreseen, several fragmentation shells having burst too close to the L-13 for comfort. Mathy opined further that the poor results of the preceding night's raid by the army were attributable to this fact. He conjectured that "heavy ground fire had forced the army zeppelins to fly too high and maybe to so rush their bomb-aiming that precision was lost." Increased British resistance had not dulled Mathy's appetite for action, however, for that same day he bragged to Karl von Wiegand, the Berlin correspondent of *The New York Times,* that he would bomb London three times successively or "die in the attempt."

Four nights later he was airborne again, searching for London and striving to hold his course in a gale-whipped rainstorm. Despite his best efforts, the L-13 was blown northward over Harwich. Unsure of his exact whereabouts, Mathy was surprised by a sudden salvo from below, one shell ripping through two gas cells. Dumping his bombs and whatever else could be spared, he tilted

[7] Dudley: *op. cit.*

the zeppelin's nose and climbed away to seaward. Landing in Belgium, his ship scraped the ground and was still further damaged. During the five days it took to restore the L-13 to servicable condition, Mathy was nagged by the memory of his fatuous boast to Wiegand. Fortunately, he had not suffered the penalty which he had himself stipulated for failure—namely, death—but it had been a narrow enough squeak to teach him the wisdom of humility, or so he stated in a letter he mailed to his father in Mannheim.

CHAPTER XV

❦ *Captain Strasser's Crusade* ❧

SUMMER 1915 WAS DRAWING near its end, and, after eight months of air raids, nothing of any real military or political advantage had been accomplished by the zeppelins. The wholesale panic that the Germans had anticipated among the people of England never materialized. A few incidental outbreaks of distemper had occurred during and immediately in the aftermath of the earlier raids—some bricks were hurled through windows of shops bearing German-sounding names, for instance, and an elderly widower walking his pet dachshund was on that account insulted as a "Hun lover" and badly beaten—but nothing like pandemonium had ensued in London or elsewhere. Auguring further frustrations for the German airship fleet was the ever-increasing capability of the British home defense, particularly in and around London.

Taking over in Churchill's stead as First Lord of the Admiralty, Arthur Balfour had assigned the job of handling London's antiaircraft defenses to Admiral Sir Percy Scott, a crusty, tough-minded, self-starting dynamo of a man whose gunnery experience was probably the widest in the Royal navy. Scott's appointment reflected the Admiralty's faith in the gun as the effective antidote to the zeppelin, and he expeditiously formulated his project for an augmented, well-armed, and better-organized defense force. He moved swiftly and directly, hewing away a great pile of dead wood and letting the chips fall where they may. Recruiting personnel to be trained and overseen by naval specialists, charting new sites for gun emplacements and searchlight stations, unraveling knots in his lines of communication, instituting discipline and cultivating an *esprit de corps* where lacking, he not only enlarged and suitably equipped the force but altered its complexion radically. Scott, indeed, soon began to irritate the First Lord by his almost abusive enthusiasm. It was not

371

long before he wrote to Balfour, threatening to resign unless given a free hand in getting what he wanted. Denigrating the pom-pom gun as useless and dangerous, he submitted a detailed proposal for new batteries which would require an additional 104 high-angle fixed cannon and at least fifty more searchlights. He induced Balfour to sequester this matériel from the fleet arsenal, which, he insisted, contained a surplus of smaller caliber guns.

Scott appreciated the need for a self-propelled gun capable of firing a high-power shrapnel shell, and he heard of one the French had been using with good results. Accordingly, he sent an aide, Lieutenant Commander A. Rawlinson, to Paris with orders to bring back a sample of the latest such gun in production. In early September, after a two-week stay in France, Rawlinson returned with a long-barreled 75-mm piece mounted on a motorized bed. This gun, called the French Automobile Cannon and manned in London by ratings from the armored-car squadrons that Scott disbanded, was the nucleus of the antiaircraft mobile section that was formed under Rawlinson's charge. It was this gun that almost hit the L-13 during the night of September 8, and so convinced Captain Mathy that subsequent sorties over the capital would be met with harsher opposition. Through the remainder of 1915, Rawlinson's guns played a busy part in helping to repel German dirigibles. By the year's end six similar cannon—manufactured by the Vickers company and mounted upon Lancia truck chassis—were in use, along with several mobile searchlights. Upon receipt of a raid warning, the guns, with their caissons in tow, rolled to pre-allotted positions about the city; when it was found which neighborhood was being bombed, they converged on that area posthaste.

Although setting great store by his gun crews, Scott quickly recognized the potential worth of the airplane. He urged that night flying by the R.N.A.S. on the east coast should be taken more seriously in hand, and that special planes should be developed for antizeppelin warfare. Airplanes, he said, when their design had been enough advanced, were going to be "the zeppelin's worst enemy." They would, in the future, figure more prominently in the protection of London than people thought. Citing past airplane attacks on the zeppelin sheds in Belgium, and the memorable foray against the Friedrichshafen works, and recalling Lieutenant Warneford's victory over the LZ-38, Scott theorized that the defense of London by aircraft began on the continent and that the defense by gunfire as well as aircraft commenced at the British coast. "We," he said, meaning his metropolitan guard, "are, so to speak, in the last ditch."

Scott maintained that a coastal barricade of guns and planes was needed to turn back any attempted aerial attack. But he held the prudent view that although no zeppelin should ever be allowed to reach London, there should be sufficient guns in and around the capital to "hit anything bigger than a sea gull at seven thousand feet." In his thoroughness, detailing every available factor of air-raid prevention, he even disinterred for re-evaluation an earlier plan for cordoning the eastern shoreline with giant kite balloons and stretching from one to the next a vertical net, many miles long, the object being to entoil low-flying zeppelins.

At Scott's plea, thirty airplanes were reserved to the London area for the specific purpose of securing the city against surprise attack. Borrowing an idea from the Paris defense, he inaugurated the practice of dusk-to-dawn patrols above London. Except in adverse weather, at least four planes were flown above the capital at any given hour of darkness. Scott also saw to it that the R.N.A.S. increased the number of planes patrolling the coast each night. Only this—the rather sizable levy of men, guns, aircraft, warships, munitions, and other supplies required to shield the British Isles against zeppelins—justified to some extent the enormous expense and risk incurred by the Germans.

Strasser and Scott became distal antagonists, fencers as it were, the one lunging with his zeppelins, the other parrying with his guns. On October 13, Strasser attacked, sending five dirigibles against London. The program worked out by Strasser, who accompanied Peterson in the L-16, was for a three-pronged assault, Mathy and Boecker plotting their courses so that the former crossed the city from the southwest, the latter from southeast, while the remaining trio traveled due west together along the Thames. Strasser's plan looked very neat on paper, but in execution it became something else again. Running through sporadic clumps of fog, the three zeppelins in formation were soon separated from one another. Peterson got no farther than Hertford before dropping his bombs on what both he and Strasser were positive was London. Buttlar, in the L-11, strayed far to the north and bombed some villages around Norwich. Mathy got lost between St. Albans and Guildford, but sorted himself out in time to bring the L-13 over Woolwich, on the easternmost edge of London; believing himself to be above the Victoria docks, he expended four bombs and twenty-eight incendiaries, which did little property damage, although one person was killed and twelve injured. Because of the fog, Mathy twice almost collided with the L-14, Boecker's ship, the two of them on intersecting courses. Boecker, an unusually candid fellow, later admitted that he was not sure where his bombs had been dropped. In fact, they had come down innocuously on some country estates near the suburban town of Bromley.

One zeppelin alone found the heart of London that night, the L-15, commanded by Captain Joachim Breithaupt, a handsome, yellow-haired, thirty-three-year-old hero who had received the Iron Cross. At about half-past ten he maundered over Waterloo bridge and from eleven thousand feet aimed his first parcel of explosives at the Admiralty. Although he plainly saw his target, he missed it by almost half a mile, the blame belonging to his bombsight which, later investigation revealed, was defective. Had he been luckier and hit the Admiralty, he might have cut short the career of Sir Percy Scott, who was there in his office, telephone in hand, shouting instructions to his gun teams.

Overflying their objective, Breithaupt's bombs cascaded into the Strand, London's theatrical district. One of them blew in the stagedoor of the Lyceum theater, where a rehearsal was in progress; at the sudden explosion, several actresses and the director fainted. Other of Breithaupt's bombs disrupted performances at the Strand theater, which was presenting Fred Terry in *The Scarlet Pimpernel;* at the Aldwych, where the gripping third act of Hall Caine's *The Prodigal Son* was just then turning its lachrymose climax; and at the Gaiety, which was showing the American musical comedy, *Tonight's the Night.* The district's theaters and vaudeville houses were crowded to capacity that night. At none but these three was there more than a moment's interruption on stage. And in the Opera House, its rafters ringing with an exuberant aria from *Madame Butterfly,* no one on either side of the proscenium heard the din of two bombs exploding outside.

The L-15, as soon as its missiles had been delivered, became the target of concentrated ground fire. Four planes, feeble-powered BE-2's, climbing laboriously toward the zeppelin, were spotted by Breithaupt's crew, but none of the would-be interceptors got close. Nevertheless, when he was advised of the planes' presence, the L-15's commander ordered more altitude.

Breithaupt had decided it was time to leave for home. With the Thames pointing his course, he came over Woolwich, where Mathy had lately been. He saw there a small warehouse burning alongside the river. After assuring himself that his aerial pursuers had been evaded, he headed downward to let go the remainder of his bomb load. He brought the L-15 to a hover at eight thousand feet and ordered his bombardier to make ready. However, before the release lever could be pulled, Breithaupt felt the shock of a shell exploding beneath the zeppelin. Looking out, he saw the flash of a second burst, a little closer than the first, he estimated, and only about seven or eight hundred feet short of its mark. Although too low to score a shrapnel hit, it was the highest-reaching shot he had yet witnessed, and he realized it was from a special kind of weapon. A third detonation shook the L-15 as Breithaupt off-loaded his water ballast and reared the zeppelin's nose in a frantic grab for altitude. He simultaneously ejected the last of his bombs, which fell aimlessly, killing a wagoner and his horse in Cable Street in the city's east end.

Where adverse luck had balked his attempt on the Admiralty, Breithaupt was luckier now than he guessed. The automobile gun—which had been rushed to Woolwich earlier to meet Mathy's assault but had arrived too late— possessed one shortcoming, which its French designers never did, or could, explain. Its highest angle of elevation was eighty-three degrees. The L-15 was directly overhead, an easy target for Rawlinson's next shot, when his crew chief reported that the gun would no longer bear. A fuming Rawlinson could not fire again until the zeppelin was well out of range, almost swallowed in mist and darkness.

From their inimical viewpoints, neither Scott nor Strasser was much pleased with the outcome of that night's action. The London defense head, with re-doubled vigor, continued to agitate for more antiaircraft guns, more airplanes for the night patrol, more airfields. As for Strasser, vexed by the formidable opposition his zeppelins had encountered, he knew but a single answer: bigger and better airships that could attain altitudes far surpassing the reach of any enemy guns or planes. Promised by Dr. Eckener that a new type of zeppelin would soon enter production, one that would satisfy his requirements, Strasser, throughout the winter of 1915–1916, refrained from raiding the British capital. London enjoyed a welcome respite, which time Scott turned to practical advantage, placing more than three dozen additional guns about the city and establishing auxiliary airfields at Northolt, Farningham, Black-heath, Romford, and Wimbledon.

For the ensuing three and a half months, not only London but the entirety of England was spared the visitation of zeppelins. The theory took hold that Germany, whether for reasons of economy or conscience, was done with bombing the British Isles. But this comforting illusion was dispelled on the night of January 31, 1916, when nine zeppelins in formation crossed the central east coast between Marblethorpe and Skegness. Strasser had been merely husbanding his resources while awaiting delivery of the new super ships he had been promised. Fidgeting with impatience, he had received another half dozen of the older model zeppelins but none of the improved type by mid-January, and so—to keep his crews occupied and afford them experience—he decided to lash out at England's industrial Midlands. Liver-pool, which he rated as the next big prize after London, was the prescribed objective of the January-31st raid, and one zeppelin, the L-21, commanded by Captain Max Dietrich, did reach Liverpool, although his bombs did little more than frighten the local populace. The other eight dirigibles, thrown off their course by fog, zigzagged all over the countryside, dropping bombs indiscriminately, killing seventy people, injuring 113, with considerable damage to private property. Manchester and Sheffield, by blind chance more than intention, were among the places hit. Of sixteen R.N.A.S. pilots who took off in search of the raiders, not one saw a zeppelin, and two were fatally injured in crash landings.

Again choosing the L-16 as his flagship, Strasser himself went along on this, the most ambitious mission he had so far tried. On his return to Nordholz he was welcomed by a throng of newspapermen and the station band playing "See What Comes There from on High," a stirring hymn that often greeted the zeppelins when they landed. Shouting jubilantly above the music's blare, Strasser informed the reporters that the English would now have to attend to their Midland defenses and those, too, of the northern and western reaches of the island. This alone, quite apart from the destruction and terror the raids were accomplishing, he declared, warranted an expanded program of zeppelin attacks.

There and then, although he had only fragmentary reports—preliminary estimates radioed from his commanders—on which to rest his assessment, Strasser characterized the raid as an "unqualified success," boasting that Liverpool and "other strategically vital areas" had been dealt a "paralyzing blow." Apropos of standing policy, the follow-up stories issued from government propaganda mills exaggerated the importance of this raid still further. It was, of course, a fact that the English had ample cause for alarm, what with the unprecedented toll of civilian casualties, nine zeppelins arriving en masse, and one of them making the distance to Liverpool. It was by far the bloodiest night's work yet achieved by the German lighter-than-air fleet; nevertheless, as a military operation, since nothing of any real strategic or logistic value had been destroyed, the raid failed. In no palpable way was the British war effort weakened. Moreover, as Strasser had yet to learn while prating of his "unqualified success," one of his zeppelins was lost at sea with all hands.

The fate of the missing airship, the L-19, with Captain Loewe its master officer, remained a perplexing riddle for several weeks. The enigma was solved when the Swedish yacht *Stell Smogen* picked up a bottle with a note inside. The message was addressed to Strasser at Nordholz and duly forwarded to him. It said: "With fifteen men on the upper platform, roof and body of the L-19, minus cars, drifting at about longitude three degrees east, I am trying to write a final report. With three engine breakdowns and a light headwind on the homeward leg, my return was delayed, and I got into fog over Holland, where we met heavy rifle fire. Ship became very unwieldy and three of our engines stopped running simultaneously. February 2, 1916, about noon, probably our last hour. Loewe." [1]

Two more messages in bottles were subsequently found washed up on a beach in Norway. One contained a succinct farewell note from Lieutenant Erwin Braunhof, the L-19's observation officer, to his clergyman-father in Hannover. The other contained last words from a noncommissioned officer to his wife and mother. Both these notes made mention of a British steamship, the *King Stephen* out of Grimsby, refusing assistance to the zeppelin crew during their second day adrift.

In his letter of condolence to Loewe's widow, Strasser asserted that "the British merchantman ruthlessly declined to rescue your husband and his crew . . . a blatant violation of the rules of warfare, seamanship and simple human decency." Left at that, Strasser's accusation would seem well founded. The official British account, though, offers another aspect to the incident which, if true, exonerates or at least mitigates the guilt of the captain in question. Here, verbatim, is the finding of an investigatory board appointed by the Admiralty to look into the matter:

> The commander of the airship hailed the skipper of the *King Stephen* with a request that the airship crew be taken on board,

---

[1] Dudley: *Monsters of the Purple Twilight.*

but the skipper replied: "No, if I take you on board you will take charge," for it was his conviction that his few hands could, and would be easily overpowered by the Germans, even if they were unarmed. He therefore steamed off to find and report to a patrol boat, but it was not until he had put into the Humber, on the morning of February 3, that he found a vessel to receive his report. Then it was too late. A search failed to locate the airship, which is presumed to have gone under with no survivors.

On March 5, and again on March 11, Strasser repeated his attacks on the Midlands and both times inflicted light damage on villages and hamlets in rural Lincolnshire. On the last night of that month a raid was undertaken against the Norfolk-Suffolk coast. Four zeppelins participated. Leaving together from Nordholz, they became dispersed while bucking blusterous winds at sea, whereupon each proceeded alone to work whatever mayhem it could. In the L-15, finding himself above the mouth of the Thames, Captain Breithaupt was bitten by an impulse to try a sneak assault on London. He got as far toward the capital as Rainham, then was met with a stiff barrage from high-angle guns at Purfleet, Abbey Wood, Plumstead, and Erith. Unloading bombs as he went, Breithaupt evasively swerved north, his ship glistening in the full glare of searchlights. Breithaupt later remarked that his opposition was keener this night than ever previously, which statement cannot be disputed, for a couple of weeks earlier, the Lord Mayor of London, Colonel Sir Charles Wakefield, had offered a bounty of five hundred pounds to any gun crew that should bring down a zeppelin on domestic soil; incentive was thus stronger than usual among the defenders. So eager were they that many joined in the shoot from beyond practical range of their weapons, indulging in a great waste of ammunition. Finally, an antiaircraft gun in Wellington Marshes scored two hits under the L-15's bow, which caused the huge vessel to tilt up precariously on its tail for a few seconds.

Recovering as best he could, his lamed ship unable to maintain altitude, Breithaupt found his situation further complicated by the sudden appearance of a BE-2. The assailing biplane was piloted by Lieutenant C. A. Ridley, who managed to pump twenty machine-gun slugs into the L-15's envelope before the zeppelin slipped out of the searchlight beams and was lost to view. Half an hour later, while patroling about three-quarters of a mile offshore, Lieutenant Alfred de Bath Brandon, in his BE-2, chanced to glimpse the L-15 looming toward him. To his excited delight, it was possible to attack from above—a rare opportunity. Flying over the shadowy vast monster, he dropped a stick of incendiary bombs without any visible effect. Near the end of a long coastwise patrol when he encountered the dirigible, so that he had barely enough fuel left to reach the closest landing strip, he now faced no rational alternative but to abandon the chase. His plane having not yet been fitted with a Lewis gun, he drew his pistol and fired seven quick parting shots.

Minutes after Brandon withdrew, right there in the Thames estuary, its two forward gas compartments empty and three others punctured, the L-15 crunched into the water, the impact breaking its back.

Already submerged amidships and gradually sliding deeper beneath the surface, its nose and tail sections jutting upward at steep angles, with the crew clinging to its flaccid skin for dear life, the wrecked zeppelin was promptly ringed by British naval craft. The cutter *Olivine* ventured alongside with gunners poised at the ready, although it was immediately obvious that the shivering figures crouched on the zeppelin would do no more fighting for the Fatherland. Breithaupt waited until his men were all safely aboard the *Olivine*, only then permitting himself to be rescued. Welcomed by the British skipper, Breithaupt snapped to attention, saluted smartly, and spoke in faultless English: "I wish to state for the record that I accept full responsibility. My men are innocent." An officer-gentleman of the old school, he was referring to the responsibility for having killed and maimed civilians during his raids, and it was with astonished relief that he and his men learned that they would not be prosecuted as murderers, but treated as ordinary prisoners of war. A tug took the zeppelin hulk in tow. It kept sinking lower in the water, however, until the towline had to be severed. By morning, except for some flotsam bobbing along a sinuous oil slick, nothing could be seen of the defunct airship.

A few days later, no little consternation was aroused in the War Office by the arrival of a letter claiming the Lord Mayor's prize. The letter had been sent by Captain John Harris, officer in charge of the Purfleet battery. Declaring that his gunners had scored a direct hit on the L-15, and acting on their behalf, Harris suggested that the bank draft be written to his order and that he would distribute equal cash shares to the men in his command, himself excluded. Harris' letter was passed like a hot potato to the top brass, who had some sticky questions to answer. Not only was there some doubt about the propriety of awarding cash prizes to military personnel for merely acquitting their duty, but also there was the puzzle as to which battery actually did finish off the L-15. Almost every antiaircraft gun around the lower Thames had been banging away at the zeppelin that night, and two prior hits had been achieved from Wellington Marshes. After much soul-searching and many conferences, some anonymous Solomon in the War Office ruled that the victory belonged jointly to all the gun crews in the area, and that the reward money should be divided evenly among them, which amounted to less than two guineas per man. That decision made, the Lord Mayor was consulted. He regretfully advised that the prize was meant only for volunteers of the civilian defense. Members of the armed forces, he explained, were ineligible. As a concession, though, he agreed to use the money to strike a commemorative medal, which the gunners later received in a colorful ceremony attended by the royal family. The medal bore this inscription: "L-15. Well hit. March 31–April 1, 1916."

In April Strasser attempted three raids that also proved ineffective. The last of these, undertaken on the night of April 24, saw ten zeppelins used in conjunction with a massed force of surface vessels on a sortie aimed against Lowestoft and Yarmouth. The plan was to lure elements of the British fleet into the jaws of a pincer by bombarding these places from the sea, as well as by nocturnal air attack. A bold, imaginative idea, it was frustrated by an unforeseen change in the weather, a violent storm compelling the surface force and eight of the zeppelins to turn back. Those hardy airshipmen— buffeted by wind, lashed by intermittent rain, their visibility destroyed by a solid mat of low clouds—who did make England, dropped their explosives with no sure knowledge of their whereabouts. Their victims numbered two. A Norfolk farmer was killed in his bed, and in Southwold, a woman succumbed to shock when a bomb fell near her house.

The following evening, five Belgium-based army zeppelins embarked for London. Success eluded them, too, although Captain Linnarz, now commanding an example of the army's latest type, the super-sized LZ-97, skulking inland by way of the Blackwater River, reached Seven Kings. He was repulsed —or to be precise, scared off—by six airplanes, one of which the soon-to-be-famous Lieutenant W. Leefe Robinson piloted. A few long-range shots, Robinson testified, seemed sufficient to convince Linnarz that the moment was ripe for clearing out. His cargo of bombs intact, he made about for Belgium and beat a hasty retreat.

On May 2, Strasser, joined for the first time by an army zeppelin, the LZ-98, tried another foray on the Midlands of England, guiding the operation as usual from aboard Peterson's ship. Two of the eight participating dirigibles straggled north into Scotland. Commanding one of these wayward-flown craft, Captain Buttlar erroneously reckoned himself to be over Firth of Forth when he was actually gazing down at the river Tay. Dumping every bomb he carried, he hit none of the structures below; some riverside cottages were damaged only to the extent of a few broken panes of glass. The other straggler, a Captain Stabbert, who commanded the L-20, no sooner described Loch Ness than the weather hemmed him in; although he hung about over Scotland for almost five hours, his bombs were strewn haphazardly and ineffectually. On the way home, Stabbert became woefully confused in his navigation and wound up crashing on a hillside in Norway, where he and his crew were interned for the remainder of the war.

Yet another airship, the old and outmoded L-7, was lost to Strasser two days later, when the Royal navy staged a surprise attack on the zeppelin sheds at Tondern. Scheduled to take part were eleven pontoon-equipped Sopwiths from the seaplane-tenders *Vindex, Engadine*, and *Campania*. However, owing to various problems, only one Sopwith reached the target, its pilot loosing a pair of sixty-five-pound bombs, the effect of which he could not determine because of a thick ground mist. The purpose of the venture was to draw a German flotilla away from inshore waters and across a wide shoal of freshly planted mines. First, though, the Zeppelin L-7, commanded by a Lieutenant Schubert, came forth to size up the British force. A shell from one of H.M.S. *Galatee's* six-inch guns caught the zeppelin broadside, staved in its ribs, and sent it flaming into the sea. Seven survivors were taken prisoner by a British submarine, which also scuttled the wreck with five or six rounds from its foredeck gun.

Almost half a year had now elapsed since Strasser demanded and was promised a bigger, more dependable type of dirigible. His impatience had been heightened and his resentment incurred in early spring when the army—exerting it considerable influence in Berlin—received the first two of the so-called super zeppelins produced. In mid-May, his countenance beaming like a child's on Christmas morn, Strasser finally set eyes on one of the new giants coming to berth at Nordholz. Designated the L-31, a sleek, silver, spindling colossus that seemed to span the sky, it was entrusted to Captain Mathy's able command. But Strasser's happiness was soon spoiled. To his utter exasperation, he was informed that the next delivery would be delayed two, possibly three months. The initial three craft were prototypes, built largely by hand, and before regular production could be started, the factory at Friedrichshafen required extensive alteration and retooling.

Since the nights of late May, June, and most of July were neither long nor dark enough to accommodate Strasser's aggressive ends, Mathy found ample time for familiarizing himself and his augmented crew with the formidable-looking L-31. On July 28, the date that marked the resumption of the zeppelin campaign against England, the L-31 flew together with nine other dirigibles to bomb interior targets in Norfolk and Suffolk. Limbering up now for his long-anticipated destruction of London, Strasser was critically interested in the L-31's first performance. But, as had happened so often before, the attack was thwarted by fog, Mathy never even crossing the enemy coast. Ironically, the sole raider to penetrate any distance inland was the L-13, taken over from Mathy by a novice commander, Lieutenant Franz Proelss.

Mathy flew the L-31 on two more raids in the following week, failing both times to achieve results. On the second of these raids, undertaken on the night of August 2, five zeppelins accompanied the L-31, but only two of them found anything worth bombing. The L-11, dropping more than three hundred pounds of explosives on Harwich, produced nothing worse than a slightly injured child and a lot of shattered window glass. The L-21, meanwhile, bombed Thetford airdrome, doing little damage, although the field was conveniently outlined with flares in readiness for a returning patrol of naval planes.

Strasser's cherished plan for razing London from the air, which of necessity had for so many months been held in abeyance, now began to monopolize his mind. Colored by this quenchless desire, his interpretation of events led him to believe that the propitious moment was close at hand. During that first week of August he experienced a stimulus to action when another of the super zeppelins was delivered to Nordholz. Although of later manufacture than the L-31, this sister ship was numbered L-30; placed in Captain Buttlar's charge, it underwent its operational baptism on August 8, venturing forth that night as one of eleven dirigibles bent upon attacking the British east coast at various points between Norfolk and the river Tweed in Scotland. Again, the attack was defeated by heavy mist, but there was, too, on this occasion, a certain timidity exhibited by the zeppelin commanders—a cautiousness that Strasser, flying in the L-16, realized was not without reason. More and more British antiaircraft defenses were springing up, protecting targets from north to south and east to west. No less sinister were the airplanes that had been encountered on the last four consecutive raids. Quite some while had passed now since Strasser's last trip over London, and the thought occurred to him that, if the outlying regions were so efficiently defended, the capital itself was probably more securely screened against air attack than he remembered.

Digesting all the signs and portents and relying almost as much on intuition as hard evidence, he decided that he must soon strike his knockout punch with his new giant dirigibles before even they were outmatched by opposing aircraft that not only could attain increased altitudes, but also, he suspected, carried ever deadlier armament. This hunch of his was uncannily correct; although a well-kept secret, the R.N.A.S. had, in fact, recently adopted two types of improved incendiary ammunition, the Pomeroy and Brock bullets, both especially designed to pierce the outer envelope of a zeppelin and then explode on contact with the inner hyrogen bags.

Strasser, having unalterably committed himself to destroying London, scrutinized his situation vis-à-vis the high command. Summer 1916, had become a bitter season for the German armies in France. Verdun, after many months of unremitting siege, had not capitulated; its blood-bedraggled defenders were rallying, beginning to push back the high tide of the German assault. For the French, their appalling losses notwithstanding, Verdun shone as an epic of resistance. But the Germans had paid dearly, too, and gained nothing. The sanguinary episode represented a costly debacle for the German military, and for the German people a depressing, even sickening, spectacle of failure. All this adversity had been compounded by the Allied offensive in the Somme, which had massacred the front line of German infantry and drained entire divisions from the Verdun front, thereby erasing any dim hope that Verdun could yet be conquered. As they related to his plan, Strasser overlooked none of these considerations. In this grave hour of crisis, he speculated, the high command might be easily convinced that the Fatherland was yearning for a dramatic, telling blow at the enemy's nerve center—a massive aerial attack on London, even a brutal, frightful onslaught that would bring the English begging on their knees for an end to it and thus retrieve victory from despair.

Despite a professed abhorrence for bombing cities, Strasser was after all a military pragmatist who could calm his feelings of guilt with the usual excuses of his kind. On the afternoon of August 24, he wrote to his mother:

> Please do not worry about me. Nothing ever happens to me, and if anything should happen one day, my adjutant would notify you immediately. We are enjoying pleasant weather here, and we are marching against England. . . . We who strike the enemy where his heart beats have been slandered as "baby killers" and "murderers of women." Such name-calling is to be expected from enemy quarters. It is maddening to learn, however, that even in Germany there are simple fools and deluded altruists who condemn us. What we do is repugnant to us, too, but necessary. Very necessary. Nowadays there is no such animal as a noncombatant; modern warfare is total warfare. A soldier cannot function at the front without the factory worker, the farmer, and all the other providers behind him at home. You and I, Mother, have discussed this subject, and I know you understand what I say. My men are brave and honorable. Their cause is holy, so how can they sin while doing their duty? . . . If what we do is frightful, then may frightfulness be Germany's salvation.

A few hours after composing this sop to his and his mother's consciences, Strasser opened his grand campaign. As soon as the day began fading, he sent out twelve zeppelins toward London in an operation that he termed a tentative probe. The outcome of this mission would have discouraged a less dedicated individual. Hampered yet again by fog, only four of the airships crossed the British coast, and just one—Mathy's L-31—reached the city outskirts, where nine victims died and forty were injured in the ensuing bedlam of bursting bombs and shrapnel. Of the other three raiders to find England, none prowled so far upriver as Mathy; instead, with a wary regard for the glutinous murk that blanked their visibility, they dawdled about the Thames estuary and deposited their missiles blindly along its north shore; a few telephone poles were knocked down, and great gobs of untenanted earth were gouged, but not enough damage was done to compensate for the cost of a tiny fraction of the fuel they consumed that night.

If the chief of the Imperial navy's airship service entertained any misgivings about the prodigality of this raid, let alone many previous ones, he betrayed no hint of it. On the contrary, his determination to smash London was bolstered that week when another of the big new zeppelins, the L-32, was ceremoniously commissioned at Nordholz. With three of the giant aerial warships in his fleet, and two more flying with the army in Belgium, Strasser marked out the second night in September for what he called the "climactic raid" on London. As it turned out, his choice of adjective was apt, but also, from his viewpoint, infelicitous. The raid did indeed prove climactic, though not in the sense Strasser meant.

After soliciting the army's cooperation, which was gladly tendered, the airship chief prepared his plan of attack. His calculations were made with stop-watch precision. Split-second timing would be essential to success, for Strasser had to coordinate a force of at least sixteen zeppelins—maybe more, depending on how many the army would furnish—and he wanted all of them to arrive over London simultaneously. Since the raiders would be leaving from widespread localities in Germany and Belgium, their departure times had to be staggered according to a carefully computed schedule. The army twice changed its mind as to the number of dirigibles it would commit, which precluded Strasser from crystallizing the details of his plan until the very eve of the appointed day, when he was at last assured that he could count definitely on six of the Belgium-based airships taking part in the operation. This afforded him a total combined task force of twenty ships, of which five were super zeppelins. Eighteen of the available craft were assigned to strike London in concert, while the remaining pair, both outdated naval types, had orders to stage a feint attack over the Humber.

Strasser, if he suffered a bad case of jitters on that important September 2, had some excuse. Here he was, contemplating the biggest gamble of his career, with twenty dirigibles and some three hundred experienced crewmen— virtually the sum and substance of Germany's lighter-than-air fleet—primed for the momentous mission, with the frankly skeptical eyes of the army's as well as the navy's senior commanders focused squarely on him, with the fate of the Fatherland perhaps at stake, and all Strasser could see through his office window that day was a low-hung ceiling of somber cloud and a steady, drenching downpour. Luck had merely teased him, however, not forsaken him, for the late afternoon brought widening blue seams in the overcast and an end to the rain, and with dusk came the torpid calm of a warm evening mist, dense and unbroken at ground level, but thinning out at flight altitude so that stars might be glimpsed between feathery patches of cirrus higher above.

Still using the L-16 as his aerial command post, Strasser crossed the Norfolk coast with his main body at about ten o'clock and veered toward London, expecting to converge with the army formation above the capital. It happened, though, that just two army ships reached England that night. One had been withdrawn an hour or so before takeoff because of an ailing engine, and three others, for reasons never divulged, turned back a few miles off the Thames inlet. Only Lehmann, in the LZ-98, and an inexperienced but courageous young officer commanding the SL-11, Captain Wilhelm Schramm, fulfilled their share of the army's bargain with Strasser. Somewhat rashly, considering that his ship was an obsolescent Schutte-Lanz, Schramm traveled the more strongly defended route to London that lay north of the Thames.

Shrewd veteran that he was, Lehmann approached the city from the south-east.

As usual, the Admiralty was topmost on the agenda of priority objectives. High on the list, too, was the Bank of England, the destruction of which, so Strasser had been led to believe, would occasion a collapse of the pound sterling and create an economic strife from which the enemy power would not soon recover, possibly even bankrupting its entire war effort. Each of the naval raiders had been delegated a particular target, although if a commander could not locate the desired target, or was somehow prevented from attacking it, his contingent instructions were to "make the best of opportunity" —in other words, to drop his bombs anywhere on the city that he was able. Barring life-or-death exigencies, a commander would on no condition be forgiven the folly of returning to base with so much as a single unused bomb aboard ship.

Midnight found Strasser's armada strung out pretty much along an east-west line, a spectral phalanx drawing toward the northern environs of London. Lehmann, all by himself, was moving in from the city's southern flank, and Schramm, seeing ahead of him one of the naval zeppelins turning upriver, had just ordered the SL-11's navigation lights to be blinked in recognition. Schramm's signal was a needless, thoughtless, not to say stupid act. And it was to result quickly in disastrous consequences, laden with significance.

London, the city proper and its circumjacent towns and countryside, all the way to the mouth of the Thames, had been blacked out since about half-past ten, when the preliminary alarm was sounded. As the zeppelins neared the British coast, thanks to their need for wireless intercommunication, their presence was discovered and their movements crudely tracked. The seat of this detection system was situated in the older wing of the Admiralty building, behind the locked doors of Room 40. Here, under the strictest security cover, worked a department of naval intelligence. None but the highest authorities knew what went on in this secluded chamber. Those army and navy officials privy to its secrets were few enough to be counted on the fingers of one hand, and in their official papers they alluded to it simply as "Room 40" to conceal its function. On the civilian side, only the Prime Minister and his confidential aides were even aware of its existence.

Inside this room a group of master cryptographers was kept busy around the clock interpreting enemy radio transmissions that had been overheard and relayed by the several listening posts then in operation along the east and south coasts. Because the zeppelins maintained radio contact with each other and their bases while approaching England, Room 40 was alerted to impending raids and so could forewarn the home defense force and the various authorities responsible for public safety.

September 2, in England, as on the opposite side of the North Sea, had been a wet, sullen day. The weather was so foul that the air patrol had to remain grounded until almost ten o'clock, when the night sky finally began to clear. A few planes were already airborne by the time the oncoming zeppelins were detected and the alert given. At about quarter to eleven, as soon as he could fuel his BE-2 and warm its engine, Lieutenant Leefe Robinson, of No. 39 Squadron, took off from Sutton's Farm to patrol the sector between there and Joyce Green. Flying at ten thousand feet, he saw nothing for more than an hour. But then, almost exactly on the stroke of midnight, he saw— wiping his goggles clean to make sure he was really seeing—a miniature constellation of winking red and green and white lights. Off a few miles, Robinson estimated, to the south of him, they appeared to be at the same elevation as he, give or take a thousand feet. "I was frankly mystified," he said later. "It was a spooky sight, a cluster of lights suspended in midair like that twinkling on and off in merry rhythm. The thought occurred to me that it might be a Hun dirigible, but what kind of fool was in command to reveal himself in such conspicuous fashion? I doubted anyone could be so asinine, although I did not discount the possibility altogether." Robinson was on his way over to investigate when all his riddles were solved by the sudden advent of searchlight rays stabbing upward from the blackness below. Ground observers had noticed the pulsating dots of color, too. Within a few seconds the beams fastened upon the hull of an airship, the SL-11. Robinson did not recognize it as a Schutte-Lanz, referring to it as a "Zeppelin"—with a capital Z—in his report on the action that followed. Of course, under these circumstances, the distinction was immaterial. Robinson's work was plainly cut out for him; shoving his throttle open as far as it would go, he sped toward the prey.

Leefe Robinson, wounded as an aerial photographer on the western front before winning his pilot's rating, was a lanky, fair-complexioned youth whose six-foot stature made him taller than most of his fellow airmen. Beneath his unconformably dark brows, his blue eyes held a steady stare in his serious moments. His flaxen mustache seemed misplaced on a face as boyish as his, but mustaches were then considered stylish among British officers. Robinson's demeanor was modest to the point of timidity, except when he was at the controls of an airplane. The villagers of Hornchurch, over which he regularly flew from nearby Sutton's Farm, pegged him as an inveterate daredevil who sooner or later would perform one stunt too many. He once dumbfounded the locals by looping his flimsy BE-2 six times in spectacular succession, and often were the occasions when they stood brandishing fists at him as he whisked over their cottages, missing the roofs by inches they swore. But it was his favorite trick to balance his plane almost vertically on its tail, then to flip over and swoop in a screaming nosedive at a regal oak that shaded a road at the edge of town. Robinson loved flying. He relished its thrills. While too diffident ever to say so, he was a better pilot than most and probably knew it. But still, as he closed now toward the SL-11, he felt his stomach knotting.

He felt the clammy moisture of nervous sweat soaking into his shirt. "I was a bit of what you might call boiled-up," he afterward told a newspaperman.

The SL-11, when pinioned by searchlights, was running at some twelve thousand feet of altitude. The guns of the London defense immediately began thundering their bolts of destruction at the illuminated predator. Captain Schramm—in such a mental dither, apparently, that he forgot to douse the lights that had first attracted enemy attention—fled northward, aimlessly dumping most of his bombs. Robinson, ignoring the heavy antiaircraft barrage, kept up his pursuit. Judging the airship to be eight hundred or so feet above him, he decided to sacrifice speed in order to climb. As he was boring slowly upward in its wake, however, the SL-11 slinked into a cloud and out of sight. Robinson searched for fifteen minutes in vain, then disgustedly resumed his patrol.

About half an hour later, as he skirted the northeast fringe of London, Robinson looked off his port wing and beheld a glinting reflection in the distance. He made toward it. It gradually assumed the shape and substance of a dirigible, the identical ship, he realized, that a little earlier had eluded him. Determined this time not to be cheated of his quarry, he rushed straightaway to the attack. Suddenly, before he came within shooting range, some searchlights picked the long silvery raider out of the darkness, which in turn brought several gun batteries to bear on it. Robinson flashed his lights, a signal telling those on the ground that he was at hand, ready to pounce. The searchlights were promptly put out, and the gunfire ceased. Just then, the SL-11 vanished behind a smoke screen of its own making. Minutes of breathless waiting passed, with Robinson circling the area, fearing that he had again been bilked. But there was a good wind blowing, and it soon divested the airship of its concealment. What happened next is taken from Robinson's report to his squadron commander:

> Remembering my last failure, I sacrificed height (I was still at 12,900) for speed and made nose down in the direction of the Zeppelin. I flew about eight hundred feet below it from bow to stern and distributed one drum along it (alternate Brock and Pomeroy). It seemed to have no effect; I therefore moved to one side and gave another drum distributed along its side—without apparent effect. I then got behind (by this time I was very close—five hundred feet or less below) and concentrated one drum on one part (underneath rear). I was then at a height of 11,500 feet when attacking Zeppelin. I had hardly finished the drum before I saw the part fired at glow. In a few seconds, the whole rear part was blazing.
>
> When the third drum was fired, there was no searchlight on the Zeppelin, and no antiaircraft was firing. I quickly got out of the way of the falling, blazing Zeppelin, and being very excited, fired off a few red Very lights and dropped a parachute flare. Having

very little oil and petrol left, I returned to Sutton's Farm, landing at 1:45 A.M.

On landing, I found I had shot away the machine-gun wire guard, the rear part of the center airfoil section, and had pierced the rear main spar several times. . . .

The huge, burning body of the SL-11 lit the heavens brightly enough, according to a contemporary account, to enable a retired sailor residing in Billericay, fifteen miles distant, to read a befitting verse from his naval hymn book. "Oh, happy band of pilgrims," the verse began, "look upward to the skies, where such a light affliction shall win so rich a prize." Not since the Great Fire had London witnessed such brilliant illumination. Hundreds of thousands gaped in astonished silence, shading their eyes against the glare, craning their necks to watch the immense bubble of hydrogen gas being devoured by hungry flames. The stricken dirigible hung in place for more than a minute, a sizzling, undulating inferno from which blazing fragments showered like meteors. By slow increments, the SL-11's tail sagged and drooped, pulling the rest of the ship after it. Once started, it took three minutes descending to earth. As it fell, a mounting chorus of cheers roared out of the night. Horns and whistles from factories, from vessels in the Thames, from railway locomotives, from lorries and cars, shrieked and bellowed until the joyous cacophony recalled the pandemonium of a prewar New Year's Eve in Piccadilly.

The last scene of the drama unfolded at the Hertfordshire village of Cuffley, "enriched and made immortal," suggested an American journalist, Jane Anderson, in the following Sunday's *Weekly Dispatch,* "by the spectacle and wondrous miracle of a flaming airship hurtling from the sky into a green meadow beside a church." The SL-11 had crashed into a plot of coarse grass and unkempt hawthorn bushes, a neglected acre set apart from the church grounds by a moss-encrusted stone fence hidden in the damp shadow of a row of poplars, a field where young boys played at mock wars. The wreckage burned hotly almost till sunrise, and smoldered through the next afternoon. Daybreak found the roads to Cuffley already clogged with traffic as people from miles around thronged to view the ruins, which lay beneath a pall of malodorous smoke. Corpses could be seen amid the debris, bodies crisped and battered beyond human semblance, grisly lumps of blackened flesh and bone strewn in hideous poses. It was a sight sensational to see, and with each passing hour the influx swelled, thousands arriving in every kind of vehicle, the railroads providing special trains to accommodate the rush. Ankle-deep with mud from the previous day's rain, the narrow lane running alongside the field became choked with cars and buses, trucks and tractors, bicycles and motorcycles, donkey carts, elegant carriages and rude farm wagons. Some budding entrepreneurs of the village, peddling food, drinks, and souvenirs, pocketed handsome profits. Families picnicked at the site; many pitched tents and camped there overnight. Homes were converted into jampacked boarding houses, charging exorbitant prices. A gala spirit prevailed. It was like Derby Day.

Frederick William Wile, formerly the Berlin correspondent to the *Daily Mail,* wrote:

> Notwithstanding the carnival atmosphere even those who felt most bitterly about the brutality of raids upon unarmed civilian populations could not refrain from pity at the gruesome tableau. . . . It is a tradition of the Hohenzollerns that the King of Prussia must ride across the battlefields on which his soldiers have fallen and look his dead men in the face. Trench warfare and a decent regard for his own skin have prevented William II from carrying out this ghoulish rite in his war. But I wish some cruel Fate might have taken the Kaiser by his trembling hand yesterday morning and led him to that rain-soaked meadow in Hertfordshire, and bade him look, as I looked, at the charred residuum which a few hours before was the crew of an Imperial German airship. I wish Count Zeppelin, the creator of the particular brand of Kultur which sent the baby-killers to their doom, might have been in the Supreme War Lord's entourage. I wondered, standing there by the side of that miserable heap of exposed skulls, stumps of arms and legs, shattered bones and scorched flesh, whether the Kaiser would have revoked the vow he spoke in the Black Forest eight years ago, when he christened the inventor of airship frightfulness, "the greatest German of the twentieth century."

The results of the SL-11's fiery dissolution were momentous. The immediate effect on the rest of Strasser's fleet was crushing. Already apprehensive, having themselves encountered a more powerful opposition than they had been warned to expect, the awful sight of one of their companion dirigibles erupting into flame completely disconcerted them. A peculiarly phlegmatic sort to begin with, Lehmann was the sole exception. "There," he wrote, describing the arena that was London that horrific night, "I saw searchlights more numerous and more powerful than I had ever seen before. The big guns had increased in number, too, and their range was greater. London sprawled beneath a luminous mist, dotted everywhere with the incessant flickering and flashes of bursting shells, the countless searchlights combing frantically to and fro, their incandescent beams a maze of crisscrossing feelers from the enemy below." He snatched glimpses of other zeppelins sidling into the attack, only to sheer off again when brushed by a sweeping shaft or two of light. "To distinguish much of anything in that dazzling confusion was difficult. It was like being suspended above a brightly illuminated stage in a theater with the auditorium darkened." The LZ-98 had scarcely arrived over the city—Lehmann was studying a map in the chart room, orienting himself in relation to his chosen target, the Royal arsenal and its adjacent dockyard—when a frenzied voice crackled through the intercom. "Looking north . . ." Lehmann wrote, "I saw a tremendous sheet of fire, high up at our own level, somewhere near the city limits. It hung in the air for fully a minute, casting its lurid glow to the horizon, tincturing the entire encompassment with a coppery glaze. Parts were breaking loose and falling faster than the main body. Poor fellows, trapped like that in a burning ship, they had no chance."

Although his bombs did negligible damage, Lehmann retained his composure and proceeded directly to strike his planned objective, only then eloping from the scene. But his colleagues, upon seeing the SL-11's terrible fate, were not so impassive. The sky above and around London was swarming with dirigibles when the SL-11 was hit; within ten or fifteen minutes, they were gone, every last one. The L-23, for example, was poised to spill its lethal load over the Shoreditch district when its commander, a Captain Gayer, saw the SL-11 blossom into flame. His courage deserting him, Gayer ordered his bombs away without bothering to aim, and swiftly fled. All the rest of the fleet followed suit, except that they delayed dropping their bombs until well away from London. Captains Mathy and Hallermund, even these seasoned campaigners, joined the headlong exodus. Mathy's missiles were indiscriminately dumped on Foulness Island and by naked chance sank a small coasting smack; Buttlar, to his profound sense of shame, returned to Nordholz with his cargo intact.

The far-flung communities of Thaxted, Retford, Cromer, and Yarmouth were among the places raked by bombs hastily jettisoned from routed airships. Mostly, though, the distraught Germans were more concerned with disencumbering themselves of their bombs than they cared about hitting worthwhile targets, the result being that they succeeded merely in churning up large tracts of open country. Official British reports the next day confirmed that a Schutte-Lanz airship had been brought down near London, and that casualties—one man and one woman killed, eleven men and two children injured—and damage had been incredibly disproportionate to the number of zeppelins employed in the raid.

Not until September 5 was Lieutenant Robinson identified as the widely celebrated "dirigible destroyer," the "Cuffley hero," to use just two of his headlined sobriquets. His name was finally disclosed in the morning newspapers, where it was formally announced that King George had been "graciously pleased to bestow the Victoria Cross on Lieutenant W. Leefe Robinson for most conspicuous bravery." "He attacked an enemy airship under circumstances of great hardship and danger," declared the palace communiqué, "and sent it crashing to the ground as a blazing wreck."

Robinson's momentous deed brought him other rewards besides honor and notoriety. Various cash prizes totaling almost four thousand pounds had been awaiting the first airman to destroy an enemy dirigible over England, and this tidy sum he collected. As always, the War Office took a jaundiced view of servicemen realizing monetary profits for their heroism; although Robinson was allowed to keep his bounty, a regulation was quickly adopted to preclude any recurrence of such uncouth goings-on. Emboldened, apparently, by his newfound wealth, Robinson that month announced his betrothal to the comely young widow of a regimental captain who had fallen in France during the early weeks of the war.

Seven months later, on April 5, 1917, recently promoted to his captaincy and leading a flight of six Bristol fighters on their inceptive sortie over the western front, Robinson had the misfortune to cross the path of Germany's peerless ace, Baron Manfred von Richthofen, accompanied by four members of his crack Jagdstaffel. A savage combat ensued. In this, their first dogfight, Robinson and three of his comrades were shot down. Surviving a crash in enemy territory, Robinson was captured and incarcerated in the British officers' prisoner-of-war camp at Holzminden. His stay here was a hellish ordeal, for he came under the vengeful eye of the camp boss, Captain Karl Niemeyer, a notorious sadist who scoffed at him as "the English Richthofen" and swore to make him suffer for having caused the death of Schramm, the late skipper of the SL-11. By the unlikeliest coincidence, Schramm and Niemeyer had been townsmen of warm mutual admiration. Robinson compounded his warder's hatred of him by trying repeatedly to escape, which cost him a long stretch of solitary confinement in a cubicle so cramped that he could neither stand erect nor lie down. Classified as an incorrigible, he was transferred to even tougher camps, eight in all. By the second week of December 1918, when he was repatriated, Robinson was a haggard victim of the cruelties he had endured. So wasted was his health that on New Year's Eve, just seventeen days after his homecoming, he died of influenza. According to his obituary in the *News of the World:* "Although he never spoke of his sufferings, during a delirium which preceded his last breath, Robinson was haunted by the vision of the German arch-brute and his guards. He imagined that Niemeyer and sentries with fixed bayonets were standing by his deathbed. Several times he cried out to be protected from the fiends." [2]

Leefe Robinson, in that transcendent moment of his short life when he set fire to SL-11, had singlehandedly quashed the most ambitious air raid ever attempted. It can be certified as well that he there and then administered the first of a series of setbacks that would soon relegate the dirigible to a less aggressive role in the war, and ultimately to the military scrap heap. Robinson's victory figures as a pivotal factor in the history of wartime aeronautics, for it presaged the fast-evolving era in which winged flying machines would altogether outstrip the lighter-than-air variety. One who forthwith grasped the significance of the SL-11's ugly fate was Strasser, the *luftschiffen führer* himself, who watched the whole sickening episode from aboard his aerial flagship, the L-16.

[2] Dudley: *op. cit.*

At that gravid instant when the SL-11 went ablaze, the L-16 was hovering over Hyde Park with Captain Peterson drawing a bead on the Admiralty nearby. Even the coolly competent Peterson forgot the purpose of his mission upon seeing that great flower of flame blossom off his port beam. With Strasser grim-faced beside him, he turned abruptly northeastward and headed back the way he had come. Strasser said nothing to deter him. Dropping his bombs on Ware and Hertford before departing seaward over Lowestoft, Peterson the next day revealed in a letter to his wife: "It was an execrable night . . . a disgraceful failure. I was deeply worried about [Strasser's] mental state on the trip home. He simply sat and stared, not saying a word. I would have thought him a stone statue except that he kept clenching his jaw during the whole trip. His thoughts were as black as the night outside. . . . He seemed utterly desolated."

Strasser, having just seen his dream reduced to ashes along with the SL-11, was indeed disquieted. It was not to be expected, though, that the ruination of a single airship would put a full stop to the attacks on London. For one thing, too much German money, pride, and reliance had been invested in the dirigible arm. For another thing, Strasser was too hardy and resilient a character to admit defeat merely because it lurked somewhere in the offing. He was a self-avowed diehard. In a conversation he had once had with Dr. Eckener, he spelled out his philosophy in this regard, saying that "one does not concede defeat until one has been conclusively defeated."

Accordingly, in the week following the loss of the SL-11, Strasser conferred at length with his army counterpart, Lehmann. It was agreed that raiding London from heights of ten to twelve thousand feet was no longer practical in view of the improved defense. In future, they decided, a minimum altitude of sixteen thousand feet would be the strict rule. However, only the latest-model zeppelins, those of the super class, could maintain such an altitude without a considerable reduction in bomb capacity; the older ships, therefore, were to steer clear of London and attack secondary targets that were less strongly defended. Strasser saw fit also at this juncture to reshuffle some of his officers and crews. Among other changes, he placed Peterson, his protégé, in command of the L-32, leaving Buttlar and Mathy in charge of the remaining super zeppelins, the L-30 and L-31. Another ship of the new giant class, the L-33, delivered to Nordholz in midmonth, was turned over to Captain Boecker, ex-master of a Hamburg-Amerika Lines' trans-Atlantic steamer, the *Imperator,* and holder of the second most coveted naval order, Hausordern von Hohenzollern.

Utilizing his four ultra-sized dirigibles and six of the smaller types, Strasser sallied against England again on September 23. In accordance with his revised *modus operandi,* the quartet of super ships assailed London, while the others ranged farther north between the Wash and the Humber. Yielding to a last-minute whim, Strasser went along this time with Mathy instead of accompanying Peterson in the L-32. Maybe, as a few occult-minded historians have gratuitously inferred, he was responding to some vague presentiment of the horror that befell Peterson in the course of this action.

It happened on the north side of the Thames, a little to the east of London, shortly after midnight, when Lieutenant John Sowrey R.F.C., saw the L-32 caught in a cone of searchlights, maneuvered his BE-2 into a position underneath it, and peppered its vast belly with three canisters of Lewis-gun ammunition, a combination of Brock, Pomeroy, and tracer bullets. Watching from a couple of miles away, Lieutenant A. de B. Brandon afterward reported that it looked as if the zeppelin was "being hosed with a stream of liquid fire." Some of Sowrey's shots pierced one of the cylindrical fuel tanks located along the L-32's central gangway. Immediately there was an eruption of flame which raced around the airship's huge hull. Glissading slowly to earth, the L-32 finally came to rest at Snail's Hall Farm in Great Burstead, the twisted skeleton lying athwart a hedge with its lattice framework impaled on an oak tree. A reporter of the London *Times* graphically described the scene next morning. After noting that all hands had perished, he described how "the frightfully disfigured lay huddled together, smelling foully; nothing of the majesty of death; only its gruesomeness and terror in the most abominable shapes. Lying on the ground," he continued, "was a red-leather cushion. This covered the engineman's seat, and the ghastly evidences . . . showed that he had died at his post. . . . There were remains of an air mattress and a blanket, perhaps the bed for one of the night shift when off duty. Curious evidences of the crew's breakfast still remained. There were slices of bacon and hunks of brown greasy Kriegsbrod with delicately sliced potatoes."

Peterson's mangled corpse lay some three hundred feet from where the command car landed, which raises the probability that he threw himself from the car with a good deal of lateral momentum, that he leaped rather than simply fell to his death. As with all the many wretched victims who jumped from flaming aircraft during the four years of the first air war, it is impossible to know for certain whether he did so deliberately—that is, as a rational alternative to the agonies of being burned to death—or whether he flung himself overboard in a maddened fit of fear. An act of moral courage or cowardice? If it matters to the record, the likelihood seems to be that Peterson did panic, an assumption based—albeit somewhat tenuously—on the fact that another, more merciful means of suicide was presumably at hand: the vial of instant-working poison issued to him, as to every German airshipman, for just this awful contingency.

Strasser averted his eyes from the sight of the L-32's destruction, but Mathy, always the impassive objectivist, watched the doomed dirigible plunge to its end. "Poor Peterson," Strasser muttered over and over again, until Mathy asked his orders. The edge on Mathy's voice was sharp enough to prick the numbness from Strasser's brain. Wanting desperately to avert a repetition of the hysteria that had emanated from the loss of the SL-11 during the last foray, Strasser took the precaution of radioing instructions to Buttlar and

Boecker, explicitly ordering them to execute the raid on London as planned, which was done with rather telling effect. Meanwhile, the L-17, one of the six zeppelins operating farther north, bombed Nottingham, the others failing to reach their targets. Damage and casualties in Nottingham were comparatively light. Of the thirty-nine Britons slain and 131 injured that night, all but three resided in the capital metropolitan region.

The score did not end there, however. About an hour after seeing Sowrey destroy the L-32, Lieutenant Brandon had an opportunity himself to bag a super zeppelin. Encountering the L-33 over Chelmsford, he hung behind its tail for most of thirty minutes and shot at it at every chance. He saw his tracers entering the envelope again and again, but the airship would not oblige by bursting aflame. His fuel running low, Brandon at last turned off his attack and headed back to base, disgruntled. Captain Boecker, when told of his assailant's departure, whispered his thanks to God; the zeppelin, he thought, had been spared any serious impairment. A little while later, though, he learned otherwise, for the vessel grew increasingly heavy by the stern as it lumbered seaward, a sign that too many bullet holes had been drilled through the after ballonets. To conserve altitude, he began jettisoning his ballast and whatever equipment was not bolted to the deck or bulkheads. But the punctured cells were spouting gas at an excessive rate, rapidly diminishing the L-33's buoyancy, so that Boecker finally decided to make about for land, preferring captivity to drowning.

Its brief operational career of a single mission ignominiously terminated, the L-33 sank gently to earth near Colchester at about three o'clock in the morning. Boecker, flustered and wondering what else to do, glumly marched his men toward town. They were met along the road by a local constable who, alone and unarmed, had bicycled out to find them. Boecker meekly surrendered, whereafter he and his crew became inmates of a detention camp at Stobs, in Scotland. (Nearly a year later, in August 1917, six of Boecker's men escaped and managed to steal a small sailboat, but a patrolling destroyer found them becalmed at sea, and they were sent right back again to Stobs.) The L-33, recovered intact by the British authorities, proved an invaluable source of useful information to the island's defense force. By neglecting to set fire to his stranded airship, Boecker was guilty of a gross dereliction of duty; there is no calculating the extent of his disservice to his nation's war effort in general and to his fellow airmen in particular, but it was considerable.

Two of Germany's newest and biggest zeppelins had thus come to grief in a single action. Here was a dramatic demonstration that the airplane was fast developing into a creditable instrument of domestic defense, much to the relief of the whole British public. Typical of many cheerful editorials in the home press was one which appeared in the *News of the World*. "The flea," it observed archly, "has been shown capable of becoming the elephant's nemesis. Lest the analogy remain obscure, we refer to our airplanes and their splendid success of late against prey hundreds of times their own size, namely, zeppelins."

Our gallant aviators have brought down three giant raiders within this month,
two in the same night. . . . If it be yet premature for unbounded optimism, it
must be remarked that the prospect does look positively brighter."

Nothing of the real import of this news, of course, was divulged to the
German public, whose morale was already depressed by the sinister turn of
events at Verdun and the Somme, and by a worsening scarcity of food, clothing, coal, and other basic commodities. Because the zeppelin now began to
figure as a last illusion of German invincibility, very little of a dismaying nature
was being published in the German press about the airship fleet. Among the
dirigible crews themselves, the prevailing mood was one of intermingled disappointment, apprehension, and obdurate hope. As for Strasser, he was keenly
aware that his stock with the high command had taken a pronounced downswing. And, no doubt, it was partly for this reason—to redeem himself, at
least in some measure, before his prestige slumped to rock bottom—that he
resumed his aerial crusade against England just as soon as circumstances
permitted.

A spell of nasty offshore weather delayed him for a week, which at first
irritated him. "But it has been for the best, after all," he wrote to his mother
on September 27, "for a new ship has been received which will augment our
striking power when the weather turns favorable. . . . Mathy has advised me
not to go along on any more raids. He says I am irreplaceable, which is
flattering nonsense. We are all expendable. Nothing will happen to me, anyhow.
I have gone on these raids often, and I have come back every time. . . . I
sometimes think a guardian angel watches over me."

Strasser, in another letter that week, recounted a discussion he had had
with Mathy as to whether or not the raids should be halted until the Zeppelin
works could perfect a ship able to cruise at even greater altitudes. In a meeting
with factory representatives, he had learned that such a ship would require at
least six months to be put into production. He apprised Mathy of this fact,
and asked him: "Should we delay resuming the raids until next spring?"
Mathy replied with an emphatic "No!" To cease the attacks at this time, he
argued, would be interpreted by the high command as an admission of defeat.
"Furthermore," he said, "for so long as our troops are fighting and dying on
the western front, it will remain our job to tie up enemy resources in England."
Strasser could not have heard more agreeable words. Mathy's argument was
exactly his own.

There was, however, a strong counterargument that could not be lightly
dismissed, for it was gaining ever more currency in top command circles. It
rested on the fact that Strasser himself employed a force of some seven
thousand men in the air and on the ground, a force that his critics claimed
could be more advantageously deployed. Although a growing faction of admirals was exhibiting symptoms of disenchantment with Strasser's gasbag fleet,
his loudest detractors were high-placed army officers who resented the gen-

erous appropriations of money and vital matériel—fuel, for instance, and munitions—going to such a questionable purpose when crucial problems at the front were forever being complicated by shortages of supply. "The airship," noted the general staff in a secret memorandum dated September 12, 1916, "has not yet vindicated itself as an offensive weapon, nor does it promise to do so in the foreseeable future. Airship operations against enemy cities, especially in England, should therefore be curtailed drastically, or discontinued altogether."

With the unflagging hope of yet allaying the gathering wave of condemnatory opinion, Strasser launched eleven dirigibles against England in the afternoon of October 1, just hours after his meteorologists reported that offshore conditions had improved. Four ships—the L-13, L-22, L-23 and the supersized L-30—turned back with mechanical troubles before reaching the British coast. The L-14, L-16, and L-21 did no more than waste their bombs over rural Lincolnshire, and the L-17 and L-24 attacked Harwich and Lowestoft. Strasser flew with Captain Dietrich aboard the L-34 on its maiden run. His presence pleased the crew, who had come to look upon him as a lucky charm after Peterson's tragic experience. Cruising above ten thousand feet was cold work, and Strasser, like the rest of the men, wore paper underclothing beneath his uniform, a concession to Germany's dwindling store of wool and cotton.

The L-30 having turned back, only two super zeppelins remained for an assault on London, the virgin L-34 and the L-31, skippered by Mathy, whom Strasser had dubbed "the maestro," and who intended to live up to his billing this time out. At twenty minutes before midnight, in the vicinity of Chesham, repeated salvos of intense ground fire compelled him to scramble for additional height, but not until he had loosed thirty high-explosive missiles and a couple of dozen incendiaries on a crowded residential area; six persons were killed, thrice that number were injured. Still determined on a crack at London, Mathy wended westward, twisting and swerving, dipping and climbing to dodge the searchlights and popping shrapnel, as he sought out the familiar landmarks that marked his route to the west side of the city.

Earlier that evening, Lieutenant W. Joseph Tempest, R.F.C., had been dining with friends when a telephone call had fetched him in a hurry to North Weald, at which airdrome his BE-2 biplane was hangared. He was airborne by ten o'clock, scanning the sky in hopes of intercepting the zeppelins reported to be marauding to the north and east of the capital. He searched futilely until almost midnight, when, at fourteen thousand feet, he noticed a group of searchlights near Chesham concentrated in an enormous pyramid. Perched at the apex was a cigar-shaped object, the first zeppelin that Tempest had actually ever seen. Estimating it to be about fifteen miles away, he set off at full speed in pursuit, passing through, he later said in his action report, "a very inferno of bursting shells." When still some five miles off, his automatic fuel-pressure pump broke and "I had to use my hand pump. . . . This exercise at so high an altitude was very exhausting, besides occupying an arm and thus giving me 'one hand less' to operate with when I commenced shooting."

Despite this handicap and the barrage, he persevered until he got within range. The L-31, traveling its eccentric evasion course, was at this moment mounting rapidly. "I accordingly gave a tremendous pump at my petrol tank and dived straight at her," Tempest related, "firing a burst into her as I came. I let her have another burst as I zoomed under her, and then banked my machine over, sat under her tail and, flying along underneath her, threw lead into her for all I was worth. As I was firing, I noticed her begin to glow red." Having consigned the L-31 to flames, Tempest found himself in imminent peril of being engulfed by his victim. "She shot up about two hundred feet, paused, and then came whooshing down straight on to me before I had a chance to get out from under. In just the nick of time, with the zeppelin tearing after me, I nosedived. . . . I put my machine into a spin and managed to corkscrew out of the way as she hurtled past me, roaring like a furnace."

Breathing easier, Tempest, absorbed in the pyrotechnics he had started, stayed to circle the area. It was a fantastic spectacle. A massive festoon of rampant flame, the plunging zeppelin trailed long streamers of fire in its wake, some to flare gorgeously for an instant and evanesce, others to smolder and waft higher on the wind, while still others, many of them, slithered down to disappear again in the radiance of the parent conflagration. Then, with a concussive force that, according to Tempest, "quaked the heavens," the huge blazing carcass burst asunder, "spewing a mountainous shower of sparks." Tempest waited until nothing was left to see except burning remnants scattered about the ground, "and then I proceeded to fire off some green Very lights in the exuberance of my feelings."

During his homeward flight, when the handle broke off his manual pressure pump and rendered it inoperable, Tempest's giddy satisfaction was displaced by heart-chilling dread. His engine, starved for fuel, coughed, sputtered, and died, necessitating a deadstick descent in utter darkness and an emergency landing that luck alone would govern. As it happened, he pancaked into a field of stubbled wheat, the BE-2 skidding crazily on its belly, and slamming into a tree stump, which impact flipped it over onto its back. Although his machine was totally ruined, Tempest walked away with only a superficial cut on his forehead. Thumbing a lift to his airfield in a motorcycle sidecar, he arrived to a glad and boisterous welcome as the fourth pilot in less than a month to have destroyed a zeppelin.

At Potters Bar, where the main section of the L-31 had fallen, Mathy was found lying alongside his scorified control car, miraculously still alive. A bed was provided for him at a nearby inn. Despite a medical team's earnest labors, he never regained consciousness and died of internal injuries before the sun rose. The only disfigurement was a slight distention of his face, that of a blondish, balding, affable-looking gentleman in his early thirties. Over his

leather jacket and breeches he wore a camel's-hair greatcoat, smelling of gasoline, oil, and latex (which substance was used to mend leaks temporarily in
the hydrogen sacks), and around his neck a thick woolen scarf, probably
knitted by his wife, who had shared his quarters at Nordholz.

In his birthland Heinrich Mathy had reigned supreme among dirigible captains as a popular hero, achieving the status almost of a legend. His name and
deeds were so widely advertised that his colleagues had sometimes teased him
as "der Volksheld . . . das Wunderkind . . . the glamour boy," which had
always summoned a chuckle from him or a wisecrack in reply. The shock to
the German people on learning of his grievous fate was kindred to that caused
by the death of Max Immelmann several months previous, and barely less
than the sorrow felt four weeks later, on October 28, when the extravagantly
beloved Oswald Boelcke was killed in a freakish midair collision with one of
his own pilots.

As a result of Mathy's death, the popular image of the zeppelin—as a
sublime fruition of German genius, a marvel of modern war technology, a
veritable basilisk dealing wholesale devastation to the German foe—received
a serious setback. The people's faith in the airship had already begun to waver
in spite of the censorship of news concerning the raids on England, and
Mathy's loss served to undermine further a fading confidence. What had been
only a gnawing suspicion, a vague sense of misgiving, was amplified into overt
dismay by the knowledge that even such a virtuoso as Mathy could be fatally
destroyed by enemy defenders.

Almost anyone intelligent enough to keep abreast of events was capable of
detecting discrepancies in the official dispatches. All one had to do was pry
between the printed lines, interpret things said and unsaid, assemble particles
of data, draw obvious inferences, add this shred of fact and that bit of surmise
to the growing mound of evidence. Indeed, it was difficult for the most casual
observer not to perceive at least a faint glimmer of the truth. Losses incurred
on the raids, for example, were invariably described as being modest, but the
casualty list would usually be published on the very same page to compromise
and sometimes belie this assertion, and the list of known dead, moreover, was
often boxed with a black border, thereby snatching the reader's immediate
attention and predisposing him to doubt. Similarly, whereas each and every
zeppelin sortie was declared to have inflicted considerable damage to London
or whichever other city had been attacked, these places—after nearly two
years of aerial attack—had yet to be decimated or, for that matter, even dis-
ordered to any apparent degree. Unless the press had been so inconceivably
remiss as to have neglected mentioning it, London had suffered nothing like
the obliterating bombardment once prophesied.

With an increasing public appreciation of these harsh realities, mutterings
of disillusionment were more and more being heard. Wherever friends met, a
hushed dialogue was apt to derive from the "zeppelin question"—*sotto voce*
because many still considered it unpatriotic, if not downright treasonable, to

denigrate such a hallowed symbol of national might and majesty. It was a topic that only the unwise discussed within eavesdropping distance of strangers.

Among those in high-command circles who were privy to the facts, the proponents of continued zeppelin assaults on England had by this time, naturally enough, dwindled to a small minority. Even so, a rather bizarre situation arose to reprieve Strasser's aggressive policy from immediate cancellation. There developed now a distinct schism over the conduct of zeppelin strategics, the army on one side, the navy on the other, and in the middle, squirming uneasily, the Kaiser. The controversy had long been simmering beneath the surface. It boiled up to a head when the general staff lodged a singularly outspoken appeal with the Emperor and begged his influence in stopping the raids. Formerly, all interservice discussion of this subject had been couched in circumspect language, but the generals had lost patience for any further polite pandering to the navy. They submitted to the Kaiser, in so many blunt words, that the airship, insofar as it was being misused, had become an unsupportable extravagance, a thriftless and debilitating indulgence in false dreams. They conceded its utility for offshore patrol and certain kinds of transport and liaison work; however, in its glorified guise as a long-range attack craft, they likened it to a voracious white elephant that the German war economy could no longer feed. One of the general staff's memoranda in this relation went so far toward acrimony as to condemn the zeppelins as a *"damnosa hereditas"*—a burdensome inheritance.

An invidious issue had thus been raised that impugned the competence of naval leadership, and Kaiser Wilhelm—so his behavior tends to show—preferred to sidestep rather than embroil himself in an interservice quarrel. If his prime motive was to avoid any implication of favoritism, his dodge was both clumsy and transparent. Indeed, instead of leading toward a satisfactory solution, his evasiveness further vexed the problem. Expressing absolute trust in the wisdom and fairness of his admirals, he passed along to them—verbatim— the army's plea, much against the army's expectations or wishes. Perhaps, had this not occurred, the navy would of its own volition have terminated the raids in the autumn of 1916, the almost unanimous consensus of admirals having already gone sour on Strasser's activities. Maybe too, if His Imperial Highness had been tactful and foresighted enough to soften the tenor of the army's complaint before letting the navy see it, the consequences would have been less baleful, for the admirals were incensed by what they read. Accusing the general staff of rudely meddling in naval affairs, the German sea lords— jealous of their prerogatives—assumed a posture of righteous indignation. They icily replied that the army, considering the mess it had made of things in France, ought to rectify its own faults before appointing itself the navy's judge. And in a scathing rejoinder they refused to proscribe the lighter-than-air fleet from bombing England until they themselves were good and ready to do so.

Huffed and pettish as they were, though, the admirals retained enough perspective toward the truth of the situation to impose a drastic restriction on

Strasser's scope of authority. Until now, not according to official prescript but in routine practice, he could plan and prosecute raids entirely at his discretion. There had been the formality of notifying headquarters of each prospective raid, but an understanding had existed whereby his request for clearance was tantamount to clearance granted, so that he had embarked on many a sortie before receiving technical sanction; hearsay maintained, furthermore, that in several instances he had first carried through the mission and then, upon his return to Nordholz, filed the appropriate preliminary papers, an anomalous procedure that, if rumor be true, evinced no censure from the powers above. But the days of his autonomy were past. Until mid-November, when the squabble with the army was arbitrarily settled if not reconciled, only those zeppelins on local training flights and those patrolling coastal waters found employment, and practically all but Strasser's sleeping time was spent in consultation with his none too sympathetic senior officers. The upshot of these many meetings was a ruling by which future bombing expeditions would be mapped out and scheduled at the next higher command level; these projections would then have to be reviewed and endorsed at the top naval echelon prior to their implementation. Strasser's sole say in such matters was to be that of a bottom-rung adviser. The airship chief, in something more than a figurative sense, had had his wings clipped.

Accordingly, then, before the close of 1916, the rigid airship had begun to slip from German grace as a tool of war (although not as a commercial transport, as peacetime evolvements later demonstrated). If Strasser was yet unconvinced of the zeppelin's obsolescence, if he cherished hopes of somehow resurrecting its reputation, he faced profound disappointments in the months ahead. For one thing, as he bitterly learned, his ambitious scheme for blitzing London had come to naught; despite his persistent requests for permission to resume bombing the enemy capital, no dirigible ever again attacked that great city. Strasser was also distressed by the fact that German airship production, although continued right up to the Armistice, underwent periodic reduction at the request of the War Ministry during the last two years of fighting. Only one more major improvement was incorporated in the basic production model, a slightly bigger and better-powered ship—a sort of super-super zeppelin—emerging in the spring of 1917, the progenitor of this new class being the L-42.

There were dirigible attacks on England until August 1918, but they were confined to targets along the east coast and in the industrial midlands. These attacks, moreover, steadily diminished in force and frequency, and, as always, they were attended with inordinate losses. For example, on the raid succeeding that in which Mathy had died, an eleven-ship foray undertaken on the night of November 27, 1916, the L-21, commanded by a Lieutenant Frankenberg, and the recently commissioned L-34, commanded on this trip by a Captain Erlich (since Dietrich was absent on liberty), were both shot down by R.F.C. interceptors. And on the following March 16, when the Humber-bound L-36 drifted over Normandy with its engines frozen, it was destroyed by French artillerymen. On the next raid after that, the L-48 met its end at the hands of two British aviators, Captain R. H. M. S. Saundby and Lieutenant L. P. Watkins. The L-48 crashed in flames near Therberton, in Suffolk, and its crew—all of whom perished—were buried in the local churchyard, upon their common gravestone being inscribed the text: "Who art thou who judgeth another man's servant? To his own master he standeth or falleth."

It was during the night of October 27, 1917, however, that the airship fleet suffered its worst disaster of the war. Of seven ships departing to strike Harwich and Yarmouth that night, four never touched German soil again. Two, the sister ships L-44 and L-45, were brought down by antiaircraft fire after a terrific gale blew them many miles southward over the British lines in Artois. The L-49 and L-50 likewise drifted across France, the former being forced to earth near Neufchâteau, where it was captured intact. About midday, when the wind abated, the L-50 attempted to land behind the German trenches. Attracting a heavy barrage from the Allied positions and trying hurriedly to reascend, it grazed the top of a wood and lost its forward car. Thus lightened and out of control, it bounded skyward and soon disappeared. Spotted the next morning high above Toulon, a helpless rider on the seaward wind, the L-50 was chased by a whole swarm of French airplanes to no avail. The planes at last had to turn back, leaving the zeppelin to an unknown fate far out over the Mediterranean.

Spring 1918, found Strasser chin deep in difficulties. But still, despite the disinterest or outright opposition he met from almost everyone in Berlin, he kept the remnants of his fleet operating. Nothing stayed him in his purpose, not even the great toll of casualties he had incurred since the advent of war. That he was wide awake to these gruesome statistics is sure; in March that year, at the instance of the naval bureau, he prepared a summary report on his losses to date. By his own tally seventy officers and more than 250 non-commissioned officers and men had died, and an additional 150 had been wounded or taken prisoners of war. He revealed further that approximately a third of his airships had been knocked out by enemy action, that almost as many had fallen forfeit to the weather, and that eight had accidentally caught fire or, in two cases, possibly had been sabotaged. Stated in simple numerical terms, the price paid in German lives may have seemed small compared to the mass annihilations that had occurred—and would again—on the western front, but Strasser's figures actually represented a casualty rate in excess of 40 percent!

The financial expense of his dubious enterprise can be quickly assessed when one remembers that the average manufacturing cost of a zeppelin was something equivalent to half a million dollars, which in those days was a large sum for even a government to spend. Nor was it cheap, either, to support an airship division as a going concern. The overhead was tremendous; Strasser's monthly budget would have easily sustained a couple of infantry brigades in the field for twice the time. Nevertheless, apparently unfazed by the horror story he had just translated into a synopsis of abstract symbols, he signed his report with a bold, assertive hand. As an afterthought, he inserted a comment about the morale of his commanders and crews, certifying it to be at the optimum. Whatever *esprit de corps* remained, however, could only be ascribed to the leader's infectious enthusiasm and adamant conviction that his crusade would yet be crowned with success.

Keeping his zeppelins busy as always on coastal and offshore reconnaissance, Strasser gave his novice skippers every opportunity to gain experience and confidence. Though it afforded him less personal gratification than he derived from bombing England, the work of his airshipmen on the North Sea Patrol was beyond reproach—the redeeming accomplishment, in fact, of the entire airship effort.

For nearly two years the lighter-than-air machines had kept a sharp watch on Allied shipping with virtual immunity. The best available high-angle guns were difficult to aim accurately from pitching decks at sea. During the summer of 1917, however, there were a number of occasions when the flying boats from both Felixstowe and Great Yarmouth were able to make attacks on zeppelins and drive them upward to the shelter of the clouds. But this was neither good enough—nothing short of destruction was required—nor frequent enough. Because they had to stay above the effective reach of shipboard guns, about sixteen thousand feet, the airships only rarely attempted to sink or disable an enemy with bombs. More often, upon seeing a convoy, they summoned U-boats or motor torpedo boats to attack. In less than a year, from August 1917, through June 1918, the zeppelins had played a major role in the destruction of twenty-six cargo ships, plus a half-dozen naval craft. An additional forty-odd freighters had been damaged, some beyond repair.

No real defense against the scouting zeppelins seemed feasible. It was left to Captain C. R. Samson, who was in command of Great Yarmouth air station, to evolve a new manner of using the Sopwith Camel, the only really suitable machine for the task. After conferring with a panel of aerodynamics experts, Samson believed he had devised a method for launching a normal fighter plane at sea. A small lighter barge was requisitioned and modified to his specifications. Along with its engine room, its superstructure was removed. Thirty feet long and half as wide, a flat deck was boarded athwart its gunwales. Lashed to the rear of this platform was a Sopwith Camel, its two wings overhanging the beam of the barge.

The flying-off arrangement consisted of two wooden troughs in which skids attached to the chassis of the plane were fitted. The barge, after its conversion to a miniature aircraft carrier, was to be towed upwind by a destroyer at a speed of thirty knots. This, the experts had calculated, would be fast enough to get the Sopwith airborne without a takeoff run. With his engine turning at full throttle, the pilot merely had to yank a wire catch in the cockpit to unfetter the Sopwith, at which it would fairly leap into the air. Unfortunately for Samson, however, when he tried it out, the launching system did not work according to plan. The Sopwith's starboard skid slipped its groove, and this caused the entire undercarriage to collapse. The plane went slithering off the bow into the sea. Onlookers were dumb with shock as they watched the barge ram the wrecked aircraft and plow it under. Four agonizing minutes elapsed before the aviator bobbed back to the surface, unconscious. Besides soaking his lungs with salt water, he had suffered a fractured rib, three broken fingers, and a nasty skull concussion.

At Samson's pleading, naval higher-ups reluctantly consented to give the scheme one more chance. From his own station Samson picked a lanky, nineteen-year-old Canadian ex-cowboy, Lieutenant Stewart D. Culley, to attempt another test. Blaming a slight crosswind for his mishap, Samson directed Culley to employ a Sopwith with regulation wheels instead of skids, figuring that the traction afforded by rubber tires would hold the plane steady even if one wing should lift a little ahead of the other. While a new flight deck was being laid on the barge, Culley devoted four hours a day to practicing short-field takeoffs and slow-speed maneuvers. It was time well used, as became evident when he managed to fly his machine from its tiny sea-going platform and land it safely at a nearby airfield. Later, of course, in the actual operation, hundreds of miles from any Allied territory, he would be required to ditch, hopefully alongside a British vessel. Culley did not relish the prospect.

The experiment successfully concluded, preparations for the real thing were set in motion. Ten days afterward, in the evening of August 10, the Harwich Light Cruiser Force put out from harbor on a special operation. Culley was quartered aboard the *Redoubt,* a squat, four-funnel destroyer, with his makeshift aircraft carrier in tow astern. Dawn, August 11, found the flotilla steaming through the summer-calm waters of the Heligoland Bight. The ships were bearing eastward in close formation, skirting the Frisian Islands off the coast of Germany, staying barely outside the range of hostile shore batteries. For several hours now, despite the proximity of enemy guns, the ships' radios had been broadcasting a steady flow of genuine-sounding, but phony, messages in a code that German intelligence was known to have deciphered. The signals were a thinly disguised invitation to any zeppelin commander in the vicinity. Past experience had proved the Germans would not ignore a target as choice as this.

The deception worked. At daybreak, revealed in the slanting rays of the new sun, a hovering airship, the L-53, was spotted by the British lookouts. Culley rushed to the *Redoubt's* bridge and gazed thoughtfully upward at the supernal monster come to sniff the bait. When the order was given him to launch the plane from the barge, he was—he later wrote—"nauseous with apprehension." Culley had felt from the beginning that the scheme was as zany as it was hazardous, and no one in the Harwich Force would have argued with him. He knew that among the shipboard personnel a great deal of sea pay was being wagered on the outcome of his mission, and he also knew that most

France's supreme ace, the conceited, unpopular, but exquisitely skilled Captain Réné Fonck. (*U.S. War Dept. General Staff*)

Sergeant Raoul Lufbery smiles from the cockpit of his Nieuport, painted with the Indian-head insignia of the Lafayette Escadrille, at Cachy airdrome in 1916. Sergeants Robert Soubiran *(left)* and Didier Masson are playing with Whiskey, the squadron's lion cub and mascot. *(U.S. Air Force)*

OPPOSITE, TOP—Four of the American volunteers in the Lafayette Escadrille figure out the best way to cross Fritz' lines. They are *(left to right)* Walter Lovell, Edmund Genet, Raoul Lufbery, and James McConnell. *(U.S. Air Force)*

OPPOSITE, BOTTOM—Some of the pilots of the Lafayette Escadrille admiring their two pet lions, Whiskey and Soda. *(U.S. Air Force)*

Holding the rank of adjutant in 1917, Raoul Lufbery was the leading ace of the Lafayette Escadrille. *(U.S. Air Force)*

Funeral of Edmund Genet, killed in aerial action on April 16, 1917. Genet, a pilot-volunteer of the Lafayette Escadrille, was the first American to die in battle after the United States entered the war. *(U.S. Air Force)*

OPPOSITE, TOP—Forward control car of the *Schwaben,* one of Count Zeppelin's prewar airships. Naval personnel here prepare to take off on a training flight. *(Library of Congress)*

OPPOSITE, BOTTOM—The *Victoria Luise* being taken from its hangar at Oos in September 1914, just before entering war service. *(Library of Congress)*

Count Ferdinand Zeppelin, Imperial Germany's "Man of the Century," whose mammoth airships struck terror into the hearts of the Allies. *(Smithsonian Institution)*

A zeppelin lumbers across Belgium on the way to bomb London in 1915. *(Library of Congress)*

Wreck of the Zeppelin L-20 near Stravanger, Norway. Blown off course while returning from a raid on England in May 1916, the L-20's crew was rescued by Norwegian fishermen and interned until the end of the war. *(U.S. Air Force)*

Wheelhouse of Zeppelin L-49 after it was brought down and captured intact by the French. *(U.S. Air Force)*

Dwarfing the house in the background, the charred framework of Zeppelin L-33 lies athwart a field near Colchester; it had been shot down after bombing London. *(U.S. Air Force)*

Captain Treusch von Buttlar Brandenfels, a veteran zeppelin commander who participated in many raids against the British Isles.

An unidentified zeppelin over London in 1917. *(U.S. War Dept. General Staff)*

Zeppelin L-70, flagship of the German lighter-than-air fleet in the summer of 1918. Captain Peter Strasser, commander of zeppelin operations, was among the casualties when the L-70 was shot down in August. *(U.S. War Dept. General Staff)*

Ground crew loads 100-pound bombs on a Gotha. *(U.S. War Dept. General Staff)*

Germany's big twin-engine Gotha bomber demonstrated the superiority of airplanes over airships in long-range strategic raids. *(U.S. Signal Corps)*

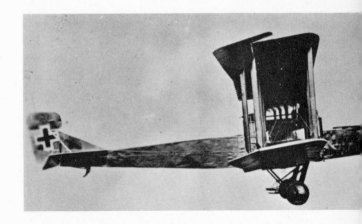

Leergewicht:
Nutzlast:
zul. Gesamtgewich
Auf rech

Fokker triplane takes off in search of prey. (*Library of Congress*)

Captain Hermann Goering in the cockpit of the Albatros D-5 he flew as commander of Jasta 26. (*Library of Congress*)

OPPOSITE—Forward gun of a Gotha bomber. Note oxygen tube in gunner's mouth. (*U.S. War Dept. General Staff*)

German observation balloon, heavily defended by unseen guns on the ground below, was no easy target. (*U.S. War Dept. General Staff*)

OPPOSITE, TOP—All-white Fokker D-7 was sometimes used by Goering after he assumed command of the Richthofen geschwader. (*Library of Congress*)

OPPOSITE, BOTTOM—"The Balloon Buster," Lieutenant Frank Luke, Jr., second on the list of American aces, poses with the Spad in which he blazed a name for himself along the Toul and Chateau-Thierry sectors of the front. (*U.S. Signal Corps*)

When observation balloon came under attack, the observer parachuted to safety. *(U.S. War Dept. General Staff)*

Typical identification card for American pilots in World War I, this one belonging to Lieutenant Harlan R. Sumner. *(U.S. Air Force)*

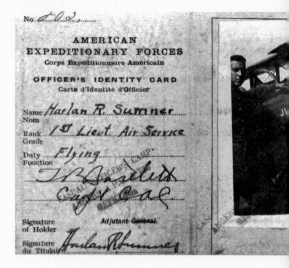

Aerial vista of a large air park near Paris. *(U.S. Air Force)*

Colonel William (Billy) Mitchell *(left)* beside his two-seater Spad after one of his frequent reconnaissances. The man with him is probably his French liaison officer, Adjutant Fumat. *(U.S. Army Air Forces)*

French-built Breguets of the U.S. 96th Bombardment Squadron head for daylight bombing assault on German territory. *(U.S. Air Force)*

His face bloodied, Unteroffizier Hans Marwade *(center)*, a five-victory ace, is taken prisoner by American doughboys after falling in combat. *(U.S. Signal Corps)*

A gaudily decorated Spad of the U.S. 94th Pursuit Squadron and its pilot, Captain Reed Chambers. An ace in his own right, with seven victories, Chambers became a postwar business partner of his famous squadron commander, Captain Eddie Rickenbacker. *(U.S. Army Air Forces)*

America's top ace, Captain Edward Vernon Rickenbacker, commanding the famed "Hat-in-the-Ring" squadron, achieved the unique distinction of shooting down twenty-six enemy planes and balloons in less than eight months flying at the front. *(U.S. Signal Corps)*

of the money was odds-on against his ever getting the Camel airborne. Perhaps the prevailing attitude in the flotilla had been most eloquently summed up by the nameless comedian aboard the *Redoubt* who had left a pair of galoshes on Culley's bunk. Tied to the overshoes was an unsigned card which said, "So you won't get your feet wet."

Slowing its headway, the destroyer began rolling on the gentle swells as a longboat was lowered over the side. In it were seven men: Culley, his two mechanics, and four seamen who silently stroked the oars, pulling the boat toward the barge. When the longboat had drawn up alongside the barge, Culley and his pair of assistants—a sergeant and a corporal of the Royal marines—clambered onto the small flight deck and tore the tarpaulin from the snub-nosed Camel. While the mechanics gave the engine a final inspection and wiped the dampness from the electrical joints, the pilot strapped himself into the cockpit and tried the controls. In another minute the sergeant started rotating the propeller to prime the cylinders with fuel.

Culley advanced the magneto switch to the "on" position and waited for the engine to spark. Traveling into a thirty-knot headwind on the slippery platform, the crewmen were in nearly as much danger as the aviator. The corporal kneeled between the landing-gear struts and held the wheel chocks in place while the sergeant swung the propeller. The latter, if he lost his footing, faced the double danger of falling overboard or, worse, into the whirling propeller blades after the engine was running. When the moisture-fouled engine finally did wheeze to life, the mechanics dived for the edge of the deck and hugged themselves flat to it, each with a chock rope in hand. As Culley revved up the big Bentley radial to a full-throated roar, he watched the tachometer needle slide past the red warning mark on the dial and listened with a critical ear. The engine was dropping revs badly. He warmed it for five minutes while he checked and rechecked his gauges and repeated his testing of the magneto switches.

When he was ready to take off, he raised his left fist and opened it with a nervous flourish. At his signal, the mechanics yanked the chocks from under the wheels of the straining Sopwith. The plane's power plant snarled at the sudden load. The Sopwith slung itself forward and lifted shakily from the deck. It bounced back hard, sprang upward again, hesitated on the verge of a fatal stall, and gradually took a grip on the air. Besides his imperative need for airspeed, Culley had to contend with the turbulence kicked up by the destroyer's superstructure, which loomed before him like a mountain. Flying with scarcely enough speed to retain control, he cautiously nudged his left wing down and banked precariously away from the destroyer. He skimmed the water and labored to an altitude of maybe a hundred feet. Nosing down slightly, he gathered precious speed, circled the *Redoubt* once, and then commenced the long climb toward his quarry.

Heading generally away from the zeppelin in order to lessen the chances of being seen from above, Culley took the better part of a half-hour to attain the L-53's altitude. He was about ten miles away to the east when he leveled out of his ascent, and keeping the sun at his tail, took up his attack course. "It was," he recalled in later years, "the unbelievable size of the thing that most impressed me as I drew toward it. . . . It was painted metallic silver, so that it resembled a giant mirror of reflected sunlight which some divine miracle-worker had suspended in the sky." As long as the dirigible continued hovering languidly in place, Culley knew he had not been observed. The prospect of tangling with a Sopwith would have induced the enemy commander to climb, and climb fast, for refuge. Culley knew it was essential, therefore, to pounce as suddenly as possible.

He was a bit lower than the zeppelin and about a quarter mile away. Tightening his grip on the control stick and easing it back between his knees, his thumb resting in readiness on the trigger button, he raised the Sopwith into a shallow climb toward the L-53's starboard forequarter and closed in for his first pass. Culley laid his gunsight against the bulging wall of fabric and let go with his two guns. After fifteen rounds No. 1 gun jammed, but No. 2 continued firing until its ammunition was exhausted. There was no visible sign that the zeppelin was damaged; but as he turned away, he saw over his shoulder small red patches developing where his shots had entered the envelope of the zeppelin. With volcanic energy, the gap erupted into a huge, fiery, orange flower of destruction, shattering the hull of the L-53 before those on board could have realized their fate. The flash of the explosion was seen from the German mainland, fifty miles distant—in broad daylight.

This was Culley's first witnessing of death wholesale. "Maybe, had I not glimpsed their faces when I flew by the gondola, I would have been less affected by their ghastly fate," he later wrote. "Without so vivid a reminder, it was easy for a pilot to forget that enemy machines contained flesh-and-blood men such as himself, men whose fatal sin it was to be born German. . . . I was horrified and sickened by what I had wrought. The memory of those frightened faces haunted me for weeks afterward, and even nowadays"—this in 1959—"sometimes still does."

When the zeppelin exploded, the Sopwith was in a forty-five-degree dive. The blast threw the tiny biplane violently upward and momentarily dazed Culley. Acting from reflex more than reason, he shoved the stick forward and dived the plane quickly from the area of burning debris.

Nursing the plane out of its screaming nosedive, Culley remained a few minutes, lamely circling, in order to view the spectacular end of his victim. Now Culley focused his thoughts on the ticklish business of finding the Harwich Force in order to land by his towing destroyer, the *Redoubt*. In order to fix his position, he flew to the Dutch coast and turned south until he recognized Texel. Then he flew on a known course to the rendezvous, fixed at the Terschelling Bank. When he arrived there, with scarcely any fuel left, he could see nothing but cloud. Through a gap he saw a Dutch fishing boat and decided to land alongside this as he could now no longer reach the coast again.

But as he broke cloud he saw the whole of the Harwich force awaiting him, and after a short display of exuberance he picked out his destroyer and prepared for his ditching.

Because his takeoff had been too critical to tolerate an ounce of superfluous weight, there was no flotation equipment in the Sopwith, and Culley was, by his own estimate, "a contemptible swimmer." He planned his approach path, accordingly, to a point along the northern flank of the Harwich Force, close abeam and in front of the *Redoubt*. Here he put the Camel down as gently as he could and scrambled out of the cockpit as soon as the machine came to rest and settled in the water. With the usual efficiency of the navy, the longboat picked him up and transferred him to the safety and warmth of the destroyer. Moreover, the machine was quickly hoisted out of the water before it could sink and deposited back on the lighter from which it had taken off such a short time before.

Except for some bruises about his head and a livid welt caused by the seat strap across his legs, Culley was none the worse for wear. Two months later, just a day before the Armistice, he was awarded the Distinguished Service Order for the action.

Although the destruction of the L-53 made sensational reading in the British press, not a solitary account touched upon the real significance of the episode. It was, indeed, to quote typical commentary from the *News of the World* and the London *Times* in turn, a "scintillating exploit of intrepid ingenuity" and a "thrilling feat of uncommon imagination, resourcefulness and daring." The newspapers all did point out that Culley's victory demonstrated at last a workable method to deal with enemy airships out of reach of land-based fighter aircraft. Had hostilities lasted longer, barge-borne fighter planes would no doubt have become fixtures in Allied convoys or squadrons in waters menaced by zeppelins. In effect, Culley's guns had sounded the death rattle of warrior dirigibles. There and then, in that thunderous instant above the North Sea, the zeppelins became relics of bygone wars. Moreover, Culley's pioneering takeoff from the barge pointed clearly to the aircraft carrier of future wars—a far cry from the crude barge with its postage stamp of a flight deck.

Peter Strasser was spared the humiliation of this final blow to his once-vaunted aerial armada. Less than a week earlier, during the night of August 5, Strasser had been killed in action, which was the mode of death his ideology had taught him to prefer over any other. Poignantly poetic, perhaps, is the fact that he lost his life in what turned out to be the final raid on England, aboard the very last zeppelin to enter wartime commission—the unique and shortlived L-70.

This dirigible, the hundred and nineteenth produced by the Zeppelin company since the beginning of the war, was a prototypic giant among giants, its 694-foot length surpassing that of any seagoing vessel, German or Allied, then in naval service. Lifted by 2,196,000 cubic feet of hydrogen, driven by four

Maybach 245-horsepower engines, the L-70 was designed specifically to fly at extreme altitude. Instructions provided by the Maybach factory advised that the engines should not be turned on full until an altitude of six thousand feet had been attained. The only one of its kind to see action (the Armistice precluded the commission of others), the L-70—with fifty-one tons of weight aboard—could maintain a headway of from seventy to seventy-five miles per hour in the rarefied atmosphere above twenty thousand feet. With an estimated range of nearly eight thousand miles, as Strasser keenly appreciated, the superlative-sized dirigible could be expected to cross the Atlantic Ocean both ways, nonstop. Sensibly painted black instead of silver, the L-70 was placed under the command of a Captain Lossnitzer, an eager officer to whom Strasser had promised an important assignment.

Upon receipt of orders to dispatch five ships on a foray of the British Midlands, the L-70 was chosen to lead the pack. There was a few days delay because of inclement weather, but August 5 dawned without a cloud in the sky. At Nordholz, the flag denoting the commencement of priority operations was unfurled, and the base was soon bustling with the activity that always preceded a takeoff. One by one, with painstaking care, the zeppelins were removed from their sheds to the parking apron, where they sat in a row, straining at their mooring lines, undergoing final preparations. By three o'clock in the afternoon, the raiders were ready to depart. Scarcely audible above the din of the idling engines, the naval band played a medley of patriotic anthems. Captain Lossnitzer, having assured himself that all was right with his black leviathan of an airship, stood at the top of the boarding ladder and looked for Strasser, who, if he was not going along on the mission himself, always came to wish his commanders godspeed before they left. Strasser arrived at the L-70 just a few minutes before departure time and, to Lossnitzer's surprise, climbed into the gondola saying, "Let's get going." By half-past three, the zeppelins were airborne, maneuvering into *V* formation as they headed westward above a glass-smooth sea.

Five hours later, the first watch aboard the Lehman Banks lightship spotted the zeppelins making landward toward Yarmouth, thirty-five miles away. In response to the lightship's radio report, more than two score airplanes roared off from fields all up and down the Norfolk–Lincoln coast to search out and accost the enemy intruders in the upper darkness. Among the hunters was Lieutenant Egbert Cadbury, piloting a DH-4 two-seater. Handling the rear gun was Lieutenant R. Leckie. An experienced pilot whose own plane was laid up for repairs, Leckie was afraid he would be cheated of some excitement and so had talked Cadbury into letting him substitute for the regular gunner.

Cadbury jettisoned his bombs to increase the DH-4's rate of climb. He had coaxed the plane up to 16,500 feet and was somewhere north and east of the Wash when he saw four airships in the distance, silhouetted against an exceptionally bright corona of moonlight. In the half hour it took for him to fly up close to them, he observed the fifth airship far behind the main formation. Thinking this laggard ship might be having engine trouble, Cadbury considered attacking it instead of a nearer one. But then he noticed that the vanward zeppelin was larger than the others and guessed that it was the command ship, which made up his mind for him. He attacked slightly to port ahead, so as to clear any obstruction such as a radio antenna or observation car that might be suspended from the hull. Passing under the nose, Leckie fired a sustained burst of explosive bullets at a spot immediately forward of the zeppelin's wheelhouse, tearing a great hole in the fabric which soon began spurting flame. The fire spread quickly within the envelope, so that the entire ship glowed like a bar of red-hot metal before blazing up and plunging seaward.

The commander of the L-63, a Captain Freudenreich, in his report the next morning, described it vividly:

> The L-70 was on my starboard bow, bearing southwest, perhaps three miles off. My altitude was, if I remember correctly, about 17,800 feet. . . . I was nearing the coast when we suddenly saw an outbreak of flame on the L-70, admidships or a little aft. Then the whole ship was on fire. One could see flames all over her. It looked like a huge sun. Then she stood up erect and went down like a burning shaft. The whole thing lasted thirty, maybe forty-five seconds. I guessed it had been done by airplanes, so I altered course, ascended to 21,300 feet, crossed the coast later on, and dropped my bombs on a battery which was shooting at me.

Actually, as did the other three remaining dirigibles, the L-63 fled upward and away as fast as it could and spilled its bombs at random, doing damage to nothing. Cadbury tried to attack another of them, but it easily outclimbed his DH-4 and got away. Although he did not learn until almost a week later that he had occasioned Strasser's death, Cadbury was profoundly moved by the fiery dissolution of the L-70. The morning after his victory, in a letter to his father, he wrote: "Another zeppelin has gone to perdition, sent there by a perfectly peaceful, live-and-let-live citizen who harbors no lust for blood or fearful war spirit in his soul. It all happened very quickly and very terribly." Both Cadbury and Leckie received the Distinguished Flying Cross for their handiwork.

The flaming zeppelin had fallen a few miles offshore from Wells-next-the-Sea. For a long time after, bits and pieces of the wreckage were washed ashore nearby, but no bodies were ever recovered except that of the observation officer, a man named Kruger, whose badly decomposed remains were beached by the tide along the Frisian coast in late November. Three days subsequent to the L-70's doom, the naval directorate in Berlin released this bulletin: "During the night of August 5–6, Captain Strasser, Führer der Luftschiffe, with one of our zeppelin squadrons again successfully attacked the east coast and Midlands of England, conducting bombing raids on Boston, Norwich, and military fortifications around the mouth of the Humber. He probably, together with his brave officers and crew, died a hero's death in action. His ship was leading the squadron. All other zeppelins which participated in the mission returned home without loss, despite fierce enemy resistance."

Never for a moment had Strasser's faith in zeppelin warfare faltered. The months before his death had seen him suffer still more crippling blows, yet he remained to the end a steadfast believer in the efficacy of lighter-than-air craft. As had the year before, 1918 brought a succession of calamities for the airship division. On January 5, for example, at Alhorn, a shed housing the L-51 caught fire. A brisk wind foiled efforts to contain the blaze, and soon the whole place was enveloped in a swirling tempest of flame and smoke, zeppelins and storage tanks of hydrogen exploding in deafening chorus. Five airships—the L-46, L-47, L-51, L-58, and SL-20—were reduced to molten skeletons. Frantic crews and officers strove manfully to save their ships, fifteen dying in the attempt and ninety-odd being injured. The fire was of mysterious origin, an official investigation producing no explanation apart from Strasser's gratuitous allegation that sabotage by enemy agents had taken place, a theory plausible but never substantiated with real evidence.

There occurred, on March 12, a small-scale, moderately successful raid on the Midlands in which no zeppelins were lost, although Captain Buttlar's L-54 was hit amidships by an artillery shell and made it home only because an alert-minded rigger had secured the damaged framework with ropes to prevent the hull from breaking in two. The real benefit of this raid lay in the relief it provided to a dismal record of reverses. Whatever good auspices Strasser may have divined in this change of luck, however, swiftly evaporated. In that same week, at Nordholz, a training zeppelin was wrecked while trying to land during a squall. And, on May 10, off the Heligoland Bight, the L-62, commanded by one Captain Manger, was stalked for three and a half hours by a British flying boat and then shot down with no survivors. The victorious co-pilots, Captains T. C. Pattinson and A. H. Mundy, related that they had been able to overtake the zeppelin when its portside engine inexplicably stopped functioning. Two more dirigibles were lost to Strasser on July 19, seaplanes from the H.M.S. *Furious* staging a dawn attack on the hangars at Tondern, destroying the L-54 and L-60 in their berths.

The day before this excitement at Tondern, Strasser was in Berlin to keep an audience with Admiral Reinhard Scheer, the powerful chief of naval operations. The specter of inevitable defeat dogged his every footstep, but the iron-willed airship *führer*—emboldened by the acquisition of his latest super-dreadnought, the L-70—was sure of his ability to persuade Scheer to allow a resumption of raids against London. At their meeting, the admiral listened to Strasser's arguments in an indulgent silence, which the latter misconstrued as a sign of agreement. As he continued talking and as Scheer maintained what was meant to be noncommittal taciturnity, Strasser began overestimating his salesmanship. Everything seemed to be going so well that he purposefully digressed from his announced topic, London, and made a little ceremony of withdrawing some papers from his brief case. Placing them on Scheer's desk, he explained glibly that here was a plan by which to launch a bombing attack on—Strasser paused for histrionic effect—the United States! To be precise, New York City!

The admiral's face became a mask of astonishment. Before Scheer could find voice, Strasser was vigorously expounding reasons to circumstantiate the practicability of a transoceanic foray. In the foregoing autumn, he reminded the admiral, the L-59, in order to supply German forces in East Africa, had flown nonstop from Bulgaria to the Sudan and back. The new L-70 boasted a range superior to the intermediate-sized L-59's, a range easily embracing the distance both ways across the Atlantic. Another two ships like the L-70 were already in production, and a flight of three such zeppelins would be capable of dropping enough bombs on New York to incapacitate the city, physically and psychologically. Imagine, Strasser beseeched, what a coup this would be for the German cause. How devastating to the smug Americans in their remote fastness, deluded as they were in the belief that German retaliation would never reach so far across the sea.

Perhaps, had the zeppelin raids on London been more successful, Scheer would have manifested some curiosity at the least. As it was, he asked Strasser to leave the papers with him for further study. This was, on the admiral's part, a tactful alternative to stating his point-blank rejection, or so it may be inferred from the fact that he sent the papers back to Strasser within twenty-four hours, apparently unread. Two weeks later, following Strasser's fatal voyage in the L-70, they were discovered among his personal effects. On the flyleaf had been penciled the initials R.S., below the one stark word, *"Nein."*

When Strasser died, the most fanatic disciple and practitioner of zeppelin warfare passed from existence. There remained only Dr. Hugo Eckener and a dedicated coterie of dirigible commanders to preach the doctrine of armed lighter-than-air craft. They tried to push ahead construction of the L-70-type zeppelins, although just one more, the L-71, was completed before the end of the war. It proved unsound in its flight tests and required extensive modification. Feverish efforts were exerted to rush the L-72 through production, and three more mammoth airships were listed to follow, but Germany's defeat brought a finish to all this. Also nullified, incidentally, were the sinister intentions of Captains Lehmann and Dietrich, each of whom—without the knowledge of the other—had contrived a wildcat scheme for flying the L-71 secretly to America.

CHAPTER XVI

·°❦ *Wings Across the Channel* ❧°·

IMMEDIATELY AFTER the capitulation of Germany, nine zeppelins were surrendered by their commanders. Two went to the British, three to the French, two to the Italians, one to the Belgians, and another was dismantled and shipped piecemeal to Japan. Most of the remaining zeppelins were junked, though not quite all. At Scapa Flow, in June 1919, German sailors scuttled their ships rather than humbly cede them to the Allies, and this action revived the last vestige of Strasser's defiant spirit in the cadre of zealots who had served with him. The next morning Lehmann, Dietrich, Buttlar, and others deliberately destroyed seven of the last airworthy zeppelins, five in their hangars at Nordholz and two at Wittmundhaven.

"It was not as easy as might be suspected," Buttlar recounted. "We had no more gas. The ships were deflated. Otherwise, of course, a cigarette would have done the trick. But there were other means." At Nordholz, the L-14, L-41, L-42, L-63, and L-65 were hanging inert from their shed roofs. The suspension tackle was abruptly released, at which the zeppelins collapsed to the floors, each a pile of mangled girders and shredded fabric. The L-52 and L-56 at Wittmundhaven were demolished in similar fashion. "It gave us a genuine feeling of physical anguish," Buttlar recalled, "to think that we would be obliged to raise a hand against our own beloved ships. But we said never a word. Why betray to each other that we were choking with tears? . . . And thus they died, our proud aerial cruisers! Thus died Germany's aerial fleet! We had done our duty."

Buttlar omitted one sordid detail from his story. He and his accomplices were aided in their petty rebellion by a certain Royal Air Force staff-captain named Vivian Stranders, a member of the Inter-Allied Commission to Germany. Stranders, whose task it was to supervise the transfer of the zeppelins,

410

turned out to be a covert sympathizer of the disgruntled airshipmen. Had he not forewarned them of the commission's impending arrival, they probably would have been prevented from their vandalism. Stranders' political leanings were eventually uncovered, and a warrant was issued for his arrest should he ever set foot again in England. A few years later, apprehended in Paris, he was convicted as an agent of the German secret service and sentenced to a short prison term. His subsequent career consisted of writing anti-French stories of espionage for German publishers, and in the period leading up to and during World War II, he was a passionate Nazi.

In the final analysis, once the propaganda was ignored, the zeppelins had proved themselves to be largely an empty threat, and the adventures of those who flew them were but an unavailing exercise of courage and skill, a monumental waste of talent. Including the Schutte-Lanz species, 140 German dirigibles were used on operations during the war, of which roughly two-thirds were destroyed or captured in action, or wrecked by storms or mischance. They were a negligible factor both on the western and eastern fronts. As for the campaign of "frightfulness" unleashed upon the British Isles, Strasser's force actually executed forty raids, dropped 220 tons of bombs, killed 557 persons, injured 1,538, and caused nearly thirty million dollars worth of property damage, a third of which was wreaked on London. That was something on the credit side, and the usefulness of zeppelin patrols over the North Sea was something more, but everything considered, the lighter-than-air fleet had accomplished too little to offset its cost in manpower, money, and materials.

Better results might conceivably have been obtained. Had the airship division of the German army possessed a leader of Strasser's zeal and vision, had the zeppelins struck massively as a unified fleet and early in the war, before the enemy could build up his defenses to confront them, they might have altered the course of events. But even with energetic, organized planning and unvacillating adherence to a policy of ruthless terrorism, luck and weather would also have been necessary. The whole zeppelin concept—a tremendous envelope of volatile gas presenting an easy target to any enemy gun, its uneconomical bulk in relation to its payload, its handling difficulties on the ground, and its vulnerability to the weather—constituted a nightmare that could never have long competed with the rational use of heavier-than-air bombers and reconnaissance machines.

Always in the history of warfare, a new weapon has been swiftly countered by a specific defense. A means of opposing the zeppelin was readily available in the form of antiaircraft ordnance and the airplane, both of which, as they were generally improved and refined to particular purpose, compelled the zeppelins to fly even higher. With the science of bomb-dropping then still in its infancy, the dirigible's usefulness as a raider decreased proportionately with every increase of service ceiling. Not only was accuracy impaired by this resort to remote heights, but the crew was obliged to endure oppressive cold and the lack of oxygen, the engines were more prone to troubles, and the ship became increasingly at the mercy of unpredictable atmospheric conditions. Navigation problems were never solved; ludicrous and sometimes ruinous errors were made by commanders drifting on strong winds at extreme altitudes at night, which accounted for many of the more fanciful reports of success.

All the luck, then, and technological advantage lay with the defenders, whereas in the opposite camp—with one notable exception—the promoters of zeppelin strategy refused to learn from the early lessons of blood and fire. Only Count Zeppelin himself appeared to recant from his earlier beliefs. Although the German public never heard of it until after the war, the seventy-eight-year-old count, shortly before he died on March 8, 1917, had confessed a growing doubt about the military value of his *luftschiffe*. He expressed this disillusionment during a visit to General Hindenburg's headquarters at Pless, which event Hindenburg mentioned in his memoirs: "Count Zeppelin, too, was among my honored guests . . . and the touching simplicity of his manner deeply affected us all. Even then, early in 1917, he regarded his airships as an antiquated weapon in warfare. In his judgment, the airplane and not the airship will, in future, dominate the sky. The Count died soon after this visit, and so he was spared the misfortune of his Fatherland . . . fortunate man."

In the nascent days of the war, Zeppelin had shared all the hopeful expectations of the German people as to the effects of air raids. He could not, however, really adjust himself comfortably to the thought that women and children might be hurt or slain by bombs dropped from his airships. "Nobody regrets more than I," he told Wiegand, *The New York Times* correspondent, in February 1915, "that noncombatants have been killed, but have not noncombatants been killed by other countries as well? Why is England pouring forth this cry of outrage against us just now? Actually, England is feeling outrage because she is afraid that the zeppelins will abolish her 'splendid isolation.' The British are outraged, furthermore, because they have not constructed anything comparable to the Zeppelin airship."

The elderly count, for a man of his background, was surprisingly parochial in his understanding of the Weltpolitik. A loyal German was expected to hate England as the Fatherland's cardinal enemy—"Gott strafe England!"—and Zeppelin naturally adopted this attitude along with his fellow patriots. He, the busy inventor, had never had time to ponder the psychology of other nations, and so—as might truly have characterized the well-regimented Germans were the situation reversed—the British were objecting to air raids more from motives of envy and military embarrassment than because civilians were being uselessly killed in cities and towns far removed from the battle zone. Zeppelin's preoccupation with airships seemed to throw his view of the war entirely out of focus. Unwilling at first to admit that his dirigibles could possibly fail in war service, he seldom discussed anything else connected with the war. The interview with Wiegand, in fact, was one of very few occasions when Count Zeppelin bared a personal opinion concerning wartime government policy, and he showed himself as naïve in that as he was wrong in his initial assessment of the airship's armipotence. "Aerial warfare, like submarine warfare, has come to stay. The future of war in the air," he assured Wiegand, "depends upon the technical advancement of the Zeppelin airship."

Exactly two years later, at Pless, he expressed a contrary conviction, a testimony of bitter disenchantment, to General Hindenburg. These last two years of his life were full of disappointments, and Zeppelin suffered them with practiced grace. As the war raged on every side, he spent more and more of his time at the factory in Friedrichshafen, devoting himself almost exclusively to his work. His living quarters occupied an entire wing of the Kurgarten Hotel, just a short drive from the factory. His rooms contained simple, modern furniture, and pictures of his airships adorned every wall. Displayed in a large cabinet were many of the medals, cups, plaques, and similar tokens of esteem that had come to him from the government and nearly all of the major cities, universities, civic clubs, and scientific societies in the country. It was here that he preferred to spend his leisure. Once in a while he would visit his country house, Obergirsberg, only a few miles distant, but practically all his attention was devoted to the mammoth creatures of the air he had created. When not traveling, his time was about equally divided between the study in the hotel and the workshop in the great plant that was constantly growing. "To find him," wrote Captain Lehmann, a frequent caller, "one had to search the buildings. If he could not be found in one of the hangars or along the assembly line, he might be in the drafting studio; if not there, then in the research laboratories. There was always something going on which he wanted to direct or desired to observe personally. Indeed, despite his advanced age . . . he was continuously walking about, so that it was difficult to locate him in any one spot."

Rudolf Stratz, a German journalist who often visited Zeppelin in Friedrichshafen, described their first meeting thus:

> A small, thin man with a white mustache, wearing a dressing-jacket, arose from behind the table. He was a very old man, yet spry as a youngster. His eyes were strangely bright and a little moist. His nose was slightly curved. There was an aloofness in his gaze—the fanaticism of a discoverer of new worlds. A sacred fanaticism. In other ways, he looked like the typical, reckless old hussar. And yet, for all that, he looked the impeccable gentleman from head to toe—the diplomat, the general, the landowner, the aristocrat. And he was invested by that aura of perfect unconscious assurance which seems to surround all really great men.

Although Zeppelin was more active during than before the war, becoming thoroughly absorbed in the accelerated tempo of development and production, he doubtless yearned for the days of peace when he would be able to resume his commercial airship service, which was, after all, closer to his mind than the construction of military ships. He was sure now that no one would ever again question the practicability of dirigible transports. He was certain that, once the war had been won, all the principal cities of the globe would be linked by giant airships carrying upwards of a hundred passengers apiece. In his ambitious plans and calculations for the postwar years, however, he over-looked one vital consideration, namely that—owing to the many disasters to which his airships fell heir—their average life was unblessedly short. In 1924, *Nature,* a British scientific weekly, compiled an analysis of the Zeppelin air-ships' past performances: even dismissing those shot down in battle, they were found to have had a life expectancy averaging less than eighteen voyages in eighteen months. It was a mercy for Zeppelin that he was not by temperament statistically minded. Stratz, who came to know him well, wrote of the count that "he was able to bear the practical failure of his airships during the war because he was confident, absolutely confident, that they would be the primary means of passenger travel when peace was restored to Europe."

If Zeppelin was a stubborn man, he was also a realist, honest to himself. At first his faith in his airship as a military asset had been unaltered by the adverse experiences of the lighter-than-air fleet, but gradually, as the airplane was developed and perfected, he was constrained to think of aerial conflict— although not peacetime transportation—in terms of heavier-than-air craft. He was no stranger to this other realm of flight. If only because it had emerged as a potential rival of his huge rigids, he had watched the evolution of winged flying machines with intense interest and a slow-dawning, reticent approval. By 1912, he was satisfied that airplanes had earned a permanent place in the scheme of things—a place subordinate, of course, to the airship's—and that year he established the Flugzeugbau Friedrichshafen, a company to design and manufacture seaplanes for the Imperial navy.

As the size of his dirigibles demonstrated, Zeppelin was disposed to equate size with success in an aircraft. Before the end of 1913, his chief engineer at the Flugzeugbau, Theodor Kober, brought out the FF-30, a large twin-engined landplane retrospectively designated the G-1, which did not go into production. This plane was to serve as the forerunner of a whole family of Friedrichshafen bombers that worked on medium-range missions through the latter half of the war. Introduced into action in late 1916, the Friedrichshafen G-2, built under franchise by the Daimler concern, flew in limited number throughout 1917. But it was in operational employment only six months when it began to be phased out of service and supplanted by the much-improved G-3 model. A sturdy, well-balanced machine, carrying almost a half ton of bombs and armed with Parabellum guns at the nose and behind the wings, the Fried-richshafen G-3 was produced in much greater quantity than its predecessor, and it figured prominently in the strategic picture. That summer of 1917, for example, in a series of night attacks on the British installations at Dunkirk, a force of these bombers pounded the dock facilities to virtual uselessness, im-mobilizing a major Allied supply port for weeks. And during the ensuing winter and spring, successive waves of G-3's and new G-4's terrorized Paris after dark. Hence, the curious and ironic fact is that Count Zeppelin contributed directly to the creation of the very machines destined to eclipse and finally to supersede his dirigible raiders.

Not only did he lend a hand in producing the Friedrichshafen bomber; he also aided in the creation of Germany's R-type aircraft, one version of which was developed under his aegis and manufactured under his name. The designative initial "R" stood for "Riesenflugzeug"—giant airplane—and it was no misnomer. Although Zeppelin did not live long enough to see it happen, the capacious-sized, multi-engined R-plane, truly a prodigy of the period, proved decidedly superior to the airship as a long-distance raider. It was, in fact, an ancestor of those heavy bombers that were to revise all the classic theories of warfare before midcentury.

The planning of the R-planes commenced immediately after war was declared. Having always been skeptical of the airship's promise as an instrument of destruction, the German high command agreed to sponsor the development of a giant bombing plane after inspecting some blueprints submitted in September 1914, by Hans Forssman, an aeronautical engineer working for the Siemens-Schuckert combine. Since the authorities were none too optimistic about airplanes either, this patronage took the form of a relatively small money grant, on receipt of which Siemens-Schuckert began constructing a tri-engined biplane based on Russian Sikorski designs. It happened in the meanwhile that the industrialist, Robert Bosch—trading on the prestige of his partner in the enterprise, Count Zeppelin—petitioned the government for a similar subsidy. A modest sum was again bestowed, and under the count's personal supervision, on a site furnished by the Gothaer Waggonfabrik, which company wished to diversify into aircraft manufacture, there was organized in November the Versuchsbau Gotha Ost—the East Gotha Experimental Factory—with the aim of evolving a long-range heavy bomber. With Zeppelin's active collaboration, the designers, Gustav Klein and Helmut Hirth, had a monster biplane ready for testing in the following April. Completed that month also was the Siemens-Schuckert prototype, a monster in its own right, and not by virtue of size alone. A comparison of the two machines showed the Siemens-Schuckert to be inferior in every respect of performance, although it did embody some novel and futuristic ideas, such as an enclosed cabin, internally installed powerplants, and a rear fuselage that was split into twin tapering booms of triangular cross section, one above the other. Its weird appearance was no less striking than its unusual size.

The Siemens-Schuckert company had twice invaded the aeronautical field in prewar years, first to make airships and then heavier-than-air craft, but in neither instance did it achieve a marketable design. With its R-plane, the firm did only a little better, bringing forth seven machines in the next twenty-three months and then closing its shops. Except as trainers, these planes saw no service. Their undoing was their poor performance alongside that of the competitor from East Gotha, where results were propitious from the start.

The first model at East Gotha, the V.G.O. I, was built for the German navy and given the serial number RML-1. It was quite an orthodox example of aircraft layout and construction technique for its time, size being its only claim to unconventionality. With wings spanning nearly 140 feet, it was propelled by three Maybach 240-horsepower engines driving one tractor and two outboard pusher airscrews. Subsequent to trials, it flew operationally with the Imperial navy against Russia. A later model, one similar in configuration to the RML-1, completed trials six months later and also was used in the eastern theater of war—possibly to offset the effect of the Russian Sikorskis. A third and yet more estimable aircraft, the R-3, undergoing trials in January 1916 (when the "R" or "Riesenflugzeug" category was adopted into the official nomenclature), rewarded the experimenters with a generous measure of success. Driven by three sets of tandem-paired 160-horsepower Mercedes engines, and crewed by seven men, the R-3 carried five Parabellum machine guns for defensive armament, which prompted Count Zeppelin to praise it as a "winged fortress." Encouraged now to begin full-scale production, the East Gotha development team moved to Staaken, near Berlin, where a large factory was tooled up by midsummer. Liberally funded with government contracts, the organization was rechristened the Zeppelin Werke Staaken, which name would soon spell bad news to the British.

Its association with the Zeppelin group concluded, the Gothaer Waggonfabrik had not been sitting idle all this while. In return for the use of its facilities, the company enjoyed free access to the engineering concepts worked out by Klein, Hirth and Zeppelin. After wasting his talent on a variety of maladroit landplanes and seaplanes, Gothaer's head aircraft designer, Karl Rosner, contrived a prototype medium bomber of great merit, the Gotha G-2. This plane's debt to the Zeppelin R-type was apparent at a glance; though not a slavish copy, it much resembled a scaled-down R-3, and Rosner candidly acknowledged that he had, indeed, borrowed many ideas from the Zeppelin product, as he was entitled to do. The Gotha G-2, emerging in early 1916, was a squarish-looking biplane with considerable rake to its wings. Twin 220-horsepower Benz engines, housed in interplane nacelles, drove pusher airscrews. Ring mountings for Parabellum guns were positioned at the nose and behind the wings, the after cockpit having shields of wire mesh to protect the gunner from the propeller blades. A three-seater of seventy-eight-foot wingspread and hauling a thousand pounds of bombs, its performance was marvelously nimble for a plane of its kind. While not as fast in level flight as, say, the Friedrichshafen G-type—making seventy-eight miles per hour as against the latter's eighty-four miles per hour—the Gotha had more versatility in maneuver. And its flying range exceeded that of any comparable machine then in the air. The original design, in fact, was sound enough that it changed but slightly in the process of development, Rosner modifying only the aileron mechanism, the landing gear, the fuel tanks, and the armament in follow-up models.

Unveiled in late spring, the G-3 version so excited the enthusiasm of War Ministry representatives that a purchase order was placed for fifty machines. The Berlin customers were doubtless captivated by an unusual feature of the G-3, a ventral gun tunnel that permitted the rear gunner to fire downward under the tail. This arrangement did away with the so-called blind spot, that vulnerable area below the fuselage that in most aircraft could not be covered by a gunner, lest he risk shooting apart the empennage of his own machine. Re-equipped with larger fuel tanks that increased its flight endurance to seven hours, the "Gun-Tunnel Gotha" was given a G-4 designation and entered into assembly-line production.

The end of 1916 was approaching, and the German high command—by now acutely aware that airship raids on England were unreliable and much too costly to be continued as a regular thing—decided to try the new long-distance bombers that would soon be at its disposal, the Gotha G-4 and the Zeppelin R-plane. To this purpose, Bombing Group No. 3, later nicknamed the "England Geschwader," was deployed at Ghent, about 170 miles from London, with orders to prepare to attack the British capital. Thirty Gothas were scheduled for delivery to the unit in February 1917. Due to factory delays, the planes did not begin arriving until the middle of May. No time was wasted in putting them to use. On June 13, a formation of fourteen, led by Captain Ernst Brandenburg, attacked London in daylight and caused more casualties than all the airship raids had inflicted on the entire county of London up to that date. Seven tons of explosives fell into the city; 594 persons were killed or injured. Some sixty fighter planes scrambled aloft to repel the invaders, but only five got within machine-gun range, and these did nothing else than engage in a futile skirmish after the bombs had been dropped. Flying in diamond formation so that every plane was protected by several of its sisters, no matter what an adversary's angle of attack, the Gothas were a formidable match in air-to-air combat. They operated, furthermore, at upward of eighteen thousand feet, beyond the reach of antiaircraft fire and any but the ablest pursuit craft. On this first outing all the Gothas returned to Ghent untouched.

Strategic air power had suddenly, after a fitful upbringing, come of age. Its astonished foster parents, the German war lords, awoke to the realization that they had been nursing the wrong baby in their early concern for the airship; that upstart brat, the airplane, was the one earning its keep. "Hearing of the recent successful attack . . . by our lads in aviation," wrote the Führer der Luftschiffe, Captain Strasser, a bit wistfully to his mother, "my officers and I anticipate some real competition from them in seeing who can work the greater punishment on England. We in airships will do our utmost, and let the chips fall where they may. I wish the aviators well. Whether they do better than we, or we better than they, the loser will be England." Magnanimous sentiment notwithstanding, Strasser found that his relations with the high command, which were already strained, had not been improved by the stunning triumph of the Gotha bombers.

The Germans always claimed, with some justification, that the French were the first to bomb an open city and that subsequent German attacks of such nature were but retaliatory measures. Actually, in January 1915, French pilots did hurl down a few hand grenades on Freiburg, a city well removed from the battle line. This incident has been cited in almost every pro-German chronicle of World War I as a vindication of more than two hundred air raids on Allied population centers, including London and Paris. Precisely what was meant by the term "open city" was not clear. The capital of a warring power can hardly be presumed inviolable when it shelters, as did London, all the machinery of government and many of the staff directing military and naval operations. It is an obvious assumption that the British and French would have attacked Berlin had the means to do so been available, for in 1917, the epoch of total warfare had begun in earnest. Inasmuch as geography precluded the Allies from bombing Berlin, it was easy and politic for them to play the role of raped innocents and to solicit help from the Americans and other sympathetic neutrals. Beneath this façade, however, lay a considerable desire to repay German attacks with compound interest.

This desire for revenge afforded some of the incentive that made the British rush into service a large bomber—the Handley-Page 0/100—six months before the Germans did. Extravagantly described as "the answer to the Zeppelin airship," the Handley-Page was an angular biplane powered by twin Rolls-Royce engines with tractor propellers, its top wing spanning exactly a hundred feet. About midway in size between the enemy Gotha and R-type bombers, it made its operational debut with the R.N.A.S. Fifth Wing at Dunkirk in November 1916, whereafter it was flown in raids against the U-boat lairs at Bruges, Ostend, and Zeebrugge, and in support of the army, later, in Flanders. By mistake, while ferrying one of these planes to France, a pilot landed at Laon and presented the Germans with a factory-fresh example of the latest British handiwork. The seeds of a myth were hereby sown. The Handley-Page, besides a Lewis gun at the nose and one behind the wings, carried a third gun mounted to fire through a hatch in the underside of the fuselage; since the Gotha appeared soon afterward with much the same provision for defending its tail, British propaganda defamed the Gotha as an imitation of their Handley-Page. Although it was smart policy, the accusation was baseless, and there are documents extant that testify to the originality in the Gotha. Nevertheless, through all the intervening years since World War I, some aviation historians have persisted in portraying the Gotha as more or less a copy of the somewhat inferior Handley-Page. These same historians at the same time have totally ignored the Gotha's affinity to the Zeppelin R-plane, its outsized cousin.

That the British did not immediately use the Handley-Page to implement a long-range bombing campaign against Germany can be attributed to two factors: (1) a lack of concerted initiative that would later be sorely regretted and (2) a judicious regard for American opinion while the United States wavered on the verge of announcing its cobelligerency with the Allied nations. As early as June 1916, when the Handley-Page was accepted by the Admiralty for service in limited quantity, there had been talk in London of opening an aerial offensive against the enemy homeland, of avenging the zeppelin raids and gaining strategic dividends in the same bargain, but nothing was soon done toward effecting this. General Hugh Trenchard, commanding the R.F.C. in the field, requisitioned that summer ten squadrons of the new heavy bombers; but it was more than a year later, in October 1917, that the first such R.F.C. squadron was established in France, at Ochey. The Handley-Page was not ordered into full production until after the Gotha and R-plane raids had induced a crisis situation in England. Nor did Handley-Page squadrons strike at any targets inside Germany until the spring of 1918, when they began bombing the Saar and Rhineland with telling, if belated, weight and frequency.

The building up of a powerful British strategic bomber force was impeded by the difficulty of reconciling the great need of the armies in France for maximum air support with the relatively small supply of aircraft and crews. Trenchard, his tactic of "direct action" having markedly enhanced the efficiency of Allied combat squadrons at the front, at first supported the British commander-in-chief, Sir Douglas Haig, in his constant request for more squadrons to aid his armies. The political difficulties and arguments that assailed the various Air Boards, the exhausting rivalry between the R.F.C. and the R.N.A.S. for the available supplies of aircraft, engines, and skilled manpower, clouded the issue hopelessly. Although the purpose of the strategy was clearly visible to many of the best air commanders, the pressure of events on the western front concentrated everyone's gaze upon it. It is not incurious that it was the Germans themselves, as if on cue, and with an obliging touch of brutality that shook Whitehall to its foundations, who provided the impetus to a change of vision on that bitter thirteenth day of June 1917.

Nobody in London was prepared for the descent in broad daylight of a formation of Gotha bombers. The raid, claiming nearly six hundred casualties at no loss to the raiders, dealt a staggering blow to British morale. Where the domestic defense had at last proved effective against marauding dirigibles, it was shown to be inadequate for warding off this new menace. This revelation, to say nothing of the ensuing public outcry, led the government to react vigorously. Not since early 1915 and the advent of the airship raids had this unsettling aspect of the expanding air war been rammed home so forcibly. Trenchard was recalled from France for urgent consultation. The flying corps' chief came armed with a four-point appreciation of the general aviation picture, which he expounded at a special cabinet session on June 20. His exposition was constructive and concise, shirking none of the questions then agitating the politicians and people, and yet embodying principles of air power that have since lost little of their grim validity.[1]

Trenchard advocated, first, that the Belgian coast be wrested from enemy control. This "most effective step of all," he explained, would not only lengthen the distance to be traversed, but it would also compel the German raiders to fly across Allied-occupied territory when going or returning, or else to overpass neutral Holland, where British agents could spot them and radio advance warnings.

The "next most effective step" was to inflict the greatest possible damage on the enemy's bases and machines behind the western front. The amount that could be accomplished, he indicated, would be governed solely by the number and capability of planes and pilots available in France. An increase in this tactical effort, or "direct action," would serve the twofold purpose of assisting the armies in overcoming the foe and, at the same time, reducing his capacity to send expeditions to England. To the Germans, Trenchard asserted, "this reply would be very discommoding."

The third item on Trenchard's agenda related to the home defense.

> Any system of patrols . . . would entail the use of a great number of machines and pilots. To insure any hope of such a system being effective—except by sheer luck—the number of pilots and machines required would be entirely beyond our present power of supply. . . . As a temporary measure, a modified system of patrols might be tried, working on both sides of the English Channel. To give this its best chance of success, an extensive system of communications, by wireless and other means, would be needed. And it is imperative that there should be unity of command over the whole system of patrols and communications.

Trenchard closed his discourse with a plea for the long-range bombers which the War Office had seen fit to withhold from the R.F.C. He was careful here to counsel that bombing objectives in Germany should preferably be confined to factories and legitimate military facilities.

> Reprisals on open towns, although we may be forced to adopt them, are repugnant to British ideas. It would be worse than useless to do so, however, unless we are determined that, once adopted, they will be carried through to the end. The enemy would almost certainly reply in kind—and unless we are resolved and prepared to go one better than the Germans, whatever they may do and whether their reply is in the air or against prisoners or otherwise, it will be infinitely wiser not to attempt reprisals at all. At present we are not

[1] Boyle: *Trenchard.*

prepared to carry out reprisals effectively, being unprovided with suitable machines.

The prime minister proposed that Mannheim should be bombed forthwith. Trenchard retorted that such an effort could not possibly succeed. Personally he disapproved of theatrical countermeasures intended merely to appease the popular lust for retaliation. Though he had no scruples about attacks on German industrial plants—and was, in fact, eager to bomb them—he pointed out that none could be reached from his bases in northern France. For that matter, Mannheim was scarcely within flying radius of French airfields farther south. Still, as a demonstration of his readiness to initiate a vigorous campaign of strategic bombing when the appropriate aircraft became available, Trenchard offered to take up immediate negotiations with the French for the lease of some of their more conveniently located bases in eastern central France.

That much agreed upon, the Cabinet insisted that at least two crack fighter squadrons should be pulled from the front for daylight defensive patrols above the English Channel, disregarding Trenchard's admonition that the Germans would strenuously exploit a weakened R.F.C. in France. Events proved him right. No. 66 Squadron, equipped with Sopwith Pups, and the renowned No. 56 Squadron, its experienced pilots flying SE-5's, were ordered home to help guard London, whereupon the Gothas bombed with relative impunity several towns behind the British lines, as well as trenches, roads, dumps, and depots. For ten consecutive days the Gothas rampaged, and Richthofen's boys, who seldom ventured across no-man's-land, displayed a new aggressiveness in holding off R.F.C. attackers while the raids were in progress, the Red Baron himself claiming two victories, his fifty-fifth and fifty-sixth. With the British army in the midst of marshaling its resources for a push toward Ypres, the Gotha forays could not be allowed to go on. Accordingly, after patrolling the Kentish coast for nearly a fortnight, the two squadrons were returned to their former stations in France at the adamant behest of the War Office. The Germans responded with an alacrity that betrayed their ruthless simplicity of aim. No sooner had the R.F.C. fighters ceased picketing the Channel than the Gothas were dispatched from Flanders to assail London again.

They appeared above the capital again at mid-afternoon, July 7. When the alert sounded, the members of the Air Board left their offices and from the balconies of the Hotel Cecil watched the Gothas—twenty-two of them disposed in duplicate diamond formations—circling three miles and more overhead, easily beating back the few home-based planes that struggled up high enough to attempt interception. Once more leading the German bombers, Captain Brandenburg was surprised to find the city as ill-defended as on his previous visit; anticipating fiercer opposition, he had lightened the bomb loads to afford the Gothas an extra measure of speed and altitude. But, as he noted in his action report afterward, "it was a needless precaution. We encountered only token resistance, a few decrepit two-seaters firing at us from, at their nearest approach, a thousand meters below. . . . Although none with me was hit by enemy fire, one of our machines . . . developing engine trouble on the inbound flight, crashed into the sea with no sign of survivors." When the Gothas departed, London was left with 252 casualties.

The fiery horror of this second daylight raid within a month gave rise to near-hysteria. The press reacted with anger and consternation, affecting the people with black dismay. The Cabinet convened a few hours after the all-clear, but the mood of the ministers was gloomy and recriminative. The ministers glumly faced up to the fact that domestic defenses were helpless to cope with this new menace. Of paramount necessity was, obviously, an exhaustive reappraisal and overhaul of the defensive establishment. But first, to wipe the egg off their red faces, the Cabinet members decided that the two squadrons borrowed from the R.F.C. and prematurely returned to France should now be brought home again to resume their watch along the southeast coast. It was decided further that a reprisal raid should be flown against Mannheim, provided this could be done without cramping preparations for the impending Ypres battle.

The R.F.C. fighters flew north at once to home defense, but the citizens of Mannheim were left unmolested. As Trenchard advised the Air Board president, Sir William Weir: "We must stop the bombing of London, but the only way to do it is to knock out completely the German aviation here. . . . At the same time, there is no doubt that we ought to do bombing, and directly you can obtain for me a squadron of DH-4's with B.H.P. engines, I shall recommend that we start bombing the factories of Mannheim."

Somehow, Trenchard had been misinformed as to the status of the B.H.P. engine. Introduced by the Beardmore company specifically for long-range assignments, the engine was still in its experimental stages, so that none were available; indeed, another six months elapsed before the B.H.P.'s teething troubles were cured. Whereas Trenchard would have dearly preferred Handley-Pages to DH-4's, he knew there was no point in asking for them, the promised production of these planes for the flying corps having not as yet been set in motion. Trenchard was too conditioned by past disappointments of this nature to make an exhibition of his frustration. This current predicament was merely a domestic variation on the theme of "too little and too late," which had haunted him since his accession to command. As he probably guessed would be the case, Mannheim was not quaked by R.F.C. bombs until the better part of a year had passed.

Where they had failed with their monster dirigibles, the Germans, with just two airplane sorties, had convulsed the vital plexus of the British Empire, and now His Majesty's government decided to combine all the components of defense under a single authority. Brigadier General E. B. Ashmore, then com-

manding artillery in the line north of Ypres, was selected to head the new
defense organization. Ashmore's expertise in artillery was his main qualification for the post, the exigent need being for improved, higher-reaching antiaircraft guns in and around London. But Ashmore would also share in the
management of a sizable force of home-defense airplanes. A stranger in this
province, he had the good sense to confer at length with Trenchard, whose
cogent diagnosis of affairs he endorsed.

Once he had been made aware of the prime goals of German air strategy,
Ashmore tried his best to conform his policies with Trenchard's. Intrinsic in
their relationship, however, was a conflict of interest that would eventually
drive a wedge between them. Ashmore did, however, always concur in principle with Trenchard's viewpoint, and until the constraints of his own position
left him no alternative but to go against Trenchard's counsel, he endeavored
to cooperate in every way with the R.F.C. commander. For example, at a time
when many politicians and newspapermen were urging withdrawal of additional squadrons from the front, Ashmore opposed such a move. As Trenchard had shown him, the raids on London were deliberately meant to attenu-
ate British air strength in France. The Germans hoped to impose a defensive
role on the R.F.C. and to rob it of its striking capacity. The raids were a
diversion, a well-timed side blow, intended to drain off and contain enemy
detachments out of all proportion to the effort involved.

Ashmore, listening to Trenchard, had his eyes opened to the inherent advantage conferred by extreme tactical mobility upon a winged attacker, who
is, in effect, always on interior lines. The German bomber group then stationed in Belgium, with a radius of action of three hundred miles, could cover
almost a full semicircle of hostile territory. It could reach any point on a cir-
cumference of nearly a thousand miles, or in an area approximately seventy
thousand square miles, and elements of it could simultaneously hit objectives
as much as six hundred miles apart. No master geometrician was required to
calculate that even if defending fighters had equivalent range, even if they
could get information the moment the bombers took off, and even if a given
number of fighters could repulse a comparable number of bombers, it would
still be necessary to retain precious many aircraft within the semicircle to
oppose each and every potential attacker. Since none of these postulated conditions prevailed—which is to say that *all* the benefits of the situation redounded to the Germans—the British found themselves in a serious dilemma,
much like a one-armed boxer who, should he block a left jab, bares his chin
to a right uppercut.

If the criterion of success be the size of the attacking force in relation to
the enemy force it holds in check, the German airplane forays across the
Channel must be counted among the most successful diversionary moves in
the annals of warfare. Never did the bombers employed against England—
Gothas and R-planes taken together—exceed forty-three in number. So small
a contingent as that compelled the British to hold at home almost eight hun-

dred aircraft, of which about half were first line. It is true that there was, in addition, the possibility of a revival of the airship raids, but offsetting that is the fact that by no means the whole of German bomber strength was directed against England. As a conservative estimate, it is probably fair to say that the military effort expended respectively by attacker and defender was somewhere in a ratio of one to twelve—a singularly worthwhile operation for the Germans.

The activities of these few German bombers, miles away from the scene of the real battle, had both immediate and long-continuing effects on the subsequent course of hostilities in the central arena. Not only was Trenchard divested of two of his finest squadrons at a most crucial period, just prior to the third battle of Ypres, but supplies of Sopwith Camels—then the latest-type of single-seater, desperately needed in France to cope with the new and formidable Albatros D-5 fighter—were kept back from the front and used to re-equip units of the home defense. It was on this issue that Trenchard and Ashmore came to loggerheads. The R.F.C. chief complained wrathfully at being deprived of the Sopwiths. Ashmore understood why, but his appointed responsibility was, after all, the safekeeping of London, and he was "pained by the necessity to set myself at odds with my esteemed friend." The R.F.C., as a result of this privation, lost the initiative in the Ypres sector, and the Germans seized the opportunity to intensify their local air strikes. British bombers were perforce diverted from objectives deemed to have a direct influence on the important operations then impending and to attack instead the enemy airfields—particularly those at St. Denis Westrem and Gontrode—which housed the German night raiders. The immediate price of protecting London, therefore, was a loss of air superiority at a time and a place that could scarcely have been more inconvenient.

This so nicely applied squeeze on British resources had long-term repercussions that, though indeterminable, can only be described as enormous both in their scope and character. The hundreds of fighter planes locked up in domestic defense, had they been present in France, unquestionably would have enabled the R.F.C. to secure the Flanders sky against enemy aircraft. The absence of these planes prevented the R.F.C. from attaining a degree of ascendancy that could have materially shortened the war. As a certainty, the third battle of Ypres would have been less grim an ordeal for the unfortunate troops of the British Fifth Army who spearheaded the attack. Their opening advance bogged down for days by torrential rains, they were hammered incessantly by German artillery, and choked and hideously blistered by mustard gas which mixed with the mud and water to cause, long after its release, persistent casualties. Things got no better when the weather cleared, for then the toiling British troops were strafed and bombed by wave after wave of enemy planes. Outnumbered, their machines often outclassed, the overworked airmen of the R.F.C. fought back valiantly, but with little practical effect. The Germans, thanks to the vigilance of their flying observers, were long-since ready and waiting for the siege to begin. Among other preparatives, they had concentrated the bulk of their air force behind the Ypres salient and used it, once the battle started, as their forward line of resistance. Never before had they or anybody else used the airplane as a frontal assault weapon with such murderous efficiency. The British Fifth Army, almost destitute of air support until autumn, suffered terrible losses. On no other battleground of the war did so many soldiers fall victim to air attack.

The Germans, however, neglected to press their strategic advantage as unremittingly as they should have. Immediately preceding, and during, the clash in Flanders, they ought to have increased the frequency and magnitude of their airplane attacks on England, especially in light of the inadequacy of British home defenses. But they failed to step up the pressure at a time when the threat of raids would have played havoc with British plans. Apart from detaining men and matériel from the front, such bombings caused serious slowdowns in British war production. Winston Churchill, who had become Minister of Munitions, informed the Cabinet that after one raid on London, only 27 percent of the workers in the important small-arms plant, Woolwich Arsenal, had reported for duty, and that only 64 percent showed up the following day. Churchill found that after every raid, whether by planes or airships, the absentee rate soared among workers engaged in vital industry and that many tons of war goods were thus lost to troops in combat. Then, too, there was the business of replacing London's antiaircraft guns. Those in use were of early 1915 vintage that, besides lacking sufficient range, had an average life of only fifteen hundred rounds. A sturdier model, capable of reaching the high-flying raiders, was quickly developed under Ashmore's guidance, but its production required the reconversion of plants that had been making fieldpieces and automatic weapons for the front.

Why, if their bomb-dropping runs on England were so damaging to the enemy war effort, did the Germans not send more planes across the Channel? The explanation is that, although they knew their air attacks were vitiating British strength, they did not realize to what extent. They grossly underestimated the value of the raids, partly because of wrong intelligence reports, but mostly because of a hidebound infatuation with the traditional way of doing things and a blind distrust of new ideas. Never before the invention of self-propelled flying machines had a strategic diversion of this kind, encompassing hundreds of miles, been feasible in warfare. So it was rather a novel departure from classic military scripture, and the German generals—a conventional class by training—were predisposed to suspect its efficacy. Not wishing to risk too much on, nor to be too closely identified with, such a speculative proposition, they remained conservative and casuistic in their assessment of the results. And their attitude was reflected in the fact that the relatively small number of bombers used against England stayed more or less static, never exceeding forty-three, and also in the fact that even these bombers were not utilized frequently enough to impair the British war effort as greatly as they might have.

This reluctance to intensify the raids did immeasurable damage to the German cause. Before the end of September, the R.F.C. in Flanders was receiving substantial allotments of long-overdue and sorely needed equipment—including the latest Sopwith and SE-5 fighters—along with scores of new pilots, and the struggle for mastery in the sky reached a savage pitch. Employing the combat techniques pioneered by Albert Ball and his contemporaries, and developed by Edward "Mick" Mannock and James McCudden, a fresh crop of heroes got their first taste of action here. As the outstanding example: Lieutenant (later Major) William "Billy" Barker, a Canadian who opened his account by destroying two Albatros D-5's on October 16. Like a sniper who notches his rifle butt, Barker had a small white flash painted on the struts of his Sopwith Camel to denote each of his k'lls; when hostilities ended, a year later, his plane carried fifty-six of these marks, which placed him seventh-best among British aces. He and his fellow novices, after every day's flying and fighting above Flanders' plain, were required to attend lectures in which their more experienced comrades imparted to them practical knowledge won in the world's newest battle arena. They took down notes, studied instructional bulletins, watched demonstrations. "Deflection shooting," "cloud concealment," "decoys," "Beware the Hun in the sun"—the jargon of the new martial trade became their accustomed language. They learned their lessons fast and well, as they had to, and before long they were turning the tide against the German airmen.

Ashmore, meanwhile, had begun ringing London with his improved anti-aircraft guns, which proved so effective that the Germans decided to end their daylight raids and resorted to night bombing. By May 1918, the Gothas and accompanying R-planes were meeting punishment so severe that cross-Channel operations were discontinued, after which the Gothas flew against French targets exclusively and the giant Zeppelin machines were reclassified as general utility craft. All told, German airplanes had carried out fifty-two attacks on Great Britain and dropped seventy-three tons of explosives—by actual count, 2,772 bombs—which killed 857 persons and injured nearly three times as many. Egregious enough from the British standpoint, it could have been decidedly worse. Irresolution, misjudgment, a fearful approach toward novel methods, and plain and simple shortsightedness led the Germans to rely on half measures. They had not struck hard enough nor persistently enough when the chance was theirs. After flustering the British with their initial blows, they had failed to follow up, thereby allowing the British time to recover their equilibrium and hit back. The strategic concept underlying the raids was valid, but its execution was inept, yielding nothing more tangible than a few weeks of air superiority at the front. Although British casualties at Ypres were about double the German losses, due in part to the bombings on London, the latter were losses Germany could ill afford. And a major battle that might have been won, an Allied offensive that might have been turned back in complete defeat, was merely fought to a standstill.

But the raids had one significant aftereffect. Caught flatfooted in this emergency, the British authorities—and the press and public—at last perceived the wasteful confusion that had resulted from the existence of two separate and distinct air forces, the R.F.C. and the R.N.A.S. Owing largely to their lack of mutual regard and a sense of rivalry that allowed for only the most perfunctory kind of cooperation, the situation become so muddled that both forces suffered embarrassing consequences. In competitive haste, each had made more than its permissible share of blunders. In 1916, for example, the War Office placed orders helter-skelter for aircraft long out of date, including such obsolete types as the Farman and Bleriot two-seaters. On another occasion, three thousand Sunbeam engines were purchased despite the manufacturer's warning that they were of an untried design incorporating aluminum parts that might be difficult to cast properly. Two large factories were devoted entirely to filling this order, and when the engines were delivered, their aluminum cylinders and valve lifters did, in fact, prove to be impractical. Likewise, the Deasy company sold a large consignment of engines to the flying corps with 90 percent of the cylinder blocks defective. The two-hundred-horsepower Hispano-Suiza, manufactured under license by the Wolsley company, was at first unsuccesful due to a faulty crankshaft, although War Office engineers did not discover this fact until some twelve hundred units had been accepted and paid for. Eventually, all of these would be modified and corrected, but the right time for experimentation was prior to government order and purchase.

The Admiralty's record in this connection was not much better than that of the War Office, although the navy avoided many blunders by contracting with Rolls-Royce, whose engines were, as a matter of company policy, rigorously inspected before delivery. The two air services were in constant competition for priority on the production of planes and powerplants. They worked at cross purposes, often wastefully duplicating each other's efforts. They bickered and wrangled, not only between themselves, but with their respective departments in the War Office and the Admiralty, whose knowledge of aviation problems was often clouded by prejudice and inexperience. And both were frequently at odds with the Air Board, which had a loose power of recommendation and no executive function at all.

The Admiralty made a habit of giving short shrift to the R.N.A.S. Accordingly, when the R.N.A.S. sought the necessary funds to buy some Hispano-Suiza engines from a French concern, a chair-borne admiral objected to the size of the order on the remarkable premise that every belligerent nation, Great Britain included, would be so exhausted by the end of 1917, its military stores so depleted, that the war would just peter out, so that "to be left with a surplus of airplanes would be inconvenient."

All this internal squabbling, of course, did not conduce to a smooth, uninterrupted flow of top-grade matériel from factory to front. The situation, as brought into focus by the Gotha raids, was intolerable. The need for reformation was heralded in the press and discussed in Parliament. Obviously, the only sensible solution was to unite the air services under a single ministry. But both the Admiralty and the War Office resisted any move to take away their sovereignty. Sir Douglas Haig, speaking on behalf of the War Office, warned the Cabinet against what he called "the grave danger of an autonomous aviation command which would assume control with a belief in theories not in accordance with practical experience." Since its birth aviation had been treated as an unwanted child by the army and navy alike. It had been under-fed and carelessly treated through all its developmental years. But suddenly now, as it approached maturity, neither of its foster parents could bear the thought of its going forth on its own.

It was too late for making amends, however. On August 17, 1917, that doughty Boer, Lieutenant General Jan Smuts, at the request of the British Prime Minister, submitted to the Cabinet his "Report on Air Organization," which has been described officially as "the most important paper in the history of the creation of the Royal Air Force." Smuts advocated the establishment of a unified, independent aviation arm, to be directed by an Air Ministry and Air Staff. This principle was accepted by the Cabinet a week later, and the Air Force Bill, 1917, received the Royal Assent on November 29. Thus, after many birth pangs and with the sentimental regrets of many members of the R.F.C. and R.N.A.S., the Royal Air Force was ushered into being.

Setting up a new ministry as a functioning organism required time. In the interim, to correct immediately the damage done by all the confusion and downright poverty of perception, the Cabinet instituted an Aerial Operations Committee to adjudicate the whole matter of procurement. Smuts was appointed chairman and Winston Churchill was seated at his right hand. There was no appeal from any decisions made by this board, which presented no problems as it worked out, for the wisdom, solicitude, and absolute impartiality of Smuts was duly appreciated by both the War Office and the Admiralty. The board was soon renamed the War Priorities Committee, and its scope was broadened. Through its efforts an Air Ministry would be established to unify and command the air services. And so was born, just seven months before hostilities ceased, the R.A.F.

It is certain that the founding of the R.A.F. would have been delayed for several more years had not the Gotha raids on London aroused so much apprehension and disapproval that the heads of the R.F.C. and R.N.A.S. found themselves constrained to bury their differences and become better partners in the fight against a common foe.

CHAPTER XVII

·❧ *A Red Eagle Falling!* ❧·

W ITH THE ADVENT of the new year, 1918, none who shaped the conduct of the war had any illusions about what lay in prospect. After seventy-five months of unremitting attrition, the testing time was now at hand. The great contestants, gasping and bleeding, girded for the climactic ordeal of flesh and steel they knew was coming. There would be decisive moves, as both camps realized, and a Wagnerian finale to these many godawful months of unlimited bloodshed.

By 1918, the airplane was an appreciable military factor. Little more than three years of frontline service had transformed it from a motorized boxkite into a murderous battle machine. Combat planes with speeds as high as 148 miles per hour (the Nieuport-Delage Type 29) and ceilings surpassing twenty thousand feet were in development and limited use. Its rate of progress always accelerating, aviation had become a lusty participant in all phases of warfare. Strides had been made not only in technology but also in organizational efficiency. The British army and navy wings were combined to form the Royal Air Force on April 1, and upon its severance from the Signal Corps in May, the United States Air Service was founded. After a troubled and protracted start, the so-called Independent Air Force—the long-range bombing apparatus of the R.A.F. commanded by General Trenchard—was established by the British in Lorraine during the spring. Using DH-4 day bombers and the big Handley-Page night bombers, it dropped more than five hundred tons of explosives on German factories and communications targets. Conversely, the German raids on London declined in 1918, the last coming in May, when six Gothas and an R-plane were shot down. The Gothas continued assailing Paris, however, until mid-September.

These beginnings of strategic bombing, if somewhat disappointing in total effect, did gain certain results. The raids rattled morale, increased industrial absenteeism, thereby reducing output, and caused the retention of much valuable manpower and matériel for home defense. But on the whole, this had only an oblique influence on frontline military evolutions. By contrast, air power's direct intervention in the ground battle was growing always more potent and varied. The size of the aviation forces, puny in 1914, had increased enormously. The days of lone errantry were past. The unceasing struggle for air supremacy had become an exercise of large fighter formations. By midsummer, the Allies together had more than five thousand operational aircraft in France; the Germans, according to various estimates, had between twenty-seven hundred and twenty-nine hundred planes deployed along the front. The epic battles of 1918 were everywhere accompanied by action in the air. If it was a sideshow, it was a spectacular one. Sometimes the sky swarmed with hundreds of machines twisting and turning in combat, the chatter of their guns an infernal serenade, and here and there a streak of smoke to mark a loser's fall.

Out of the tiny Lafayette Escadrille, composed of impatient American volunteer flyers who fought for the French a year before the United States entered the war, grew an air service of more than a quarter-million men. American pilots trained largely in Curtiss JN-4's—the famous "Jenny," built and flown on stateside—but less than one-fifth, 1280 out of 6300, of the planes delivered to the American Expeditionary Force were produced in the United States, and all of them were of foreign design. In observation balloons the United States achieved a better record. It produced 642 and actually used 389 in France. Among others, such American airmen as Eddie Rickenbacker and Frank Luke quickly became aces; theirs was a short life expectancy with never a dull moment. Of 2698 planes flown in battle by A.E.F. pilots, less than one-half were still in service at the Armistice. With 750 confirmed kills, the "flying doughboys" tallied better than two victories for each of their losses. But like the American ground forces, they did not shoulder the main burden of the war—their more numerous, more experienced French and British allies did.

Arriving at the eleventh hour, the American aviator found himself involved in air action that had attained terrific pitch in combat, as well as maturity in technology and tactics. The Germans, in the forepart of the year, bolstered their superior offensive ground capabilities with their excellent pursuit planes —the Albatros D-5's, Fokker triplanes and D-7's, and Pfalz single-seaters. Beginning in July, however, and continuing throughout the great Allied drives to victory, the Germans were overwhelmed by sheer weight of numbers as the biggest air concentrations of the war—British, French, and American—reconnoitered, directed artillery fire, strafed, and bombed. The tables had been thoroughly turned against Germany. Within ten months the German forces on the ground and in the air had fallen from what had seemed the brink of triumph to the pit of defeat.

The German grand strategy for 1918 was simple: to concentrate maximum effort on the western front and to achieve victory, or at least a favorable peace, before American reinforcements could tip the scales. The British and French had anticipated this. The Allies were in no condition in the early part of the year to mount an offensive. Ludendorff, now chief engineer of the German war machine, contemplated a gigantic breakthrough on the Somme, to be followed, if need be, by a series of sledgehammer assaults to widen the breach and drive a wedge between the battle-weary French and British. As spring came to the long swathe of shell-scarred ground that stretched across France, the German general staff seemed justified in its optimism. There were but six combat-ready American divisions in Europe—with supply troops, less than 300,000 men—by March. And on the right flank of the British armies along the Somme, seventy-one German divisions, with some 2500 large-caliber guns, faced twenty-six British divisions, which possessed fewer than a thousand pieces of artillery.

The second battle of the Somme began in morning darkness, March 21, the Germans opening their drive along a forty-five-mile sector from La Bassée to La Fère. The British batteries were drenched with gas and soon silenced, their earthworks were shattered by booming siege guns, and under cover of a fog the onrush made rapid progress. Three elite armies, carefully rehearsed to new tactics, comprised the spearhead. As shock troops, they had been taught to forget all they had so painfully learned about trench warfare and to adapt themselves to mobility. Short, intensive artillery preparations, a creeping barrage, the bypassing of strong points, massive infiltration, sustained forward momentum at almost any cost—these were the ingredients of Ludendorff's hope for a quick and conclusive victory. By such bold tactical measures, he confidently expected to smash through the British lines, wheel northward toward the sea, and chew up the enemy armies. And he very nearly succeeded.

Although the Allies knew the assault was coming, and approximately where, they underestimated its power. Once in motion, the square-helmeted host surged ahead fourteen miles in four days, achieving the longest advance in the western theater since 1914. By March 25, Ludendorff believed the battle won. His troops were in Peronne, back again in the devastated area they had been forced to evacuate during the previous year. The vital rail center of Amiens was threatened, and the Allies were scraping up divisions from other sections of the front and funneling them frantically toward the Somme, once more a valley of death.

At this crucial point a unique German weapon and an incident of Allied disharmony seemed to provide the makings for disaster. In Paris, a mysterious explosion killed some people. It was followed by others. Aerial bombardment was blamed at first, but then it was discovered that the Germans were lobbing eight-inch shells into the city, from a distance of more than seventy miles, with an extraordinary gun they called "Big Bertha"—a macabre compliment to Frau Berta, wife of Alfred Krupp von Bohlen und Halbach, head of the

Krupp munitions works, where the gun had been produced. "Big Bertha" created more panic than havoc with the huge bolts she hurled into the French capital; coupled with the German success on the Somme, however, she represented one more incident of raw terrorism that did not benefit Allied morale.

If less visible to the worried layman, a far worse danger arose from the misapprehensions and divergent views of the British and French military commanders, Haig and Pétain. The rapid German advance came very close to causing the two forces to become separated in the manner that the Germans hoped to achieve. Diverging retirements would have meant almost certain defeat. This severe crisis led to the appointment of sagacious old Marshal Ferdinand Foch as commander-in-chief and coordinator of all the Allied forces in France. It was a more restricted title than it sounds, so that Foch often had to accomplish by tact and persuasion what he could not do by decree, but at long last, out of emergency, was born a unified command.

Ludendorff kept reaching toward Amiens, but a staunch British stand turned him back, seven miles from that town's valuable rail junction, and the second battle of the Somme ended on April 5. It had been a near thing. The British had lost about 160,000 men, including ninety thousand prisoners, and their confidence and that of their French partners, who suffered more than seventy thousand casualties, had been dealt a nasty jolt. The Germans had captured tremendous booty. They had reestablished the old Noyon salient. But they had also brought about what Allied deliberations had not been able to effect in three long years—a central Allied headquarters.

Pausing only to catch their breath, the Germans let loose their second mailed fist. Twelve miles wide, it struck south of Ypres and was aimed at the Channel ports of Dunkirk, Boulogne, and Calais. The battle of Lys, as it was called, started auspiciously for its devisers. A skittish division of Portugese infantry—one of two combat units sent by Portugal to France—had the misfortune to be camped across the Germans' path. It precipitously relocated, leaving a gap that Haig had to plug with British soldiers still resting and recovering from the severe fighting in the Somme valley. By April 12, Ludendorff had achieved a ten-mile penetration and was closing on his initial objective, Hazebrouck, a key rail center. The British had little room for maneuver. Haig issued an order to his troops: "With our backs to the wall and believing in the justice of our cause, each one must fight on to the end." The ensuing collision was a frenzied chaos. Ludendorff's charging phalanx overran most of Messines Ridge, and the British gave up that bloody glacis, so dearly bought. However, when the fighting extended into the coastal lowlands, the Germans were stopped short. After the arrival of seven French divisions to reinforce the British line, the first tangible result of Foch's unified command, the contest was all over by the end of April.

There came a lull after the battle of Lys, the communiqués reporting, "All quiet on the western front." Then, without warning, on May 27, Ludendorff unleased yet another offensive. This, his third great blow in less than ten weeks, was leveled at the French-held sector on the Aisne River. His object was to pin down the French and draw away their reserves from Flanders, where he envisaged a final annihilation of the tattered and spent British armies. The third battle of the Aisne began when nineteen German divisions, with twenty-two additional in close support, moved out abreast along a twenty-five-mile line. The Chemin des Dames, which had cost so many French lives to take, was quickly recaptured, and the Aisne was crossed. Within eight days, the Germans reached the Marne at Château-Thierry, a scant fifty-five miles from Paris. A salient thirty-five miles deep at its extremity, with a base of fifty miles, had been gouged into the French lines. In the emergency, Foch looked about desperately for reinforcements. The only troops not yet committed were of the American Expeditionary Force; more than half a million men were by now in France, but hardly a third of them had completed their advanced training and their performance in battle was an unknown quantity.

But Foch was hard-up for men, so he prevailed upon General John Pershing to supply them. Pershing responded with the Second and Third U.S. Infantry Divisions, with a brigade of marines attached. The doughboys and leathernecks were hurried to the Marne in trucks and buses, a motorcade reminiscent of the 1914 "taxicab army" that had reprieved France at this same river. The untested Yanks, as they neared the combat zone, could hear the ominous orchestration of war—the rolling thunder of barraging cannon, the strident rataplan of machine guns, the intermittent snap and crackle of rifles. Though not the first of Pershing's men to join the conflict—the First U.S. Infantry was then seeing heavy action near Amiens, and four other divisions were in the lines at various sectors—no Americans had ever reached the front at a more critical moment.

Apprenticed to the French, the Americans helped in no small measure to reduce the German bridgehead at Jaulgonne, for which they earned high praise from Foch and Pétain. The Second Division, on the attack throughout June and early July along the western flank of the salient's apex, took Vaux and Bouresches and Belleau Wood in hard-fought, bloody engagements. The marine brigade—"devil dogs" the enemy called its men, 40 percent of whom fell killed or wounded—won its immortality in nineteen days of gruelling combat. Anyone who had wondered how well the Americans could fight now had his answer. The crucible of battle had found them inexperienced, but brave and apt pupils. These debut appearances of A.E.F. units in active sectors of the front had the double-edged effect of restoring hope to the tired Allies and instilling fear in the enemy. The Americans had come to the rescue. They were jaunty and eager, almost childishly eager, and there were millions more where they came from. This was salvation for the western powers, since only the United States could redress the unfavorable balance of strength in France, where some 162 Allied divisions faced, as of June 1, more than two hundred German divisions. The French and British pleaded this fact to Washington and asked that another one hundred American divisions, roughly four million men, be shipped across the Atlantic before Christmas.

Ludendorff saw his opportunity slipping away. While he retained the advantage, the sole chance for victory or even a decent compromise hinged on his ability to beat into submission the tired armies of France and Great Britain before the flow of American troops and equipment swelled to a flood. On June 9, therefore, in an attempt to expand the Marne salient and link it with the Amiens bulge, he turned thirteen divisions toward the Montdidier-Compiègne-Soissons railroad, his fourth attack in as many months. Though he made a six-mile gain—tremendous by the standards of 1915–1917—it was not enough in these last bids for success. As Ludendorff admitted to his confidants, Germany was almost done for. At home, war weariness and food shortages and subversion were undermining morale; at the front, the Americans —whom Ludendorff styled as "those grinning cowboys"—were arriving, hale and hearty, in ever-increasing numbers.

Making his last attempt, Ludendorff attacked again. This final thrust, begun on July 15, and fought to a standstill just three days later, is remembered as the third battle of the Marne, or the Champagne-Marne. Had it succeeded in pulling French forces away from the British front, as was Ludendorff's stubborn intention, he then planned to land the ultimate blow in Flanders. But the scheme misfired. One-armed, redoubtable General Henri Gouraud, commanding the French Fourth Army, had prepared elastic defenses in depth east of Rheims. These, he calculated, would absorb the initial impact of the assault, while aerial bombardment and artillery would close the enemy supply routes across the Marne bridges. As he predicted would happen, the German drive ran out of inertia and was easily arrested and reversed. France had once again been saved at the banks of the Marne.

It was the fateful turning point. Foch and Pétain and Haig and Pershing had all foreseen that the first six months of 1918 would be the days of decision. Ludendorff's full-furied "End the War" campaign was over, a monumental failure. The spring tempest had been the bloodiest interlude of the long conflict. Once again the gray-clad armies had moved almost to within sight of the spires of Paris, only to be held off at the last. The Germans had captured 225,000 prisoners and inflicted a total of nearly a million casualties, yet their triumphs were victories without reward. Ludendorff's rifle strength, decimated in the onslaught, had fallen below that of the Allies. His soldiers were groggy, discouraged, sullen. The Allied ranks were burgeoning with fresh, vigorous Americans. In mid-July, there were twenty-nine khaki divisions in France, close to a million men. A "bridge of ships" spanned the Atlantic; from 250,000 to 300,000 troops were being conveyed across it monthly; by the end of October, forty-two U.S. divisions would be "over there." The doom of Imperial Germany was sealed. It was a matter only of time and tenacity. Once they had been stopped at the Marne in midsummer, it was to be all downhill for the armies of the Kaiser.

Through the whole of that tumultuous spring the German air force was called upon as never before. Ludendorff, progressive in his ideas on the uses of aircraft, relied heavily on tight tactical overhead support. The fluidity of his maneuvers, which finally broke the stalemate on the western front, laid a premium on winged cavalry. Massed bayonet charges across open terrain were canopied by low-flying Fokkers and Albatroses. The planes made repeated passes at enemy fortifications, their bullets and bombs tearing at concertina wire and abatis and gabions. This disorganized the defense and drove it deeper into its ditches and burrows. Radio-equipped two-seaters were directed against troublesome pillboxes, machine-gun nests, mortar and howitzer positions. Strafing and bombing became daily chores of the German aviator. French, British, American, and Belgian pilots replied to the challenge manfully. The resultant air battles had no previous compare. The airplane figured prominently, heroically, in the final battles.

Conspicuous, as always, in the German air effort was Jagdgeschwader No. 1 —Baron Manfred von Richthofen's celebrated "flying circus." Shortly before the start of the great spring offensives the illustrious Red Knight and his three squadron commanders, along with several other senior commanders of Germany's air service, were Ludendorff's dinner guests at army field headquarters. The general had arranged the occasion to impress upon them the importance that was being attached to aviation in the impending campaign. He prescribed that, in the three weeks remaining until "Der Tag," pilots should be conditioned for working in close cooperation with the infantry. By way of a prolix toast to victory, General Hoeppner, commander-in-chief of the air force, delivered a pep talk to his "eagles," as he called them, and vowed to Ludendorff that "our planes will guarantee your success." An inveterate cynic, Ludendorff is reported to have permitted himself an ambiguous smile and to have said to Hoeppner: "Don't you think, Herr General, that our six million foot soldiers will be useful also?" [1]

These were tense days for Richthofen. The corrosive strain of almost three years of combat flying, the extraordinary demands on him as a national war idol, the compelling need to accumulate kills and maintain his primacy among aces, and the onerous pressures of running a geschwader had exacted a terrible toll from the ambitious young man whom Oswald Boelcke had recruited from the eastern front and nursed to greatness. Not yet twenty-six, Richthofen had survived the hazards and travails of a hundred ordinary lifetimes. Faced now with the culminating crusade, he was worn out. He ate without appetite. When a party was thrown by one of the squadrons at the field, which was often, he never stayed long. "This is no place for me," he once explained.

[1] Actually his riflemen numbered about two million.

"The boys will soon get into the right mood when I'm not here." He slept fitfully, his dreams perhaps inhabited by an old and intimate acquaintance: Death. If he was haunted by any sinister harbingers of his own destiny, it seemed to blunt the hard edges of his character. "M. von R. is a different man . . ." a pilot of Jasta 11 wrote home. "He has mellowed."

They all remarked how the baron had become more charitable in his assessments of his pilots and how solicitous for their safety and welfare. He had developed an almost maudlin anxiety about his brother, Lothar, so much so that he wept when the latter was shot down on March 13. After bagging two Bristols that morning in a series of dogfights above the lines between Cambrai and Le Cateau, Lothar was bested by his intended third victim, another Bristol, piloted by Captain G. F. Hughes, with Captain H. Claye in the gunner's cockpit. A prolonged burst from Claye's twin Lewis guns sent Lothar's triplane spiraling erratically to earth. Manfred broke off combat and watched, horror stricken, as the tiny machine crashed. Returning to the airdrome at Avesnes-le-Sec, he was told that Lothar's injuries were grave. "The baron's eyes flooded," a witness wrote. "It was touching to see his tears, for they showed him to be human after all. Those of us who knew him from his early days at the front had kept our doubts . . ."

Rushing to the hospital, Richthofen was visibly relieved to hear that Lothar was not as badly hurt as at first had been feared. The doctors had suspected the worst when they found him spitting blood, but it was blood swallowed from a severely lacerated nose and jaw. A sprained ligament in his left leg required bed rest. During his convalescence he was visited daily by his brother.

Lothar was back in the air again within a fortnight, flying and fighting as recklessly as ever. By the Armistice he would shoot down thirteen additional adversaries, to bring his total score to forty, which tied him with Boelcke and Lieutenant Franz Buchner for ninth place among the German aces. In 1919, he married the Countess Doris von Keyserling, the daughter of an old privy counsellor to the Kaiser, but they soon separated. Three years later, on July 4, 1922, Lothar and a film actress, Fern Andra, and the latter's manager were flying from Hamburg to Berlin in an old ex-military airplane. There was engine trouble, an emergency landing, an unseen telephone wire, and a crash in which the gallant war ace lost his life and his two passengers suffered serious injuries.

On that day of Lothar's almost fatal smash-up at the front, his famous brother—during the twilight patrol—engaged a Sopwith Camel in even battle and shot it down in flames. The loser, Lieutenant John Millett, a Nova Scotian lad recently come to No. 73 Squadron, R.F.C., had earlier in the day noticed Lothar's triplane in distress and harried it all the way to the ground. Manfred had seen the Sopwith on Lothar's tail, but whether he recognized it that evening as the same aircraft and singled it out for combat will never be known. In any case, Millett paid with his life for the lamentable distinction of becoming the Red Knight's sixty-fifth victim.

Although Manfred von Richthofen flew at least two patrols on each of the next five days, during which there occurred frequent encounters between large numbers of hostile planes, he did not take his sixty-sixth victim until March 18. He was flying at the head of Jasta 11 that morning, followed closely by Jasta 6 and Jasta 10, when he spotted British formations crossing the lines toward Le Cateau. Both he and Lieutenant Siegfried Gussmann, a newcomer to Jasta 11, dived at the same machine, their guns blazing in unison. The Bristol fell. Gussmann, later, dared not claim a victory that Richthofen might think his own, but the baron—a changed man, indeed—entered a report which credited Gussmann with the kill. Nor did Richthofen's sudden magnanimity end there. Moving over to another flock of Bristols, he again found one of his pilots attacking the same machine at which he was firing. Drawing aside, he left the *coup de grâce* to Lieutenant Erich Loewenhardt, who thus achieved his thirteenth victory. Loewenhardt, before he died in a mid-air collision just a month prior to the Armistice, raised his score to fifty-three, which qualified him as the third-ranking German ace of World War I.

After seeing Loewenhardt finish off the Bristol, Richthofen joined with others of his geschwader in a melee against ten SE-5's and nine Sopwith Camels. As a Sopwith flashed across his sights, he fired and missed. To his surprise, the Sopwith made an abrupt turn and climbed at him with both its guns chattering. Its occupant, Lieutenant William G. Ivamy of No. 54 Squadron, realizing that the all-red triplane belonged to the notorious Baron Richthofen, could not resist the temptation to try himself against Germany's *wunderkind*. But he went at it too impetuously. Richthofen merely rolled into a downward bank. When the Sopwith was framed in the arc of his propeller, he opened fire, scoring hits on both its fuel tanks. Ivamy, landing without a scratch, was taken prisoner. Nine years later, he wrote an account of that day's action which appeared in Floyd Gibbons' biography of Richthofen, *The Red Knight of Germany*. Explaining that the SE-5's and Sopwiths had been detailed to escort a naval bombing squadron of DH-4's on a raid against the German airdrome at Molain, Ivamy—under the faulty impression that Richthofen had deliberately selected him from the crowd to attack—described the episode in these words:

> As we were following the bombers, the German planes were in position on four sides of us and above. Directly the DH-4's had dropped their bombs, they turned for home, and this evidently was the signal for the Germans to attack, and the lot of them came down on us with a bang.
>
> Their plan of attack was to get anyone with streamers on. As deputy flight commander, I flew these streamers from my wing struts, and being in the rear of the flight and highest up, I can't say that I had much of a fight with his highness the baron, as I was slightly handicapped almost from the start, having an explosive

bullet in the petrol tank and the emergency tank being punctured.

I was saturated and blinded with petrol and sitting up there with a dead engine. There was nothing to do but descend, which I did in a veering nosedive. I have a faint recollection of the speed indicator going off the scale, but the old Sopwith hung together, and I made the best landing I ever made—up the side of a hill among a bunch of German infantry who were training for the big push. They appeared none too friendly with their rifles. By the time I could get out of the bus, three German planes were buzzing around over it, and the scrap up above seemed to be over.

I looked up and saw that the SE-5's had pulled away a bit to the north, so that we were rather in the soup. We lost five of our nine: the flight leader, two deputy flight leaders, and two new fellows, three of them prisoners and two killed. The SE-5's lost two and the bombers one, and I don't know what the German casualties were. It was just two days after this that the big German push of March, 1918, began, and this accounts for the number of German machines that were in the air that morning. That was the end for me, as I was a guest of the Kaiser till the Armistice.

Ivamy was spared any regrets about not having time in which to destroy his plane. His captors did the job for him. The German soldiers, upon hearing that he had been brought down by Richthofen, tore the Sopwith to shreds in their mad desire for souvenirs. Not that it really mattered, for a lack of replacement parts precluded the Germans from using the plane anyway, and as for learning the fine details of its construction, several captured examples of the Camel fighter had already been thoroughly examined and flight-tested by German technicians. What was left of Ivamy's machine was carted to a dump and stripped of any reusable fittings. As usual, every ounce of salvable copper and brass was also removed from the airframe.

As the quickening tempo of German air activity signified, zero hour for the great spring offensive was drawing near. At noon, March 19, a motorcycle courier arrived at Avesnes-le-Sec bearing sealed orders for Richthofen. The baron read them in his office where—as had lately become his habit—he ate lunch alone. The orders stipulated, first, that a detachment from Jagdgeschwader No. 1 should be in position at the advanced airfield at Awoingt, ready to take off at an instant's notice, by the eve of the offensive. The orders, neatly typed above General Hoeppner's signature, went on to advise that two additional squadrons, Jastas 5 and 46, were being placed under Richthofen's command. As the baron already knew from conversations with Hoeppner, his augmented geschwader would operate on the northern half of the German Second Army front, while to the immediate south would be six jastas commanded by a gifted executive officer, if not a distinguished combat aviator, Lieutenant Walter Kohze. Richthofen drew some comfort from the knowledge that he would be flying over familiar terrain. It was his old stamping ground from the summer of 1916 and the first battle of the Somme, and he remembered it with the instinct of a hawk as well as a man.

Germany's fierce legions were arrayed in readiness as the hour of attack drew near. The wait was tense, a trial of men's patience. Then, a little before five o'clock in the morning of March 21, the suspenseful silence was shattered by a thundering chorus of artillery. German gunners began laying down a tremendous barrage of high-explosive and gas shells along the British front. Three hours later the first wave of infantry moved out toward Saint-Quentin. At their airdromes the pilots of J.G. 1 breakfasted to the echoic peal of cannon. Their planes were prepared for takeoff at an instant's notice, and they ate in their flying clothes, anxiously awaiting the call to action. But none was received. That morning's dense fog kept them grounded, sulking about the base, bitterly disgusted at being deprived of the excitement of this long-awaited day. By early afternoon, however, the fog had thinned a bit, and word was received that the British had floated a couple of observation balloons. Two pilots of Jasta 10, Lieutenants Loewenhardt and Fritz Friedrichs, went out and shot them down. A few tentative patrols were flown before dark, but poor visibility ruled out any chance for a proper combat. There was only one engagement, a brief exchange of fire over Bourlon Wood that gave nobody a victory.

Lingering mist and intermittent rain continued to hamper aerial operations until March 24, when the weather cleared. Meanwhile, the German advance on the ground reached almost to the strategic prize that was Amiens. The fighting had spread all along the Somme from Ham to Hem, and the British retreat—fourteen miles in four days—was beginning to take on the complexion of a rout. Such it might have become but for the heroic services rendered by British airmen on that fourth day of the battle.

The magnitude of that day's air action was unprecedented. At every point along the local front, from dawn until dark, the heavens resounded with the clamor of guns and the roar of engines as the opposing air forces, fresh from their days of inactivity, came together in full strength and ferocity. When it was over, forty-five German aircraft had been claimed by the R.F.C., whose own losses comprised eleven missing, fifty-one wrecked, and three abandoned after being forced to land between the lines. Risen to fame that afternoon was a Sopwith pilot of No. 43 Squadron, Lieutenant J. L. Trollope, who alone accounted for six crashed Germans, an R.F.C. record at that time. Four days later, with a total of eighteen victories to his credit, Trollope was shot down and taken prisoner. Mutilated by an explosive bullet, his right arm had to be amputated by German doctors.

The flyers of both sides would long remember that March 24 as "the day of the great battle." For those of Richthofen's circus, though, it was an unhappy day to recall. In more than a hundred individual sorties, which cost the lives of seven of its pilots, Jagdgeschwader No. 1 claimed but a solitary victory—and that by Richthofen himself. Leading twenty-five machines in a new red triplane, he challenged ten SE-5's of his oft-encountered enemies of No. 56 Squadron. The ensuing tussle lasted over an hour. It was a running fight, the outnumbered Britons trying to break away toward their lines and the Germans trying to stop them. Richthofen scored on his first sweep, shooting the wings from the plane of Lieutenant Wilson Porter, Jr., a youthful Canadian of limited combat experience. The plane disintegrated as it fell, so that parts and pieces were scattered over a wide area, the engine thudding to earth near Combles, while Porter's body was found, still strapped to the cockpit seat, more than a mile away. But Porter's death was amply avenged. Despite the numerical odds against them, his squadron mates dispatched three of their pursuers before the contest ended. They achieved their salvation by drawing the Germans westward, always closer to the R.F.C. security patrols over British-held territory. When he saw other machines speeding to the aid of the SE-5's, Richthofen turned for home, waggling his wings, which was the signal for his pilots to withdraw.

On the next day Richthofen was again the sole member of J.G. 1 to score, this time a Sopwith Camel. In common with most R.F.C. fighter units that day, the Sopwiths of No. 3 Squadron were committed to low-level strafing in an all-out endeavor to stem the German advance toward Amiens. Richthofen, accompanied by five aircraft of Jasta 11, spotted a flight of these Sopwiths above the Albert-Contalmaison road at about four o'clock in the afternoon and promptly dived on them. The British planes were slowed by the Cooper bombs they were carrying. Evidently, Richthofen hit one of them before its pilot, Lieutenant Donald Cameron, was sufficiently aware of danger to release his bombs, for several explosions were seen to go off as the machine went earthward in a wreath of smoke and flame.

The next day, March 26, a new personality was welcomed to the jagdgeschwader, a man whom Richthofen had personally invited to join his elite band. A week prior to the Somme offensive, the baron had made a tour of aviation facilities in the Second Army region. At a field near Le Cateau, where Jasta 37 had just that morning moved in readiness for the coming campaign, he sought out the squadron commander, Lieutenant Ernst Udet, of whom he had heard glowing reports. Meeting Richthofen was for Udet a milestone in life, and he described it later in his autobiography, *Ace of the Black Cross:*

> On March 15, the squadron received its orders to move. . . . We realized that the long-expected offensive was due to commence.
>
> As soon as we arrived at our new airdrome, we set to work erecting the big marquees for our planes by the side of the road leading to Le Cateau. It was raining, a penetrating drizzle that was slowly and surely coating everything in liquid mire. . . .
>
> I had pulled on a leather jacket and was helping my mechanics to drive in the tent pegs when a motor car came by. So many cars

passed us that we took no notice of it. We continued our work, silently and doggedly.

Then I felt a tap on the shoulder and, turning around, I saw—Richthofen. Rain trickled from the peak of his cap and ran down his face.

"How d'you do, Udet," he said, negligently acknowledging my salute. "Nice weather we're having today."

I looked at him and noted the calm expression and the cold eyes, half-shaded by heavy lids. He looked older than I had imagined, older than the newspaper and postcard photos showed him to be, older than a man of his age ought to look. But he was the fighter who had already brought down no fewer than sixty-eight enemy aircraft—our best ace.

His car was waiting alongside the road, and he had climbed down the embankment to speak to me. I waited.

"Udet," he asked me, "how many have you shot down to date?"

"Nineteen recognized, one waiting for confirmation," I replied.

He raked the mud with the tip of his walking stick.

"Hmm, twenty," he commented. Then he raised his eyes and scrutinized me for a while. "That about qualifies you to join us. Would you care to?"

Would I care to? It was the most attractive suggestion anybody had ever put to me. If it had rested with me, I would have packed up and gone with him at that very moment. There were many good outfits in the German air service, and Jasta 37 was by no means the worst of them. But there was only one Richthofen geschwader.

"Jawohl, Herr Rittmeister," I said, scarcely able to contain my elation.

We shook hands and he left.

I watched him—a slender, fragile-looking fellow—as he climbed back up the slippery embankment. He then jumped into his car and soon vanished in the wet, gray distance.

Udet had ahead of him a career replete with excitement. In the remaining months of battle he attained rare heights of glory. Of all airmen, only Richthofen was more venerated in Germany. But unlike Richthofen, Udet survived the conflict, and he went on to fresh fame. Through another two decades he figured conspicuously and glamorously in aviation. He became the German champion of flight, a cynosure of national pride, a legend of his generation. Ultimately, though, he rambled astray into the jungle that was Nazi politics, and in the end, unjustly disgraced and wallowing in despair, he committed suicide.

As a flying fighter of J.G. 1, Udet became the second highest-scoring German ace of the war, bringing his sum of victories to sixty-two. He shot down forty-two adversaries in the half-year between March 26, 1918, when he first flew with Richthofen, and September 26, on which day he was wounded after destroying a pair of American DH-4's. In the uneasy peace that followed, he earned his living primarily as a stunt pilot, barnstorming the globe, gaining worldwide acclaim for his sensational aerobatic feats. He was featured in several films, one of which—*The White Hell of Pitz Palu*—remains a classic both of the cinema and of aerial technique. When the Nazis rose to power, Udet was disinclined to cast in his lot with them; only at the outbreak of World War II, as a proper patriot, did he rally to Hitler's Luftwaffe. Because of his immense popular appeal, he was ceremoniously placed in high position. Accorded the rank of general and put in charge of aircraft production, he chose to style himself as the nation's chief test pilot, a guise better suited to his romantic image. Although he could judge a sound design, he proved less than expert at assessing operational capabilities.

A cheerful extrovert, thoroughly charming, he was generally well liked as an individual. As an officer of the Third Reich, however, he became the butt of harsh and invidious criticism on two accounts—his politics, or rather his lack of them, and his inveterate hedonism. Udet's devotion to Nazism was transparently superficial, and it was not long before his artless recusancy aroused the suspicion and antipathy of some influential party zealots. This, together with his libertine improprieties, immersed him at last in deep trouble. He loved elegant food and wine, and could never resist a pretty face. His erotic capers were a constant source of gossip among Berlin's Nazi society. At his home he provided his friends with lavish entertainments of a type about which they discreetly did not want to tell their wives. Even when in debt, which was often, he maintained his reputation as a gay, generous, and in-defatigable *bon viveur*. He was spared any flagrant scandal for this, censorship being what it was, but his wild and merry indecorum made him vulnerable to his detractors in the Nazi party, and they finally conspired to ruin him. How they did it was to make him the scapegoat when it became obvious that the vaunted Luftwaffe had been ignominiously defeated over England by the few men and machines of the R.A.F. Aware of the conspiracy and doing nothing to thwart it was Hermann Goering, an old comrade of Udet's from 1918, now one of Hitler's closest colleagues and the Nazi air minister. The "Fat Man," as Udet called him behind his back, was understandably eager to load the blame for the Luftwaffe's failure on someone else, and Udet happened to be the most vulnerable. Unnerved by the intrigues against him, Udet, in November 1941 shot himself with his own pearl-handled Luger automatic. "You will see," he prophesied on the eve of his self-extinction, "they'll say I died of a heart attack and give me a state funeral."

The import of his prediction was correct. The official explanation of his death was that he had been accidentally killed in the discharge of his duty, while testing a new weapon. Staged under the Führer's personal direction, the funeral was of the opulent kind reserved for only the "noblest of Aryan heroes"—and Udet was so eulogized by the very men who had insidiously coerced him into taking his own life. "Your death will strengthen us," said Goering. "And now I can only say: Farewell, my best friend." And Hitler too, fully aware of the plot against Udet, mouthed eloquent laments at his passing.

Ernst Udet, eighteen years old when World War I began, was the curious product of an insensitive father's authoritarian abuse. As a small child, Ernst was shy, introspective and delicate. He showed early artistic talent and temperament. His father, fearing for the boy's masculinity, sternly repressed his aesthetic proclivities and goaded him into more "manly" pursuits, such as athletics and mechanical science. For the rest of Ernst's life, the specter of his domineering parent never ceased to haunt him. It affected his every decision and always put him on his mettle to prove his manhood. Although he retained his talent for drawing and used his sketchbook throughout the war for portraits of his fellow aviators and pictures of air battles (which have since commanded high prices from collectors of World War I memorabilia), he always needed a few stiff drinks before yielding to his muse. "Liquor sharpens the artist's perception," he once declared. Perhaps it also washed away, for a little while at least, the ingrained dread of paternal censure.

Before the war, one of the few things he did with his father's blessing was learn to fly. That was in 1913, when he joined the aero club in Munich. Since it entailed honest courage to pilot an airplane in those days, his father deemed aviation to be a manly business, and he not only gladly paid for Ernst's lessons, but when the club needed money, he donated more than enough to save it from insolvency. Strange to say in view of later events, Ernst saw little future in aviation and soon lost interest. It was the furthest thing from his mind that next summer when Germany went to war. Enlisting in the infantry, he served as a motorcyclist with the 26th Württemberg Reserve Division, stationed in Strasbourg. In the last week of August, upon the division's being ordered into battle, Udet penned a terse, revealing note to his father. "You have often accused me of cowardice," he wrote, "but I think you were wrong. I am off tomorrow to the front, and I hope that I shall soon win the Iron Cross. If I happen to be killed, then my frivolous life will have met a worthy end."

Two weeks later, on a road outside the village of St. Die, Udet's motorcycle was shot from under him by a French patrol that had infiltrated the lines. Regaining consciousness next morning, he found himself back in Strasbourg—in a hospital ward. Released after ten day's convalescence, he heard that his division had been sent to Belgium. He set out to find it, but neither at the headquarters in Namur nor Saint-Quentin was there any word of its whereabouts. No one seemed able to direct him to the division from Liège either, so he reported to the local transport center and was assigned a job delivering mail.

It was dull, easy, safe work. Udet, nagged by the compulsion to prove himself, was ashamed of having been reduced to a postman. His solace was the excellent cuisine at the Hotel Dinant, where he was very comfortably billeted. Here, at supper one evening, he made the acquaintance of a young army aviator, a Lieutenant Waxheim, whose reconnaissance squadron was based nearby. Partial to French cooking, Waxheim dined at the hotel frequently, sharing a table with Udet. The two of them were soon pals. They talked mostly of airplanes. Udet spoke of his flying experiences in Munich, and Waxheim related his adventures as a military pilot and told of the comforts and privileges of the German airmen in luxury billets well behind the lines. He was wise enough also to emphasize both the danger and the love of flying. Upstairs in his bedroom that night Udet composed a letter requesting his immediate transfer to aviation.

Having thus steered Udet toward his remarkable destiny, Waxheim was killed six months later. Death came to him out of a lovely blue spring sky. It was his second patrol that day at the head of three other observation machines. They were flying at nine thousand feet, traveling west across a scrollwork of French trenches below. The observer in the forward seat had just given the signal to turn for home when they sighted a small French monoplane speeding straight at them. Though mildly surprised by this, Waxheim felt no anxiety. The sun was behind his formation, and as long as the Frenchman flew toward them, what was there to worry about? The Germans carried revolvers and Mausers aboard, but these were meant for use only in case of a forced landing on enemy ground. Airplanes were not yet fighting machines. This was April 1, 1915.

The monoplane held its course. Waxheim stared at the glistening disc of its propeller, and his eyes opened wide in astonishment. With this bewildered expression on his face, he died. His plane twisted crazily to earth, and even before it crashed, another was falling in its wake. The two other German pilots fled in panic. They had seen what no one had ever seen before—an airborne machine gun firing bullets between the blades of a whirling propeller. They had seen the gun mounted in front of the Frenchman's cockpit, and they had seen the fiery tongue at its muzzle as it shot out a steady stream of bullets.

The faces of the remaining two airmen still registered their astonishment when they returned to base. Nobody believed their story. It was utter fantasy, or so everyone thought until it happened again. And again, and again. Always it seemed to be the same Frenchman, the same monoplane, the same accursed gun. The news spread like wildfire from airfield to airfield. Now, each time a suspect monoplane was sighted in the air, the German airmen wisely avoided it.

When he learned of all this, Udet was at Heiligenkreuz, near Colmar, where he had been posted after getting his wings. He saw Waxheim's name on the monthly casualty list in *Flugsport* magazine. Only then did he realize that his late friend had been shot down by the notorious Frenchman, for Waxheim was one of just two German aviators lost that April 1, and the both of them had fallen to the Frenchman and his uncanny weapon. Udet and his observer, Lieutenant Bruno Justinus, flew daily in good weather. For three weeks they saw nothing of the monoplane; then, while returning home from a long reconnaissance, they spotted it. The Frenchman, about a thousand feet below them, was strafing a railway station and dropping explosive darts. Abruptly, the monoplane's propeller stopped. It was gliding, losing altitude rapidly. Udet caught up with the disabled craft and came close enough to recognize the machine gun on its nose. As Udet followed it down, Justinus stood in his cockpit and shouted exultations. The monoplane glided to a landing in a meadow on the outskirts of Hulste. Circling at low level, Udet and Justinus saw a German cavalry troop gallop toward the machine and take the pilot into custody.

Udet, though yet unaware of it, was witnessing a fateful event. The Frenchman was, of course, Roland Garros—the forerunner of all fighter pilots. The capture of his Morane-Saulnier and its crudely contrived forward-firing machine gun brought about a radical change in the pattern of military aeronautics. Unsafe, undependable, and unwieldy, the weapon system that Garros had improvised nevertheless inspired Anthony Fokker to perfect, on Germany's behalf, a far superior device for mechanically synchronizing a standard automatic gun to shoot through an airscrew ahead. Thus armed, the Fokker E-1 became the first fighter plane deserving such description, and aerial warfare—as a heavy toll of Allied airmen attested—was revolutionized overnight.

Later in his career, Udet crossed the path of another star of French aviation, the inimitable Georges Guynemer. It was early June 1917, when these two experts chanced to meet in the air. The resulting combat was for Udet the most memorable of his whole experience. Since each was flying by himself, it was a personal duel. They were evenly matched in skill, but Guynemer had the better plane, inasmuch as an Albatros D-5—such as Udet was piloting—was prone to shed its wings in a steep power dive. Udet, paradoxically, was saved by his own gun stoppage. After about twenty minutes of intricate maneuver and countermaneuver, neither man scoring a hit, Guynemer noticed his opponent's inability to fire. Full of admiration for this German's courage and exceptional skill, the chivalrous Guynemer waved a farewell and turned away. (That such quaint concepts of gallantry had, and have still, no place in twentieth-century warfare is a sad truth underlined by the fact that Udet, who then had six victories to his credit, went on to destroy fifty-six additional Allied aircraft.) Udet was deeply perturbed by the incident. It left him with a sense of humiliation so acute that he was unable to concentrate on his responsibilities as a flight leader in Jasta 15, and he therefore put in for an extended furlough. Upon his return to duty, he was reassigned to Jasta 37 as that squadron's commanding officer. Here he came into his own, recording fourteen kills in the next seven months and earning the high compliment of being asked by Richthofen, in the week before the 1918 spring offensive, to join the elect association of aces in J.G. 1.

And so Udet, on that March 26, handling his first Fokker triplane, accompanied Richthofen and three members of Jasta 11 on a combat patrol. When he sighted a British two-seater, an unescorted RE-8, soon after he took off, Udet left the formation, shot the enemy down as a matter of routine, and then took his place again behind the baron. In another few minutes they espied some low-flying Sopwith Camels. They all dived to the attack, and their startled victims never quite knew what hit them. One Camel each fell to Richthofen and Lieutenant Gussmann. The surviving trio fled in confusion.

Barely was this flurry over when the baron spotted an RE-8 scuttling away from under. It was down at treetop level, where its pilot evidently hoped to escape detection. Its topside camouflage blended almost perfectly with the background foliage, but not so perfectly as to fool Richthofen's sharp and practiced eye. Due to the desperate circumstances of the German offensive having thrown Haig's armies back almost to Amiens, the R.F.C. was obliged to use even these pathetically outclassed two-seaters for the most hazardous kinds of low-altitude work. The instructions at this time to certain R.F.C. units were explicit: "Very low flying essential . . . all risks to be accepted." (This order was in one case carried out to the extreme, for the diary of the German 8th Grenadier regiment records an officer being run over by a British SE-5!) Also, although the Allies enjoyed a numerical superiority in the general theater, the Germans actually had the larger aviation force at the Somme at this early stage of the battle. By siphoning away from other regions all the men and machines that could be spared, they had allocated a total of some 820 planes to the critical sector before unleashing their massive assault. The Allies, at the end of March, had exactly 645 planes in the area, and about a fourth of these were obsolete two-seaters—rickety old "Harry Tates" (RE-8's) and "Fees" (FE-2's).

The occupants of the machine Richthofen was stalking had been sent out to locate and size up German reserve strength, which information No. 15 Squadron had been delegated by headquarters to provide. The observer, seeing the red triplane swooping out of the sun, waited coolly until it was well within range and then fired a series of short snap bursts. Here was the tactic of an experienced hand, and Richthofen appreciated it as such. Bagging this RE-8, he knew, was not going to be the usual child's play. Since there was not enough altitude for him to get under its tail and take advantage of its blind spot, he came down at it from above and ahead. He gauged his angle of attack with exquisite precision, positioning himself so that the British gunner was prevented from shooting at him by the obstruction of the RE-8's top wing. Although the pilot had a synchronized Vickers on the port side of the fuselage, it was situated so far back from the nose that he would have had to pull up sharply to bring the gun to bear on his antagonist. Either way, the clumsy two-seater was set up for the kill—testimony, indeed, to Richthofen's detailed knowledge of opposing aircraft. Closing at half throttle, purposely reducing his rate of descent in order to get off the maximum number of rounds and better ensure a hit, he let go with both barrels. The RE-8 burst into flames. It flipped over, roared like an exploding meteor into a small grove, and exploded. Scattered hunks of burning wreckage, and the broken bodies of two young lieutenants, were all that remained.

With four enemy planes destroyed and none of his own so much as touched by a bullet, any other flight leader would have returned to base bubbling with delight, but Richthofen, sober-faced as a deacon, remarked only that he was "satisfied." That he was something more than satisfied with his new man, Udet, was demonstrated a couple of days afterward, when the latter was named to command Jasta 11. As for the war-weary baron, who seemed too jaded to care, his name was again on every front page in Germany, for he had run his total victories up to an even seventy. Having scored four times in three days, it was his finest performance in almost a year, and that, too, was heartening news. The statistics, however, if they made him look like his old self, were misleading. If he flew and fought as deftly as ever, it was not with the same gusto. All the joy had gone out of it. When his pilots suggested that a celebration should be held to mark his seventieth kill, he declined. He was animated now only by his loyalty to duty. He spent much of his time in the solitude of his hut, where sometimes he lay for hours, staring abstractedly at the ceiling. Perhaps there was a foreboding in him. His adjutant, Lieutenant Karl Bodenschatz, had already been given a sealed envelope by Richthofen, whose instructions were that it should be opened in the event he failed to return from a sortie.

But the baron's marvelous ability as both commander and air fighter seemed uncontaminated by his melancholy ruminations. After his double victory on March 26, he followed up next day with a triple victory—claiming a Sopwith Camel in the morning and two Bristols in the afternoon. A new strategy was adopted this day by the geschwader. Hitherto, the prime mission had been to assist the advancing infantry by furnishing umbrella protection and by assailing enemy defense points. Because of the ferocious determination with which R.F.C. fighters were concentrating on ground attack, the Richthofen circus was retained behind the German van positions in an interdictory role. The object now was to engage the incoming British aircraft, and this was work that the specialists in Richthofen's troupe much preferred to strafing roads and trenches. Between sunrise and nightfall an unprecedented 118 sorties— seek-and-destroy missions—were flown, and counting those victimized by the baron, thirteen British planes were blasted out of existence, while not a single casualty was suffered by J.G. 1. It was altogether a bad day for the R.F.C. Apart from the reduction of performance imposed on their planes by the carriage of bombs, British pilots—operating at meager altitudes and preoccupied with finding targets below—were miserably handicapped. "Our job has always been dangerous," one of them wrote that week. "As things now stand, it is all but sheer suicide."

Richthofen continued his victory spree on the following day, March 28, chasing an Armstrong Whitworth FK-8 biplane and setting it ablaze with two or three well-aimed bursts. The baron derived a certain gratification from this, his seventy-fourth kill. This was the first (and only) machine of its type to fall under his fire; huntsman that he always was, he felt that special flush of pride which infects his breed when a new species of game has been vanquished.

Shooting down an FK-8, moreover, was nowhere near as easy as might be thought from the plane's appearance. Many a German flyer—even one so adept as Lieutenant Erwin Bohme, the veteran leader of Jasta Boelcke who had twenty-four victories—died while under the false assumption that the FK-8 framed in his gunsight was a clay pigeon. The Germans carelessly confused it with the RE-8, and the consequences of this misidentification were all too often disastrous, for the FK-8 was by far the more challenging quarry. A hefty two-seater that entered service at the beginning of 1917, the "Big Ack," as it was affectionately called by its crews, did excellent work throughout the rest of the duration. Although slow, it could maneuver tightly and so put up a good defensive fight. Significantly, it seldom figured on German score cards. The fact that the greatest German fighter of them all accounted for only one example speaks eloquently enough for the virtues of its design.

On the day Richthofen claimed his FK-8, three other victims fell to his predatory pack. From then until the end of the month, much to the relief of British airmen, rain and dense overcast curtailed operations. The baron did not welcome this layoff. It broke the continuity of his and his group's splendid performance of late. It upset a favorable rhythm in this day-to-day campaign and threatened to throw his squadrons off their stride. This spell of enforced idleness, furthermore, was difficult for him to endure in his frazzled state of mind, and the morning of the third day found him in an evil humor. Stomping into the pilots' mess during breakfast, he made a cruel spectacle of cashiering three men from the geschwader, loudly berating them in front of their comrades and then, before they had even finished eating, bundling them off to the reserve pool for reassignment. After relatively long service with the geschwader, only one of these three had chalked up a single victory, so their dismissal was neither undue nor surprising—it had customarily been the price a man paid for his failure to meet the leader's exacting standards—but the curt, humiliating manner of their expulsion was most uncharacteristic of the baron. Always in the past, when it became necessary to cull an undesirable from his personnel, he had done it in such a way as to spare the feelings of the individual involved as much as possible. For the one being banished, of course, it was invariably an affair attended by degradation and chagrin. Worth remarking, however, is that such unpleasantness occurred less frequently under Richthofen than under the commanders who succeeded him after his death. This was so primarily because Richthofen was more selective in his recruitment.

The weather cleared again on April 1, the founding day of the Royal Air Force, the day when the long-awaited amalgamation of the R.F.C. and R.N.A.S. finally went into effect. A merger that enthused neither entity, it was marked with feeble fanfare. At the front, except for the official announcements tacked to squadron bulletin boards, the reformation was accorded little notice. After all, as the events of that day woefully indicated, nothing had in fact changed for these hard-used British aviators at the Somme. The German drive having exhausted its initial impetus, there was little fighting on the ground, but in the air, especially at low altitudes, the battle raged again in full heat and ruthlessness. Out to do some early morning strafing, No. 65 Squadron lost two Sopwith Camels. Three bombing runs over Bapaume cost No. 58 Squadron two of its DH-4's. No. 56 Squadron, in the thick of it as always, lost three SE-5's. A Bristol fighter of No. 20 Squadron failed to return, and No. 100 Squadron—unfortunate enough to be still equipped with FE-2's so late in the war—lost four planes. An additional thirty-eight machines were damaged, some beyond repair, in accidents and emergency landings. A dismal beginning for the R.A.F., and the Richthofen geschwader had a big hand in making it so. Of British losses over the lines, J.G. 1 claimed half.

Both the opposing air forces were hampered at this time by restrictions of supply. The British problem was logistics rather than any real shortage. Since their fuel and repair depots were in danger of being overrun by the German incursion, these facilities were removed to the rear as a precautionary measure. Getting the goods to forward airfields thus became a hardship, albeit only a temporary one. The German problem was more basic, and it would progressively worsen. Fuel stores had dwindled to the point where pilots were admonished, under threat of court-martial, "to make no unauthorized flights . . . [and] to avoid any needless deviation from prescribed missions." Ammunition and aircraft replacement parts were growing ever scarcer. Food stocks, in quality if not yet quantity, had sharply declined, and luxury items were at a premium even for the pampered aces of J.G. 1. Tobacco, for instance, was unprocurable at field canteens. Udet wrote that "unless we could beg, buy or filch our smokes from British prisoners, we had no choice but to content ourselves with ersatz tobacco, the best of which one resourceful fellow in Jasta 11 concocted of dried beech leaf and a wondrous assortment of aromatic weeds and herbs."

On April 2, another advance base was established for J.G. 1 at Harbonnières. As a "temporary expedient," the main body of the geschwader was to fly here each morning from Léchelle, where maintenance services and billeting were provided, and to operate from the new airfield throughout the hours of daylight. The plan presented a twofold advantage in that it increased the unit's combat capability while at the same time effecting an appreciable economy in its operations. Except for those detached to Awoingt, Richthofen's men had been averaging three or four sorties daily to and from the lines; by working out of Harbonnières, in closer proximity to the field of action, a considerable amount of fuel would be conserved. An increase in the geschwader's tactical value would also result from its being stationed nearer to the front, both because it could range farther up and down the lines while consuming the same amount of fuel and because it was able to respond with greater immediacy to enemy moves.

The field at Harbonnières was a hastily converted pasture and looked it. Except for a platoon of riflemen entrenched around its fringe, the only permanent personnel consisted of a couple of cooks, their assistants, and about a half dozen mechanics. In a glade alongside the field were a small camp kitchen, a few tents for storage and shelter, some tank trucks and ammunition wagons, all well camouflaged. "What surprised me most," Udet recalled in his autobiography, "were the pilots' seats on the field. They were an idea once advocated by Boelcke, Germany's master airman, and the scheme was now adopted by Richthofen, his prize pupil. A few kilometers behind the front, within easy reach of enemy shells, we sat . . . in deck chairs in the middle of the field. Our machines stood close by, ready for instant use. As soon as a hostile plane showed itself above the horizon, we took off. Sometimes only one of us went up, and at other times an entire flight hustled into the air. When the chase was over, we landed and again reclined in our chairs, scanning the sky with binoculars, waiting for our next chance." With this to keep them occupied between their scheduled patrols, their days at Harbonnières were full and arduous, beginning before dawn with the long trip from Léchelle and winding up after dark, back at Léchelle, with a late supper. But the result more than compensated their effort.

Their first day at Harbonnières was rewarded with the destruction of five British machines, Richthofen himself shooting down an RE-8. With the halting of the German drive along the Somme, it became the turn of the R.A.F. to revise its tactics and instead of concentrating on ground attack, to grapple with the formations of black-crossed fighter planes that were sweeping the lines. J.G. 1, however, due to rain and cloud in its sector, attained only one victory on April 3. Two days of inclement weather intervened; then, on April 6, the geschwader laid claim to ten victories, the baron again accounting for one. It was his seventy-sixth score, and that evening a telegram, relayed through General Hoeppner, informed him that he had been invested with the Order of the Red Eagle (Third Class) with Crown and Swords, a coveted decoration hitherto awarded exclusively to royalty, ranking aristocrats, and general officers. As if to celebrate, Richthofen scored a double victory the next day, when he brought down an SE-5 and a Nieuport Type 27 (which he erroneously identified as a Spad). Four other British planes were destroyed that day by J.G. 1.

The geschwader was riding high. In its four operational days at Harbonnières, twenty-two enemy aircraft had been knocked out. Further to this success was the fact that casualties in J.G. 1 had been nil. It was with some perturbation, then, that Richthofen—on the showery morning of April 8, when the geschwader remained weathered-in at Léchelle—received instructions to move his squadrons to Cappy. The baron's agitation was excusable, for Ludendorff had already opened the second phase of his offensive and the main sphere of action shifted northward to Flanders, where the battle of Lys was at full pitch. On this very day, in fact, Haig promulgated his memorable "backs to the wall" injunction to his beleaguered troops. The British were being hard pressed, and aviation was a vital factor, yet the Richthofen circus, the most potent element of the German air force, was being held back from the Flanders front. Why? The rationale behind this decision never came to light, neither then nor since. But why was the unit to be shunted to Cappy? Because, as the incredulous commander of J.G. 1 read in his orders, his advanced airfields at Awoingt and Harbonnières were "inadequate for prolonged use." More permanent accommodations were deemed advisable, and Cappy afforded them. Since this explanation avoided the central issue by leaving unanswered the question of why the high-scoring geschwader was being relegated to a relatively quiet sector, Richthofen felt obliged to fabricate a story for the benefit of his pilots. He told them that they needed a short rest before launching into the final campaign ahead, which sounded plausible and calmed their indignation for the time.

The move required several days to complete, and through it all, Richthofen's frustration mounted. For one thing, he was badgered by orders and counterorders. Daily he anticipated a cancellation of the transfer to Cappy and a call instead to the embattled plain of the Lys. Because of this expectation, he actually delayed for a couple of days the conveyance of equipment to Cappy. And he did receive the desired order, although only to hear of its rescission a few hours later. Twice again the geschwader was alerted for a move to the north; twice again the order was rescinded. And so the Red Knight, in the week before his death, found himself and his elite troupe relegated to the wide bog of Somme mud that was Cappy airdrome during the spring rains.

The place itself contributed to his depression and did nothing to alleviate the black mood of his men. The accommodations at Cappy were strictly utilitarian. The surrounding towns and villages, what was left of them after the shellings they had endured, were even less inviting than the airdrome barracks. Five straight days of downpour added to a pervasive aura of gloom, an atmosphere that almost reeked of impending disaster. But if Richthofen harbored any dire premonition, he did not let it obsess him. He spent these days—the last of his life—writing an essay on air fighting in which he endeavored to update the already classic Boelcke Dicta in accordance with recent developments. The principal subjects covered were: (1) unit oganization, (2) rules governing the employment of single and multiple squadrons, and (3) techniques of combat with special reference to the leader's signaling system. The essay contained little that was new, however. Possibly it was motivated by a desire to divert his thoughts from morbid paths. Certainly there is no reason to suppose that Richthofen was immune to fear. Aside from his great talent as a fighting pilot, he was quite an ordinary man, susceptible to all the frailties of humankind. Whatever anxiety he did feel was empirically justified. The odds were to be reckoned with, he knew well, after so many months of action; compared to most frontline aviators, he was a patriarch, even a relic. To dislodge him from the air, moreover, was the highest ambition of every enemy he met. Despite his marvelous skill, there were risks in each encounter, and the law of averages is inexorable as it is irrepealable.

On the morning of April 20, the penultimate day of Richthofen's life, the rain finally began to slacken. At the invitation of the late Werner Voss's father, Richthofen had planned to leave this morning for a two-day vacation at the Voss hunting lodge in the Schwarzwald. The prospect of woodcock shooting had raised his morale a bit. But there was other game much more to his liking, and when he saw the weather improving at Cappy and realized that a fling at the enemy might soon be feasible, he sent a wire to Herr Voss postponing the visit indefinitely. After almost two weeks of deprivation, he craved action. He was by now thoroughly addicted to the incomparable excitement of combat.

Most of the morning he spent in a hangar with his ground crew, readying a new triplane for its first operational flight. Outside the rain steadily abated. A little before one o'clock, when the rain stopped, the baron, together with a select few from Jasta 11, took off on an offensive patrol. No hostile aircraft were seen. None was yet abroad, for an unbroken ceiling of gray cloud, hardly fifteen hundred feet high, still shaded the front, brushing the hilltops with tendrils of mist, while pockets of fog obscured the river lowlands. Returning to base, he fidgeted about the communications hut, where he waited impatiently for reports of enemy air activity. The weather continued gradually to improve. By late afternoon the overcast had broken up into isolated cloud banks, and Richthofen, despite having heard nothing of any R.A.F. planes in the area, decided to undertake another patrol. This time a formation of six Sopwiths was sighted before the lines were reached. Richthofen, accompanied by five of his best pilots, attacked. The British leader spotted the oncoming triplanes and turned his formation to meet them head-on.

Two flights of six machines each from No. 3 Squadron, R.A.F., had set out together on the evening patrol, only to become separated amid the patchwork of heavy cloud. C Flight, that which Richthofen accosted, was led by Captain D. Bell, an Australian ace, and included among its number the squadron commander, Major R. Raymond-Barker, who had tagged along, he told his adjutant before take-off, "to have some fresh air." As soon as the shooting started, Richthofen banked around smartly and fired a quick burst at the major's machine, which instantly went out of control and plunged, trailing smoke, into a wood near Villers Bretonneux. The baron wasted no time in his eagerness for prey. His speedy Fokker, with red wings, red fuselage, red hood, red tail, red wheels, responded to his will as a thing alive. He swerved toward another Sopwith and opened fire. Its pilot, nineteen-year-old Lieutenant D. E. Lewis, attempted every evasive trick he knew, but to no avail. A bullet ignited his emergency fuel tank and he went down, landing before the flames consumed his entire plane. His was the unpleasant distinction of becoming Richthofen's eightieth—and last—victim.

"Except for minor burns and bruises," Lewis recounted in a postwar memoir, "I was unhurt. . . . The following articles were hit by Richthofen's bullets: the compass, which was directly in front of my face; my goggles, where the elastic joined the frame of the glass (these went over the side); the elbow of my coat, and one slug through the leg of my trousers. . . . The rest of my flight was saved from annihilation by the timely arrival of a squadron of SE-5's. Before he departed, Richthofen flew down to within one hundred feet of the ground and waved at me." [2]

The baron returned to Cappy in a jubilant mood. Safely landed, he jumped spryly from his cockpit without the assistance of the smiling riggers and mechanics who surrounded him. "Eighty!" he exclaimed, rubbing his gloved hands together in a gesture of self-satisfaction. "That is really a decent number!" His companions of the flight congratulated him. In the mess they raised their cups and toasted him as "our leader, our teacher, and our comrade, the ace of aces." They drank to him again, dubbing him "the one-man army"—a facetious allusion to a recent statement by Ludendorff asserting that Richthofen was worth three divisions of infantry to the German effort. Rarely of late had they seen him so happy. His wide grin reflected not only the merriment about him, but the pride he felt in his accomplishment. Eighty was indeed a tidy sum, a fat, substantial, nicely rounded number. There was nothing about it that sounded fortuitous; rather it seemed a goal that had been thoughtfully ordained, and now it was fulfilled. On the last night of his life, Richthofen went to bed a contented man.

Next morning, April 21, two young aviators rolled out of their bunks and took a look at the weather. They stood in chill barracks, about thirty miles apart, one at Cappy and the other at Bertangles, and between them stretched an expanse inhabited by two mighty legions locked in death grips. One of the young men was a Canadian. He was twenty-four years old and a member of Squadron No. 209, R.A.F. He awoke with a queasy stomach and unsteady nerves. After more than a year of uninterrupted combat service with the lately disbanded R.N.A.S., and twelve victories, he was tired and sick. He should have been in a hospital or at some rest camp back home in Canada, but there was no leave for any Allied soldier who was not an actual casualty in these difficult days, so he got along as best he could. A captain now three weeks, his name was Roy Brown.

The other man was twenty-five-year-old Rittmeister Manfred, Freiherr von Richthofen, the highest-scoring fighter pilot of the war. Rejuvenated by his feat of the previous day, his ears still tingling with the congratulations of his

[2] Gibbons: *The Red Knight of Germany.*

admiring pilots, he felt better than he had in weeks. The morning air was crisp, but a glimmer in the sky gave promise of sunshine later, a propitious sign that cheered the baron even more. He had never heard of Brown, but Brown had heard plenty about Richthofen.

Spirits that spring morning at Cappy were ebullient as those pilots detailed for morning duty lounged around awaiting their orders. For the first time in almost a month, Richthofen left his quarters and ate breakfast with his men. Afterwards he joked and laughed with them in the squadronroom, and even indulged in some horseplay, tipping over a cot on which Lieutenant Richard Wenzl, a recent arrival, was dozing peacefully. Another pilot set up the cot again and sprawled upon it for a nap. But Richthofen mirthfully spilled him to the floor, too. A few minutes later the baron's pet hound, Mortiz, came bounding up to his master in a state of great agitation, dragging a wheel chock that had been tied to his tail. The two officers whose repose had been upset by their playful commander had exacted their revenge. "But why make poor Moritz suffer for my crimes?" asked Richthofen, trying to look stern. "Because," Wenzl replied with a grin, "it would be improper to hang a weight from the tail of a superior officer." No one had seen Richthofen laugh so heartily in many months.

At about midmorning, to everyone's surprise, a regimental band came goose-stepping across the airfield and halted in front of the barracks to play a medley of patriotic marches. It had been sent over by a neighborhood division commander, who offered this serenade with his congratulations upon the baron's eightieth victory. Horns blared, drums thumped, and cymbals clanged, but Richthofen did not enjoy the music. He said it was too loud. With his amused pilots behind him, he walked away from the band, and together they went to the hangars where their planes were being fueled and inspected preliminary to takeoff. One by one the diminutive Fokkers were rolled out upon the tarmac, nine of them. A moderately strong breeze was blowing in from the east, which was not so good, for it meant that a crippled German machine limping home would have to face a headwind; usually it was the other way around, with prevailing westerlies disadvantaging Allied airmen. Before boarding his plane, the baron paused for a chat with his cousin, Lieutenant Wolfram von Richthofen, who had joined the geschwader a couple of weeks ago and was now about to fly in company with his famous kinsman for the first time, and the last. Their tête-à-tête lasted but a minute or two, the veteran ace presumably confiding a few words of advice and encouragement.

The Red Knight was standing alone beside his plane and buttoning his coat collar, when someone with a camera clicked his picture, the last ever taken of him alive. That snapshot reinforced a superstition, long held among German war pilots, that it is bad luck to be photographed just before departing on a mission.

A sergeant edged forward from among the mechanics with a postcard addressed to his son back in Germany. He asked Richthofen to autograph it for him. "What's your hurry?" the ace inquired with mock seriousness. "Are you afraid I won't return?" The sergeant blushed and stammered, at which Richthofen chuckled as he signed his name for the last time.

The adjutant, Bodenschatz, left for the observation tower after relaying word that weather conditions, despite a lingering morning haze, would permit take-off. From there he saw six machines dart into the air, Richthofen's scarlet beauty at the lead, heading west along the Somme canal toward the front. Three more machines followed a half-minute behind. Today's patrol beat extended along a line from Marceux to Puchevillers, the primary object being to prohibit enemy reconnaissance flyers from investigating the countryside north of Hamel, where preparations were being made for a local offensive.

Meanwhile, No. 209 Squadron R.A.F., consisting of three flights of five planes each, had already set out from Bertangles airfield. The first flight flew in a close *V* formation, with the unit commander, Major G. H. Butler, at the point. Flanking the major's group on the right and a little to the rear, in another *V* formation, was Captain Brown's flight, he being Butler's second in command. A similar formation was on the left rear flank. This was the squadron's battle stance. It was out for trouble, and it was flying straight for the sector that Richthofen's circus had been ordered to secure against intrusion.

As the British squadron was enroute northeastward toward the Somme River, Richthofen and his contingent made a prearranged rendezvous with Jasta 5, which was at full strength, and proceeded thence to his appointed area. The paths of the enemy formations converged above the road running between Hamel and Sailly-le-Sec, about a half-mile south of the river. Inasmuch as they were traveling at different altitudes on a hazy day with scattered low cloud, they might never have sighted each other, however, had it not been for two RE-8's of No. 3 Australian Squadron that were bumbling along at seven thousand feet on a photographic mission. The momentous fight started shortly before eleven o'clock, when four Fokkers peeled off from the main bunch to dispose of these antiquated crates. The occupants of the first RE-8 attacked, Lieutenants T. L. Simpson and E. C. Banks, were caught by surprise because of the poor visibility. Banks, the observer, began shooting at almost point-blank range, using up two canisters of ammunition before Simpson won a zigzag race for the sanctuary of some clouds. Cheated of this kill, the triplanes went hawking after Lieutenants S. G. Garrett and A. V. Barrow in the other two-seater. Manning the paired Lewis guns in the back cockpit, Barrow greeted them with several long bursts of withering fire. One of the Germans was plainly hit and wheeled earthward, whereupon the remaining trio hauled off to rejoin their crowd upstairs.

During this engagement, with an east wind blowing, the attacking Fokkers were wafted over the lines. British antiaircraft opened up, the shells popping with their characteristic white puffs. These drew Brown's attention to the detached triplanes and he led his flight in against them. Off to the east and higher up, Richthofen spotted the Sopwiths and turned his entire formation to meet them. Major Butler, seeing the enemy swarm descending on Brown's group, brought the rest of No. 209 Squadron toward the impending clash. The opposing forces streaked directly at one another, and in a few seconds the troops on the great natural grandstand of the Morlancourt ridge were spectators of a first-class air battle. Standing in muddy pits and trenches, they lifted their helmet-framed faces and strained to watch the ferocious, quarterless battle that swirled above their heads. They could not see the whole show, for much of it was hidden by the haze. But the tremendous din of shrieking engines and barking guns told much of what they could not actually see.

Brown opened first fire at one of the isolated triplanes. With the slipstream howling past the struts and bracing wires of his cherry-nosed Sopwith, he dived at a blue-tailed three-winger and—a split-second too soon—pressed the trigger button under his thumb. His intended victim veered away, only to run into a hail of bullets from Lieutenant F. J. W. Mellersh. The riddled triplane lunged into a vertical fall, then flattened out and started limping back toward Cappy, crashing along the way. Mellersh had tried to tag after it, but the other two triplanes had in turn followed him, forcing him to spiral down to hedgehopping altitude. They kept up the chase for a considerable distance. After eventually shaking them off, Mellersh happened to see a bright red Fokker glide to a rude landing about a mile and a half west of Sailly-le-Sec. Flying over to have a close look, Mellersh noticed Captain Brown's plane circling the site. The captain wobbled his wings. "It was more than a recognition signal," Mellersh later asserted. "By its exuberance I could tell it was a victory sign." He said further: "Although I knew, of course, that Richthofen flew a pure red 'tripe,' it just never occurred to me at the time that I was witnessing the baron's final exit."

The dogfight that had developed saw twenty-five German machines, mostly triplanes and a few Albatroses, pitted against the fifteen British Sopwith Camels. Lasting from twenty to thirty minutes, depending on which of various conflicting accounts is to be believed, it comprised a chaotic whirligig of planes weaving in and out of one another's track, banking, looping, slipping, rolling, climbing, diving, often almost scraping noses as pilots maneuvered madly for a fractional moment's vantage. Richthofen milled about with the rest.

First to drop out was a Sopwith pilot, Lieutenant W. J. Mackenzie, who was wounded in the back. Before withdrawing, however, Mackenzie managed to spray a triplane that went down trailing smoke. Suffering excruciating pain, he was lucky to reach Bertangles again and land his plane in one piece, enemy shots having dislodged an engine support, severed three longerons, and shredded the stabilizer and elevators.

Among the pilots in Brown's flight was a newcomer, Lieutenant Wilfred R. May. He, too, was Canadian and an old pal of Brown's from their school days in Edmonton, Alberta. This being his baptismal outing across the lines, May was under strict orders not to involve himself in any combat he could avoid. Doing as he had been told, he remained circling at twelve thousand feet, watching what he could see of the affray in the lower haze. When an enemy machine flew by underneath him, he allowed it to pass unmolested, still obeying instructions. But when a second one came by, he could not longer resist temptation. May swooped at it, fired, missed, and tailed it down right into the midst of the fight, where he attacked it again. "Through lack of experience," he wrote, "I held one of my guns open too long. It jammed and then the other. I could not clear them, so I spun out of the mess and headed west by the sun. When I had leveled off, I looked around, but nobody was after me—or so I thought. Feeling pretty good at having extricated myself, the next thing I knew I was being fired at from behind! All I could do was try and dodge my assailant, which was a red triplane. Had I known it was Richthofen, I probably would have fainted on the spot!" [3]

Brown, meanwhile, had just eluded a couple of gaudy-hued machines near the fringe of the melee when he saw May emerge with Richthofen in his wake. Beginning a race to May's rescue, he saw the baron overtaking the Sopwith, dogging its every evasive move. May tried everything he knew to get away. He pulled on the stick, kicked over the rudder, reared up hard, pirouetted, sideslipped and reversed his direction, only to find the snarling Fokker still bearing down on him. The frantic *pas de deux* continued, the pursued and the pursuer—a greenish blur followed by a red streak—hurtling down the wind as they twisted and turned at full throttle. Richthofen steadily gained. Now the Sopwith was centered in his sights again. The touch of a sure finger on the trigger sent two shafts of bullets spouting from the Spandau barrels. Bullets whined and snapped around May's head. Chunks of mutilated wood sprang from the struts before him. A neat row of holes was stitched along the fabric of the bottom starboard wing. One bullet traversed the flesh of his right arm, but the pain was forgotten in the fever of the moment.

Straight ahead of the downrushing pair were the emplacements of some Australian field batteries on the slope of the Morlancourt ridge. The artillerymen watched with bated breath the plunging, churning forms of Richthofen and the harried quarry. May was contour flying, hugging the ground and striving to beat his antagonist over the crest of the hill. From below, suddenly, a machine gunner blurted a volley at the German plane. Others, farther up the rise, threw quick bursts at it as it whisked over their positions. They could see their bullets gouging splinters from the woodwork of the Fokker. Later they demanded credit for Richthofen's defeat—and perhaps partial credit is owed them—but the consensus of history, except in Australia, is that the baron was killed by Captain Roy Brown, R.A.F. A postmortem examination of Richthofen's body left little room for argument, since it indicated that the fatal shot could only have been fired from aloft. Such was the opinion of three of the four doctors who performed the autopsy, the lone dissenter

[3] Nowarra and Brown: *Richthofen and the Flying Circus.* The author owes much to this most authoritative work, and here acknowledges his debt.

being an Australian who proposed that the wound could conceivably have been inflicted from the ground while Richthofen was banking his machine. Against this possibility, though, is the fact that neither plane, according to eye-witness reports, was seen to bank or in any way alter course while zooming toward the brow of the ridge.

The baron was so absorbed in the chase, apparently, that he failed to notice Brown's approach. The latter, closing in a forty-five-degree power dive, came almost directly over his target. In order to give a damaging burst, Brown found it necessary to turn. Precious time was lost. He saw himself dropping behind and fired hastily with no real expectation of a hit, but hoping at least to distract Richthofen's attention from Lieutenant May. Some of his shots nevertheless went home—and the illustrious Red Knight of Germany, the incomparable *kampfflieger,* the remorseless vanquisher of four score courageous adversaries of war, began his last descent to earth.

Slanting gently downward, the triplane stayed airborne for more than a mile. It lowered smoothly, gliding as though its dying, if not already lifeless, pilot was still in complete control. Without slowing, it crunched against the shell-pocked crust of a once green meadow, the impact smashing its undercarriage, and it careened on its belly to a stop in a shallow crater alongside the Bray-Corbie road.

A standing order forbade the troops in the area from exposing themselves on or near the road, which was under enemy observation, but in their curiosity they violated this order and thronged around the wrecked aircraft. An officer ascertained that the pilot was dead, then unhitched the safety harness and, with the help of others, lifted the limp body from the cockpit. The handsome Nordic face, what could be seen of it below the strapped helmet and shattered goggles, was lathered in blood. The body was laid on the ground and searched for papers. "My God, it's Richthofen!" the officer exclaimed. "Christ," a tommy gasped, "they got the ruddy baron!" While some stood gawking at the inanimate terror of the air, the rest, stampeding for souvenirs, tore and hacked the Fokker to pieces. The propeller was removed and was being cut into shares when an officer intervened, but the stripping of fabric went on until the German artillery delivered a barrage that sent everyone dashing for cover. By now the machine was little more than a tattered skeleton with engines and guns, most of the instruments having also been ripped out as mementos. That afternoon, while the barrage intermittently continued, a chaplain circulated among the troops and prevailed upon them to surrender any personal belongings they had taken from the dead ace. One of the articles returned was a gold pocket watch bearing an inscription from his parents on the occasion of his eighteenth birthday.

A salvage party was organized in No. 3 Australian Squadron to collect the remains. While there was yet some languishing daylight, Corporal C. C. Collins, a mechanic, crept out and recovered the body. After nightfall, in the concealing darkness, the tattered airframe was brought in on a trailer. Richthofen's body was retained overnight in one of the squadron's hangars at Poulainville. Toward morning, when the contradictory claims of the R.A.F. and the Australian gunners were regarded at headquarters, the telltale postmortem was performed. The finding was that Richthofen had been killed by a single bullet passing obliquely through his chest, glancing off his spine, penetrating his heart, and issuing from the opposite side of his chest.[4] Only after the cause of death had thus been determined was Captain Brown officially credited with the victory.

After medical examination the shrouded body was laid upon a bed of flowers on the platform of an open truck that proceeded slowly along the road to nearby Bertangles and corps headquarters. An escort of six R.A.F. captains walked behind the truck. At Bertangles the body was placed in a hangar of No. 209 Squadron and prepared for interment. A burial detail was already digging a grave in the village churchyard, where a choice plot had been selected in the shade of a lordly hemlock. Through most of the day, Richthofen reposed in state while hundreds of his former enemies, pilots and ground personnel from the entire region, filed past the bier in thoughtful, reverential silence. As one of them reflected years later in a published reminiscence: "Our last respects were tendered with mixed emotion. . . . You become accustomed to your daily enemies. They are as much a part of life as family and friends. So, when a staunch foe of long standing passes on, you find you strangely miss him. . . . With [Richthofen] out of it, a certain piquancy was found lacking in the ensuing weeks of action."

Late in the afternoon of April 22, Richthofen was buried with the military honors befitting his rank. His plain wooden coffin was carried by the six captains to a Crossley tender, a light utility truck that had been painted black and reserved for use as a hearse. Decked around the coffin were the various wreaths which had accumulated during the day. One bore the dedication: "To our gallant and worthy foe." On command from the presiding officer, who wore a black armband, the cortege moved off with a fourteen-man firing

---

[4] The fact that the bullet struck Richthofen in the chest, although Brown was shooting from behind and off a bit to one side, has moved several historians to question whether Brown fired the fatal shot. The controversy rages to this day among researchers. What has often been lost sight of, however, is that several witnesses to the action, including Brown himself, have stated that they saw Richthofen rise in his seat and turn his body in order to have a backward look, and that he did so at the same instant Brown opened fire, or perhaps a split second after. It could be that the Australian gunners below had hit the rear of his plane and he wanted to check the damage; it might also be that Brown's shots caused him to look back. Whichever the case, Richthofen's torso was twisted far enough around so that one of Brown's bullets could have done the grisly job described in the autopsy. Moreover, it seems impossible that a shot from the Australian positions could have killed Richthofen, unless he were flying with his wings nearly vertical to the ground, which was not so. Accordingly, since the bullet hit him at a small angle, it could only have been fired from the same level or a little above. That the exit wound was found to be about two inches higher than the entrance wound can plausibly be explained by the fact that the bullet, when it bounced off the spinal column, was as likely to rebound in a slightly upward direction as any other.

party in the lead, walking two abreast, their rifles reversed in the traditional expression of mourning. Next came the tender, followed by the pallbearers, then a platoon of infantry. It was a beautiful April day. The solemn procession, crawling along a sunlit lane toward the cemetery, passed trees and hedgerows budding with new life.

The firing party halted at the cemetery gate and formed into two ranks, each facing the other. The burdened pallbearers, preceded by a chaplain of the Church of England, moved between them. As the coffin passed, they stood with their rifles at salute. Watched by a large audience of soldiers and townspeople, the graveside rites were simple but impressive. When prayers and eulogy had been spoken, and Richthofen's remains were being lowered, the rapt stillness was broken by a crisp voice ordering the firing party to attention. Then came the commands—"Load! Present! Fire!"—and three volleys rang out in timed succession. Concluding the ceremony was the playing of the last post, that most haunting of all bugle calls.

Next morning a cross was planted at the head of the grave. Fashioned of a disused propeller with three blades lopped, it bore a small brass plaque on which was engraved, along with his name, rank, and age (erroneously given to be twenty-two), a concise statement of where and when and how Richthofen had died. All could see that the great German hero, a fierce enemy in life, had in death been laid to rest as a comrade.

Bertangles, however, was not his last resting place. Soon after the end of hostilities it became a policy to reinter the war dead in special cemeteries according to nationality. Richthofen's body was removed to Fricourt cemetery, there to lie among some eighteen thousand of his German brethren in arms. Row upon row of uniform white crosses gave witness to their sacrifice—a silent witness, its true meaning too readily forgotten. Forgotten as well, except as the stuff of cheap patriotic slogans and perfunctory laments, were the decaying bones beneath. But Richthofen was remembered. Bolko, his youngest brother, on a chill November morning in 1925, walked among the crosses at Fricourt seeking Manfred's grave. His errand was a doleful one. Arrangements had already been settled for exhuming the body and transferring it to a richly appointed, zinc-lined casket. The intention was to ship the chest to the churchyard at Schweidnitz, where lay the father, Albrecht, who had peacefully expired soon after the war. Lothar reposed there, too, in native Silesian soil. But when the German authorities learned that the body was to be sent home, they respectfully claimed it for the nation. Many thousands attended the ceremony when the hero-aviator's remains were entombed in the Invaliden, a memorial shrine to the Fatherland's most prominent sons.

On the same day Richthofen was killed, a communiqué from German headquarters proclaimed the confirmation of his seventy-ninth and eightieth victories. While congratulations were pouring in at Cappy, the high command in Berlin, apprised of the fact that Richthofen was missing, found itself faced with the problem of how best to convey this bombshell of bad news to the public. The loss of a personage so idolized could not for long be concealed; the British, as soon as they had identified their victim, whether he be dead or alive, would surely publicize Richthofen's fall. Since, in any case, the next of kin had a right to be told before any disclosure was made to the press, a telegram was sent to Major Albrecht, Freiherr von Richthofen. There were no tears when he read of his son's disappearance, no outward sign of anguish or even mild distress. Father and son were soldiers, uncompromising Prussian soldiers, whose duty was dearer than life, whose fealty to emperor and country transcended any personal concerns, whose creed maintained that dying for the glory of the Reich was a sublime privilege.

Albrecht, when the dismal message came, was at his desk in a field command tent. Practicing the rigid stoicism he had so often preached to his sons, he read the telegram twice, nodded a moment in private meditation, folded it into a pocket, and then, according to one of his subordinates, "busied himself again in his work. He said nothing about it to any of us at that time or afterward." A few days later, when Albrecht received a consolatory letter from the new commander of J.G. 1, Captain Wilhelm Reinhard, he wired back this reply, addressing it to all geschwader members: "My son still lives as your model."

On the morning of April 23, the day after the funeral at Bertangles, it was not yet known on the German side whether Richthofen had survived, and news from neutral sources was being assiduously scanned for a clue. A terse bulletin, factual and noncommittal about the flyer's fate, had been issued in the interim. "Rittmeister von Richthofen failed to return," it blandly revealed, "from an aerial mission over the Somme, April 21." Having learned that much, the populace waited with dread for further information. The authorities were no less anxious. While the people prayed and speculated and wondered, government propaganda geared up for any eventuality.

The first definite word on what had happened to Richthofen was provided to the Germans by the R.A.F. at the earliest opportunity. A little before noon on April 23, a British plane flew over Cappy airdrome and dropped a metal container attached to a streamer. Enclosed was a photograph of the burial ceremony, together with a note bringing this message:

TO THE GERMAN FLYING CORPS
Rittmeister Baron Manfred von Richthofen was killed in aerial combat on April 21, 1918. He has been buried with all due military honors.
From the British Royal Air Force

The desolating news was immediately communicated to Second Army headquarters, whence it was forwarded to Berlin. Across a stunned nation the story broke in the evening papers, quoting not only the R.A.F.'s informal aviso but also an official British communiqué that, during the previous night, Reuters had flashed to the neutral press. Relayed to Berlin via diplomatic channels, the communiqué ran: "After a long spell of inclement weather which greatly hampered aerial work, the morning of April 21 brought a change and our airplanes could be seen in the air all day long. . . . The pilot of one of the hostile machines brought down in combat was the well-known German airman and fighter, Rittmeister von Richthofen, who claimed to have shot down eighty Allied machines. His body has today been buried with full military honors."

His death was global news. Papers in nonbelligerent countries devoted whole pages to recounting his deeds and downfall. The British press—decently refraining from any triumphant glee at his misfortune—headlined lengthy obituaries of the fallen ace. "While probably not as brilliant as Captain Ball," the *Times* observed, "all our airmen concede that Richthofen was a great pilot and a fine fighting man." Commented the influential aeronautical weekly, *The Aeroplane:* "Richthofen is dead. All our airmen will be pleased to hear that he has been put out of action, but there will be no one amongst them who will not regret the death of such a courageous nobleman. . . . Anybody would have been proud to have killed Richthofen in battle, but every member of the R.F.C. [sic] would have been proud to shake his hand had he been captured alive. . . . His death is bound to have a depressing effect on the German flying service, for obviously the younger and less intrepid will argue that if a Richthofen cannot survive, their chances must be small. Equally his death is an encouragement to every young French and British pilot. . . . [Richthofen] was a brave soldier, a clean fighter and an aristocrat. May he rest in peace."

Not all Britons subscribed to this lofty sentiment. Following the publication of pictures of Richthofen's funeral, a spate of letters to editors decried such ceremony on behalf of an enemy aviator, especially one who had singlehandedly consigned eighty Allied aircraft to destruction. A heated controversy thereby arose in the correspondence columns of various newspapers, a discussion echoing that in 1916 about the burial in English churchyards of the crews of zeppelins brought down while raiding London and the east coast. Judging from all evidences, however, those who would have denied this Christian courtesy to the enemy dead were in a small minority.

As was only to be expected, there was bitterness in the German press, too. Regarding the funeral pictures, a writer in the *Deutsche Tagezeitung,* for example, contemptuously repudiated any presumption that the British had conducted the rites in good faith. "This homage," he sneered, "is simply the latest British self-advertisement of sportsmanship and knightliness. . . . We cannot look upon the ceremony shown here as sincere. The Allied press is full of this cant as it goes on in the same old trite fashion, beating the big drum of absurd British magnanimity. But nothing is mentioned of how many and how large were the cash prizes for the one who succeeded in killing Richthofen. The sum must have been enormous. What else explains the ghoulish quarrels that raged around the body? . . . A fortune awaited the man who inflicted the fatal wound. The very flying officers who bore the coffin to the grave were paid off with blood money!"

This was spiteful nonsense, of course, and it was espoused only by that faction of journalists given to chauvinistic rabble rousing. On the whole, the press in Germany was more sedate and philosophical than acrimonious or malicious. Typical was the obituary by Dr. Max Osborn in the *Berliner Zeitung am Mittag,* wherein Richthofen's virtues as a man and his prowess as a warrior were poignantly eulogized, and the reader was implored to "revere the memory of this *grosser kriegsheld* . . . who shall exemplify forever the perfect standard of German manhood." "Hearing of his tragic fate, our first reactions are shock and anger," Osborn continued, "but then comes a profound sadness. . . . Richthofen, we realize, was more to us than just a symbol. He was the able and high-minded type of young man on which the nation must rely for its future progress and prosperity. . . . Alas, they who possess the best human qualities are the ones readiest to sacrifice their lives for the ideals they cherish. The cream of our male population, most of an entire generation, is thus immolated on the battlefield."

As implied by the tenor of Osborn's writing, many Germans were moved almost to contrition by the loss of yet another exalted hero. The editor of an evangelistic monthly became so exercised in his bereavement that he drew an analogy, however tenuous or inapt, between the mode of Richthofen's death and the crucifixion of Christ. "An airplane, seen against the sky from below, appears as a cross," he moralized, "and on such a cross as this have Richthofen and a multitude of other brave martyrs, friend and foe alike, paid awful atonement for humanity's sins of war."

An interesting epilogue to Richthofen's death was that his conqueror, Captain Roy Brown, retired from active service two days later. After ailing for weeks and forcing himself to duty, Brown reported to the medical officer on April 23, complaining of intolerable stomach cramps. He was found to have a severe case of ulcers. Rushed to a hospital for emergency treatment, he was subsequently invalided back to England, where he remained for the remainder of the war and up until his discharge in April 1919. If today, half a century later, the men who fly supersonic fighter jets in No. 209 Squadron, R.A.F., cannot recall him by name, they remember well the historic deed with which Brown was credited, for their unit insignia depicts a red eagle—falling.

CHAPTER XVIII

Götterdämmerung

ON THE MORNING AFTER Richthofen's death his aide, Lieutenant Boden-schatz, awoke from a fitful sleep and left earlier than usual for the clapboard hut that housed the command center of Jagdgeschwader No. 1 at Cappy airfield. There were yet two hours until dawn. Except for the sentries on their solitary rounds, coming and going like phantoms in the calm darkness, none but Bodenschatz was astir. Hunched in his flannel greatcoat, he strode briskly past the row of hangars toward his office. Entering, he first carefully covered the windows in accordance with blackout regulations. Then he yanked on the pullcord of a naked bulb that dangled by its wire from the ceiling. Its wan yellow light imparted a sepulchral chill to the room, or so it seemed to Bodenschatz as he stood and stared forlornly at the desk and the empty chair alongside his own. His anguish swelled within him. He felt his composure melting. Straining to keep hold of himself, he sat and donned his reading glasses. From a drawer he took the sealed envelope that Richthofen had en-trusted to him to be opened when and if he, Richthofen, was killed or cap-tured. Although the baron's fate was not yet known on the German side of the lines, he had been missing now for almost sixteen hours. Distressing as Boden-schatz found it to accept, the only realistic conclusion was that the far-famed ace, the choice and master spirit of the German flying corps, was either a British prisoner or he was dead.

Bodenschatz lay the envelope on his desk and regarded it quizzically. To open it would be to concede the probability that Richthofen was not going to return, but the grieving adjutant knew that what he had come to do had to be done. Nervously he unsealed the envelope and withdrew its contents—a single sheet of personal stationery on which the baron had written his testamentary recommendations for the succession in command of J.G. 1. Bodenschatz had always prided himself on his ability to anticipate the group leader's desires and decisions, yet he was completely flabbergasted to find that Captain Wilhelm Reinhard was the man whom Richthofen had nominated to inherit his command. When the news got out later in the day, it surprised everyone. The most amazed of all was Reinhard, who, when he was told, thought he was being kidded and indignantly reproached what seemed an unspeakably boorish prank under the circumstances. Convinced finally that he was not being hoaxed, he could only ask: "But why me?"

Richthofen furnished no explanation. Nevertheless, his reasons for selecting Reinhard, although essentially unexpressed, can at least be tentatively surmised.

Whereas Reinhard was well qualified as far as seniority was concerned, and here was a consideration weighed heavily by the authorities in ratifying his accession to geschwader command, something more than that was obviously required by Richthofen. Uppermost in his mind, needless to say, were both the welfare and the continued efficiency of the fifty or so elite airmen whose lives were in daily peril. An officer less dashing and less publicized than the average in J.G. 1, but who was canny and undaunted in any situation and inspired confidence, would prove a more effective leader than a flashy performer with a bent for heroics. Relevant in this connection was Richthofen's habit of dividing his pilots into two species: the "hunters" and the "shooters," as he labeled them. The first kind were prudent and calculating in battle; ever heedful of the odds, they shunned extravagant risks. By contrast, the second kind were an impulsive, temerarious breed, whose mercurial passions tended to overrule their discretion and whose success derived as much from their stunning bravura as from any refined talent. Although Richthofen appreciated the uses and usefulness of each, he generally admired a "hunter" above a "shooter," especially in his assessment of an individual's qualifications for leadership. And by this yardstick, Reinhard measured up as an eminently eligible candidate.

A three-year flying veteran who had achieved sixteen victories and would have four more before his death in mid-June, when he crashed while testing an experimental fighter plane at Adlershof, Reinhard was by temperament and technique a "hunter." He was good, albeit unspectacular, as a pilot. His superior marksmanship, more than his airmanship, accounted for his successes in combat. Shrewd, methodical, thoroughly dependable, never one to lose his head or his nerve, he was every inch the professional *kampfflieger*. Increasing his favor in Richthofen's estimation, no doubt, was the fact that having recently reached his twenty-seventh birthday, Reinhard was older than anyone in the outfit. Not merely his age, but his demonstrated maturity, must have appealed to the baron.

But Reinhard had his flaws as a flight commander. The staidness which Richthofen had discerned in him as an asset was, in his case, a trait that impaired the competence to lead. Some in the circus criticized the new ringmaster for an almost slavish adherence to textbook tactics. He was too conservative and predictable, they complained. He lacked an ability to adapt to varied and ever-changing combat conditions. He was neither flexible nor versatile enough to improvise as the occasion demanded. What was more, he seemed unable to maintain firm control over a large formation aloft. To his great credit, however, he unashamedly owned up to his faults and delegated others to take charge when the enemy was encountered. In early May, a couple of days after Lieutenant Hans Weiss was shot down in his white triplane, Reinhard wrote of him: "He had the makings of an outstanding leader, and in the air I yielded to his guidance." Others beside Weiss acted as surrogate commanders in battle, Reinhard taking a back seat in preference to running a poor show at the cost of lives and victories. Hence it was by his probity, his common sense, and his selfless candor, rather than any edifying skill as a combat leader, that Reinhard earned the respect and loyalty of men who were his equals, most of them, and his betters, some of them, in the execution of their grim, exacting task.

J.G. 1 had a busy time of it during Reinhard's brief stewardship, and several good pilots were lost. But victories, amounting to fifty-four in his less than nine weeks of command, outnumbered casualties in a lopsided ratio of six to one! With the coming of May, scoring opportunities grew more plentiful every day above the Somme. On May 10, for instance, eleven kills were bagged without a loss. And on May 15, again without loss, thirteen British machines were blasted out of action. Aside from the familiar patrols of Sopwith Camels, SE-5's, and Bristols, the circus was engaging French Spads and Breguets that began operating in the sector about the end of April, when the Allies were compelled to redistribute their power to cope with Ludendorff's furious, slashing, shifting, multiaxial "win the war" campaign. There were also more and more De Havillands of the so-called Independent Air Force—the newborn strategic bombing arm of the R.A.F.—overflying the Somme front on their way to pummel the industrial Rhineland.

The geschwader was having one of its most successful periods, yet none among its members were sorry when, on May 20, a move was ordered to Guise. For their part, they could not get away from Cappy soon enough. The place had been a misery to them from the moment of their arrival. During their six-week stay, because the field was so often waterlogged, they found themselves grounded for days at a stretch; since the camp and nearby villages offered meager comforts and divertissements, the tedium was sometimes maddening to endure. Except for the excitements they met in the air, their first two weeks at Cappy, although a trial of boredom, were yet a pleasure compared to the last four weeks of their stay, for Richthofen was killed and the airfield abounded with reminders of him; the thought of their great loss had unsettling effects. Despite all the victories they won while based there, Cappy would remain in their memories as a chapter of miseries. Their eagerness to be gone was summed up by Lieutenant Hans Kirschstein, the commander of

Jasta 6 and a twenty-seven-victory ace when he crashed to his death two months later, who wrote to his parents on the evening of May 19: "Tomorrow we leave this dismal place and I could not be happier if I were being paroled from hell itself. . . . We have shot down many of the enemy since coming here, but the loss of Richthofen cries for a hundred British lives in retaliation, or maybe a thousand would be more like it."

On the morning of their departure, shortly before takeoff, a telegram was received from General Hoeppner, advising that the unit had been redesignated as Jagdgeschwader Freiherr von Richthofen No. 1. The news came as no real surprise, for almost since its inception, the unit had been popularly known everywhere as the Richthofen geschwader or Richthofen circus. Like the Jasta Boelcke before it, this larger association of picked specialists was a superlative instrument of warfare, organized and administered by a singularly gifted genius, and to distinguish it by his name was the natural, the inevitable, action. In its composition and workings, the geschwader was a unique product of its founder and foster spirit. That it should be officially dedicated as a living monument to him was foreseeable. The German military had a tradition of thus remembering its conspicuously brave and victorious commanders.

Passing from the jurisdiction of the Second Army to that of the Seventh, the geschwader was transferred to Guise in preparation for the offensive that would soon be directed across the Aisne toward the Chemin des Dames. Situated in a prime staging area, its ancient castle and many of its private residences having been converted into barracks, Guise fairly teemed with soldiers. But the town stood relatively unscathed by the war, and, despite its crowded condition, it seemed a paradise after Cappy. With six weeks of privation behind them, the geschwader pilots were treated regally as guests at the various officers' clubs in town. Aside from plenty of good food and drink, they enjoyed the attentions bestowed upon them by the amiable "hostesses" who graced these clubs. After two days and nights, the geschwader's morale had visibly perked up. However, because the local airfield was too small to accommodate the whole troupe, the circus was redeployed. Only Jasta 6 and a detachment of headquarters personnel were fortunate enough to remain at Guise, Jasta 4 going to Longchamps, Jasta 10 to Etreux, and Jasta 11 to Lamotte Ferme. (Jastas 5 and 46, attached to J.G. 1 throughout the Somme campaign, had stayed with the Second Army.)

The forthcoming offensive, the third of Ludendorff's sledgehammer blows that spring, was scheduled to begin on May 27. In the five days preceding the zero hour, the geschwader was almost entirely reequipped with new aircraft— Fokker D-7 biplanes, the first examples off the assembly line—and the changeover aroused considerable consternation. Although destined to be acclaimed as unquestionably the finest all-around German fighter plane of World War I, and notwithstanding the fact that Manfred von Richthofen himself, after testing the prototype at Adlershof in January 1918, had insisted that his unit be the one to introduce the D-7 into operational service, the new biplane was accorded an icy reception at the geschwader airfields. That it did not find ready acceptance among triplane pilots betrayed a normal reluctance on their part to discard a combat-proved machine of good maneuverability and an unsurpassed rate of climb. But their prejudice was heightened by the many rumors they had heard of the D-7. The plane was badly maligned by the false gossip that preceded it to the front. The source of these malicious stories was never determined. It was Anthony Fokker's theory that they had been set afoot by Allied agents in Berlin, and he might have been right.

Whatever the reason, J.G. I was not alone in its pessimistic appraisal of the untried Fokker. All during June, the D-7 arrived as an unwanted thing at German air bases in France. So strong was the initial bias against this aircraft, which he knew to be his best design to date, that Anthony Fokker made a tour of frontline squadrons for the purpose of demonstrating its merits and to convince pilots of its superiority. And they discovered by watching him put it through its paces and by trying it out themselves that, contrary to the rumors so widely circulated, it was an extremely easy plane to handle.

Beautifully balanced, sturdily constructed, responsive to every movement of the controls, yet forgiving of pilot error, the D-7 had no terrors for the rankest beginner. It was as tractable as a trainer but more airworthy. If any D-7's could ever have been spared away from the front, in fact, the type would have served at army flight schools where advanced combat tactics were taught. Such a plan was endorsed by the aviation command, but circumstances prevented its implementation—unfortunately for the Germans. The benefits of this training would have been tremendous, for the D-7—as the Richthofen circus learned upon introducing it to the enemy in late May at the third battle of the Aisne—was second to none as a fighting machine. If it could not quite match the triplane's climbing speed, its service ceiling—ranging upward of 22,000 feet—was more than half a mile greater. Indeed, its forte was its maneuverability at high altitude, an almost awe-inspiring aerobatic agility that afforded a nice margin of advantage over the opposition. Making a top speed of about 125 miles per hour with either a 180-horsepower Mercedes or a 185-horsepower BMW inline water-cooled engine, the D-7 was faster in level flight than the triplane at any altitude. Thanks to its rugged airframe and inherent stability, it also made a better gun platform. Being bigger than the triplane, and some four hundred pounds heavier, the D-7 was scarcely affected by the recoil of its twin Spandaus. The triplane, carrying the same armament, was known to shake violently when both its guns were fired in a sustained burst; the D-7 never did more than vibrate gently, almost imperceptibly, which resulted in surer shooting and calmer nerves.

In other ways, too, the D-7 was conducive to an aviator's peace of mind. For all its speed and combat capability, it imposed no premium on piloting skill. Unlike the machine it supplanted, it could be counted on to emerge from a steep power dive with its wings intact. Nor did it stall with the treacherous alacrity of the triplane. To pull the temperamental three-winger through a tight turn and bank or to maintain it in a sharp nose-up attitude was to risk an unintentional spin—and in the heat of battle a man could not always be as careful as was necessary to avoid losing control in this fashion. Of course, the D-7 also stalled when deprived of sufficient thrust and lift, but never as readily and always with enough forewarning to allow the pilot to take corrective action. That German airmen came to esteem the new biplane, and Allied airmen to fear it more than any other single-seater they faced, was no wonder. By midsummer, there was a saying in the German flying corps that the Fokker D-7 transformed greenhorns into heroes. Nobody on the other side would have quibbled with that notion after engaging the plane in a combat or two. The D-7 was considered so outstanding that it was specified by type to be surrendered to the Allies under the terms of the Armistice.

Following their first encounters with the new Fokker, several British and French flyers commented in their reports that its rather cumbrous appearance completely belied its performance. The plane was neither sleek nor pretty. To look at it was to see a structure of contrasting curves and angles that promised nothing of speed and spry maneuverability; yet from its prowlike nose to its somewhat outsized tail unit it was a creation of functional purity, deceptively well streamlined for its time. Viewed from any perspective, the D-7 was not to be mistaken for any other aircraft. It was instantly identifiable from above by the protruding of the ailerons beyond the upper wing tips and the scalloped trailing edges of both wings. From head-on, the frontal radiator, which looked as if it had been snatched off an automobile, was unmistakeable. From either side its distinctive profile gave it away, especially the long triangular stabilizer that merged into the high ellipsoidal rudder. The notable feature viewed from below was the large fairing that enclosed the axle and acted as an airfoil and also provided some extra lift. The fuselage, tail, and undercarriage, as well as the interplane and cabin struts, were uniformly constructed of welded steel tubing. The wooden-framed wings were cantilevered with box spars. The design thus lent itself to mass production. The demand for D-7's finally became so great, however, the Fokker factory could not keep pace. Contracts for its manufacture were therefore issued to the Albatros works in Germany and Austria, and that company's own D-plane, after long and excellent service, was discontinued as obsolete. The D-7 was built in such quantity that by autumn it was being used by the majority of German pursuit squadrons on the western front.

Superb as the D-7 was, Anthony Fokker topped it with another design before hostilities ceased, a small parasol monoplane. The Fokker E-5, as it was originally designated, later becoming the Fokker D-8, took eight months to get from the drawing board to the battle zone. Beginning in October, just five weeks prior to the Armistice, it was supplied in small numbers to the various geschwader, where it flew alongside the D-7. The "Flying Razor Blade," as it was christened by the British, hardly had a chance to prove itself. Although trickier to handle than the D-7, and despite a tendency to wing failure, which necessitated several modifications and production delays, the D-8—slightly faster than the D-7 both in level flight and rate of ascent but limited to a nineteen-thousand-foot ceiling—had more than its smart performance to recommend it. It was happily cheaper to manufacture and operate. Fokker, moreover, had been having difficulty obtaining engines for his biplane. According to him, Albatros was enjoying priority treatment from Mercedes and BMW alike:

> It became increasingly evident that unless immediate steps were taken to correct the situation, I would be squeezed out of the manufacture of combat planes, even though I designed them. Looking over the engines available, I discovered that a large surplus of Oberursel rotaries had accumulated. I decided to build a cantilever wooden wing monoplane around the Oberursel, despite the fact that my first ship along these lines had been rejected a year and a half before. The D-8 monoplane . . . had the exact shape and wing for which I had been ridiculed. But in the period since my original failure to convince the army experts, the cantilever wing, with its box spars, had shown its reliability in the D-7. The wings were almost invulnerable under the hottest fire. Bullets shooting away struts and guy wires left ordinary wings in a state of collapse, but scarcely damaged box spars.

The D-8 was a first-class combat machine, yet its crowning virtue was the appreciable economy it rendered to a war industry ridden with shortages, and it would have certainly replaced the D-7 if hostilities had lasted through the 1918–1919 winter. But, as Fokker recorded, "this final pursuit type hardly figured in front-line conflict, for just when the factory commenced large-scale production of the monoplane, the Armistice was invoked. Some forty D-7's, and a few D-8's, either captured or delivered after the truce, were brought back to McCook Field, at Dayton, by the United States Army Air Corps. They were flown for experimental purposes there, and gained a solid reputation for me among aeronautical engineers."

Fokker's star, risen in a wartime firmament, continued ascending in the ensuing years of peace. His trimotor transports of the 1920's revolutionized and greatly hastened the progress of commercial aviation. A giant among pioneer aircraft designers, he retained his stature as a forward-thinking and prolific producer right up until his death in 1939. Though he learned to dislike his employers in World War I, he never apologized for working in Germany. He had, he later submitted, "served not the Germans so much as man's ambition to fly ever swifter, ever higher, and ever more safely." Some irony resides in the fact that, when the Nazi legions overran Holland shortly after his death, they seized the Fokker Aircraft Works in suburban Amsterdam and kept it operating with forced labor, so that the fruits of his genius—

this time under less congenial circumstances—served a second generation of German militarists.

Fokker began his development of the D-8 monoplane in February 1918, after one of his test pilots successfully flew a D-7 minus its bottom wing. The D-7 was then reproportioned and fitted with a 140-horsepower Oberursel rotary engine, which was housed in a horseshoe-shaped aluminum cowling adapted from that of the triplane. Like the triplane and the D-7 before it, the monoplane had a supplementary airfoil incorporated into its landing gear and was armed with a pair of synchronized Spandau guns. The new wing devised for the D-8 was noteworthy not only for its improved cantilever construction but because the ailerons were cleanly recessed entirely in the trailing edge instead of extending to the wing tips or beyond, as was then the standard arrangement on all late-model aircraft. This feature, as well as the graceful and modernistic configuration of the wing, represented yet one more advance to Fokker's credit.

In June, at Adlershof, the D-8 was entered into competition with rival prototypes for army acceptance. Among the pilots invited to try the various new machines and evaluate their potential was Captain Reinhard, recently promoted to command the Richthofen circus. His enthusiastic estimate of the D-8 was confirmed by all who took it aloft, and it was ordered into limited production for further trials. The army, however, desired some changes in the wing frame. Fokker, against his better judgment, complied. What resulted was a long comedy of errors that delayed the plane's debut at the front by several months. The wing as the army wanted it was unsafe. Only after some sixty machines had been fitted with the faulty wings and scrapped as useless, was Fokker's original design accepted.

On July 3, the day after he tested the prototype D-8, Reinhard met his death. Taking off in an unorthodox aircraft conceived by the later-eminent Dr. Claudius Dornier and built by the Zeppelin company, Reinhard was climbing rather steeply past three thousand feet when a strut broke, causing the top wing to buckle. Reinhard was mortally injured in the crash. The man who had flown this plane immediately before him was the commander of Jasta 27, Lieutenant Hermann Goering. Since Goering succeeded Reinhard at the head of J.G. 1, it was an eerie coincidence that wove their destinies together that afternoon at Adlershof. Had their turns to fly the ill-fated machine been reversed, the subsequent history of J.G. 1 might have been altered to a significant degree. And so also, considering Goering's later career, his prominence and sway in the Nazi regime, his close ties to Hitler, and the prime part he played in organizing and commanding the Luftwaffe, the course of World War II might have been greatly affected if Goering, not Reinhard, had perished on that spring day in 1918.

With Reinhard gone, temporary command of J.G. 1 went to Captain Udet, only to be taken away from him the next day, without explanation, and given instead to Captain Loewenhardt. Udet, outraged by this move, suspected Loewenhardt of underhandedness, whereby an already existing rivalry between them was sorely aggravated. These two high-scoring aces—Udet leading Jasta 11, Loewenhardt leading Jasta 10—were engaged in intense rivalry to become the supreme air fighter and to outdo Richthofen's eighty victories.

This seesaw contest continued at full pace until Loewenhardt fatally crashed in August, and although neither he nor Udet ever openly acknowledged it, the contest had been the talk of the whole German flying corps. Such internal strife was unheard of while Richthofen was alive, for the baron demanded teamwork of his pilots and brooked no disobedience of that rule. The competition between Udet and Loewenhardt developed in the weeks following Richthofen's death, Reinhard's permissive style of command affording them the freedom to pursue their hunting. Each had considered himself the heir apparent to Richthofen's job, only to find it bequeathed to Reinhard. Now that Reinhard was dead, Udet and Loewenhardt felt certain, as did everybody else in the outfit, that one or the other of them would be installed as the new geschwader chief. At first, when he was nominated for interim command, it looked as if Udet had prevailed. Barely twenty-four hours later, though, when Udet was summarily deposed in favor of Loewenhardt, the latter seemed certain to step into Reinhard's boots. The formality of an order from army headquarters was all that remained to settle the affair.

For three days, no such confirmation was received. Then, on the morning of July 7, Lieutenant Bodenschatz, emerging excitedly from his office, waved a paper over his head to beckon attention. Pilots and mechanics came running. When they had congregated around him, Bodenschatz read out a message from Berlin: Order No. 178654. 6.7.18. Lieutenant Hermann Goering . . . presently commanding Jasta 27 . . . is hereby appointed *Kommandeur* of Jagdgeschwader Freiherr von Richthofen No. 1."

None who heard it quite believed his ears. Not Loewenhardt, not Udet, but a *fremde*—a stranger—was going to take over the geschwader. The idea was at once incredible and galling. And when he arrived a week later to assume his coveted new command, Goering was greeted with polite but heartfelt coolness. If any in the geschwader reflected on it, they must have realized that the decision to bring in an outsider probably owed to the rampant jealousy between Udet and Loewenhardt, and to the fear that dissension would result if either was granted preference over the other.

Goering's relations with the geschwader quickly went from bad to worse, for he ruled with an iron hand. A stricter disciplinarian than Richthofen had ever been, he tolerated nothing less than absolute submission to his authority in the air. Combats were to be fought in narrow conformity with his prescribed tactics, which were radically different from those of his predecessors. He laid this down as dogma on the day after his arrival, when the entire complement of J.G. 1 pilots was assembled in a hangar at Guise to hear an address. The proceedings began with a short ceremony in which Bodenschatz, as adjutant, presented the new leader with the so-called *geschwaderstock*—the blackthorn cane that Richthofen and then Reinhard had carried. Goering accepted it with all the gravity of a prince at coronation receiving the royal scepter. He then delivered his introductory speech. He told them—these veterans and victory-rich aces, the flower of the German flying corps—what they had been doing wrong. Then he told them how he was going to institute the necessary reforms. The old order was changing, and the new—as outlined by Goering—was not to the liking of his audience.

Individualism in the air, which had been curbed to a judicious extent by Richthofen, was effectually abolished by Goering. The late, now more than ever lamented, baron had never imposed regimentation in combat. Once he had given the signal for attack, his pilots were each on his own. Richthofen had complete faith in them. They had been recruited by him on the basis of courage and skill, and he personally had further schooled them to a rare degree of proficiency. As this suggests, Richthofen's confidence in them reflected an even greater confidence in his own faculties as both a judge of men's merit and as a battle leader. To grant them such freedom of action required of him, in his role as leader, an almost uncanny ability to keep track of almost everything that went on around him in even the wildest melee. Richthofen possessed this ability. As for Reinhard, a man of decent acumen, if not a flyer of conspicuous address, he lacked the prestige and self-assurance to assert himself, but the exceeding excellence of his men more than compensated for his flaccid leadership. Goering, in contrast to his two predecessors, was an overweening autocrat. For example, where Richthofen and Reinhard had relied on the *freie jagd*—the "free hunt," which perhaps should better be translated to mean a general free-for-all—Goering, a born organizer and leader who jealously exercised all the prerogatives of his command, flatly discountenanced these tactics. His authoritarian mentality balked at such anarchic methods. So long as he was boss, nobody but Lieutenant Goering would dictate the where, when, and how of geschwader operations.

Although the pilots' antipathy toward him eventually softened, due undoubtedly to the disarming affability he displayed in his man-to-man dealings, they never quite forgave him his posture as the infallible dictator. His was in many respects the classic personality of the ostensibly benevolent despot. Suave, amiable, ingratiating in his social bearing, he was imperious and self-opinionated in wielding his authority. For all his magisterial conceit, however, few could resist his conciliatory charm, and he was a facile manipulator of people. Goering, in fact, shared these traits with Adolf Hitler, on whose coattails he later rode to a historic place in world affairs, achieving powerful office, enormous affluence, and—in the end—everlasting infamy.

In common with Hitler, Goering believed himself elected by destiny to a messianic mission. Perhaps he was seduced by this notion as a boy at his father's knee, hearing again and again of his illustrious family background, of the kings and queens among his ancestors, of how he had sprung from a

lineage reaching back to the ancient royal houses of Hohenzollern and Wittels-
bach. Young Goering was intoxicated by the thought that the blood of sov-
ereigns flowed in his veins. It imbued him with a sense of innate superiority
and with the will to command. The subject never lost its fascination for him.
In 1937, the Nazi government published the "authorized" geneology of the
Air Minister, the Premier of Prussia, and the Führer's right-hand man,
Colonel-General Hermann Wilhelm Goering. Charted on the pages of that
elegant volume was indeed an imposing pedigree. A diligent scholar, Professor
Baron Otto Dungern, had traced Goering's patrilineal forebears back to the
twelfth century. The professor's research was probably valid, although his
book appeared as one in a series of family histories of prominent Nazis, and
some of the other works in the series—most notably that purporting to de-
lineate Hitler's ancestry—were deliberately falsified to avoid embarrassments.
The racial laws were now in force in the Third Reich, and investigations into
the antecedents of the famous and nonfamous, even of the insignificant, developed into a thriving commerce; every fervent patriot and frightened bour-
geois was anxious to prove himself of pure Aryan extraction. In Goering's
case, there was nothing to hide. He was related, for example, to the descendants of the great German poet and thinker, Johann Wolfgang von Goethe,
and to the grandchildren of Bismarck, the "Iron Chancellor," and appropriately, to Count Zeppelin, who had given his name to the erstwhile marvel
of German aeronautical science. Through the Hohenzollerns, Goering was
even a kinsman to Queen Victoria and Kaiser Wilhelm II. Monarchs and
noblemen fruited many branches of his family tree.

The vanity induced in him by these family connections colored his whole
life. Born in January 1893 to Heinrich and Fanny Goering, he always
attributed his love of soldiering to his descent from a long line of military
leaders, adding that this hereditary inclination was fortified by the atmosphere
in his father's home. Actually, he did not live with his parents until his sixth
year. As a career diplomat with the Foreign Office, his father—after distinguished service in England and German Southwest Africa—was managing
the consulate in Haiti when Hermann was begot. Haiti was not a place where
Europeans gladly risked bringing a baby into the world. So Fanny Goering
voyaged to Germany and, in the Marienbad Sanitorium at Rosenheim, Bavaria,
delivered her fourth child, the second son, Hermann. When he grew up,
although he was of Prussian-Austrian stock, he liked to pass himself off as a
Bavarian. He rose to high station as a member of the "Bavarian Group" of
the Nazi Party, and many who knew him, including his closest associates,
were later surprised to discover the Prussian elements in his character.

In 1938 Hermann Goering played an active role in the Anschluss of
Austria. Among the refugees who fled from Vienna was Sigmund Freud, whose
delvings into human mental phenomena had revealed a relationship between
infant experience and adult behavior. Goering was living proof of many of
Freud's findings. Had the Nazi Air Minister submitted himself to examination

by a psychoanalyst, he would have been told of the severe trauma he suffered when he was abruptly parted from his mother only six weeks after his birth. Fanny Goering, the dutiful wife, left her son to return to her husband and three older children in Haiti. The island, she decided with justification, was no fit place for a babe in arms. The natives were surly, disease was rampant, earthquakes and hurricanes shook the ramshackle abode of the consul-general, giant ants and scorpions wandered indoors and menaced the household. Hermann, therefore, was left in the care of Frau Graf, a friend of the family, whom he called "Mother" as soon as he learned to speak.

Most psychologists would agree, and some have stated, that Goering exhibited the typical symptoms of a person who had been weaned too soon from his mother's breast. Subconsciously he was always trying to recapture the maternal love he had missed in early childhood. There is also evidence to show how sorely aggrieved he was by the separation. As a youngster, feeling himself abandoned by his family, he bitterly envied his brother and sisters who had shared their parents' life in the far, exotic lands beyond the sea. He needed a sense of importance, and to get it he invented stories that would impress his little friends. He fabricated such preposterous tales about himself and was so overbearing in telling them, moreover, that the neighborhood children shunned him. Frau Graf, an elderly and austere widow, had no patience with or understanding of him. Starved for affection, his first six years of life were cold and lonely.

Then came the time for the Goering family to return to Germany. Hermann was reunited with the mother he could not remember and the father he had never known. They settled down in a comfortable, modest home in Berlin. Father Goering worked a while longer at the Foreign Office before retiring to a life of slippered ease. He was complacent in his well-being and doctrinaire in his patriotic sentiments. His friends were of his class, civil servants and army officers, and they endorsed his view that German culture would ultimately impose its order on the world. It was in this atmosphere that young Hermann acquired his superiority complex and his mania for the military life. His father lectured on the proud heritage of his family line, and he found here a ready-made rationalization with which to repress the feelings of rejection and insecurity that accrued from his years with Frau Graf. At the dinner table and in the parlor of his father's home there was constant talk of past wars, of the "French enemy," of Germany's greatness and the power of her arms. In later years, Hermann often told a nostalgic story of how, as a boy, he had fondled the glittering helmets and shining swords his father's guests had deposited in the foyer. On Sundays, Father Goering would take his brood to Potsdam to watch the troops parade. The atmosphere of martial grandeur completely enthralled them, especially Hermann. He amassed a large collection of toy soldiers and played with them at every chance. Whenever he deplored his miniature armies, he placed a large mirror behind the battlefield. His father once asked him why he did this, to which he proudly replied that the mirror enabled him to double his forces. It was a stroke of strategic genius much like that he exhibited in the final stages of World War II, when the Luftwaffe was about twice the size on paper that it was in reality.

Goering's education was a stormy and unavailing trial for everyone concerned, until he was enrolled in military college. Then twelve years old, he had been expelled or tactfully and timefully summoned home from five schools, and his parents decided he needed the stern discipline of an army institute. His exaggerated ideas of self-importance had turned him into a teacher's nightmare, unruly, defiant, and mulishly impenitent. Apart from his father and mother, the only authority he respected wore a brass-buttoned uniform. The boy was jubilant when he was enlisted in the Karlsruhe Academy. It was exactly what he wanted. Book learning took second place in Karlsruhe; the emphasis was on military training. There were no more complaints. He was a good soldier. He made quick progress. Everything was order and precision, and that gave him the emotional security he craved. He became a cadet officer, and his deep-seated urge to boss others was gratified. Though it never healed, the bruised ego of childhood was salved.

According to the writings of one who attended the academy with him, Goering underwent a marked personality change after his promotion to cadet officer. From a tense, laconic, unsociable type, he suddenly became a very personable, witty, and convivial fellow. It was a veneer he wore through the rest of his life—just so long as things were going right and he had a voice in running them. Goering, the love-impoverished infant turned adult, suffered an insatiable hunger for solicitude and approval. He desperately needed friends, yet enjoyed few genuine friendships. He was too guarded with his sincerity to accomodate the demands of an honest camaraderie, too much afraid that his trust would be betrayed. He feared being hurt as he had often been hurt in boyhood, and to allay that fear, he tried a friendship a dozen different ways before accepting it. The handful of indulgent sympathizers who passed the test were set upon pedestals so towering and durable that to inscribe the legend "Mama" thereon would have been superfluous. They were his confidants, his consolers and applauders. "Speaking in a figurative and Freudian sense," wrote an anti-Nazi pamphleteer in Germany in 1932, "Goering is a breast-sucker."

The friends he did find, he clung to for as long as they let him. Ernst Udet was one. He met Udet, of course, in J.G. 1 and occasionally barnstormed with him as a stunt pilot in the postwar decade. When Udet served under Goering again, as a Luftwaffe general during the Nazi heyday, he learned to detest the "Fat Man." In 1941, when the Nazi Party needed a sacrificial goat to blame for the Luftwaffe's failure to bomb England into submission, Udet was made to wear the horns. He was less culpable than Goering, really, and yet, disgraced and vilified, driven to suicide, he neither expected nor received any defense from the "Fat Man." Goering had long ago detected Udet's alienation. Feigning a sad face, he stood by and watched his old comrade's ruination.

Karl Bodenschatz, Goering's adjutant in J.G. 1, remained his friend, too. Bodenschatz was probably his most sycophantic satellite, joining his staff in 1933, and soon thereafter becoming a general of the Luftwaffe. At the Nuremberg Trials in 1946, where Goering shared the dock with twenty other high Nazi officials accused of "crimes against humanity," Bodenschatz was among a few of his intimates and collaborators who testified in his behalf, extolling him to the heavens as a misunderstood and viciously maligned boy scout. One of these witnesses for the defense, Paul Koerner, who had served as Hitler's Secretary of State, described Goering as "the last remaining Renaissance figure"—at which the prisoner beamed appreciatively.

Clad in a faded Luftwaffe uniform without insignia, Goering was obviously pleased that he had been given the number-one seat in the dock, for that represented a recognition of his place in the Nazi hierarchy now that the Führer was dead. Fourteen of the defendants at Nuremberg were sentenced to the gallows. Goering was among them. In English, French, Russian, and German simultaneously, the judgment was read to the courtroom. The whole grim record of his Nazi past was recited. Concentration camps . . . purge . . . mass liquidation . . . Gestapo . . . the Anschluss . . . Poland . . . genocide . . . aggressive wars . . . slave labor . . . spoliation of conquered countries . . . the persecution of Jews. "There is nothing to be said in mitigation," the voice concluded, "for Goering was often, indeed almost always, the moving force, second only to his leader. . . . His own admissions are more than sufficient to be conclusive of his guilt. His guilt is unique in its enormity. The record discloses no excuse for this man. The Tribunal finds the defendant Goering guilty on all counts."

But Goering—the handsome, dashing air hero of World War I, who had grown obese feeding off his own corruption, who had wallowed in pomp so ludicrously grand that he was ridiculed behind his back, who had reveled in the luxuries of an Oriental potentate, who had become a man with the mannerisms of a fop and the characteristics of a hysterical woman—this absurd, pathetic, sinister egomaniac could not face the humiliation of dying in the style of a vulgar criminal. If they had condemned him to some more dignified mode of execution, he might possibly have faced it. A firing squad would have honored him as a soldier. A headsman's axe would have been a death befitting a patrician of his august pedigree and the last of the Renaissance princes. It was a matter of pride for him to cheat the hangman, and he managed to do so. Two hours before it would be his turn to hang, he swallowed a vial of poison that had been smuggled into his cell. Like his Führer, Adolf Hitler, he succeeded at the last hour in choosing his own way of leaving the earth on which he, in league with the other, had made such a murderous impact.

A third crony of Goering's from World War I days later became a general in the Luftwaffe along with Udet and Bodenschatz. His name was Bruno Loerzer, and although his friendship was esteemed above any other by Goering, he declined to appear in the Air Minister's defense at Nuremberg. Loerzer's perfidy wounded Goering deeply, for their careers had run together for some thirty-two years. They were lieutenants of the same infantry regiment and shared similar duties during the early battles of World War I. But Goering came down with an ailment that threatened to end his precious career almost as soon as it had started. Complaining of a painful stiffness in his legs, he was sent to the hospital at Freiburg. The diagnosis—rheumatoid arthritis—confirmed his worst fears. It meant that his days as an infantry officer were over. Whenever the disease acted up, he could walk only with great difficulty. But his friend, Loerzer, who was attending a nearby flight school, hatched a scheme whereby Goering might still see action in spite of his infirmity. They decided that when Loerzer qualified for his pilot's certificate and received his posting to the front, Goering would go along with him as his observer. When the time came, Goering sneaked out of the hospital; reported away without leave, he was tried in absentia by a miltary court and sentenced to three months' confinement, but the verdict never caught up with him. With great cheek, he and Loerzer actually obtained an airplane without permission and passed themselves off as a trained crew. After much dickering with the authorities, they reached a frontline airfield.

Feldfliegerabteilung No. 25 was their first unit. The commanding officer, since he had a full complement of observers but not enough pilots, wanted to retain Loerzer and reassign Goering elsewhere. They persuaded him to change his mind, however, and the two devoted friends were allowed to fly together. They became known around the barracks as the "curious couple"—but their work was good. They even succeeded in shooting down a French plane one day over Verdun.

Goering's vaulting ambition spurred him onward and upward. He trained as an aviator. For a short time, piloting C-type two-seaters, he chauffered artillery spotters over the lines. Then he graduated to single-seaters and rejoined Loerzer, who in that year of 1916 was named to head Jasta 26. Goering was made subcommander of the squadron, much to the annoyance of Loerzer's brother, Fritz, whose lugubrious appearance earned him his name of the "Flying Pastor" and who eventually acquitted himself as an eleven-victory ace. Goering received a thigh wound in one of his first dogfights, but he was hospitalized for only a week, railing to get back into cockpit harness. His enthusiasm, his grasp of tactics, and his keen managerial flair soon brought to him the command of his own unit—Jasta 27. Still he and Loerzer were together, for their squadrons shared the same field. Their reputations grew apace, Loerzer's more as an expert flyer-fighter than a leader, Goering's not so much as the deft pilot than as a shrewd and effective director. Their scores reflected that difference in their respective aptitudes. Loerzer finished the war with forty-one victories, Goering with twenty-two (only two of which he acquired while in command of J.G. 1). Participating in the great air battles that preceded the German offensive of March 1918, both men were decorated with the exalted Order Pour le Mérite. When, in June, after Captain Reinhard's death, a replacement was sought to take charge of the Richthofen geschwader, Loerzer as well as Goering was considered for the job by the supreme command. Since Goering was the candidate chosen, it seems safe to infer that heavier stress was laid upon leadership than individual skill in the air. This is not to imply that Loerzer was not a good leader, for he subsequently took over Jagdgeschwader No. 3 and administered it brilliantly. Hindenburg himself addressed a letter of commendation to Loerzer in September, which was followed by a promotion to captain. Goering remained an oberleutnant.

But it was Goering's splendid privilege to command Germany's finest group of battle flyers. Arriving at Guise that July morning, a little plumper than when he originally entered the army, a little shorter than most of the pilots around him, his square jaw jutting, his blue eyes hard and steady, he had reached the pinnacle of an airman's wartime career. Just four months later, Germany capitulated. J.G. 1 was based at Tellencourt when the dreadful news came. Orders, on Armistice Day, were to fly to Darmstadt to await further instructions. There, as in many German cities, Communist revolutionaries had created trouble by exploiting the national crisis in an attempt to usurp control. The civil situation had degenerated into chaos, and Red soldier-councils confiscated the weapons of the first section of J.G. 1 to land. When Goering heard of this, he issued an ultimatum—the return of the weapons or an attack on the town by the whole unit. They received back their weapons, then flew on to Aschaffenburg for disbandment. That was the end of the famous, already legendary Richthofen circus, commanded in its last days by an incipient madman whose name became only too well known to the world not many years later.

Goering attained the peak of his World War I career at an inauspicious moment. The history of J.G. 1 after his assumption of command—the history of German aviation as a whole in those final seventeen weeks of war—tells of a hopeless struggle against ever-mounting odds. On July 15, a week after Goering received the *geschwaderstock* of J.G. 1, General Ludendorff launched his final offensive. As in 1914, the gray hordes swept toward Rheims and Paris, but this time their blow had no chance of success. Once again the Marne valley became a mass grave for Germans as Joffre's old rallying cry— "They shall not pass!"—sounded above the roaring guns. Ludendorff's attack ended in gory disaster. Blasted by artillery, bombed and strafed from the air, driven by bayonet, grenade, and rifle, the Germans fell away from the Marne, their regiments decimated, their divisions shattered. By July 18, the pendulum had swung away from the German side. The Allies' turn had come to hit back. The combined might of France, Great Britain, and the United States— a vast, untapped reservoir of men, machines, munitions, and food—was now poised against a depleted, weary, disheartened German army. Ludendorff had dealt his last card and the *Götterdämmerung* lay inevitably ahead for Imperial Germany. It was a question only of time.

From July 18, when Marshal Foch counterattacked at the Marne, throughout the remainder of the war, the Allies conducted a continuous series of overwhelming onslaughts up and down the western front. The opening thrusts were directed at the great salients the Germans had hammered into the Allied lines since March: the Aisne-Marne; the Amiens-Somme-Noyon; the Lys-Ypres; and Saint-Mihiel. After the reduction of these bulges, the final drives were aimed at breakthrough and triumph. In some sectors the Americans led the assault; in others, the British or French. On August 8, behind four hundred tanks and a tremendous barrage, the British struck east of Amiens. Years later, Ludendorff called it "the black day of the German army," for it was the beginning of the end. A gaping hole was torn in the German lines, and the exultant tommies raced through. Tanks roved the German rear. The penetration was so deep that a trainload of Ludendorff's reinforcements was captured en route to the front. When a detachment of British surprised a divisional staff at supper, they found among their prisoners a pair of thoroughly disgusted generals. The British incursions unbraced German morale from the top to the bottom of the ranks. For the first time, German soldiers were disobeying orders, straggling, deserting under fire, surrendering in large numbers. Reserves moving forward were greeted with hoots of derision and exhorted to stay back from the front by disorderly units trudging rearward. Discipline was coming apart at the seams. In an emergency conference at Spa in mid-August, the Kaiser and his military pundits decided that feelers should be extended to explore the possibility of a peace bargain.

Ludendorff endured another black day on August 28, when the advancing line of British and French infantry was widened to form a solid front reaching from Arras to Soissons. The cost of gaining a few yards had been appalling in 1917, and now the Allied armies were rolling up whole miles. The Somme was crossed. On into September the Allies continued the multiple blows against the buckling enemy wall. The pressure became unbearable, and the wall gave way. The Germans vacated the Lys-Ypres salient, and backed out of the Noyon bulge, retreating across devastated earth to the Hindenburg line, from where they had started in the spring. The withdrawal was stubborn and coordinated, but it was designed mainly to secure time in which to augment and bolster the long-prepared and already formidable field fortifications of the Hindenburg line. By September 25 the retirement was completed. The Allies were confronting the last German stronghold. Meanwhile, fighting now as a cohesive army—since General Pershing had insisted that his troops must go into battle under American command—the men of the A.E.F. captured Saint-Mihiel. The campaign was directed by Pershing himself, wielding the U.S. First Army, which had been organized on August 10 and which incorporated fifteen American divisions, with four French divisions in support roles. In the battle of Saint-Mihiel, almost half the artillery pieces were manned by the French, and all the guns and tanks and aircraft were of French or British manufacture. Almost fifteen hundred aircraft—the largest concentration of aircraft ever mustered—participated in the attack. More than half of them were flown by French and British pilots, but the officer in command was Colonel (later Brigadier-General) William "Billy" Mitchell. The Germans were far outnumbered at Saint-Mihiel. It was, in fact, a rear-guard defense they put up, for they had already begun evacuating the salient when the Americans attacked. The victory was quick and comparatively easy. Although not too important in the overall picture, it was a satisfying success for the confident but unproven novitiates, and Clemenceau and a host of others sent congratulations.

From Saint-Mihiel, the Americans streamed northward and at the end of September linked up with the French and British to help smash the Hindenburg line. There were now thirty-nine U.S. divisions in France, 102 French, sixty British, twelve Belgian, two Italian, and two Portuguese—a total of 217 —opposing 193 German and four Austrian divisions, many of them undermanned and undersupplied. But the huge American divisions were twice as large as the French, almost twice as large as the British—and four times the size of the emasculated German divisions. In terms of miles of front, the Americans held about one-fourth of the total. Pershing consented to six of his divisions staying under French and British command; the rest were grouped in the U.S. First Army, under General Hunter Liggett, and in a new Second Army, created on October 12, under General Robert Bullard.

The U.S. First Army, with the French Fourth Army on its flank, started the final drives of the war on September 26, with an offensive in the Meuse-Argonne—the severest test of American arms to that time. On the following day, the British unreeled a massive assault in Picardy, between Peronne and Lens. And on the next day after that, King Albert of the Belgians attacked in the coastal lowlands. Everywhere the action was brutal. The Germans yielded ground slowly, doggedly. They offered savage resistance, delaying the Allies with mortars, machine-gun nests, and skillful rear guards, protecting their vital routes of supply. In the first week of October, however, Ludendorff saw that all hope was gone. He told Hindenburg, who fully agreed, that the hour had come to sue for peace. The new German chancellor, Prince Max of Baden, asked President Wilson if an armistice might be arranged on the basis of the American leader's "Fourteen Points." Wilson referred him to Marshal Foch. "An armistice," said Wilson, "is the business of the military."

The war dragged on. Some of the fiercest fighting lay ahead. All along the western front, from Verdun to the sea—for the first time in four long years—the Allied line was advancing. The Germans were staging their bitterest defense in the Argonne, against the Americans. The A.E.F. covered three miles on the first day of the campaign, meeting light opposition. But soon they were slowed by murderous fire in the tangled maze of the Argonne forest and around the stark heights of Montfaucon. Absorbing heavy casualties, they crashed their way across about one-half of the forest by October 3, had taken Montfaucon, and their right flank rested south of Brieulles-sur-Meuse. The battle then reached a frenzied pitch. Through the rest of that month, at a frightful cost of flesh and blood, the Americans inched their way slowly through the stygian gloom of the forest. Back home, front pages were monopolized by lurid descriptions of the "super battle." For days the country waited breathless to learn the fate of the "Lost Battalion"—the First Battalion, 308th Infantry, 77th Division—which had become detached and was surrounded by the Germans. An air drop, the first ever of any magnitude, was undertaken by the American flying corps in an attempt to sustain the battalion until it could break out or be rescued from its predicament. Billy Mitchell discussed the episode in his memoirs:

> I ordered chocolate and concentrated food and ammunition dropped off to [the battalion]. Our pilots thought they had located it from the [signal] panel that it showed, and dropped off considerable supplies. The battalion held out and rejoined its command, but I later found out that they had received none of the supplies we had dropped off. The Germans had made up a panel like theirs and our men had calmly dropped off the nice food to the Germans, who undoubtedly ate it with great thanksgiving.

Hard-won though it was, American success in the Argonne was assured. Pershing's ranks were replenished and augmented by a constant flow of reinforcements; furthermore, they had all the battle hardware they needed. The Germans, on the other hand, could not replace their losses. Day by day they grew fewer in number, shorter in supply, and less disposed to fight. The Americans surged relentlessly onward against a faltering, groggy enemy. By November 1, they had cleared the awning heights of the Meuse and secured Grandpré. The Hindenburg line was breached on a wide front, and the Argonne was behind them. The German defenses were unhinged, and from then until the Armistice the Americans swept forward in great leaps. When hostilities ceased, the 42nd Division, Brigadier General Douglas MacArthur commanding, was on the outskirts of Sedan, and the French held Mézières. In the north, the Belgians had liberated Bruges and Ghent and were marching toward the Scheldt; the British controlled the rail junction at Maubeuge; the Canadians occupied Mons.

The final chapter of hellish fury at the close of World War I compressed much agony and turmoil into a few weeks' time. Prince Max's appeal for an armistice to President Wilson in early October was followed by exchanges of notes and statements of conditions. But the vise was clamping on Germany, and soon she could impose no conditions. Bulgaria was forced out of the war in September. Next to collapse was the Turkish Empire, when the Sultan's forces in Palestine were routed. In the concluding action British planes annihilated an entire Turkish army trapped in a narrow passage through the hills near Nablus; it was the first large-scale victory won by aircraft over ground troops. The Turks begged for peace and an armistice was signed on October 31.

Only four days later, Austria—her provinces racked by rebellion—surrendered. Germany was alone. The great monolith of *Kultur* that Bismarck had alchemized of "blood and steel" was crumbling. The disintegration began with a splintering of the general staff into quarreling factions. Ludendorff, who was prone to panic in a crisis, resigned on October 27. And in the navy, sailors of the High Seas Fleet refused to obey orders for a final sortie against the British Isles. Their dissidence flared into mutiny; the mutiny became insurrection and spread throughout the land. In every part of Germany, mobs rioted against the war and the emperor. Bavaria erupted into a full-scale revolution, led by Russian-style soviets. The end could not be long delayed though the German army was continuing its senseless resistance. On November 9, Kaiser Wilhelm II abdicated his throne as armed crowds, carrying red banners, paraded through Berlin. When garrison troops, called out to quell the mobs, joined them instead, even haughty Wilhelm knew his sun had set. Hours after his abdication, Germany was proclaimed a republic, with a socialist, Friedrich Ebert, at the helm. The Kaiser, on November 10, fled across the Dutch frontier to live out his years in moody exile. Meanwhile, representatives of the new government met with Marshal Foch and other Allied military heads. A railroad coach, drawn on a siding in the forest of Compiègne, was the scene of the conference. Signed at five o'clock in the morning was an armistice treaty to become effective six hours later on that same day, November 11.

And so, at the eleventh hour, eleventh day, eleventh month, 1918, the war ended. A loud silence fell across the swath of battle-ravaged wasteland that stretched from the Alps to the distant beaches of the North Sea. Men emerged from their burrows and ditches, and each, whether victor or vanquished, in his own way celebrated the gladness of survival, some with prayer, some with antic rejoicing, and some with cigarettes and drinks accepted from the former foe.

Among the factors that contributed to Germany's downfall—for example, the incalculable cumulative cost of a monstrous war of attrition; the gradual economic strangulation resulting from the British sea blockade; the ever-worsening shortages of food, fuel, and other essentials; the virus of Bolshevik revolutionism; a sheer exhaustion of human spirit and patriotic fervor; the people's disaffection from an autocratic regime that had brought the nation to disaster—the one underlying all the rest was an insensate strategy born of grandiose delusions. Taking too literally the concept of *"Deutschland uber alles,"* the German general staff mapped out a war of inordinate scope and unlimited aims. Theirs was an impossible dream of conquest; for Germany it became a nightmare, with half the world at her throat. Though they fought bravely and well, her armies were engaged in a hopeless crusade, doomed to ultimate defeat as they strived toward an unattainable goal—a goal evolved from the imperious conceit of a military-monarchial hegemony and its scornful disparagement of the enemy. Since Bismark's day, the German war-lovers had contemptuized the French and British as the "lesser breeds." Such callous disregard for the dignity of other men is a fatal defect in peace as in war.

Goodbye Broadway, Hello France

I T WOULD BE naïve at best, chauvinistic at worst, to assert (as some American historians have asserted) that the war was won and the Allies saved by the timely intervention of the United States. What might have been the outcome if America had remained neutral? No one can say, of course, although the likelihood of a German victory—considering the limited success of Ludendorff's spring, 1918, offensives—seems remote. But to dwell on this question would be to rehash old arguments to no practical purpose, for the hard fact is that the United States did enter hostilities and did thereby ensure an Allied victory—which, to draw a critical distinction, was not the same as winning it for them.

The French and British had already withstood almost four years of bitter attrition and stalemate when American forces, fresh and robust and boyishly eager, stepped in to help administer the knockout punch to a haggard and despondent German army. The Americans had barely time in which to flex their stupendous muscles before the fight was over. Their factories were just beginning to catch up with demands. A year and a half had passed since America declared war, yet little had been provided in the way of matériel. And even in human terms, the United States paid a comparatively small price. Two million Americans sailed "over there" to "keep the world safe for democracy," and they fought well and valiantly. In two hundred days of battle, some 116,000 Americans were killed, and some 235,000 wounded. Of the total force mobilized—four million men, half of whom served in France—the American casualty rate was approximately 8 percent. A lot of spilled blood, to be sure, and a sad enough loss, but only a small part of the grievous total that made up the World War I casualty lists.

France, besides having a third of her land devastated, incurred a casualty rate of 73 percent! Of 8,410,000 French combatants, more than half were wounded. Nearly 1,500,000 were slain.

The British Empire had a casualty rate of 36 percent, comprising a million dead and twice that many wounded.

More than two million Russian soldiers perished, and almost five million were wounded, giving a casualty rate of 76 percent!

The remaining Allied powers—Italy, Belgium, Greece, Roumania, Portugal, Montenegro, and Japan—lost about a million men.

On the other side, Germany suffered a casualty rate in excess of 65 percent, with 1,800,000 dead, 4,216,000 wounded, and at least a million more missing.

Austria incurred the highest casualty rate of all the belligerents: 90 percent! Of her eight-million-man army, nearly a fourth did not survive the war.

Between Turkey and Bulgaria, another half million lives were spent.

Hence, a total of at least ten million men in uniform were killed in battle or died of injuries or disease. At least 21,250,000 others were wounded. Civilian casualties caused by military action and by famine, disease and the civil wars and disorders that attended World War I, are numbered in additional but uncounted millions.

The statistics of Armageddon. Numbers so astronomical that the mind staggers in the attempt to grasp their magnitude. Numbers that bespeak a horror of such enormity that it beggars description or graphic perception. Virtually an entire male generation in Europe was wiped out. A huge convulsion had disrupted the affairs of man, and its profound effects—political, economic, and military—are still being felt.

The military lessons were many. Among the most obvious was that war, in an era of rapidly advancing technology, had become "too important to be trusted to the generals." World War I, unlike any previous war, involved entire populations in its meshes. The battle extended to the heartland of every belligerent nation—to its homes and industries and farms. Newspapers, magazines, and posters were exhorting civilians to do their part as "troops" on the "home front." But if it was a war of peoples, it was also a war of the "big factories." The fate of Imperial Russia demonstrated the folly of trying to fight a modern war with inadequate industrial means. The "big battalions" meant nothing in the final analysis without the vast productive resources necessary to supply and sustain them. The United States discovered the meaning of "industrial mobilization." Millions of soldiers were not enough; an army could not be equipped overnight. Time to prepare, time for the conversion of factories from peacetime to wartime production, was an essential factor in victory.

America's plans were grandiose, but its performance disappointing. Twenty-three thousand tanks, for example, were ordered from American factories; scarcely two dozen were completed by war's end. Only 130 artillery pieces out of 2,250 used by American troops in battle were produced in the United States. Of the nearly nine million artillery shells expended by the A.E.F. in

France, just 208,327 were stamped "Made in U.S.A." So it went down through the entire list of combat commodities.

A source of particular embarrassment, since boastful promises had been loudly noised by the national authorities, was aircraft production. The great fleet of twenty thousand and more planes that was going to "darken the skies of Europe," the vast aerial armada that was going to "bridge the Atlantic" and "crush the Teuton," never materialized. Nor did a single plane of American design ever reach the front.

The one American-built warplane to see action abroad was the DH-4 two-seater, manufactured by license from the British De Havilland company and powered by the much-publicized, but quite inferior, Liberty engine that a group of Detroit automobile makers had hurriedly developed. By the Armistice, a total of 3,227 Liberty DH-4's had been turned out, 1,885 had been shipped to France, and 667 to the advance zone. Although they had been projected as fighters by the American air command, the DH-4's were good only for bombing and reconnaissance. Most of those built in Detroit proved defective when they finally arrived overseas, and further delay resulted from the need to rebuild them at the A.E.F. aircraft repair center at Romorantin. But another feature of their construction made them a national disgrace. They had been equipped with flammable fuel tanks. The twelve squadrons whose misfortune it was to fly these machines immortalized them as "flaming coffins." "None of us in France," noted an American pilot in a postwar magazine article, "could understand what prevented our great country from furnishing machines equal to the best in the world." Despite the enormous sums expended on aircraft, declared General Halsey Dunwoody, director of aviation supply, "we never had a single plane that was fit for use."

It took exactly eleven months from the declaration of war to put the first American-trained pilots in the air at the front. No one was more disgusted at this delay than the young Air Service volunteers themselves. Like the rest of the nation, they believed General Squier in June, 1917, when he forecast the dispatch of "myriads of airplanes over the German lines to teach Germany that we have come to win." The first class of cadets graduated from the ground schools in the United States one month later. By mid-October 1917, nearly seven thousand cadets had entered the ground schools; more than three thousand had graduated, and five hundred of them had completed flight training in the United States. Then a situation developed that greatly damaged the morale of the aviation branch. Representatives of the Air Service in France requested that five hundred cadets be sent overseas every month immediately after the completion of ground training, to be breveted as pilots in the French military flying schools in the latest types of French planes. The privilege of prompt transfer to France was restricted to honor graduates of stateside ground schools, those cadets who stood at the top of their classes. By December 1917, some eighteen hundred had been shipped overseas.

The plans for rapid flight training in France did not work out, however.

An order was received in December to send no more cadets abroad. Later, this order was canceled, and men were again sent to France. These men, having been graduated from flight schools in the United States, received their commissions and went to war as lieutenants. Their unlucky predecessors— the eighteen hundred honor students—had not been commissioned. In fact, many of them had no opportunity to receive flight instruction for six months after their arrival in France. Most of them, to quote Colonel Hiram Bingham, "found themselves confined for months at a time in concentration and mobilization camps far from the sight or hearing of an airplane, forced to study over and over again the very subjects which they had mastered with so much enthusiasm at American ground schools, treated by despairing officers as though they were 'draft-dodgers' who needed military discipline and who deserved reprobation rather than sympathy." It did not improve their spirit to realize that the men whom they had surpassed in studies were now their superiors in rank and authority. They were the victims, said Colonel Bingham, of "serious and exasperating delays, disappointments, and 'new deals' which tended to break their morale and destroy their self-respect." When these facts finally became public, many Americans were inclined to agree with Bingham that the story was "the worst page in the history of the Air Service."

But those officer-pilots who arrived in France for their advanced training met disappointment also. Learning to fly in a Curtiss "Jenny"—as they had done in the United States—did not qualify them to undertake immediate combat work in the fast French planes that the Air Service had procured. The army had set up at Issoudun—which Pershing was once heard to describe as "the worst muddle in France"—a flight school that covered an area of fifty square miles and eventually had twelve large airfields. It was contemplated that Issoudun would be used to give pilots a brief "finishing course" before sending them against the enemy. As things worked out, however, it became not only an advanced, but a primary, training facility for all branches of flying. Because of the uncertainty that prevailed about the procurement of operational aircraft, officers who had already earned their wings back home were now required to master at least six different types of French planes to qualify for frontline duty.

Such scandalous bungling as this, on the very highest levels, did not end there. Recognizing that it was "in no sense a logical branch of the Signal Corps," General Pershing very early established the Air Service as a separate and distinct entity within the A.E.F. Although a number of excellent officers were transferred to it from both line and staff, their lack of knowledge impaired their usefulness. Pershing soon found that differences in their viewpoints were often irreconcilable. There was bitter factionalism over the most petty issues. Grudges arose among the senior officers; none enjoyed the good will of all the others. This resulted in a series of quick turnovers in command personnel, and a confusing sequence of reorganizations.

By February 1918, Pershing was "seriously concerned." His timetable required that sixty squadrons be at the front by July and twice that many by November. Yet only nine squadrons were anywhere near combat readiness. According to the official Air Service historian, Lieutenant Colonel H. A. Toulmin: "At the beginning of May, an aggregate of some thirty thousand enlisted men and officers, in France, England, and Italy, were planeless and purposeless. . . . [The Air Service] was a practical failure; was facing the possibilities of disaster in the accomplishment of any phase of its then un-fixed program, and was faced with moral and mental disorganization and disarrangement, which was insidiously wrecking the very integrity and the morale of the entire service."

At this juncture, Pershing placed the Air Service in the command of Major General Mason M. Patrick, who later confessed that he was completely taken aback by the appointment "inasmuch as I had never before seen an airplane, save casually." The new aeronautics chief had been a classmate of Pershing's at West Point; as an officer of the engineer corps, he had supervised the vast construction projects of the A.E.F. in France. Notwithstanding his un-familiarity with aviation, Patrick instituted reforms which saved the Air Service from wholly disastrous mismanagement.

But still there were serious blunders. For example, when the 94th Pursuit Squadron arrived at the front, its pilots were distressed to find that their Nieuports had not yet been equipped with guns. Since the French had agreed to train the tyros of the 94th in combat over the lines, a couple of experienced French pilots accompanied them on patrols. Two full weeks passed before the French patrol leaders discovered—to their utter amazement—that the Americans were flying unarmed machines. No one thought it very funny ex-cept the pilots of the 94th, who considered it a splendid hoax to have perpe-trated. The dangers of such tomfoolery, however, became tragically evident a few weeks later, when a pilot in the 95th Pursuit Squadron, Captain James Miller, was shot down while flying a Nieuport that his French combat instruc-tor erroneously assumed had proper armament. A pilot wrote: "Us boys are finally in it. We've got nice planes to fly, but somebody forgot to put guns on them. After so many months of waiting, nobody wants to draw too much attention to this oversight, 'cause then they'll ground us and we'll be waiting again, this time for guns, and that might take a year or two the way things are run around here. We can't shoot at the Heinies, but there's nothing in the rules against thumbing our noses at them."

Their grievances did not end there. High on their list was a gripe they held against Pershing personally. This was the issue of extra rank and pay they had been led to expect and felt they deserved. These inducements to Air Service volunteers had been held out by the War Department in the early days of the mobilization, when the general staff still believed it would be difficult to recruit aviation trainees. An act of Congress, passed at the army's instiga-tion, entitled cadets to commissions as first lieutenants upon completion of their primary training; they were also to receive a 25 percent pay increase when put on flying duty. As their proficiency improved and a prescribed series of tests was passed, they were entitled to further advances in rank and pay.

Pershing, who refused ever to ride in an airplane himself, subscribed to the notion that aviation was no more hazardous than any other branch of the armed forces, and he tried to convince Congress that the law should be revised. Now that the Air Service was being thronged by eager volunteers, Pershing told the Military Affairs Committee of the Senate that there was no longer any need to offer enticements. He added that the increments in rank and pay that had already been authorized for airmen should be retroactively revoked. Although his proposals got nowhere in Congress, he nevertheless accomplished his purpose insofar as A.E.F. pilots were concerned. He did this by resorting to a legal technicality. For many months he held back the orders necessary to place pilots officially on "flying duty." Of course, they were flying every day, but this high-handed stratagem of Pershing's deprived them of their due. The resulting resentment was soon heightened when the general conferred the grade of military aviator on officers of the regular army transferred to the Air Service to fill administrative jobs on the ground. These desk-chair pilots were paid double and triple the salaries received by the men who daily faced death in the sky. The airmen complained that their good faith had been shabbily abused. They were incensed by the conviction that Pershing was deliberately discriminating against them. And they were indignant that the senior posts in the Air Service were reserved to officers of the regular army who never flew or wanted to, and that these officers were entrusted with the shaping of aviation policy.

The situation often had ludicrous side effects. At one large airfield a new commanding officer on his first tour of inspection was disturbed at seeing some crumpled planes stacked as junk behind a shed. Aware that they had only recently been received from the factory, he inquired as to the cause of their condition. "Rough landings," he was sarcastically informed. The new commander promptly got out a directive forbidding any more rough landings.

In charge at another field was a cavalry officer who conducted his inspections on horseback; when his steed was frightened by the noise of aircraft engines being warmed up, he barked the order to "stop those fans!"

And there was the infantry major, the commandant of a flight school, who heard that the student pilots disliked the Caudron biplanes in which they trained. These obsolete machines had a wing-warping device instead of ailerons. Upon hearing that "wing warping" accounted for the students' dissatisfaction, this brilliant administrator ordained that all planes must be hangared when not in use. "Under no circumstances," his order decreed, "should the machines be allowed to sit in the sun where their wings may warp."

Many pilots felt that old-line army officers, especially those of staff, begrudged the Air Service its growing popularity at home. If the military heads were not yet enthused over aviation, a keen Congressional and public interest was being manifested, and the press was full of the exploits of daring airmen. One result of the staff officers' dudgeon was, according to Colonel Bingham, "the failure on the part of the army to realize that different standards of work and discipline should be expected of a highly technical and purely voluntary service like aviation, where individual initiative and high morale are so necessary." Pershing did indeed fail to discern the special nature and requirements of the Air Service. Except for administrative purposes and its role in battle, the general made no distinction between the aviation branch and, say, the infantry. It was his theory that the strict methods he had learned at West Point should be applied equally to all the forces under his command, aviation included. The tangible consequences of this stolid attitude convinced the long-suffering airmen of the A.E.F. that the top brass was prejudiced against them. Why else, they wondered, did the general staff require them to wear regulation blouses with high, snug, starched collars? Thus attired, they often returned from combat patrols with their necks chafed raw. In the air, over the lines, they had to keep constantly turning their heads to look out for enemy planes: A surprise attack could come from behind, below, or above, and there was a lot of sky to watch. The uniforms in all other air forces—including that of the U.S. Navy—were provided with soft roll collars for safety as well as comfort, since a sore neck did not contribute to a fighter pilot's efficiency. When some squadron commanders at the front, concerned for the welfare of their men, permitted the use of nonregulation blouses with roll collars, they were harshly reprimanded. And the pilots, perhaps coming in from a vicious dogfight, were not pleased to be met by some pompous martinet of an officer with a lecture on the rules of military dress. Contributing further to their discontent was the knowledge that aviators in other armies were accorded every befitting consideration. The French and British refrained from galling their pilots with a lot of ritual nonsense, for they recognized that the exceedingly perilous and nerve-straining duty of the battle flyer warranted some special dispensations in the matter of military punctilio. The effect of such enlightened policy, as Captain Eddie Rickenbacker observed, was "to produce a morale and esprit in the Royal Air Force that has not its equal in the world."

By the early summer of 1918, only three months after its first squadrons were posted at the front, the Air Service had demonstrated its military value. Even Pershing conceded its importance. "The usefulness of our Air Service during this period could hardly be overestimated," he declared, "as previously the enemy had seemed to have the superiority whenever he cared to use it." Marshal Foch, speaking as the supreme Allied commander, had advised Pershing that he should vigorously exploit aviation in battle. He also informed Pershing that large numbers of planes would be essential in subsequent operations. Accordingly, extraordinary preparations were made prior to the Saint-Mihiel offensive.

In August, General Patrick attached to the new U.S. First Army all the American air units at the front, and placed them under the tactical command of Colonel William Mitchell. Additional units were borrowed from the French, bringing Mitchell's total force to forty-nine squadrons, which he divided into three wings: pursuit, observation, and bombardment. He also had the cooperation, but not the control, of nine British bombing squadrons. Though he had nearly fifteen hundred planes at his disposal, the greatest concentration of air power to that time, Mitchell felt himself robbed by fate when, shortly before the offensive began, a rather incredible occurrence lost him the use of an entire flight of bombers.

"Our bombardment group was not in good condition," he noted in his memoirs. "It was poorly commanded, the morale was weak, and it would take some time to get on its feet. This was largely due to the fact that when I was away in Château-Thierry, the 96th Squadron was left behind in the Toul area. The officer [Major Harry K. Brown] who was then in command of the 96th flew over into Germany with what ships he had available for duty. He lost his way in the fog and landed in Germany with every ship intact. Not one single plane was burned or destroyed, and the Germans captured the whole outfit complete. This was the most glaring exhibition of worthlessness we had had on the front. The Germans sent back a humorous message which was dropped at one of our airdromes. It said, 'We thank you for the fine airplanes and equipment which you have sent us, but what shall we do with the major?'

"I know of no other performance in any air force in the war that was as reprehensible as this," Mitchell grumbled. "Needless to say, we did not reply about the major, as he was better off in Germany at that time than he would have been with us."

For the assault on the Saint-Mihiel sector in September, Mitchell devised an aerial campaign of unprecedented scope. One-third of his command was assigned to various tasks in conjunction with army operations. The remainder was reserved as a strategical strike force. His objectives were to gain an ascendancy in the air; to attack German troops, lines of communication and supply, installations of all kinds; to bomb the enemy's airfields in order to compel his airmen to engage in combat or else suffer the destruction of their machines on the ground. He split his strategical reserve into two brigades of five hundred planes each. Alternately, and sometimes simultaneously, these attacked the flanks of the salient, as well as its base, squeezing the Germans between. For the first time the American army had numerical superiority in the air, and Mitchell exploited it fully. He used his reserve brigades not only to destroy installations, but to bomb and strafe retreating German columns and turn their routes of withdrawal into avenues of withering fire. In so doing, he introduced a tactic that later became known as "blitzing," whereby direct aerial action affords complete initiative to the infantry. In effect, Mitchell's winged brigades became pivots of maneuver that secured the flanks of the First Army as it closed in and wiped out the Saint-Mihiel bulge. German aviation waged a savage resistance. Compared to losses on the ground, the casualty rate among airmen was disproportionately high on both sides. But Mitchell's operation was a thorough success, and it opened many eyes to the effectiveness of large offensive air formations.

After the Saint-Mihiel front was consolidated, the A.E.F. moved into the Meuse-Argonne sector for the next planned assault, launched on September 26. Promoted to brigadier general a few days later, Mitchell employed much the same strategy as before, but with a smaller force of about eight hundred planes, of which three-fourths were manned by American pilots. Since he had to rely mainly on his own squadrons in this campaign, he was particularly annoyed to find that fewer than two hundred Liberty-powered DH-4's, out of more than six hundred received from stateside, were fit for duty. Before the offensive opened, a tremendous congestion developed along the army's lines of communication. If the Germans seized the chance to strike from the air in superior strength, they would inflict awful punishment on American divisions and compound the confusion that already reigned. Mitchell therefore struck before the Germans could capitalize on the situation. By bombing their key defensive positions he forced them to defend these. As a result he quickly gained advantage in the air.

Massing his squadrons as he had so successfully done in the Saint-Mihiel battle, Mitchell hurled them against the enemy rear. The largest raid of the campaign occurred on October 9, when 253 bombers, with 110 fighters in escort, went over the German lines in two great echelons. The target was a mobilization area where the enemy was staging for a counterattack. Over thirty tons of explosives were dropped in spite of fierce opposition by German interceptors. During the engagement, twelve German planes were brought down out of control, while only one American plane was lost. The success of this and other large raids must be credited in goodly measure to the aggressive patrols carried out by Mitchell's pursuit units. He called them battle squadrons and instructed them to stay low and invade the enemy's backyard, there to attack targets of opportunity: troops, fortifications, truck convoys, supply depots, and especially airfields. During a period of less than two weeks, American pilots claimed over a hundred German planes and twenty-one balloons.

The superiority of the aviation forces commanded by General Mitchell was obvious to the Germans. They realized that the Allies had obtained a supremacy in the air that could not be overturned or long endured. They believed that within nine months the American Air Service would have a total of 202 squadrons at the front. Their intelligence apparatus in the United States had reported that by the spring of 1919, American factories would deliver a minimum of thirty thousand aircraft to the war zone—a larger, more powerful aviation force than any nation had ever conceived as possible. These facts were among the principal considerations that persuaded the German high command that defeat was inevitable.

Nineteen months after the United States declared war, a phenomenal change

did take place in American military aviation. From a stunted branch of the
Signal Corps having sixty-five officers and about a thousand enlisted men,
there had been developed an Air Service of twenty thousand officers and
170,000 enlisted men. At the Armistice there were forty-five American squadrons on the front, with a strength of 740 planes, almost eight hundred pilots,
and five hundred observers. They had carried out 150 bombing raids, dropped
about 140 tons of explosives, and penetrated as deep as 160 miles behind
the German lines. They shot down 781 enemy planes and seventy-three balloons, scoring three victories for each of their losses. Thus, from a state of
utter—and shameful—unpreparedness in 1917, through the growing pains of
complete reorganization and the problems of rapid mobilization of equipment
and personnel, the budding Air Service was able to put an effective team into
combat. Had the war lasted longer, the Air Service would no doubt have
produced an even better record of achievement and perhaps to a greater
extent vindicated most of the earlier arguments made on behalf of military
aviation. Chief among its prophets—before, during, and after the war—was
Billy Mitchell.

Few histories of World War I, even air histories, have very much to say
of Mitchell. They mention that he commanded the American Air Service in
the concluding battles of the war, and some add almost parenthetically that,
to quote one, he did a "good job." Yet here was a man who—with the possible exception of his friend and admirer, General Trenchard of the R.A.F.—
knew better than any of his contemporaries what aerial warfare was all about.
Long before the United States became involved in hostilities, Mitchell had
preached the wisdom of building up a strong military air arm. As early as
August 1913, Mitchell, testifying before the House Military Affairs Committee, pointed out that "we are behind all other major powers in the matter
of aviation." He went on from there to propose the establishment in Washington of a "permanent authority" to foster the development of army and navy
aeronautics, and he urged that inducements be offered to officers to take up
flying.

He was then a captain and, at thirty-two, the youngest man ever assigned
to the general staff. In July 1915, Mitchell prepared a detailed paper for the
Army War College under the title "Our Faulty Military Policy." In this paper
he described America's entry into the European war as a certainty. He advocated immediate mobilization, citing compulsory selective military service as
"the only fit defensive organization for a democracy." "The military policy of
the United States is and has been," he maintained, "to prepare for war *after
such war has actually broken out* [Mitchell's emphasis], and to have practically
no machinery in time of peace with which an army could be created with
rapidity." As a vital part of the mobilization he envisaged, Mitchell again
recommended an accelerated program for shaping a large, modern air force.

Aware of the rapid strides that aviation was making in European war skies,
Mitchell decided to learn how to fly. During the winter of 1915-1916, he

attended the Curtiss school at Newport News and qualified for his pilot's certificate. Soon thereafter he was promoted to the rank of major and appointed as the head of the Signal Corps' puny aviation section. He laid elaborate plans for expanding the air force. He encountered, however, very early the opposition of the conservative element in the War Department. Seeing the futility of his effort, and unwavering in his belief that the country was bound to become embroiled in the World War, he arranged to go to Europe as an official observer. A week after his arrival in Spain, America proclaimed her belligerency. Mitchell rushed directly to the war front and presented himself to General Pétain. It became his distinction to be the first regular American officer to participate in an attack with the French, as well as the first to cross the German lines in an airplane and the first to be decorated with the Croix de Guerre for duty on the field of battle.

Mitchell's imperative responsibility, as he saw it, was to learn all he could of Allied strategy and techniques in the air. He toured the French escadrilles, studied their machines, asked questions, went along on operational flights over the front. At Chalons one night, he experienced his first air raid. "No one can ever tell me that there is nothing in airplane bombing," reads the account in his diary. "It will have a great effect on all the operations, if efficiently carried out. Many buildings were hit and destroyed in Chalons that night. . . . At the place of amusement there were assembled fifteen or twenty men who had been safely through hundreds of battles; practically all of them were killed." The raid led him to make this penetrating analysis of the demoralizing effect of aerial bombing: "It is a menace from an entirely new quarter. Fighting on the ground and on the water has gone on since the beginning of time, but fighting in the air has just started, and several generations will have to be born and pass away before people can adopt and maintain the same attitude toward this form of warfare as they exhibit toward the old familiar ones."

The rapid development of mechanized weapons convinced Mitchell there and then that the Germans had to be defeated in the interests of the United States as well as of France and Great Britain. "With the present means of electric communication which can encircle the globe in an instant, with aircraft, submarines and automotive transportation," he surmised, "they can forge a world empire and hold it indefinitely under their heel."

In the years following World War I, right up until his death in 1936, Mitchell devoted his whole energy to educating an indifferent public and a hidebound military establishment to the fact that America's geographical isolation was no longer a safeguard against attack from a potential enemy. He championed a unified command for the armed forces, and above all, a strong arm of aviation. "The only real defense against aircraft," he wrote, "is other aircraft." But the generals and admirals learned none of the lessons that World War I taught about air power, and Mitchell's preachments in the postwar years rocked their cozy bureaucratic boat in a storm of controversy. He was ordered to keep quiet, to quit teaching his "ridiculous heresies and romantic fictions," but he neither could nor would be silenced, and his army career ended, of course, with his famous court-martial in 1925. But Mitchell continued his crusade until time ran out on him. On his deathbed, where he was visited by one of his former airmen, Colonel Homer Berry, Mitchell spoke out: "Homer, the American people will regret the day I was crucified by politics and bureaucracy." Less than seven years later, Japan unleashed her surprise attack on Pearl Harbor. It happened exactly as Mitchell had predicted in 1925.

"Air power"—what does it mean? This question, which remained a subject of sharp dispute until World War II settled every doubt, already challenged Mitchell in April 1917, when he found all the accepted laws of warfare shaken to their foundations by his direct experiences with aviation at the front. The ancient military theories had brought the war to a stalemate in which millions of armed men, burrowed into the ground, were fighting on and on with no decision in sight. How was such a decision to be won? Did the airplane hold this promise? It opened up unforeseen vistas and ever-wider horizons. But who could point the future path of air power with authority? Mitchell thought he knew the man.

In early May he went to R.F.C. headquarters in northern France to call on General Trenchard, the father of British attack aviation, who was, as Mitchell noted in his diary, "a creative strategist of the air." Probably no one throughout his life had a greater influence on Mitchell's aviation views than Trenchard. Their first meeting was awkward, since Mitchell arrived at an inconvenient moment. Trenchard was just leaving to inspect outlying squadrons when his unexpected caller barged in demanding to see the general. The R.F.C. commander stared quizzically at the businesslike, absurdly boyish-looking intruder. He had known other American officers on "fact-finding" trips to the front, and he gritted his teeth. "What can I do for you?" he asked, fearing the usual fatuous reply. But Mitchell bluntly explained that he had come to learn all he could about the British flying corps, its organization, equipment, system of supply, and conduct of operations. Trenchard remarked that this was quite a large order. "Do you suppose," he asked, "that I have nothing better to do than chaperon you and answer your questions for the next couple of weeks?" Mitchell grinned his winning smile and replied that he would need only a day or two of the general's time. Trenchard was amused and intrigued by Mitchell's good-natured impudence. "All right," he said. "Come along with me, young man. I can see you're the sort who usually gets what he wants in the end."

For the better part of three days, Mitchell seldom left the general's side. An intent listener and a shrewd interrogator, he made no apology for "picking other men's brains." He visited artillery and fighter squadrons, watched the bombers of the headquarters wing take off after dark to strike behind the enemy lines, rode along as a passenger on several patrols, and went away convinced that everything the French had told him of Trenchard's leadership was an understatement. "His judgment inspired my immediate confidence and his whole personality my deep respect," Mitchell wrote of Trenchard in his diary, "and we became fast friends at once." Here was an officer not bound by tradition, and Mitchell prized that. He recorded Trenchard's saying that "the great captains are those who think out new methods and then put them into execution. Anybody can always use the old methods."

"An airplane is an offensive and not a defensive weapon" was the keynote of Trenchard's doctrine of "forward action," and Mitchell proved himself an alert and proficient disciple. "A man after my own heart," Trenchard said of him. They met officially and unofficially several times again before the war ended. Twice during August 1918, Mitchell called to let Trenchard run a paternal eye over the preliminary details of his first big "air show" in support of the U.S. First Army at Saint-Mihiel. Trenchard fully approved. He considered Mitchell's plan to be "boldly and ingeniously conceived." He found few other kindred spirits in the A.E.F. He condemned American staff officers, including Pershing, for being "too army-minded." Indeed, Pershing confessed to Trenchard that he had placed regular army officers in charge of the Air Service because "natural airmen have a visionary faith in three-dimensional warfare that owes more to intuition than to the teachings of West Point." Trenchard, now commanding the Independent Air Force, was responsible for British bombing operations during the final phase of the war. When he complained to Mitchell that Pershing's air advisers were making a botch of it, Mitchell sadly agreed. He had already written rebelliously in his own diary: "The general staff is now trying to run the Air Service with just as much knowledge of it as a hog knows about skating. It is terrible to have to fight with an organization like this."

By the time Pershing's advisers repented, it was too late to make much difference. Mitchell's boost to brigadier general and his appointment, on October 1, as operational chief of the Air Service—which was the top berth of authority for aviation in the A.E.F.—could no longer influence the outcome of a war already racing to a victorious climax on land.

Just six weeks before the Armistice, then, Billy Mitchell achieved overall command of American aviation in France. He had in his aegis the air groups of the U.S. First and Second Armies. A third army was being prepared for action, and it was Mitchell's task to muster a flying force for that army. On top of all these duties, he bargained endlessly with the French and British for additional aircraft and the loan of their squadrons to bulk out his own force. He even busied himself with public relations of a kind. "It was practically impossible," he noted, "to impress the men in the ranks, through their own officers, as to the value of aviation. They did not even know what the insignia on our planes was. . . . They had been taught in the United States that our airplane insignia was a star on the undersurface of the plane, whereas the insignia of all Allied aviators was round concentric circles, with the colors of the country they belonged to. Wherever possible, we took the infantry battalions back of the line to our airdromes and took the noncommissioned officers and other soldiers up in the air. This impressed them with the necessity of cooperating with the airmen as much as possible, and they transmitted it on to the privates."

Mitchell also had the following leaflet dropped to all American infantry positions:

FROM THE AMERICAN SCRAPPERS IN THE AIR TO
THE AMERICAN SCRAPPERS ON THE GROUND

DOUGHBOYS—

While you are giving the Boche hell on the ground, we are helping you to the limit in the air.

The artillery are behind you anxious to help with their shells.

Headquarters is trying through us to keep in close touch with you and to render aid whenever you are checked or outnumbered.

Keep us posted at all times as to where your front lines are, either with Bengal lights, panels, or—if nothing else is available— wave a white towel or any white cloth.

Your signals enable us:

To take news of your location to the rear.

To report if the attack is successful.

To call for help if needed.

To enable the artillery to put their shells over your head into the enemy.

We prevent the enemy planes from telling the enemy artillery where you are; we bomb and machine-gun enemy troops whenever the chance offers.

If you are out of ammunition, and tell us, we will report it and have it sent up.

If you are surrounded, we will deliver the ammunition by airplane.

We do not hike through the mud with you, but there are discomforts in our work as bad as mud, but we won't let rain, storms, Archies nor Boche planes prevent our getting there with the goods.

Do not think that we are not on the job when you cannot see us—most of our planes work so far in front that they cannot be seen from the lines.

Some enemy planes may break through our airplane barrage in front of you, and may sometimes bomb and machine-gun you, but in the last month we have dropped ten tons of bombs for every one the Boche has dropped. For every Boche plane that you see over you, the Boche sees ten Allied planes over him. For every balloon that he burns, we burn eight.

Our losses of aviators correspond to your losses, but for every one that we lose, the Boche has to pay with heavy interest.

Whenever a Boche plane is brought down in your sector, do not collect souvenirs from it; you may remove an article or marking that would have given valuable information to us. If Boche aviators are not dead when they land, wait ten minutes before approaching within one hundred feet of the plane after they have left it; sometimes they start a time bomb. DO NOT TOUCH ANYTHING IN A BOCHE PLANE—they sometimes carry innocent-looking infernal machines.

Use us to the limit, show your panels, burn the signal lights, wave a cloth; anything to tell us where you are and what you need.

After reading this, pass it along to your buddie, and remember to show your signals.

YOUR AVIATOR

Undertaking such jobs as this in addition to his manifold duties as operations chief, Mitchell found little time for flying over the lines himself, as he loved to do. Formerly, he had made numerous reconnaissances across the lines, in recognition of which he received the Distinguished Service Cross. The citation specified "acts of extraordinary heroism in action" at Noyon in March, at the Marne in July, and in the Saint-Mihiel salient in early September. He was a flying officers' flying officer, and the men in his command revered him. They liked his casual style, his commonsensical disdain of military punctilio, his aversion to red tape and his marvelous ability to slice through it. He was accessible to any man's complaint or suggestion. A frequent visitor to frontline squadrons, he enjoyed the society of his pilots and joined in their conversations as "one of the boys." He knew the majority of them on a first-name basis. "They did their brave deeds as much in a desire to please Billy Mitchell," one of his biographers has opined, "as to get the war over with and go home."

Balloon-busting stole the show on the American air front during the weeks preceding the Meuse-Argonne offensive, and Mitchell was on hand to witness a special performance. A pair of skilled pilots of the 27th Pursuit Squadron, Lieutenant Frank Luke, Jr., a shy lad from Arizona, and Lieutenant Joseph Wehner, a big, cool, athletic youth from Massachusetts, became friendly rivals in picking off the enemy *drachen*. One day Luke had bagged two in succession, making a score of eight balloons in five days, and there was great rejoicing on the ground. Wehner asked the squadron commander, Major Harold E. Hartney, for permission to go after the only German balloon then left in the air, which he destroyed. Hartney had just heard from headquarters, where Luke's feat had made quite an impression, that Mitchell was on his way over to congratulate the outfit.

"Mitchell was proud as punch," Hartney wrote. "He then questioned us about the plan for strafing balloons in the dusk of evening. I called for Luke—it was his idea. Poor Frank was quite flabbergasted as he came before the general in his untidy uniform and cloth puttees. He was bashful and silent.

Colonel [Thomas De Witt] Milling"—who was Mitchell's chief of staff—"a great diplomat, soon had Luke at ease. And Luke put forth his plan." He and Wehner would stage a special balloon-busting show for the general at a fixed hour the following evening.

Mitchell arrived for the promised spectacle in his Benz staff car. "We had a spot of coffee, then, looking at our wrist watches, sauntered out in the evening shadows to the brow of a nearby hill," Hartney wrote. "Slowly the hands on our watches crept up to zero hour. Darkness was beginning to fall, and a strange sort of peace, broken only by the distant rumblings of artillery, was settling over the countryside. The balloons, swinging lazily yet menacingly in the evening breeze, could be discerned through the gathering mist off in the distance, over Verdun way."

Hartney described the action vividly: "At exactly two minutes before seven o'clock, a tongue of flame shot into the sky over by Spincourt, followed by a huge burst of fire as the fast-burning hydrogen practically exploded the entire balloon. I knew the observer was somewhere out there in a parachute, trying desperately to reach the earth before the sparks caught him, and the crew on the winch were running for their lives, lest the flaming bag settle quickly over them and roast them alive. The second bag was going down rapidly as the winch crews worked feverishly to save it."

Mitchell was impressed and greatly excited by the efficient timing of the operation, and when he had regained his composure, he asked Hartney how Luke and Wehner were going to land in the dark.

Mitchell was led to a crude two-by-four-foot platform raised above the headquarters shack. Probably the first structure of its kind for the control of night flying, it functioned by receiving a short signal from the pilot intending to land, who would then be provided with a limited, indirectly illuminated surface for the space of one minute. If he missed, he was required to climb again and continue circling for ten minutes. All the while there was a lighted dummy airfield four miles down the road, serving as a decoy to deceive the Germans if they followed the American pilots home at night.

By this time Wehner and Luke were back on the ground. Milling proposed to Mitchell that he ought to examine their planes for damage. It was Luke's fifth and Wehner's third machine in combat. "Mitchell took his swagger stick," Hartney wrote, "and with a zip pulled huge chunks of fabric off Luke's left lower wing, and then off Wehner's fuselage. Literally, those planes had been all but shot out from under them. Each had at least fifty bullet holes and was useless for further service without a complete overhaul."

Before that month was over, both pilots met their deaths. Luke was attacked by six Fokkers. Wehner rushed to his comrade's defense and saved him, but sacrificed himself in doing it. Brooding to the point of distraction, Luke was advised to take leave in Paris. He went, but returned early and insisted on flying. He was determined to avenge Wehner's death. On September 26, he again sought combat, this time in the company of Lieutenant Ivan Roberts.

Although Luke scored, Roberts was shot down. His depression deepened by this loss, he went absent without permission, for which he was verbally reprimanded. Next day, on an unauthorized flight, he burst a balloon near Batheville. He spent that night with the famous French aces of a Stork escadrille at a nearby airfield, again without leave. When Luke reported for duty on the following afternoon, Major Hartney restricted him from further flying until he could sort himself out emotionally. Angered, Luke defied orders. He took off in his Spad, flew to a forward field to take on fuel, and then headed for enemy territory. Just before sunset, he buzzed the American balloon section at Souilly and dropped a note which read: "Watch three Hun balloons on the Meuse." It was signed "Luke."

He caught the first balloon at Dun-sur-Meuse, igniting it before its defenders on the ground realized there was a hostile plane in the semidarkness above. The great explosion alerted the whole German line to his presence, however, and Luke had to penetrate a ring of withering fire to get the second balloon. His Spad was riddled, and he was badly wounded, yet he scored again. He passed through another screen of fire to bring down the third balloon in flames near Milly. Although weak from loss of blood, and with his plane billowing smoke, he strafed German troops in the streets of Murvaux before crash landing on the edge of the village. Dragging himself from the cockpit, he propped himself against a tree for cover and waited there for the Germans to come after him. They surrounded him, demanding that he give himself up. Luke answered with his pistol. He shot eleven of his would-be captors before one of them put a Mauser slug through his heart.

Frank Luke, with twenty-one victories, was the second highest-scoring American ace of World War I. For his "gallantry in action and intrepidity above the call of duty," he was posthumously awarded his nation's greatest military decoration, the Congressional Medal of Honor. He had zoomed almost meteorlike over the western front that summer, and in only seventeen days of spectacular aerial combat he became an American legend.

Wehner, who tallied eight victories before he was killed, was Luke's closest companion and teammate. They became friends while training at Issoudun, perhaps because they were so much alike. Both shy and reticent, they felt ill at ease among their fellow airmen—a boisterous, ebullient lot—and so found immediate rapport with one another. Both were of German parentage, and both had earlier been investigated, and Wehner arrested, by the Secret Service as potential spies. But any lingering doubt of their patriotism was soon erased after they got overseas.

A more formidable fighting team did not exist. Luke performed his most memorable feat on September 18, and it was in the course of this action that Wehner was killed. During a dusk patrol together, they spotted a couple of balloons over Labeuville. While Wehner stayed above for protection, Luke dived and destroyed both gasbags. Then he looked up to see a flock of six Fokkers speeding down at him, with Wehner on their tails. A frantic dogfight developed in which Luke dispatched two of the enemy and sent the rest scurrying for safety. Losing sight of Wehner and thinking he had gone back to base, Luke headed for the lines again. Southeast of Verdun he saw a bunch of Spads preparing to pounce upon a lone Halberstadt. Finding himself in good firing position, he attacked and shot down the two-seater. Luke—having claimed two balloons and three planes within only ten minutes—had accomplished the fantastic. His elation turned to gloom, however, when he landed and discovered that Wehner, in protecting him, had fallen victim to one of the Fokkers. Just eleven days later, on Sunday, September 29, Luke died while trying to expiate the torturing guilt he felt for Wehner's death.

Luke was, and has been named in history as, the American "balloon buster." It was a high calling at the front in those days, for there was no riskier job on wings than blowing up these hydrogen-buoyed observation posts. It required no expert marksmanship, but to fly through the defensive barrier of bullets and shrapnel around a balloon demanded foolhardy courage and nerves of plaited steel. The handful of pilots who made a specialty of this suicidal sport were held in awe. Celebrated by the Germans as their *"Drachen-streifer"* was the commander of Jasta 15, Lieutenant Heinrich Gontermann, who, in six months at the front, won every medal a German flyer could win, including the coveted "Blue Max," as the Order Pour le Mérite became known. Between Easter Sunday morning 1917, when he exploded his first gasbag, and the following October 30, when he crashed to his death, Gontermann destroyed eighteen Allied balloons—as well as twenty-one planes.

But the greatest balloon-buster of them all was Lieutenant Willy Coppens de Houthulst of the Belgian flying corps, who survived the war as his nation's foremost ace, scoring all but nine of his thirty-seven victories against enemy balloons. That Coppens survived even a week of combat, let alone two years of it, was no slight miracle. His daring, as all who flew with him emphatically testified, verged on the maniac. A short, slightly built, rather homely man, in a roomful of aviators he resembled a sparrow amid an array of handsome peacocks. But in the air he was a raging eagle. Fear seemed to have no meaning for him; time and time again, he flaunted himself in the face of almost certain death. Once, for example, he volunteered to attack a balloon behind the German lines at Bovekerke, which usually floated at about three thousand feet and, as Coppens knew, was very heavily defended. Escorted by a flight of fighters, he tested the one gun on his plane and found it inoperative. Instead of calling off the mission, he dived on the balloon anyway, braving an inferno of antiaircraft fire. As the German crew hurriedly pulled the balloon down, Coppens executed a magnificent loop right in the midst of the flak. The leader of the protecting fighters thought Coppens had gone mad, and said so in his report. But the reckless Belgian surpassed even that breathtaking *coup de théâtre* a few weeks later, when he ran the wheels of his plane across the top of a German balloon. "I had to do something," he explained. "I was out of ammunition and if I turned around and did not go in close—well, what would the Boches have said of Belgian courage?"

The idea of shooting down balloons obsessed him. That he destroyed twenty-eight of them speaks more of his prowess than any words. He was not interested in personal glory; in fact, when it came his way, he poked fun at it. In May 1917, he was cited in dispatches for escaping an ambush by four enemy fighters while flying a reconnaissance in a Sopwith 1½-Strutter and returning to base with vital intelligence. The dispatches further praised him for bringing back his aircraft with thirty-two bullets still lodged in its frame. "What a stupid text," he commented. "Of course I had to bring it back. I needed it to take me home!" In his opinion, the funniest incident of his wartime career occurred on September 7, 1918. That morning he was told to put on full dress with helmet and sword. He thought this pretty ridiculous, but he complied, for he was to receive the Legion of Honor from Georges Clemenceau himself. To Coppens' great amusement, Clemenceau—a tall man —had to bend down to pin the medal on his tunic. Solemn as the ceremony was, Coppens barely kept from laughter when the French premier banged his august head on the steel helmet and gasped an audible "Ouch!"

Coppens' balloon-busting feats become all the more remarkable when it is realized that he—and his fellow Belgian airmen—flew and fought under a handicap, since their machines were hand-me-downs from the British and French. Except for a half-dozen Sopwith Camels they acquired in the summer of 1918, the Belgians were stuck with obsolescent and inferior aircraft throughout the war. Not until March 1917, did they scrape together enough armed single-seaters to field a three-squadron pursuit group, and it was equipped with a motley miscellany of planes, mostly outdated Nieuports, which the French and British had already phased out of service. That July, Coppens considered himself lucky to get hold of a Hanriot HD-1 biplane, a machine that found few willing pilots in any of the Allied air forces. Coppens, who had it painted blue because the original finish reminded him of a varnished toy snake that had given him nightmares as a child, flew the Hanriot until mid-October 1918, when, while attacking a balloon, he was hit in the leg by shrapnel, lost control and crashed. When he recovered consciousness, his wounded leg had been amputated.

Coppens never complained about flying a second-rate aircraft. It was small, very maneuverable if none too fast, and afforded good visibility. Only its light construction was to be deplored, since no more than a single machine gun could be safely borne aloft, and that was a disadvantage that few pilots happily abided. But Coppens' worries did not end there. He literally had to plead for the incendiary ammunition he needed to kindle enemy balloons. Finally, the French gave him an allowance of twenty incendiary bullets per month. These he husbanded carefully, making it a rule to use only four rounds at a time, and only when within fifty yards of his target. Yet he destroyed more balloons than any other pilot of the war—and, miraculously indeed, lived to write his memoirs.

America's ace of aces, the "head man" as his pilots called him, Captain Eddie Rickenbacker accounted for four balloons among his twenty-six victories. With the exception of one time, when he was unsuccessful, he never went out looking for balloons to shoot down, but rather attacked them as the opportunity presented itself. Rickenbacker was daring and fearless, but never reckless. The one occassion when he did go balloon hunting was the beginning of the Argonne offensive, when he took off shortly before zero hour at the lead of his entire squadron. The operation had been carefully planned by Rickenbacker and approved by Colonel Mitchell. Its object was to destroy a line of enemy observation balloons precisely at the moment when the American infantry went "over the top." By shooting down the balloons, Rickenbacker and his pilots would deprive the German artillery of its eyes and so spare the lives of many doughboys in the initial advance across no-man's-land. Rickenbacker, in the week preceding the action, had briefed his pilots on where the balloons were located, what kind of protective barrage to expect, and how to penetrate such a barrage to place a few good bursts into one of the fat "sausages."

"We went up before daylight," Rickenbacker wrote, "and hung around until we saw our targets. Each pilot knew the balloon he was to get, and I saved one for myself. Then I flew over the front, which was like a giant switchboard with all the guns going off." The scene below—twinkling with myriad flashes of cannon fire—so fascinated him that he momentarily forgot his purpose. Then a whistling shell narrowly missed his plane, shaking him from his reverie, and he started for his balloon. Another man shot it down, however, before Rickenbacker got in close enough to open fire.

Of the aces to emerge from the air war in that climactic year of 1918, none exceeded Rickenbacker's record. No pilot, before or since, ever accumulated so many victories in such a limited period—four months of actual combat.

Born in 1890 in Columbus, Ohio, the son of William and Elizabeth Reichenbacher, forced to quit school as a twelve-year-old boy to help support his widowed mother, Rickenbacker found a job with the Frayer-Miller Air-Cooled Car Company, where he began to learn all about the newfangled "horseless carriage." By 1917, earning $40,000 a year, he was famed as one of the top racing drivers in the world. When the United States entered the war that spring, he was in England to organize a racing team for the Sunbeam Motor Company. He returned to America full of enthusiasm over a scheme that had occurred to him—he would form a flying squadron entirely of racing drivers. He reasoned that their quick reflexes, their knowledge of engines, and their familiarity with high speeds would qualify them as excellent battle pilots. Not surprisingly, his idea received a stony reception at the War Department.

During his stay in Washington, however, he was introduced to General Pershing, and accepted his invitation to join the army and serve as the general's driver in France. Before enlisting he Anglicized the spelling of his name; nevertheless, like many whose names sounded German, he was annoyed on several occasions by Secret Service agents. In England, in fact, he had been detained by Scotland Yard until his identity papers were verified by the American embassy.

Rickenbacker reckoned that taking a job with Pershing would give him a shortcut to the front. It did, indeed, for he would never have been able to find his way into aviation without Pershing's assistance, because he did not meet the educational requirements. Several of his applications for pilot training were already rejected before Pershing wangled him into a flight unit. He became an engineering officer and for many months his commanding officer, Major Carl A. Spaatz, refused to allow him to become a combat aviator because his services were so valuable. In March 1918, he was finally assigned as a pilot to the 94th Pursuit Squadron at Villeneuve. He saw his first enemy for combat on April 25. Four days after that, he scored his first kill, shooting down a single-seater near Baussant. Some confusion exists as to the make of the German machine. In his book *Fighting the Flying Circus,* Rickenbacker calls it a Pfalz; officially, however, it is listed as an Albatros.

The action occurred after Rickenbacker and Captain James Norman Hall went up in their Nieuports to intercept an enemy two-seater which a forward observation post reported to be heading in over the lines. Rickenbacker was flying on Hall's right side when he noticed, high off to his right, a large plane on the same general course as their intended prey was said to be traveling. Assuming it to be the German plane they had set out to engage, he drew Hall's attention to it and started climbing for the attack. But Hall, instead of following, continued on toward the front. Inexperienced as he was, Rickenbacker figured that Hall was generously granting him the opportunity to score a singlehanded victory. It was not until five minutes later, as he was closing in on his quarry, preparing to fire, that Rickenbacker realized his mistake. The plane was indeed a two-seater, and perhaps the one observed earlier from the ground, but it had French markings.

Thoroughly ashamed of himself, he dived quickly away and began searching about to rejoin Hall. An antiaircraft barrage behind the German lines caught his eye, and there amid the bursting shells he saw Hall performing aerobatics. "Evidently he was waiting for me to discover my mistake and then overtake him," Rickenbacker wrote, "for he was having a delightful time with the Archy gunners, doing loops, barrels, sideslips and spins immediately over their heads to show his contempt for them, while he waited for his comrade." They were flying baseward a few minutes later when they spotted an enemy fighter coming directly at them.

Before the German saw them, they banked and climbed into the sun. While

Hall dived to the attack, Rickenbacker stayed above and maneuvered for a position from which to cut off the German's retreat in case Hall's shots failed to strike home. In a lucky blunder, Rickenbacker inadvertently flew out of the sun's glare and revealed himself to the enemy pilot, who promptly pulled up the nose of his plane and began racing for altitude. Only then did he see Hall's Nieuport swooping at him, which caused him to wheel over into a steep descent. Anticipating this move, Rickenbacker was already diving in the German's wake, rapidly narrowing the space between them. After leveling off, the German tried no evasive measures but hoped to outrun his antagonist. It was a case of bad judgment, probably induced by panic. He seemed unaware that the Nieuport was swiftly gaining on him.

Rickenbacker opened fire from a distance of about five hundred feet and saw his tracers raking the rear fuselage and tail of the German machine. Lifting his nose slightly to correct his aim, he triggered off another burst. A fiery stream of bullets poured into the enemy pilot's cockpit. When the black-crossed machine began weaving erratically from side to side, Rickenbacker realized that its rudder was no longer in control. Coming up closer, he looked again and—with mixed feelings of elation and regret—saw his victim slumped forward in his seat. The unpiloted plane now curved gently earthward. With Rickenbacker following it down, ignoring the heavy ground fire that greeted him as he crossed over the enemy lines, the plane crashed near the edge of a small woods, about a mile behind the trenches.

While climbing back toward the French lines, Rickenbacker was met by Hall, who displayed his pleasure over their success by executing a series of loops. The Germans, meanwhile, were sending up a furious barrage at the two cavorting Nieuports. Rickenbacker, as he wrote, had had quite enough excitement for one day. He went along with Hall, however, when the latter headed deliberately toward a battery of gunners to stage yet another show of incredible stunts right above their cannon muzzles. "Jimmy exhausted his spirits about the time the Huns had exhausted all their available ammunition," Rickenbacker wrote, "and then we started blithely for home."

News of Rickenbacker's victory preceded him back to the airdrome. When he landed, every pilot and mechanic of the squadron welcomed him with a handshake, which moved him deeply. "There is a peculiar gratification in receiving congratulations from one's squadron for a victory in the air," he later wrote. "It is worth more to a pilot than the applause of the whole outside world. It means that one has won the confidence of men who share the misgivings, the aspirations, the trials and the dangers of airplane fighting. And with each victory comes a renewal and recementing of ties that bind together these brothers-in-arms. No closer fraternity exists in the world than that of the air fighters in this great war. And I have yet to find one single individual who has attained conspicuous success in bringing down enemy airplanes who can be said to be spoiled either by his successes or by the generous congratulations of his comrades. If he were capable of being spoiled, he would not have had the character to have won continuous victories, for the smallest amount of vanity is fatal in airplane fighting. Self-distrust rather is the quality to which many a pilot owes his protracted existence."

By the end of May, Rickenbacker was a five-victory ace. As he had known it would, his experience as a racing driver stood him in good stead. He was accustomed to danger, to wind-whistling speed, to making a quick decision in an instant of peril; he was skilled in watching the actions and estimating the intentions of an antagonist. These characteristics afforded him advantage over his opponents in this new game he was playing, where the prize was not a loving cup overflowing with money, but one's very life. His familiarity with these elements of the game steadied him and gave him self-confidence. Above all, he was impressed with one valuable principal—"never take an unnecessary risk." He had already made up his mind on this by his seventh week at the front, when a mastoid infection sent him to the hospital in Paris for two months. Returning to action in the middle of September, he made his big impact and swiftly rose to the top of the Air Service's list of aces.

From the beginning, the 94th Pursuit Squadron was commanded by expert combat flyers. Major Lufbery was its first commander and, at his death, the unit was taken over by another veteran of the Lafayette Escadrille, Captain Hall, who was shot down and captured by the Germans in early May 1918. On September 25, a day in which he scored a double victory and raised his total to nine kills, Rickenbacker was placed in charge of the 94th, the celebrated "Hat-in-the-Ring" squadron. The man who picked him for the job was Lieutenant Colonel Hartney, as he had now become, the First Pursuit Group commander. He selected Rickenbacker over several superiors because he thought Rickenbacker was more mature, had a better knowledge of engines, and was an exceptional air fighter. General Mitchell had some reservations about the appointment. He said he did not like the notion of bypassing men with seniority in grade and service; possibly he also remembered Rickenbacker's close ties with Pershing and feared some sort of collusion. Nevertheless, he gave his approval on Hartney's insistence. "Just been promoted to command of 94th Squadron," noted Rickenbacker in his diary. "I must work harder now than I did before."

As good as his word, he amply vindicated Hartney's faith in him by developing into one of the best squadron commanders of the war, shooting down seventeen additional aircraft himself and guiding his unit to victories and honor. At the cessation of hostilities, the squadron led all others in the Air Service with sixty-nine confirmed victories—more than a third of these Rickenbacker's. It has been said that in no other squadron in France was there so much loyalty to a leader, so much fraternalism, such subordination of the individual to the organization. Believing that his men should learn to look after each other, Rickenbacker taught and practiced the "buddy system" in combat. He promised himself that "I shall never ask a pilot under me to go on a mission that I won't go on." Contrary to the practice in some other units, he made no attempt to stimulate rivalry among members of the group, appealing instead to the competitive spirit of the squadron as a whole against other squadrons. He established a forum in the mess for discussion and comparison of engagements and tactics. He and his men fought together, honing their skills into precision teamwork. He personally logged more hours above the lines than any other American airman. He combined courage, resourcefulness, and natural leadership ability with a rare appreciation of the fine points of aerial combat. He led, rather than drove, his pilots, and made his "Hat-in-the-Ring" squadron the most lethal American pursuit unit at the front; his own victory skein was still growing when the Armistice came.

"You know," he wrote nearly a half-century later, "I was the only pilot, to my knowledge, on the front at the zero hour of eleven when the war ended. We'd all been ordered to stay on the ground the night before. But I wanted to see the war end, and you could only do that by getting out to the front. It was a foggy morning at the base, and I wiggled my way out just a half minute before eleven o'clock. I was flying down no-man's land, between the trenches of the opposing forces, and they were shooting at each other just as madly as they could. And then the hour of eleven struck. The shooting stopped, and gradually men from both sides came out into no-man's land and threw their guns and helmets into the air. They kept talking to each other and shaking hands and doing something for the men who had been hit. That was one of the hazards. I had a chance to see the war end with my own eyes. I was only up about a hundred feet over no-man's land. I got out to see what I went out to see and went back home and that was it." [1]

[1] *Esquire*, August 1964.

APPENDIX I

AIRCRAFT OF
WORLD WAR I

For easy reference, the following fifty-five side-view drawings are arranged in alphabetical order. Included are all the important operational planes mentioned in the foregoing text, as well as the Curtiss "Jenny" trainer and three prototype fighters of the United States. The data describe each plane as it was produced in largest quantity, although modified versions, with alternate engines, were available in many cases. The span of the top wing only is given for biplanes.

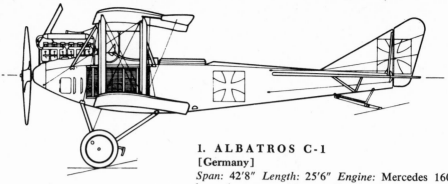

1. ALBATROS C-1
[Germany]
Span: 42′8″ *Length*: 25′6″ *Engine*: Mercedes 160
h.p. *Armament*: ½ mg. *Bomb Load*: 200 lbs.
Speed: 85 m.p.h. *Ceiling*: 11,100 ft.

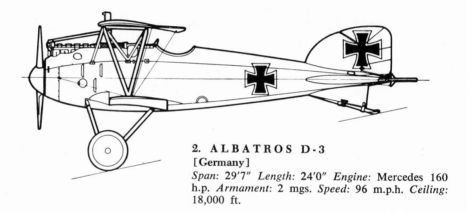

2. ALBATROS D-3
[Germany]
Span: 29′7″ *Length*: 24′0″ *Engine*: Mercedes 160
h.p. *Armament*: 2 mgs. *Speed*: 96 m.p.h. *Ceiling*:
18,000 ft.

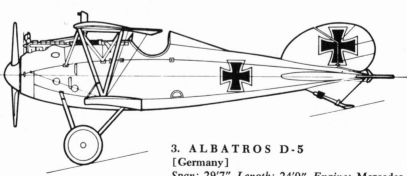

3. ALBATROS D-5
[Germany]
Span: 29′7″ *Length*: 24′0″ *Engine*: Mercedes 180
h.p. *Armament*: 2 mgs. *Speed*: 99 m.p.h. *Ceiling*:
20,500 ft.

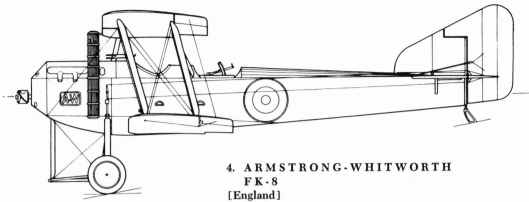

4. ARMSTRONG-WHITWORTH F K - 8
[England]

Span: 43'6" *Length:* 31'0" *Engine:* Beardmore 160 h.p. *Armament:* 2 mgs. *Bomb Load:* 160 lbs. *Speed:* 98 m.p.h. *Ceiling:* 13,000 ft.

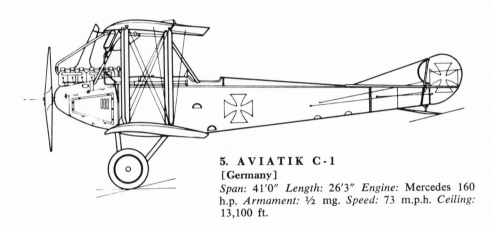

5. AVIATIK C - 1
[Germany]

Span: 41'0" *Length:* 26'3" *Engine:* Mercedes 160 h.p. *Armament:* ½ mg. *Speed:* 73 m.p.h. *Ceiling:* 13,100 ft.

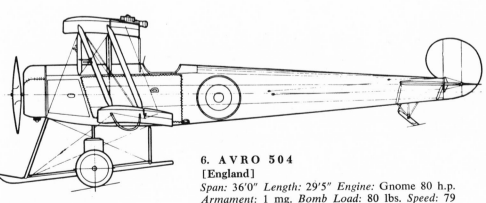

6. AVRO 504
[England]

Span: 36'0" *Length:* 29'5" *Engine:* Gnome 80 h.p. *Armament:* 1 mg. *Bomb Load:* 80 lbs. *Speed:* 79 m.p.h. *Ceiling:* 12,000 ft.

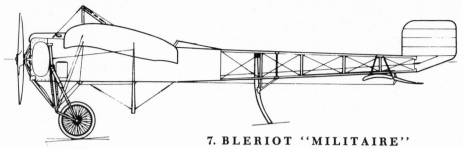

7. BLERIOT "MILITAIRE"
[France]

Span: 29'2" *Length*: 25'7" *Engine*: Gnome 50 h.p.
Armament: None *Bomb Load*: 50 lbs. *Speed*: 58
m.p.h. *Ceiling* 6,000 ft.

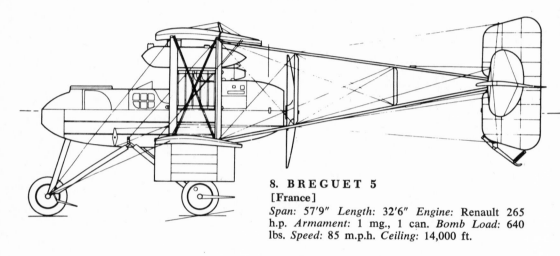

8. BREGUET 5
[France]

Span: 57'9" *Length*: 32'6" *Engine*: Renault 265
h.p. *Armament*: 1 mg., 1 can. *Bomb Load*: 640
lbs. *Speed*: 85 m.p.h. *Ceiling*: 14,000 ft.

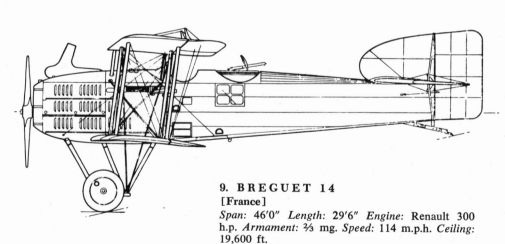

9. BREGUET 14
[France]

Span: 46'0" *Length*: 29'6" *Engine*: Renault 300
h.p. *Armament*: 2/3 mg. *Speed*: 114 m.p.h. *Ceiling*:
19,600 ft.

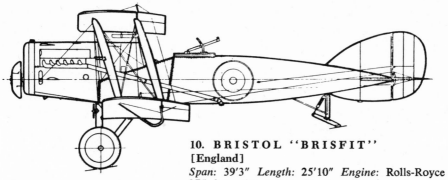

10. BRISTOL ''BRISFIT''
[England]

Span: 39'3" *Length*: 25'10" *Engine*: Rolls-Royce
275 h.p. *Armament*: ⅔ mg. *Speed*: 122 m.p.h.
Ceiling: 20,000 ft.

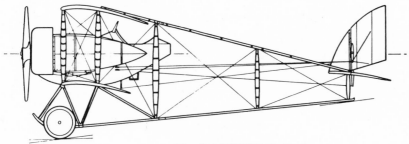

11. CAUDRON G-4
[France]

Span: 56'4" *Length*: 23'6" *Engines*: 2 Le Rhone
80 h.p. *Armament*: ½ mg. *Bomb Load*: 250 lbs.
Speed: 83 m.p.h. *Ceiling*: 14,000 ft.

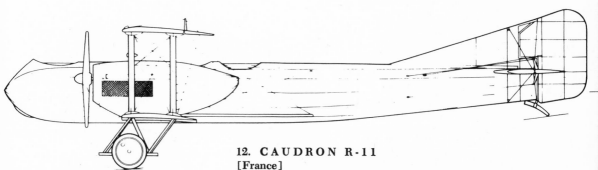

12. CAUDRON R-11
[France]

Span: 58'10" *Length*: 36'11" *Engines*: 2 Hispano-
Suiza 220 h.p. *Armament*: 5 mgs. *Bomb Load*: 265
lbs. *Speed*: 114 m.p.h. *Ceiling*: 19,500 ft.

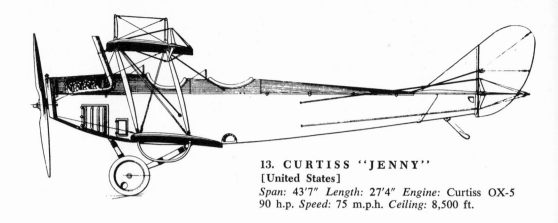

13. CURTISS "JENNY"
[United States]
Span: 43'7" *Length*: 27'4" *Engine*: Curtiss OX-5
90 h.p. *Speed*: 75 m.p.h. *Ceiling*: 8,500 ft.

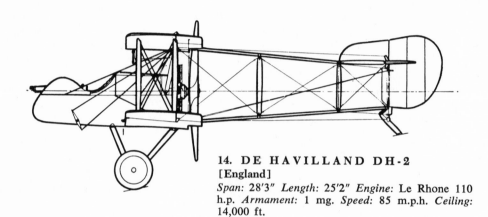

14. DE HAVILLAND DH-2
[England]
Span: 28'3" *Length*: 25'2" *Engine*: Le Rhone 110
h.p. *Armament*: 1 mg. *Speed*: 85 m.p.h. *Ceiling*:
14,000 ft.

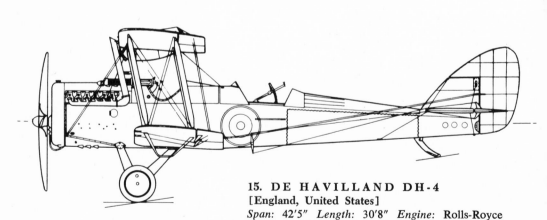

15. DE HAVILLAND DH-4
[England, United States]
Span: 42'5" *Length*: 30'8" *Engine*: Rolls-Royce
375 h.p. (Liberty 400 h.p. in U.S. version) *Armament*: ⅔ mg. *Bomb Load*: 460 lbs. *Speed*: 125
m.p.h. *Ceiling*: 22,000 ft.

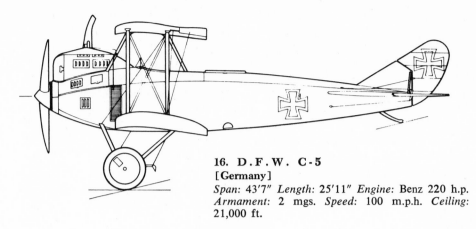

16. D.F.W. C-5
[Germany]
Span: 43'7" *Length*: 25'11" *Engine*: Benz 220 h.p.
Armament: 2 mgs. *Speed*: 100 m.p.h. *Ceiling*:
21,000 ft.

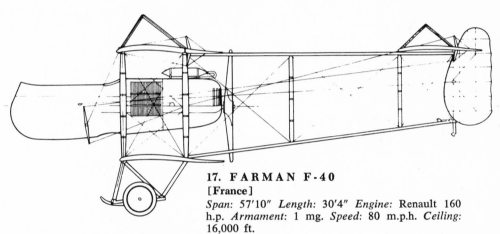

17. FARMAN F-40
[France]
Span: 57'10" *Length*: 30'4" *Engine*: Renault 160
h.p. *Armament*: 1 mg. *Speed*: 80 m.p.h. *Ceiling*:
16,000 ft.

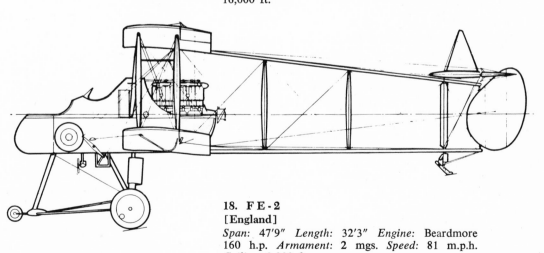

18. FE-2
[England]
Span: 47'9" *Length*: 32'3" *Engine*: Beardmore
160 h.p. *Armament*: 2 mgs. *Speed*: 81 m.p.h.
Ceiling: 9,000 ft.

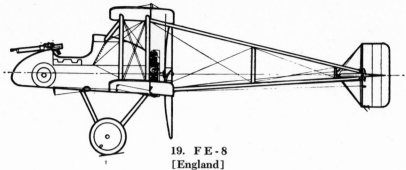

19. FE-8
[England]

Span: 31'6" *Length:* 23'8" *Engine:* Gnome 100
h.p. *Armament:* 1 mg. *Speed:* 94 m.p.h. *Ceiling:*
14,500 ft.

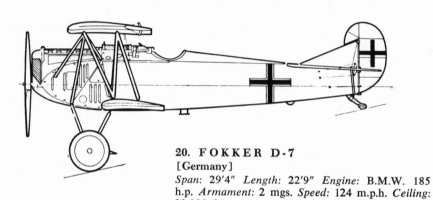

20. FOKKER D-7
[Germany]

Span: 29'4" *Length:* 22'9" *Engine:* B.M.W. 185
h.p. *Armament:* 2 mgs. *Speed:* 124 m.p.h. *Ceiling:*
22,900 ft.

21. FOKKER D-8
[Germany]

Span: 27'3" *Length:* 19'5" *Engine:* Oberursel 140
h.p. *Armament:* 2 mgs. *Speed:* 125 m.p.h. *Ceiling:*
21,000 ft.

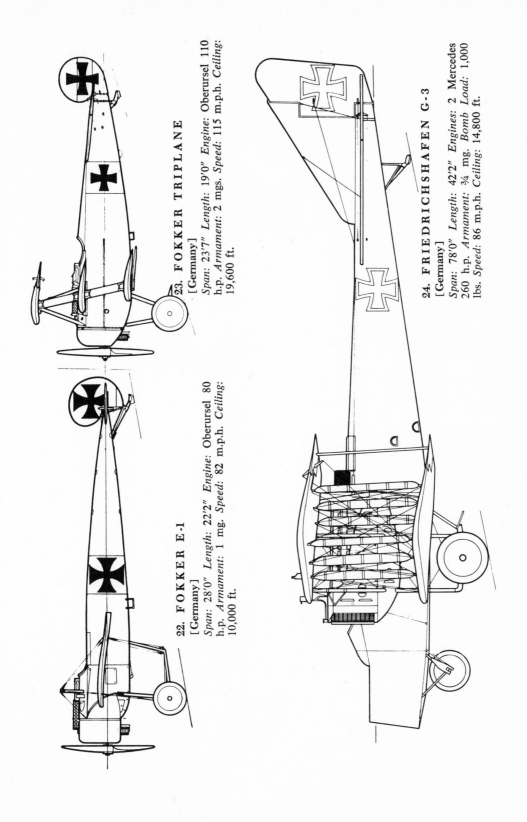

23. FOKKER TRIPLANE
[Germany]
Span: 23'7" Length: 19'0" Engine: Obenursel 110 h.p. Armament: 2 mgs. Speed: 115 m.p.h. Ceiling: 19,600 ft.

22. FOKKER E-1
[Germany]
Span: 28'0" Length: 22'2" Engine: Obenursel 80 h.p. Armament: 1 mg. Speed: 82 m.p.h. Ceiling: 10,000 ft.

24. FRIEDRICHSHAFEN G-3
[Germany]
Span: 78'0" Length: 42'2" Engines: 2 Mercedes 260 h.p. Armament: ¾ mg. Bomb Load: 1,000 lbs. Speed: 86 m.p.h. Ceiling: 14,800 ft.

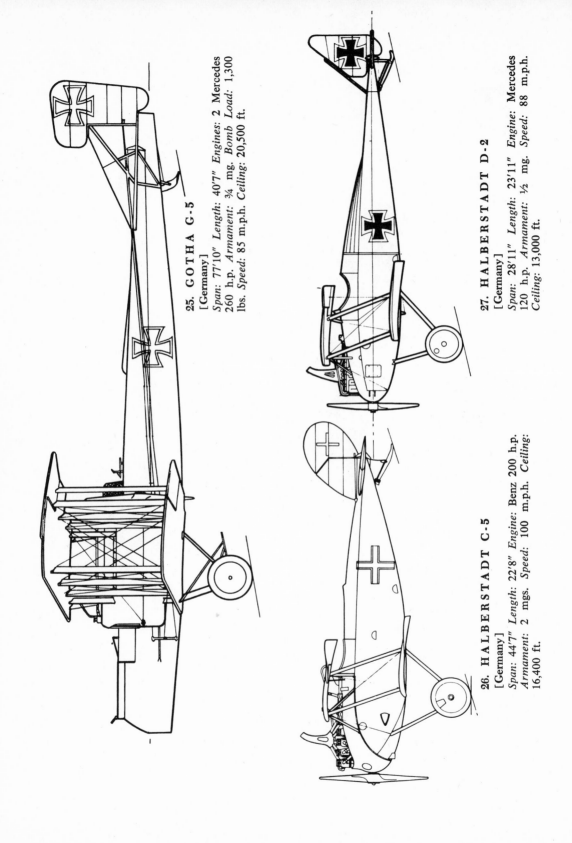

25. GOTHA G-5
[Germany]
Span: 77'10" *Length:* 40'7" *Engines:* 2 Mercedes
260 h.p. *Armament:* ¾ mg. *Bomb Load:* 1,300
lbs. *Speed:* 85 m.p.h. *Ceiling:* 20,500 ft.

27. HALBERSTADT D-2
[Germany]
Span: 28'11" *Length:* 23'11" *Engine:* Mercedes
120 h.p. *Armament:* ½ mg. *Speed:* 88 m.p.h.
Ceiling: 13,000 ft.

26. HALBERSTADT C-5
[Germany]
Span: 44'7" *Length:* 22'8" *Engine:* Benz 200 h.p.
Armament: 2 mgs. *Speed:* 100 m.p.h. *Ceiling:*
16,400 ft.

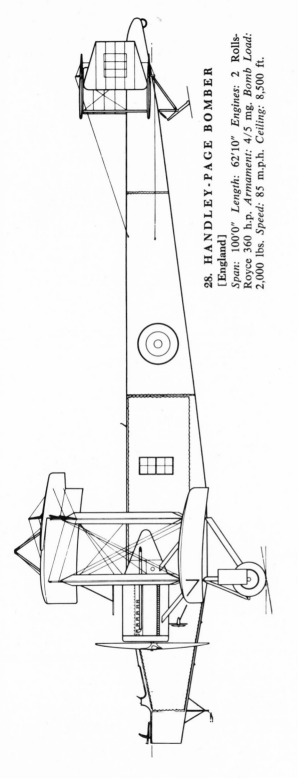

28. HANDLEY-PAGE BOMBER
[England]

Span: 100'0" *Length:* 62'10" *Engines:* 2 Rolls-Royce 360 h.p. *Armament:* 4/5 mg. *Bomb Load:* 2,000 lbs. *Speed:* 85 m.p.h. *Ceiling:* 8,500 ft.

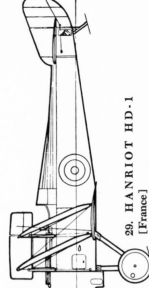

29. HANRIOT HD·1
[France]

Span: 28'6" *Length:* 19'2" *Engine:* Le Rhone 130 h.p. *Armament:* 1 mg. *Speed:* 112 m.p.h. *Ceiling:* 23,600 ft.

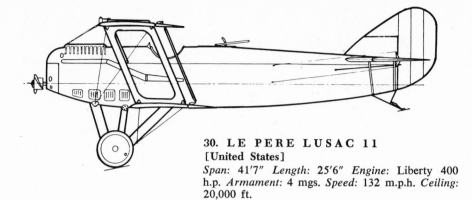

30. LE PERE LUSAC 11
[United States]
Span: 41'7" *Length*: 25'6" *Engine*: Liberty 400
h.p. *Armament*: 4 mgs. *Speed*: 132 m.p.h. *Ceiling*:
20,000 ft.

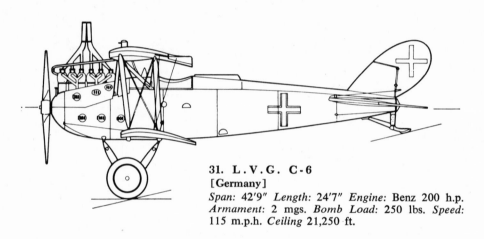

31. L.V.G. C-6
[Germany]
Span: 42'9" *Length*: 24'7" *Engine*: Benz 200 h.p.
Armament: 2 mgs. *Bomb Load*: 250 lbs. *Speed*:
115 m.p.h. *Ceiling* 21,250 ft.

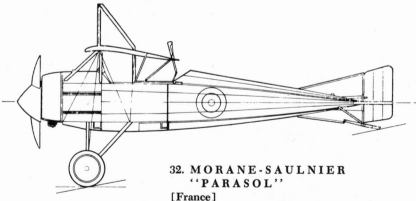

**32. MORANE-SAULNIER
    "PARASOL"**
[France]
Span: 36'9" *Length*: 23'7" *Engine*: Le Rhone 110
h.p. *Armament*: ½ mg. *Speed*: 97 m.p.h. *Ceiling*:
16,000 ft.

33. MORANE-SAULNIER TYPE-N
[France]

Span: 27'3" *Length*: 22'0" *Engine*: Le Rhone 110 h.p. *Armament*: 1 mg. *Speed*: 102 m.p.h. *Ceiling*: 13,000 ft.

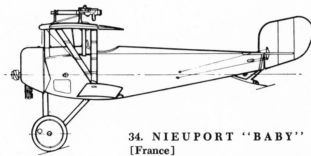

34. NIEUPORT ''BABY''
[France]

Span: 24'9" *Length*: 18'8" *Engine*: Le Rhone 80 h.p. *Armament*: 1 mg. *Speed*: 97 m.p.h. *Ceiling*: 18,000 ft.

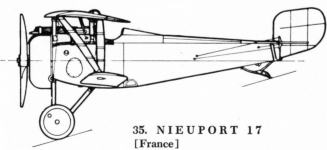

35. NIEUPORT 17
[France]

Span: 26'10" *Length*: 18'11" *Engine*: Le Rhone 110 h.p. *Armament*: ½ mg. *Speed*: 107 m.p.h. *Ceiling*: 17,400 ft.

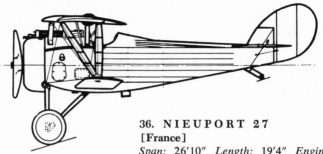

36. NIEUPORT 27
[France]

Span: 26'10" *Length:* 19'4" *Engine:* Le Rhone 120 h.p. *Armament:* 2 mgs. *Speed:* 116 m.p.h. *Ceiling:* 18,200 ft.

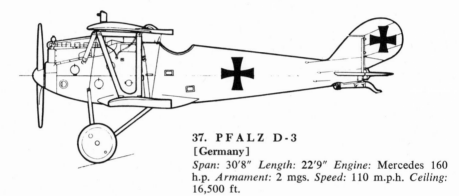

37. PFALZ D-3
[Germany]

Span: 30'8" *Length:* 22'9" *Engine:* Mercedes 160 h.p. *Armament:* 2 mgs. *Speed:* 110 m.p.h. *Ceiling:* 16,500 ft.

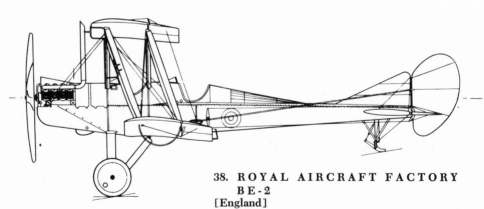

38. ROYAL AIRCRAFT FACTORY BE-2
[England]

Span: 40'9" *Length:* 27'3" *Engine:* R.A.F. 90 h.p. *Armament:* ½ mg. *Bomb Load:* 100 lbs. *Speed:* 88 m.p.h. *Ceiling:* 8,500 ft.

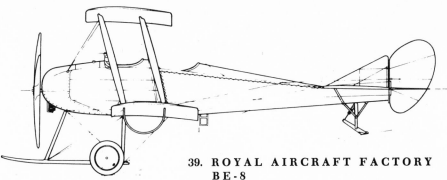

**39. ROYAL AIRCRAFT FACTORY
BE-8**
[England]
Span: 37'8" *Length:* 27'3" *Engine:* Gnome 80 h.p.
Armament: None *Bomb Load:* 100 lbs. *Speed:* 77
m.p.h. *Ceiling:* 7,500 ft.

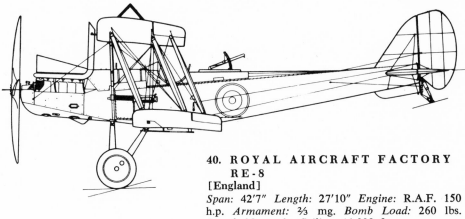

**40. ROYAL AIRCRAFT FACTORY
RE-8**
[England]
Span: 42'7" *Length:* 27'10" *Engine:* R.A.F. 150
h.p. *Armament:* ⅔ mg. *Bomb Load:* 260 lbs.
Speed: 98 m.p.h. *Ceiling:* 11,000 ft.

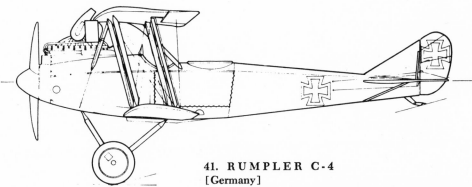

41. RUMPLER C-4
[Germany]
Span: 41'7" *Length:* 27'6" *Engine:* Mercedes 260
h.p. *Armament:* 2 mgs. *Speed:* 106 m.p.h. *Ceiling:*
21,000 ft.

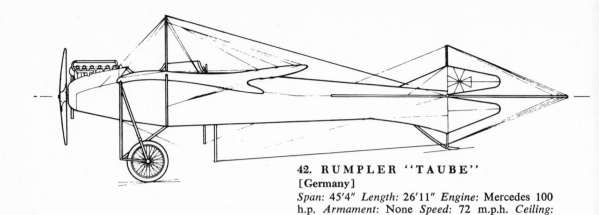

42. RUMPLER "TAUBE"
[Germany]
Span: 45'4" *Length*: 26'11" *Engine*: Mercedes 100
h.p. *Armament*: None *Speed*: 72 m.p.h. *Ceiling*:
8,500 ft.

43. SALMSON 2
[France]
Span: 38'7" *Length*: 27'11" *Engine*: Salmson 260
h.p. *Armament*: ⅔ mg. *Speed*: 116 m.p.h. *Ceiling*: 20,500 ft.

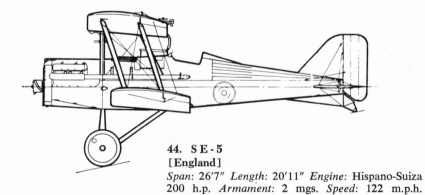

44. SE-5
[England]
Span: 26'7" *Length*: 20'11" *Engine*: Hispano-Suiza
200 h.p. *Armament*: 2 mgs. *Speed*: 122 m.p.h.
Ceiling: 22,000 ft.

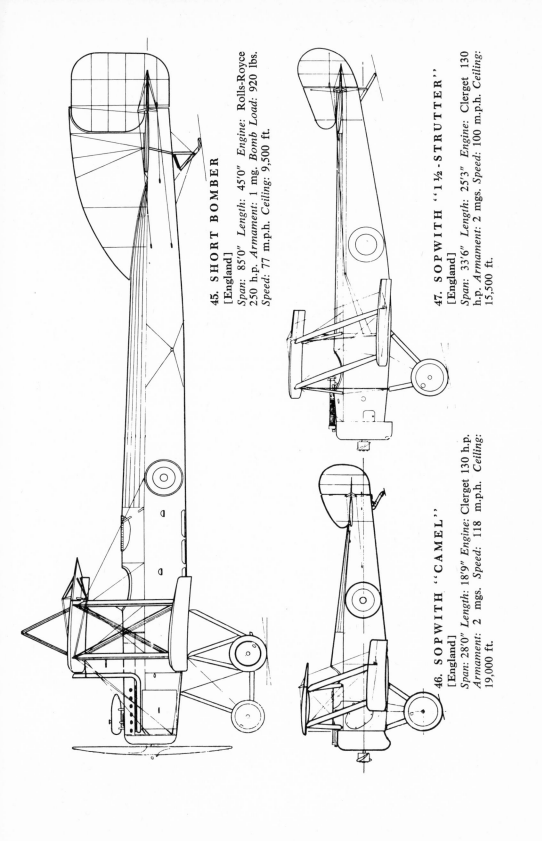

45. SHORT BOMBER
[England]
Span: 85'0" *Length:* 45'0" *Engine:* Rolls-Royce 250 h.p. *Armament:* 1 mg. *Bomb Load:* 920 lbs. *Speed:* 77 m.p.h. *Ceiling:* 9,500 ft.

47. SOPWITH "1½-STRUTTER"
[England]
Span: 33'6" *Length:* 25'3" *Engine:* Clerget 130 h.p. *Armament:* 2 mgs. *Speed:* 100 m.p.h. *Ceiling:* 15,500 ft.

46. SOPWITH "CAMEL"
[England]
Span: 28'0" *Length:* 18'9" *Engine:* Clerget 130 h.p. *Armament:* 2 mgs. *Speed:* 118 m.p.h. *Ceiling:* 19,000 ft.

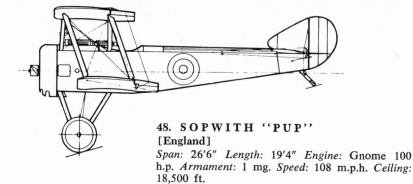

48. SOPWITH ''PUP''
[England]

Span: 26'6" *Length*: 19'4" *Engine*: Gnome 100 h.p. *Armament*: 1 mg. *Speed*: 108 m.p.h. *Ceiling*: 18,500 ft.

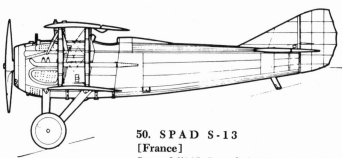

49. SOPWITH TRIPLANE
[England]

Span: 28'6" *Length*: 23'2" *Engine*: Hispano-Suiza 150 h.p. *Armament*: ½ mg. *Speed*: 120 m.p.h. *Ceiling*: 20,500 ft.

50. SPAD S-13
[France]

Span: 26'11" *Length* 20'8" *Engine*: Hispano-Suiza 200 h.p. *Armament*: 2 mgs. *Speed*: 130 m.p.h. *Ceiling*: 22,300 ft.

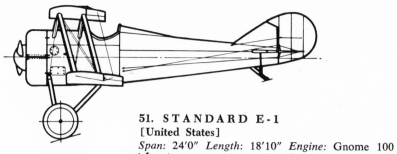

51. STANDARD E-1
[United States]

Span: 24'0" *Length:* 18'10" *Engine:* Gnome 100 h.p. *Armament:* ½ mg. *Speed:* 98 m.p.h. *Ceiling:* 15,500 ft.

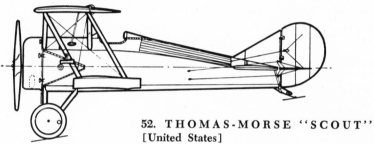

52. THOMAS-MORSE "SCOUT"
[United States]

Span: 26'6" *Length:* 19'10" *Engine:* Gnome 100 h.p. *Armament:* ½ mg. *Speed:* 95 m.p.h. *Ceiling:* 15,000 ft.

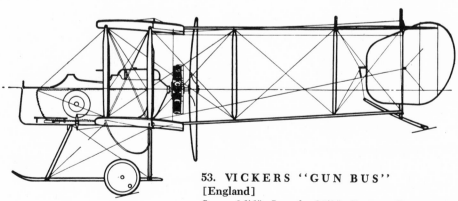

53. VICKERS "GUN BUS"
[England]

Span: 36'6" *Length:* 27'2" *Engine:* Gnome 100 h.p. *Armament:* 1 mg. *Speed:* 74 m.p.h. *Ceiling:* 9,000 ft.

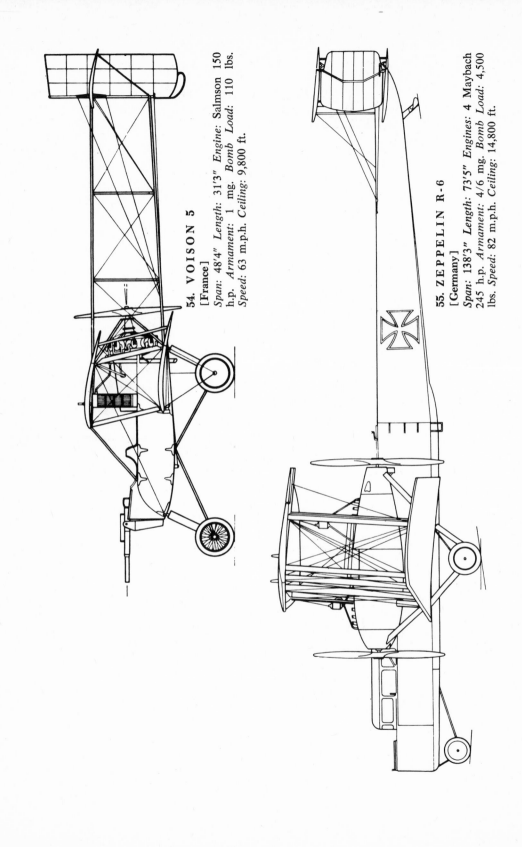

54. VOISON 5
[France]

Span: 48'4" *Length:* 31'3" *Engine:* Salmson 150 h.p. *Armament:* 1 mg. *Bomb Load:* 110 lbs. *Speed:* 63 m.p.h. *Ceiling:* 9,800 ft.

55. ZEPPELIN R-6
[Germany]

Span: 138'3" *Length:* 73'5" *Engines:* 4 Maybach 245 h.p. *Armament:* 4/6 mg. *Bomb Load:* 4,500 lbs. *Speed:* 82 m.p.h. *Ceiling:* 14,800 ft.

APPENDIX II

LEADING ACES OF WORLD WAR I

BRITISH ACES

Maj. E. Mannock	73	Capt. W. G. Claxton	39
Lt. Col. W. A. Bishop	72	Maj. R. S. Dallas	39
Maj. R. Callishaw	60	Capt. F. R. McCall	38
Maj. J. T. B. McCudden	57	Capt. H. W. Woollett	35
Capt. A. Beauchamp-Proctor	54	Capt. F. G. Quigley	34
Capt. D. R. McLaren	54	Maj. G. H. Bowman	32
Maj. W. G. Barker	53	Maj. A. D. Carter	31
Capt. R. A. Little	47	Capt. J. L. M. White	31
Capt. P. F. Fullard	46	Capt. M. B. Frew	30
Capt. G. E. H. McElroy	46	Capt. C. E. Howell	30
Capt. A. Ball	44	Capt. S. M. Kinkead	30
Capt. T. F. Hazell	41	Capt. A. E. McKeever	30
Capt. J. I. T. Jones	40		

(NOTE: *An additional 512 pilots of Great Britain and the British Empire qualify as aces, each having shot down five or more aircraft.*)

FRENCH ACES

Capt. R. P. Fonck	75	Capt. A. Pinsard	27
Capt. G. Guynemer	53	Lt. R. Dorme	23
Lt. C. Nungesser	45	Lt. G. Guerin	23
Capt. G. F. Madon	41	Lt. C. M. Haegelen	23
Lt. M. Boyau	35	Lt. P. Marinovitch	23
Lt. M. Coiffard	34	Capt. A. Heurtaux	21
Lt. J. Bourjade	28	Capt. A. Deullin	20

(NOTE: *An additional 145 French pilots qualify as aces, each hav-ing shot down between five and nineteen aircraft.*)

AMERICAN ACES

Capt. E. V. Rickenbacker	26	Capt. F. E. Kindley	12
Lt. F. Luke	21	Lt. D. Putnam	12
Maj. R. Lufbery	17	Capt. E. W. Springs	12
Lt. G. A. Vaughn	13	Maj. R. Landis	10
Lt. F. Baylies	12	Capt. J. N. Swaab	10

(NOTE: *An additional seventy-eight U.S. pilots qualify as aces, each having shot down between five and nine aircraft. Five of them, like Lt. F. Baylies, served only with the French flying corps.*)

BELGIAN ACES

Lt. W. Coppens	37	Capt. F. Jacquet	7
Adj. A. de Meulemeester	11	Lt. J. Olieslagers	6
Lt. E. Thieffry	10		

GERMAN ACES

Capt. M. von Richthofen	80	Capt. E. R. von Schleich	35
Lt. E. Udet	62	Lt. J. Veltjens	34
Lt. E. Loewenhardt	53	Lt. H. Bongartz	33
Lt. W. Voss	48	Lt. O. Koennecke	33
Lt. F. Rumey	45	Lt. K. Wolff	33
Capt. R. Berthold	44	Lt. T. Osterkamp	32
Lt. P. Baumer	43	Lt. E. Thuy	32
Lt. J. Jacobs	41	Lt. P. Billik	31
Capt. B. Loerzer	41	Capt. K. Bolle	31
Capt. O. Boelcke	40	Lt. G. Sachsenberg	31
Lt. F. Buchner	40	Lt. K. Allmenroder	30
Lt. L. von Richthofen	40	Lt. Degelow	30
Lt. H. Gontermann	39	Lt. H. Kroll	30
Lt. K. Menckhoff	39	Lt. J. Mai	30
Lt. M. Muller	36	Lt. U. Neckel	30
Lt. J. Buckler	35	Lt. K. Schaefer	30
Lt. G. Dorr	35		

(N O T E : *An additional 327 German pilots qualify as aces, each having shot down five or more aircraft. Conspicuous among them are Lt. M. Immelmann, with fifteen victories, and Capt. H. Goering, with twenty-two victories.*)

BIBLIOGRAPHY

Anonymous. *Airpower to 1919*. Gunter Air Force Base, Ala.: Extension Course Institute USAF, 1959.

Anonymous. *War Birds: Diary of an Unknown Aviator*. New York: Doran, 1926.

Archibald, Norman. *Heaven High, Hell Deep*. New York: Boni, 1935.

Bartlett, Robert M. *Sky Pioneer: The Story of Igor I. Sikorsky*. New York: Scribner's, 1947.

Berget, Alphonse. *The Conquest of the Air*. New York: Putnam, 1911.

Biddle, Charles J. *The Way of the Eagle*. New York: Scribner's, 1919.

Bingham, Hiram. *An Explorer in the Air Service*. New Haven: Yale, 1920.

Bishop, William A. *Winged Warfare*. Toronto: McClelland, Goodchild & Stewart, 1918.

Boelcke, Oswald. *An Aviator's Field Book*. New York: National Military Publishing Co., 1917.

Bordeaux, Henry. *Guynemer: Knight of the Air*. New Haven: Yale, 1918.

Boyle, Andrew. *Trenchard*. New York: Norton, 1962.

Buttlar, Treusch von. *Zeppelins Over England*. New York: Harcourt, Brace, 1932.

Chandler, Charles deForest, and Lahm, Frank P. *How Our Army Grew Wings*. New York: Ronald, 1943.

Channing, Grace Ellery (ed.). *War Letters of Edmond Genet*. New York: Scribner's, 1918.

Chapman, Victor. *Victor Chapman's Letters from France*. New York: Macmillan, 1917.

"Contact" (Alan Bott). *Cavalry of the Clouds*. New York: Doubleday, Page, 1918.

Coppens, Willy. *Days on the Wing*. London: Hamilton, 1934.

Cross & Cockade Journal. Vols. I–V. Santa Ana, Calif.: The Society of World War I Historians, 1960-1964.

Cuneo, John R. *Winged Mars: The German Air Weapon, 1870-1914.* Harrisburg, Penn.: Military Service Press, 1942.

Cutlack, F. M. *The Australian Flying Corps, 1914-1918.* Sydney: Angus and Robertson, 1933.

Doerflinger, Joseph. *Stepchild Pilot.* Tyler, Texas: Longo, 1959.

Draper, Christopher. *The Mad Major.* London: Air Review, 1962.

Driggs, Laurence La Tourette. *Heroes of Aviation.* Boston: Little, Brown, 1927.

Dudley, Ernest. *Monsters of the Purple Twilight.* London: Harrap, 1960.

Farre, Henry. *Sky Fighters of France.* Boston: Houghton Mifflin, 1919.

Fokker, Anthony H. G., and Gould, Bruce. *Flying Dutchman.* New York: Holt, 1931.

Freudenthal, Elsbeth E. *Flight into History: The Wright Brothers and the Air Age.* Norman: University of Oklahoma, 1949.

Frischauer, Willi. *The Rise and Fall of Hermann Goering.* Boston: Houghton Mifflin, 1951.

Gauvreau, Emile, and Cohen, Lester. *Billy Mitchell.* New York: Dutton, 1942.

Gibbons, Floyd. *The Red Knight of Germany.* Garden City, N.Y.: Doubleday, 1927.

Goerlitz, Walter, *The German General Staff.* New York: Praeger, 1953.

Goldsmith, Margaret. *Zeppelin, A Biography.* New York: Morrow, 1931.

Grahame-White, Claude, and Harper, Harry. *Aircraft in the Great War.* London: Unwin, 1915.

Grey, Charles G. *The History of Combat Airplanes.* Northfield: Norwich University, 1941.

Gurney, Gene. *Five Down and Glory.* New York: Putnam, 1958.

Hall, Bert. *En l'Air!* New York: New Library, 1918.

Hall, Bert, and Niles, John R. *One Man's War.* New York: Holt, 1929.

Hall, James Norman. *High Adventure.* Boston: Houghton Mifflin, 1929.

Hall, James Norman, and Nordhoff, Charles Bernard. *The Lafayette Flying Corps.* Boston: Houghton Mifflin, 1920.

Hall, Norman S. *The Balloon Buster: Frank Luke of Arizona.* New York: Doubleday, Doran, 1928.

Hart, B. H. Liddell. *The Real War, 1914 to 1918.* Boston: Little, Brown, 1930.

Hatch, Alden. *Glenn Curtiss: Pioneer of Naval Aviation.* New York: Messner, 1942.

Hearne, R. P. *Aerial Warfare.* London: Lane, 1919.

Heinkel, Ernst. *Stormy Life.* New York: Dutton, 1956.

Herlin, Hans. *Udet: A Man's Life.* London: Macdonald, 1960.

Heydemarck, Haupt. *Double-Decker C.666.* London: Hamilton.

Immelmann, Franz. *Immelmann, Eagle of Lille.* London: Hamilton.

Jones, Ira. *King of Air Fighters: Biography of Major "Mick" Mannock.* London: Nicholson and Watson, 1934.

Kelly, Fred C. (ed.). *Miracle at Kitty Hawk: The Letters of Wilbur and Orville Wright.* New York: Farrar, Straus and Young, 1951.

Kiernan, R. H. *Captain Albert Ball.* London: Hamilton, 1933.

Knappen, Theodore M. *Wings of War.* New York: Putnam, 1920.

Lamberton, W. M. *Fighter Aircraft of the 1914-1918 War.* Letchworth: Harleyford, 1958.

Lamberton, W. M. *Reconnaissance and Bomber Aircraft of the 1914-1918 War.* Letchworth: Harleyford, 1958.

Lehmann, Ernst, and Mingos, Howard. *The Zeppelins.* New York: Sears, 1927.

Levine, Isaac Don. *Mitchell: Pioneer of Air Power.* Cleveland: World, 1944.

March, Francis A. *History of the World War.* Philadelphia: Winston, 1918.

McConnell, James R. *Flying for France.* New York: Doubleday, Page, 1917.

McCudden, James Thomas Byford. *Five Years in the Royal Flying Corps.* London: The "Aeroplane" and General Publishing Co., 1918.

Millis, Walter. *Road to War.* Boston: Houghton, Mifflin, 1935.

Mitchell, William. *Memoirs of World War I.* New York: Random House, 1960.

Molter, Bennett A. *Knights of the Air.* New York: Appleton, 1918.

Morris, Lloyd, and Smith, Kendall. *Ceiling Unlimited.* New York: Macmillan, 1953.

Mortane, Jacques. *Guynemer: The Ace of Aces.* New York: Moffat, Yard, 1918.

Musciano, Walter A. *Lieutenant Werner Voss.* New York: Hobby Helpers, 1962.

National Geographic Magazine. A special issue devoted to the air war. January 1918.

Nordhoff, Charles Bernard. *The Fledgling.* Boston: Houghton Mifflin, 1919.

Nowarra, H. J., and Brown, Kimbrough S. *Richthofen and the Flying Circus.* Letchworth: Harleyford, 1959.

Oughton, Frederick. *The Aces.* New York: Putnam, 1960.

Parsons, E. C. *The Great Adventure.* Garden City, N.Y.: Doubleday, Doran, 1937.

Pemberton-Billing, Noel. *Defence Against the Night Bomber.* London: Robert Hale.

Pierce, W. O'D. *Air-War.* New York: Modern Age, 1939.

Poolman, Kenneth. *Zeppelins Against London.* New York: John Day, 1961.

(Prince, Norman.) *Norman Prince: A Volunteer who Died for the Cause He Loved.* Boston: Houghton Mifflin, 1917.

Reynolds, Quentin. *They Fought for the Sky.* New York: Rinehart, 1957.

Richthofen, Baron Manfred von. *The Red Air Fighter.* London: The "Aeroplane" and General Publishing Co., 1918.

Rickenbacker, Edward V. *Fighting the Flying Circus.* New York: Stokes, 1919.

Roberts, E. M. *A Flying Fighter.* New York: Harpers, 1918.

Robertson, Bruce (ed.). *Air Aces of the 1914-1918 War.* Letchworth: Harleyford, 1959.

Rockwell, Paul A. *War Letters of Kiffin Yates Rockwell.* Garden City, N.Y.: Country Life Press, 1925.

Roosevelt, Kermit (ed.). *Quentin Roosevelt: A Sketch with Letters.* New York: Scribner's, 1921.

Rosinski, Herbert. *The German Army.* Washington, D.C.: Infantry Journal, 1940.

Roustam-Bek, B. *Aerial Russia.* London: Lane, 1916.

Saunders, Hilary St. George. *Per Ardua: The Rise of British Air Power.* London: Oxford, 1945.

Sigaud, Louis A. *Douhet and Aerial Warfare.* New York: Putnam.

Slessor, J. C. *Air Power and Armies.* London: Humphrey Milford, 1936.

Smith, Laurence Yard. *The Romance of Aircraft.* New York: Stokes, 1919.

Sullivan, Alan. *Aviation in Canada, 1917-1918.* Toronto: Rous and Mann, 1919.

Taber, Sydney Richmond. *Arthur Richmond Taber: A Memorial Record Compiled by his Father*. Privately printed, 1920.

Udet, Ernst. *Ace of the Black Cross*. London: Newnes, 0000.

Veil, Charles (as told to Howard Marsh). *Adventure's a Wench*. New York: Morrow, 1934.

"Vigilant." *French War Birds*. London: Hamilton.

"Vigilant." *German War Birds*. London: Hamilton, 1933.

Voison, Gabriel. *Men, Women and 10,000 Kites*. New York: Putnam, 1963.

Wagner, Ray. *American Combat Planes*. Garden City, N. Y.: Hanover House, 1960.

Walcott, Stuart. *Above the French Lines*. Princeton: Princeton University Press, 1918.

Wellman, William A. *Go, Get 'Em!* Boston: Page, 1918.

Winslow, Carroll Dana. *With the French Flying Corps*. New York: Scribner's, 1917.

Wortley, Rothesay Stuart. *Letters from a Flying Officer*. London: Oxford, 1928.

INDEX